Politics in the Republic of Ireland

**Edited by
John Coakley and Michael Gallagher**

Third edition

Published in association with

PRESS

London and New York

First published 1992 by PSAI Press
Second edition 1993 by PSAI Press

Third edition 1999
by Routledge in association with PSAI Press
11 New Fetter Lane, London EC4P 4EE

Simultaneously published in the USA and Canada by
Routledge
29 West 35th Street, New York, NY 10001

Reprinted 2000

Routledge is an imprint of the Taylor & Francis Group

Typeset in Baskerville by Curran Publishing Services
Printed and bound in Great Britain by
St Edmundsbury Press, Bury St Edmunds, Suffolk

British Library Cataloguing in Publication Data
A catalogue record for this book is available
from the British Library

Library of Congress Cataloguing in Publication Data
Politics in the republic of Ireland / [edited by] John
    Coakley and Michael Gallagher. – 3rd ed.
    336 pp. 15.6 x 23.4 cm.
    Includes bibliographical references and index.
    1. Ireland–Politics and government–1949–
    I. Coakley, John. II. Gallagher, Michael, 1951–
JN1415.P65 1999
320.9417'09'045–dc21   99–31724
                                                  CIP

ISBN 0–415–22193–5 (hbk)
ISBN 0–415–22194–3 (pbk)

Contents

14   Democratic politics in independent Ireland   350

TOM GARVIN

Appendices   364

JOHN COAKLEY

Boxes and figures

Tables

Glosssary of Irish terms

Áras an Uachtaráin (*aw*-rus un *ook*-ta-rawn) Residence of the President
Ard Chomhairle (ord *ho*-er-le) national executive of Fianna Fáil
ard-fheis (ord-*esh*) national convention (of a political party)
Bunreacht na hÉireann (*bun*-rokt ne *hay*run) constitution of Ireland
Cathaoirleach (ka-*heer*-luck) chairperson (of the Senate)
Ceann Comhairle (kyon *kohr*-le) speaker or chairperson (of the Dáil)
Clann na Poblachta (clon ne *pub*-lak-ta) 'party of the republic' (party name, 1946–65)
Clann na Talmhan (clon ne *tal*-oon) 'party of the land' (party name, 1939–65)
comhairle ceantair (*koh*-er-le *kyon*-ter) district council (in Fianna Fáil)
comhairle dáilcheantair (*koh*-er-le *dawl*-kyon-ter) constituency council (in Fianna Fáil)
cumann (*kum*-man) branch (of a political party or other organisation); plural **cumainn**
Cumann na nGaedheal (*kum*-man ne *ngale*) 'party of the Irish' (party name, 1923–33)
Dáil Éireann (dawl *ay*-run) national assembly of Ireland; plural Dála
Éire (*ay*-reh) Ireland
Fianna Fáil (*fee*-an-a *fawl*) 'soldiers of Ireland' (party name)
Fine Gael (*fin*-a gale) 'Irish race' (party name)
Gaeltacht (*gale*-tuckt) Irish-speaking districts
garda (síochána) (*gawr*-da shee-*kaw*-ne) (civic) guard, policeman; plural **gardaí**
Oireachtas (*ih*-rock-tus) parliament
Saorstát Éireann (*sayr*-stawt *ay*-run) Irish Free State
Seanad Éireann (*sha*-nad *ay*-run) senate of Ireland
Sinn Féin (shin *fayn*) 'ourselves' (party name)
Tánaiste (*taw*-nish-deh) deputy prime minister
Taoiseach (*tee*-shuck) prime minister; plural Taoisigh
Teachta Dála (*tak*-tuh *dawl*-uh) Dáil deputy, TD
Uachtarán (*ook*-ta-rawn) president

Note: A number of the party names above have a range of alternative translations; see John Coakley, 'The significance of names: the evolution of Irish party labels', *Études Irlandaises* 5, 1980, pp. 171–81. The pronunciation system indicated above is approximate only, and follows in part that in Howard Penniman and Brian Farrell (eds), *Ireland at the Polls: a Study of Four General Elections* (Durham, N.C.: Duke University Press, 1987), pp. 265–6. Italics indicate stressed syllables.

Acronyms

AIM	Action, Information, Motivation (family law reform group)
AMS	additional member system (of PR)
C&AG	Comptroller and Auditor General
CFSP	Common Foreign and Security Policy (of the EU)
CNG	Comhhdháil Náisiúnta na Gaeilge (language association)
CRG	Constitution Review Group
CSF	Community Support Framework
ESRI	Economic and Social Research Institute
IBEC	Irish Business and Employers Confederation
ICTU	Irish Congress of Trade Unions
IFA	Irish Farmers' Association
IMRO	Irish Music Rights Organisation
INOU	Irish National Organisation for the Unemployed
IRB	Irish Republican Brotherhood
MSG	Ministers' and Secretaries' Group (co-ordinating policy towards the EU)
NESC	National Economic and Social Council
NFA	National Farmers' Association
NSSB	National Social Service Board
NWCI	National Women's Council of Ireland
OEEC	Organisation for European Economic Cooperation
PCW	Programme for Competitiveness and Work (1994–96)
PESP	Programme for Economic and Social Progress (1990–93)
PFP	Partnership For Peace
PNR	Programme for National Recovery (1987–90)
PR	proportional representation
RIC	Royal Irish Constabulary
RTÉ	Radio Telefís Éireann
RUC	Royal Ulster Constabulary
SDLP	Social Democratic and Labour Party
SIPTU	Services Industrial Professional Technical Union
SMI	Strategic Management Initiative
STV	single transferable vote (PR system)
TD	Teachta Dála (Dáil deputy)

Note: £ = Irish pounds (equivalent to 1.27 Euros, around £0.83 sterling, in July 1999)

Contributors

John Coakley is a lecturer in politics at University College Dublin and Secretary General of the International Political Science Association. He has published extensively on Irish and comparative politics, and has edited *The Social Origins of Nationalist Movements* and *The Territorial Management of Ethnic Conflict* as well as a special issue of the *International Political Science Review* on the resolution of ethnic conflict.

Eileen Connolly lectures in government in Dublin City University. Her research interests include feminist theory, gender and the Irish state since the 1950s, and the politics of European integration. Her most recent publications include chapters in Galligan *et al.* (eds), *Contesting Politics: Women in Ireland, North and South* and in Philip Norton (ed.), *Parliaments and Pressure Groups in Europe*.

Robert Elgie is Senior Lecturer in politics at the University of Nottingham. He is author of *Political Leadership in Liberal Democracies* and editor of *Semi-Presidentialism in Europe*. He is conducting a research project on the Taoiseach in conjunction with John Stapleton of the University of Limerick.

Michael Gallagher lectures in the Department of Political Science at Trinity College Dublin. He is co-author of *Representative Government in Modern Europe*, and co-editor of *Candidate Selection in Comparative Perspective: the Secret Garden of Politics* and *The Referendum Experience in Europe*. His current research interests include a survey of the backgrounds, attitudes and roles of party members, and comparative warlordism.

Yvonne Galligan is a lecturer in the Department of Political Science at Trinity College Dublin. She is author of many publications on Irish politics and policy making, including *Women and Politics in Ireland: From the Margins to the Mainstream,* and is co-editor of *Contesting Politics: Women in Ireland, North and South*.

Tom Garvin is Professor of Politics and Head of the Department of Politics at University College, Dublin. He is the author of many publications on Irish politics, including *The Evolution of Irish Nationalist Politics* and *Nationalist Revolutionaries in Ireland 1858–1928*.

Patrick Keatinge is former Jean Monnet Professor in European Integration at Trinity College, Dublin. He has written several books and many articles on Irish foreign policy. He edited *Ireland and EC Membership Evaluated* and *Ireland and Maastricht: What the Treaty Means*; his most recent book was *European Security: Ireland's Choices.*

Lee Komito is a College Lecturer in the Department of Library and Information Studies, University College Dublin, and was Senior Lecturer in the Information Technology and Society programme at Manchester Metropolitan University. Recent publications include articles in *The Information Society, Economic and Social Review* and *Journal of Information Technology.*

Brigid Laffan is Jean Monnet Professor in European Politics at University College Dublin. She has written extensively on European integration. Her recent publications include *The Finances of the European Union* and she is co-author of *Europe's Experimental Union: Re-thinking Integration.*

Michael Laver is Professor of Political Science at Trinity College Dublin. He is author of a range of books and articles on the politics of party competition in different contexts. His most recent books include *Playing Politics: the Nightmare Continues* and *Private Desires, Political Action.*

Peter Mair is Professor of Comparative Politics at Leiden University, and co-editor of the *European Journal of Political Research.* He is author or co-author of *Identity, Competition and Electoral Availability,* which was awarded the Stein Rokkan Prize in Comparative Social Research, *Representative Government in Modern Europe,* and *Party System Change.*

Michael Marsh is Head of the Department of Political Science and a Fellow of Trinity College Dublin. He is author of a wide variety of articles on parties and electoral behaviour. Co-edited books include *Candidate Selection in Comparative Perspective: the Secret Garden of Politics* and most recently *How Ireland Voted 1997.*

Gary Murphy is a lecturer in government at Dublin City University. He has published widely on interest group politics in Ireland and the European Union. He is currently working on a major study of Irish interest groups in the policy process and is review editor of *Irish Political Studies.*

Eunan O'Halpin holds the Paddy Moriarty Chair of Government at Dublin City University. His current research interests include 20th century Irish political development, Irish defence and security policy, and the role of intelligence in interstate relations. He is chairman of the Documents on Irish Foreign Policy project, and joint editor of *Documents on Irish Foreign Policy: Volume 1, 1919–1922.* His most recent book, *Defending Ireland: the Irish State and its Enemies since 1922,* was published by Oxford in 1999.

Richard Sinnott is Associate Professor of Politics at University College Dublin. He is the author of *Irish Voters Decide: Voting Behaviour in Elections and Referendums since 1918,* co-author of *People and Parliament in the European Union: Participation, Democracy, and Legitimacy,* contributing co-editor of *How Ireland Voted: the Irish General Election 1987, How Ireland Voted 1989,* and *Public Opinion and Internationalized Governance.*

Preface to the first edition

This book arose out of a shared feeling among a number of teachers of courses on Irish Politics at universities and other third-level institutions in Ireland and further afield that there was no book that matched satisfactorily the course they taught. Existing texts were either out of date or did not give adequate coverage of some central elements in the Irish Politics courses that were actually offered. The problem was becoming particularly acute given the steady growth of interest among students and the rapidly expanding numbers taking such courses.

Ironically, this shortage of material coincided with an increase both in the output of research into many aspects of Irish politics and government and in the number of academics who had built up an expertise in particular areas of the subject. It was only a matter of time before the logical solution was arrived at: a collaborative effort that would draw on the wide range of expertise among Irish political scientists to produce the book that we, as teachers of Irish politics and government, have been looking for.

The emergence of the book owes a lot to the existence of the Political Studies Association of Ireland (PSAI), the body that draws together and represents those engaged in the professional study of politics in and of Ireland. Its meetings and conferences have provided the opportunity for the establishment of informal networks between those teaching at different institutions, for comparing notes on our experience with existing textbooks and for discussing alternatives. It is fitting that the book is published by the Association's publishing house, the PSAI Press, with any profits being ploughed back into financing further publications and activities of the Association.

Planning for the book began in 1991 and the final outline was sent to contributors in November of that year. The target of having the book ready by September 1992 was thus highly ambitious, even with the benefits of desktop publishing and the fast turnaround guaranteed by our printers, and there were those who doubted whether the schedule was realistic. The fact that the book has appeared by the target date is due primarily to the thirteen contributors, who accepted with equanimity the news that they would not receive any royalties for their efforts, applied themselves enthusiastically to the task, and did not protest too vigorously at the constant harassment to which they were subjected by the editors.

As well as writing their own chapters, several contributors have been especially helpful to the project by suggesting improvements to the overall plan or to individual chapters. In particular, Brian Farrell has been an enthusiastic backer of the project from the start as has Michael Laver, who can also take credit for the cover design, for producing the financial projections that convinced first the committee and then the 1991 annual general meeting of the PSAI that paying for the start-up costs of a book such as this was likely to be a sound investment, and for his energetic pre-publication efforts to ensure that it would be. Others who have helped by commenting on one or more chapters include Brian Keary, John Logan, Brian Mercer Walker and Bernadette Whelan.

The aim throughout has been to produce a book that combined real substance and a readable style. It is aimed particularly at undergraduates at third-level institutions, but we hope that it will also meet the needs of the wider public interested in the politics and government of Ireland. In addition, since no country's politics can be understood in isolation, the authors have written their chapters with a comparative (especially a western European) dimension very much in mind. The venerable generalisation that 'Ireland is different', so there is no need to make the effort to compare its politics with those of other countries, is no longer adequate. It is a well-worn observation that Ireland has become a more outward-looking country since the 1950s, and its academic community has not been unaffected by this development. *Politics in the Republic of Ireland* is among the fruits of these broader horizons.

John Coakley and Michael Gallagher
Limerick and Dublin, August 1992

Preface to the third edition

The first edition of *Politics in the Republic of Ireland* was published in 1992, and since that time the book has been extensively used as a textbook on Irish Politics courses in universities and colleges in Ireland and elsewhere. The second edition, which appeared in 1993, marked an updating of the material, and for this third edition the book has been thoroughly revised. New chapters have been introduced and the other chapters have been thoroughly rewritten, in response to both feedback from readers and the unstoppable march of events.

Producing the third edition has been an exciting challenge for authors and editors alike. Although for many years the Republic of Ireland had the image of being a place where, politically speaking, not much of interest happened, this perception was never accurate and, in any case, the image changed greatly in the 1980s and 1990s. Ireland is now seen as a country of cultural vitality, economic dynamism and rapid social change, and its politics reflect this new air of liveliness. Unprecedented patterns of government formation, challenges to the established political parties, ever-deepening if sometimes ambivalent involvement in the process of European integration, and sustained discussion of gender issues are among some of these developments, along with evidence, revealed by several tribunals of enquiry, that Irish politics are not so free of corruption as many had assumed.

As with previous editions, a number of people have helped by giving their comments on one or more chapters or in other ways, and we should like to thank particularly Sean Donnelly, Gerard Hogan, Keiko Kinjo, members of the staff of the Houses of the Oireachtas, and many others who in various ways have facilitated the publication of this book.

Previous editions of *Politics in the Republic of Ireland* were published by PSAI Press, the publishing house of the Political Studies Association of Ireland, and profits from the book have been ploughed back into financing further publications and other activities of the Association. In order to secure as wide a readership as possible for the third edition, the PSAI has linked up with the major international publisher Routledge. We should like to thank Routledge's political science editor Mark

Kavanagh for his enthusiasm for the book and his expeditious shepherding of it to publication. Our hope is that this third edition of *Politics in the Republic of Ireland* will contribute to a fuller understanding of the endlessly fascinating Irish political process.

John Coakley and Michael Gallagher
Dublin, July 1999

1 The foundations of statehood

John Coakley

To many people, 'Irish politics' conjures up images of calculating politicians being investigated by expensive tribunals of enquiry, state institutions failing to ensure that the law is evenly applied, and disillusioned voters waiting to take their revenge – though never quite managing to do so. It is undoubtedly the case that such images form a prominent feature of political life in Ireland, as elsewhere. But this is by no means the full story: as in other western democracies, the political system is extremely complex, and the human beings who operate it vary enormously in all aspects of their characters.

In this book, our starting point for the analysis of Irish politics is the state itself. As in the case of other states, it is impossible to understand the contemporary position without an understanding of the past. Although political histories of Ireland often start at 1922 and conventional wisdom stresses the 'new era' that then began, significant elements of continuity underlay the sharp political break that took place at the time that the state was founded. Before looking at the establishment of the state itself and at subsequent developments, then, we must examine the legacy of the old regime.

In the first section of this chapter, we look at institutional developments and political processes of the pre-independence period that were to prove of enduring significance in Irish political life. Many of these are rather different from the political events that were important at the time, and that form the subject matter of conventional historical studies (for more general histories of the period see Lyons, 1973; Foster, 1988; Girvin, 1989; Lee, 1989; Keogh, 1994; Harkness, 1996; and Townshend, 1999). The second section discusses the political background to the establishment of the independent Irish state. We move on in the third section to examine the political themes of the post-independence period, linking them with earlier developments.

The prelude to statehood

The apparatus of the modern state first developed in Ireland under the tutelage of the English monarchy. Prior to this, Gaelic Irish society, though attaining a high degree of cultural, artistic and literary development in the early medieval period, had shown few signs of following the path of contemporary European political development. The Norman invasions that began in 1169 and the establishment of the Lordship of Ireland that followed (with the Norman King of England exercising the functions of Lord of Ireland) marked the beginning of rudimentary statehood. Although Norman or English control was little more than nominal for several centuries, the vigorous Tudor dynasty subjugated the island in the sixteenth century, a process whose beginning was marked by the promotion in 1541 of the Lord of Ireland to the status of King. The Kingdom of Ireland continued thereafter to have its own political institutions, though a much more profound degree of British influence followed the passing of the Act of Union in 1800, which created a new state, the United Kingdom of Great Britain and Ireland (UK).

In looking at the legacy of this system of government to independent Ireland, we may identify three areas in which spillover effects were important. First, at the *constitutional* level, certain roles and offices that had evolved over the centuries provided an important stepping stone for the builders of the new state. Second, at the *administrative* level, the development of a large civil service bequeathed to the new state a body of trained professional staff. Third, at the *political* level, Irish voters and politicians had for some decades before 1922 been accustomed to increasingly democratic political practices and had been part of a political culture whose assumptions bore some similarity to those of today.

The constitution of the old regime

In an era when travel was slow, difficult and dangerous, it was neither sensible nor practical for expanding dynasties to seek to govern all of their territories from a fixed centre or capital. In common with the peripheral areas of other medieval states, then, Norman Ireland acquired a set of political institutions that were gradually to evolve into modern ones. The hub around which political life revolved, at least in theory, was the King's personal representative in Ireland, the Lord Lieutenant. The Lord Lieutenant was advised on everyday affairs of government by a 'Privy Council' made up of his chief officials, and on longer-term matters by a 'Great Council' or Parliament that met irregularly.

The evolution of the Irish Parliament followed a path similar to that of the English Parliament (see Farrell, 1973). It first met in Castledermot, Co Kildare, in 1264, and for the next four centuries it continued to assemble from time to time in various Irish towns, with Dublin increasingly becoming dominant. By 1692 it had acquired the shape that it was to retain up to 1800. Its House of Commons consisted of 300 members (two each from thirty-two counties, from 117 cities, towns or boroughs and from Trinity College, Dublin), and its House of Lords of a small but variable number: archbishops and bishops of the established (Protestant) Church of Ireland

and lay members of the Irish peerage. The Irish Parliament thus resembled its English counterpart closely, despite the earlier existence of a third house (this contained representatives of the clergy; such a house was common in continental Europe).

By adopting the Act of Union of 1800, this parliament voted itself out of existence, opting instead for a merged or 'united' parliament for all of Great Britain and Ireland. In the new House of Commons there were to be 100 Irish MPs (about 15 per cent of the total), while the House of Lords would receive thirty-two additional members: the Irish peerage would elect twenty-eight of its number for life, and four members of the Irish Protestant episcopate would sit in the House of Lords in rotation.

Although the legislative branch of government thus disappeared completely from Ireland, the executive branch did not. Throughout the entire period of the union (1800–1922), the existence of a 'Government of Ireland' was recognised, a critical weakness in the scheme for Irish integration with Britain (Ward, 1994, pp. 30–8). The Lord Lieutenant, as representative of the sovereign, was formal head of this government. This post was always filled by a leading nobleman who, in addition to his governmental functions, was 'the embodiment of the "dignified" aspects of the state, the official leader of Irish social life' (McDowell, 1964, p. 52). He left the actual day-to-day running of the process of government, however, to his principal assistant, the Chief Secretary. This official had responsibility for the management of Irish affairs in the House of Commons and, although he was not always a member of the cabinet, he was at least a prominent member of the governing party. Over the decades, effective power passed from the Lord Lieutenant to the Chief Secretary, following the pattern of a similar shift in power in Britain from the King to the Prime Minister. (Significantly, the Lord Lieutenant's official residence, the Viceregal Lodge in the Phoenix Park, has now become the President's residence, Áras an Uachtaráin, while the Chief Secretary's Office in Dublin Castle went on to become the core of the Department of the Taoiseach.)

Even after the union, Ireland remained constitutionally distinct from the rest of the UK. Although all legislation was now enacted through the UK parliament, in many policy areas (including education, agriculture, land reform, policing, health and local government) separate legislation was enacted for the different components of the United Kingdom. For example, the parliament of 1880–85 passed seventy-one acts whose application was exclusively Irish (out of a total of 422 acts, the rest being 'English', 'Scottish', 'United Kingdom' or other). Electoral reforms illustrate the extent to which Ireland was treated in a distinctive way even in the matter of representation at Westminster: it was only in 1884 that a uniform electoral law was adopted for all parts of the UK.

The question of electoral reform indeed has a central place in the process of constitutional evolution. It has been assumed since the late nineteenth century that democratic elections have four characteristics, and these are frequently written into modern constitutions: voting is *direct*, the process is *secret*, all votes are of *equal* weight and suffrage is *universal*. Elections to the old Irish House of Commons and to its post-union successor always operated on the basis of direct voting: electors selected their members of parliament without the intervention of any intermediate electoral college, so the first of the four conditions was met.

The second condition was met rather later. Traditionally, voting was open: a public poll was conducted at a central place in the constituency, and voters declared publicly the names of the candidates for whom they wished their votes to be recorded. This obviously permitted intimidation by influential groups such as landlords and clergy, but the Ballot Act (1872) abruptly and permanently changed these practices: in future voting was to be carried out by secret ballot, except in the case of illiterates and other incapacitated persons.

Third, in the old Irish House of Commons, voters' voices were of unequal weight; large counties (such as Cork) and small boroughs (such as Tulsk, Bannow and Ardfert) were all represented by two MPs each, with complete disregard for their greatly varying populations. This position was rectified in three principal stages. In 1800 the smaller boroughs were abolished; in 1885 all seats were redistributed to conform more closely to the distribution of the population; and in 1922 the new constitution guaranteed that all votes would be equal.

Fourth, although in many countries extension of the right to vote was characterised by a number of major reforms and the proportion of those enfranchised increased in stages, the process in Ireland was more complex. This may be seen in Box 1.1. The most sweeping early changes were the extension of the right to vote to Catholics (1793) and the abolition of the county 'forty-shilling freehold' (1829), one greatly extending, the other greatly reducing the electorate. The reforms of 1832, 1850 and 1868 (unlike the English reforms of 1832 and 1867) had an incremental effect only. The major reforms were those of 1884, associated with the birth of modern politics in Ireland, 1918, linked with another episode of electoral revolution, and 1923, which completed the process. (For an illustration of the impact of these reforms on the proportion of the population entitled to vote, see Figure 1.1 and discussion on pages 10–11.)

Emergence of state bureaucracy

Underneath the political superstructure of the Irish government, the modern Irish civil service developed gradually. It consisted of a number of departments, offices and other bodies that employed considerable numbers of officials and were established from time to time as the need was seen to arise. Formal control of these bodies was normally collegial rather than individual: they were directed by 'boards' or 'commissions' or groups of 'commissioners', generally overseen by the Chief Secretary. The extent of the

Box 1.1 Extension of voting rights, 1793–1973

Act	Major effect
Catholic Relief Act, 1793	Extension of vote to Catholics
Parliamentary Elections (Ireland) Act, 1829	Raising of county qualification from £2 to £10
Representation of the People (Ireland) Act, 1832	Minor extension of borough franchise
Representation of the People (Ireland) Act, 1850	Lowering of county qualification
Representation of the People (Ireland) Act, 1868	Lowering of borough qualification
Representation of the People Act, 1884	Uniform householder and lodger franchise
Representation of the People Act, 1918	Universal male and limited female suffrage
Electoral Act, 1923	Universal suffrage
Electoral (Amendment) Act, 1973	Reduction of voting age from 21 to 18

Chief Secretary's influence was not uniform; it was decisive in the case of the Local Government Board (founded in 1872), for instance, but indirect in the case of others, such as the Board of National Education (1831). There were twenty-nine of these bodies by 1911, employing a staff of 4,000 (see Box 1.2).

In addition to these 'Irish' departments answerable to the Chief Secretary, a number of departments of the 'Imperial' civil service also had branches in Ireland. These were controlled ultimately by the relevant British cabinet ministers, and in some cases employed very large staffs in Ireland. The pre-union Post Office (1785) was merged with its British counterpart (1831), and underwent rapid expansion in the late nineteenth century. The old Irish revenue boards also survived the union, but were merged with their British counterparts following the Anglo-Irish customs amalgamation of 1823; they also developed considerable staffs (see Meghen, 1962; McDowell, 1964). By 1911 these bodies, eleven in all, had some 23,000 employees in Ireland, of whom 20,000 worked in the Post Office.

By the beginning of the twentieth century, then, Ireland already had a very sizeable civil service, with more than 27,000 employees spread over

Box 1.2 Civil service continuity, 1914–24

Board/department in 1914	*Location in 1924*
Irish government departments:	
Department of Agriculture and Technical Instruction (1899) Land Commission (1881) Congested Districts Board (1891)	Department of Agriculture
Local Government Board (1872) Registrar General's Office (1844)	Department of Local Government and Public Health
Commissioners of National Education (1831) Commissioners of Intermediate Education (1878)	Department of Education
General Prisons Board (1877) Public Record Office (1867) Registry of Deeds (1708)	Department of Justice
United Kingdom government departments in Ireland:	
Inland Revenue Commissioners Registrar of Friendly Societies Ordnance Survey	Department of Finance
Post Office	Department of Posts and Telegraphs

Note: A considerable number of additional boards and departments have been omitted from this list.

twenty-nine Irish and eleven UK departments. In addition, there were large field staffs in certain other areas: two police forces, the Dublin Metropolitan Police (established in 1787) with about 1,200 and the Royal Irish Constabulary (1836) with about 10,700, and the body of national teachers, numbering some 15,600. Together, these amounted in 1911–13 to about 55,000 state employees, not including the large numbers of army and naval personnel stationed in Ireland.

Finally, it is necessary to consider the system of local government. In urban areas this had consisted of sixty-eight cities, towns and boroughs whose local administrations survived the Act of Union, each governed by a council or corporation headed by a mayor, 'sovereign', 'portreeve' or 'provost'. Although some of these bodies were open to limited forms of election, most were not; a report in 1835 showed that most were oligarchic and self-perpetuating, that almost all were exclusively Protestant, and that only one (Tuam) had a Catholic majority. Comprehensive reform took place with the Municipal Corporations (Ireland) Act, 1840, which abolished all of these bodies and replaced those in the ten largest cities by corporations elected on a limited franchise. A second set of urban elective bodies was set up under acts of 1828 and 1854: towns with a certain minimum population were allowed to elect Town Commissioners to make provision for lighting of streets, paving and other local infrastructural purposes.

In rural areas the principal authority was the county grand jury, made up of large property owners selected by the county sheriff (an official appointed, in turn, by the Lord Lieutenant) and responsible for most of the activities that we associate with county councils today. As public intervention grew in the nineteenth century, however, most notably in the areas of poor relief and health, responsibilities were delegated to other bodies. In 1838 the country was divided into 130 Poor Law Unions, each governed by a Board of 'Guardians', of whom some were elected and some held office *ex officio*. The 'union workhouses' through which they administered poor relief still form a prominent feature of the local urban landscape (though they have been converted to serve a variety of other uses today); the dispensaries through which they attended to public health survive to the present; and the rating system by which they were funded formed a lasting basis for local taxation, though much of it was dismantled in the 1970s.

The final stage in the modernisation of the local government system came with the Local Government (Ireland) Act, 1898. This drew up the basis of the system of local government that has survived with some changes to the present by transferring the administrative functions of the county grand juries to new, elected county councils. It also further democratised the franchise for elections to the Boards of Guardians of Poor Law Unions, and introduced a new, lower tier of local government. This consisted of rural district councils (corresponding to the rural portions of poor law unions, except when these crossed county boundaries, in which case the portions of the unions in different counties became separate rural districts) and urban district councils in the larger towns; in the smaller towns, the town commissioners continued. The only significant change in this system before independence was the introduction of proportional representation in 1920 (see Roche, 1982).

The birth of modern party politics

Although the impression is sometimes given that modern party politics began in Ireland in 1922, or at the earliest with the foundation of Sinn Féin a few years before that, this is misleading. The reality is that modern party politics began in the 1880s, and had earlier roots. The growth of party politics in nineteenth century Ireland, indeed, follows closely a pattern of evolution identified elsewhere (Sartori, 1976, pp. 18–24). Three phases in this growth may be identified; the transition between them was marked by significant changes in levels of electoral mobilisation.

In the first phase, political life was dominated by *parliamentary parties,* defined as groups of MPs without any kind of regular electoral organisation to provide support at election time. In so far as parties existed before the 1830s, they fell into this category. These were not parties in any recognisably modern sense; instead, Irish MPs allied themselves after 1800 to one or other of the two great English groupings, the Tories and the Whigs. Already during this period, however, the linkage between the Tory party and the Protestant establishment was beginning to find expression in geographical terms, as Tories achieved a much stronger position in the north than in the south. This may be seen in appendix 2a, which summarises the results of the thirty-one elections that took place under the Act of Union (because of the large number of uncontested elections, we have to rely on distribution of seats rather than of votes for an indication of party strengths). This point emerges even more clearly from Table 1.1, which is based on this appendix: in the ten elections before 1832, Tories already controlled 74 per cent of the seats in the present territory of Northern Ireland, but only 45 per cent of those in the south.

In the second phase we see the appearance of *electoral parties,* consisting not merely of loosely linked sets of MPs but rather of groups standing for some more or less coherent policy positions and supported by constituency organisations that enjoyed a degree of continuity over time (see Hoppen, 1984). This phase began around 1830 and lasted for approximately five decades. It was characterised by the metamorphosis of the Whigs into the Liberal Party, which increasingly became the party of Catholic Ireland, and of the Tories into the Conservative Party, which quickly became the party of Protestants. The members of these parties in parliament were supported by organisations at constituency level. These support groups used such names as 'Independent Clubs' on the Liberal side and 'Constitutional Clubs' on the Conservative side. From a comparative perspective, this was unusual in two respects. First, constituency organisations developed at a remarkably early stage in the Irish case. Second, the content of the liberal–conservative polarisation, with its sectarian overtones, contrasted sharply with the issues at stake behind similarly named instances of polarisation elsewhere in Europe, where constitutional issues (such as conflict between the monarchy and parliament) were to the fore. In particular, the association between Catholicism and liberalism appears anomalous in a European context where liberalism was associated with anticlericalism.

In the context of an electorate restricted to the wealthy (who were disproportionately Protestant), Irish Conservatives (though reduced from their position of overall dominance, especially in the south where they now

Table 1.1 Irish parliamentary representation, 1801–1918

Group (Number of elections)	1801–31 (10)	1832–80 (12)	1885–1910 (8)	1918 (1)
North:				
Tories/Unionists	73.6	78.6	69.5	80.0
Whigs/Liberals	14.1	18.5	2.5	0.0
Nationalists, etc.	—	0.0	28.0	10.0
Others	12.3	2.9	0.0	10.0
(Number)	(220)	(276)	(200)	(30)
South:				
Tories/Unionists	44.5	24.4	3.7	4.0
Whigs/Liberals	41.4	39.6	0.0	0.0
Nationalists, etc.	—	35.3	96.3	2.7
Others	14.1	0.7	0.0	93.3
(Number)	(780)	(980)	(624)	(75)
All Ireland:				
Tories/Unionists	50.9	36.3	19.7	25.7
Whigs/Liberals	35.4	35.0	0.6	0.0
Nationalists, etc.	—	27.5	79.7	4.8
Others	13.7	1.2	0.0	69.5
(Number)	(1,000)	(1,256)	(824)	(105)

Source: Calculated from appendix 2.

Note: Party strengths are indicated as percentages of seats won. Before 1832 party affiliations are approximate only. 'Tories/Unionists' includes Liberal Unionists; 'Nationalists, etc.' includes independent nationalists; in 1918, 'others' refers to Sinn Féin MPs. The north is defined as the present area of Northern Ireland, the south as the Republic. The number of MPs returned by constituencies in the north was twenty-two, twenty-three and twenty-five in the first three periods; in the south it was seventy-eight in the first and third periods and eighty-two in the second period, except for the last two elections, in 1874 and 1880, when the number was eighty.

controlled only 24 per cent of the seats) enjoyed solid support throughout most of this period. The relationship between the Liberals and the Catholic vote was, however, much less secure, and was open to challenge from parties representing specifically Irish interests. The most significant of these were O'Connell's Repeal Party in the 1830s and 1840s, the Independent Irish Party in the 1850s, the rather amorphous National Association in the 1860s and, most importantly, the Home Rule Party from 1874 onwards.

The third phase was marked by the birth of modern *mass parties*. These took the form of tightly disciplined parliamentary groups resting on the support of a permanent party secretariat and a well-oiled party machine: thousands of members were organised into branches at local level, with provision for constituency conventions to select candidates and for a national convention to elect an executive and, at least in theory, to determine policy. This development took place first on the Catholic side, with the formation of the Irish National League (1882) as the constituency organisation of the Home Rule or Nationalist Party. This was modelled on an earlier agrarian organisation, the Land League (1879); another organisational predecessor, the Home Rule League, founded in 1873, had followed the model of the electoral party. On the Protestant side a similar development took place in 1885 with the formation of the Irish Loyal Patriotic Union (from 1891, the Irish Unionist Alliance), to represent southern Unionists, and a range of similar organisations, eventually brought together under the Ulster Unionist Council in 1905, to represent northern Unionists. These parties were prototypes of the party organisations that appeared after 1922 in the south (see chapter 6), while the Ulster Unionist Council continues to the present to constitute the organisational apex of the Ulster Unionist Party in Northern Ireland.

The 1885 election marks the birth of modern Irish party politics. It was characterised by a strict polarisation between Protestant and Catholic Ireland in which the Liberals were completely eliminated, being decisively defeated by the Nationalist Party in competing for Catholic votes. In the territory that was to become the Republic of Ireland, Nationalists won virtually all of the seats. In the north, a geographical balance between Nationalists and Unionists was established that was to persist to 1969, a phenomenon of electoral continuity without parallel in Europe (after 1969, the Nationalists were replaced by the Social Democratic and Labour Party and the Unionists were seriously challenged, most notably by the Democratic Unionist Party).

Nationalist domination of the south lasted for more than thirty years, for most of this period in single-party form (the most important exceptions were the deep divisions within the party in 1890–1900 precipitated by the issue of the leadership of Charles Stewart Parnell and the creation of a small breakaway party, largely confined to Co. Cork, by William O'Brien in 1910). The Irish National League indeed suffered serious consequences from the Parnellite split (the more electorally successful anti-Parnellites setting up their own rival Irish National Federation); but when the two wings of the party reunited in 1900 they adopted a new organisation, the United Irish League, as their constituency body. Nationalist Party dominance in the south was consolidated at local level by the 1898 reforms.

Two important points need to be made about the background to the emerging Irish party system. The first is the relationship between electoral reform and political mobilisation. The appearance of significant new political forces has often been associated with major waves of franchise extension; indeed, it is obvious that new groups that target unenfranchised sections of the population can win their electoral support only if these groups are actually given the vote. Franchise extension alone, however, does not necessarily bring about electoral mobilisation, as the Irish experience vividly illustrates. This may be seen by looking at political mobilisation in the context of changes in the proportion of the population actually entitled to

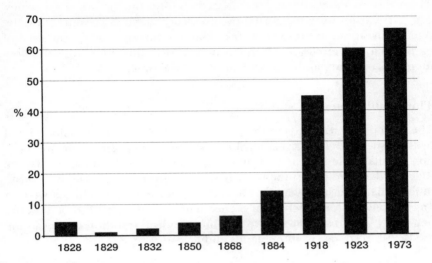

Figure 1.1 Electorate as percentage of population, 1828–1973
Source: Coakley, 1986.
Note: The data refer to all of Ireland up to 1918, but only to the south in 1923 and 1973.

vote, as summarised in Figure 1.1. Thus, the enormous expansion of voting strength that followed from the Catholic Relief Act of 1793 had a negligible political effect; instead, landowners simply had more voters to manage at election time. By contrast, the first appearance of modern electoral parties began in 1830, *after* the huge disenfranchisement of 1829 and *before* the reform of 1832. Again, the wave of electoral rebellion that began in the late 1870s and that marked the birth of modern mass politics took place a few years before the 1884 reform; it was to be seen vividly at the level not only of parliamentary but also of local elections (Feingold, 1975). The major reforms of 1884 and 1918 may, in fact, be seen as permitting the consummation of new voter–party alliances rather than as making the match in the first place. This political mobilisation was not confined to the electoral level; it extended also to the formation of new organisations with mass membership in the economic, cultural, sporting and other domains, and to the growth of a more radical press (see Legg, 1998).

Second, divisions between the main Irish parties corresponded closely to social divisions. Irish political life was dominated by three principal relationships in the 120 years after the Act of Union came into effect: between Ireland and the United Kingdom, between Catholics and Protestants, and between tenants and landlords. By the 1880s the two major parties had adopted fairly unambiguous positions on these issues: the Nationalist Party stood for Home Rule for Ireland, for defence of Catholic rights and for the principle of state intervention to promote the interests of tenant farmers.

The Unionist Party adopted a contrary position on each of these issues. The two parties were supported by two clearly defined communities, the line of division coinciding with the religious cleavage. As an instance of early electoral mobilisation behind monolithic ethnic blocs, this development was without parallel in the Europe of the time.

The establishment of statehood

The Irish political agenda of the pre-independence period was dominated by the issue of Ireland's relationship with the United Kingdom, and election results made it clear that most voters endorsed the policy of 'Home Rule' or devolved government for Ireland. It was not, however, the constitutional nationalist movement but rather a more militant alternative that was responsible for the chain of events that led to the establishment of the new state. We must turn now to this more radical tradition and examine the British response to its demands and activities.

1916 and the republican ideal

For an important section of Irish public opinion, the efforts of the Nationalist Party to win Home Rule for Ireland were not merely futile but rested on a flawed interpretation of the nature of Irish–British relations. This more radical strand shared with mainstream nationalism an interpretation of Irish history that cast the neighbouring island in a negative light: the British presence in Ireland was based on a process of conquest in which foul means had overshadowed fair ones; the lands of Irish Catholics had been confiscated and the Catholic religion had been suppressed; British trade policy had sought to stifle nascent Irish industrialisation in the eighteenth century; the Act of Union had been procured by bribery and corruption; and Britain's indifference to the terrible problems of Irish poverty had been highlighted most vividly in a failure to intervene effectively in the catastrophic famine of 1845–49, in the course of which a million people died and a million emigrated. While there was some substance to these charges, of greater importance than their objective truth or falsity is the fact that they were generally believed: there was a widespread acceptance among Irish Catholics of a version of Irish history that associated British rule with evil, and that largely ignored such material benefits as it had brought. This ideological package was disseminated in the oral tradition and in popular literature and – in a rather bizarre development in the last two decades of British rule – through the national school system, a network of state elementary schools established in 1831 that eventually permeated Irish society.

While Irish Catholic opinion in general drew the conclusion from this version of history that some form of self-government for Ireland was a necessary antidote, the more radical strand referred to above went further. Since British rule in Ireland had been achieved by military force, the argument ran, it could only be reversed by the same means: by armed rebellion, not by parliamentary or constitutional means. Furthermore, since Britain's presence in Ireland was seen as entirely illegitimate, the ultimate goal became a complete break and the establishment of a separate Irish republic. This perspective was reinforced by powerful cultural arguments: among other organisations, the Gaelic Athletic Association (1884) and the Gaelic League (1893) emphasised, respectively, the distinctiveness of Ireland's sporting traditions and its language, and sought to cultivate these to combat English influence.

The most obvious representative of political separatism was the Irish Republican Brotherhood (IRB), established in 1858 and committed to setting up an independent republic by force of arms. In this it followed a tradition of revolutionary activism that could be traced back to the Young Ireland movement that had attempted a rebellion in 1848; it also claimed the United Irishmen of the 1790s as its ancestors, even though their movement and their rebellion in 1798 were Protestant-led and were influenced by the values of French radical democracy rather than Irish ethnic nationalism. Although the IRB's attempted insurrection in 1867 was a failure, it was not without sympathisers in prominent places: many members and supporters of the parliamentary Nationalist Party may well have seen Home Rule as a half-way house to the complete separation of Ireland from Great Britain, and MPs with IRB associations were occasionally elected. Nevertheless, extreme nationalist organisations were unable to challenge the electoral machine of the Nationalist Party. This is clear from the experience of Sinn Féin, a radical nationalist group founded in 1905 by the journalist Arthur Griffith. Its objective was to establish a separate Irish state linked to Great Britain only through a shared head of state, the King; but such electoral success as it had was confined to local level.

A spiral of paramilitary developments began in the years immediately before the First World War. The first stage was the formation in January 1913 of the Ulster Volunteers, organised by the political leaders of Ulster unionism and committed to opposing Home Rule for Ireland. The National Volunteers were founded the following year to support Home Rule, and they quickly came under the control of the Nationalist Party. Although members of both forces joined the British Army in their thousands in the course of the First World War, a breakaway section of the National Volunteers – the Irish Volunteers – engaged in rebellion in Dublin in April 1916 (the Easter Rising) under IRB leadership, declaring Ireland to be an independent republic with the IRB Military Council as its provisional government. The rebellion was crushed within days and appears to have had little popular support, but the circumstances under which its leaders were executed and the harsh treatment of other suspects alienated public opinion. This alienation was reinforced by the government's threat to introduce conscription in 1918 and by a pan-European climate of political radicalism in the closing months of the war. The main beneficiary was Sinn Féin, reconstituted in 1917 as a broad nationalist front under the leadership of Eamon de Valera, the senior surviving commander of the 1916 rebels. Despite military defeat, the 1916 rebels were elevated to the pantheon of Irish nationalism, and Patrick Pearse and the other executed leaders were for long to be regarded as the spiritual fathers of independent Ireland.

As Table 1.1 shows, Sinn Féin gained an overwhelming electoral victory in the 1918 general election, when it won seventy-three of Ireland's 105 seats. Although it is true that a significant number of voters supported the Nationalist Party, demoralisation within the party itself and the fact that the electoral system caused minorities to be under-represented left it with only two seats in the south and four in the north. Sinn Féin won almost all of the remaining seats in the south (see Coakley, 1994).

Hardly surprisingly, Sinn Féin took this result as a mandate to pursue a separatist policy. Its members refused to take their seats in the British Parliament, and instead established their own revolutionary assembly, Dáil Éireann, in January 1919 (see Farrell, 1994). The Dáil ratified the 1916 rebels' proclamation of Ireland as an independent republic, set up its own government under de Valera and in 1919–21 accepted responsibility for a guerrilla war fought by the Irish Republican Army (IRA), reconstituted from the Irish Volunteers, against the security forces. These efforts were reinforced by an attempt, which inevitably had strictly limited success, to set up a separate state and to obtain international recognition for it, especially by bringing American pressure to bear on the British. The Dáil could not hope to control the official Irish government agencies, and its efforts to secure the running of its writ were confined by the size of its own tiny civil service, and by the fact that this could not operate openly. Nevertheless, after the local elections of 1920 it was able to detach the loyalty of most local authorities from the Local Government Board, and it enjoyed some success in establishing a network of local courts (see Garvin, 1996, pp. 63–91).

From Home Rule to partition

One of the reasons advanced to explain the rapid electoral advances of the militants is the failure of the British to make sufficient concessions to constitutional nationalists. It is true that the British had belatedly brought forward Home Rule proposals for Ireland (O'Day, 1998). The first such bill had, however, been defeated in the House of Commons in 1886. A second Home Rule Bill was passed by the House of Commons but was blocked by the House of Lords in 1893. The third Home Rule Bill had to wait until the Nationalist Party again held the balance of power after the 1910 election. Introduced in 1912, it eventually became law in 1914. It proposed to establish a bicameral parliament in Dublin that would legislate in areas of domestic concern (essentially, those covered by the 'Irish' government departments described above), with a separate Irish executive or cabinet.

Ireland would continue to send MPs to Westminster, but their numbers would be greatly reduced.

The implementation of the Home Rule Act was postponed because of the outbreak of war but also for a more fundamental reason: opposition in Ulster. The Protestant population of Ireland did not share the view of Irish history described above, perceiving itself as being connected by a wide range of historical ties to Britain, from where many Irish Protestants had come as colonists in the seventeenth century. In addition to seeing the British link as a guarantee of civil and religious liberties in a Catholic island, many Protestants, especially in the north east, regarded the Act of Union as having brought significant economic benefits and as having assisted the industriali-sation of Belfast and its hinterland; these benefits, they believed, would be threatened by Irish autonomy (see Laffan, 1983; Fitzpatrick, 1998).

Determined political pressure and threatened paramilitary resistance in Ulster, together with support from within the British Conservative party, was sufficient to ensure that the terms of the Home Rule Act would have to be changed. The result was the partition of Ireland by the Government of Ireland Act (1920). This broadly reproduced the 1914 Act but instead of concentrating power in a single capital it made provision for parallel institutions in Belfast (to govern six north-eastern counties that contained 71 per cent of the Irish Protestant population) and Dublin (to govern the remaining twenty-six counties). The Act came into effect in 1921, and was successfully implemented in one of the new states that it created, Northern Ireland, where it formed the basic constitutional document until 1972.

Although the Act proved largely ineffective in the south, its provisions for the government of 'Southern Ireland' formed an important precedent for constitutional development. Alongside the Irish government there was to be a parliament of two houses. The House of Commons was to consist of 128 members elected by proportional representation by means of the single transferable vote. The Senate was to consist of sixty-four members, of whom three were *ex officio* members (the Lord Chancellor and the Lord Mayors of Dublin and Cork), seventeen were to be nominated by the Lord Lieutenant to represent commerce, labour and the scientific and learned professions and forty-four were to be elected by five other groups (the Catholic bishops were to elect four of their number, the Protestant bishops two, southern Irish peers sixteen, privy councillors eight and county coun-cillors fourteen). In the first election to the House of Commons in 1921, Sinn Féin won 124 seats, all uncontested, and interpreted this election and that to the Northern Ireland House of Commons as elections to the 'second Dáil'. Since only four MPs turned up for the first meeting of the legally constituted house (all from Trinity College, Dublin) and two for the sec-ond, it adjourned *sine die*. Although attendance at the Senate was better (eighteen senators attended at least one of its two meetings) it suffered the same fate, and, in the absence of support from any significant group, the Act ceased to have real effect in the south.

It is worth noting that although it has been called the 'partition act', the Government of Ireland Act also sought to make provision for all-Irish institutions. Irish unity would continue to be symbolised by the continuance of certain offices, including that of the Lord Lieutenant, and provision was made for a forty-member inter-parliamentary Council of Ireland, with thirteen members from each House of Commons and seven from each Senate. The responsibility of the Council was confined to a small range of matters initially, but provision was made for it to become an embryonic Irish parliament. Due to opposition from the South, the Council never came into existence and the proposal was formally scrapped in 1925.

The Treaty and the new state

The deadlock between the Dáil and the British government was finally broken following the conclusion of a military truce in July 1921. In the subsequent negotiations between the two sides, a 'Treaty' was agreed in December 1921. This went much further than conceding Home Rule, but stopped well short of permitting complete separation. Instead, a state would be established that would be almost fully independent, but which would be a member of the British Commonwealth and would recognise the King as its head. There would be a representative of the crown to stand in for the King in Ireland, and constitutional provision would be made for a parliamentary oath of allegiance to the constitution and fidelity to the King. Partition would remain, but the location of the boundary line would be determined by an intergovernmental commission; the British would also retain naval facilities in certain seaports. Since two of the six counties and other border areas had Catholic majorities, the Irish negotiators believed that this would result in a major revision of the line of the border, and that this in turn might undermine the viability of the northern state.

Although the Treaty was narrowly ratified by the Dáil in January 1922 by a majority of sixty-four to fifty-seven, the division that it generated was bitter and saw the resignation of de Valera as head of government and the departure of his anti-Treaty supporters from the Dáil. The constitutional position that followed was complex. First, the second Dáil continued to exist, though only pro-Treaty Sinn Féin members now attended. On 10 January 1922 Arthur Griffith was elected President of the Dáil government in succession to de Valera and a new Dáil government was appointed; on Griffith's death on 12 August 1922 he was succeeded as President by William T. Cosgrave. Second, the Treaty made provision for a meeting of 'members of parliament elected for constituencies in Southern Ireland', who duly came together on 14 January for their one and only meeting; at this they formally approved the Treaty and elected a Provisional Government with Michael Collins, guiding force of the IRA campaign and head of the IRB, as its Chairman. On Collins's death on 22 August 1922 he was succeeded as Chairman by Cosgrave. Although

Cosgrave's succession to both of these posts helped to disguise the anomalous existence of two governments, both pro-Treaty, the reality was that there was not complete overlap in the membership of the two. A general election took place in June 1922, however, and when the new (third) Dáil eventually met on 9 September 1922, again in the absence of the anti-Treaty deputies, it removed this anomaly by electing Cosgrave to the single post of President. The Dáil also approved the new constitution on 25 October 1922, and when this came into force Cosgrave became President of the Executive Council (yet another title for the prime minister) on 6 December 1922.

The consolidation of statehood

The new state, then, did not have a particularly easy birth. The remaining chapters in this volume look at the kinds of political structures and patterns of behaviour that have evolved in Ireland since independence. Since the authors have where appropriate set their examinations of contemporary politics in historical context, a detailed overview of post-1922 politics is not needed here. It is nevertheless necessary to review a number of themes that link contemporary politics with the events and institutions already discussed. First, the nature of the independence struggle left the new state with a series of challenges to its legitimacy. Second, a steady evolution took place in the content of political conflict. Third, however, the administrative structures inherited by the new state provided an important bedrock of stability.

Problems of legitimacy

The new Irish state was faced with a formidable challenge to its legitimacy (MacMillan, 1993, pp. 165–85; Prager, 1986). It would be forced to work within the framework of the Treaty while at the same time presenting itself as authentic heir to the republican tradition. This was reflected in the curious anomaly described above: the coexistence for several months in 1922 of a President of the Dáil Government (Griffith) and a Chairman of the Provisional Government (Collins). This was a deliberate attempt by the new regime to claim legitimacy in the eyes of both Irish republicans and British politicians and to fudge the essential incompatibility between these positions; the post-1922 President of the Executive Council could claim continuity with the republican tradition. Partial symbolic success in this is reflected in the fact that, to the present, each Dáil is numbered on the basis of a recognition of the Dáil of 1919 as the first one (the Dáil elected in 1997, for instance, was designated the 28th Dáil even in official circles, though it was only the 26th since the state came into existence in 1922).

This attempt to turn two ways at once presented the state with fundamental challenges from both directions. At one extreme, its birth upset those who remained loyal to the United Kingdom: the sizeable unionist population, which had wished to maintain the political integrity of the British Isles, and the significant population that had supported the Nationalist Party in the 1918 election and would have been happy with devolved government for Ireland within the United Kingdom. Since the union appeared irretrievably dissolved, however, and the spectre of de Valera and the Republicans appeared to be the main alternative to the Free State, many former Unionists and Nationalists switched to a position of neutrality towards (or even support for) the new regime.

At the other extreme, and more seriously, the new regime also offended those Republicans who took the view that the proclamation of a republic in 1916 and its confirmation by the Dáil in 1919 were irreversible. They regarded the Irish Free State as a hideously deformed alternative to 'the Republic', deficient not only because it represented a truncation of the 'national territory' but also because it retained important links of subordination to the United Kingdom, at least at a symbolic level. This issue split the IRA, whose pro-Treaty wing became the core of the new national army; it eventually spilled over into open armed conflict, during a civil war that lasted from June 1922 to May 1923 (see Garvin, 1996). In the course of this, many hundreds died as a consequence of armed clashes, executions and assassinations. In the early stages of the civil war, the anti-Treaty Sinn Féin members sought to undermine the constitutional position of the pro-Treaty side. They asserted that the 1922 general election was not legitimate since the second Dáil (elected in 1921) had not dissolved itself, declared themselves to be the 'second Dáil' and met on 25 October 1922 to elect de Valera once more as 'President of the Republic'. Even after the civil war, this group (now known simply as Sinn Féin) continued to abstain from the Dáil. This fundamental challenge to a new state was not unique to Ireland: in the emerging postwar states of Finland, Estonia, Latvia and Lithuania similar civil wars were fought, though these had a more obviously social content, pitting left against right (see Coakley, 1987).

The building of the new state and its institutions was in the hands of a group of people who supported the political and economic status quo either through conviction or out of political realism. Their cornerstone was the constitution of 1922, which, ironically, they designed and amended in such a way that their rivals could dismantle it after 1932 (by extending the period during which the constitution could be amended by legislation from eight to sixteen years, they in effect gave any parliamentary majority free rein to make fundamental changes; see chapter 3). The core of the new political elite was made up of pro-Treaty members of Sinn Féin, who reorganised under the label Cumann na nGaedheal in 1923 (this had been the name of a precursor of the old Sinn Féin, organised by Arthur Griffith in 1900). Led by Cosgrave, its character was shaped by other strong political figures of a broadly conservative disposition, a conservatism that was reflected in a new, close relationship with the Catholic church. Although the

1922 constitution was an entirely secular document, the new government quickly moved to show its deference to Catholic moral values. Thus divorce was prohibited, restrictions were placed on the sale of alcohol, and censorship of films and publications was greatly intensified. Yet not all policy areas were dominated by conservatism: state intervention in the energy production sector was represented by the initiation in 1925 of the Shannon hydro-electric scheme, for instance, and, in a rather different area, the new government sought vigorously to promote the Irish language.

Although Cumann na nGaedheal struggled to protect the autonomy of the new state and even to extend it in a Commonwealth context, its conservatism in the constitutional arena and its increasingly unreserved defence of the Treaty had two kinds of consequence for political realignment in the 1920s. First, those who had accepted Collins's argument that the Treaty was 'a stepping stone to the Republic' became disillusioned, and broke with the party. This issue was used as a pretext in the 'Army Mutiny' of 1924, when a group of senior officers demanded action from the government to end partition (though other motivations were also present; see Lee, 1989, pp. 96–105). Another division took place on the leaking of the report of the Boundary Commission in 1925 (set up under the terms of the Treaty, the commission recommended that only marginal changes be made to the line of the border). The latter occasion, incidentally, resulted in an agreement between the Irish, British and Northern Irish governments to 'freeze' the border as it stood, and to shelve the idea of a Council of Ireland. Second, however, former supporters of the now-defunct Nationalist and Unionist parties increasingly came to identify with Cumann na nGaedheal, especially after 1927. Many of the former had briefly given their support to a short-lived party, the National League, in 1927; the latter had either remained detached, voted for independent candidates, or, in the 1920s, supported two smaller parties, the Farmers' Party and the Business Men's Party.

One of the most significant developments in the normalisation of the new state occurred following a major split within Sinn Féin in 1926. Support for the party had been dropping off in the mid-1920s as it continued its policy of abstention from the Dáil, and de Valera resolved on an alternative strategy. At the party's 1926 ard-fheis (convention), he proposed a resolution to the effect that, in the event of the removal of the oath of allegiance, abstention from the Dáil would become a matter 'not of principle but of policy'. The resolution was defeated, and de Valera and his supporters broke with Sinn Féin and immediately founded an alternative republican party, Fianna Fáil. The popularity of this move became obvious in June 1927, when a general election gave Fianna Fáil forty-four seats, to Sinn Féin's five.

There were two further stages in this process of political normalisation. On 10 July 1927 a leading minister, Kevin O'Higgins, was assassinated. Among the measures adopted in response by the government was a bill requiring all future parliamentary candidates to declare that, if elected, they would take the oath of allegiance. This left abstentionist parties with a difficult choice: either to enter parliament or to be wiped out. Fianna Fáil decided on the former course, and de Valera and his supporters took the oath in August 1927 in what they described as an empty gesture. Ironically, by thus forcing Fianna Fáil into the Dáil, the government changed the balance of political forces there and, facing defeat, called a second general election in 1927 at which both Cumann na nGaedheal and Fianna Fáil gained, at the expense of smaller parties (see appendices 2b and 2c).

The ultimate stage in political normalisation followed the next election, in 1932. Fianna Fáil became the largest party and, although it did not have an overall majority, it was able to form a government with Labour Party support. This peaceful transfer of power by the victors in the civil war to the vanquished was an important milestone in the consolidation of democracy in Ireland. Within a year, a new general election gave Fianna Fáil an overall majority, and it was to remain in power without interruption until 1948 (see Dunphy, 1995; for later developments within Fianna Fáil see Hannan and Gallagher, 1996).

The early years of the new Fianna Fáil government were characterised, not surprisingly, by vigorous moves to dismantle some of those elements in the constitution that republicans found objectionable. Thus, the oath of allegiance, the right of appeal to the Privy Council in London (a limited but symbolically important restriction on the sovereignty of the Irish judicial system) and the Governor-General's right to veto legislation were abolished in 1933. Although these amendments were strongly opposed by the British on the grounds that they violated certain provisions of the Treaty, the context within which they took place had changed considerably since 1922. A series of Commonwealth Conferences in the 1920s had been moving in the direction of giving Commonwealth states greater independence from London, and these culminated in the Statute of Westminster (1931), which authorised any Commonwealth state to amend or repeal British legislation that affected it.

The character of the constitution was even more fundamentally altered in 1936, when the Senate was abolished and the sudden abdication of King Edward VIII was used as an opportunity to remove almost all references to the Governor-General from the constitution. This left the way open for the adoption of a new constitution, which, although it stopped short of declaring Ireland a republic, made no mention of the Commonwealth and was intended to symbolise the completion of the process of Irish independence, at least for part of Ireland (see chapter 3).

Opposition to a British role in Ireland also extended to the issue of 'land annuities', payments due to the British exchequer from Irish farmers as a consequence of loans taken by them to purchase their holdings under the provisions of the Land Acts of the pre-1922 period. On coming to power in 1932, de Valera simply retained the repayments for the Irish exchequer. An Anglo-Irish trade war followed, with each side imposing import duties on selected goods from the other; it was concluded by a trade agreement in 1938 and British acceptance of a once-off lump sum payment. The second issue was that of the naval facilities that the British had been allowed to retain under the terms of the Treaty. This issue was settled more amicably, also as part of the 1938 settlement: the British ceded control of the ports, thus laying the ground for the policy of neutrality that the Irish government was able to follow during the war.

As these changes proceeded, the original pro-Treaty forces found themselves increasingly impotent. The spectre of extreme republicanism raised by the Fianna Fáil victory in 1932 and the polarised climate of the 1930s formed the background for the formation of a fascist-type movement in Ireland. This was born as the Army Comrades' Association (1931), transformed in 1933 into the National Guard (popularly known as the Blueshirts) led by the former head of the police, General Eoin O'Duffy. The parallels with fascist movements in continental Europe were close: the fascist salute, the wearing of a distinctive shirt as a uniform, anti-communist rhetoric and, most importantly, an authoritarian nationalist ideology. The movement was suspicious of parliamentary government and sympathetic towards a reorganisation of the state along corporatist lines, where the primary divisions would not be between parties but rather between different socio-economic segments, such as agriculture, industry and the professions (see Manning, 1987; Bew, Hazelkorn and Patterson, 1989, pp. 48–67; Cronin, 1997). This development was followed by a further realignment of anti-Fianna Fáil forces. In 1933 a demoralised Cumann na nGaedheal merged with the Blueshirts and another small party, the National Centre Party, to form the United Ireland Party, which quickly became better known by its Irish name, Fine Gael. Led initially by O'Duffy, the party came increasingly to resemble the old Cumann na nGaedheal party, especially after William Cosgrave replaced O'Duffy as leader in 1935. Fine Gael, however, was no match for Fianna Fáil in electoral terms, and its share of the vote dropped until 1948. Then, in an ironic development, its worst-ever electoral performance was followed by its entry into a coalition government; and, even more ironically, this government moved to break the last remaining links between Ireland and the Commonwealth, with the decision in 1948 to declare the state a Republic.

By this stage, then, the anti-Treaty side no longer objected to the terms of the Treaty with its old vehemence, and the pro-Treaty side had actually declared the country a republic. While one might have expected this to copper-fasten the legitimacy of the state, a problem remained. The rump of Sinn Féin and the IRA that survived after 1926 remained adamant in their hostility to the state, which they continued to reject as an illegitimate, British-imposed institution. Instead they continued to give their allegiance to the 'Second Dáil', and then to the Army Council of the IRA, to which the remnants of the 'Second Dáil' transferred their authority in 1938. While this might appear to be of importance only in the world of myth, myths can be of powerful political significance. It is precisely in terms of this myth that the reborn IRA and Sinn Féin were able after 1970 to claim legitimacy for their struggle to oust the British from Northern Ireland (see chapter 2 for a discussion of the concept of legitimacy).

Political issues in the new Ireland

The most visible political conflicts in the new Irish state have already been discussed above; during the 1920s and the 1930s these focused largely on constitutional matters, or on matters pertaining to Anglo-Irish relations. On these issues, the principal line of division was between the pro- and anti-Treaty splinters from Sinn Féin. Other political interests also sought, however, to force alternative issues onto the political agenda, and the pro-portional representation electoral system permitted them to gain significant Dáil representation (see chapter 4 on the electoral system; for an overview of the parties' electoral strengths, see appendix 2b, and Sinnott, 1995; on the contemporary Irish political system see also Chubb, 1992; Hazelkorn and Murray, 1995; Collins and Cradden, 1997; Dooney and O'Toole, 1998; Collins, 1999).

The most significant of these other groups in the long term was the Labour Party, which had been conceived by the Irish Trades Union Congress in 1912 and was finally born in 1922 as a party committed to a moderate policy of defence of workers' rights. The party was marginalised by debates on the national question, on which it was unable to adopt a distinctive posi-tion, and moved quickly into the role that it has retained ever since: that of third party in a three-party system (see Gallagher 1982). In the absence of a significant classical revolutionary left, the consistent weakness of Labour has been remarkable in a European context (see chapter 5).

A second important issue was that of agriculture. In 1922 a Farmers' Party appeared, drawing its strength from the large farmers of the south and east. The Farmers' Party found it difficult to maintain an identity separate from that of Cumann na nGaedheal, and it faded away after 1927. A suc-cessor party with a similar support base, the National Centre Party (founded in 1932 as the National Farmers' and Ratepayers' League), was one of the parties that, as we have seen, merged to form Fine Gael. In 1939 a farmers' party of a rather different kind appeared. This was Clann na Talmhan, originating among the small farmers of the west, which won significant support in the elections of the 1940s and even participated in two governments but which was unable to prevent its voters from drifting back to the two large parties subsequently.

Three other types of political force also fought for Dáil seats. First, espe-cially in the 1920s and the 1930s, a considerable number of independent deputies represented diverse opinions, including those of former unionists and nationalists. Increasingly, however, the support base of deputies of this kind was mopped up by the larger parties. Second, former nationalists made a more determined attempt to regroup through the National League (founded in 1926), which won eight seats in the June 1927 general election. In fact, following Fianna Fáil's entry to the Dáil, the prospect of a minority Labour–National League coalition government, with Fianna Fáil support, appeared to be a realistic possibility. The calling of a snap second election in 1927 put paid to the prospects of this party, however; it lost all but two of its seats. Third, there have been dissident republican parties caused by divisions within Cumann na nGaedheal in the 1920s (the National Group in 1924 and Clann Éireann in 1925) and within Fianna Fáil in the 1970s (Aontacht Éireann in 1971 and, to the extent that it may be seen as a separate party, Independent Fianna Fáil in Donegal from 1973). In contrast to these small groups, another republican party, Clann na Poblachta, founded in 1946 by Seán MacBride, a former IRA chief of staff, appeared destined for greater things (Rafter, 1996; MacDermott, 1998). This party was able to capitalise on post-war disillusion with Fianna Fáil and win ten seats in the 1948 election. But following bitter internal disputes, most notably over the 'Mother and Child' scheme for the provision of comprehensive postnatal care in the social welfare system (on which the party's health minister, Noel Browne, had clashed with the church), its support collapsed in the 1951 election and never subsequently recovered (for minor parties generally, see Gallagher, 1985, pp. 93–120; Coakley, 1990).

It was, indeed, precisely the intervention of Clann na Poblachta in the 1948 general election that ushered in a new era in Irish politics. Fianna Fáil was unable to form a government after the election, and was replaced in office by a five-party coalition supported also by independent deputies, the first 'Inter-Party' government (McCullagh, 1998). In this Clann na Poblachta sat alongside its principal enemy, Fine Gael, together with Clann na Talmhan, Labour and the National Labour Party (a group of deputies that had broken with Labour and maintained a separate party in the years 1944–50). Headed by Fine Gael's John A. Costello, this coalition broke up in disarray in 1951, to be replaced by a Fianna Fáil government. Costello was nevertheless back in 1954, this time heading a three-party coalition of Fine Gael, Labour and Clann na Talmhan. Following the 1957 election, however, Fianna Fáil returned for a second sixteen-year period in office.

The fact that a single party was in power for this lengthy period disguises the extent of change that took place between 1957 and 1973. The period began under de Valera's leadership with a cabinet still made up largely of activists of the 1919–23 period; after a transition under Seán Lemass (1959–66), one of the youngest of those involved in the independence movement, it ended with a younger cabinet led by Jack Lynch and consisting of ministers without direct experience of the civil war (see chapter 9 for an assessment of recent government leaders). The ghosts of the civil war were, however, disturbed by the outbreak of the Northern Ireland 'troubles' in 1969. In a dramatic incident in May 1970 that became known as the 'arms crisis', Lynch dismissed two ministers, Neil Blaney and Charles Haughey, for alleged involvement in the illegal purchase and supply of arms to Northern Ireland nationalists, and, in related developments, he accepted the resignations of two more. Together with the ensuing trial, this incident was to haunt Fianna Fáil for over two decades.

Although the Northern Ireland problem thus ensured that certain traditional issues would remain on the agenda, the post-war period was in general characterised to an increasing extent by conflict over economic rather than constitutional matters. Protests over high rates of unemployment and inflation in the 1950s forced these issues into the political arena, though without translating them into votes for the left. The principal policy shifts were, indeed, a consequence of civil service decisions rather than of public debates; the outstanding example was the pursuit of foreign investment rather than reliance on traditional Sinn Féin-type policies of encouragement of indigenous industry. The most notable landmarks were the announcement of the first Programme for Economic Expansion (1958), the signing of the Anglo-Irish Free Trade Agreement (1965) and the decision to join the European Community (1972).

The sixteen unbroken years of Fianna Fáil rule that ended in 1973 were succeeded by sixteen years of alternation between Fine Gael–Labour coalitions and single-party Fianna Fáil governments; the pattern was broken in 1989, when Fianna Fáil entered a coalition for the first time (for a list of governments, see appendix 3). Some election results of the period were decisive, such as that of 1977, in which Fianna Fáil emulated its 1938 performance by winning a majority not only of Dáil seats but also of popular votes (though ironically party leader Lynch's popularity ebbed quickly afterwards, and he was replaced in 1979 after an intense internal party campaign by Charles Haughey). All subsequent election results were less decisive, however, and brought a new element of unpredictability to electoral competition.

Although the old political issues lived on until the end of the century, new ones arose (see Crotty and Schmitt, 1998). In particular, moral issues acquired increased prominence. Despite the weakness of the secular tradition in Irish society, politicians were increasingly forced to take positions that might place them at odds with the Catholic church. In the 1970s the sale of contraceptives was finally permitted; in the 1980s the issues of abortion and divorce found their way into the public forum, though in both cases referendum results delivered conservative verdicts. The 1990s witnessed more radical constitutional and legislative change. In 1992 the Supreme Court ruled that abortion was permitted by the constitution under certain limited circumstances (see chapter 3), and a proposed constitutional amendment later in the same year designed to negate this interpretation was defeated at a referendum. In 1993 the sale of contraceptives was further liberalised and homosexual activity was decriminalised. Finally, in 1995 a referendum narrowly approved a constitutional amendment removing the prohibition on divorce legislation, and the law was subsequently changed to permit dissolution of marriage on a relatively restricted basis.

These changes coincided with increasing prominence for the issue of women's rights and women's representation in the political domain towards the end of the century (see chapter 12; Galligan, 1998; Galligan, Ward and Wilford, 1999).

If changes reflecting the new secularism of Irish society were the most visible manifestations of the demise of certain values of the old Ireland, they were not the only ones. The changes described above were in part facilitated by a transformation in Irish social structure, itself a consequence of the unprecedented pace of economic growth and the development of levels of wealth undreamt of by earlier generations. Economic development was, in turn, a function of Ireland's changing relationship with Europe. Popular endorsement of the Single European Act, of the Maastricht treaty and of the Amsterdam treaty in 1987, 1992 and 1998 paved the way for Irish participation in a new, European state structure, and implied substantial Irish support for the restriction of formal Irish sovereignty (however imperfectly the issues may have been understood). A sea-change appears also to have taken place in another aspect of traditional nationalist values: in 1998 voters supported by an overwhelming majority a proposal to drop the constitutional claim on Northern Ireland, as part of the Good Friday Agreement of April 1998 (see chapter 13). This was accompanied by an increasing level of southern Irish intervention in the affairs of Northern Ireland, even if this took place in the context of firm guarantees regarding the constitutional status of Northern Ireland as part of the United Kingdom.

All of these developments were reflected not only in policy changes within the traditional parties but also in the appearance of new parties. On the left, the Labour Party was challenged by a form of transformed republicanism. The remnants of the Sinn Féin movement that had survived the 1926 split had been reactivated in the 1950s and the 1960s; in 1970 this small party again split, with a more activist wing breaking away as 'Provisional Sinn Féin' and becoming a major political force in Northern Ireland in the 1980s. The remaining 'official' Sinn Féin was gradually transformed into a radical-left party of secular and, strangely, anti-nationalist orientation, and was renamed the Workers' Party in 1982. After steadily building up its Dáil strength to seven deputies in 1989, this party split in turn in 1992, six of its seven Dáil deputies breaking away to form the Democratic Left. Following losses in the 1997 election, however, the Democratic Left began to reconsider its position, and in January 1999 it merged with Labour.

On the right, a new liberal-type party, the Progressive Democrats, appeared in 1985. Although the immediate cause of the party's appearance was a deep division within Fianna Fáil on Northern Ireland policy and on the issue of Charles Haughey's leadership of the party, the new party managed quickly to establish a distinctive niche for itself: conservative on economic policy, liberal on social policy and moderate on Northern Ireland. It became the first party to form a coalition with Fianna Fáil, after the 1989 election. Although this coalition collapsed in 1992, the party re-entered coalition with Fianna Fáil in 1997. Its small size and declining electoral strength, however, make the future uncertain for the Progressive Democrats, with the party's absorption by Fianna Fáil a real possibility.

The new flexibility within Fianna Fáil and its willingness to contemplate coalition marks a decisive shift in the dynamics of Irish party competition (see chapter 5). Albert Reynolds, who succeeded Haughey as leader of Fianna Fáil in 1992, negotiated an historic coalition with the Labour Party in 1993. In an even more remarkable development, when this coalition collapsed in 1994 it was replaced, without a general election, by a 'rainbow coalition' of Fine Gael, Labour and Democratic Left. Under Bertie Ahern (who succeeded Reynolds as leader of Fianna Fáil in 1994), the strategy of openness regarding coalition possibilities has if anything been accentuated.

Although the more open attitudes to coalition formation and the new issues in Irish politics echo those in continental Europe, the kind of political forces that we find elsewhere in Europe have been weak or absent. In a political system dominated by two successors of a nationalist party and with only a weak Labour Party, there has been little room for the appearance of alternative political forces. It is true that farmers' parties have appeared from time to time, but these proved ephemeral. The most characteristically European phenomenon has been the Green Party, which has established a foothold for itself since 1989. At the opposite pole, the most distinctive phenomenon on the Irish electoral landscape has been the independent deputy; during the 1990s, indeed, it appeared as if independents were to enjoy a new period of influence, as insecure governments turned to them for politically expensive support in time of need.

The administrative infrastructure

If the pattern of politics in post-1922 Ireland shows strands of continuity beneath seemingly dramatic political changes, stability is even more strikingly a characteristic of the administrative system that has lain underneath. As we have seen, the old regime had already built up a formidable administrative infrastructure before 1922, and this was to serve the new state well.

The central bureaucracy continued with little change. Officials transferred from the old regime constituted the core of the new civil service, which for many years consisted of about 20,000 employees. The small number of members of the Dáil civil service (of whom 131 were transferred) made little impact on this, and the character of this body changed very slowly as new staff were recruited. In 1922, 98.9 per cent of civil servants had been recruited under the old regime; by 1927–28 this figure had dropped to 64.3 per cent, and as late as 1934 a majority (50.1 per cent) of civil servants had been recruited to the pre-1922 service (calculated from Commission of Inquiry into the Civil Service, 1935, pp. 3, 9, 138). The fact that so large a body of civil servants could adapt to working in an entirely different state structure owes much to the 'greening' of the Irish civil service that had been taking place steadily since the advent of open competition for recruitment to lower ranks of the civil service in 1876. There had been a deliberate policy of appointing or promoting nationalist-oriented civil servants to senior ranks from 1892 onwards, at least under Liberal administrations (MacBride, 1991; see also O'Halpin, 1987).

The external staff associated with certain departments posed particular problems. Surprisingly, the Department of Education had little difficulty with its body of teachers and inspectors, even though these had been recruited and trained under the old regime. The shift towards ideals of Irish nationalism was not difficult for teachers, since they had allegedly been spreading such ideas even before 1922; the main problem lay in raising their proficiency in the Irish language to a level that would allow them to become effective agents in the state's language revival policy. Matters were different in the area of security. Although the Dublin Metropolitan Police continued until 1925, the more politicised, paramilitary Royal Irish Constabulary (RIC) was disbanded in the south and renamed the Royal Ulster Constabulary (RUC) in the north. The new, unarmed Civic Guard (Garda Síochána) was an entirely new force established in 1922, though it used the administrative structures, buildings and other property of the RIC. It eventually settled into a force of more than 6,000. There was a similarly complete break in the military domain: the withdrawing British army was replaced by an Irish army built up around a nucleus of the pro-Treaty members of the IRA. It expanded rapidly in response to civil war needs, and by the end of March 1923 had some 50,000 soldiers. This number had dropped to 16,000 by the following year, and after 1926 further rapid reduction brought this figure to 6,700 by 1932. Apart from temporary expansion during the Second World War, the army was to remain at this size until the end of the 1960s. Then, following the outbreak of the Northern Ireland troubles and with increased crime in the south, the size of both the defence forces and the police was increased by about 50 per cent in the 1970s, though the role of the former continued to be defined in minimalist terms (see O'Halpin, 1996).

In terms of its structure, the new civil service was a rationalisation of the old one (for case studies of the departments of the Environment and of Finance, respectively, see Daly, 1997 and Fanning, 1978). The twenty-nine 'Irish' departments were reorganised into a smaller number of new departments; but in areas associated with 'imperial' departments the state, while it inherited thousands of civil servants, had to create new structures on the British model (in foreign affairs, defence and finance, for instance). The formal organisation of the new system was defined in the Ministers and Secretaries Act, 1924; subsequent changes (such as the transfer of areas from one department to another, or the creation of new departments) were on a smaller scale, but their cumulative effect was to increase the number of departments under the control of individual ministers from ten in 1922 to fifteen by the end of the century. Of these, six core departments have continued with little change other than in name: those of the President of the Executive Council (renamed Taoiseach, 1937), Finance, External Affairs (renamed Foreign Affairs, 1971), Home Affairs (renamed Justice, 1924), Defence, and Education. The other four core departments of the early service (Local Government, Industry and Commerce, Posts and Telegraphs, and Agriculture) had been replaced by the end of the century by nine departments with rather unstable boundaries. These cover various areas of economic development and planning, management of the public sector, health and welfare, and culture and recreation.

At the level of local government, continuity was even more obvious. The old system continued after 1922, still governed by the principles of the 1898 Act, with only incremental change. In terms of formal structures, the most significant changes were the abolition of poor law unions and their boards of guardians (1923) and of rural district councils (1925), and the transfer of their functions to county councils. This left the state with a system of local government sharply different from the European norm, where local government has typically been two-tiered: an upper level consisting of a small number of counties or provinces, modelled on the French *départements* and acting largely as agencies of the central government, and a lower level consisting of a very large number of communes or municipalities of greatly varying sizes, each one with a local council and considerable administrative powers. Especially after 1925, the latter level was largely missing from Ireland, and the main focus of local representative government was on the county level. While a restructuring of local government was being discussed up to the end of the century, only minor changes were actually implemented.

Post-independence governments have also been disposed to exercise central control to a much greater degree than their predecessors. This may be seen in the first place in a willingness to suspend local authorities and replace them by appointed commissioners (especially in earlier years, allegations of corruption against local authorities were often used as a justification for this). This was the fate of several councils in the 1920s, including those of the cities of Dublin and Cork; Dublin city council was again suspended in 1969. Second, from 1942 a system of 'county management', implemented earlier in the cities, gave considerable executive power at local level to an official appointed by the Local Appointments Commission, itself a central body. Third, although the term of office of all councils was extended in 1953 from three to five years, the elections are regularly postponed by the government. Thus elections should have taken place every five years since 1965, but they have normally been deferred for lengthy periods; instead of end-of-decade and mid-decade elections, they have taken place in 1967, 1974, 1979, 1985, 1991 and 1999.

One of the most significant changes in the area of state intervention lay in the creation of 'state-sponsored bodies' to carry out a range of functions, many of them connected to economic development. The number of such bodies, over which government has only indirect control, increased steadily from an initial four in 1927 to well over 100 by 1990. In part under the impact of European Union legislation designed to encourage competition, however, the substantial dismantling of this semi-state sector commenced in the 1990s, as major public sector organisations began to be sold off to private investors.

Conclusion

It is obvious that the birth of the new Irish state marked a decisive or even cataclysmic shift in Irish political development, but we should not ignore the extent to which its political institutions built on pre-1922 roots. Although there was a sharp break both in constitutional theory and at the level of the political elite, narrowly defined, there was little change in much of the administrative infrastructure. While local government was radically restructured, the civil service, the judicial system and the educational system were merely overhauled; but all continued to be staffed by much the same personnel after 1922 as before.

In this the Irish experience is not greatly different from that in other post-revolutionary societies. Radical though some strands in the independence movement may have been, it was the more cautious, conservative wing that ultimately won power in the new state and shaped its character during the early, formative years. Although Fianna Fáil's victory in 1932 led to some far-reaching changes, the most obvious, long-term effects of independence on the system of government were superficial: the faces and accents in Dublin Castle were different, but the business of government itself was little changed. Indeed, to the extent that the ethos of Dublin Castle is a barometer for the Irish system of government, the twenty-first century may bring further significant change, as the accents of Belfast and Brussels intrude tentatively on the former preserve of Mayo and Kerry.

References and further reading

Bew, Paul, Ellen Hazelkorn and Henry Patterson, 1989. *The Dynamics of Irish Politics*. London: Lawrence and Wishart.

Chubb, Basil, 1992. *The Government and Politics of Ireland*, 3rd ed. London: Longman.

Coakley, John, 1986. 'The evolution of Irish party politics', pp. 29–54 in Brian Girvin and Roland Sturm (eds), *Politics and Society in Contemporary Ireland*. London: Gower.

Coakley, John, 1987. 'Political succession during the transition to independence: evidence from Europe', pp. 59–79 in Peter Calvert (ed.), *The Process of Political Succession*. London: Macmillan.

Coakley, John, 1990. 'Minor parties in Irish political life, 1922–1989', *Economic and Social Review* 21: 3, pp. 269–97.

Coakley, John, 1994. 'The election that made the First Dáil', pp. 31–46 in Brian Farrell (ed.) *The Creation of the Dail.* Dublin: Blackwater Press.

Collins, Neil and Terry Cradden, 1997. *Irish Politics Today*, 3rd ed. Manchester: Manchester University Press.

Collins, Neil (ed.), 1999. *Political Issues in Ireland Today*, 2nd ed. Manchester: Manchester University Press.

Commission of Inquiry into the Civil Service, 1935. *Final Report with Appendices.* Dublin: Stationery Office.

Cronin, Mike, 1997. *The Blueshirts and Irish Politics.* Dublin: Four Courts Press.

Crotty, William and David E. Schmitt (eds), 1998. *Ireland and the Politics of Change.* London: Longman.

Daly, Mary E., 1997. *The Buffer State: The Historical Roots of the Department of the Environment.* Dublin: Institute of Public Administration.

Dooney, Sean and John O'Toole, 1998. *Irish Government Today*, 2nd ed. Dublin: Gill and Macmillan.

Dunphy, Richard, 1995. *The Making of Fianna Fáil Power in Ireland, 1923–1948.* Oxford: Oxford University Press.

Fanning, Ronan, 1978. *The Irish Department of Finance, 1922–58.* Dublin: Institute of Public Administration.

Farrell, Brian (ed.), 1973. *The Irish Parliamentary Tradition.* Dublin: Gill and Macmillan.

Farrell, Brian (ed.), 1994. *The Creation of the Dáil.* Dublin: Blackwater Press.

Feingold, W. F., 1975. 'The tenants' movement to capture the Irish poor law boards, 1877–1886', *Albion 7*, pp. 216–31.

Fitzpatrick, David, 1998. *The Two Irelands 1912–1939.* Oxford: Oxford University Press.

Foster, Roy, 1988. *Modern Ireland 1600–1972.* London: Allen Lane.

Gallagher, Michael, 1982. *The Irish Labour Party in Transition 1957–82.* Manchester: Manchester University Press.

Gallagher, Michael, 1985. *Political Parties in the Republic of Ireland.* Dublin: Gill and Macmillan.

Galligan, Yvonne, 1998. *Women and Politics in Contemporary Ireland: From the Margins to the Mainstream.* London: Pinter.

Galligan, Yvonne, Eilís Ward and Rick Wilford (eds), 1999. *Contesting Politics: Women in Ireland North and South.* Boulder, Colo.: Westview; Limerick: PSAI Press.

Garvin, Tom, 1996. *1922: The Birth of Irish Democracy.* Dublin: Gill and Macmillan.

Girvin, Brian, 1989. *Between Two Worlds: Politics and Economics in Independent Ireland.* Dublin: Gill and Macmillan.

Hannan, Philip and Jackie Gallagher (eds), 1996. *Taking the Long View: Seventy Years of Fianna Fail.* Dublin: Blackwater Press.

Harkness, D. W., 1996. *Ireland in the Twentieth Century: Divided Island.* Basingstoke: Macmillan.

Hazelkorn, Ellen and Tony Murray, 1995. *A Guide to Irish Politics.* Dublin: Educational Company of Ireland.

Hoppen, K. T., 1984. *Elections, Politics and Society in Ireland 1832–1885.* Oxford: Clarendon Press.

Keogh, Dermot, 1994. *Twentieth Century Ireland: Nation and State.* Dublin: Gill and Macmillan.

Laffan, Michael, 1983. *The Partition of Ireland, 1911–25.* Dundalk: Dundalgan Press, for the Dublin Historical Association.

Lee, J. J., 1989. *Ireland 1912–1985: Politics and Society.* Cambridge: Cambridge

University Press.

Legg, Marie-Louise, 1998. *Newspapers and Nationalism: The Irish Provincial Press, 1850–1892*. Dublin: Four Courts Press.

Lyons, F. S. L., 1973. *Ireland Since the Famine*. London: Fontana.

MacBride, Lawrence W., 1991. *The Greening of Dublin Castle: The Transformation of Bureaucratic and Judicial Personnel in Ireland, 1892–1922*. Washington, D.C.: Catholic University of America Press.

McCullagh, David, 1998. *A Makeshift Majority: The First Inter-party Government 1948–51*. Dublin: Institute of Public Administration.

MacDermott, Eithne, 1998. *Clann na Poblachta*. Cork: Cork University Press.

McDowell, R. B., 1964. *The Irish Administration 1801–1914*. London: Routledge and Kegan Paul.

MacMillan, Gretchen M., 1993. *State, Society and Authority in Ireland: The Foundation of the Modern State*. Dublin: Gill and Macmillan.

Manning, Maurice, 1987. *The Blueshirts*, new ed. Dublin: Gill and Macmillan.

Meghen, P. J., 1962. *A Short History of the Public Service in Ireland*. Dublin: Institute of Public Administration.

O'Day, Alan, 1998. *Irish Home Rule 1867–1921*. Manchester: Manchester University Press.

O'Halpin, Eunan, 1987. *The Decline of the Union: British Government in Ireland 1892–1920*. Dublin: Gill and Macmillan.

O'Halpin, Eunan, 1996. 'The army in independent Ireland', pp. 407–30 in Thomas Bartlett and Keith Jeffery (eds), *A Military History of Ireland*. Cambridge: Cambridge University Press.

Prager, Jeffrey, 1986. *Building Democracy in Ireland: Political Order and Cultural Integration in a Newly Independent Nation*. Cambridge: Cambridge University Press.

Rafter, Kevin, 1996. *The Clann: The Story of Clann na Poblachta*. Cork: Mercier.

Roche, Desmond, 1982. *Local Government in Ireland*. Dublin: Institute of Public Administration.

Sartori, Giovanni, 1976. *Parties and Party Systems: a Framework for Analysis*. Cambridge: Cambridge University Press.

Sinnott, Richard, 1995. *Irish Voters Decide: Voting Behaviour in Elections and Referendums since 1918*. Manchester: Manchester University Press.

Townshend, Charles, 1999. *Ireland: The 20th Century*. London: Arnold.

Ward, Alan J, 1994. *The Irish Constitutional Tradition: Representative Government and Modern Ireland, 1782–1992*. Dublin: Irish Academic Press.

2 Society and political culture

John Coakley

It used to be argued that the politics of a particular country can be fully understood by reference to its constitution and to the political institutions for which it makes provision. It is true that in most societies what the constitution says has an important effect on political life; but the constitution does not operate in a vacuum. It is given substance by the set of political values and expectations that are dominant in the society within which it operates. The term *political culture* has been coined to describe this set of attitudes; it refers to fundamental, deeply held views on the state itself, on the rules of the political game and on the kind of principles that should underlie political decision making.

This chapter begins with a discussion of the concept of political culture and an examination of its importance in political life. This will show that political cultural values do not exist in isolation; they are influenced by the social backgrounds and life experiences of those who hold them. We continue, therefore, by looking at the context within which Irish political cultural values have been acquired: we examine the evolution of certain aspects of Irish society. We go on to examine the extent to which this pattern of evolution has generated a characteristic set of political cultural values. Finally, since it is clear that no political culture is homogeneous, we need to consider the divisions within Irish political culture and the impact of the rapid pace of social evolution over recent decades.

Political culture and its importance

It is now taken for granted that political stability depends on compatibility between political culture and political institutions: the way in which a society is governed must not deviate too far from the system of government favoured by the politically conscious public. The political culture of a particular society need not, of course, be supportive of democratic institutions; idealistic attempts to impose liberal democratic constitutions in societies that do not share the kind of thinking that underlies them may well end in failure. This was what happened in many of the new states that appeared in central and eastern Europe after the First World War, in areas outside Europe (for instance, in the British Commonwealth) after the Second World War, and in certain post-communist societies after 1989. What is important is that there be a match of some kind between political institutions and political culture; even authoritarian government presupposes a supportive political culture unless it is to rely entirely on rule by force, as the collapse of the Communist regimes in central and eastern Europe in 1989 showed.

It has been rightly pointed out that 'political culture is one of the most popular and seductive concepts in political science; it is also one of the most controversial and confused' (Elkins and Simeon, 1979, p. 127). The widespread use of the term and the creation of a more systematic theory arguing its central importance in the political process date from the publication in 1963 of *The Civic Culture* by two American scholars, Gabriel Almond and Sydney Verba (see Almond and Verba, 1989a). Although their work has been subjected to extensive criticism on methodological grounds and certain of its theoretical assumptions have been undermined (see Almond and Verba, 1989b; Welch, 1993; Eatwell, 1997), the term 'political culture' has been assimilated into the everyday vocabulary of political science. It is therefore appropriate to look at the kinds of area in which political cultural values have most importance.

A useful starting point is the suggestion by Almond, Powell and Mundt (1993, pp. 9–11, 55–9) that the political system has three principal levels and that these offer an appropriate framework for mapping the contours of its political culture. Furthermore, it appears that these three levels correspond approximately to three layers of values that a person acquires through the process of political socialisation.

- The *system* level refers to the state itself as a geopolitical structure and to people's attitudes towards it. This touches on a person's *core* values, absorbed during childhood and early adolescence, relating to such matters as national identity.
- The *process* level refers to the rules of the political game – the basic constitutional principles that determine how decisions are taken – and the public's view of these. Attitudes to these typically constitute a deep, *inner layer* of values, acquired during adolescence and early adulthood, relating to fundamental principles of government.
- The *policy* level refers to the actual outcomes of the decision making process – the pattern of public policy that is followed by the state – and the extent to which it matches citizens' expectations. This corresponds to an *outer layer* of values, acquired for the most part in adult life, relating to day-to-day political issues.

Research on political socialisation (which examines the processes and agencies by which the individual arrives at these values, through the influence of the family, school or peers, for instance) suggests that core values are almost unalterable, that inner layer values are extremely difficult to dislodge and that even outer layer values (such as a commitment to a particular political tradition, party or ideology) tend to remain relatively unchanged within the individual.

While it might be possible to confine ourselves to describing Ireland's political culture in terms of this framework, it is important to remember that no political cultural pattern comes about simply by accident. The same kinds of forces help to shape it as influence political life more generally. We may group these into three broad dimensions. First, the shape of a country's path of *socio-economic development* is of great importance: the extent to which society has industrialised, the nature of this industrialisation and its effects on social structure. The second dimension is the pattern of *cultural evolution*: the degree to which particular values (such as religious ones) have come to be dominant and the extent to which these are challenged by alternative values (such as loyalty to distinctive ethnic or linguistic groups). Third, a country's *long-term political experience* needs to be considered: external influences, patterns of past domination by distinctive groups and other consequences of the course of history may be of great significance.

In what ways, we might ask, have these factors helped to shape Irish political culture? We can picture their impact at all three levels mentioned above. First, people's perceptions of the legitimacy of the state, especially with reference to their satisfaction with the way in which it reflects their feelings of national identity, are likely to be strongly influenced by all three background factors. Variations in the pattern of socio-economic development, cultural (and, above all, linguistic) homogeneity, and particular aspects of political experience (such as a period of colonial rule) will probably have an impact on people's loyalty to the state. Second, the level of socio-economic development has a major bearing on the form of government adopted in the constitution (more specifically, liberal democracy is said to require a relatively advanced level of development); this is also related to cultural factors (such as religious denominational membership or, more clearly, level of literacy); and, once again, political experience may cause certain systems of government to be regarded as more 'normal' than others. Third, attitudes towards more concrete public policy issues are also obviously related to social background factors. Rapid economic development may promote interclass tensions and therefore conflicting views on public policy, for instance; religious fragmentation may promote conflict over moral issues; and diverging perceptions of history may cause divisions over other policy areas, such as foreign relations.

The pattern of political activity in any society is, then, in large measure a product of the political culture of that society; and political culture is, in turn, a product of a complex interplay of more fundamental societal factors, rather then being an immutable undercushion that shapes behaviour (Garvin, 1981, p. 177). It should not be assumed from this, however, that causation is entirely in one direction. It is true that political culture gives substance to the institutions of state; but the direction of causation may also be reversed. Few states are merely passive victims of their political cultures; most attempt – some with exceptional vigour – also to shape their citizens' political values. This may be done through speeches and other direct cues from political leaders, through central control or manipulation of the mass media or, most powerfully of all, through the education system. The teaching of such subjects as history and civics, in particular, may be a very effective mechanism for attempting to influence or even remould a political culture. Debates about the manner in which Irish history should be taught in schools constitute a good example (Coakley, 1994). Even more fundamentally, a state may in the long term seek to transform its own socio-economic infrastructure or to convert its citizens from one religion to another (and, indeed, sociologists since Max Weber have been conscious of the mutual influence of these two underlying dimensions, socio-economic development and religion).

The Irish state, as we have seen in chapter 1, came into existence in difficult circumstances at the same time as certain short-lived democracies in central and eastern Europe. Since it also shared many structural and historical characteristics with these states, it is important to ask why democratic institutions were apparently able to flourish here. We may find at least part of the answer in Ireland's political culture: in the set of deeply ingrained attitudes that caused Irish people to see democratic institutions and practices as normal and legitimate. This set of attitudes has had a double effect. On the one hand, the close conformity between political culture and political institutions reinforced the structures of the state. On the other hand, precisely because political cultural values normally change slowly, it is likely that these very values will act as an obstacle to future political evolution and that they will have an essentially conservative effect.

In the two sections that follow we look in turn at these two sets of characteristics: first at the set of long-term societal trends that have been relevant for Irish political culture, and then at the nature of this political culture itself. While the starting point of this discussion will be a set of generalisations that have been commonly accepted about Irish society and political culture, we qualify this by looking at the enormous changes that have been taking place in recent decades. This approach oversimplifies the position by temporarily overlooking the heterogeneity of Irish political culture; the last section of the chapter seeks to compensate by turning to the issue of social and political cultural fragmentation.

Stability and change in Irish society

When the first systematic attempts to examine aspects of Irish political culture got under way in the early 1970s, it was still possible to describe Ireland as 'an agricultural country of small, scattered family farms'; the Irish people as being strongly attached to the Catholic church and as adhering to a religion of 'an austere and puritanical variety that is somewhat cold and authoritarian'; and Irish society as being insulated from Europe by an all-pervasive British influence

(Chubb, 1970, pp. 51, 53, 46–7; see also Farrell, 1971, pp. ix–xx; Schmitt, 1973). These characteristics, authors suggested, combined to produce a distinctive political culture which was characterised by such features as nationalism, authoritarianism, anti-intellectualism and personalism. Before going on to speculate in the next section about the extent to which such features survive in contemporary Ireland, we examine in the present section the background characteristics in Irish society that are likely to have had a major impact on political values. The pattern that we will encounter will be one of relative stability until the 1970s, but of accelerating change since then in each of the three domains that we have already discussed: economic transformation, cultural secularisation and geopolitical reorientation (on long-term Irish economic development, see Ó Gráda, 1995, 1997; on Irish society, Breen *et al.*, 1990; Clancy *et al.*, 1995; Goldthorpe and Whelan, 1992).

Socio-economic development

The outstanding characteristic of socio-economic development in Ireland, viewed over the long term, has been a radical change in socio-economic structure. Ireland has not been unique in this; researchers from different disciplines and ideological perspectives have pointed to the central importance of the revolutionary socio-economic transition through which all western societies have progressed, whether this is described as a transition from agrarian (or preindustrial) to industrial society, from feudal (or precapitalist) to capitalist society, or from traditional to modern society. This change may best be appreciated by considering 'ideal types' (theoretical descriptions that do not necessarily exist in reality) of the two kinds of society. It should be noted that these types refer to more or less integrated packages of characteristics spanning a wide range of areas rather than being confined exclusively to economic change as implied in the narrow sense of the word 'industrial'. It has been argued that many western societies have indeed progressed beyond this, into a later 'postindustrial' phase, whose implications for political culture need also to be borne in mind; but our present focus is on the great historical transition from agrarian to industrial society.

Agrarian society has been typified as that in which the population, by definition, is overwhelmingly agrarian (with peasants relying on mixed subsistence agriculture, and the minuscule industrial sector being confined to small-scale cottage industries and crafts); with predominantly rural settlement patterns; mainly illiterate, and with an oral tradition dominated by village-based or regional dialects; with only a restricted transport network; and with poorly developed communications media. In industrial society these characteristics are reversed. The population is overwhelmingly involved in the industrial or services sectors (with large-scale, machine-dependent industry and a small, surviving agricultural sector of specialised commercial farmers); with predominantly urban settlement patterns; mainly or even universally literate in a modern, standardised language; and with a high degree of mobility of people and goods, and of ideas.

A yet more profound difference between the two types of society takes place in the area of social relations. In agrarian society the individual is born into a particular rank in society, kinship group and village, and faces a fixed set of occupational options. Mobility prospects are restricted not just by society itself but also by the individual's own acceptance of his or her existing role as inevitable and natural. In industrial society, by contrast, regardless of the position into which an individual is born, the prospects for spatial and occupational mobility are much greater not just because society is open to this, but because the individual's own perspective allows him or her freely to contemplate such roles. In contrast to agrarian society, where the existing order and the individual's role within it are accepted, in industrial society the typical individual has a capacity to envisage himself or herself occupying an unlimited range of roles.

Where does Ireland fit between the poles of agrarian and industrial society defined above; or might it even have developed so far that it is better described as postindustrial? The data on occupational structure and urbanisation in appendix 1 are summarised in Figure 2.1, which also considers two other variables, language and literacy. If economic development was relatively slow, with Irish society long remaining rural and agrarian, the pace of other aspects of social change was relatively rapid. Although secondary education, in Ireland as elsewhere, was left to private interests or to the church until recent decades, and third level education was of negligible impact until recently, the state intervened at an early stage in primary education. After 1831 an ambitious network of 'national schools' was established throughout the country, and by the end of the nineteenth century the great bulk of children of school-going age were attending these schools. The impact of this system and of the efforts of other agencies on levels of literacy was dramatic, as Figure 2.1 shows. Furthermore, between the 1880s and 1920s the stark cleavage between landlords and tenants (a common feature of agrarian societies) was overcome as the process of state-sponsored land purchase established and consolidated the principle of peasant proprietorship and led to the disappearance of traditional landlords as a class.

The level of educational development in Ireland and the growth of literacy, then, proceeded much more quickly than the more retarded pace of economic development would have suggested. This anomaly draws attention to one of the hazards of viewing socio-economic development in isolation from external relationships and influences, especially those of dependence. Although Ireland (or at least the south) was an economically backward periphery, it formed until 1922 part of one of the world's most advanced industrial states. The British government was prepared to promote a separate agenda for Ireland, overseeing the establishment there of an advanced primary education system and of a developed transport infrastructure that included thousands of miles of roads and railways.

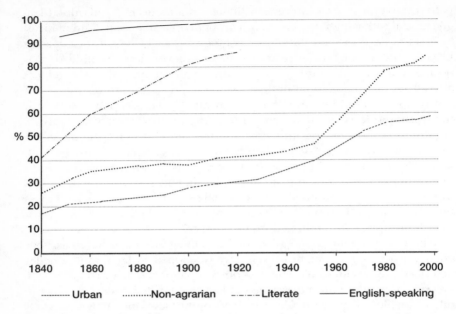

Figure 2.1 Urban population, non-agrarian population, literacy and language, 1841–1996
Source: Census of Ireland, various years, 1841–1996.

British educational policy in Ireland was not disinterested: it also contributed to the anglicisation of the country. The earliest reliable information on the linguistic structure of the population dates from 1851, and shows that already at that time almost all of the population (94 per cent of those in the present territory of the Republic) were able to speak English, and that a considerable majority (61 per cent) were able to speak English only. As the nineteenth century progressed the trend towards anglicisation continued, with the result that by the beginning of the twentieth century virtually the entire adult population was familiar with a single language of wider communication, English.

The right-hand side of Figure 2.1 points to a more recent and particularly striking phenomenon: it shows clearly that, after many decades of relative stability, the period since 1960 has been characterised by economic and social change that is almost revolutionary in scope. The proportion of the workforce engaged in agriculture has been plummeting and the urban population has expanded. The character of the non-agricultural workforce has been changing rapidly. Although the labour force engaged in manufacturing industry increased only slightly between 1966 and 1996 (from 200,000 to 250,000), traditional food and clothing related industries accounted for 52 per cent of this in 1966, but only 28 per cent thirty years later. Over the same period, chemical and metal related industries (incorporating new high technology manufacturing) increased from 20 per cent to 45 per cent. Furthermore, there has been a rapid growth in the services sector: over the three decades after 1966, the insurance, finance and business services sector increased five-fold, while professional services more than doubled (indeed, the rate of increase was even more dramatic within certain high-profile professions: the number of lawyers increased by 275 per cent and the number of accountants by 500 per cent). All of this has been associated with yet another development that is also likely to have a considerable social effect: the growing wealth of Irish society. GDP per capita has been rising more rapidly than in the United Kingdom since 1960, and it has grown faster than the EU average since 1973. As a result, GDP per capita increased from about 60 per cent of the EU average in 1960 to about 85 per cent in 1997, having overtaken the UK level in 1996 (Haughton, 1998, pp. 27–28).

Dramatic though the statistics may be, they do not tell the full story: qualitative changes have also been taking place. The decline in the agricultural sector of the population, for example, does not mean simply that there are fewer farmers; the character of farming is being transformed from a way of life into just another enterprise, as small family farms are replaced by larger agribusinesses. Indeed, rural Ireland as it was traditionally conceived is disappearing as villages in the hinterland of larger urban settlements become dormitory towns. At the end of the 1990s, the national rail/bus service interpreted the Dublin commuter area as being enclosed in a semicircle whose circumference was defined by towns almost 100 km from Dublin: Dundalk, Carrickmacross, Mullingar, Tullamore, Portlaoise, Carlow and Gorey. This erosion of urban–rural divisions is reflected in travel-to-work statistics: by 1996, 44.5 per cent of the working population was travelling five miles or more to work daily.

There are other respects in which the quality of Irish life has been changing. A communications revolution has occurred, with an explosion in access to a new, powerful medium, television, and greatly enhanced geographical mobility as a consequence of the increased availability of cars. The extent of these changes is indicated in Table 2.1, which covers the period 1960–96. The most useful yardstick for interpreting these data is the number of households per hundred people. In 1991, there were 28.5 households for every 100 people, a relatively stable figure; by 1990 the proportion of telephones had reached this figure, and the proportion of cars had reached it by 1996.

The extent of these changes is to be seen also in the educational revolution, which fuelled economic growth as well as being in part its consequence. By 1996 the third level student population numbered more than 100,000, having increased six-fold since 1966. The significance of this figure may be assessed by expressing it as a share of those aged eighteen to twenty, the typical third-level age group: the 1996 student population was 55 per cent of this figure, by comparison with 12 per cent thirty years earlier. The most compelling evidence of change in the level of education of the Irish population

Table 2.1 Telephones, televisions and private cars, 1960–96

| | Telephones | | Television licences | | Private cars | |
	Number	*Per 100 population*	*Number*	*Per 100 population*	*Number*	*Per 100 population*
1960	148,818	5.3	(92,675)	(3.3)	169,681	6.0
1970	291,478	9.8	415,918	14.0	440,185	14.8
1980	650,000	18.9	642,751	18.9	735,760	21.4
1990	967,000	27.4	806,055	22.8	796,408	22.6
1996	1,341,719	37.0	889,358	24.5	1,057,383	29.2

Source: Computed from *Statistical Abstract of Ireland,* 1963–1997.
Note: The earliest data on television licences refer to 1962. To place these figures in context, it should be noted that the number of houses per 100 population in 1991 was 28.5.

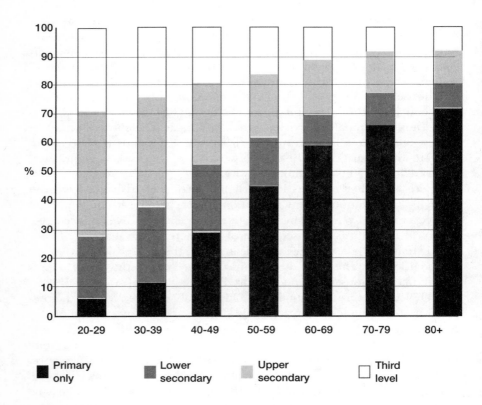

Figure 2.2 Education levels by age cohort, 1996

Source: Calculated from Census of Ireland, 1996.
Note: The data refer to all whose full-time education has been completed.

is presented in Figure 2.2, which depicts the share of each decennial age cohort in 1996 that had completed a particular level of schooling. The level of education increases from cohort to cohort, from those in their twenties (of whom 70 per cent had completed higher secondary education, and many had also completed third level education) to those aged eighty or more (of whom 70 per cent had received primary education only).

Religion and secularisation

In terms of religious affiliation, a great majority of the population belongs to the Catholic church (see appendix 1a). The Protestant population, which in the nineteenth century constituted 25 per cent of the population of the island, amounted to a minority of only 10 per cent in the south after partition. Furthermore, many members of this community had been killed in the First World War; many had been strongly associated with the old regime, and left after 1922; many were landlords who lost their estates or who were subjected to intimidation at around the same period, and who also left; the remaining Protestant population had shrunk to three per cent by 1991. This was a consequence of continued emigration, a low rate of natural increase (in fact, for many decades Protestant deaths outnumbered births) and assimilation to the Catholic community especially through mixed marriages (the children of which have typically been brought up as Catholics).

The position of the Catholic religion within Irish society has been rather remarkable. Unlike the position in central and eastern Europe (the most obvious part of the continent in which to look for comparable societies in an historical perspective), it was along lines of religious denomination rather than of language that political mobilisation took place in the nineteenth century. This arose in part from the perceived (but, in reality, imperfect) coincidence between the two main religions and two ethnic traditions: Catholic Irish natives, and Protestant British settlers. It was also related to the fact that the institutional Catholic church in Ireland up to the nineteenth century was not a major landowner, was not linked with the old regime, and was neutral or sympathetic on the issues of democratisation and nationalism, rather than being suspicious or hostile, as in continental Europe.

In any case, Irish history offers many illustrations of the grip of the Catholic church on the people. Even before the famine of 1845–49, when evidence suggests that only a minority of Catholics attended weekly mass, the church had become intimately involved in political movements, first in the movement for Catholic emancipation, then in that for repeal of the Act of Union, both led by Daniel O'Connell. This involvement continued and intensified in post-famine Ireland. In what has been described as a 'devotional revolution', weekly mass attendance rates began to approach 100 per cent. Already before the new state was founded, Ireland was noted for the remarkable loyalty of Catholics to the church and for the absence of a tradition of anticlericalism (Whyte, 1980, pp. 3–8). This relationship was cemented through the educational system, in which the Catholic church has had an unchallenged role. Catholic identity – the self-perception of Catholics as an oppressed group, with both clergy and laity discriminated against by the state – became an important element of Irish national identity. Like all processes of collective mobilisation, of course, the political integration of the Catholic population had a negative aspect, its differentiation from others; in this case, the excluded group was the Protestant population.

The significance of interdenominational differences for an important aspect of development that has already been discussed, education, needs to be underscored. Historically, a preoccupation with education was characteristic of Protestant, not Catholic, societies; in the former, particular emphasis was placed on the need of every individual to be able to read the Bible and, hence, it was seen as imperative for all to be provided with rudimentary schooling. Evidence abounds from Europe of the enormous differences in Catholic and Protestant literacy levels, and the same trends are apparent in nineteenth century Ireland. In 1861 in the present territory of the Republic, for instance, 47 per cent of Catholics were illiterate, as against only 12 per cent of Protestants. While these figures must be treated with some caution since Protestants were also, in general, of a higher social status than Catholics (and are for this reason more likely to have been exposed to education), they do draw attention to an important aspect of the interplay between cultural evolution and socio-economic development.

It is clear that until the 1970s the level of commitment to traditional Irish Catholicism was extremely high. This was reflected not just in the character of public debate but also in objective indicators such as church attendance, participation in church activities and clerical vocations. The pace of change in the 1980s and 1990s has, however, been dramatic. Those attending church at least once weekly amounted to 91 per cent in 1973–74, but this figure had dropped to the low 60s by the end of the 1990s, by which time only a minority of those aged eighteen to twenty-four were weekly churchgoers. Between 1970 and 1995 the number of clergy had fallen from 33,000 to a little over 21,000, a drop of 35 per cent; but these figures hide a profound crisis in clerical recruitment. In 1996 there were only 111 vocations to religious life, a drop of 92 per cent over a thirty-year period (Inglis, 1998, p. 212). Since a considerable number of those who respond to a religious vocation drop out before taking final religious vows, and since the general pattern is one of decline in religious vocations, the Catholic church has already reached a point where it no longer has the personnel to staff its schools – or, in places, even its churches. Since the age profile of the Irish clergy is rapidly becoming older, the problem of staffing parishes is likely to become progressively more acute. Given the traditional centrality of the priest not just as a religious but also as a social leader in Ireland, the impact of this trend on the character of Irish life will be considerable.

It must be assumed that the decline in clerical recruitment and the lapse in lay involvement reflect changes in underlying patterns of belief. One useful classification of the belief systems of Irish Catholics identified three types:

- *magical-devotional practices*, in which material goals are pursued through traditional prescriptions and formulas, such as prayer, penance and pilgrimages, the predominant type until the nineteenth century;
- *legalist-orthodox beliefs*, in which the emphasis is on strict adherence to Church rules and regulations (as summarised traditionally in the catechism), which became the dominant type in the early twentieth century; and
- *individually principled ethics*, in which an individually reasoned set of ethical guidelines is followed, an approach that began to make inroads in Irish Catholicism at the end of the twentieth century (Inglis, 1998, pp. 12, 20–4).

Inglis argues that elements of all three types co-exist today, though their balance changes over time. The decline in the first element is indicated by falling numbers at novenas, prayer vigils and outdoor processions (notwithstanding an upsurge in popular devotion to Our Lady in summer 1985, when thousands of people congregated at statues said to have been associated with miraculous events), while of 3,000 holy wells recorded, no more than 200 were still in use by the 1990s (Inglis, 1998, pp. 24–30). The number of visitors to St Patrick's Purgatory, an island in Lough Derg that has been famous as a destination for pilgrims since the middle ages, declined from 27,000 in 1988 to 13,000 in 1997 (Irish Catholic Directory, 1998, p. 11). The shift to the third type in the 1980s and 1990s has been marked, and has included 'a reformation of the Catholic Church, or a Protestantisation of Catholic belief and practice', in the sense that Catholics are increasingly guided by conscience rather than by church teaching; and this has been accompanied by a secularisation of Irish social life (Inglis, 1998, p. 204).

Survey evidence records change in the second element in Irish Catholicism, that of legalist-orthodox belief. Agreement with the monolithic package of beliefs enshrined in the Catholic catechism appears to be breaking down; while 96 per cent of Irish respondents in 1990 stated that they believed in God, only 77 per cent believed in life after death and 50 per cent in Hell (Ashford and Timms, 1992, p. 40), figures that would have been inconceivable thirty years earlier. Even the centrality of God in people's lives has been declining, as we may see from Table 2.2: the pace of decline in a perception that God is very important was much more rapid in Ireland than elsewhere in western Europe during the period 1986–94, with only about half of Irish respondents seeing God as very important in 1994.

Table 2.2 Perceptions of importance of God in one's life, 1985–94

Response	Ireland			European Union		
	1985	1994	change 1985–94	1985	1994	change 1985–94
Very important	74	51	-23	43	37	-6
Fairly important	16	22	6	16	16	0
Not very important	5	17	11	16	18	2
Not important at all	5	10	5	25	29	4

Source: Computed from *Eurobarometer* no. 24, 1985, p. 50; *Eurobarometer* no. 42, 1995, p. B60.
Note: Respondents were asked 'How important would you say God is in your life', and were asked to pick a position on a 10-point scale ranging from 1 (not important) to 10 (very important). Responses 1–3, 4–5, 6–7 and 8–10 have been grouped to correspond to the four degrees of importance reported in the table; 'don't know/no answer' excluded.

The decline in religious belief and practice recorded above may be in part a function of the socio-economic changes already discussed. Religious leaders themselves have not been immune from the pattern of value change in Irish society, and scandals associated with the clergy are likely to have further undermined the teaching authority of the church; but it must also be remembered that the falling trust in the church in Ireland is matched by a similar decline in trust in other major institutions (see Hardiman and Whelan, 1998, pp. 82–5). The extent to which traditional church teachings in the domain of sexual morality and the family have been ignored is indicated in Figure 2.3. This shows the sharp increase in the proportion of births outside marriage that began in the 1980s; by the end of the 1990s, more than a quarter of all births were to unmarried women, and this proportion increased in the younger age groups (in the third quarter of 1998, for example, 75 per cent of births to women aged under twenty-five and 50 per cent of births to women aged under thirty took place outside marriage). Notwithstanding the increased availability of contraceptives, the number of abortions has been increasingly steadily (though here our data are based on women having abortions in England and Wales but giving Irish addresses). Marriage breakdown has also been on the increase, and the phenomenon of separated people entering new unions without the sanction of the church has been growing.

Political experience

The dominant element in Ireland's political experience, viewed over a long time span, has been the legacy of British rule, which appears to have left a lasting impact on the Irish political mentality. This is not surprising, given the centuries-long British presence on the island. Whether or not Ireland was a willing recipient, Britain bequeathed to its neighbouring island its dominant language, much of its culture, many of its social practices

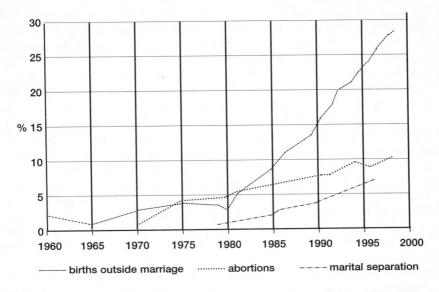

Figure 2.3 Births outside marriage, abortion and marital separation, 1960–1998

Source: Statistical Abstract of Ireland, various years; Office for National Statistics, Series AB no. 24, 1997, *Abortion Statistics for England and Wales; Census of Ireland,* 1979, 1981, 1986, 1991, 1996.
Note: Births outside marriage are expressed as a percentage of all births; abortions (based on British statistics for women having abortions in England and Wales and giving an Irish address) are expressed as a percentage of this figure plus total births in Ireland; marital separation refers to those who have been divorced, separated legally or otherwise or deserted, or whose marriages have been annulled, expressed as a percentage of the ever-married population.

and, most importantly for present purposes, its political vocabulary, concepts, institutions and patterns of behaviour. A large volume of Irish emigration to (and a smaller volume of reverse migration from) Britain has been characteristic of Irish population movement patterns. For long after independence a close economic relationship also remained, with the two countries sharing a common currency until 1979 and with a remarkably high degree of Irish trade dependence on the British market: for several decades after 1922 the greater part of Ireland's imports came from Great Britain, and approximately three-quarters of Irish exports were destined for Britain.

One of the most obvious aspects of the British legacy has been in the domain of language, as we have already noted. The British may have failed to assimilate the Irish to their religion; but where religious proselytism failed, anglicisation succeeded. The Irish language was in a very weak position by 1922, notwithstanding the energetic activities of revivalists. Little effort was made by the new state to halt its decline in Gaeltacht areas, though enormous resources were devoted to providing children in English-speaking Ireland with a rudimentary knowledge of the Irish language. While official statistics thus show a steady rise in the proportion claiming a knowledge of Irish (from 18 per cent in 1911 to 44 per cent in 1996), the language has continued to decay to the point of extinction as a living language. By 1996, less than 43 per cent of the population of the Gaeltacht areas used Irish on a daily basis (calculated from *Census of Ireland*, 1996, vol. 9). From a comparative point of view, the position of the Irish language has been unique and extraordinary. It has been given a powerful constitutional and legal position because of its status as the perceived ancestral language, yet most of the population fail to understand it and very few speak it on a daily basis. Although the language issue was used by the early nationalist movement, it was important as a symbol of Irish identity rather than as a medium of communication. The language revival movement was, strangely, made up overwhelmingly of people whose home language was English, and, by sharp contrast to the position in central and eastern Europe, the language boundary in Ireland did not separate two ethnic groups: speakers of the two languages felt equally Irish.

Geographical proximity and community of language thus continued to promote British influence in Ireland even after 1922. It was not only goods and people that travelled freely to Ireland from the neighbouring island; ideas could also do so. British newspapers have always circulated widely in Ireland. They accounted for at least 10 per cent of daily newspaper circulation in Ireland in 1968, and 21 per cent in 1992 (not including the Irish edition of the *Star*, with 14 per cent); of Sunday newspapers, British titles accounted for at least 40 per cent in 1968, though this figure had dropped to 31 per cent by 1992 (calculated from Chubb, 1970, pp. 124–5; Wilson Hartnell, 1992, pp. 17–18). Irish people's first familiarity with radio and with the powerful medium of television came from Britain, and even with the development of Irish services competition from Britain has been intense, especially on the east coast. In 1997 it was estimated that 98 per cent of Irish homes had television with access to the domestic stations, RTÉ1 and Network 2, and that 70 per cent had access also to four British terrestrial channels. In this 'multichannel land', the market share of British stations was estimated at 56 per cent, compared to 44 per cent for the two RTÉ stations. However, because of the imperfect penetration of multichannel TV, RTÉ's overall market share in the state was 59 per cent, to 41 per cent for the British channels (calculated from *MAPS Directory* 1998, p. 5).

British influence has been imperfectly balanced by countervailing influences from elsewhere. The enormous Irish diaspora in the United States and in other English-speaking countries has had only occasional impact on attitudes at home. Links with the nearer countries of continental Europe, intense by contemporary standards until the eighteenth century, were rather weak in the nineteenth and early twentieth centuries; it is clear from data on the destinations of Irish emigrants that they were oriented almost entirely to the English-speaking world rather than to continental Europe. It is likely that American culture has been making inroads through the powerful medium of television (since the Irish channels carry a relatively high proportion of syndicated American material), but in this the Irish are likely to be only slightly ahead of the British and their other fellow-Europeans.

Paradoxically, the impact of the European Union, which in general has had the effect of breaking down borders between neighbouring countries, has had the opposite effect on Anglo-Irish relations. While the signing of the Anglo-Irish Free Trade Agreement in 1965 represented a further rap-prochement between the two countries and might have been expected to lead to closer bilateral economic ties, Ireland's accession to the EC in 1973 acted as a counterbalance. There was a great increase in travel in general, and especially, in so far as we can measure it, in travel between Ireland and the continent. In 1960 a little more than a million passenger movements out of Ireland took place by ship and aeroplane, and only 7 per cent of them were to destinations other than Great Britain; by 1996 this figure had increased sixfold, and the proportion travelling directly to non-British des-tinations had increased to 28 per cent (calculated from *Statistical Abstract of Ireland*, 1961 and 1997). In addition, Ireland's trade relationships changed dramatically. In 1960, 46 per cent of Irish imports and 61 per cent of Irish exports were from or to Great Britain; by 1996 these proportions had dropped to 32 and 22 per cent, respectively (calculated from *Statistical Abstract of Ireland*, 1961 and 1997). Ironically, although in the long term the significance of the UK–Irish border is likely to diminish, over recent decades it has actually increased: different VAT rates, excise duties and the impact of the break in parity between the Irish and British currencies rein-forced the border. Ireland's participation since 1999 in a European monetary union from which the United Kingdom has stayed aloof is likely to reinforce this trend, if only in the short term. These developments have had implications not only for the British–Irish relationship, but also for the North–South one. The Northern Ireland civil unrest that began in 1968, and in particular the increasingly detached southern attitude towards it, also drew attention to the extent of the gap that had grown even between north and south after two generations of partition.

Ireland's changing political culture

The long-term economic and social processes discussed above have pro-duced a society in which particular patterns of political cultural values are likely to flourish. We consider these at the three levels outlined at the beginning of this chapter:

- the issue of national identity, typically a core value with implications for the geopolitical status of the state (we will examine the extent to which *nationalism* is a key component in Irish political culture);

- the question of attitudes towards democracy and decision making processes, which are typically deeply embedded in the political psychological makeup of the citizen (we will assess the extent to which a commitment to *democratic values* is characteristic of the Irish); and
- the domain of policy preferences, where people's values are less immutable (we will consider three areas, though rather more briefly than in the case of the more deeply embedded values discussed above: *conservatism*, a disposition to support socially and economically non-interventionist policies, *clericalism*, a tendency to defer to the political leadership of the church, and *isolationism*, a preference for a strategy of non-alignment in the area of foreign policy).

It is not our argument that Irish political culture can be reduced simply to these five features; indeed, this list is far from exhaustive. Rather, we will use these as a framework for discussing Irish political cultural values, illustrating the extent to which change has taken place over time in each one. In each case, the discussion begins with an examination of the meaning of the term and its general implications, and continues with an assessment of such empirical evidence as is available: historical evidence of various kinds, electoral evidence and survey evidence. In each case, also, an effort is made to account for this particular feature in Irish political culture.

Nationalism

Although the term is elastic, *nationalism* implies at a minimum a sense of loyalty to one's nation, a type of community with which one primarily identifies. To the extent that this entails a willingness to sacrifice individual interests for the good of the community, this seems socially desirable, but it begs the question as to how the community is defined. If the community or nation with which people identify does not coincide with the state, then loyalty to it is likely to conflict with loyalty to the state (the collapse of the Soviet Union and of Yugoslavia were among the more drastic consequences of this form of conflict). Furthermore, when taken to excess, national loyalty can threaten other forms of human affiliation and can conflict with other ethical and political values (the ethnic 'purification' of Nazi Germany through the extermination of national minorities is an example).

It is clear that as Irish people mobilised politically in the nineteenth century the idea of an 'Irish nation' based in those who were of Catholic, Gaelic background became a central political ideal; its political programme entailed autonomy (or possibly even independence) for the island of Ireland. At this time, Irish nationalism was essentially separatist, and increasingly rejected the legitimacy of the United Kingdom government. The ultimate expression of this attitude followed Sinn Féin's victory in the 1918 general election, when a majority of Irish MPs refused to attend parliament and succeeded ultimately in establishing a separate state. Had the goals of Irish nationalism been fully achieved, it is possible that nationalist sentiment would have faded away or been transformed. As we saw in chapter 1, however, full formal independence was achieved only in 1949, and even then this did not extend over the whole island.

Irish nationalism after 1922 thus became in large measure *irredentist*: achieving territorial unification through annexation of Northern Ireland was a central aim. This was written into the constitution in 1937 in the form of a definition of the national territory as comprising 'the whole island of Ireland, its islands and the territorial seas', and the irredentist policy was vigorously pursued, apparently with significant popular support, in the 1940s and the 1950s. The growing violence in Northern Ireland in the 1970s appears to have convinced policy makers that this form of nationalism was actually subversive of the state; through their efforts, but also as a consequence of other social changes, the intensity of irredentism gradually diminished in the last quarter of the century. Furthermore, a progressive redefinition of the community appears to have taken place: identification with the population of the Republic of Ireland appears to be gradually replacing a form of identification that extended to people living North of the border. It remains to be seen whether the tolerance of other groups (including those differentiated by race) that is associated with the national self-image as a non-colonial state which is a net exporter of people can survive the transition to membership of a post-imperial club in which greatly increased immigration is likely to be the norm.

Electoral evidence broadly supports this interpretation. Even in the turbulent 1920s, support for parties that rejected the new state never significantly exceeded 25 per cent, and the main anti-treaty party's growing electoral success in the later 1920s and in the 1930s coincided with its increasingly moderate stance on the national question. Since 1922, parties organised on an all-Ireland basis have been marginal; notwithstanding rhetorical flourishes at times of emotion or in party constitutions, the mainstream parties appear to be increasingly content with the status quo of partition. By the end of the 1990s it is likely that the irredentist strand in Irish nationalism was on its last legs, in the South at least. The decision by Sinn Féin to abide by the terms of the Good Friday Agreement of 1998 (for which see Box 13.1), to accept the right of Northern Ireland to determine its own future and to grant full recognition to the institutions of government of Northern Ireland, and the party's success in bringing the great bulk of its electorate with it in this remarkable shift, marginalised fundamentalist nationalism. The results of the May 1998 referendums in Northern Ireland and the Republic (in which respectively 71 per cent and 94 per cent voted in favour of the agreement) not only provided a popular mandate for the settlement but also symbolically revoked what fundamentalist republicans had regarded as the irrevocable decision of the Irish people in 1918 in favour of an independent, united Irish republic.

Survey evidence permits us to explore further the character of contemporary Irish nationalism. We may use this, and supplementary information from other sources, to address a number of questions:

- *Irredentism*: to what extent is the demand for territorial unity a continuing feature of Irish nationalism?
- *Patriotism*: in what respects is Irish nationalism a force that is supportive of the state?
- *Ethnocentrism*: to what extent are external groups regarded with hostility?

Perhaps inevitably, one legacy of partition has been increased differentiation between communities on either side of the border. Especially over the past two decades, the psychological gap between the South and Northern Ireland appears to have grown. Although majorities in public opinion surveys still claim to desire a united Ireland, at least in the long term, support for this appears to lack the intensity it once possessed, and measures proposed to bring a degree of unity to the island (such as the creation of an all-Ireland police force) have evoked a hostile reaction in the South. Public reaction in the Republic to violence in Northern Ireland and to its overspill into Great Britain suggested that the former sympathy with the Catholic population of Northern Ireland was dead or dying, and that many southern Irish found it easier to empathise with victims of paramilitary violence in Manchester than in Belfast. There is evidence, however, that following the declaration of the IRA ceasefire in 1994 the psychological distance that separated southerners from the North has lessened, even if years of censorship of militant nationalist perspectives 'left huge gaps in understanding and many unrealistic expectations' (Ruane and Todd, 1996, p. 255).

Survey evidence from 1988–89 confirms the North–South gap, though comparison with an earlier survey in Dublin in 1972–73 suggests that this re-orientation pre-dated the 1980s; there were few differences between the two sets of data. Irish people, it appears, felt considerably closer to English (or British) people than to the Northern Irish of both communities, in terms of willingness to contemplate marriage relationships, close friendship or neighbourliness. Indeed, large numbers felt that Northern Ireland and the Republic were two separate nations (49 per cent agreed, 42 per cent disagreed) and that 'Northerners on all sides tend to be extreme and unreasonable' (35 per cent agreed, though 46 per cent disagreed) (Mac Gréil, 1996, pp. 225, 234).

When we turn to examine the extent to which the character of Irish nationalism may be supportive of the state, it is true that we uncover patterns of patriotism that are in some respects stronger than those elsewhere in western Europe, and that in other respects are weaker. In surveys in 1981 and 1990 the Irish were significantly more likely than other Europeans to claim that they would be willing to fight for their country in the event of war, and a much higher proportion (76 per cent in 1990) declared themselves to be 'very proud' of their nationality; the average for other European countries was 37 per cent (Ashford and Timms, 1992, p. 90). On the other hand, it would be unwise to attribute too much significance to these figures, since in another survey in 1988 only 13 per cent of the Irish (but 30 per cent of those in the European Community overall) felt that 'defence of country' was a great cause worth the trouble of taking risks and making sacrifices for (*Eurobarometer* Special, 1989, p. 5), while observers have also questioned expressions of willingness on the part of citizens of small countries to fight for them (Therborn, 1995, p. 281).

It is, perhaps, the process of European integration that will pose the greatest challenge in the longer term to Irish nationalism. Survey evidence seems to point to the Irish as enthusiastic Europeans. Surveys since 1973 have shown consistently high levels of support in Ireland for EC/EU membership and for the process of European integration, which implies a diminution of the proclamation of sovereignty in the constitution, and the referendum results in 1972, 1987, 1992 and 1998 confirmed this. This tolerance of political realignment appears to extend even to rapprochement with the 'ancient enemy'; closer diplomatic ties since the early 1980s were crowned by the creation of an Anglo-Irish Inter-Parliamentary Council, which the suspicious could see as symbolising the unity of the British Isles, with few signs of public disquiet or even interest. In the late 1990s, and especially since the signing of the Good Friday Agreement, there were signs that surviving anglophobia has receded further. Yet it would be unsafe to conclude that Irish identity is simply being submerged in an emerging European one; the process is much more complex, with Europe providing even for many Irish nationalists an attractive counterbalance to British dominance (see Laffan and O'Donnell, 1998, pp. 173–6). As Table 2.3 shows, there are few signs of Irish people adopting a primarily European identity, and the small portion who do (7 per cent) are comparatively fewer than in the European Union overall (11 per cent).

In Ireland, as elsewhere, there is a darker side to nationalism: it can easily lead to racism and intolerance of non-nationals. Early survey evidence presented a mixed picture. Analysis of a large-scale survey in Dublin in 1972 suggested that there was a 'relatively high level of dormant or latent racialism' (Mac Gréil, 1977, p. 530). Although this had diminished by 1988, the level of ethnocentrism (prejudice against persons belonging to a nationality or culture other than one's own) had actually increased – rather ironically, but not surprisingly, since this coincided with efforts to bring the peoples of Europe together, which itself can aggravate inter-group tensions (Mac Gréil, 1996, pp. 128–32). Of course, mistrust of other races tends to be related to the visibility of racial minorities: a 1990 survey

Table 2.3 Perceptions of national identity, 1998

Identity	Ireland	Britain	European Union
Irish [British, etc.] only	53	60	44
Irish [British, etc.] and European	37	25	41
European and Irish [British, etc.]	4	5	6
European only	3	5	5
Don't know	4	5	4

Source: Computed from *Eurobarometer* no. 49, 1998, p. B26
Note: Respondents were asked 'In the near future, do you see yourself as Irish only, Irish and European, European and Irish, or European only?' (with corresponding questions in other countries).

showed the Irish to have a more tolerant attitude towards immigrants than the typical European one (Ashford and Timms, 1992, p. 14). This was confirmed in a 1993 survey of attitudes towards non-EC immigrants as well as people from other EC countries (*Eurobarometer* no. 39, 1993, pp. A51–4). As late as 1997, surveys continued to convey the impression of Irish tolerance of ethnic minorities. Only 12 per cent said that they would not accept people seeking political asylum in the European Union (lower than the overall figure of 18 per cent for the EU as a whole), while only 19 per cent felt that there were too many foreigners living in Ireland (the corresponding figure in other EU countries averaged 45 per cent; *Eurobarometer* no. 48, pp. 70–1). The reality, of course, is that the proportion of foreigners in Ireland is considerably lower than that in the typical European state, and it remains to be seen how far ethnocentrism remains under control as the number of immigrants attracted by the 'Celtic tiger' increases.

Historical explanations of Irish nationalism have generally referred to the factors considered in the first section of this chapter: Ireland's slow pace of economic and social development was juxtaposed with a much more developed Britain in a relationship of dependency; Catholics resented their heritage of oppression, and the church could see in self-government for Ireland a buttress against 'godless' ideas from across the Irish Sea; and Britain may be said to have governed Ireland with insufficient wisdom to secure Irish loyalty to the united state established in 1800. While these factors have had an obvious and lasting impact on attitudes in Northern Ireland, elements of them appear also to have survived, if in less acute form, in the south; 'normalisation' of nationalist attitudes has proceeded only to the extent that the effect of these factors has faded away. It appears undoubtedly to be the case that self-confidence arising from the Republic's undisputed statehood and economic success has contributed to the erosion of traditional anglophobia, and that the territorial identity of the Republic has been further reinforced by a growing social psychological barrier coinciding with the border.

Democratic values

The existence of a political culture in which *democratic values* are dominant is clearly of central importance for the maintenance of democracy. By this we mean that those who are involved politically must be reasonably well informed about politics and be broadly supportive of democratic institutions. While observers of Irish political culture are agreed that a basic commitment to democratic values is a central feature, they disagree on the extent to which this is modified by other values of a more traditional character.

One book-length analysis of Irish political culture identified authoritarianism as one of its central characteristics (Schmitt, 1973, pp. 43–54); a strong pressure towards political conformism, especially in rural areas, has been noted (Gallagher, 1982, pp. 19–20); and loyalty (to leaders in church and state) and anti-intellectualism (in which a consensus on religious and political values was able for long to continue virtually unchallenged) have been seen as key elements, especially in the past (Chubb, 1992, pp. 18–20). These terms belong to a common category to the extent that each of them implies commitment to opinions received from above, and a suspicion of those who are not prepared to accept these. (The term 'authoritarianism' is used here in a very specific and, perhaps, unusual sense; it is taken to refer not to a particular system of government but rather to a distinctive type of attitude that combines deference to the views of established leaders with intolerance of those who dissent from these views. The source of authority is not necessarily the will of the majority but some principle held to be objective and absolute, transcending individual preferences.)

The second set of political cultural features whose implications for democracy are rather negative appears at first sight to be incompatible with the set just discussed: *personalism* (Schmitt, 1973, pp. 55–64) and *individualism* (Gallagher, 1982, pp. 16–20). Personalism has been defined as 'a pattern of social relations in which people are valued for who they are and whom they know – not solely for what technical qualifications they possess' (Schmitt, 1973, p. 55). This is a more general articulation of the traditional maxim about recruitment: 'it's not what you know that matters, it's whom you know'. It also implies a tendency to evaluate and respond to persons in positions of power (such as the President, the Taoiseach or a local Dáil deputy) in terms of their personal character rather than in terms of the authority associated with their office. Its principal aspects include a closely integrated pattern of social and political relationships, and brokerage politics (see chapter 8). It is entirely compatible with the broader concept of individualism, defined as 'a preference for individual action as opposed to cooperation' (Gallagher, 1982, p. 16), and has the same political consequences. This characteristic is similar to the 'amoral familism' detected by Edward Banfield (1967) in village life in southern Italy – a suspicion of and sense of competition with all those outside the immediate family, attributable to a low level of economic development and a legacy of foreign rule – features also of the Irish experience.

One of the strongest pieces of historical evidence that has been cited in support of the apparently strong commitment of the Irish to democracy has been the very survival of the liberal democratic institutions that were created in 1922. The prospects for democracy in the new states that appeared in Europe after the First World War were not bright: collapse was more common than survival (see Coakley, 1986). In Ireland, objective indicators (such as socio-economic development and political experience) were not promising. The very fact that the state and its constitutional system managed to survive so difficult a birth (see Prager, 1986) is clearly related to the pattern of existing political cultural values, even if this provides only a partial explanation (see Kissane, 1995). Irish voters adopted the country's democratic basic law, the constitution, in 1937, at a time when democracy was collapsing elsewhere in Europe. No significant voice has been raised against democratic institutions and practices, though certain fringe groups and personalities in the 1930s and the 1940s did advocate alternative forms of political organisation incompatible with democracy as we know it.

Electoral evidence relating to the character of Irish democratic values is also positive. Support for anti-democratic parties of the right and left has been negligible, and although individual deputies within the established parties may have wavered at times in their commitment to democracy, the parties themselves have remained firmly within the liberal democratic framework. Data relating to voting turnout confirm the similarity between the pattern in Ireland and that in other democracies. While a larger proportion of Irish people typically abstain from voting than is the case in continental Europe, Ireland compares favourably with other English-speaking countries, with an average turnout rate of 73.2 per cent in the sixteen general elections over the period 1948–97. The evidence for commitment to local democracy is less convincing. Apart from lower turnout levels (a characteristic shared with other western democracies), observers have commented on the high degree of public acquiescence in decisions by governments to postpone local elections, or even to suspend local councils and replace them by appointed commissioners, and one observer has commented that 'the public is relatively unconcerned about local democracy' (Collins, 1987, p. 51).

Survey evidence in general bears out the view that the Irish are relatively supportive of liberal democratic government. The most useful evidence of this kind comes from polls that allow us to look at Ireland in a comparative context. The first such survey, dating from 1970, replicated questions from the classic study of political culture published originally in 1963 (Almond and Verba, 1989a). The researchers found that in certain areas Ireland was to be grouped with countries that had a political culture said to be conducive to democracy (Great Britain, the USA and, to a lesser extent, Germany), though the evidence covered very limited areas: perceptions of the impact of national and local government on everyday life, and expectations of fair treatment by the police (Raven and Whelan, 1976, pp. 22, 24, 46). In other areas, however, the same body of evidence suggested that Irish people have a more relaxed attitude to democracy. In a comparative context, their level of 'subjective competence' (sense of having the capacity to influence the political process at local and national levels) was found to be low (Raven and Whelan, 1976, p. 26).

More recent survey evidence confirms the similarity between Irish attitudes and those in other European states. We may assess this in terms of three areas:

- *Knowledge about politics*: how well informed is the Irish public?
- *Trust in political institutions*: how do the Irish regard the major state institutions?
- *Political tolerance*: to what extent are the rights of minorities and individual rights generally accepted?

Some indicators of Irish people's knowledge of politics are reported in Table 2.4. This shows that the Irish tend to rank higher than Europeans in general in knowledge about political matters. Reported interest in politics was slightly lower than the European average, however, being challenged by religion, which Europeans regarded as being of lesser importance (the

Table 2.4 Knowledge of politics, 1993, and daily news exposure, 1998

	Ireland	EC/EU	Irish–EC/EU difference
Political knowledge, 1993			
Can identify correctly:			
the national capital	99	94	+5
the name of the prime minister	95	94	+1
the role of the head of state	84	81	+3
the capital of the EC	78	72	+6
the number of countries in the EC	49	53	-4
the name of the President of the EC Commission	44	38	+6
Exposure to news, 1998			
watches news every day on television	67	73	-6
listens to news every day on radio	65	42	23
reads news every day in newspaper	45	45	0

Source: Eurobarometer no. 39, June 1993, pp. A32–4; no. 49, September 1998, pp. 11–12.
Note: All figures are percentages.

Irish, and Europeans generally, regarded work, the family, friends and leisure as much more important than politics; *Eurobarometer* no. 39, June 1993, p. A48). Irish people also tend to follow the news as eagerly as their European counterparts, as Table 2.4 also shows, though there is one striking difference: radio seems to be a rather more important source of news than is the case elsewhere in Europe.

In most important respects the Irish are significantly more favourably disposed towards major institutions than their European counterparts. Thus, a 1981 survey showed that the Irish were more likely than the 'average' European to express confidence in the police, the civil service, parliament and the press (Fogarty, Ryan and Lee, 1984, pp. 179, 243). These findings were confirmed from the opposite perspective in a 1990 survey: the Irish were much less likely than the 'average' European to express lack of confidence in these same institutions, except the press; furthermore, Irish people's sense of subjective competence appeared now to be higher (Ashford and Timms, 1992, pp. 16, 98). By 1997 the position had changed, as we may see in Table 2.5: trust in parliament was low, comparable with the position elsewhere in Europe, and trust in political parties was lower still: 72 per cent distrusted them. While the survey from which these findings are derived took place after the first wave of investigation of potential political scandals in Ireland had begun, it is to be assumed

Table 2.5 Trust in selected institutions and in the media, 1997

	Ireland trust	mistrust	EU trust	mistrust	Irish–EU difference (trust)
Institutions:					
Army	83	8	61	27	22
Police	78	19	62	31	16
Charities	65	25	55	32	10
Civil service	61	25	40	49	21
Justice/the legal system	59	33	43	49	16
Church	58	34	50	38	8
European Union	57	18	37	41	20
Trade unions	54	29	38	48	16
Big companies	39	44	36	50	3
The government	39	52	37	54	2
Dáil/parliament	38	52	40	48	-2
Political parties	20	72	16	75	4
Media:					
Radio	73	24	63	29	10
Television	69	29	56	39	13
Press	37	59	40	54	-3

Source: Eurobarometer no. 48, pp. B4-6, B27.
Note: All figures are percentages.

that the scandals that were later uncovered will lead to higher levels of mistrust and cynicism. Interestingly, levels of trust in television and radio are high, as elsewhere in Europe, but the print media are treated with some suspicion.

The cumulative impact of political developments on perceptions of the political system has been relatively positive. A series of surveys carried out regularly since 1973 has shown that a clear majority of those questioned has normally been satisfied with 'the way democracy works' (*Eurobarometer trends* 1974–1993, pp. 27–36, and information from later Eurobarometers). Over the period 1973–89 this proportion (those declaring themselves either 'very' or 'fairly' satisfied) has been relatively stable: it has averaged 53 per cent in Ireland, and 51 per cent in the EU overall. After a once-off dramatic drop in Ireland in March 1991 (to 33 per cent; 65 per cent expressed themselves dissatisfied with the way in which democracy worked at that point), confidence recovered dramatically in the later 1990s. From 1992 to 1998 the level of satisfaction with democracy in Ireland averaged 66 per cent, fully 20 percentage points above that for the EU as a whole. Most surprisingly of all, this level peaked at 75 per cent in spring 1998, at a time when work relating to two tribunals of enquiry into possible political impropriety by senior politicians was getting under way – or, perhaps, because of this very fact.

We have already raised the question of the level of political tolerance that is characteristic of the Irish. Early evidence suggested that this was relatively low. A survey in 1970 found that 61 per cent believed that they would be justified in imposing on others 'something which one believes to be good and right' and 78 per cent agreed that 'certain political groups must be curbed when they abuse freedom of speech' (Raven and Whelan, 1976, pp. 47–8). A large survey in Dublin in 1972–73 led to the conclusion that there was a 'relatively high level of dormant or latent racialism, and a moderately high degree of intolerance against political and social outgroups', as well as 'a considerable degree of general intolerance and authoritarianism' (Mac Gréil, 1977, p. 530). If this were the case in Dublin, it might well be that such attitudes were even more common in rural Ireland. Indeed, as may be seen in Table 2.6, although levels of intolerance in Dublin had dropped by the end of the 1980s, overall levels of intolerance on certain topics continued to be high, and had presumably been even higher in the early 1970s. Some confirmation of these findings emerged in a 1990 poll, where Irish respondents very interested in politics came close to the bottom of a group of ten western democracies in terms of their tolerance of the right to protest (Johnston, 1993, p. 16). Analysis of Irish survey respondents' views on such issues as respect for authority, protection of free speech and the existence of clear guidelines about what is good and evil suggest that 'the level of authoritarianism in Ireland, on these measures, is significantly above the average European level' (Hardiman and Whelan, 1994a, p. 126).

Table 2.6 Authoritarian attitudes, 1972–3 and 1988–9

	Dublin 1972–3	Dublin 1988—9	Ireland 1988–9
Communism should be outlawed in Ireland	54	42	53
A thing is either right or wrong and none of this ambiguous woolly thinking	48	39	52
Men whose doctrines are false should not be allowed to preach in this country	44	42	48
Punks and skinheads should be locked up	39	8	13
Gardaí should be armed always	32	24	30
There should be very strict control of RTÉ	29	38	40
Student protest should be outlawed	25	12	21

Source: Mac Gréil 1996, pp. 390–1.
Note: All figures are percentages agreeing with the propositions.

Since authoritarianism can rest on non-democratic processes of decision making, it is often accompanied by a willingness to rely on mechanisms other than the ballot box to give effect to political decisions. The cult of political violence has, indeed, played a significant role in Irish history, but the evidence suggests that the Irish have buried the rifle. A 1970 survey showed that while a majority clearly opposed the use of force, a large minority (20 per cent) agreed that the use of force was at least sometimes the only way to advance an ideal (Raven and Whelan, 1976, p. 49), while a survey carried out in 1978 suggested that 21 per cent supported IRA activities (Davis and Sinnott, 1979, pp. 97–9). On the other hand, despite the long tradition of revolutionary violence in Ireland, regular surveys since 1976 have shown that Irish people's attitudes to political change are not greatly different from those in other parts of the EC/EU: only tiny minorities are prepared to endorse attempts to change society by revolutionary means (*Eurobarometer trends* 1974–1993, May 1994, pp. 43, 48–9). Survey data from 1990 show that Irish respondents are remarkably similar to those elsewhere in Europe in terms of their attitudes towards conventional forms of protest behaviour (such as signing a petition or attending a lawful demonstration) as opposed to unconventional ones (such as unofficial strikes and occupation of buildings or factories; see Hardiman and Whelan, 1994a, pp. 112–17).

How can we account for these characteristics of Irish political culture? The discussion earlier in this chapter of the impact of socio-economic development implies that the dissemination of such values depends on the transition to industrial society. To the extent that this process was developed, it 'explains' the openness of Irish society to democratic values; to the extent that this process had not been completed, it 'explains' the persistence of authoritarian values. The net effect of the dominance of the Catholic church and of its influence through the educational system is likely to have been a strengthening of authoritarian values. This influence was probably both direct (through the teaching of the value of obedience) and indirect (through a transfer from religious into political life of authoritarian values). Unlike the Protestant churches, the Catholic church is strikingly undemocratic and hierarchical in structure, with instructions issuing from the Pope through bishops and priests to the laity. The source of these precepts is itself sharply different from that in the Protestant churches, with their emphasis on the individual's discovery of the truth in the Bible and decision on action in accordance with conscience; in the Catholic tradition the emphasis is on an objective morality, on which the church is authoritative arbiter, and on collective compliance with rules. One comparative study of the political cultural implications of Catholicism, Islam, Hinduism and Buddhism concluded that it was remarkable that 'the one Western religion among the four is the least conducive to an open, democratic political culture' (Smith, 1970, p. 178).

Finally, the British influence was paradoxical. On the one hand, much of Irish political history was dominated by an Irish nationalist struggle against the British; on the other, this was accompanied by a strong (and in some areas uncritical) admiration for the British way of life and for British political models. It is possible that Ireland's relationship of dependence on Great Britain indeed left a deep mark: nationalist political mobilisation took place at an extremely early stage in the nineteenth century, and it was characterised by passionate loyalty to 'strong leaders' such as O'Connell and Parnell, a tradition that may well have survived. We should also recall that some of the most authoritarian attitudes and most slavish patterns of leadership adulation have developed in 'modern' industrial societies.

Of course, in many respects Irish society is now postindustrial and it is increasingly secular. To a growing extent, it is a 'typical' west European society, and, while survey evidence may point to certain respects in which the Irish deviate from other west Europeans in terms of their attitudes towards democracy, these exceptions must be seen in the context of the overwhelmingly reality that the broad thrust of Irish views in this area is typically European.

Conservatism?

By *conservatism* we mean a leaning in the direction of support for traditional values and in particular, in the context of liberal democracy, a suspicion of state intervention. Conservatives generally support the existing social and political order, favour low rates of taxation and prefer free enterprise to state involvement in the economy.

The historical balance sheet is rather ambiguous on the question of Irish conservatism. In the nineteenth and early twentieth centuries the major political forces in Irish society were radical by European standards: they stood for a dismantling of the existing system of land ownership and for the pursuit of redistributionist policies. Radical egalitarian ideology was reflected in the 1916 proclamation and in the 'democratic programme' of the first Dáil, adopted in 1919. This was widely shared in the new state, especially on the anti-Treaty side. But it is one thing to call for redistribution of wealth when the privileged group can be portrayed as an alien minority whose riches were gained by conquest; it is quite another to continue this call when members of the former underclass have enriched themselves through their own efforts. Egalitarian or socialist rhetoric has been notably muted in Irish society since the new state consolidated its position. On the other hand, conservative ideology has not been vehemently and coherently articulated either; instead, policy makers experimented pragmatically with far-reaching policies of state intervention, and public opinion appears in general to have accepted this.

Electoral evidence indeed points towards conservative tendencies in Irish society, or, at least, towards the relatively underdeveloped state of radicalism. Over the sixteen elections from 1948 to 1997, the two largest parties – both relatively conservative in orientation – have won on average 76 per cent of the first preference vote, compared to 12 per cent for the Labour Party (the rest of the left has been insignificant). It might be more accurate to interpret this as evidence of the weakness of the left rather than of the strength of the right. It is true that Fianna Fáil and Fine Gael identify themselves at European level as parties of the right (they are members, respectively, of the conservative Union for Europe group and the European People's Party, a group made up mainly of Christian Democratic parties), but both parties span a wide range of ideological positions, and neither can be seen as an archetypal conservative party.

Survey evidence has consistently shown that when Irish respondents are asked to identify where they are located on the left–right spectrum they place themselves significantly further to the right, on average, than other Europeans. Although it has been argued that the connotations of these terms may not be the same in Ireland as elsewhere, there is evidence of a close convergence between Ireland and the rest of Europe in terms of the correlation between left–right self-placement and other values classically associated with being on the 'left' or the 'right' (Hardiman and Whelan, 1994b, pp. 162–3). On the other hand, surveys provide little evidence of commitment to ideologies of the extreme right. Indeed, survey data from 1979–83 placed the Irish in clear second position after the Greeks among EC peoples in their willingness to endorse classic economic policies of the left; many more of them were in favour of reducing income inequality (90 per cent), of more government management of the economy (72 per cent) and of more nationalisation of industry (64 per cent) than was the case in other west European states (Inglehart, 1990, p. 255). Data from 1990 position the Irish somewhere in the middle of a group of ten western democracies in terms of their attitude towards heavier taxation of the wealthy (supported by 83 per cent) and provision of jobs by the government for all who want them (71 per cent), though Ireland was close to the top when it came to the view that the government has too much power (51 per cent; Johnston, 1993, p. 13). There appears also to be considerable support for the kind of interventionist policies that have created so large a public sector in Ireland. While the political conservatism of the Irish is, then, undoubted, it coexists ambiguously with a rather pragmatic attitude towards economic development and an egalitarian attitude towards the distribution of resources.

In an obvious sense, this complex mixture of values may be related to the Irish path of socio-economic evolution, with the early disappearance of the traditional landed class, the installation of a strong farming class, late industrialisation and retarded development of class consciousness. It is also undoubtedly the case that the Catholic church, with its traditional horror of communism and suspicion of socialism, has reinforced conservatism; in this context, the recent re-orientation of leading members of the church in the direction of support for more egalitarian educational and social welfare systems has probably come too late to have much impact on deeply ingrained popular values.

Clericalism?

By *clericalism* we mean acceptance of the view that the teaching of the Catholic church possesses such authority that it should be reflected in state legislation: it is argued that the political views of the clergy should be heeded, that the laws should reflect Catholic moral and social teaching, and sometimes that the church itself should be given a special place in the constitution. In continental Europe, clericalism was a political force opposed to the great liberal movement that dated from the time of the French revolution, a movement that stood for the complete separation of church and state and protection of the individual against both.

Historical evidence of the significance of clericalism in Irish political life and its impact on social policy is so well documented that it needs little further comment (see Gallagher, 1982, pp. 12–16, Girvin, 1986, and Girvin, 1989, for short discussions, and Whyte, 1980, for a more extended analysis). For many decades into the life of the new state, public policy was firmly guided by Roman Catholic principles. The Labour Party dropped the expression 'Workers' Republic' from its constitution in 1940 and the government refused to support Noel Browne, Minister for Health, in his ambitious welfare programme in the so-called 'Mother and Child' controversy in 1951, in response to pressure from the Catholic bishops. More significant than the effect of episcopal intervention, however, is the fact that it has had to be used so rarely. On other occasions public opinion was sufficiently supportive of the Catholic position to make clerical intervention unnecessary, and when the bishops did intervene in the two cases mentioned their position was compatible with dominant lay opinion.

Towards the end of the twentieth century, however, the phenomenon of Irish clericalism appeared to be seriously under threat. Although the 1983 and 1986 referendums on abortion and divorce respectively resulted in conservative decisions, the very fact that these matters were subjected to a constitutional poll and the size of the minority vote were themselves indicators of change, and pointers to the ultimate narrow majority in favour of divorce at the 1995 referendum. The liberalisation in 1993 of the laws relating to the sale of contraceptives and to homosexual practices would have been inconceivable in 1973, or, perhaps, even in 1983. The authority of the Catholic bishops in speaking on matters of public morality was undermined by a pattern of social change linked with a climate of public opinion in which the press felt free to reveal that a prominent bishop had fathered a child in the course of a long-running affair. It suffered further as a consequence of a series of scandals relating to sexual abuse of children by clergy.

Electoral data do not readily lend themselves to indicating levels of clericalism in Irish society. In the past, the only parties which were avowedly anti-clerical, such as the Communist Party, were electorally insignificant. Almost all votes were cast for parties that were essentially clericalist; and to the extent that change has taken place, it has occurred within these parties, as first Labour, then Fine Gael and finally Fianna Fáil began to adopt positions that could be seen as being in conflict with official church views. Rather strikingly, fundamentalist Catholic parties altogether failed to make inroads into the space vacated by the secularising major parties in the 1990s.

We scarcely need survey evidence of the intensity of Irish clericalism in the past. Even in the late 1980s, although the authority of the church to express its views in political areas began to be questioned, there remained significant differences between the perceptions of Irish people and of other Europeans on areas in which it was appropriate for the church to speak out: the Irish were much more favourably disposed to the expression of church views (Ashford and Timms, 1992, pp. 34–5). However, it is clear from public opinion polls that many people hold positions of which the church has traditionally been critical, notably in the areas of divorce, abortion and availability of contraceptives, and impressionistic evidence would suggest that popular support for the view that church leaders should be listened to with particular attention has been seriously eroded. An attitude scale on the issue of church–state relations based on 1990 data, indeed, shows little difference between Irish respondents and those in other western democracies (Heath, Taylor and Toka, 1993, pp. 58–9). Given the declining significance of religion in people's lives, as discussed above, it is likely that the decline of clericalism will accelerate. This may be due in large measure to the effects of economic growth and new wealth on individual psychological makeup, but it probably also reflects the greater exposure of Irish society to external influences. The conditions in which the Catholic church could offer spiritual consolation to a poor but happy Irish nation, and provide moral guidance in its struggles in an often hostile world, have been changed out of all recognition.

Isolationism?

As with 'authoritarianism', we use *isolationism* here in a rather special sense: not to refer to a characteristic of the state but rather, for want of a better word, to refer to a predisposition to support a neutral position in the domain of foreign policy (see also chapter 13). This feature, in Ireland as elsewhere, is derived from more profound values, such as nationalism.

Although the new state was anxious after 1922 to maximise international recognition by extending its external involvement in such bodies as the League of Nations and the United Nations, it always stopped short of any hint of participation in an external military alliance. While the justification for this (as expressed in rejection, for example, of NATO membership) was rooted in specific hostility to Britain because of its role in maintaining the partition of Ireland, in time the policy of military neutrality became valued in its own right, and it appears to have been transformed into a canon of Irish public opinion.

Much of the evidence relating to Irish feelings on this subject is indirect. It is notable, though, that political parties have been reticent in tackling the issue of security cooperation, which is an inevitable concomitant of deepening European integration. The frequency with which politicians call for a 'debate' on neutrality but indicate their own views only tentatively suggests a distinct nervousness on the issue, and possibly a perception that people's commitment to the principle is deeply rooted. However, it is true that the dominant parties have been moving to a more accommodating position on the issue of pan-European military alliances, while those parties which adopt an uncompromising policy on neutrality are weak in terms of electoral support, even if they are rather vocal on the issue.

Survey evidence has consistently shown that Irish respondents want control over security and military matters to be retained at national level. A clear majority of Irish respondents in a 1993 survey (71 per cent) wanted decision making in the sensitive areas of security and defence to remain at national level, while this position was supported by only 42 per cent of Europeans (Eurobarometer no. 39, 1993, pp. A26–7). By 1998, the position had scarcely changed: 67 per cent of the Irish, but only 44 per cent of Europeans overall, wanted this form of decision making to remain under national control (Eurobarometer no. 49, 1998, pp. B24–5). Additional survey evidence confirms this commitment to neutrality, even if it is linked to other foreign policy attitudes that imply a willingness to cede sovereignty.

It is probable that this rather complex feature of Irish political culture arises from the country's distinctive 'colonial' and 'post-colonial' experience. But as this experience recedes into the more distant recesses of the collective memory, and as the full geopolitical implications of membership of an increasingly integrated European Union become clear, the depth of Irish commitment to traditional values of neutrality will be put to the test. At elite level, it appears as if there is a much greater willingness than in the past to contemplate participation in military alliances; it remains to be seen how long it takes for these ideas to achieve mass support, or at least acceptance.

A divided political culture?

The discussion up to now has focused on the 'typical' Irish person's political cultural values. Society, of course, is made up of individuals holding a great range of values; while the discussion so far in this chapter has drawn attention to areas where certain values are dominant or where the Irish adopt distinctive positions, we need to turn now to look at those who do not subscribe to these values and examine the extent of fragmentation in Irish society and in its political culture.

Social cleavages

Clearly, economic and social development did not proceed at a uniform pace in Ireland, or in any other society; some groups always lagged behind others, and the process itself created some divisions while perhaps rendering others irrelevant. In the Irish case this process, at least in its later stages, appears to have been associated with elements of a rural–urban and agrarian–industrial clash. It has also promoted divisions within each of these sectors, though many of these remain latent. On the agrarian side, although agricultural labourers, small subsistence farmers and large, commercially oriented farmers have conflicting interests, these are now rarely articulated. On the industrial side, an urban proletariat slowly developed, but levels of politicised class conflict remained low by European standards (though the level of industrial disputes was high). The spurt of economic growth that has contributed to new levels of wealth in Irish society at the end of the twentieth century was not, however, accompanied by any diminution in the gap between rich and poor, and social inequalities remain endemic (see Hardiman, 1998).

In the religious domain, the most obvious historical division was that between Catholics and Protestants, and this survives, even though the Protestant minority is now of negligible size. Within the Catholic community recent decades have seen the growth of secular values; although there is nothing corresponding to the secular subcultures of continental Catholic Europe, tensions between traditional Catholics and those with more liberal beliefs are likely to grow (see Girvin 1997a; 1997b).

Contrasting perceptions of the past were also strongly held by different groups, with unionist, moderate nationalist and republican versions of history coexisting. Similarly, the degree of exposure to British, European and other influences tends to vary with region, class, occupation and level of education. We might expect these features, like the ones discussed in the last two paragraphs, to promote conflicting currents within Irish political culture; to what extent is there evidence for this?

Political cultural cleavages

The most fundamental political cultural cleavage faced by the new state related to the question of *nationalism*. In the early years, a strong 'republican' subculture struggled against the dominant values of the ruling group but, as we have seen, these two sets of values were largely accommodated to each other by 1948 at the latest. On the other hand, it could be argued that as Irish nationalist values became less strident a fundamentalist nationalist subculture, comprising those loyal to the old ideals, has been increasingly clearly defined. The core beliefs of this subculture include rejection of the institutions of government of Northern Ireland, since partition was illegitimate, but also of the institutions of the South, for the same reason (fundamentalist nationalists often refer to the South as 'the Free State'). This ideology rested on the assumption that the Irish people had made an irreversible decision in 1918 in favour of independent statehood, and that armed resistance to anyone who opposes this decision is justified. Many hold to this set of beliefs with passionate commitment (extending to a willingness to engage in an armed struggle or to die on hunger strike).

While it is clear that these views have extensive support among Northern Ireland Catholics, their attractiveness to people in the South is less clear. If measured in terms of support for Sinn Féin in national or local elections, the tradition appears to be marginal. Although the party won four Dáil seats in 1957, that election represented the height of its success in the south. Two candidates were elected to the Dáil in 1981 on a 'H-Block' ticket during hunger strikes in Northern Ireland, but Sinn Féin was unable to hold their seats subsequently, and it was not until 1997 that another Sinn Féin deputy was elected. In any case, the motivations of those who vote for Sinn Féin in the south are complex; in those areas of Dublin where Sinn Féin has done well in local elections, for instance, local issues rather than metaphysical discussion of 'the Republic' are likely to have been crucial. The traditional argument that the Dáil is an illegitimate, British-imposed institution, though attractive to the purists, is likely to have won few votes. In particular, the Good Friday Agreement of 1998 is likely to have brought a large block of fundamentalist nationalists into a position of support for the two existing states, and to have further marginalised those who adhere to the traditional ideology. In any case, as the example of Northern Ireland shows, the cleavage between constitutional nationalism and Irish republicanism pales into insignificance beside the Catholic–Protestant cleavage over national identity. The history of Northern Ireland provides a good example of the force of this cleavage; why has conflict of this kind been so strikingly absent in the south?

A number of contrasts between the northern and southern minorities help to explain this divergence between the two parts of Ireland. In demographic terms, the southern Protestant minority is much smaller and is shrinking rather than increasing as a proportion of the total population. In the socio-economic domain, this minority has traditionally been associated with a position of relative advantage, and has occupied more prestigious positions in a type of cultural division of labour. Politically, it was associated with a programme (maintenance of the union with Great Britain) that was quickly seen to be entirely unrealistic after 1922. Most significantly of all, however, it appears to have been ethnically assimilated to the dominant group. Whereas at the beginning of the twentieth century southern Protestants were a national minority with their own ethnic symbols, myth of history and political programme, today they are essentially a denominational minority, distinguished from the majority mainly in terms of religious practice and belief (Coakley, 1998). In all of these respects, the position of the Catholic minority in Northern Ireland has been the reverse of this.

On the matter of democratic values, there appears to be a considerable degree of consensus, and challenges from groups adhering to sources of authority other than 'the people's will' have been few and weak. Nationalist authoritarianism – the belief that 'the nation' has a collective destiny which must be protected by an elite, if necessary against the wishes of a majority – largely disappeared in the south after the 1930s. Religious authoritarianism – the belief that no electoral or political majority has a right to contravene the 'natural law', as defined, in an Irish context, by the Catholic church – may, however, come to the fore as Catholic values are subjected to increasing challenge. Ironically, though, up to the early 1990s Catholic activists relied on public opinion and referendum results to defend their position, whereas their more 'progressive' rivals sought to bypass these and to use the courts and parliament to bring about change. The ease with which the will of the greater number may be translated into the dictatorship of the majority has not yet become the subject of public debate.

In terms of attitudes towards public policy, there are predictable divisions within Irish society. First, there is clearly a division between left and right, one side supporting interventionist economic policies, the other advocating privatisation and the free market. While the boundary between the two sides is not very precise, and does not correspond entirely with social class or with party political divisions, the two tendencies are none the less real. Second, there is an emerging division between secular and clerical forces, ranging Protestants, liberal Catholics and the non-religious against those disposed to accept church teaching more fully (Girvin, 1993; 1996). Third, there are elements of a division between cosmopolitan and isolationist views, the former arguing for a redefinition of Ireland's relationship with Europe and a reassessment of its policy of military neutrality, the latter defending the traditional position in these respects.

Conclusion

While political culture is an elusive concept and our instruments for measuring it are poor, the survey evidence reported in this chapter is sufficiently compatible with other evidence and with the perceptions of observers to allow us to make some generalisations about the nature of Irish political culture. First, there appears to be a consensus among the population in terms of core values relating to national identity: there is virtually universal agreement on one of the cardinal principles of Irish nationalism (the need for a separate Irish state), and the legitimacy of the Republic of Ireland is therefore now virtually unchallengeable. Second, commitment to democratic values appears to be solidly rooted within people's inner values. The challenge from authoritarianism is weak; nationalist authoritarianism has receded in recent decades, and religious authoritarianism has not yet been articulated in such a way that it constitutes a serious challenge to democratic principles. Third, in terms of people's values relating to principles of public policy, we can detect elements both of stability and of conflict. On socio-economic issues, conservatism appears to be dominant, even if the manner in which it is articulated has changed. On foreign policy issues, there may well be an emerging tension between positions that may be labelled isolationism and cosmopolitanism. Most obviously of all, however, on social and moral issues conflict between clericalism and secularism has emerged as a characteristic phenomenon of Irish life.

Political culture in Ireland, then, resembles that in other west European states rather closely, despite a significant lag in socio-economic development in this country. While the legacy of history and preoccupation with British dominance may have been a particular influence in the past, it is probably the pattern of underlying religious values in a slowly secularising society that will be responsible for the most distinctive elements in Irish political culture in the future.

References and further reading

Almond, Gabriel A, G. Bingham Powell and Robert J. Mundt, 1993. *Comparative Politics: a Theoretical Approach.* New York: HarperCollins College Publishers.

Almond, Gabriel A. and Sidney Verba, 1989a. *The Civic Culture: Political Attitudes and Democracy in Five Nations*, new ed. London: Sage.

Almond, Gabriel A. and Sidney Verba (eds), 1989b. *The Civic Culture Revisited*, new ed. London: Sage.

Ashford, Sheena and Noel Timms, 1992. *What Europe Thinks: a Study of West European Values.* Aldershot: Dartmouth.

Banfield, Edward, 1967. *The Moral Basis of a Backward Society*, new ed. London: Collier-Macmillan.

Breen, Richard, Damien F. Hannan, David B. Rottman and Christopher T. Whelan, 1990. *Understanding Contemporary Ireland: State, Class and Development in the Republic of Ireland.* Dublin: Gill and Macmillan.

Chubb, Basil, 1970. *The Government and Politics of Ireland.* Stanford: Stanford University Press.

Chubb, Basil, 1992. *The Government and Politics of Ireland,* 3rd ed. London: Longman.

Clancy, Patrick, Sheelagh Drudy, Kathleen Lynch and Liam O'Dowd (eds), 1995. *Irish Society: Sociological Perspectives.* Dublin: Institute of Public Administration.

Coakley, John, 1986. 'Political succession and regime change in new states in inter-war Europe: Ireland, Finland, Czechoslovakia and the Baltic republics', *European Journal of Political Research* 14:1/2, pp. 187–206.

Coakley, John, 1994. 'The Northern conflict in Southern Irish school textbooks', pp. 119–41 in Adrian Guelke (ed.) *New Perspectives on the Northern Ireland Conflict.* Aldershot: Avebury.

Coakley, John, 1998. 'Religion, ethnic identity and the Protestant minority in the Republic', pp. 86–106 in Crotty and Schmitt, 1998.

Collins, Neil, 1987. *Local Government Managers at Work: the City and County Management System of Local Government in the Republic of Ireland.* Dublin: Institute of Public Administration.

Crotty, William and David E. Schmitt (eds), 1998. *Ireland and the Politics of Change.* London: Longman.

Davis, E. E. and Richard Sinnott, 1979. *Attitudes in the Republic of Ireland Relevant to the Northern Ireland Problem.* Dublin: Economic and Social Research Institute.

Eatwell, Roger, 1997. 'Introduction: the importance of the political culture approach', pp. 1–12 in Roger Eatwell (ed.), *European Political Culture: Conflict or Convergence?* London: Routledge.

Elkins, David J. and Richard E. B. Simeon, 1979. 'A cause in seach of its effect, or what does political culture explain?', *Comparative Politics* 11:2, pp. 127–45.

Farrell, Brian, 1971. *The Founding of Dáil Éireann: Parliament and Nation-Building.* Dublin: Gill and Macmillan.

Fogarty, Michael, Liam Ryan and Joseph Lee, 1984. *Irish Values and Attitudes: the Irish Report of the European Value Systems Study.* Dublin: Dominican Publications.

Gallagher, Michael, 1982. *The Irish Labour Party in Transition, 1957–82.* Dublin: Gill and Macmillan, and Manchester: Manchester University Press.

Garvin, Tom, 1982. 'Theory, culture and Fianna Fáil: a review', pp. 171–85 in Mary Kelly, Liam O'Dowd and James Wickham (eds), *Power, Conflict and Inequality.* Dublin: Turoe Press.

Girvin, Brian, 1986. 'Nationalism, democracy, and Irish political culture', pp. 3–28 in Brian Girvin and Roland Sturm (eds), *Politics and Society in Contemporary Ireland.* Aldershot: Gower.

Girvin, Brian, 1989. 'Change and continuity in liberal democratic political culture', pp. 31–51 in John Gibbins (ed.), *Contemporary Political Culture: Politics in a Postmodern Age.* London: Sage.

Girvin, Brian, 1993. 'Social change and political culture in the Republic of Ireland', *Parliamentary Affairs* 46:3, pp. 380–98.

Girvin, Brian, 1996. 'Church, state and the Irish constitution', *Parliamentary Affairs* 49:4, pp. 599–615.

Girvin, Brian, 1997a. 'Ireland', pp. 127–38 in Roger Eatwell (ed.), *European Political Culture: Conflict or Convergence?* London: Routledge.

Girvin, Brian, 1997b. 'Political culture, political independence and economic success in Ireland', *Irish Political Studies* 12, pp. 48–77.

Goldthorpe, John H. and Christopher T. Whelan (eds), 1992. *The Development of Industrial Society in Ireland: the Third Joint Meeting of the Royal Irish Academy and the British Academy*. Oxford: Oxford University Press.

Hardiman, Niamh, 1998. 'Inequality and the representation of interests', pp. 122–43 in Crotty and Schmitt, 1998.

Hardiman, Niamh and Christopher Whelan, 1994a. 'Politics and democratic values', pp. 100–35 in Christopher T. Whelan (ed.), *Values and Social Change in Ireland*. Dublin: Gill and Macmillan.

Hardiman, Niamh and Christopher Whelan, 1994b. 'Values and poltical partisanship', pp. 136–86 in Christopher T. Whelan (ed.), *Values and Social Change in Ireland*. Dublin: Gill and Macmillan.

Hardiman, Niamh and Christopher Whelan, 1998. 'Changing values', pp. 66–85 in Crotty and Schmitt, 1998.

Haughton, Jonathan, 1998. 'The dynamics of economic change', pp. 27–50 in Crotty and Schmitt, 1998.

Heath, Anthony, Bridget Taylor and Gabor Toka, 1993. 'Religion, morality and politics', pp. 49–80 in Roger Jowell, Lindsay Brook and Lizanne Dowds with Daphne Arendt (eds), *International Social Attitudes: the 10th BSA Report*. Aldershot: Dartmouth.

Inglehart, Ronald, 1990. *Culture Shift in Advanced Industrial Society*. Princeton, N.J.: Princeton University Press.

Inglis, Tom, 1998. *Moral Monopoly: the Catholic Church in Modern Irish Society*, 2nd ed. Dublin: UCD Press.

Irish Catholic Directory, 1998. *Irish Catholic Directory*. Dublin: Veritas.

Johnston, Michael, 1993. 'Disengaging from democracy', pp. 1–22 in Roger Jowell, Lindsay Brook and Lizanne Dowds with Daphne Arendt (eds), *International Social Attitudes: the 10th BSA Report*. Aldershot: Dartmouth.

Kissane, Bill, 1995. 'The not-so-amazing case of Irish democracy', *Irish Political Studies* 10, pp. 43–68.

Laffan, Brigid and Rory O'Donnell, 1998. 'Ireland and the growth of international governance', pp. 156–77 in Crotty and Schmitt, 1998.

Mac Gréil, Mícheál, 1977. *Prejudice and Tolerance in Ireland*. Dublin: Research Section, College of Industrial Relations.

Mac Gréil, Mícheál, 1996. *Prejudice in Ireland Revisited*. Maynooth: Survey and Research Unit, St Patrick's College.

MAPS Directory, 1998. *MAPS Directory 1998/1999*. Dublin: Association of Advertisers in Ireland.

Ó Gráda, Cormac, 1995. *Ireland: a New Economic History, 1780–1939*. Oxford: Clarendon Press.

Ó Gráda, Cormac, 1997. *A Rocky Road: the Irish Economy since the 1920s*. Manchester: Manchester University Press.

Prager, Jeffrey, 1986. *Building Democracy in Ireland: Political Order and Cultural Integration in a Newly Independent Nation*. Cambridge: Cambridge University Press.

Raven, John and C. T. Whelan; Paul A. Pfretzschner and Donald M. Borock, 1976. *Political Culture in Ireland: the Views of Two Generations*. Dublin: Institute of Public Administration.

Ruane, Joseph and Jennifer Todd, 1996. *The Dynamics of Conflict in Northern Ireland:*

Power, Conflict and Emancipation. Cambridge: Cambridge University Press.

Schmitt, David E., 1973. *The Irony of Irish Democracy: the Impact of Political Culture on Administrative and Democratic Political Development in Ireland.* Lexington: Lexington Books.

Smith, Donald Eugene, 1970. *Religion and Political Development: an Analytic Study.* Boston, Mass.: Little, Brown.

Therborn, Goran, 1995. *European Modernity and Beyond.* London: Sage.

Welch, Stephen, 1993. *The Concept of Political Culture.* Basingstoke: Macmillan.

Whyte, J. H., 1980. *Church and State in Modern Ireland 1923–1979,* 2nd ed. Dublin: Gill and Macmillan.

Wilson Hartnell, 1992. *The Irish Market: Facts and Figures,* 8th ed. Dublin: Wilson Hartnell Advertising.

3   The changing constitution

Michael Gallagher

Constitutions play an important part in determining the nature of politics
in liberal democracies. They lay down the ground rules about how political
power is attained and how it can be exercised, about what governments
can do and what they cannot. They also set out rights of the citizens and,
in addition, often specify certain values, held to be central to the country's
political culture, and deem it the duty of the state to aim to promote or
defend them. Although most countries – Britain, Israel and New Zealand
are among the best known exceptions – possess a document called 'The
Constitution', in practice every country's constitution contains both a written and an unwritten component. That is, there are aspects of a country's
political system that, perhaps through precedent and convention, have
acquired the status of firm rules, even though they are not explicitly written into 'The Constitution'. For this reason, we cannot expect to get a full
picture of the way in which a country's politics operate just by studying its
written constitution, which often, for example, takes little or no cognisance
of central features of modern politics such as large and disciplined political
parties. Consequently, in this chapter we shall not examine constitutional
features that regulate, for example, relations between government and
parliament, or the rules governing the election of parliament – these are
covered in other chapters of this book – but will concentrate on the evolution of the constitution.

Constitutionalism – that is, the idea that the rulers are bound by rules
that are not easy to change, and that certain fundamental rights of the
citizens are protected absolutely, or almost absolutely – is an integral feature
of contemporary liberal democracies, and yet in some ways there is an
inherent tension between constitutionalism and democracy (Murphy,
1993, pp. 3–6; Holmes, 1988, pp. 196–8). Constitutionalism prevents the
people, or their elected representatives, from carrying out certain policies
that might have majority support, and can be criticised as 'rule by the
dead', whose values the constitution embodies. Critics of constitutionalism
such as Martin Shapiro (quoted in Holmes, 1988, p. 197) argue that
when we examine a law we should ask not 'is it constitutional?' but 'do
we want it to be constitutional?'; we should not be guided by 'certain

dead gentlemen who could not possibly have envisaged our current circumstances' but instead should be guided by our collective decision
about what sort of community we want to become. Defenders of the principle argue that there are certain rights that are so fundamental that they
should be protected even against the wishes of a majority that wants them
set aside. Although most liberal democracies feel that they have established a reasonable balance between constitutionalism and democracy,
the tension undoubtedly exists, and has at times clearly manifested itself
in Ireland.

The background: the Irish Free State constitution

Ireland's constitution (Bunreacht na hÉireann) dates from 1937 and,
despite significant innovations, marked a development of previous constitutional experience rather than a decisive break with it. Its precursor, the
1922 Irish Free State constitution, was drawn up under the terms of the
Anglo-Irish Treaty, and so the British government insisted on modifications
to the version that had been produced by the Provisional Government,
so as to ensure that it contained nothing that conflicted with the Treaty
(for the Irish Free State constitution see Ward, 1994, pp. 167–238). As a
result, the final document was rather different from what the Irish government would have wanted (for an overview, see Farrell, 1988b). This
British pressure manifested itself particularly in those articles that provided for a Governor-General, representing the Crown, and for the terms
of an oath that all members of the Oireachtas (parliament) had to take,
swearing to 'be faithful to HM King George V, his heirs and successors'.
The Free State was declared to be a member of the British
Commonwealth, and the constitution provided for an upper house, the
Seanad, that was designed to give strong representation to the Protestant
minority. Moreover, the introductory section of the Act establishing the
constitution stated that if any provision of the constitution was, even after
the British government's legal officers had scrutinised the document
with a fine toothcomb, in conflict with the Anglo-Irish Treaty, that provision was 'absolutely void and inoperative'.

Apart from these articles representing the result of arm-twisting by the
British, the broad outlines of the governmental system also showed a
strong British influence, as the constitution provided for government by a
cabinet (the Executive Council), chaired by a prime minister (the
President of the Executive Council). There were none of the rhetorical
flourishes to be found in the 1937 constitution, and, unlike that document,
the Irish Free State constitution was explicitly neutral as between religious
denominations and, despite pressure from some quarters to make it so,
could not have been described as a 'Catholic constitution'.

But although in some ways the constitution marked an attempt to codify
some central aspects of the Westminster model of government, it by no

means represented a slavish acceptance of British practice. Mainly due to a desire to avoid an over-centralisation of power in the cabinet, the constitution contained some features designed to make the parliament more accountable to the people, and the government more accountable to the parliament, than was the case in the United Kingdom.

One of these was a proportional representation (PR) electoral system (the background to its adoption in Ireland is outlined in chapter 4). There was also provision for referendums on both laws and constitutional amendments, for the 'legislative initiative' (under which, if enough voters signed a petition calling for a particular change in the law, the Oireachtas would have either to make the change or to submit the issue to a referendum), and for judicial review of the constitution. In addition, the constitution allowed for the appointment of ministers who were not required to be members of the Dáil, an option that, had it been made use of, would have brought Ireland into line with the mainstream in western Europe. These 'extern ministers', as they were termed, would be appointed by the Dáil and answerable directly to it. However, apart from PR, most of these devices proved to be of little significance. No extern ministers were appointed after 1927, and even those who were appointed before then were all members of the Dáil. In 1928, the government used its parliamentary majority to abolish both the legislative referendum and the initiative, after Fianna Fáil took the first steps towards forcing a popular vote on the oath of allegiance (Gallagher, 1996, p. 87). It was characteristic of the Cumann na nGaedheal government's decidedly non-populist style that it abolished articles that might have enjoyed some support in the electorate while doggedly defending the most unpopular ones, such as those relating to the oath and the Governor-General.

The provision for judicial review did not prove much of a check on the government. For one thing, the Oireachtas itself could amend the constitution at will. The original version allowed it to do this (provided that any amendment came within the terms of the Treaty) for a period of eight years after 1922, after which amendment would require a referendum. But since this article itself could be amended, a simple extension of the period from eight to sixteen years in 1929 ensured that the document was under the control of the Oireachtas throughout its unhappy life. Moreover, although constitutions are usually more powerful than ordinary legislation, so that if the two conflict it is the constitution that prevails, the Irish Free State constitution was a weak document. Laws that contradicted the constitution, far from being thereby invalid, could simply incorporate a declaration that they amended the constitution to the extent necessary to render them constitutional (Casey, 1992a, p. 13; Kelly, 1994, pp. 1168–70; MacMillan, 1993, p. 196).

When Fianna Fáil came to power in 1932, it moved rapidly to remove those parts of the constitution that offended it most. In 1932 it abolished the oath, and in 1936 the Seanad and the office of Governor-General went the same way (Sexton, 1989, pp. 165–6). By this time, it might have been imagined that the resulting document was to Fianna Fáil's liking. Instead, it satisfied no-one. Fianna Fáil had always viewed it with distaste, while even those who had clung so faithfully to it during the 1920s could not have felt much affection for it by 1937. Apart from the substance of the changes made by Fianna Fáil, the very fact that the document had been amended so many times (forty-one of the eighty-three articles had been changed) gave it a moth-eaten look. In any case, for Fianna Fáil the Irish Free State constitution was inherently illegitimate no matter how it read. Eamon de Valera in particular felt the need for the state to have an entirely new constitution, and to this end he initiated the process of drafting one in 1935 (Fanning, 1988; Hogan, 1997a; Keogh, 1988a). The resulting document was debated and finally passed by the Dáil in June 1937 (the vote on the final stage was sixty-two to forty-eight). Although legally and constitutionally this new constitution could have been enacted by the Oireachtas as one long amendment to the existing constitution, that would have defeated the whole point of the exercise; it was vital symbolically to seem to make a new beginning, and to have the Irish people confer the new constitution on themselves. Accordingly, it was put to the people in a referendum on 1 July 1937, the same day as a general election. It was passed by 57 per cent to 43 per cent and came into effect on 29 December 1937 (see appendix 2h on results of referendums).

The constitution has been the subject of two major reviews since it came into being. The first systematic assessment was made in 1966–67, when an all-party Oireachtas committee, which included former Taoiseach Seán Lemass, examined it article by article and issued a report that recommended certain changes and assessed the merits of other possible amendments. The bipartisan approach adopted by this committee was brought to an abrupt end when Fianna Fáil went ahead the following year with its second attempt to change the electoral system, and little came of its work. In 1995–96 a root and branch assessment of the constitution was conducted by an expert committee, the Constitution Review Group (CRG), whose 350,000-word report can be read as an informed analysis of the constitution as well as an assessment of the arguments for change (CRG, 1996).

The main features of the constitution

The promulgation of a new constitution was not purely symbolic, for despite the high degree of continuity, the 1937 constitution differed significantly in some respects from its predecessor in terms of both its scope and its substance. We shall now examine some of its main features, without going in any depth into areas, especially those concerning the operation of government and parliament, that are covered in other chapters of this book.

Nation and state

Articles 1 to 3 relate to 'The Nation' and Articles 4 to 11 to 'The State'. These articles emphasise the importance attached to the constitution's role as a statement of the independence of the Irish state. Articles 1 and 5 both contain affirmations of sovereignty, and Article 6 says that all powers of government derive from the Irish people, emphasising that the institutions of the state should not be seen as having been in any way bestowed on the people by the British in 1922. Among this group of articles, Articles 2 and 3 caused most controversy over the years. Article 2 defined 'the national territory' as 'the whole island of Ireland, its islands and the territorial seas'. Article 3 declared that, notwithstanding this, the laws enacted by the state shall, 'pending the re-integration of the national territory', apply only to the twenty-six counties, but by referring to the 'right' of the state's parliament and government to exercise jurisdiction over the whole of the national territory it affirmed a clear claim to Northern Ireland. Changes to these articles were demanded by northern unionists as part of the 1998 Northern Ireland Agreement, and, in a referendum in May of that year, the Irish people voted overwhelmingly to replace them by new articles. The new Article 2 declared it the entitlement of everyone born in Ireland to be part of the Irish nation. The new Article 3 declared it to be:

> the firm will of the Irish nation, in harmony and friendship, to unite all the people who share the territory of the island of Ireland, in all the diversity of their traditions, recognising that a united Ireland shall be brought about only by peaceful means with the consent of a majority of the people, democratically expressed, in both jurisdictions in the island.

Implementation of these constitutional changes was made conditional on a declaration by the Irish government that the 1998 Good Friday Agreement (which is discussed further in chapter 13 below) had come into effect; until then, the changes to Articles 2 and 3 would remain in suspension.

The state was described as sovereign, independent and democratic. Its name remains unclear to many. Article 4 reads 'The name of the State is Éire, or in the English language, Ireland'. The 1948 Republic of Ireland Act refrained from giving a name to the state, so as not to violate this article; instead, its formulation is that 'the description of the State shall be the Republic of Ireland'. In different contexts, the state is now known as 'Éire', 'Ireland', 'the Republic of Ireland', and even 'the Irish Republic', a confusion that the constitution does not entirely resolve.

Political institutions

Articles 12 to 33 deal with political institutions. As far as the operation of government was concerned, there was little major change from the Irish

Free State constitution. There was to be an Oireachtas, consisting of a President and two houses. The office of the President was a major innovation, and is discussed further in chapter 9 below. The lower house of parliament, Dáil Éireann, was to be directly elected by proportional representation, using the single transferable vote (see chapter 4) as before. The re-emergence of the upper house, the Seanad, which de Valera had abolished only a year earlier, was surprising; given the nominally vocational basis of the Seanad (see Box 7.2 below), this may have been an adroit move to make a token concession to the transient clamour for the introduction of a vocationalist system of government (Lee, 1989, p. 272). The prime minister was now termed the Taoiseach, and his or her dominance within the government was strengthened in a number of ways; for example, the power to call a general election belonged now to the Taoiseach alone rather than to the government as a whole as before (see chapter 9). It is clear, though, that for the most part the constitution merely reflected and summarised what had become existing practice rather than enforcing a change in that practice.

Constitutions are often frameworks, setting the parameters within which the institutions must operate, rather than codes specifying the details of precisely what must occur at every step (Elazar, 1985). Thus the Irish constitution does not spell out, for example, exactly how the Taoiseach comes to be Taoiseach, or make any mention of the existence of coalition governments. The absence of detailed rules to cover every possible situation means that there are some lacunae. For example, when a Taoiseach is defeated in a vote of confidence, but the Dáil is unable to elect anyone else as a replacement, the Taoiseach is required to resign unless the President grants a dissolution (Article 28.10) yet continues in office until a successor is appointed (Article 28.11). The 1996 Constitution Review Group recommended that in such situations the outgoing government should conduct the state's business on a 'care and good management basis' only, for example refraining from making any non-essential appointments (CRG, 1996, pp. 98–9), but the constitution does not make it clear just what powers a caretaker government and Taoiseach have.

The rights of citizens

The articles of the 1937 constitution that deal with citizens' rights (40–45) differed significantly from those of its predecessor. Like the earlier document, the new constitution guaranteed the usual liberal democratic rights – habeas corpus, free association, free speech, inviolability of dwellings, and so on – though (as is the case in most constitutions, and in the European Convention of Human Rights) almost invariably the ringing enunciation of a right is followed by a qualifying clause or paragraph asserting the power of the state to curtail it if justified by, for example, 'public order' or 'morality'. The main difference was that the 1937 constitution also included rights articles that were strongly influenced by Catholic social thought (Whyte, 1980, pp. 51–6; Keogh, 1988b). Two clauses of Article 44 gave Roman Catholicism a unique status. Article 44.1.2 read 'The State recognises the special position of the Holy Catholic Apostolic and Roman Church as the guardian of the Faith professed by the great majority of the citizens', while, in Article 44.1.3, the State merely 'recognised' a list of other and presumably less significant religions. Moreover, Article 41.3.2 prohibited the legalisation of divorce. These articles apart, admittedly, in many cases there is nothing visibly Catholic about the phraseology to the uninformed eye; only those familiar with Catholic social thought of the period would be able to identify the genesis of the expressions used.

The impact of Catholic thought on the constitution has led to its some-times being branded a narrowly confessional document. However, in the context of its time it could even be seen as liberal. The final formulation of Article 44 met with the approval of all the non-Catholic religions, while many in the Catholic church were clearly disappointed. They had hoped that theirs would be recognised as 'the one true church' and were reluctant even to accept that the word 'church' could validly be claimed by other religions (Keogh, 1988b, pp. 111–17). The first large scale protests against the religious articles came, twelve years later, not from non-Catholics but from the ultra-Catholic Maria Duce group, which wanted Article 44 amended to recognise the Catholic church as the one true church (Whyte, 1980, pp. 163–5). De Valera, far from imposing a sectarian constitution on a pluralistic society, was steering a middle course between non-Catholics on the one hand and triumphalist Catholics on the other, and he displeased the latter more than the former. Moreover, as Lee (1989, p. 203) observes, the explicit recognition given to the Jewish congregations was 'a gesture not without dignity in the Europe of 1937'.

Since 1937 the constitution has evolved in two ways. First, the constitution has been amended, initially by parliament and then by the people. Second, it has been developed by judicial interpretation.

Amendment of the constitution

The Irish constitution, like most constitutions, is more rigid – that is, less easily amended – than ordinary legislation. The constitution was amendable by parliament for a short period, but since then any amendment has required the consent of the people.

Amendment by parliament

The constitution contained, in Articles 51–63, transitory provisions to cover an interim period. These articles are no longer included in official texts of the constitution (they can be found in Kelly, 1994, pp. 1167–1181) but continue to have the force of law. Article 51 permitted the Oireachtas to amend the constitution for a period of three years after the first President entered office, which meant up to 25 June 1941, though the President had the right, if he chose, to refer any such amendment to the people for them to decide the matter by referendum. Any subsequent amendment would require the consent of the people. The loophole left in the Irish Free State constitution was addressed: Article 51 prevented the three-year transition period from being extended by the Oireachtas.

Two packages of amendments were made in this way. The first, made in September 1939, altered only one article (28.3.3, the 'emergency' article), while the second, in May 1941, amended sixteen different articles simultaneously. Some of the changes made in 1941 were minor 'housekeeping' changes, merely ironing out defects that had been detected in the articles affected. Other changes were more significant (though the President chose not to put the package to a referendum), such as those relating to Articles 26 and 34, and especially to Article 28.3.3, which now looked quite different from the version approved by the people in 1937 (the annotated constitution in Foley and Lalor (1995) shows which sections were added by the Oireachtas). This article was designed to protect emergency legislation from scrutiny by the courts. In its original form, the article had stated that nothing in the constitution could be invoked to invalidate legislation designed to secure public safety and the preservation of the state in time of war or armed rebellion. The two amendments widened the scope of the article in circumstances where each House of the Oireachtas passes a resolution declaring that a national emergency exists affecting the vital interests of the state. After amendment, the article now says that 'time of war or armed rebellion' can include a time when an armed conflict is taking place that affects the vital interests of the state, even if the state is not directly involved, and a time after the war or armed rebellion has ceased but during which the Oireachtas takes the view that the emergency created by the conflict still exists. The Oireachtas declared a state of emergency after the outbreak of the Second World War in 1939, and this emergency remained in existence up to 1976, being lifted only by a resolution that simultaneously declared a fresh emergency arising 'out of the armed conflict now taking place in Northern Ireland', an emergency that was finally lifted in February 1995.

While it could plausibly be argued that the state's vital interests were indeed affected by the Second World War, in a way that persisted for some time after that war formally ended, it is easy to see that this article could potentially set at nothing all the rights guaranteed elsewhere in the constitution. At least at first sight, it appears that in order to pass any legislation it chooses, a government that has effective majority support in parliament, as most governments have, need only have the houses of the Oireachtas pass a resolution declaring that an emergency exists and then secure the passage of the legislation by declaring it to have the purpose of securing the public safety and preserving the state. In this way, it seems, legislation that, for example, proscribed opposition parties, abolished elections or prescribed draconian penalties for even minor transgressions of the law would be immune from scrutiny by the courts.

However, a significant judgment of the Supreme Court in 1976, when it pronounced the Emergency Powers Bill constitutional, tempered the potential effect of Article 28.3.3. While not disputing the right of the Oireachtas to enact any legislation it saw fit in order to preserve public safety and the state once an emergency had been declared, the court said that it 'expressly reserves for future consideration' the question of whether it had the right to consider whether the Oireachtas was justified in declaring that a national emergency existed. No case has arisen subsequently to test the extent to which the courts' thinking on this issue has developed, but the warning shot sounded in 1976 may have counterbalanced to some extent the action of the Oireachtas in 1939 and 1941 in widening the scope of Article 28.3.3. Both constitutional review committees recommended that a law declaring an emergency should have effect for three years only and should require annual renewal thereafter (Committee on the Constitution, 1967, pp. 37–9; CRG, 1996, p. 94).

Amendment by the people

Ireland is one of the few countries where every constitutional amendment requires the consent of the people, a feature that in western Europe it shares only with Denmark and Switzerland. Article 46 lays down that a proposal to amend the constitution must be passed by the houses of the Oireachtas and then be put to a referendum. Up to June 1999, twenty-two proposed amendments had been put to the people, of which seventeen had been approved (see Box 3.1 and appendix 2h; for an overview, see Gallagher, 1996; O'Mahony, 1998). Of the twenty-two, seven related to moral or religious issues, seven to voting, and four to the European Community/Union. One was on Northern Ireland, and the other three (in 1979, 1996 and 1997) were on relatively minor and technical matters that did not engender high turnouts.

Box 3.1 Major changes made to the Irish constitution since it was adopted in 1937

Changes to the constitution have been made to allow:

- Ireland to take a full part in the process of European integration (1972, 1987, 1992 and 1998)
- Recognition of the 'special position' of the Roman Catholic church to be removed (1972)
- Divorce to be legalised (1995)
- Ireland to fulfil its part of the Northern Ireland Agreement (1998).

Of the seven referendums on moral or religious issues, the first proposal was passed comfortably, with the backing of all the parties and the opposition only of conservative Catholic groups (Cardinal Conway, the Catholic primate, had already given his blessing to the amendment). It removed from Article 44.1 the two subsections, already referred to, that recognised the 'special position' of the Catholic church and the mere existence of a number of other churches. It was ironic, and an indication of the change in attitudes, that the article amended was the very one that all the churches had approved in 1937 (Keogh, 1988b, p. 118). The two referendums of the 1980s were much more heated affairs, with deep divisions apparent within as well as between the parties. The first, in 1983, inserted what its proponents termed a 'pro-life' amendment, to the effect that the state 'acknowledges the right to life of the unborn' and undertakes 'by its laws to defend and vindicate that right' (Article 40.3.3). The second, in 1986, would have made it possible for the Oireachtas to legalise divorce in restricted circumstances, but was decisively rejected by the voters (Girvin, 1987).

The next three 'moral issue' referendums were held in November 1992 in response to the Supreme Court decision in the 'X' case (see page 86 below). Amendments stating that Article 40.3.3 does not limit either freedom to travel outside the state or freedom to obtain information about services lawfully available in another state were passed with the support of both 'liberal' and 'centrist' voters and of all the political parties (for the complex background to these issues see Kennelly and Ward, 1993). A third proposal, which would have permitted abortions only in cases where a continued pregnancy would have meant a risk to 'the life, as distinct from the health, of the mother' (except where the risk to life arose from the possibility of suicide), was defeated, as both liberal and conservative voters opposed it, along with all the political parties except Fianna Fáil. In 1995 there was a second vote on divorce, and this time the decision was, albeit very narrowly, in favour of legalisation (Girvin, 1996). The pattern of voting was very similar at each of these referendums, with a great deal of consistency as to which constituencies were the most liberal and which were the most conservative. The Pearson correlations between voting patterns at each pair of these referendums are exceptionally high; for example, the correlation between the patterns at the 1983 abortion referendum and the 1995 divorce referendum is 0.96 (Gallagher, 1996, p. 97). These moral issue referendums all brought to the fore the liberal–conservative cleavage in Irish society, as discussed in chapter 2.

Of the seven proposals concerning voting, two, in 1959 and 1968, were unsuccessful attempts by Fianna Fáil to replace the PR-STV electoral system by the single-member plurality system (these referendums are described at pp. 102–4 below). On the second occasion, this proposal was coupled with one that was designed to permit rural voters to be over-represented at the expense of urban voters. The other four referendums caused little controversy between the parties. In 1972, there was all-party backing for lowering the voting age, and in 1979 an amendment to allow the university seats in Seanad Éireann to be reorganised got strong support among those sufficiently motivated to vote on the issue. In 1984 a proposal to permit the Oireachtas to extend the vote to non-citizens received general endorsement, and in 1999 voters agreed to a constitutional amendment that recognised the existence of local government and stipulated that local elections must take place at intervals of no more than five years.

Membership of the European Community (EC) and European Union (EU), with the progressively greater degree of integration entailed by developments within the Community, has been responsible for four referendums (these are discussed further in chapter 13 below). Joining the EC in the first place required a referendum because the obligations of membership would otherwise have been in conflict with the constitution. As well as the symbolic declaration of sovereignty, the constitution gives the Oireachtas a legislative monopoly, declaring that 'no other legislative authority has power to make laws for the State' (Article 15.2.1); it makes a similar assertion in the judicial area, stating that 'the decision of the Supreme Court shall in all cases be final and conclusive' (Article 34.4.6). These articles seemed incompatible with belonging to the EC, since the Community's institutions have the power to make laws for the state and the EC's Court of Justice has the power in certain circumstances to overturn decisions of the Supreme Court. However, the decision was taken in 1972 not to amend these or other articles over which EC membership might cast a shadow but instead to introduce a catchall amendment, by adding a new subsection (Article 29.4.3) allowing the state to join the EC and adding that

> No provision of this constitution invalidates laws enacted, acts done or measures adopted by the State necessitated by the obligations of membership of the Communities or prevents laws enacted, acts done or measures adopted by the Communities, or institutions thereof, from having the force of law in the State.

The 1987 amendment allowed the state to ratify the Single European Act, and the 1992 amendment allowed it to ratify the Maastricht agreement (McCutcheon, 1992; Holmes, 1993). The 1998 referendum on the anti-climactic Amsterdam Treaty, which lacked a clear focus, was overshadowed by the simultaneous referendum on the Northern Ireland agreement, and the vote in favour reflected diffuse support for the EU rather than enthusiasm for the contents of the Amsterdam Treaty specifically (Gilland, 1999).

The referendum requirement in Article 46 has been a powerful check on governments wanting to make changes that do not have broad support across the political spectrum. On only one occasion (the referendum to approve the constitution in 1937) have the people approved a proposal not backed by the major opposition party, and even then the second opposition party, Labour, adopted a neutral position. Since 1937, when governments have put forward proposals not supported by the main opposition party – Fianna Fáil's attempts in 1959 and 1968 to change the electoral system and in 1992 to restrict the circumstances under which abortion could be made legal, and the Fine Gael–Labour coalition's proposed legalisation of divorce in 1986 – the people have rejected them.

The requirement that no changes can be made without a referendum may well enhance the status of the constitution, whose contents remain under the control of the people. Consequently, any proposed change to the method of amendment – for example, allowing amendment to take place without a referendum in cases where there is a four-fifths majority in parliament – has little chance of being approved by the people, and is thus unlikely to be put to them. The referendum requirement also means that such changes as are made, however controversial – for example, on divorce, Northern Ireland, or the EU – have a legitimacy that they would not have if the decision was made by politicians alone.

However, the referendum requirement does have some drawbacks. One is that the expense involved in holding a referendum to make even the most insignificant and uncontentious amendment inhibits the process of change. A second concerns the modalities of the referendum process itself. Before 1995, the government of the day felt free to use public funds to promote its side of the case exclusively. In the McKenna judgment of November 1995, the Supreme Court decided that this was unconstitutional, leaving the body politic with the dilemma of how to create a level playing field in future. At the low-profile referendums of 1996 and 1997 no public money was involved, leaving many electors feeling under-informed. Before the 1998 referendums the government created a 'Referendum Commission', which was given £2.5m to present information to the public. Its approach, which consisted of gathering arguments from groups on both sides and presenting simplified versions of these in television, radio and newspaper advertisements, was widely seen as unsatisfactory. The requirement that both sides of the argument be given equal prominence was also criticised as inequitable in the context of the Northern Ireland agreement referendum campaign, which was opposed by only 6 per cent of voters, and it seemed that the Commission felt itself obliged to publicise some far-fetched claims simply because someone had made them.

Judicial development of the constitution

Given that a constitution lays down rules about what government and parliament can and cannot do, someone is required to keep an eye on them to make sure that they are obeying the rules, and this role is commonly performed by a judicial body. Judicial review can be defined as the power of a court to declare any law, any official action based on a law, or any other action by a public official, to be in conflict with the constitution and hence invalid (Abraham, 1996, p. 70). In many European countries, such as

Austria, Germany, Italy and Spain, there is a special constitutional court, but in common law countries such as Ireland and the USA this function tends to be carried out by the regular courts. The importance of judicial review in Ireland marks the country's gradual divergence from British practice, for whereas judicial review is significant in many countries, it plays little part in the governance of the United Kingdom.

The judges cannot alter the text of the constitution, but they decide what the text means. This power to interpret the constitution is considerable, since judges can, if they are so minded, 'discover' meanings that were never envisaged or intended by anyone initially; in the USA Charles Evans Hughes, who later became Chief Justice, bluntly declared in 1916 that 'the constitution is what the judges say it is' (Abraham, 1998, p. 356). Similarly, in an important Irish constitutional case in 1993, Mr Justice McCarthy observed that 'It is peculiarly within the jurisdiction of the courts to declare what the Constitution means' (Morgan, 1997, p. 32). In a number of European countries, the significance of judicial review is such that the judges could be counted among the policy makers (Gallagher, Laver and Mair, 1995, pp. 64–75). In Ireland, judicial review has proved to be the main method by which the constitution has been developed.

Constitutional cases can reach the courts by one of two routes. First, the constitution makes provision for a priori *abstract* review; that is, the constitutionality of a bill can be considered before it has become law and without reference to any specific case. Such review can be brought about only by a presidential referral of the bill to the Supreme Court. Second, there is provision for *concrete* review: it is open to anyone affected by a law to challenge its constitutionality before the High Court, with the possibility of appeal to the Supreme Court. The court decides whether the law is valid or whether it must be struck down. In addition, any other act of the government (such as the signing of an agreement with another government) may be challenged in the courts as a violation of the constitution. In order to take a constitutional case, citizens must show that they have *locus standi*: that is, that they are in some way affected by the action or statute they are complaining about and are not merely busybodies.

Presidential referrals

The president of Ireland usually signs bills into law, but she or he has the power, under Article 26 of the constitution, instead to refer a bill to the Supreme Court for a decision on its constitutionality. In this event the Supreme Court hears arguments from lawyers assigned to put the case for and against the constitutionality of the bill, and delivers its judgment. If it decides that the bill is 'repugnant to the constitution', the president may not sign it into law.

This presidential power was employed on twelve occasions up to the end of 1998; on six occasions the Supreme Court found the bill constitutional,

and on the other six it found that the bill, or sections of it, were unconstitutional. The merit of this procedure is that the constitutionality of bills
about which doubts have been raised can be definitively established before
they become law; it prevents an unconstitutional law being in force until
successfully challenged, a situation that could have consequences difficult
ever to put right (CRG, 1996, p. 75).

However, there are two difficulties with the procedure. One is that
Article 34.3.3 enshrines for all time a positive judgment in such cases: it
states that the validity of a bill (or any part thereof) that is cleared by the
Supreme Court after referral by the President may never again be questioned
by any court. Even if the views of Supreme Court judges change over
time, as of course they do, or if operation of the Act reveals aspects that
no-one had detected when the bill was argued about in abstract form, the
Act is immune from all further challenge. The CRG thus recommended
that Article 34.3.3 should be deleted (CRG, 1996, pp. 76–80). This particular presidential power is certainly best confined to bills raising, as
Casey (1992a, p. 270) puts it, 'a pure question of constitutional interpretation'. The other difficulty is the opposite; it is that a bill may be struck
down too readily, because the Supreme Court is not confined to the facts
of any particular case. Whereas in the normal course of events the constitutionality of a law can be challenged only by an individual with a
specific case to argue, in an Article 26 referral hypothetical suppositions
can be conjured up and a bill could be found unconstitutional because
of a possibility that might never arise in practice (Hogan, 1997b; cf
O'Higgins, 1996, pp. 281–2).

Judicial review

Once a bill is on the statute books, it is open to challenge by anyone whom
it affects, and the courts are responsible, under Article 34.3.2, for delivering
an authoritative decision on the constitutionality of legislation or the actions
of public bodies. Judicial review has become more significant since the
mid-1960s. Before then, the courts tended to interpret the constitution in a
'positivist' or literal manner, sticking closely to the letter of the document
and taking the view that there was no more to it than the words it contained.
The position then began to change, reflecting a 'general rise in the level
of judicial activism observed in the western democracies since the 1960s'
(Holland, 1991, p. 10). Due partly to the accession of a new generation of
judges and partly to the general changes taking place in society and political
culture at that time, the Irish judiciary began to adopt a more 'creative'
approach (see Casey, 1992a, pp. 300–49; Chubb, 1991, pp. 60–78). This was
seemingly encouraged by the Taoiseach of the day, Seán Lemass, who in
1961 privately urged two newly-appointed Supreme Court judges to be
more activist in their approach to interpretation of the constitution
(Sturgess and Chubb, 1988, p. 144). Judges began to speak of the general

tenor or spirit of the constitution and of the rights that those living under such a constitution must by definition, in their view, enjoy.

An important article in this process turned out to be Article 40.3.1: 'The State guarantees in its laws to respect, and, as far as practicable, by its laws to defend and vindicate the personal rights of the citizen.' Although this may appear to be merely a pious declaration without much substance (as may, indeed, have been the intention), it has proved to be of great significance. Until the 1960s, it was assumed that the 'rights' referred to in Article 40.3.1 were only those specifically listed in Articles 40–44, but a landmark judgment in 1963 changed that. The plaintiff in the case of Ryan v Attorney General argued that the fluoridation of water violated her right to bodily integrity, a right not mentioned anywhere in the constitution. In his judgment, Mr Justice Kenny accepted her contention that she – and by extension every other citizen – did indeed have such a right (unfortunately for her, he didn't accept that putting fluoride in the water violated it), and said: 'The personal rights which may be invoked to invalidate legislation are not confined to those specified in Article 40 but include all those rights which result from the Christian and democratic nature of the State'.

Subsequently, as the number of constitutional cases brought to the courts increased, judges 'discovered' many more 'undisclosed human rights' in the constitution (for a list of eighteen such rights see CRG, 1996, p. 246). One of the most dramatic judgments came in 1973, when the Supreme Court (in the case of McGee v Attorney General) accepted the plaintiff's claim that she had a right to marital privacy, and accordingly struck down the 1935 legislation banning the importation of contraceptives. Given de Valera's strongly Catholic views, and since it was his government's legislation that was being declared unconstitutional, it was apparent to all at this stage that the constitution was not, as indeed it never really had been, 'de Valera's constitution', the name sometimes applied to it. His creation now had a life of its own, and it was for the courts, not for any politician, to decide what its words meant. It is generally believed, inci-dentally, that de Valera did not anticipate judicial review being anything like as significant or extensive as it has proved, and indeed the Irish courts have proved much readier to identify unenunciated rights than their American counterparts (Beytagh, 1992).

The seemingly bottomless well of unenunciated rights that might reside in Article 40.3.1 has some self-evidently undesirable features. One is that the Oireachtas, striving as it always will not to pass legislation that violates the constitutionally-protected rights of the citizens, is placed in a position of uncertainty if it has no way of knowing exactly what these rights are. Another is that it seems to give considerable and perhaps undue power to the unelected judiciary, a point to which we return later in this chapter. Accordingly, the CRG recommended the replacement of the existing 40.3.1 by a comprehensive list, which would include those rights identified by the courts to date, together, perhaps, with those set out in the European

Convention on Human Rights and the International Convention on Civil and Political Rights, and other rights as well (CRG, 1996, pp. 257–65). The revised article would 'confine further recognition of fundamental rights by the courts to those necessarily implicit in the rights expressly listed' (p. 259). Whether this formula would bring about the certainty at which the CRG was aiming seems questionable, though, since it would still lie with the judiciary to decide which further rights are, in fact, 'implicit' in those listed.

Since 1973 the courts have made a number of decisions that have had major political implications, and we can give several examples (details of the main cases can be found in Doolan, 1994, pp. 289–385; Beytagh, 1997, pp. 43–111). First, they have defined and seemingly redefined the circumstances when the 'political offence' argument can be used by a defendant to avoid extradition. Second, in 1987, the Supreme Court, by its decision in the Crotty case, prevented the state from ratifying the Single European Act until the

---

Box 3.2 The 'X' case of 1992

The 'X' case, which arose early in 1992, concerned a 14-year-old girl who had become pregnant, allegedly as a result of being raped. She intended to travel to Britain to obtain an abortion, but the Attorney-General, the legal adviser to the government, obtained a High Court injunction to prevent her travelling out of the country, on the ground that she intended to terminate the life of her unborn child, which he believed would be contrary to Article 40.3.3 of the constitution (the 'pro-life amendment' inserted by referendum in 1983). This decision caused an uproar in Ireland and earned the country wide unfavourable international publicity.

In March 1992 the Supreme Court overturned this injunction. It declared that Article 40.3.3 did in fact confer a right to an abortion on a woman whose life would be threatened by continuing with a pregnancy, including cases where this risk arose from the possibility of suicide by the mother.

This decision was welcomed by pro-abortion groups, and liberals in general, though there was concern that the Supreme Court had not explicitly affirmed that a woman had the right to travel out of the country no matter what her reasons for wanting to do so. It was bitterly criticised by anti-abortion groups, who complained that when the Irish people voted in 1983 to add the 'pro-life' amendment, they had intended this to have the effect of completely outlawing abortion. The judges, in their view, had undemocratically imposed their own idiosyncratic interpretation of the article in question. However, in the words of Charles Evans Hughes quoted on page 83, 'The Constitution is what the judges say it is'.

constitution was amended to permit this (see Casey, 1992b; McCutcheon, 1992; Thompson, 1991). Third, in March 1992 in the 'X' case the Supreme Court declared that abortion was legal in certain circumstances (see Box 3.2). Fourth, in August 1992, the Supreme Court decided that the constitutional reference to collective cabinet responsibility (Article 28.4) entailed an absolute ban on all disclosure of discussions at cabinet meetings (Hogan, 1993). Fifth, in 1995, as mentioned earlier, in the McKenna judgment it decided that governments could not use public funds to promote only their own side of the case at referendums.

Furthermore, in addition to high-profile judgments such as these, there have been many less spectacular but none the less significant judgments in which the courts, relying on their power to interpret the constitution, have effectively changed the law. To give one from many possible examples: in the McKinley v Minister for Defence case of 1992, the plaintiff claimed that injuries (for which she held the defendants responsible) to her husband had deprived her of certain conjugal rights. Under common law, only a husband could claim compensation for the loss of these rights, and the state argued that this common law right was unconstitutional, discriminating as it did against married women, and hence had not survived the enactment of the constitution in 1937. Instead of taking this course, the Supreme Court 'developed' the rights in question so as to vest them in a wife as well. The cumulative effect of such judgments in invalidating old and unreformed statute and common law embodying anomalies or injustices should not be underestimated.

When delivering judgments on the constitutionality of post-1937 Acts of the Oireachtas, the Supreme Court is prevented by Article 34.4.5 from giving more than one opinion, or even disclosing the existence of opinions other than the one delivered (Article 26.2.2 makes exactly the same stipulation concerning bills referred to the court by the President for a decision on their constitutionality). This 'one judgment' rule not only means that dissenting judgments are suppressed; it also poses problems if judges have reached the same conclusion but for different reasons, a difficulty to which former Chief Justice Tom O'Higgins has attested (O'Higgins, 1996, pp. 281–2). This restriction is unpopular with jurists; the former senior judge Brian Walsh maintained that it 'seriously hampers the development of our constitutional jurisprudence' (in the foreword to Casey, 1992a, p. xi). The argument in favour of the rule is that however fascinating jurists might find a plethora of different judgments, the rest of the political system requires certainty from the Supreme Court, and the disclosure of minority views might undermine the authority of the majority decision. This would apply especially if the minority opinions were generally felt to be more persuasive than those of the majority, as has happened on some occasions where the one judgment rule did not apply because the issue did not concern a post-1937 law. Examples include the 1987 Crotty case and the 1992 cabinet confidentiality case, though it cannot be said that these judgments were any less effective or authoritative as a result. The CRG recommended the deletion of Article 34.4.5, but saw an argument for retaining Article 26.2.2 because of the special character of presidential referrals (CRG, 1996, pp. 80–5).

The power of judges

Provision for judicial review clearly carries potential dangers in a democratic state, because it puts significant power into the hands of unelected individuals who are not accountable or answerable to anyone. It is true that under Article 35.4 judges can be dismissed by majority vote of the Dáil and Seanad for 'stated misbehaviour or incapacity', but the possibility of invoking this provision has only very rarely been considered. One such occasion came about in November 1994, when the Taoiseach belatedly realised the disastrous political consequences of a particular judicial appointment, but the government accepted that dismissing a judge was impossible unless there were 'solid reasons'.[1] A second arose in April 1999, when disquiet about apparent irregularities behind the reduction of a sentence on a convicted drunk driver led to an investigation, at the government's request, by the Chief Justice, whose report on the affair contained strong criticism of the behaviour of two judges. The government immediately made it clear that it wished the judges to resign, and there seemed no doubt that the Oireachtas would have debated and passed a motion removing them from office under the terms of Article 35.4 had they not reluctantly resigned within four days of the government making its view known.

Mr Justice Kenny once said that 'judges have become legislators, and have the advantage that they do not have to face an opposition' (Kelly, 1994, p. 757n63); he might have added that neither do they have to face the people, as politicians do. Judges in Ireland share a number of characteristics with their counterparts elsewhere: they are not elected, they enjoy substantial autonomy from control or scrutiny by elected representatives, and they are secretive as to how they work. Their power to interpret the constitution makes them even more powerful than judges in many other countries. All of this raises the questions of who judges are, how they come to be appointed, and what values they hold.

By law, Irish judges must be barristers of at least twelve years' standing. They are appointed by the government, though in practice it seems that only the Taoiseach and the Minister for Justice (together with the other party leader(s) in the case of a coalition government) are involved in the selection, the rest of the government simply being informed of the name of the chosen person.[2] This being so, a record of support for one of the parties in government has, not surprisingly, always been an important factor. Until 1996 the procedure was an informal one, under which the names of appointees reached the government by a secret process involving the taking of soundings, with political connections playing an important role. Since 1996 aspiring judges have had to apply to the Judicial

Appointments Advisory Board, which draws up a shortlist and presents this to the government, which makes the final selection. Concerns have been expressed that, even with this reform, the pool from which judges are drawn remains very narrow, and, moreover, legal academics seem not to be considered for appointment, in contrast to the practice in many other countries (Beytagh, 1997, pp. 148–9). The only detailed study of judges' backgrounds was made over thirty years ago, and it found that most judges had a background of support for the party that appointed them (Bartholomew, 1971, p. 48). Most were from upper middle class backgrounds, over a quarter were sons of lawyers, and all were men; indeed, even up to 1998 only one woman has been appointed to the Supreme Court and only four other women have become High Court judges (see p. 303 below). A later study of judicial appointments confirmed that governments not only looked for appointees of the right political background but took into account the views of those under consideration. In the mid to late 1960s the government, and especially the Department of Justice, was disturbed at the flurry of 'creative' decisions being made by the courts, and the Department decided to ensure that less activist judges were appointed in future (Tóibín, 1985, pp. 17–20).

Most of this is characteristic of judges almost everywhere. Across western Europe generally, judges tend to come from relatively privileged backgrounds, and appointment of judges is highly politicised. Irish practice is unusual in that the government alone appoints judges; the more common approach, used by most countries for their constitutional courts, is that cross-party agreement is needed for appointments, which means in effect that the process becomes a carve-up among the main political parties (Gallagher, Laver and Mair, 1995, pp. 66–7). The result of the judicial appointment process seems to be broadly similar everywhere: although the process itself varies from country to country, 'the men and women selected to judgeships almost always hold safe, sound, middle-of-the-road opinions', and are characterised by 'moderation and attachment to regime norms' (Jacob, 1996, pp. 390–1).

There is little or no research into the question of whether the political and socio-economic background of Irish judges is related to the judgments that they deliver. No-one has suggested that judges with a record as supporters of a particular party view elevation to the bench as an opportunity to conduct 'politics by other means' (cf Chubb, 1992, p. 295). But even if Fianna Fáil (or Fine Gael) supporters appointed to the bench do not see themselves as Fianna Fáil (or Fine Gael) judges, with a mission to use their positions to continue their political activities, it might still be true that the values that led judges to join one or other of the parties in the first place will inform the decisions they make. This sometimes seemed to characterise judgments in cases in the 1980s involving extradition of alleged members of republican paramilitary groups to Northern Ireland; judges with a background in Fine Gael tended to be less sympathetic to a 'political offence' line of defence than did those whose background was in Fianna Fáil.

How far, it might be asked, do the personal values of judges determine their judgments? In the USA, critics have accused the judges of being as goal-oriented as political actors, using the constitution 'as a kind of letter of marque authorizing them to set sail at will among laws, striking down any they find displeasing' (quoted in Hodder-Williams, 1992, p. 16). In this perception, judges use the constitution simply to legitimise their own preferences when reaching a decision; as trained barristers, they are well able to make a plausible case for whatever judgment they wish to deliver. Reviewing the decisions made by the judiciary in constitutional cases, Hogan points to the absence of any consistent approach on the part of the judges, with a strong suspicion that they utilise 'whatever method might seem to be most convenient or to offer adventitious support for conclusions they had already reached' (Hogan, 1988, p. 187; see also Morgan, 1998 and Chubb, 1991, pp. 71–3). When judges accept the existence of rights not specifically mentioned in the text of the constitution, such as the right to bodily integrity or the right to marital privacy, are they logically deducing the existence of these rights from the overall nature of the constitution, inferring them, discovering them, or calling into active life rights that, though hitherto unnoticed, have lain dormant within the constitution since 1937? Or are they, as critics might maintain, merely conjuring up or drawing out of the ether a 'right' in order to provide a convincing basis for a decision whose real progenitor is the judge's own attitude towards the case in question? Any attempt to explore this question would require a far greater depth of research into the politics of the judiciary in Ireland than has so far been undertaken.

Judges are expected to refrain from commenting on the political issues of the day, so their views on current issues are not known. One of the very few exceptions occurred when in the early 1990s Mr Justice O'Hanlon became an outspoken critic of the idea of abortion. In February 1995 he criticised proposed legislation on abortion information, saying that he could no more keep silent than he could have during the holocaust. This left little room for doubt as to how he would react if asked to pass judgment on the constitutionality of such legislation, and there were calls for his resignation, but the government let the matter rest, perhaps because he was due to retire a few weeks later.

If judges do not simply interpret the constitution to accord with their own preferences, on what basis should they interpret it? The 'originalist' perspective according to which the constitution should be interpreted in line with the intentions of the Irish people when they accepted the constitution in 1937 has obvious pitfalls: how can we know whether the people of 1937 would have felt that a law should or should not be constitutional, and, if we could know, why should the Irish people of the twenty-first century be bound by their views? Such an approach really would be akin to 'rule by the dead'. Yet, without such a constraint on the judges, the danger is that their judgments will be moored in nothing more substantial than the values and policy preferences of the judges of the day, or some vague notion of what constitutes the prevailing public attitude.

As we noted at the start of the chapter, there is an inherent tension between constitutionalism and democracy. The dilemma of judicial review is inherently unresolvable. It places a lot of power in the hands of a non-elected, unrepresentative elite answerable to no-one. But if judges were somehow made genuinely accountable to the government or parliament, they would cease to be an independent judiciary, and we would lose one of the checks and balances of a liberal democracy. Judicial review has allowed judges to make important quasi-political decisions in areas such as extradition without reference to the people or their elected representatives. However, Irish judges have not come in for the type of criticism sometimes levelled against their counterparts elsewhere. Partly this is because, on the liberal–conservative spectrum discussed in chapter 2, the judiciary has often seemed to be somewhat closer than the Oireachtas to the liberal end of the spectrum; given that public opinion has been becoming more liberal, the judiciary has been a few years ahead of, but not wildly out of line with, public opinion. For example, governments had shown no inclination to grasp the nettle of reforming the restrictive contraception laws until the courts forced their hand by the McGee judgment of 1973. One of the Supreme Court judges in this case later said that the court's judgment 'was seen by everybody, including the politicians, as having got the politicians off the hook' (Sturgess and Chubb, 1988, p. 125). The courts' view that married couples should have access to contraceptives was radical in 1973 but mainstream within ten years.

Regardless of the policy content of judicial decisions, though, the merits of the 'creative' approach taken by the courts in the 1960s, and subsequently, have been increasingly questioned. The landmark decision of Mr Justice Kenny in the 1963 Ryan case – in which the judge spoke of the unenumerated personal rights that 'result from the Christian and democratic nature of the state' and quoted a recent Papal encyclical in support of his argument – is open to innumerable criticisms (for a detailed analysis of this judgment see Hogan, 1994). Reviewing the unenumerated rights discovered by the courts over the years, Hogan concludes:

> While the protection of such various unenumerated rights – such as the right to privacy, the right to earn a livelihood and the right of an unwed mother to custody and care of her child – may well be beneficial and salutary, it is often difficult to take this jurisprudence completely at face value, since there is nothing whatever in the actual text of the Constitution to show that these rights were intended to enjoy constitutional provision.
>
> (Hogan, 1994, p. 114)

Attitudes to the judiciary often depend on 'whose ox is being gored', in the words of the American Governor Al Smith, and significantly, the strongest objections were voiced after the Supreme Court delivered its verdict in the 'X' case in March 1992 (see Box 3.2 above), when anti-abortionists criticised both the specific judgments delivered (arguing that the judges had 'lost their way') and, it seemed, the principle of judicial review. Fianna Fáil Senator Des Hanafin, chairman of the 'Pro-Life Trust', declared that

> it is wholly unacceptable and indeed a deep affront to the people of Ireland that four judges who are preserved by the constitution from accountability can radically alter the constitution and place in peril the most vulnerable section of our society.
>
> (*Irish Times*, 6 March 1992)

However, this seems to be a minority viewpoint. Calls for reform of the system of judicial appointment, for example by the introduction of US-style parliamentary assessments of proposed appointees, have up to now been voices in the wilderness, as the consensus among insiders appears to be that the present system, whatever its theoretical drawbacks, operates satisfactorily in practice. The tension between democracy and constitutionalism cannot in any case be eliminated by such devices; it can only be managed, with greater or less success, and thus far the record has not been a bad one.

The debate on constitutional change

Attitudes to the constitution have undergone a number of changes over the years. Up until the mid-1960s there was remarkably little criticism of it, and, perhaps, limited awareness of how important a constitution was as the basic law in a functioning liberal democratic society. As societal attitudes began to change from the 1960s onwards, the constitution was increasingly seen as a symbol of the past and an obstacle to progress. For many, it was regarded as a product of de Valera's Ireland, an outdated Catholic and nationalist document that sought to impose the mores of the 1930s political elite upon a changing and modernising country. Numerous demands for 'a new constitution', free of the baggage of the past, were heard. Yet, at the same time, there was a growing awareness of the merits of the constitution and, due in particular to the work of the late Professor John Kelly, of the richness of the jurisprudence that was being constructed around it. When the fiftieth anniversary of the constitution was marked in the late 1980s by a spate of assessments, the tone was celebratory and appreciative rather than critical. Brian Farrell seemed to sum up the mood:

> [Since 1937,] that Constitution, Bunreacht na hÉireann, has been amended, interpreted, re-shaped by judges, politicians, civil servants and the people. One man's document has become a political community's

common charter – a living and effective guarantee of broadly based and expanding liberties.

(Farrell, 1988c, p. viii)

At the start of the twenty-first century, the standing of the constitution has never been higher.

This change in attitudes has resulted from the development of the constitution by the judiciary and from alterations to the wording of the constitution effected by referendum. The constitution no longer seems to pose an impediment to the 'liberal agenda', the 1995 removal of the ban on divorce having pretty much completed this. The rephrasing of Articles 2 and 3 for which the people voted overwhelmingly in 1998, namely, the replacement of a claim over Northern Ireland by an aspiration to a peacefully united Ireland, similarly defused much of the criticism of the constitution as expressing old-style nationalism. This is not to say that there are no further political battles to be fought over the wording of the constitution (see Box 3.3). Article 41.2, incorporating the view that women's place is in the home, would find few defenders (see chapter 12, especially p. 309, and Dooley, 1998, for a fuller discussion), and the whole constitution contains innumerable examples of gender-specific language that the CRG (1996, p. xi) recommended should be replaced by wording based on 'the principle of gender-inclusiveness'. The preamble to the constitution still conveys a very nationalist view of history in which unionists could not recognise themselves and, along with many other areas of the constitution, has a broadly Christian, often specifically Catholic, tone that does not match the political culture of the state as well as it did in 1937. Abortion is another issue fought out on constitutional terrain: since Article 40.3.3, inserted in 1983 by a referendum instigated by anti-abortion groups, was interpreted in the 1992 'X' case as allowing abortion in certain circumstances, the pro-life movement has called, with conspicuous lack of success, for the constitution to be amended again so that abortion can be completely outlawed.

The limited scope of the rights (both enumerated and unenumerated) guaranteed by the constitution has been criticised by those who believe that the constitution should actively promote equality. The constitution guarantees equality of opportunity but not equality of outcome. Two members of the CRG argued that the constitution should have an article 'committing us to a democracy based on principles of social solidarity with the aim of eliminating poverty and promoting economic equality through a system of taxation based on principles of equality and progressiveness' (Lynch and Connelly, 1996, p. 590). Why, it is asked, should a right to adequate food, clothing, shelter, rest and medical care not be affirmed (Murphy, 1998, pp. 167–81)? However, a majority of the CRG was opposed to the inclusion of specific personal economic rights. It took the view that matters such as freedom from poverty were essentially political questions, so it 'would be a distortion of democracy to transfer

Box 3.3 Possible changes to the Irish constitution

The Constitution Review Group, which deliberated in 1995 and 1996, made a number of recommendations for change, including:

- Remove all examples of gender-specific language and ensure that the constitution contains only wording based on the principle of gender-inclusiveness;
- Insert a comprehensive list of fundamental rights and seek to prevent the courts discovering further unenumerated fundamental rights;
- Continue to allow the parliament to declare a state of emergency but stipulate that any such state of emergency shall automatically lapse after a period of three years;
- Give constitutional recognition to the office of Ombudsman (for which, see chapter 8 below).

Other changes that have been suggested include altering the method by which the upper house of parliament, the Seanad, is elected; declaring that citizens have economic rights (for example, to adequate housing and health care); qualifying the right to private property so as to tilt the balance in favour of society as a whole.

decisions on major issues of policy and practicality from the Government and the Oireachtas, elected to represent the people and do their will, to an unelected judiciary'. There was also the danger that the state would find itself compelled by the courts to pursue certain policies regardless of whether the necessary resources were available (CRG, 1996, pp. 234–6). The Irish constitution, it must be said, is very much in the European mainstream in guaranteeing the standard liberal rights while refraining from asserting that those under its jurisdiction possess justiciable economic rights.

Those sections of the constitution that deal with the institutions of government are not generally seen as in pressing need of change. The CRG recommended the introduction of the 'constructive vote of no confidence', which would prevent the Dáil voting out a Taoiseach unless it was able to vote in a replacement, and it advocated giving constitutional recognition to both local government and the Ombudsman. It considered the arguments for change in the role and composition of the Seanad, and in the electoral system, but rather than make firm recommendations it called for further consideration of both questions. Many of these subjects are discussed in the other chapters of this book. The CRG also considered possible changes of a less politically controversial and more narrowly constitutional nature. We have outlined many of these areas in this chapter already, such as the character of the 'emergency' article (28.3.3), the merits of the 'one judgment' rule (Articles 26.2.2 and 34.3.5), and the freezing for all time of the initial clearance of a bill following a presidential referral (34.3.3). The report of the CRG went to an all-party parliamentary committee on the constitution, which was set up in 1996 and re-established after the 1997 election, with the brief of undertaking a full review of the constitution. The prospects for all-party consensus are much higher at the start of the new century than in the more divided 1960s and 1970s, given that substantial agreement has been reached on the constitutional aspects of Northern Ireland and the liberal agenda, though it remains to be seen how high a political priority is accorded to what to some seems the arcane topic of constitutional reform.

Calls for a new constitution are now rarely heard. To scrap the existing constitution would risk losing the rights and liberties 'discovered' by judges in it, most of which have had the effect of enhancing the rights of citizens. Despite some past accusations that the constitution is excessively long and should be replaced by one that is confined to basics like the American constitution, in fact the Irish constitution is by no means verbose by world-wide standards; its length of about 14,000 words (in each language, i.e. in both English and Irish) compares with an estimated 15,900-word average length for 142 national constitutions examined by van Maarseveen and van der Tang (1978, p. 177). No political party advocates the drafting of a new constitution, and when the public was asked for its views in a May 1995 opinion poll, only 36 per cent wanted a new constitution as opposed to 55 per cent who wanted to retain the existing constitution and amend it as required (Market Research Bureau of Ireland, 1995, Table 1). The constitution as a whole possesses the kind of widespread acceptance and legitimacy that the Irish Free State constitution never attracted, and is likely to remain the fundamental law of the state for some time to come.

Notes

1 Comment of Brendan Howlin, a minister in the 1993–94 government, in Select Committee on Legislation and Security, 1995, column 1069, 18 January 1995. The appointment in question, of Attorney General Harry Whelehan to be President of the High Court, caused the Labour party to withdraw from the government, thus bringing about its collapse (see Garry, 1995).
2 Evidence of Ruairí Quinn, a minister in the 1993–94 government, Select Committee on Legislation and Security, 1995, columns 937, 981, 17 January 1995.

References and further reading

Abraham, Henry J., 1998. *The Judiciary: the Supreme Court in the Governmental Process*, 10th ed. New York and London: New York University Press.

Abraham, Henry J., 1998. *The Judicial Process: an Introductory Analysis of the Courts of the United States, England and France*, 7th ed. New York and Oxford: Oxford University Press.

Bartholomew, Paul C., 1971. *The Irish Judiciary*. Dublin: Institute of Public Administration.

Beytagh, Francis X., 1992. 'Individual rights, judicial review, and written constitutions', pp. 147–62 in James O'Reilly (ed.), *Human Rights and Constitutional Law: Essays in Honour of Brian Walsh*. Blackrock, Co Dublin: Round Hall Press.

Beytagh, Francis X., 1997. *Constitutionalism in Contemporary Ireland: an American Perspective*. Dublin: Round Hall, Sweet and Maxwell.

Bunreacht na hÉireann (Constitution of Ireland). Dublin: Stationery Office.

Casey, James, 1992a. *Constitutional Law in Ireland*, 2nd ed. London: Sweet and Maxwell.

Casey, James, 1992b. 'Crotty v An Taoiseach: a comparative perspective', pp. 189–200 in James O'Reilly (ed.), *Human Rights and Constitutional Law: Essays in Honour of Brian Walsh*. Blackrock, Co Dublin: Round Hall Press.

Chubb, Basil, 1991. *The Politics of the Irish Constitution*. Dublin: Institute of Public Administration.

Chubb, Basil, 1992. *The Government and Politics of Ireland*, 3rd ed. Harlow: Longman.

Committee on the Constitution, 1967. *Report* (Pr. 9817). Dublin: Stationery Office.

Constitution of the Irish Free State. Dublin: Stationery Office.

Constitution Review Group (CRG), 1996. *Report*. Dublin: Stationery Office.

Doolan, Brian, 1994. *Constitutional Law and Constitutional Rights in Ireland*, 3rd ed. Dublin: Gill and Macmillan.

Dooley, Dolores, 1998. 'Gendered citizenship in the Irish constitution', pp. 121–33 in Tim Murphy and Patrick Twomey (eds), *Ireland's Evolving Constitution, 1937–97: Collected Essays*. Oxford: Hart.

Elazar, Daniel J., 1985. 'Constitution-making: the pre-eminently political act', pp. 232–48 in Keith G. Banting and Richard Simeon (eds), *The Politics of Constitutional Change in Industrial Nations: Redesigning the State*. London: Macmillan.

Fanning, Ronan, 1988. 'Mr de Valera drafts a constitution', pp. 33–45 in Farrell (1988a).

Farrell, Brian (ed.), 1988a. *De Valera's Constitution and Ours*. Dublin: Gill and Macmillan.

Farrell, Brian, 1988b. 'From first Dáil through Irish Free State', pp. 18–32 in Farrell (1988a).

Farrell, Brian, 1988c. 'Preface', pp. vii–ix in Farrell (1988a).

Foley, J. Anthony and Stephen Lalor (eds), 1995. *Gill and Macmillan Annotated Constitution of Ireland*. Dublin: Gill and Macmillan.

Gallagher, Michael, 1996. 'Ireland: the referendum as a conservative device?', pp. 86–105 in Michael Gallagher and Pier Vincenzo Uleri (eds), *The Referendum Experience in Europe*. Basingstoke: Macmillan.

Gallagher, Michael, Michael Laver and Peter Mair, 1995. *Representative Government in Modern Europe*. New York: McGraw-Hill.

Garry, John, 1995. 'The demise of the Fianna Fáil/Labour "Partnership" government and the rise of the "Rainbow" coalition'", *Irish Political Studies* 10, pp. 192–9.

Gilland, Karin, 1999. 'Referenda in the Republic of Ireland', *Electoral studies* 18:3, pp. 430–8.

Girvin, Brian, 1987. 'The divorce referendum in the Republic, June 1986', *Irish Political Studies* 2, pp. 93–9.

Girvin, Brian, 1996. 'The Irish divorce referendum, November 1995', *Irish Political Studies* 11, pp. 174–81.

Hodder-Williams, Richard, 1992. 'Six notions of "political" and the United States Supreme Court', *British Journal of Political Science* 22:1, pp. 1–20.

Hogan, Gerard, 1988. 'Constitutional interpretation', pp. 173–91 in Litton (1988).

Hogan, Gerard, 1993. 'The cabinet confidentiality case of 1992', *Irish Political Studies* 8, pp. 131–7.

Hogan, Gerard, 1994. 'Unenumerated personal rights: Ryan's case re-evaluated', pp. 95–116 in W. N. Osborough (ed.), *Irish Jurist Vols 25–7*, 1990–92. Dublin: Round Hall Press.

Hogan, Gerard, 1997a. 'The Constitution Review Committee of 1934', pp. 342–69 in Fionán Ó Muircheartaigh (ed.), *Ireland in the Coming Times: Essays to Celebrate T. K. Whitaker's 80 Years*. Dublin: Institute of Public Administration.

Hogan, Gerard, 1997b. 'Ceremonial role most important for President', *Irish Times* 21 October.

Holland, Kenneth M., 1991. 'Introduction', pp. 1–11 in Kenneth M. Holland (ed.), *Judicial Activism in Comparative Perspective*. Basingstoke: Macmillan.

Holmes, Michael, 1993. 'The Maastricht Treaty referendum of June 1992', *Irish Political Studies* 8, pp. 105–10.

Holmes, Stephen, 1988. 'Pre-commitment and the paradox of democracy', pp. 195–240 in Jon Elster and Rune Slagstad (eds), *Constitutionalism and Democracy*. Cambridge: Cambridge University Press.

Jacob, Herbert, 1996. 'Conclusion', pp. 389–400 in Herbert Jacob, Erhard Blankenburg, Herbert M. Kritzer, Doris Marie Provine and Joseph Sanders, *Courts, Law and Politics in Comparative Perspective*. New Haven and London: Yale University Press.

Kelly, J. M., 1994. *The Irish Constitution*, 3rd ed. by Gerard Hogan and Gerry Whyte. Dublin: Butterworths.

Kennelly, Brendan and Eilís Ward, 1993. 'The abortion referendums', pp. 115–34 in Michael Gallagher and Michael Laver (eds), *How Ireland Voted 1992*. Dublin: Folens and Limerick: PSAI Press.

Keogh, Dermot, 1988a. 'The constitutional revolution: an analysis of the making of the constitution', pp. 4–84 in Litton (1988).

Keogh, Dermot, 1988b. 'Church, state and society', pp. 103–22 in Farrell (1988a).

Lee, J. J., 1989. *Ireland 1912–1985: Politics and Society*. Cambridge: Cambridge University Press.

Litton, Frank (ed.), 1988. *The Constitution of Ireland 1937–1987*. Dublin: Institute of Public Administration.

Lynch, Kathleen and Alpha Connelly, 1996. 'Equality before the law', pp. 586–91 in CRG (1996).

McCutcheon, Paul, 1992. 'The Irish constitution and the ratification of the Single European Act', *L'Irlande Politique et Sociale* 4, pp. 19–41.

MacMillan, Gretchen M., 1993. *State, Society and Authority in Ireland: the Foundations of the Modern State*. Dublin: Gill and Macmillan.

Market Research Bureau of Ireland, 1995. *Irish Times*/MRBI poll, 20–22 May. Dublin: Market Research Bureau of Ireland.

Morgan, David Gwynn, 1997. *The Separation of Powers in the Irish Constitution*. Dublin: Round Hall, Sweet and Maxwell.

Morgan, David Gwynn, 1998. 'Judicial activism – too much of a good thing', pp. 107–19 in Tim Murphy and Patrick Twomey (eds), *Ireland's Evolving Constitution, 1937–97: Collected Essays*. Oxford: Hart.

Murphy, Tim, 1998. 'Economic inequality and the constitution', pp. 163–81 in Tim Murphy and Patrick Twomey (eds), *Ireland's Evolving Constitution, 1937–97: Collected Essays.* Oxford: Hart.

Murphy, Walter, 1993. 'Constitutions, constitutionalism, and democracy', pp. 3–25 in Douglas Greenberg, Stanley N. Katz, Melanie Beth Oliviero and Steven C. Wheatley (eds), *Constitutionalism and Democracy: Transitions in the Contemporary World.* New York and Oxford: Oxford University Press, 1993.

O'Higgins, T. F., 1996. *A Double Life.* Dublin: Town House and Country House.

O'Mahony, Jane, 1998. 'The Irish referendum experience', *Representation* 35:5, pp. 225–36.

Select Committee on Legislation and Security, 1995. *Meeting of Sub-Committee, Inquiry into Events of 11 to 15 November, 1994.* Dublin: Stationery Office.

Sexton, Brendan, 1989. *Ireland and the Crown, 1922–1936: the Governor-Generalship of the Irish Free State.* Dublin: Irish Academic Press.

Sturgess, Garry and Philip Chubb, 1988. *Judging the World: Law and Politics in the World's Leading Courts.* Sydney: Butterworths.

Thompson, Brian, 1991. 'Living with a Supreme Court in Ireland', *Parliamentary Affairs* 44:1, pp. 33–49.

Tóibín, Colm, 1985. 'Inside the Supreme Court', *Magill* 8:7, February, pp. 8–35.

Van Maarseveen, Henc and Ger van der Tang, 1978. *Written Constitutions: a Computerized Comparative Study.* Dobbs Ferry, NY: Oceana Publications.

Ward, Alan J., 1994. *The Irish Constitutional Tradition: Responsible Government and Modern Ireland, 1782-1992.* Blackrock: Irish Academic Press.

Whyte, J. H., 1980. *Church and State in Modern Ireland 1923–1979.* Dublin: Gill and Macmillan.

4   The electoral system

Richard Sinnott

Electoral systems (the rules governing how votes are cast and seats are allocated on the basis of those votes) are a matter of political choice. They are also a matter of institutional design: they have more or less identifiable effects on the functioning of the political system and an electoral system can be selected or rejected with a view to achieving or avoiding certain consequences. The alleged consequences of the electoral system used in Ireland – proportional representation by means of the single transferable vote, or PR-STV – have been a recurring focus of debate and controversy.

This chapter examines the way in which PR-STV came to be adopted as the Irish electoral system in the first place and then discusses the two referendums at which, contrary to the designs of the incumbent government in each case, PR-STV was re-endorsed by the people. The chapter goes on to explain how the system works, using an actual PR-STV count to illustrate the process. Finally, it examines the question of the consequences of the system for the proportionality between votes and seats, for government stability and party cohesion, and for the role of the members of the Dáil.

The proportional representation option in Ireland

Proportional representation, in one or other of its many incarnations, is the most frequently used electoral system in democracies because the main alternative – dividing the country up into single-member constituencies and giving the seat in each constituency to the candidate with the most votes – can lead to egregiously unfair outcomes at national level. This latter system, usually known as the plurality or 'first past the post' system, is used for elections to the House of Commons in the United Kingdom (it is also used in Canada, India and the United States). The 1997 British general election illustrates its potential for bringing about an 'unfair' outcome: Labour won 43 per cent of the vote and 63 per cent of the seats, whereas the Liberal Democrats won 17 per cent of the vote and 7 per cent of the seats. Such an outcome can occur because, within each constituency, the winning party takes 100 per cent of the representation (i.e., the one and only seat) while all the other parties or candidates receive zero representation. The imbalances at the constituency level could conceivably even themselves out across the country; they are more likely to be cumulative, in which case a party with considerably less than a majority of the votes may obtain a majority of the seats in parliament, entitling it to 100 per cent of the seats in cabinet and all the power and patronage that goes with control of government. The unfairness is compounded by the fact that the bonus usually goes to the largest party or parties while the smallest suffer most.

Arguments in defence of this system stress the notion of elections as 'devices to choose viable governments and give them legitimacy' (Butler, 1981, p. 22) and maintain that the bonus given to the winning party, with all the consequences that entails, is still the best way of doing that. However, since the middle of the nineteenth century and in tandem with the democratisation of the franchise, alternatives to this 'best system' have been sought, mainly because of the non-proportional outcomes that the plurality method produces. Proponents of PR have come up with a wide range of ideas and systems, the main distinction being between list systems on the one hand and PR-STV on the other. The former were generally favoured in continental Europe and PR-STV was for a long time the favoured alternative to the prevailing plurality system in Britain.

In a list system of proportional representation, each party draws up and presents a list of candidates in each multi-member constituency, and the voter chooses between the various lists; the primary decision to be made by the voter is the choice of party. Seats are then allocated to parties on the basis of their share of the vote. In theory, a party obtaining, say, 35 per cent of the vote is entitled to 35 per cent of the seats, though how closely the outcome approaches this varies from system to system (for an overview see Gallagher, Laver and Mair, 1995, pp. 271–300). List systems vary in the methods they use to award seats to individual candidates within parties: in some, the matter is decided by the party organisation and is determined by the position of the candidates on a fixed list, while in others the voters can express preferences for specific candidates on their chosen party's list. Even in the latter systems, the fact remains that the vote cast is primarily a vote for the party and may end up assisting the election of a candidate to whom the voter is actually opposed (Bogdanor, 1983, p. 15).

In contrast, the primary focus of PR-STV is on the choice of individual representatives. Indeed, the originators of PR-STV in Britain were highly critical of political parties and of the role they played (Carstairs, 1980, p. 194). Reservations about the role of parties were also quite widespread in Ireland when PR-STV was adopted, and the party affiliation of candidates was not listed on ballot papers in Ireland until 1965. PR-STV, therefore, involves a notion of the connection between the individual representative and his or her constituency that is much closer to the notion of representation implicit in the first past the post system than to the notion of the representation of parties that underlies list systems.

PR-STV is not widely used, Malta being the only other country that employs it to elect the lower house of its national parliament (it is also used, with modifications, to elect the Australian Senate and in elections in Tasmania and Northern Ireland). How did this relatively uncommon system come to be adopted in Ireland? Developed simultaneously by Carl Andrae in Denmark and by Thomas Hare in England in the late 1850s, PR-STV was strongly advocated by electoral system reformers in Britain. In the early years of the twentieth century, the problem of minority representation in the event of Home Rule seemed to make PR particularly relevant in Ireland. A Proportional Representation Society of Ireland was formed, with Arthur Griffith, founder of Sinn Féin, among its first members. Inevitably, the views of electoral reformers in Ireland were substantially influenced by current thinking in Britain. An element of PR-STV was inserted in the abortive Home Rule Bill of 1912 and, in 1918, PR-STV was enacted for a single local council (Sligo Corporation); an election was held there under the new provisions in January 1919. The next step was the decision by the British government to introduce PR-STV for the 1920 local elections in Ireland and then for the 1921 election to be held under the Government of Ireland Act.

Thus, by 1921, PR-STV had not only been endorsed by a significant section of the nationalist movement but had actually reached the statute books. It is not surprising, therefore, that when independence negotiations were under way and the issue of representation of minorities was being considered, the desirability of PR was common ground. The result was that PR was included in the 1922 Free State constitution. The constitution did not specify the precise form of PR to be used, but it was automatically assumed that this would be PR-STV, and this was the system specified in the Electoral Act of 1923.

PR-STV has been endorsed by the Irish electorate on three occasions, though the endorsement has varied both in its degree of specificity and in its degree of commitment. The first occasion was the approval of the new constitution in 1937. De Valera opted not just to include the principle of proportional representation in his draft constitution, as the 1922 constitution had done, but to spell out that this should be proportional representation by means of the single transferable vote (see Box 4.1). The matter did not give rise to extensive debate. Fine Gael had at one stage expressed some reservations regarding PR-STV (O'Leary, 1979, pp. 25–6). However, in the debate on the draft constitution, John A. Costello of Fine Gael merely questioned why the details of the electoral system should go into the constitution rather than be left to the greater flexibility of ordinary legislation, to which de Valera replied that the matter was too important to be left to the vagaries of party warfare. Pointing to some evidence that even at that time de Valera may have had reservations regarding PR, O'Leary speculates that the reason for putting PR in the constitution may have been a fear that its omission might have mobilised the opposition and led to the rejection of the constitution

Box 4.1 The constitution and the electoral system

The 1937 Constitution is quite specific about the Dáil electoral system. The main provisions are as follows:

Article 16.2.
1   Dáil Eireann shall be composed of members who represent constituencies determined by law.
3   The ratio between the number of members to be elected at any time for each constituency and the population of each constituency, as ascertained at the last preceding census, shall, so far as it is practicable, be the same throughout the country.
5   The members shall be elected on the system of proportional representation by means of the single transferable vote.
6   No law shall be enacted whereby the number of members to be returned for any constituency shall be less than three.

as a whole (O'Leary, 1979, p. 33). De Valera may then have taken the view that if PR had to be in the constitution, it was better from a Fianna Fáil point of view that it be PR-STV, which had at least offered some bonus to the largest party (see p. 114 below). The constitution was approved (see chapter 3) and, in this omnibus fashion, PR-STV received its first popular endorsement from the Irish electorate.

Twenty years later, shortly before retiring as Taoiseach, de Valera proposed the abolition of PR-STV and its replacement by the plurality system. Although Fianna Fáil had been in power for twenty-one of the previous twenty-seven years, it had won an overall majority on only four occasions, and, unless PR were abolished, might have seemed less likely to do so in the future without his leadership. Needless to say, the government did not put the case for change in such partisan terms but in terms of two other arguments (for a useful summary of the Dáil debate, see FitzGerald, 1959). The first argument was that PR has a disintegrating effect, creating a multiplicity of parties and increasing the probability of governmental instability. The second was that, whereas the plurality system enables the electorate to make a clear choice between two competing alternative governments, PR makes the formation of government a matter for post-election bargaining among parties, depriving the electorate of a direct say.

Fine Gael stifled whatever doubts it may have had about PR-STV and led the opposition to change. As a small party, Labour had fewer doubts. The opposition counter-argument emphasised the issues of proportionality and fairness, particularly the question of the representation of minorities. Opposition speakers also attacked the proposal on the grounds that it would perpetuate Fianna Fáil rule indefinitely and undermine the parliamentary opposition. The debate in the Dáil on the enabling legislation extended from mid-November 1958 to the end of January 1959 and ran to some 600,000 words in the official report (FitzGerald, 1959, p. 1). And that was not the end of it. The bill was then debated in the Seanad, where the surprise outcome was a defeat for the government – the first defeat of a government bill in the Seanad since the reconstitution of that body in 1937 – requiring the Dáil to use its power to overrule the Seanad (for which, see p. 200 below). The government also faced an array of opposition outside parliament, including all the national newspapers except the Fianna Fáil-aligned *Irish Press* and large sections of the trade union movement.

A controversial aspect of the contest was de Valera's decision to run for election to the presidency and to hold the presidential election on the same day as the referendum. The defenders of PR argued that holding both contests on the same day was loading the dice in favour of the proposed change. In the event, whatever effect this may have had, it was not sufficient. De Valera was elected to the presidency, but his proposal to abolish PR was narrowly defeated, with 48 per cent in favour and 52 per cent against (see appendix 2h).

Obviously Fianna Fáil took some encouragement from the fact that it had lost by a narrow margin (33,667 votes). Otherwise it would be difficult to explain the party's decision to put the very same proposal to the people again just nine years later. The underlying problem for Fianna Fáil – that of securing a single-party majority – remained. Seán Lemass had had to form a minority government in 1961 and secured exactly half the seats in 1965. Lemass himself appeared to toy with the possibility of reforms other than a simple move to the first past the post system, but he retired as Taoiseach shortly thereafter, and an all-party Oireachtas committee established in 1966 to review the constitution failed to reach agreement on the question of the electoral system and simply set out the arguments for and against (Committee on the Constitution, 1967).

In the event the government opted in 1968 for the same proposal as in 1959, namely, to replace PR-STV by the plurality system. A second amendment that was proposed at the same time related to the constitutional requirement that the ratio of members of the Dáil to population in each constituency 'shall, so far as it is practicable, be the same throughout the country' (Article 16.2.3). The new proposal would have allowed a deviation of up to one-sixth from the national average. The purpose of the change was to enable rural areas with declining populations to maintain their level of parliamentary representation. It did not go unnoticed, however, that the areas that would benefit from such a change tended to be areas in which Fianna Fáil had strong and stable support.

Essentially the same forces were ranged against the government on this occasion, the only difference being that the defenders of the status quo campaigned with more confidence and conviction (for a summary of the debate see O'Leary, 1979, pp. 66–70). The outcome was also more decisive: the result on the question of PR was 39 per cent in favour of abolition, 61 per cent in favour of retention, and the voting on the other proposed amendment was virtually identical (see the table of referendum results in appendix 2h). The position of PR-STV was undoubtedly greatly strengthened by this decisive popular endorsement. Certainly, nothing more is likely to be heard about moving to the plurality system. However, plurality voting is not the only alternative and, since the 1980s, there has been a renewal of the debate about the consequences of the system and about the desirability of altering it, a major contribution to the debate being the various stages of the constitutional review process initiated by the government in April 1995 (see Constitution Review Group, 1996; Laver, 1998). Before turning to consider those consequences and that debate, it is necessary to take a detailed look at how the system actually works.

How PR-STV works

There are three distinct senses in which one can have an understanding of how PR-STV works: in terms of what is involved in the act of voting, in terms of the basic logic of the system, and in terms of the mechanics of the count. From the point of view of the act of voting, the task of understanding the system is quite simple. On entering the polling station and having established his or her identity, the voter is given a ballot paper that lists the candidates in alphabetical order and bears the instruction: 'Write 1 beside the name of the candidate of your first choice, 2 beside your second choice, and so on'. The voter has only one vote (hence the term single transferable vote); what the voter does is to issue a set of quite straightforward instructions to the returning officer as to what to do with that vote. The simplicity of PR-STV from the voter's perspective is worth emphasising because a frequent objection to the system is the claim that voters will not be able to understand it.

If one had in mind the second or third kind of understanding of the system mentioned above, this might well be so. The bulk of the voters probably have, at best, a hazy notion of the logic of the system and certainly do not understand its 'mechanics'. On this very issue, the future Taoiseach Seán Lemass argued in the Dáil debate on PR prior to the 1959 referendum: 'There are not half the Deputies in this House, much less half the electorate of the country, who can give an intelligent explanation of what happens [to] a No. 3 preference on a ballot paper. Is it not far better to give the people of the country a system of election they can understand?' (quoted in FitzGerald, 1959, p. 7). This criticism misses the point, which is that PR-STV is easily understood in the sense in which the voter needs to understand it, and this does not include knowing the different things that may happen to a No. 3 preference. All that is needed in order to use the system to the full is an understanding of the notion of ranking a set of candidates according to one's preferences. This level of understanding is even enough to enable loyal party voters to participate in the vote management strategies adopted by some parties in some constituencies (see Gallagher, 1999, pp. 141–4). For such strategies to work, the party managers need to know the subtleties of the system; the loyal party voter simply needs to know that the party wants him or her to express a particular order of preferences.

In the case of the first past the post system, the logic of the system is clear: give the seat to the candidate with most votes regardless of what proportion of the total vote this is. The majority or two-ballot system, as used in French presidential elections, introduces a refinement on this rule: in order to win a seat a candidate must reach the threshold of 50 per cent plus one, that is, an absolute majority. Again, the logic is clear. But what is the logic of PR-STV?

Understanding the logic of PR-STV is best approached by first considering how the system works when there is only a single seat to be filled, as in presidential elections and most by-elections in Ireland. Because multi-seat constituencies are an essential feature of PR – since a single seat cannot, obviously, be shared out proportionally – this is not actually PR-STV.[1] However, starting with this simpler situation allows one to examine the logic of the system by illustrating the nature of the quota and of the transfer process and by then going on to see the effect on both of the introduction of multi-seat constituencies.

Whatever the number of seats, PR-STV entails a quota: the number of votes that guarantees election. Once a candidate reaches this quota, he or she is elected. The quota is calculated as follows:

$$Quota = \frac{Total\ number\ of\ valid\ votes}{Number\ of\ seats + 1} + 1$$

Any fractional remainder is disregarded. When there is only one seat available, this formula yields a quota that is identical to that used in the French presidential election system: one more than half the number of votes. STV in a single-seat contest may be seen as a sophisticated version of the majority system. The sophistication lies in how the STV system deals with the problem that arises when no candidate reaches the required absolute majority, something that may well happen if there are more than two candidates. When this occurs in a French presidential election, all but the top two candidates are eliminated and the voters troop back two weeks later to choose between the remaining two. This amounts in effect to asking those who voted for eliminated candidates to register a second preference. STV does not, as it were, waste the voters' time by asking them to come back later to register their second choice. Instead, it collects this information, and information on third, fourth, fifth and further choices, all in one economical operation. Then, rather than disposing of all but the leading two candidates in one fell swoop, STV eliminates them one by one, reassigning the votes of each eliminated candidate according to the next preferences they contain. This has the advantage of including information on the preferences of the voters across the full range of candidates rather than, as in the case of the French presidential system, merely as between the two candidates who are in the lead after the first round.

PR-STV is not, however, simply a refined version of the majority rule procedure; it has the all-important additional feature of multi-seat constituencies. The multi-seat constituency introduces two new elements into the logic of the system. The first is the systematic reduction of the quota as the size of the constituency (in terms of the number of seats) is increased. In the single-seat situation the quota is half the votes plus one. A quick look at the formula shows that this principle can be easily extended as follows: in a two-seat constituency, the quota is one-third plus one, in a three-seater it is one quarter plus one, in a four-seater it is one-fifth plus one, and so on (see Table 4.1). Thus, as the number of seats is increased, the proportion of votes carrying an entitlement to a seat is progressively lowered: a nine-seat constituency would produce a quota of one-tenth plus one.

The second feature introduced by moving to multi-seat constituencies is the transfer of the surplus votes of elected candidates: the votes of an elected candidate over and above the quota, that is, in excess of the number needed to guarantee a seat. If no such transfer were made, those who voted for such a candidate would not get the full share of representation to which, as a group, they are entitled. For example, suppose that in a three-seat constituency just over 50 per cent of the voters vote for candidate A, and that A's supporters represent a particular point of view. Since the quota in a three-seater is 25 per cent plus one, and since therefore this quantity of votes is sufficient to elect A, if A's surplus were not redistributed, the second 25 per cent of the votes supporting this point of view would achieve no representation. The problem is solved by transferring the surplus votes to the other candidates according to the second preferences of the supporters of the elected candidate. This is the point at which the mechanics of the counting procedure become somewhat complex but, fortunately, the complexities, which will be examined below, are not strictly relevant to grasping the logic of the system.

To summarise: the logic of PR-STV is that it ensures proportionality by,

Table 4.1 Quota by district magnitude in PR-STV

District magnitude (TDs per constituency)	Quota, in per cent
1	50.0
2	33.3
3	25.0
4	20.0
5	16.7

first, lowering the threshold for electoral success by using multi-seat constituencies, each additional seat bringing about a substantial reduction in the
quota; second, eliciting and using extra information on the voter's choice,
i.e. his or her order of preference among the competing candidates; and,
third, using this information not just in a process of elimination of the lowest
candidates but also in dealing with the problem of what would otherwise
be the under-representation of those who support candidates who exceed
the quota.

Understanding the fairly complex mechanics of the system is best
achieved by working through an example. Again it is best to begin with the
simple situation: a single-seat contest and the transfer of the votes of an
eliminated candidate. The presidential election of November 1990 provides a good illustration (see Table 4.2). The valid vote in that election
amounted to 1,574,651, which, when divided by the number of seats plus
one (i.e. by two) yields 787,325.5. Disregarding the fraction and adding
one to this number gives a quota of 787,326 votes. It is clear that Brian
Lenihan was in the lead on the basis of first preference votes, but, since no
candidate had reached the quota, the returning officer proceeded to elim-
inate the candidate with the lowest number of votes (Currie) and to
distribute his votes in accordance with the second preferences indicated.
On the second count about three-quarters (205,565) of Currie's votes were
found to carry a second preference for Robinson.[2] This gave Robinson a
total of 817,830 votes or 51.9 per cent of the total valid vote. This exceeded
the quota (in this case the 50 per cent plus one rule) and Robinson was
declared elected. Lenihan received only 13.7 per cent of Currie's second
preferences, while 9.5 per cent of those who supported Currie did not
specify a second preference and their ballots appear in the 'non-transferable papers' row. Note that even if Robinson had not reached the quota,
she could have been declared elected, provided that Currie's transfers
were sufficient to put her ahead of Lenihan. This situation could have
occurred if more of Currie's votes had been non-transferable.

Counting the votes in general elections is a more complicated business
because PR-STV requires multi-seat rather than single-seat constituencies.

Table 4.2 The Irish presidential election, 1990

Candidate	First preferences	Transfer of Currie's votes	Second count result
Currie, Austin	267,902	– 267,902	
Lenihan, Brian	694,484	+ 36,789	731,273
Robinson, Mary	612,265	+ 205,565	817,830
Non-transferable papers		+ 25,548	25,548

Valid votes: 1,574,651. Quota: 787,326.

The process can be illustrated by reference to the Dublin South constituency in the 1997 election (see Table 4.3, pages 110–11). In 1997 Dublin South was a five-seat constituency and there was a valid poll of 57,986 votes. When this was divided by the number of seats plus one (i.e., by six) and, disregarding the fraction, one was added to the result, the quota was 9,665 votes. One candidate (Tom Kitt of Fianna Fáil) exceeded the quota on the first stage by a margin of 239 votes and was declared elected.

Normally the next step would be the transfer of Kitt's surplus. However, the size of that surplus was such that its transfer could not have either elected another candidate, or changed the order of elimination of the lowest candidate or candidates, or resulted in any candidate reaching one quarter of the quota (thus being able to save his or her deposit); in these circumstances, the returning officer is not required to distribute such a surplus at that point but may proceed to the elimination of the lowest candidate.[3] In fact, on this count, the four lowest candidates – Dolan, Doody, Lyons and Maher – were eliminated in one operation. This is because their combined vote (894) was less than the vote of the next highest candidate, Buckley (who then had 1,268 votes), and so, even if all of the votes of Dolan, Doody and Lyons as well as the surplus votes of Kitt, had been transferred to Maher, Maher would still inevitably have been eliminated next. Accordingly, it makes administrative sense to process all these eliminations in a single operation.[4] Note that what is examined in each case in the transfer process is what the rules call 'the next available preference'. Thus if some of Maher's votes had a second preference for Kitt, then, because Kitt had already been elected, the third preference would become operative for that particular vote. If that third preference happened to be for Dolan, then, because he was also being eliminated, the fourth preference would come into effect and so on.

At the end of the second count the difference between the two lowest candidates (Buckley and Greene) was only fifty-six votes. It was necessary, accordingly, to distribute Kitt's surplus of 239 votes at this stage. The destination of that surplus was determined by re-examining the entire set of 9,904 first preference votes for Kitt. This was done by arranging these votes in 'sub-parcels' according to the second preferences indicated on them, with votes indicating no further preference being set to one side. The total number of transferable votes was then used as the base for calculating each continuing candidate's share of the total transferable vote. These proportions were then applied to the 239 surplus votes that were actually available for transfer. Thus, if candidate X obtained 60 per cent of the transferable vote in the original 9,904 votes examined, he or she was entitled to 60 per cent of the 239 surplus votes. In this case, one of Kitt's Fianna Fáil running mates, Séamus Brennan, obtained 113 votes or 47.3 per cent of the surplus and his other Fianna Fáil running mate, Ann Ormonde, received sixty-one votes or 25.5 per cent of the surplus. The only other significant beneficiary was the Progressive Democrat candidate Liz O'Donnell, who obtained twenty-nine votes or 12.1 per cent of the surplus. The other continuing candidates got single figure increments that ranged between 1.7 and 3.4 per cent of the surplus. Note that because the base used for calculating these ratios was the total number of transferable votes in Kitt's original vote, the non-transferable vote on this count was nil.

Once the number of surplus votes going to each candidate had been ascertained, the surplus votes had to be physically transferred and the question arises as to which actual ballot papers should be transferred and which should remain with the elected candidate. The choice could make a difference to the outcome of later stages since the papers transferred could subsequently be examined for their third or lower preferences. The rule is: 'The particular papers to be transferred from each sub-parcel shall be those last filed in the sub-parcel'. The defence of this procedure is that the counting process requires that the papers be thoroughly mixed and that, therefore, the set of papers chosen in the manner described is a random sample of the entire sub-parcel. However, it has been argued that it would be worth the extra cost in time to transfer all the papers in each sub-parcel at the appropriate fraction of their value, thereby avoiding all risk of bias or distortion, as is done in the counting of votes at Seanad elections and in Northern Ireland (for discussions of this point see Coakley and O'Neill, 1984; Gallagher and Unwin, 1986).[5]

The third count did not in fact change the relative positions of Buckley and Greene and, consequently, Buckley was next to go. Not surprisingly, given her non-party status, her 1,430 votes scattered widely, though one quarter of them (356 votes) did go to Gerry Boland of the Green Party. Ninety-six votes, or 6.7 per cent of them, were non-transferable.

Still no one had reached the quota and, since Greene was now the lowest candidate, his votes were transferred on the fifth count. Though this transfer tended to benefit Fianna Fáil more than the other parties or candidates, it still left the leading Fianna Fáil contender (Brennan) 126 votes short of the quota and the lowest Fianna Fáil candidate (Ormonde) with only half a quota and in the position of being the candidate with the fewest votes. Accordingly, the sixth count consisted of the elimination of Ormonde and the transfer of her votes.

Ormonde's votes did not go as solidly to the other Fianna Fáil candidate (Brennan) as one might have expected on the basis of normal levels of Fianna Fáil party loyalty; 2,519 votes or 61.6 per cent went to Brennan but 809 (19.8 per cent) leaked, as it were, to Liz O'Donnell of the Progressive Democrats. This was quite important in terms of the outcome of the election in Dublin South because it put O'Donnell within seventy-four votes of Eithne Fitzgerald of Labour. The transfer to Brennan was, however, way more than enough to put him over the quota, leaving him in fact with a surplus of 2,393 votes. The next step (the seventh count) was the transfer of this surplus.

The approach to the distribution of a surplus that arises at this stage of the process is the same as that which applies to a surplus that arises on

Table 4.3 Counting and transfer of votes in Dublin South, 1997 general election

Electorate: 90,050;   Valid votes: 57,986;   Number of seats: 5;   Quota: 9,665

	First Count	*Second Count*	*Third Count*	*Fourth Count*
	Number of votes	*Transfer of Dolan's, Doody's, Lyons's and Maher's votes and result*	*Transfer of Kitt's surplus and result*	*Transfer of Buckley's votes and result*
Boland, G. (Green)	3,539	+241 3,780	+5 3,785	+356 4,141
Brennan, S. (FF)	8,861	+67 8,928	+113 9,041	+146 9,187
Buckley, C. (Ind)	1,268	+158 1,426	+4 1,430	-1,430 —
Dolan, G. (Ind)	75	-75 —	—	—
Doody, J. (Ind)	80	-80 —	—	—
Fitzgerald, E. (Lab)	6,147	+125 6,272	+8 6,280	+205 6,485
Greene, R.	1,431	+51 1,482	+3 1,485	+100 1,585
Kitt, T. (FF)	9,904	9,904	-239 9,665	9,665
Lyons, J. (NLP)	115	-115 —	—	—
Maher, L. (Soc P)	624	-624 —	—	—
Mitchell, O. (FG)	8,775	+54 8,829	+8 8,837	+178 9,015
O'Donnell, L. (PD)	5,444	+47 5,491	+29 5,520	+149 5,669
Ormonde, A. (FF)	3,629	+54 3,683	+61 3,744	+93 3,837
Shatter, A. (FG)	8,094	+63 8,157	+8 8,165	+107 8,272
Non-transferable	-	+34 34	+0 34	+96 130
TOTAL	57,986	57,986	57,986	57,986

Elected: Tom Kitt (FF), Séamus Brennan (FF), Olivia Mitchell (FG), Alan Shatter (FG), Liz O'Donnell (PD)

Fifth Count	*Sixth Count*	*Seventh Count*	*Eighth Count*
Transfer of Greene's votes and result	*Transfer of Ormonde's votes and result*	*Transfer of Brennan's surplus and result*	*Transfer of Boland's votes and result*
+291	+150	+236	– 4,818
4,432	4,582	4,818	—
+352	+2,519	-2,393	
9,539	12,058	9,665	9,665
—	—	—	—
—	—	—	—
—	—	—	—
+77	+105	+89	+1,402
6,562	6,667	6,756	8,158
-1,585			
—	—	—	—
9,665	9,665	9,665	9,665
—	—	—	—
—	—	—	—
+169	+158	+73	+721
9,184	9,342	9,415	10,136
+115	+809	+1,511	+966
5,784	6,593	8,104	9,070
+254	-4,091		
4,091	—	—	—
+80	+204	+103	+705
8,352	8,556	8,659	9,364
+247	+146	+381	+1,024
377	523	904	1,928
57,986	57,986	57,986	57,986

the first count, except that the votes that are examined for next preferences are not the entire 12,058 votes credited to Brennan at that stage but the votes in the 'sub-parcel last received' by him, that is, the 2,393 votes he received from Ormonde. This procedure does involve substantial savings in time and effort. Its rationale is that the 'sub-parcel last received' is what put the elected candidate over the quota and in this way created the surplus. It could equally well be argued, however, that the procedure involves a potential distortion in that the distribution of next available preferences in the vote received by Brennan from Ormonde may not correspond to the distribution of such preferences in the entire Brennan vote and that the logic of the system requires that all of the voters for an elected candidate should have a proportionate say in the destination of the surplus in question. For example, it seems likely that the 63.1 per cent transfer from Fianna Fáil's Brennan (male) to Progressive Democrat O'Donnell (female) was helped by the fact that the votes determining that transfer were all votes that Brennan had received from another female candidate, Ormonde.

The distribution of Brennan's surplus differed from Kitt's in another way. This is because the number of transferable votes in the last parcel received by Brennan was less than the surplus to be transferred. When this happens, all the votes that can be transferred are transferred (i.e. there is no need for the calculation of transfer ratios). Since the number of transferred votes is less than the surplus to be transferred, the difference is reported as 'non-transferable papers' (in this case 381). If one were to infer from this that 15.9 per cent of the Fianna Fáil vote on the seventh count plumped for that party instead of transferring to their coalition partner in the person of O'Donnell, one would in fact be underestimating the rate of Fianna Fáil plumping. This is because the actual number of non-transferable votes in a case like this is the reported non-transferable vote (381) plus the difference between the total vote in the sub-parcel last received and the surplus (2,519 minus 2,393). In short, in the parcel of 2,519 votes transferred from Ormonde to Brennan there were 507 non-transferable votes and the real rate of non-transferability in the Fianna Fáil vote at that stage was thus 21.2 per cent rather than 15.9 per cent.

Be that as it may, the effect of the transfer of Brennan's surplus was to put O'Donnell substantially ahead of Fitzgerald for the first time. Substantially ahead, but not out of reach; there were still three seats to be filled and there were four candidates in contention. The candidates, their parties and the pecking order after the seventh count were Olivia Mitchell of Fine Gael (9,415), Alan Shatter of Fine Gael (8,659), Liz O'Donnell of the PDs (8,104) and Eithne Fitzgerald of Labour (6,756). Thus, the difference between the two lowest placed contenders was 1,348; but there were 4,818 Green Party votes about to be transferred on the eighth count.

Almost thirty per cent of Boland's votes were divided fairly evenly between the two Fine Gael candidates, putting Mitchell over the quota and making Shatter quite safe for the fourth seat, though short of a quota. The fifth seat was therefore between O'Donnell and Fitzgerald. The latter received 1,402 or 29.1 per cent of Boland's vote compared to 966 (20.1 per cent) for O'Donnell, but the disproportionate shareout was not enough to close the gap. O'Donnell finished on 9,070 and was thus allocated the fifth seat without reaching the quota. Fitzgerald on 8,158 was runner-up. Given that the difference between them at the end was 912 votes, it is worth noting that 1,024 of Boland's votes were non-transferable on the last count. In other words, if one thousand or so Green voters had been persuaded not to plump for the party or for Boland and had also been sufficiently persuaded by presumed policy affinities between Labour Party policy and Green Party policy to transfer to Labour, the outcome both in this constituency and in the country as a whole would have been substantially different.

The political consequences of PR-STV

It was noted at the outset that electoral systems have more or less identifiable political effects. The qualification 'more or less' is essential because there is considerable debate about what the consequences are and it is possible to be more precise and confident in identifying some of them than others. With a view to evaluating the current Irish electoral system and to contributing to the ongoing debate about it, it is now time to consider the impact of PR-STV on the proportionality of the relationship between votes and seats, on the party system and the stability of government, and on the role of the elected representative.

Consequences for proportionality

Disproportionality is measured by comparing parties' shares of the votes with their shares of the seats and noting the discrepancies. This is not quite as simple as it seems. First of all, there are several competing measures of disproportionality (for a discussion see Lijphart, 1994, pp. 58–62). Secondly, the matter is complicated in the case of STV, given the system's focus on individual candidates rather than parties and given the way in which transferred votes and not just first preference votes are a vital part of a party's overall level of support and ultimately determine who wins the seats. These difficulties can be circumvented to some extent by using what Lijphart describes as an index that 'not only makes good sense but that . . . is the simplest possible way of measuring disproportionality'. This is the 'largest deviation' measure, i.e. the largest deviation between vote share and seat share in an election result (Lijphart, 1994, p. 62). This will usually be the 'bonus' for one or other of the largest parties but can also be the deficit suffered by a minor party. The average largest vote–seat deviation in the Irish case between 1923 and 1997 was 3.9, ranging from a low of 1.5 in February 1982 (for Fianna Fáil) to a high of 7.1 in 1997 (also for Fianna

Fáil). In a comparative study by Lijphart, Irish elections over the period 1948–89 emerge as much more proportional than those held under first past the post electoral systems. Compared to elections held under PR list systems, they were more proportional than some but less proportional than others held under PR list systems in, for example, Denmark, Finland, Germany, the Netherlands and Sweden (figures from Lijphart, 1994, pp. 160–2). Using the more exact 'least squares index' developed by Gallagher (1991, see also Lijphart, 1994, pp. 58–62), one can be more precise about Ireland's overall proportionality performance in comparison to that of other countries and other electoral systems: out of thirty-seven electoral systems, Ireland's ranked fifteenth on this index of proportionality (Farrell, 1997, pp. 146–7).

Fianna Fáil has consistently obtained a bonus in seats over votes: on average, its bonus (a party's percentage of the seats minus its percentage of the votes) has been 3.3 percentage points. Although this has varied considerably in size, it has often been enough to put the party over the crucial threshold of 50 per cent of the seats, or at least to put it in a position to form a minority government. Fine Gael has generally also benefited from the system, though not to the same extent as Fianna Fáil, either in terms of the consistency or of the average size of the bonus obtained (an average of 1.5). Labour, on the other hand, has obtained a share of the seats smaller than its share of first preference votes in eighteen of the twenty-five elections of the 1923–97 period (with an average 'deficit' of -0.8 percentage points), while the minor parties and independents have been even more consistent losers.

Proportionality is crucially affected by the actual preferences and behaviour of the voters. Thus Fianna Fáil's bonus was minimal in 1951, 1954, 1973 and in the three elections of 1981–82, elections that were all marked by relatively high levels of transfers of preference votes between its main opponents (see Gallagher, 1978 and Sinnott, 1995, pp. 208–16). On the other hand, there was quite a high level of transfers between Fine Gael and Labour in 1977, yet Fianna Fáil ended up with its second highest ever bonus in seats over votes.

This election and that of 1969 illustrate the disproportionality that can arise when constituency boundaries are gerrymandered. In Ireland, this has in the past been more a matter of arranging the number of seats per constituency to best advantage assuming certain levels of support for the party or parties doing the gerrymandering and less a matter of including or excluding groups of supporters as in the classic 'gerrymander' from which the term derives (Coakley, 1980, pp. 316–17). Such arrangements are no longer possible following the establishment of an independent boundary commission in 1980, but before then the rule of thumb was to create three-seat constituencies in areas in which the governing party or parties were presumed to be strong (around 50 per cent of the votes) and four-seaters where support for the government was only moderate (around 40 per cent). Since the quota is 25 per cent in a three-seater and 20 per cent in a four-seater, the expected outcome of such an arrangement was two out of three (or 67 per cent of the representation) in a three-seater and two out of four (or 50 per cent of the representation) in a four-seater, thus maximising the representation gained.

Of course, if the assumptions on which such a scheme was based proved to be inaccurate, it backfired. This is precisely what happened in 1977, when an arrangement of constituencies designed to suit the presumed strength of the combination of Fine Gael and Labour was upended by a major swing in votes to Fianna Fáil, making Fianna Fáil the beneficiary of the carefully crafted 'tullymander' (the term was derived from the name of the minister who devised the constituency revision, James Tully). In the 1969 election the high Fianna Fáil bonus was a product both of a combination of low transfers between Fine Gael and Labour and the advantage gained from an effective assignment of three-seat and four-seat constituencies to suit Fianna Fáil by the minister concerned, Kevin Boland. Leaving these attempts to manipulate the proportionality of the system aside as being of only historical interest, and acknowledging that the proportionality of the system can vary somewhat depending on the behaviour of the voters and the strategies of the parties, one must still conclude that the system is quite satisfactory on the proportionality criterion. As Gallagher put it in an evaluation conducted for the Constitution Review Group: 'PR-STV in Ireland delivers a high degree of proportionality, virtually as high as that produced by electoral systems that have the achievement of proportionality as their sole aim' (Gallagher, 1996, p. 519).

Consequences for the party system and government stability

The classic case against proportional representation, argued mainly on the basis of case histories of Weimar Germany, and of France and Italy in the 1950s, was that it leads to a proliferation of parties and thus to political instability or at least stalemate. These alleged effects of PR have been the subject of endless debate over the years. The 1980s saw a renewal of this debate with more assiduous attention being given to systematic evidence and generally with the use of more sophisticated methodologies. In so far as the effect of PR on the number of parties is concerned, a consensus has emerged from this research. It is summed up in Sartori's rewriting of one of Duverger's famous 'laws': 'PR formulas facilitate multi-partyism and are, conversely, hardly conducive to two-partyism' (Sartori, 1986, p. 64).

In considering this issue in the Irish case one must distinguish between the problem of the proliferation of parties and the problem of the election of independent TDs. In regard to the proliferation issue, Laakso and Taagepera (1979) have proposed an index, called the 'effective number of parties' that takes account of both the number and the relative size of the parties in a system. It is particularly useful for comparing the number of parties in different countries, or in the same country at different points in time. The effective number of parties in Ireland declined from a peak in June 1927 and remained low throughout the 1930s. It rose sharply twice in the 1940s, but then fell back and settled down at a low level from 1965 to 1982. In 1987, it began a rise that continued over the next two elections, the rise being particularly pronounced in 1992 (see Sinnott, 1995, pp. 91–4). It is clear from this that the number of parties is not simply a function of the electoral system. Ireland has had the same electoral system since the foundation of the state but the number of parties has fluctuated considerably.

The average effective number of parties in nineteen western European democracies in the early 1990s was 4.1; in Ireland the number in the same period was 3.5. This puts Ireland in joint tenth place (with Sweden) on the scale of party fragmentation. The countries with the most fragmented systems were Belgium (8.4), Italy (7.3) and Switzerland (6.7). The least fragmented were Malta, which also uses PR-STV, with a score of 2.0, Portugal and Greece (2.2) and the United Kingdom (2.3) (figures from Gallagher, Laver and Mair, 1995, p. 290). Given this ranking and given the fluctuations in the effective number of parties in Ireland over time, the most one can conclude is that PR-STV in Ireland has, in Sartori's terms, facilitated moderate multi-partyism when other factors were leading in that direction.

It should also be noted that a preoccupation with the number of parties and with the alleged problems of multi-partyism assumes that multi-party systems lead to unstable government. As the Constitution Review Group has pointed out, this is not necessarily the case because, in the post-war European experience, any dangers that might arise from the presence of small parties have been countered by effective party discipline, an experience that is confirmed by the Irish case (Constitution Review Group, 1996, p. 58). In this regard, the Irish experience would seem to run counter to the widely held theory that PR-STV leads to weaker party discipline and party organisation. Thus Taagepera and Shugart (1989, p. 28) argue that 'if strength of party organization is desired, STV is inappropriate, because either list PR (even with preference voting) or plurality (in the absence of US-style primaries) gives far more leeway to party elites in deciding who the party's representatives may be'. This, however, is a relative observation. It does seem likely that, other things being equal, a list system of PR will lead to stronger party organisation. This does not mean that parties under PR-STV will be weak in some absolute sense. On the other hand, Katz (1980, p. 34) puts forward a more absolute version of the theory, hypothesising that 'Where intraparty choice is allowed, parliamentary parties will tend to be disunited' and noting that 'In the case of small districts this will be manifested in personalistic fractionalization'.

Following Katz, Blais pushes the argument even further: 'There is strong evidence that the single transferable vote leads to a weaker party system . . . Electoral competition within the party hinders unity and cohesion. . . . the single transferable vote, like preferential voting in general, is detrimental to the development of a responsible party system' (Blais, 1991, pp.

248–9). Both authors point to the prevalence of intra-party personalistic competition in the area of constituency service as evidence for their theory. However, both are also forced to declare that the equally evident unity of Irish political parties is 'illusory' (Katz, 1980, p. 107) and 'superficial' (Blais, 1991, p. 249). Neither author explains what illusory or superficial party unity is and neither provides evidence to demonstrate its existence or its consequences. It would seem more sensible to note that intense intra-party competition in the area of constituency service can coexist with a very substantial degree of party cohesion and party discipline, and that the latter are products of constitutional structure and inherited modes of politics and are not undermined by PR-STV.

In dealing with the question of stability it should be noted that the Constitution Review Group discussion focused exclusively on parties. By ignoring the way in which PR-STV facilitates the election of independent or non-party candidates, it may indeed take too sanguine a view of the Irish situation. The fact is that three Irish governments since the start of the 1980s have been explicitly dependent on the support of independent TDs. Two of these (those formed after the 1981 and February 1982 elections) collapsed within nine months. While this threat to the stability of government is occasional, since it depends on the parliamentary arithmetic after an election, no amount of party discipline can counter it. PR-STV contributes to the threat by increasing the probability of minority governments that may be tempted to rely on the support of a few independents rather than include another party in a coalition arrangement. It also facilitates the election of independents by focusing on individual candidates, by encouraging competition in the provision of local benefits and, through the mechanism of the multi-seat constituency, by lowering the threshold of representation to a point at which it is within the reach of non-party candidates. In short, while it is true that PR-STV does not lead to unstable government by causing a multiplicity of parties or by diminishing party discipline, it does increase the probability of government reliance on independent deputies whose support may be delivered only at a disproportionate price and even then may not be durable.

Consequences for the role of the TD

The issue of whether PR-STV imposes an unbearable burden of constituency work on TDs hardly figured at all in the debates of 1959 and 1968. For example, a pamphlet by a civic-minded study group that aimed to provide an objective assessment of the arguments in 1959 devoted a page and a half to the issue of the quality of TDs, but only five lines of this dealt with the problem of constituency service (Tuairim, 1959, pp. 19–20). In contrast, the subsequent increase in the burden of constituency work led Farrell (1985, p. 14) to note in the mid-1980s that 'there is an evident consensus among deputies that the competition in constituency service has got out of hand'. The current debate focuses on the question of how far the electoral system is a cause of this. The fact that the expressions of concern are coming from present or former politicians from both major parties (see, for example, Boland, 1991; FitzGerald, 1991; Martin, 1991; Hussey, 1993) suggests that there is a prima facie case to be examined. Indeed, it is clear that the call for change is not limited to the personal reflections of backbench or retired TDs. The possibility of changing the electoral system has been raised by successive Taoisigh: by Garret FitzGerald in the 1987 election, by Charles Haughey in late 1991, and by Albert Reynolds shortly after he became Taoiseach (*Irish Times,* 29 November 1991 and 7 February 1992). Following the 1997 election, the cabinet position with direct responsibility for the conduct of elections (Minister for the Environment and Local Government) went to a TD, Noel Dempsey, with a strong personal commitment to getting rid of PR-STV.

Support for the proposition that the Irish electoral system leads to excessive emphasis on constituency work is not hard to find. Katz (1984, pp. 143–4) argues that interpersonal rather than interparty competition tends to predominate, with the result that ultimately 'competition between parties tends to be on the basis of services rendered, rather than policy differences'. Carty emphasises the fact that PR-STV allows the voter to combine two criteria at once: party and personal service. He sees the electoral system as an independent contributory factor that adds to the already-existing cultural impetus to brokerage:

> This dimension of electoral politics – local brokers competing for a party vote – has been institutionalised in Ireland by the electoral system . . . With little to distinguish themselves from their opponents (particularly party colleagues), politicians are driven to emphasise their brokerage services to constituents, thus reinforcing cultural expectations.
>
> (Carty, 1981, p. 134)

The hypothesis underlying the above views is certainly plausible. The argument goes like this: the main competition for seats is between candidates of the same party. Since such candidates cannot differentiate themselves from one another on the basis of their party's policy, record in government or leadership, they compete on the basis of service to their constituents. This involves the kind of activity discussed more fully in chapter 8 below: handling a large volume of casework relating to individual benefits, ranging from welfare allowances to cattle headage payments; holding regular 'clinics' throughout the constituency; attending meetings of residents' associations and local pressure groups of all sorts; and being seen at local gatherings and functions from sporting events to funerals.

The Report of the Constitution Review Group, which was published in 1996, is an important milestone in this debate. While, as noted already, the group's report addressed all aspects of the electoral system, it paid particular attention to the nub of the debate as it has emerged in Ireland, namely the effects of the electoral system on the role of the TD. Relying heavily on a specially commissioned research paper (Gallagher, 1996), it concluded that 'constituency work is a major and increasing load on public representatives, regardless of electoral system' (Constitution Review Group, 1996, p. 56). It also noted that PR-STV and preferential systems create incentives for politicians to compete in terms of constituency service, that the role is in part a function of public expectations and attitudes, and that the only system that would tend to reduce the responsiveness of politicians to constituency demands would be 'a non-preferential list system with large constituency sizes' (p. 57). On the question of intra-party rivalry, which the report repeatedly and perhaps somewhat dramatically referred to as 'internecine', the report concluded that changing the electoral system would simply shift this to another arena, notably the candidate selection stage (p. 57). On the recruitment effects of electoral systems, the report simply noted the varying effects of different electoral systems on security of tenure and legislative turnover, observing that in PR-STV and preferential list systems these aspects tend to be influenced by voters rather than by local or national party elites (pp. 57–8). Overall, the report concluded that 'the present PR-STV system has had popular support and should not be changed without careful advance assessment of the possible effects'. It went on to note that, if there were to be change, a list system of proportional representation or a dual system that combines proportional and non-proportional components would 'satisfy more of the relevant criteria than a move to a non-PR system' (p. 60).

A balance sheet

PR-STV is a highly distinctive electoral system. It differs fundamentally from the other two main variants of electoral systems: from the plurality system by virtue of its proportionality, and from PR list systems by virtue of putting the emphasis on individual candidates rather than on political parties. Both these distinctive features are seen as weaknesses by its critics. The first line of criticism – that it produces results that are too proportional and that are conducive to unstable government – is easily dealt with: PR-STV produces moderate rather than extreme proportionality. Proportionally representative election outcomes do not necessarily lead to government instability and have not done so in the Irish case and, in any event, high degrees of disproportionality are indefensible.

There is, however, one respect in which PR-STV does allow for choice without regard to party, namely in facilitating the election of independent, non-party candidates. Frequently this will have little or no effect on the functioning of the Dáil or on the stability of the government – frequently but not always because, as noted above, parliamentary situations can and do arise in which such independents wield disproportionate power and create a potentially serious underlying threat to the stability of government.

The second main line of criticism – that it devalues parties – raises more fundamental issues. Katz argues that:

> the choice offered by [list system] PR . . . is a choice within party, while the choice offered under STV is a choice without regard to party. The effect has been to offer voters under STV a wider choice, but one which, in terms of the arguments used by its advocates, is less meaningful.
>
> (Katz, 1984, p. 145)

Instead of PR-STV, Katz argues for a small-district PR list system, in part on the grounds that it provides 'the kind of parties needed for effective implementation of the public will'. It may be, however, that the party versus non-party dilemma is overstated by Katz in the phrase 'choice without regard to party'. It is true that the choice in PR-STV is not tied to party; rather, it is open and flexible, because it elicits more information from the voter and places less constraint on the kind of information that can be transmitted. But this means that voters can vote on a party basis if they wish, and much of the evidence from the analysis of transfer patterns suggests that they do (Gallagher, 1978, Sinnott, 1995, pp. 208–16; see also Bowler and Farrell (1991) for a development of the argument that the system actually encourages an emphasis on party rather than individual candidacy).

The other side of the coin of the alleged devaluation of parties is the allegation that PR-STV is responsible for the 'excessive' constituency orientation of TDs. That TDs do an enormous amount of constituency work is undeniable. That this is due in some definitive way to the electoral system is debatable. For one thing, it is clear that there are other causes of the constituency service role: aspects of the political culture, the small size of the society, and the nature of the administrative system, including the weakness of local government (see the discussion in chapter 8). In short, it is clear that the constituency service role is due to a number of different factors, with the electoral system probably a contributory factor but not the main determinant. It should also be noted that the constituency service role has positive as well as negative aspects: keeping public representatives in touch with the real problems of ordinary people, enhancing their input into future legislative proposals and contributing to the accountability of the system.

This is a reminder that, in evaluating the system, one must look not just at its alleged negative consequences but also at its positive aspects. The latter are summarised in the Jenkins Report, which in the course of its evaluation of the options for a future British electoral system described STV in multi-member constituencies as:

a system which has several substantial advantages. It maximises voter choice, giving the elector the power to express preferences not only between parties but between different candidates of the same party. It achieves a significantly greater degree of proportionality. It avoids the problem of having two classes of member, as is the case with the Additional Member System. It also avoids the likelihood of fostering a proliferation of small splinter parties, and does this without the need for setting any arbitrary threshold. It has long worked with on the whole beneficial results in the Republic of Ireland.

(Independent Commission on the Voting System, 1998, p. 29)

One must also look at the alternatives that might replace PR-STV (Gallagher, 1987). For a variety of reasons, the plurality system, which has been twice rejected by the electorate, is a non-starter. At the other end of the spectrum, the list system is also unattractive for two main reasons: a closed list system would by definition do away completely with the candidate choice to which Irish voters are accustomed and attached; an open or preferential list system would not do away with the intra-party competition at the electoral level which is alleged to be the main disadvantage of PR-STV. This leaves a mixed system as the only plausible alternative. The prime candidate in this category is the Additional Member System (AMS) as used in Germany, in New Zealand (since 1993) and recommended (in a limited form) by the Jenkins Commission in the United Kingdom in 1998. This is a system that combines individual constituency-based representation by means of a plurality or alternative vote system with party list representation to achieve proportionality.

The danger in the Irish case is that such a system might exacerbate the two-tier character of the Dáil and the division between those with a mainly policy making orientation and those with a mainly constituency-service orientation. Indeed, it has been suggested that this division might substantially correspond to a division between the parties, since a simulation of an AMS election based on actual election results indicates that the vast majority of constituency seats would be won by Fianna Fáil and, consequently, that the majority of list seats would go to the other parties (Laver, 1998). It is also not clear that an AMS system would eradicate interpersonal constituency level competition. Experience in Germany and New Zealand suggests that many list members aspire to become constituency members and, with this in mind, informally attach themselves to a constituency. Thus one could well have a situation in which two or even three TDs would be assiduously cultivating a particular constituency; all the evidence indicates that in Ireland such competition would mainly take the form of constituency service.

Finally, although the issue does not figure much in public or political debate about PR-STV, a balance sheet of the pros and cons of PR-STV should mention the problem of what might be described as alleged theoretical flaws in the system. The flaws are theoretical because they are identified for the most part by imagining the preferences of a small set of hypothetical voters and showing that the outcomes can vary with minor changes in the assumed preferences in ways that violate certain abstract principles of how an electoral system ought to function (see, for example, Dummett, 1997, pp. 89–108, 138–57 and Nurmi, 1997). The most important such violation is the phenomenon of 'non-monotonicity'. Monotonicity is the requirement that any increase in a candidate's vote should not diminish his or her chances of being elected. Because of the importance of the order of elimination in determining the outcome in PR-STV, the possible violation of this principle can be readily demonstrated with a hypothetical set of preferences. Furthermore, rare but real violations of the principle can be found in PR-STV election results (for example, Gallagher, 1999, pp. 145–6). In assessing the significance of such issues from the voters' point of view, one must bear in mind that they depend either on assumed or on retrospective knowledge of the order of elimination of the candidates and of the transfer behaviour of the voters. Such knowledge is not available to the voters and cannot enter into their calculations. This means that complex tactical voting under PR-STV can be imagined or retrospectively constructed; it cannot be realistically pursued by the voter. In summary, proponents of PR-STV should be wary of claiming that it is perfectly logical or that it disposes completely of the issue of tactical voting; at the same time, the problems identified remain in the realm of theory rather than practice and certainly do not justify Dummett's claim that the system is 'quasi-chaotic' (Dummett, 1997, p. 143).

Conclusion

Almost eighty years ago, PR-STV seemed to be the natural choice as the electoral system of the emerging Irish state: it offered the possibility of minority representation, it suited the anti-party mood of the time, and, most importantly, it was familiar. Having become part of the institutional apparatus of the Irish Free State, it was set out in some detail in Bunreacht na hÉireann in 1937. This constitutional embodiment meant that any change to the system would require a referendum. Change was rejected on both of the occasions on which it was attempted, and by a very substantial majority on the second occasion. However, the system remains the subject of debate, a debate that has become more formal and explicit through the work of the Constitution Review Group and that of the All-Party Oireachtas Committee on the Constitution.

PR-STV is frequently criticised on the basis that it is difficult for the voters to understand. This is not a persuasive point. First, what the voter actually needs to grasp is quite simple and, secondly, both its underlying logic and its (admittedly somewhat complex) mechanics can be made readily intelligible. It has also been argued that the system produces results that are too proportional and that, as a result, it undermines the stability of government. This argument is not sustainable. Likewise, there seems to be little support for the related argument that the system is destructive of party cohesion, though it must be conceded that it is conducive to the election of independent deputies and that this can have consequences for government stability. This brings us to the most frequent and, superficially, the most plausible criticism of the system: that it imposes an excessive burden of constituency service upon those who are elected to the Dáil. There are two problems with this criticism. The first is that, in some of its versions at least, it appears to assume that all constituency service is a bad thing, that TDs should be legislators and nothing else, and that constituency service has no positive effect on the TD's legislative role. The second and the main problem with the criticism is that, rather than being due simply and solely to PR-STV, the excessive burden of constituency service experienced by TDs is due to a range of factors: the emasculation of local government, inefficiencies in the provision of welfare and other services, archaic Dáil procedures, lack of adequate funding for research and secretarial services for TDs, inadequate civic education and, in combination with all of these, perhaps the electoral system. Rather than treating alteration of the electoral system as a panacea, the more appropriate response would be to deal with the other contributory factors first. If this were done and if TDs still could not find an appropriate balance between their legislative and constituency service roles, there would then be a case for re-examining the range of alternative electoral systems to see if one of them could do better on this and on the other criteria of a good electoral system.

Notes

1   Technically, the single transferable vote in a single-seat contest is known as the alternative vote (AV). It is worth emphasising that this is not PR because, in debate about electoral reform in Ireland, the option of 'PR in single-seat constituencies' is sometimes put forward. What is being referred to is in fact the alternative vote which, for reasons that will become clear in a moment, cannot be a proportional system. The second reason for emphasising that the alternative vote and therefore the system used in Irish presidential elections is not a proportional system is to correct the mistaken impression conveyed by the Constitution, which incorrectly describes the system under which the President is elected as 'the system of proportional representation by means of the single transferable vote' (Article 12.2.3).

2   As Tables 4.2 and 4.3 show, the counting of the votes proceeds through a number of stages. Perhaps confusingly, each stage is commonly referred to as a 'count', and that term will be employed in this chapter, to conform with common usage in Ireland.

3   The rules governing the count are specified in the Electoral Act, 1992. The relevant extracts from the Act are reprinted in the official publication of the election results (see Dáil Éireann, 1998, pp. 79–85).

4   This multiple elimination procedure is not implemented if separate elimination of any of the candidates could result in the votes of one of the other candidates in question exceeding one quarter of the quota. This restriction is necessary because candidates are entitled to have their deposits returned if

their vote exceeds this proportion. Two points should be noted about this process of multiple eliminations. The first is that the scope for multiple eliminations was expanded in the 1992 Electoral Act and the practice is now much more common than heretofore. The second point is that, while it may make administrative sense, it does result in a significant loss of transparency in the electoral process because an observer cannot know the origin of the votes that are being transferred in such a count. It could be argued that the loss in transparency outweighs the gain in administrative efficiency.

5   While on the subject of anomalies in the system it is worth mentioning the alphabetical voting phenomenon. This arises because the candidates are listed on the ballot paper in alphabetical order of their surnames and some voters, presumably indifferent as to the individual candidates put forward by their preferred party, simply vote 1, 2, 3 for candidates of the party in the order in which they appear on the ballot paper. The result is an over-representation in the Dáil of individuals whose surnames begin with letters early in the alphabet (for example, in the 28th Dáil, which was elected in 1997, no fewer than forty-five of the 166 TDs had surnames beginning with the letters A, B or C). The problem could easily be eliminated by arranging the names in a number of different randomised orders on different sets of ballot papers (see Robson and Walsh, 1974).

References and further reading

Blais, André, 1991. 'The debate over electoral systems', *International Political Science Review* 12:3, pp. 239–60.

Bogdanor, Vernon, 1983. 'Introduction', pp. 1–19 in Vernon Bogdanor and David Butler (eds), *Democracy and Elections: Electoral Systems and their Political Consequences*. Cambridge: Cambridge University Press.

Boland, John, 1991. 'Dáil can only be reformed if TDs are liberated from multi-seat constituencies', *Representation* 30:111, December, pp. 42–3.

Bowler, Shaun and David M. Farrell, 1991. 'Voter behaviour under STV-PR: solving the puzzle of the Irish party system', *Political Behaviour* 13:4, pp. 303–20.

Butler, David, 1981. 'Electoral systems', pp. 7–25 in David Butler, Howard R. Penniman and Austin Ranney (eds), *Democracy at the Polls: a Comparative Study of Competitive National Elections*. Washington D.C.: American Enterprise Institute for Public Policy Research.

Carstairs, Andrew McLaren, 1980. *A Short History of Electoral Systems in Western Europe*. London: George Allen and Unwin.

Carty, R. K., 1981. *Party and Parish Pump: Electoral Politics in Ireland*. Waterloo, Ontario: Wilfrid Laurier University Press.

Coakley, John and Gerald O'Neill, 1984. 'Chance in preferential voting systems: an unacceptable element in Irish electoral law?', *Economic and Social Review* 16:1, pp. 1–18.

Coakley, John, 1980. 'Constituency boundary revision and seat redistribution in the Irish parliamentary tradition', *Administration* 28:3, pp. 291–328.

Committee on the Constitution, 1967. *Report* (Pr. 9817). Dublin: Stationery Office.

Constitution Review Group, 1996. *Report of the Constitution Review Group*. Dublin: The Stationery Office.

Dáil Éireann, 1998. *28th Dáil General Election, June, 1997: Election Results and Transfer of Votes*. Dublin: The Stationery Office.

Dummett, Michael, 1997. *Principles of Electoral Reform*. Oxford: Oxford University Press.

Farrell, Brian, 1985. 'Ireland: from friends and neighbours to clients and partisans: some dimensions of parliamentary representation under PR-STV', pp. 237–64 in Vernon Bogdanor (ed.), *Representatives of the People? Parliaments and Constituents in Western Democracies.* Aldershot: Gower.

Farrell, David M., 1997. *Comparing Electoral Systems.* London: Prentice Hall, Harvester Wheatsheaf.

FitzGerald, Garret, 1959. 'PR – The great debate', *Studies* 48, pp. 1–20.

FitzGerald, Garret, 1991. 'The Irish electoral system: defects and possible reforms', *Representation* 30:111, December, pp. 49–53.

Gallagher, Michael, 1978. 'Party solidarity, exclusivity and inter-party relationships in Ireland, 1922–1977: the evidence of transfers', *Economic and Social Review* 10:1, pp. 1–22.

Gallagher, Michael, 1987. 'Does Ireland need a new electoral system?', *Irish Political Studies* 2, pp. 27–48.

Gallagher, Michael, 1991. 'Proportionality, disproportionality and electoral systems', *Electoral Studies* 10:1, pp. 33–51.

Gallagher, Michael, 1996. 'Electoral systems', pp. 499–520 in Constitution Review Group, *Report of the Constitution Review Group.* Dublin: The Stationery Office.

Gallagher, Michael, 1999. 'The results analysed', pp. 121–50 in Michael Marsh and Paul Mitchell (eds), *How Ireland Voted 1997.* Boulder Colo.: Westview Press and PSAI Press.

Gallagher, Michael, Michael Laver and Peter Mair, 1995. *Representative Government in Modern Europe.* New York: McGraw–Hill.

Gallagher, Michael and A. R. Unwin, 1986. 'Electoral distortion under STV random sampling procedures', *British Journal of Political Science* 16:2, pp. 243–53.

Hussey, Gemma, 1993. *Ireland Today: Anatomy of a Changing State.* Dublin: Townhouse / Viking.

Independent Commission on the Voting System, 1998. *The Report of the Independent Commission on the Voting System.* London: The Stationery Office.

Katz, Richard, 1980. *A Theory of Parties and Electoral Systems.* Baltimore and London: The Johns Hopkins University Press.

Katz, Richard, 1984. 'The single transferable vote and proportional representation', pp. 135–45 in Lijphart and Grofman (1984).

Laakso, Markku and Rein Taagepera, 1979. '"Effective" number of parties: a measure with application to West Europe', *Comparative Political Studies* 12:1, pp. 3–27.

Laver, Michael, 1998. *A New Electoral System for Ireland?* Dublin: The Policy Institute and The All-Party Oireachtas Committee on the Constitution.

Lijphart, Arend, 1994. *Electoral Systems and Party Systems: A Study of Twenty-Seven Democracies, 1945–1990.* Oxford: Oxford University Press.

Lijphart, Arend and Bernard Grofman (eds), 1984. *Choosing an Electoral System: Issues and Alternatives.* New York: Praeger.

Martin, Mícheál, 1991. 'Fianna Fáil has a problem – it's time to deal with it', *Sunday Tribune* 4 August, p. 12.

Nurmi, Hannu, 1997. 'It's not just the lack of monotonicity', *Representation* 34:1, pp 48–52.

O'Leary, Cornelius, 1979. *Irish Elections 1918–1977: Parties, Voters and Proportional Representation.* Dublin: Gill and Macmillan.

Robson, Christopher and Brendan Walsh, 1974. 'The importance of positional voting in the Irish general election of 1973', *Political Studies* 22:2, pp. 191–203.

Sartori, Giovanni, 1986. 'The influence of electoral systems: faulty laws or faulty method?', pp. 43–68 in Bernard Grofman and Arend Lijphart (eds), *Electoral Laws and their Political Consequences*. New York: Agathon Press.

Sinnott, Richard, 1995. *Irish Voters Decide: Voting Behaviour in Elections and Referendums since 1918*. Manchester: Manchester University Press..

Taagepera, Rein and Matthew Soberg Shugart, 1989. *Seats and Votes: The Effects and Determinants of Electoral Systems*. New Haven and London: Yale University Press.

Tuairim Research Group, 1959. *P.R. – For or Against?* Dublin: Tuairim.

5 Party competition and the changing party system

Peter Mair

As we have seen in earlier chapters, the Irish constitution makes provision for state structures typical of those of a parliamentary democracy. It is true that the mechanics of the Irish electoral system are rather unusual, but the political effects of the electoral system are not greatly different from those of the electoral systems of other European democracies. However, while the constitution and electoral law define the formal framework within which political parties compete, they tell us little about the content of politics or about the behaviour of politicians. It is through the study of party politics that some of the most fundamental processes in modern political life are to be encountered; the study of political parties indeed provides a key to our understanding of the manner in which modern states function in practice.

Before going on in chapter 6 to look at parties as organisations in their own right and at their relations with the electorate, we need to get an overview of the whole system of parties and party competition as it has evolved in independent Ireland. Since one of the best ways of approaching such an overview is to look at the Irish system from a comparative perspective, this chapter begins by looking at those features of the Irish party system that outside observers might regard as unusual and then goes on to examine how these features have evolved and how party competition has developed. The chapter concludes with an assessment of how the party system stands following the radical changes of recent years.

The comparative context

Although the political science literature that compares the various European party systems is enormous, with a host of studies analysing the differing origins of party systems, their patterns of change and stability and the various ways in which they may be classified and compared, it often neglects the case of Ireland. There are two reasons for this. First, Ireland's status as a small peripheral state means that it often escapes the attention of studies which have inevitably focused mainly either on the larger European states (France, Germany, Italy and the United Kingdom) or on those clusters of smaller continental countries that share common traditions and cultures (the Benelux states or the Scandinavian countries). Ireland in this sense stands alone, and has often been overlooked. Second, comparative political research has also tended to overlook the Irish case because it seems that the Irish party system 'doesn't fit' into the more widely applicable models of party systems; it has long been believed that the patterns and structures of mass politics which are evident elsewhere in Europe have little relevance to the Irish case.

This is particularly true when we look at one of the most common ways to compare European party systems, which is to focus on the origins and genetic identity of the major parties which make up those systems, and then to group them into reasonably distinct sets of 'party families', such as socialists, conservatives, christian democrats and liberals (Mair and Mudde 1998). This is of course an easy and practical way in which to compare party systems, and to group particular countries together. By following this approach, for example, it is possible to make a distinction between a group of countries which includes Austria, Belgium, Germany, Italy, Luxembourg, the Netherlands and Switzerland, on the one hand, and a second group which includes Denmark, Finland, Iceland, Norway, Sweden and the United Kingdom, on the other, in that the centre-right of the political spectrum in the former group is dominated by a christian democratic party, whereas in the latter group the dominant centre-right party is a secular conservative one. This distinction is far from accidental, since Catholics have constituted a large proportion of the population in the first group of countries, whereas they constitute only a small minority in the latter. With few exceptions, christian democratic parties tended to come to the fore precisely in those countries in which there was a large Catholic population, and in which Catholic voters were mobilised in order to defend the position of the church – as regards its influence on social policy, educational policy, and so on – against the threat of growing secularism. In addition, we can also distinguish between those countries in which the left of the political spectrum was traditionally monopolised by a large social democratic party, as in the Scandinavian countries and the UK, and those where the left was formerly divided between a social democratic party, on the one hand, and a communist party, on the other, as in France and Italy. Finally, further distinctions can be drawn between countries where there has existed a strong agrarian party (for example, Denmark, Norway and Sweden) and those in which there existed a strong liberal party (for example, Belgium, Germany and the Netherlands), as well as between those in which the left is dominated by traditional parties (for example, the UK) as against those in which social democratic parties have been challenged by the relatively recent emergence of ecology parties and new left parties (for example, Germany and Denmark).

All in all, this genetic, family-oriented approach is very useful in comparing and classifying party systems. Unfortunately, however, it has never seemed very applicable to the Irish case, for it is precisely in terms of this approach that Ireland seems so exceptional. There are a number of reasons for this. In the first place, when we look at support for parties of the political centre or the right, it can be seen that the average electoral support for such parties in Ireland far exceeds that in any neighbouring European countries. During the 1980s and 1990s, for example, an average of almost 80 per cent of the vote in the various Dáil elections was won by parties of the centre-right (Fianna Fáil, Fine Gael and the Progressive Democrats), as against an average of just over 40 per cent in all the other West European countries taken together. Indeed, the only country that came close to the Irish level during this period was the United Kingdom, where the centre-right vote averaged 68 per cent prior to Labour's resurgence in 1997. The third-ranking country was West Germany, and even here the centre-right vote is only two-thirds of that in Ireland.

Second, Ireland also records the lowest level of electoral support for left-wing parties; in the 1980s and 1990s, the Irish left (the Labour Party, the Workers' Party and Democratic Left) polled an average of around 14 per cent of the vote, as against an average of more than 40 per cent in the other west European countries. In this case, the closest approximation to Ireland is the peaceful and prosperous country of Switzerland, and even there the combined vote for left-wing parties during the 1980s was exactly double that in Ireland (Gallagher, Laver and Mair, 1995, p. 206). To be sure, the surge in support for Labour in the 1992 election did finally manage to lift Ireland off the bottom of this particular league table. Even then, however, the only country to be surpassed was Switzerland, and with a total vote of just under 23 per cent in 1992 (Labour, Democratic Left and the Workers' Party combined), support for the left in Ireland still remained well below the average in Western Europe. The traditional weakness of the Irish left was underscored in 1997, when its combined strength dropped once more, to 13 per cent.

But Ireland is not only exceptional in terms of the distribution of the vote between left and centre-right; it is also exceptional in terms of the sheer difficulty of fitting the major Irish parties into the principal European families. In general, for example, comparative treatments would seem to suggest that Fianna Fáil is best regarded as a 'secular conservative' party. This means that it is a party of the centre-right which, at the same time, is not christian democratic in character, in that it did not originate as a party seeking to defend the position of the church against anti-religious forces. Even this classification results in difficulties, however. For example, other than the new conservative groupings which have emerged in the political systems of Greece and Spain, both of which democratised in the 1970s following long periods of authoritarian government, the only other major 'secular conservative' parties in Europe are to be found in the United Kingdom and in the Scandinavian countries, and in practice neither variant is very similar to Fianna Fáil. The British

Conservatives, as well as the Danish, Norwegian and Swedish Conservatives, owe their origins to the defence of middle and upper class privileges in the nineteenth century, and to resistance to the rising tide of liberalism and socialism, and all now define themselves in opposition to the major social democratic parties in their respective systems. None has the sort of radical, popular, anti-establishment heritage so treasured by Fianna Fáil (for a discussion of the party's origins and development, see pp. 132–3 and 136–7 below, and Hannan and Gallagher, 1996); none has enjoyed such close links with the organised trade union movement; and none could, or can, even come near Fianna Fáil in its traditional claims to represent the interests of the poor and the underprivileged. Indeed, it is only in certain very specific circumstances – as, for instance, when comparing the Fianna Fáil brand of nationalism with the similar patriotic appeal of the Gaullists in France, with whom Fianna Fáil forged reasonably close links in the European Parliament – that one can identify connections between this largely idiosyncratic and very successful Irish party and some at least of its European neighbours.

Fine Gael has also proved relatively enigmatic. In comparative analyses it is often listed as a christian democratic party, not least because it is now a full member of the transnational christian democratic federation, known as the European People's Party. But there the similarities largely end, and again it is in terms of its origins that the fit is least easily made. As noted above, most European christian democratic parties emerged in countries in which Catholics constituted a large part of the population, but in which the Catholic influence on social and educational policy had been challenged by secular political forces (for example, in Belgium and Italy) and/or Protestant ones (for example, in the Netherlands). The point here is that while the proportion of Catholics in the population of countries such as Italy or Belgium was nominally very high (as it was in Ireland), those who were active or practising constituted no more than a large minority, thus leaving substantial room for the mobilisation of secular political forces, whether liberal or socialist.

This was clearly not the case in Ireland, where the vast majority of the population has traditionally been made up of active and practising Catholics (see chapter 2). Thus while in much of Europe Catholicism was either effectively eradicated by the Reformation (in Scandinavia and the UK), or was subsequently challenged by the forces of secularism and socialism (in southern Europe), political Catholicism in Ireland emerged victorious, and Catholic values were quickly and very effectively enshrined in the political system. It is for this reason that, uniquely among the Catholic countries of western Europe, christian democracy has never emerged as a distinct political movement in Ireland. Thus while it might now be possible to classify Fine Gael as christian democratic, largely if not only because of its organisational links with the other christian democratic parties in western Europe, this too stretches the argument.

Finally, and also largely as a result of the pervasiveness of Catholic values, Ireland has been exceptional in the absence of a traditional 'liberal' alternative: there has been no anticlerical party of the right in the classical southern European mould, seeking to defend the individual against state and church alike. This gap in the political spectrum was partially filled in the late 1980s with the success of the Progressive Democrats, a new style of liberal party which bears many resemblances to the more recent variety of reformist liberalism which has characterised such parties as Democrats 66 in the Netherlands and (notwithstanding its name) the short-lived Social Democratic Party in the United Kingdom. Traditional liberalism, on the other hand, which owes its origins to nineteenth century secularist traditions, has always been notable by its absence from the Irish political spectrum.

In short, at least as far as the centre-right is concerned, the origins of the Irish parties bear little or no relation to those elsewhere in western Europe, and for this reason also Ireland has tended to be regarded as a unique case. It is not surprising that this should be so. The Irish parties in fact emerged from a unique experience in the period 1916–23, during which an intra-nationalist conflict and civil war centring on the country's constitutional status followed an armed independence struggle (see Garvin, 1996). Elsewhere in western Europe, on the other hand, parties mainly grew out of social conflicts, and out of the struggles of classes and other social groups for political and later social rights. Indeed, if one were to search elsewhere for echoes of the Irish experience, then the closest parallel might well be found in the United States, where the modern party system also grew out of civil war and political conflict, and where the major protagonists are also often regarded as idiosyncratic and non-comparable.

In these terms, then, the Irish party system is a case apart, and as such it is also, in terms of much of the literature on comparative European politics, a case dismissed. Indeed, as John Whyte noted some time ago, 'it is then perhaps a comfort to comparative political analysis that Irish party politics should be *sui generis*: the context from which they spring is *sui generis* also' (Whyte, 1974, p. 648).

The origins of the party system

As we have seen in chapter 1, the two major parties, Fianna Fáil and Fine Gael, originated from a split in the original Sinn Féin party, whose success in the 1918 Westminster election led to Irish independence in 1922. A crucial factor affecting the early alignment of the Irish party system was the fact that, despite Sinn Féin's success, the nationalist issue remained unresolved, with partition and the British-imposed oath of allegiance as the most contentious elements in the Treaty settlement. The division within Sinn Féin on these issues and the 1922–23 civil war created a strong polarisation between pro- and anti-Treaty sides for at least the first decade of the new state's life.

This split in Sinn Féin was primarily political, but not solely political. As the opposing forces crystallised, a marked social and economic cleavage emerged to reinforce the political opposition, with anti-Treaty Sinn Féin (and later Fianna Fáil) tending to predominate in the economically and geographically peripheral west and south-west of the country. For some time before this, of course, the question of Irish independence had gone beyond the bounds of the purely political. Although many of the original problems which had contributed to sustaining the nationalist forces had been resolved – most notably with the shift from tenant farming to owner-occupation – this very transition had led to the emergence of new issues. In particular, there was the whole question of the emphasis to be placed on the need for economic development, industrialisation and modernisation, and the earliest policies of Sinn Féin deliberately emphasised the constraint on development which resulted from the economic as well as the political dominance of Britain. Only through political independence, it was argued, could Ireland also achieve economic independence, in that only then would it be free to adopt the protectionist measures that were necessary to nurture the domestic economy.

During the crucial period leading up to independence, the Sinn Féin emphasis on the economic side of its policy had diminished. After the civil war, however, this was to re-emerge as one of the major elements in the platform of the new, anti-Treaty forces. This platform, together with an emphasis on the need for more generous social provisions, had the initial effect of alienating the anti-Treaty Sinn Féin, and later Fianna Fáil, from the more privileged sectors of Irish society, who tended to prefer the more cautious and conservative pro-Treaty wing of Sinn Féin, later to become Cumann na nGaedheal. At the same time, however, it was a programme which enhanced Sinn Féin's (and later Fianna Fáil's) appeal among the small farmers, the poor and the working class (Rumpf and Hepburn, 1977, pp. 87–107; Garvin, 1974).

The conflict between the two sides during the 1920s was therefore sharp and polarised. Indeed, not only did it involve important political and economic issues, but it also reflected a level of enmity which had found expression, just a few years earlier, in widespread armed conflict. It is worth emphasising that in almost no other country in Europe have two sides which were originally, and literally, at war with one another then gone on as fully legitimate parties to continue that contest at the electoral level within a very short space of time. It is hardly surprising, therefore, that there were many in Ireland at the time who felt that the regime itself would be unable to survive.

Survive it did, of course, and not least because of a split in the anti-Treaty Sinn Féin, which had been the losing side in the civil war, and which initially refused to recognise the legitimacy of the new state. In 1926, led by Eamon de Valera, a minority of the party broke away to form Fianna Fáil, as we have seen in chapter 1. One year later, following the introduction of the Electoral Amendment Bill which was designed to prevent any candidate standing for election who would not declare a prior commitment to swearing the oath of allegiance, Fianna Fáil turned its back on abstentionism, and entered the Dáil.

Five years later, following its electoral victory in 1932, the new party entered government, and was to remain in office continuously until 1948. For most of the 1930s its principal opponent remained the old 'pro-Treaty' wing of Sinn Féin, which, on the merger of Cumann na nGaedheal in 1933 with two minor parties, was reborn as Fine Gael. The opposition between these two parties has persisted ever since, even though, with the passing of time, and with the succession of new generations, both the original basis of their conflict and their mutual enmity have tended to wane (on the parties and the party system generally, see Manning, 1972; Carty, 1981; Gallagher, 1985; Mair, 1987; Sinnott, 1995).

Throughout the 1920s and 1930s, Labour played the role of the third party in the system, as indeed has been the case ever since. Labour is in fact the oldest of the three parties, and, like its British counterpart, was formed as the political wing of the trade union movement; it was formally launched in 1912 and developed into a proper political organisation in 1922. The party had 'stood aside' in the crucial Westminster election of 1918 for tactical reasons. Thereafter, in the new state, it also tried to stand aside from nationalist issues, and focused principally on matters of more immediate concern to its working class constituency, made up of both urban trade unionists and farm workers. Given the importance of the intranationalist divide, however, it seemed inevitable that such a strategy would force Labour onto the margins of Irish politics, and this certainly proved to be the case. Initially, when Sinn Féin/Fianna Fáil refused to enter the Dáil, Labour did enjoy quite a large share of the political limelight as the principal 'constitutional' opposition to Cumann na nGaedheal. Once Fianna Fáil had become legitimised, however, and particularly given that the Fianna Fáil programme also contained many of the more radical social and welfarist policies which were favoured by Labour, little potential remained for the smaller party to play an independent role. Indeed, when Fianna Fáil first took office in 1932, it did so as a minority government with Labour support.

Labour's failure to develop into a major party along the lines of the prominent social democratic parties in the rest of western Europe has long constituted a focus of discussion among Irish political analysts, and there are several factors which can be cited to account for the party's Cinderella status (see Gallagher, 1982; Mair, 1992). Two of these factors are of particular importance. In the first place, and most obviously, the sheer salience of nationalist issues in the early years of Irish politics meant that there was simply little scope for a party which devoted itself almost exclusively to working-class socialist concerns. Indeed, the working class itself was small, since Irish society at the time had a largely rural and agricultural character (see chapter 2). Second, as Brian Farrell (1970) has argued, Labour's decision not to take part in the 1918 election played a crucial role in determining its subsequent poor fortunes. Given the very large proportion of newly enfranchised voters – the electorate on the whole island had increased from some 700,000 in 1910 to almost two million in 1918 (Farrell 1971, p. 46) – this can really be considered as the election which set the political terms of reference for the new state. Had Labour participated, argued Farrell, then it would have had the opportunity of placing socialist issues on what was essentially a wholly new political agenda; in fact, of course, Labour missed that opportunity, and thus in its own way it helped to pass the agenda over to almost exclusively nationalist concerns.

Both of these arguments therefore place a particular emphasis on the patterns which developed at the very early stages of mass politics in independent Ireland. In the beginning was the Treaty, the argument goes, and since then nothing has changed. Precisely because nationalism became the focus of the political agenda in 1918 and immediately thereafter, precisely because Sinn Féin/Fianna Fáil and Cumann na nGaedheal/Fine Gael proved to be the dominant actors on the political stage in the 1920s and 1930s, and precisely because Labour was marginalised throughout this period, we have the outcome which became so familiar from the 1960s to the 1990s. The pattern may be seen in Figure 5.1: a strong if now slightly weakening Fianna Fáil, a rather less strong Fine Gael, and a Labour Party that consistently takes third place. The formative years of Irish politics were therefore the crucial years, setting a pattern which has since proved almost impossible to shift. It is in this sense that people still continue to speak of the maintenance of 'civil war politics' and of the uniqueness of the Irish case.

But while the particular cleavage which divided the parties in these early years and the political context in which they were embedded may well have been unique, the more general phenomenon that very early patterns of politics become frozen into place is certainly not confined to Ireland. Indeed, as Lipset and Rokkan (1967) have shown in a now widely-cited analysis, this is precisely the pattern which has tended to prevail throughout western Europe, with the cleavage structures which were dominant around the beginning of the century, when mass suffrage was first introduced, as well as the parties which mobilised on the basis of these cleavages, tending to remain frozen in place thereafter. Writing of the west European party systems of the late 1960s, they noted that these tended to reflect, 'with few but significant exceptions, the cleavage structures of the 1920s', and that throughout Europe 'the party alternatives, and in remarkably many cases the party organisations, are older than the majority of the national electorates' (Lipset and Rokkan, 1967, p. 50). The other European countries were, of course, unlike Ireland in that their party systems froze around cleavages which tended to reflect primarily social rather than political divisions, and involved socialist,

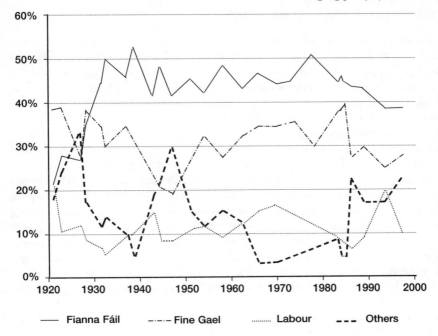

Figure 5.1 Electoral support for Irish parties, 1922–97

Source: Calculated from appendix 2b.

christian, conservative and liberal parties, rather than building on the sort of nationalist parties which were frozen into place in the Irish case; nevertheless, even though the issues were different, the process itself proved to be more or less the same.

That said, we should be wary of assuming any sense of inevitability or fatalism in our understanding of the factors which determined the development of the Irish party system. In Ireland, to be sure, as elsewhere in Europe, the formative years played a very important role. But this is not the only relevant factor, and it is certainly not the only factor which can be cited to explain the continued survival of the old civil war parties and the long-term minority position of the Labour Party.

The dynamics of party competition

In seeking to understand the evolution of the Irish party system, we need to begin with one of its most characteristic features: its domination by a single party. This feature must in turn be seen in the context of the alliance options open to each of the parties, options that were a function of two other characteristics, one arithmetical, the other ideological: the mechanics and the nature of policy competition.

The electoral dominance of Fianna Fáil

The single most important element in determining the development of the Irish party system has been the persistently dominant position of Fianna Fáil (Dunphy, 1995). As noted above, the very early and formative years of the party system were characterised by the opposition of Sinn Féin/Fianna Fáil, on the one hand, and Cumann na nGaedheal/Fine Gael, on the other, with Labour and occasional other minor parties being marginalised by this overriding contest. After 1932, Fianna Fáil began to consolidate its own pre-eminent position, not least because its governing status and increasingly moderate approach allowed the party to extend its support far beyond the small-farmer constituency in the peripheral west, and to begin to appeal to the more 'respectable' and privileged middle class (and working class) voters in the rest of the country (see Garvin, 1974), thus stealing much of the ground from under Fine Gael's feet. At the same time, support for Cumann na nGaedheal/Fine Gael itself began to slip: in 1927, when it was at its peak, the party had polled almost 39 per cent of the vote, but at the end of the 1940s, when Fianna Fáil had already been in government for sixteen years, its vote had fallen to just under 20 per cent (see appendix 2b).

Meanwhile, frustrated by the erosion of Fianna Fáil's original radical appeal, new parties had also begun to emerge in the 1940s. These included Clann na Talmhan, a party which sought to represent the interests of the small farmers, and Clann na Poblachta, which mobilised on the basis of a strong republican and socially reformist programme. Labour also managed to reach a new peak in support by 1943, although in 1944 the party temporarily split into two. By the end of the 1940s, therefore, the party system was balanced between a relatively strong Fianna Fáil party, on the one side, and a fragmented and politically diverse collection of smaller parties, on the other. This was also a period in which there perhaps existed a greater potential for political realignment and change than had been the case for almost twenty years. In moving to the centre, Fianna Fáil had abandoned much of its original radicalism and had begun to disenchant many of its former supporters. Fine Gael, on the other hand, seemed to be heading towards the margins of Irish politics, and a new, sometimes radical, politics was also afoot. In the 1948 election, the two Labour parties, the two Clann parties, and a variety of independents – all falling more or less outside the traditional mould of Irish politics – together won a total of almost 40 per cent of the vote.

The two new parties, and Labour, now had a relatively clear choice. On the one hand, they could pursue an independent line and, by mobilising an alternative politics within a system which had for some time revolved around the civil war contest, they could seek to take advantage of the problems of their established opponents, thus building the potential for a radical transformation and realignment of the party system itself. On the other hand, they could try to sink their mutual differences, and could even break bread with Fine Gael, and follow the more short-term strategy of providing an alternative government to Fianna Fáil.

In the event, it was the latter option which was favoured, and rather than turning their backs on the old civil war opposition between Fianna Fáil and Fine Gael, the various minor parties, together with some independent support, formed a loose and heterogeneous coalition with Fine Gael in an attempt to throw Fianna Fáil out of office at last. Rather than building an alternative politics, therefore, they chose instead to work towards creating an alternative government. The attempt proved successful, at least after a fashion, and the new coalition government lasted until 1951. As we have seen in chapter 1, Fianna Fáil then came back into office for three years, before being once again displaced in 1954 by a coalition of the now revived Fine Gael, the now re-united Labour Party, and the now fading Clann na Talmhan. This government also lasted for three years, with Fianna Fáil returning to office in 1957 and remaining there for a further sixteen years (see appendix 3b for a list of governments).

In retrospect, this sequence of alternating governments might not seem so important – no more than a brief flurry of change in what has otherwise been a highly predictable political balance. From another perspective, however, it was a crucial moment, for it helped to clarify the character of Irish political competition in quite an unambiguous fashion. From now on, politics no longer revolved around the contest between Fianna Fáil and Fine Gael, as had been the case in the 1920s and 1930s. Indeed, in this sense 'civil war' politics existed no more. Rather, and almost throughout the postwar period, politics instead revolved around the opposition between Fianna Fáil, on the one hand, and all the remaining relevant parties in the system, on the other (Mair, 1979). Thus while there have always been more than two parties contesting elections in Irish politics, the pattern of competition has often tended to reflect that of a straight two-party system, with a single party (Fianna Fáil) on one side and a varying collection of parties on the other. This pattern was to persist from 1948, when the first anti-Fianna Fáil coalition was formed, right up until 1989, when Fianna Fáil itself entered a coalition government for the first time in its history. There then followed, as we shall soon see, a new and less predictable pattern of potential inter-party alliances.

Strategy, policy and party competition

The most important feature of this postwar configuration involved the constraints which it imposed on party competition and party strategy, constraints which resulted from the struggle for office between Fianna Fáil, on the one side, and all of the remaining parties, on the other (see Mair, 1993). Given the size of its core electoral support and Dáil representation, Fianna Fáil was obviously the only party which was in a position to aim for a single-party majority government. As such, at least until 1989, it was also in a position to divide the party system into two camps – those who supported Fianna Fáil and those who did not – and to follow its own independent path, quite unconcerned with coalitions and alliances. If the party won a majority in the Dáil it would govern alone; if it failed to win enough seats to form a majority, then it would either form a minority single-party administration (as it did in 1951, 1961, March 1982 and 1987) or it would go into opposition (as it did in 1948, 1954, 1973, 1981, and December 1982). Indeed, in relative terms, Fianna Fáil has been one of the most successful parties in Western Europe (see Coakley, 1987, p. 159). Even in the 1980s and early 1990s, for example, at a time when the party was believed to be in trouble and to be losing its electoral grip, it still managed to win an average of close to 45 per cent of the vote, which is approximately a quarter more than that polled by the largest party in the average western European system. Only in Austria, Germany and Greece has the largest party usually managed to win a greater share of the national vote than did Fianna Fáil, although the Social Democrats in both Spain and Sweden have come very close. Moreover, because of biases in the electoral system, especially in the past, this large electoral support was also usually translated into an even larger share of Dáil seats, with the result that the party could normally hope to win a parliamentary majority on its own.

Fianna Fáil's opponents, on the other hand, were much less capable of developing a wholly independent strategy. Indeed, as far as the struggle for government was concerned, their options were relatively simple, if also unappealing: both Fine Gael and Labour could plough their own independent furrows, which would mean that they would always remain in opposition; or they could form an alliance and share office together. Thus whereas Fianna Fáil's choices through to the end of the 1980s were between government and opposition, the choices for Fine Gael and Labour were between *coalition* and opposition. In strategic terms, their hands were tied, and, to the extent that office mattered, neither could afford to go its own way.

In principle, of course, such a constraint may not appear particularly demanding. Throughout western Europe, coalition government is the norm rather than the exception (Gallagher, Laver and Mair, 1995, pp. 318–20), and most major parties usually find themselves obliged to share office with at least one of their potential competitors. But what is also striking about most of these other systems is that the parties involved usually have a choice of partners, in that coalition alliances are regularly reshuffled and changed, so that if Party A finds it difficult to forge an agreement with Party B, it can always turn around and try to fix up a deal with Party C instead.

In Ireland, however, such options were foreclosed to an unusual extent until the end of the 1980s. Precisely because Fianna Fáil chose to follow its own independent path and enjoyed a sufficient 'critical mass' of support to govern alone, it was clearly out of the reckoning in any conceivable coalition. This, in turn, meant that Fine Gael had only one potential coalition partner, which was Labour, while Labour also had only one potential coalition partner, which was Fine Gael. In effect, the dominance of Fianna Fáil therefore forced these two smaller parties together, so that their choices were not simply coalition or opposition, but were rather, and more narrowly, coalition *with one another* or exclusion from government. It is in this sense that enormous constraints had been placed on the postwar patterns of party competition.

In the three decades which elapsed between the end of the second anti-Fianna Fáil coalition in 1957 and Fianna Fáil's own first coalition in 1989, the only major element of change in the structural configuration of the Irish party system was the composition of the non-Fianna Fáil alternative. The coalition experience in the 1950s, in which both governments were led by a Fine Gael Taoiseach, was sufficient to pull Fine Gael back from the brink and to restore its previously faltering political fortunes. Labour also benefited from the experience, while the two Clann parties, and many of the independents, found that their support had waned. By the 1960s, therefore, the old parties were back in style, and by the end of that decade their total vote share had risen to almost 97 per cent: 46 per cent for Fianna Fáil, 34 per cent for Fine Gael and 17 per cent for Labour. By then, all other options had faded.

But while the old parties had consolidated their position once again, the logic of competition remained as it had been throughout the postwar period, with Fianna Fáil on the one side and a now reduced collection of opposition parties on the other. From 1957 onwards, Fine Gael and Labour did try to go their own separate ways, with each hoping, if only fancifully, that it might one day acquire sufficient support to challenge for government on its own. As far as the electorate was concerned, however, it seemed as if the choice remained either coalition or Fianna Fáil, and as long as Fine Gael and Labour were pursuing mutually exclusive strategies, this meant in fact that Fianna Fáil remained the only really feasible governing option. Thus even though Fianna Fáil did sometimes experience electoral losses, and even though it never managed to poll a majority of the votes in any election in this period, it nevertheless remained in office continuously between 1957 and 1973.

It was in 1973 that the two opposition parties once more pooled their resources and decided to recognise the fact that their most feasible strategy was to work together to establish an alternative government to Fianna Fáil. In this sense, therefore, their new strategy simply replicated that which had been pursued in the late 1940s and 1950s, when the non-Fianna Fáil parties also came together to create an alternative government. In other respects, however, there were marked differences between the two situations. In the first place, the anti-Fianna Fáil vote was now concentrated in just two parties rather than being spread over five, as had been the case in 1948, and this made the whole process of coalition negotiation that much simpler and more straightforward. Since fewer actors were involved, it was more likely that an agreement could be reached and that it would be maintained. In the second place, the new coalition was also facilitated by a change in the patterns of policy competition.

By the end of the 1960s and the beginning of the 1970s, both Labour and Fine Gael had moved to the left of the political spectrum and had begun to pursue what were essentially similar policy goals. The shift in Labour was most marked, even if largely rhetorical, and was symbolised most clearly in its slogan 'The Seventies will be Socialist'. But, perhaps surprisingly, Fine Gael had also moved to the left, abandoning many of the liberal, free-market policies which had characterised the party during the coalition period in the 1950s, and emphasising instead the need for social justice and redistribution, and for what it called 'the Just Society', which was the name given to the election programme which the party first launched in 1965. Both parties therefore shared a common ground in what was a rather moderate social democratic agenda, and a joint concern with the need for a more equitable redistribution of resources.

Fianna Fáil, on the other hand, placed progressively less emphasis on such concerns, stressing instead the need for general economic development. As Seán Lemass, party leader from 1959 to 1966, was wont to remark, 'a rising tide lifts all boats'. Such a view tended to characterise the Fianna Fáil position throughout the postwar period, in that the party's programmes usually involved an appeal to three related elements. In the first place, as the only party capable of providing single-party administrations, Fianna Fáil persistently emphasised the need for strong and capable government, arguing that coalition alliances implied both indecisiveness and ineffectiveness. Second, the party emphasised the need for economic growth, arguing that any patterns of inequality and poverty could best be eradicated by increasing the size of the national cake. Third, and perhaps most importantly, the party stressed the need for social solidarity and the need to promote 'the national interest', a plea which echoed its pre-war emphasis on territorial nationalism when it competed against Fine Gael (or, earlier, Cumann na nGaedheal), but which now, in the context of the competition between Fianna Fáil and all the other parties, became translated into an appeal for all sections of the (twenty-six-county) nation to work together in harmony. Together, these three elements combined into a more general 'corporatist' ideology, which, by emphasising the importance of the national interest, deliberately set its face against any attempts to translate social conflict into politics. In other words, it was an ideology which opposed any attempt to mobilise the interests of, say, workers against employers, or of the under-privileged against the more privileged, or of the farmers against the urban dwellers, or of secular forces against the Catholic church. According to this ideology, all sections of society should, on the contrary, work together to promote the interests of the nation as a whole, of which Fianna Fáil, in turn, was the most effective guardian (see Mair, 1987, pp. 138–206).

Policy differences between the two sides were therefore sometimes quite marked, and this helped to give the 1973 coalition programme the sort of coherence which was so noticeably absent in the late 1940s and 1950s. Against traditional Fianna Fáil corporatism, Labour and the now more left-oriented Fine Gael were promoting a moderate social democratic appeal, emphasising the particular interests of the more under-privileged sections of the community rather than those of society as a whole.

Beginning with the Fine Gael-Labour coalition of 1973–77, governments alternated along the same pattern for sixteen years, with Fianna Fáil returning in 1977, the coalition coming back once more in 1981, and then, following two short-lived alternating governments, the coalition returned to government once more in late 1982, before finally being displaced by a minority single-party Fianna Fáil government in 1987 (see appendix 3b; Penniman, 1978; Penniman and Farrell, 1987). By then, however, the common political agenda which had been forged by Fine Gael and Labour had become little more than a matter of historical memory. The deep recession of the 1980s had encouraged Fine Gael's relatively well-to-do electorate to adopt a more self-interested view of politics and had undermined much of the party's commitment to redistribution. Fiscal rectitude now became the priority issue. At the same time, Labour had witnessed the gradual erosion of its electoral support during the coalition period, with its more conservative voters drifting towards Fine Gael or even Fianna Fáil, and with its more radical supporters turning towards the newly mobilised Workers' Party. Relations between the two erstwhile allies became more and more difficult, and in January 1987, following a dispute over the budget estimates, Labour withdrew from the coalition and from government. Indeed, when Fianna Fáil returned to office in 1987, the government which it replaced was a Fine Gael minority government, a caretaker administration which had remained in office for some two months following Labour's withdrawal.

In addition to the increasing divisions between Fine Gael and Labour, the late 1980s also witnessed a renewed and quite marked fragmentation of the party system. In the midst of the recession, the political spectrum had been widened to the right as a result of the emergence of the Progressive Democrats, a party which had initially resulted from a division within Fianna Fáil over its policies in relation to Northern Ireland, but which quickly won support from elements in both major parties on the basis of its essentially conservative economic policies and liberal stance on 'moral' issues. The party made a major breakthrough in its first election in 1987, when it polled almost 12 per cent of the vote and won fourteen Dáil seats. The spectrum had also been widened on the left, with the slow but steady growth of the Workers' Party (and its later offshoot, Democratic Left), which polled almost 4 per cent of the vote in 1987 (it actually out-polled Labour in the Dublin area) and won four Dáil seats. The success of these two parties also helped to drive an even greater wedge between Fine

Gael and Labour, with the former moving to the right in an effort to stave off the challenge from the Progressive Democrats, and with the latter under pressure to move to the left in an effort to compete with the Workers' Party. By 1987, therefore, the anti-Fianna Fáil bloc, if such it may be called, had broken apart, and the parties, as well as perhaps the electorate, appeared to be more polarised than had been the case for decades.

These divisions within the non-Fianna Fáil side of the party system helped to enhance Fianna Fáil's strategic position. This relative advantage was to become even more apparent as the party attempted to move closer to the centre ground on issues relating to Northern Ireland and to church–state relations; these particular issues formerly constituted perhaps the only dimension of competition along which the various non-Fianna Fáil parties might have found common policy ground in competing against their larger opponent.

The relevance of this common non-Fianna Fáil ground had been under-scored in the wake of Mary Robinson's successful election to the presidency in 1990, and indeed it was her success which helped to shift Fianna Fáil, judiciously, closer to a more moderate position. Nevertheless, as the more conventional left–right political spectrum widened, albeit temporarily, and as the distances extended between the Progressive Democrats and Fine Gael, on the one hand, and Labour and the Workers' Party/Democratic Left, on the other, Fianna Fáil saw itself sitting increasingly happily in the centre, ready to make deals with whatever smaller party was willing to join it in coalition.

That said, the decision by Fianna Fáil to form a coalition with the Progressive Democrats in 1989 also carried certain risks for the party. As has been emphasised above, it was precisely Fianna Fáil's capacity to divide party alignments into an opposition between itself on the one hand, and all other parties on the other, which had structured and sustained the postwar party system, as well as Fianna Fáil's own position of dominance within that system. Once these constraints were loosened, however, as they were in 1989, the party system was likely to become much more volatile and unstable. The political market, in other words, was opened up, and hence those parties which had been sustained most strongly by the old alignment, especially Fianna Fáil itself, were likely to become more vulnerable (see Mair, 1990).

The consequences of this new openness were to be seen in the elections of the 1990s. Since competition was no longer structured by the opposition of Fianna Fáil against the rest, it risked ceasing, in a sense, to be structured at all. Fianna Fáil clearly suffered from this change, electorally if not strategically, with its support falling to its lowest level since 1927. Fine Gael, whose role had long been reduced to that of leadership of the anti-Fianna Fáil alliance, also correspondingly suffered, falling in 1992 to its lowest level of support since the nadir of 1948. At the same time, Labour, whose fortunes had been most seriously curtailed by the traditional alignment, finally found the space in which to begin shedding its Cinderella status, and in

1992 polled its highest share of the vote since 1922. Labour then went on to succeed the Progressive Democrats as Fianna Fáil's new junior partner in government, a move which, despite Fianna Fáil's electoral losses, did much to confirm the strategic advantage which the larger party enjoyed in the centre of the political spectrum, and which allowed it to form an alliance first to its right, and later to its left.

In one sense, of course, it can be argued that Labour's decision to enter this new coalition in 1992 was simply a repeat of the mistakes which it had made in the late 1940s and early 1970s. Then, following sporadic earlier electoral successes, the party had gone on to join new coalition governments, only to find that its identity had been undermined and its potential for further growth stymied. The position in 1992 was quite different, however. In the first place, Labour entered the coalition with a much stronger Dáil party than ever before. Second, it entered the coalition on the basis of choice rather than necessity. Indeed, for the first time in its history, Labour found itself in a position (not unlike that of the small German Free Democratic Party in the 1970s and 1980s) in which it could choose between alternative governments, and its bargaining position appeared to have become immeasurably strengthened. Third, and most importantly of all, Labour's decision in 1992 to join Fianna Fáil, rather than to try once again in some combination with Fine Gael, finally offered the possibility of ending for once and for all the old 'Fianna Fáil versus the rest' party system. It was one thing for Fianna Fáil to fracture that mould by coalescing with the newly formed Progressive Democrats, many of whose leaders were actually former members of Fianna Fáil (both Progressive Democrat ministers in the 1989–92 coalition government had formerly sat at the cabinet table as Fianna Fáil ministers). It was quite another thing for the party to reach across the traditional divide and form a coalition with one of 'the rest'. Once that had happened, everything could come up for grabs, including the possibility of a new future for Labour in which the party might finally be able to stretch its strategic muscles.

In the event, however, Fianna Fáil's relationship with Labour proved no more happy than that with the Progressive Democrats. In fact, Fianna Fáil found it difficult to adjust to coalition government and ended up by alienating both of its partners. At the end of 1994, therefore, Labour decided to abandon its experimental alliance with Fianna Fáil and to return once more to Fine Gael to form a new 'rainbow' coalition (as the first new government to take office without an intervening general election). This also brought Democratic Left into government for the first time. Following the 1997 election, however, and severe Labour electoral losses, this new coalition fell from office and was replaced by a second Fianna Fáil–Progressive Democrat coalition under the leadership of Fianna Fáil Taoiseach Bertie Ahern. Although Fianna Fáil's return to its first coalition partner has not been altogether without problems, the relationship between the two parties has been less fraught than in the case of earlier

Fianna Fáil coalitions. Quite simply, the larger party has now begun to learn how to play by the new rules (see below).

The changing party system

It will be clear from the discussion above that there have been three crucial watersheds in the overall development of the Irish party system, and that these have divided the history of the party system in rather distinctive phases. Furthermore, the transition to the current format of the party system appears to have placed institutional strains on the system itself and on its relationship with the voters. Following a summary of the major changes in the system, we will consider these strains.

The first watershed in the development of the party system came in 1927, when Fianna Fáil emerged from the wilderness and decided to take its seats in the Dáil. In so doing, the party ensured that the intense conflict which had once been fought out as a civil war would now become largely a focus for electoral competition. Politics, in this sense, genuinely became war by other means, with the major dimension of competition pitting Sinn Féin/Fianna Fáil against Cumann na nGaedheal/Fine Gael, while Labour in particular struggled to promote an alternative basis for political alignment.

The second watershed came in 1948, when the strategies chosen by the new minor parties, and by Labour, confirmed that in future the key dimension of competition would be that of Fianna Fáil versus the rest, in which the voters would simply be asked to choose whether they wished to be governed by a single-party Fianna Fáil government or by a non-Fianna Fáil coalition, a choice which remained relevant right through to the 1970s and 1980s. The waning of the civil war opposition was also later underlined in the emergence of an increasingly relevant new policy divide, which saw Fianna Fáil insisting on its guardianship of 'the national interest', as against the ever more evident social democratic appeal espoused by both Labour and Fine Gael. Despite the growing emphasis on this moderate social democracy, the constraints on party strategies imposed by this new pattern of competition were felt particularly hard by Labour, which found itself increasingly tied to the role of junior coalition partner in the anti-Fianna Fáil alignment, and therefore unable to mobilise an alternative political opposition. It is certainly the case that Labour had been weakened as a result of its marginalisation in 1918, and also as a result of the subsequent institutionalisation of civil war politics; but as Irish society modernised, and as the civil war opposition waned in importance, it was the strategic constraints imposed by an opposition pitting Fianna Fáil against all other parties which was to prove the most persistent bulwark against Labour's further progress.

In 1989, however, this decades-old pattern finally began to open up. This year marked a third watershed in the development of the party system, one that came about as a result of Fianna Fáil's decision to enter a coalition with the Progressive Democrats. This new watershed was important in two ways. In the first place, precisely because Fianna Fáil now proved willing to play the coalition game, it was no longer the case that competition revolved around Fianna Fáil versus the rest. From this point on, in fact, Fianna Fáil was to become 'just another party', bigger and more successful than its opponents, to be sure, but certainly no different from them in any other important sense. Second, by playing the coalition game Fianna Fáil opened up the possibility that it could now remain almost permanently in office. The reason for this was simple enough: as the biggest single party, and as the party which was perhaps closest to the centre of the political spectrum, it would probably always seem easier for Fianna Fáil to find a coalition partner than would be the case for most of the other parties. Moreover, unless it was to suffer a massive and quite unprecedented erosion of support, Fianna Fáil in the future, as in 1989, would be likely to need just one other coalition partner in order to achieve a majority, whereas its smaller opponents would be required to forge deals involving three if not four parties in order to control a majority in the Dáil. Thus while Fianna Fáil's electoral position might indeed have weakened, and while it might well have abandoned its old shibboleths and become just another party, nevertheless, from a strategic point of view, its decision to become available for coalition had the capacity to place it in a stronger position than it had been at any time in the two previous decades (see Laver and Shepsle, 1992).

Generally speaking, political institutions consist of recognised structures and accepted norms of behaviour. Indeed, the whole notion of institutionalisation implies a strong sense of familiarity and predictability. Norms and rules are established which then go on to develop a life of their own, and it is to these patterns and expectations that political actors will adapt. The institution of the party system is no different in this regard. In fact, the very notion of a party system implies a *patterned* set of interactions which becomes stabilised over time (Sartori, 1976, pp. 43-4), and which is recognised as such by both voters and party leaders. Breaking such a pattern can therefore be fraught with difficulties, since it implies that new norms must be developed, and that expectations may be overturned. This is precisely what had begun to happen in Ireland by the early 1990s, and two of the difficulties in particular can immediately be singled out.

The first difficulty which was confronted within the potentially novel terms of reference that followed from Fianna Fáil's first coalition in 1989 was that which concerned Fianna Fáil itself, in that it was a party which was simply unused to working within coalition, and which had had no prior experience of sharing the cabinet table with another party. Soon after becoming Taoiseach in the new coalition government, for instance, Albert Reynolds went on record to assert that 'I will not allow anybody to think that Fianna Fáil needs to get its direction from another party' (Girvin, 1993, p. 9). Increasingly, the Progressive Democrat ministers felt themselves excluded from the government decision-making processes, and came to believe that Fianna Fáil was behaving as if it were the only party in government. The withdrawal of the smaller party from the cabinet and the collapse of the government in late 1992 therefore came as no surprise (Girvin, 1993, pp. 8–12). Similar problems befell Fianna Fáil's second coalition, this time with Labour, where the potential benefits of an over-whelming and seemingly very secure Dáil majority were quickly squandered by a souring of the relationships between the two parties, and by a series of high-handed manoeuvres by Fianna Fáil which appeared to take no account of Labour sensitivities. These ultimately resulted in Labour's withdrawal and the collapse of the government in 1994 (see Garry, 1995). The result was that Fianna Fáil had to wait until 1997 to try coalition a third time, on this occasion, once more, with the Progressive Democrats. Although the Progressive Democrats were in an even smaller minority in this new administration, holding only one cabinet seat, it did seem that Fianna Fáil was intent on learning the lessons of its past, and was now more willing to recognise that this was – at least formally – a two-party government. In other words, following its previous two unhappy experiences, the party was now finally learning how to operate coalition politics. In this sense, therefore, this first difficulty has now been overcome.

The second difficulty was more fundamental, however, particularly since it also involved mass electoral expectations. Labour had spent its opposition years during the first Fianna Fáil–Progressive Democrat coalition in leading a sustained and very powerful attack on the Fianna Fáil leadership. The party also proved strongly critical of Fianna Fáil during the election campaign of 1992. For these reasons alone, it might have been expected to cast its lot in with Fine Gael in the probable event that Fianna Fáil would fail to win a clear majority in that election. More importantly, however, this was also how Irish politics was believed to work, in that for many of the party leaders, as well as for most voters, politics was still seen to revolve around the competition between Fianna Fáil and the rest. Indeed, as far as the new Fine Gael leader, John Bruton, was concerned, this could even be assumed a priori. During the 1992 campaign, without prior consultation, he suggested that a new coalition of Fine Gael, Labour and the Progressive Democrats could be formed, and that voters should therefore transfer their lower-preference votes accordingly. From one perspective, this was interpreted as simply reflecting Fine Gael arrogance, and the Labour leader, Dick Spring, was quick to disabuse his former coalition ally about taking Labour's future cooperation for granted. In fact, Spring's strategy was to keep the coalition option open, and to exploit the new and more open situation in order to gain the best possible deal for his party. From another perspective, however, Bruton's position was understandable, if somewhat maladroitly presented: in traditional political terms, after all, Labour was on Fine Gael's side.

When Labour finally did choose to turn its back on Fine Gael, and to enter a wholly novel coalition with Fianna Fáil, the reaction was therefore predictable. The party was castigated in sections of the media and by senior figures in Fine Gael as having betrayed the expectations of its voters.

Moreover, since Labour had achieved a record electoral gain in 1992, more than doubling its 1989 vote, and had done so while adopting a very critical stance towards Fianna Fáil, the accusations of betrayal achieved a particular resonance. When the alliance with Fianna Fáil broke down in 1994, therefore, and when Labour crossed the floor of the Dáil to form a new three-party coalition with Fine Gael and the Democratic Left, it was seen as marking an overdue restoration of normality and a return to the old politics of Fianna Fáil versus the rest. This sense of restoration seemed to be further confirmed by the results of the 1997 election, in that Labour's substantial losses in that election were seen, though not necessarily accurately, as at least partly reflecting the residue of electoral dissatisfaction with its initial decision to join Fianna Fáil in government. Voters were used to the old patterns of political alignment, it was argued, and they resented what had been seen as the political opportunism of Fine Gael's traditional ally. In other words, while the party leaders might have quickly adapted to the new political circumstances and to the new openness of coalition politics, the voters remained tied to their traditional expectations. As Labour had apparently discovered, the parties could confound those expectations only at great electoral cost.

In all likelihood, however, even if such popular expectations were important, they are unlikely to persist far into the future. The Dáil is now much more fragmented than before, and it will be increasingly difficult for any single party to win an overall majority. At the same time, and not least as a result of recent economic successes, policy differences between the parties have eroded significantly, and the once burgeoning polarisation of the late 1980s has now been left far behind. Within the Fianna Fáil–Progressive Democrat government that came to power in 1997, for example, a more or less clear consensus on budgetary and fiscal policy emerged, and in many respects this consensus also reached across to embrace many on the opposition benches. Moreover, the impact of European Monetary Union imposes a strong discipline on all governments, of whatever hue, leaving much less to argue about. At the same time, the old shibboleths that were specific to the Irish case are also waning in importance. In contrast to the situation which pertained through to the end of the 1980s, a clear and openly stated all-party consensus on Northern Ireland has developed, while issues concerning church–state relations and traditional morality have also largely faded from the agenda. In effect, therefore, and whether speaking about long-term ideology or short-term policy, there is now less and less to choose between the competing protagonists, and there is now less and less in principle that might prevent new forms of coalition or new governing arrangements. All parties are now coalitionable, and, what is perhaps more important, all are also now more or less capable of coalescing with all others. In other words, not only have the parties become more coalitionable, they have also become more promiscuous.

What the parties in the future are likely to value above all, therefore, is their strategic room for manoeuvre. Fianna Fáil will certainly want to keep its options open, allowing for coalition with any of the smaller parties, such as the Progressive Democrats – should they continue to survive as an independent force – or even the Greens. Nor will Fianna Fáil wish to exclude the possibility of a renewed alliance with Labour. For its part, and notwithstanding its shock defeat in 1997, Labour will also want to keep its options open, and will certainly be reluctant to remain tied exclusively to the Fine Gael option, especially after its absorption of Democratic Left in 1999. While it is now difficult to conceive of a wholly mould-breaking arrangement which might bridge the gap between the traditional poles of the party system by bringing Fianna Fáil and Fine Gael together in some new 'grand coalition', this is a possibility which also should not be excluded by definition. There is now little in terms of policy or ideology which still divides the two parties, and should the state be faced with a particular external challenge, whether provoked by an economic crisis in Europe or by developments concerning the constitutional future of Northern Ireland, old hatchets could certainly be buried.

This new politics of coalition-making is obviously something unprece-dented in Irish politics, and actually carries the Irish case further away from a British model and closer to the compromising style of party politics in such countries as Belgium, Denmark, and the Netherlands (see Mair, 1997). It also suggests that processes of government formation are likely to prove much more protracted than in the past, with post-election bargaining becoming the principal determinant of which parties end up holding office, and with voters increasingly voting in the dark, without any clear sense of which combinations are likely to form a government. What this also means, of course, is that voters will inevitably retain fewer prior expectations about how government should be formed, and this will also allow the parties greater freedom of manoeuvre. Eventually, therefore, we should see the second difficulty that was noted above – the general expectation that inter-party alignments would follow the traditional pattern – also being overcome.

Conclusion

It is certainly not easy to predict the future shape and direction of the new Irish party system. The degree of stability of party systems in general depends, among other factors, on two related elements, both of which are tied to voting patterns. The first derives from strong social cleavages, which pin voters down in particular alignments based on class, religion, region and other forms of collective identity. The second derives from a structured pattern of competition, which constrains voters by limiting the range of available alternatives. In Britain, for example, the long-term stability of the party system was sustained not only by strong ties between party and class, but also by the fact that the only realistic governing alternatives were those represented either by Labour or by the Conservatives. In Ireland, however, a country which was always characterised by a politics 'without social bases', only the second of these factors came into play, with overall stability being primarily ensured by the paramount need to choose between Fianna Fáil, on the one hand, and its opponents, on the other.

This is now no longer the case. In the first place, Fianna Fáil on its own is now less credible an alternative. In the future, it is often likely to require partners in government. Second, it is also no longer so distinct from its traditional opponents, nor they from it. If coalition with Labour is possible, then who is to argue against the future possibility of coalition with Fine Gael? It is in this sense that all the options are now open, with both the electors and the parties being less constrained and hence no longer so predictable. The terms of reference of Irish politics have finally changed, and for now, at least, the party system seems largely unstructured.

How future voters might respond to these changed terms of reference is of course difficult to foresee. If all parties are seen to be coalitionable, and if they also remain potentially politically unfaithful to their partners, then voters may have problems in choosing between them. One scenario that might therefore be envisaged is that voters will avoid the problem of choice altogether, with the new promiscuous world of Irish politics being accompanied by ever lower levels of electoral turnout. Ireland already ranks relatively low in this regard, with levels of electoral participation falling below every other west European country with the exceptions of Spain and Switzerland, and with the general election in 1997 recording the lowest ever turnout since the establishment of the party system in the 1920s. A second scenario might envisage many voters turning away from *party* politics as such, and relying more heavily on the competing personal appeals of the party leaders or even the local candidates, a tendency which already marks electoral politics in the United States, and which in the Irish case could lead to even greater successes for independent, single-issue candidates in local constituencies. Yet a third scenario would suggest that voters begin to make their choices more or less at random, with little sense of consistency over time or even between competing candidates, thus creating the possibility that electoral outcomes will be marked by ever-increasing levels of unpredictable volatility and instability.

Of course, part of the uncertainty about how voters might respond is because of the equally great uncertainty about how the parties will behave. Given that the old, established terms of reference have faded, the parties themselves must learn and develop a new language of politics. To be sure, the traditional parties are still in place, although they are now more vulnerable than before. But the political landscape which they inhabit has changed almost beyond recognition, a change which provokes both challenges and opportunities. Many, if not all of the traditional constraints which once tied down both the voters and the party strategists have now been loosened, and with them have gone many of the old certainties. It is this which makes the future shape of the Irish party system so difficult to predict. One thing is clear, however: the parties are going to have to work a lot harder and more carefully if they wish to remain key players. Success – or failure – can no longer be taken for granted.

References and further reading

Carty, R. K., 1981. *Party and Parish Pump: Electoral Politics in Ireland.* Waterloo, Ontario: Wilfrid Laurier University Press.

Coakley, John, 1987. 'The election in context: historical and European perspectives', pp. 153–72 in Laver, Mair and Sinnott (1987).

Dunphy, Richard, 1995. *The Making of Fianna Fáil Power in Ireland 1923–1948.* Oxford: The Clarendon Press.

Farrell, Brian, 1970. 'Labour and the Irish political party system: a suggested approach to analysis', *Economic and Social Review* 1:4, pp. 477-502.

Farrell, Brian, 1971. *The Founding of Dáil Éireann: Parliament and Nation Building.* Dublin: Gill and Macmillan.

Gallagher, Michael, 1982. *The Irish Labour Party in Transition, 1957–82.* Manchester: Manchester University Press.

Gallagher, Michael, 1985. *Political Parties in the Republic of Ireland.* Manchester: Manchester University Press.

Gallagher, Michael and Michael Laver (eds), 1993. *How Ireland Voted 1992.* Dublin: Folens and Limerick: PSAI Press.

Gallagher, Michael, Michael Laver and Peter Mair, 1995. *Representative Government in Modern Europe.* New York: McGraw-Hill.

Gallagher, Michael and Richard Sinnott (eds), 1990. *How Ireland Voted 1989.* Galway: Centre for the Study of Irish Elections and PSAI Press.

Garry, John , 1995. 'The demise of the Fianna Fail/Labour "Partnership" government and the rise of the "Rainbow" coalition', *Irish Political Studies* 10, pp. 192–9.

Garvin, Tom, 1974. 'Political cleavages, party politics, and urbanisation in Ireland: the case of the periphery-dominated centre', *European Journal of Political Research* 2:4, pp. 307–27.

Garvin, Tom, 1996. *1922: The Birth of Irish Democracy.* Dublin: Gill and Macmillan.

Girvin, Brian, 1993. 'The road to the general election', pp. 1–20 in Gallagher and Laver (1993).

Hannan, Philip and Jackie Gallagher (eds), 1996. *Taking the Long View: Seventy Years of Fianna Fáil.* Dublin: Blackwater Press.

Laver, Michael, Peter Mair and Richard Sinnott (eds), 1987. *How Ireland Voted: The Irish General Election 1987.* Swords: Poolbeg Press.

Laver, Michael and Kenneth A. Shepsle, 1992. 'Election results and coalition possibilities in Ireland', *Irish Political Studies* 7, pp. 57–72.

Lipset, S. M. and Stein Rokkan, 1967. 'Cleavage structures, party systems, and voter alignments: an introduction', pp. 1–64 in S. M. Lipset and Stein Rokkan (eds), *Party Systems and Voter Alignments.* New York: The Free Press.

Mair, Peter, 1979. 'The autonomy of the political: the development of the Irish party system', *Comparative Politics* 11:4, pp. 445–65.

Mair, Peter, 1987. *The Changing Irish Party System: Organisation, Ideology and Electoral Competition.* London: Frances Pinter.

Mair, Peter, 1990. 'The Irish party system into the 1990s', pp. 208–20 in Gallagher and Sinnott (1990).

Mair, Peter, 1992. 'Explaining the absence of class politics in Ireland', pp. 383–410 in J. H. Goldthorpe and C. T. Whelan (eds), *The Development of Industrial Society in Ireland*. Oxford: Oxford University Press.

Mair, Peter, 1993. 'Fianna Fáil, Labour and the Irish party system', pp. 162–73 in Gallagher and Laver (1993).

Mair, Peter, 1997. *Party System Change: Approaches and Interpretations*. Oxford: The Clarendon Press

Mair, Peter and Cas Mudde, 1998. 'The party family and its study', *Annual Review of Political Science* 1, pp. 211–29.

Manning, Maurice, 1972. *Irish Political Parties: an Introduction*. Dublin: Gill and Macmillan.

Penniman, Howard R. (ed.), 1978. *Ireland at the Polls: the Dáil Elections of 1977*. Washington, DC: American Enterprise Institute for Public Policy Research.

Penniman, Howard R. and Brian Farrell (eds), 1987. *Ireland at the Polls, 1981, 1982, and 1987: a Study of Four General Elections*. Durham, NC: Duke University Press.

Rumpf, Erhard and A. C. Hepburn, 1977. *Nationalism and Socialism in Twentieth-Century Ireland*. Liverpool: Liverpool University Press.

Sartori, Giovanni, 1976. *Parties and Party Systems: a Framework for Analysis*. Cambridge: Cambridge Universitry Press.

Sinnott, Richard, 1995. *Irish Voters Decide: Voting Behaviour in Elections and Referendums Since 1918*. Manchester: Manchester University Press.

Whyte, John H., 1974. 'Ireland: politics without social bases', pp. 619–51 in Richard Rose (ed.), *Electoral Behavior: A Comparative Handbook*. New York: The Free Press.

6 Parties and voters

Michael Laver and Michael Marsh

Parties and elections are now two sides of the same coin: we almost never find one without the other. Yet, although elections have been held for millennia, parties as we know them today date back only to the nineteenth century. Irish parties are even younger than those found in other parts of Europe, typically dating from 1922 or later, though in many other respects they resemble their counterparts elsewhere in Europe, as we saw in chapter 5.

The relationship between parties and elections is at the heart of parliamentary democracy, in Ireland and elsewhere. By offering a relatively small number of alternatives at election time, they structure the options faced by voters. They provide choices between opposing teams of politicians, as different parties nominate competing teams of candidates for the legislature and senior party politicians hold themselves out as possible government ministers. Parties may also present voters with clear-cut policy options, allowing people to select the policies as well as the personnel of government.

This chapter starts by examining party organisations: their structure, their membership and the way they are financed. In a second section we go on to look at how parties manage their internal affairs: how they make policy and select people for office. It will be seen that despite their central role in the political process, Irish parties have been very much private organisations when it comes to running their affairs,whereas in some other countries these matters are governed by law. Furthermore, in most countries, parties are very dependent upon the public purse for their income whereas Irish parties traditionally raised their own money. However, this has changed in recent years, making Irish parties rather more like public bodies than they used to be.

A parliamentary democracy such as Ireland can function effectively only if party legislators are relatively disciplined, voting for the most part according to the strategies determined by their party leaders. If they do not do this – and such a situation arose in the French Fourth Republic, for example – then governments can never be sure from day to day of their legislative majority and are likely to be very unstable. Yet party legislators behave in a disciplined manner only if party membership is valuable to them. In this event the threat of expulsion or suspension from the party is something to be taken seriously. The value of a party label depends very much upon whether voters give their support consistently to parties rather than to individual candidates. If voters support candidates rather than parties, then politicians can defy the party line and generally behave as mavericks in the knowledge that they can nonetheless hold onto their seats at the next election. The third part of this chapter, therefore, will look at what seems to influence voters when they make their choices. We will note a growing body of evidence that some, at least, of the traditional social bases of party support are beginning to change.

Party organisation

All modern political parties have a group of active supporters whose role goes well beyond the simple act of voting. These people normally join an organisation, pay a membership fee, and thereby acquire the right to participate in certain party activities. We look below at three types of decision made by Irish political parties: candidate selection, the choice of party leader, and policy formation. First, however, we look at the general organisation and financing of Irish parties. We confine our attention to the more established parties represented in the Dáil, in particular Fianna Fáil, Fine Gael and Labour. Where the experience of other parties is significantly different, we incorporate this in our discussion.

Structure

The organisational heart of Irish parties is their central office. This provides support for deputies and co-ordinates local branches scattered all over the country. Central office is staffed mostly by full-time officials in larger parties and by volunteers in smaller ones. While the size of central offices is growing, even Fianna Fáil, Ireland's largest political party, employed only twenty-one full-time staff in 1997. This lack of resources places clear limits on the exercise of central control and in many respects Irish parties are quite decentralised, with local organisations retaining a high degree of autonomy.

The local branch (called a cumann in Fianna Fáil and a local group in the Green Party) is the basic unit of any political party. These branches vary in size, but each party sets a formal minimum membership of around ten people (five for Labour in rural areas). A party normally has a number of branches in each Dáil constituency and these branches send delegates to a constituency council (variously called) which handles candidate selection and the conduct of elections. For larger parties there is also an intermediate tier at the level of the local government constituency, which deals with local elections. Irish party organisations are thus constructed from the 'grassroots' upwards.

Despite their status as the building blocks of party organisations, the real-world existence of particular party branches is often rather indefinite. Fianna Fáil, for example, estimates that it has almost 3,000 branches, although several hundred of these might not be registered in any particular year. Some branches exist only on paper, being created to allow the supporters of certain local politicians to deploy more votes in constituency councils and internal party elections. Some parties have sought to contain this practice (in 1978, for example, Fine Gael introduced new procedures into its constitution that were designed to put an end to paper branches).

At the summit of this organisational pyramid is the national conference (called an ard-fheis in Fianna Fáil and Fine Gael, and a convention by the Greens). In theory this is the supreme policy making body of the party, comprising delegates from the branches, public representatives and party officials. It is typically a large and unwieldy body meeting infrequently, usually once a year, and its meetings tend to be major social and political occasions. Whatever their limitations as policy making bodies, the national conferences function as rallies designed to reinforce the commitment of the rank and file and to allow the party to demonstrate unity and enthusiasm to the outside world. Weekend conventions are now giving way to more low-key one-day events, tailored much more to the demands of the broadcast media than to participation by delegates. While financial and media considerations provide the main justification for this, such changes also reflect the declining importance of ordinary party members.

Between one national conference and the next, management of the party rests in the hands of an executive committee of between fifty and a hundred people. Its name and precise composition vary from party to party: the National Executive in Fine Gael, General Council in the Labour Party and the Ard Chomhairle in Fianna Fáil. It typically includes a combination of party officials, national public representatives (senators and TDs) and constituency delegates drawn from party rank-and-file (for more details on party organisation in Ireland, see Farrell, 1992; Farrell 1994; Mockler 1994).

Figure 6.1 shows a typical party structure, in this case that of Fianna Fáil. It shows the cumann at the base, sending delegates to local and Dáil constituency organisations. Each of these units in turn sends representatives to the ard-fheis. Between meetings of the ard-fheis, the party is under the authority of the Ard Chomhairle, which supervises the party bureaucracy located in central office. The parliamentary party is represented strongly in the Ard Chomhairle. There are some differences of detail between this structure and those of the other Irish parties, but the essential features are the same.

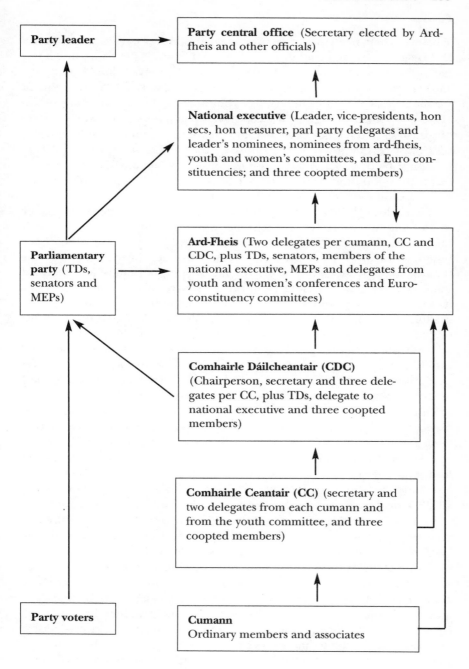

Figure 6.1 Organisational structure of the Fianna Fáil party

Finance

Whatever their organisational structure, all political parties need money and Irish parties are certainly no exception. Gone are the days when it was enough to have an army of dedicated volunteers willing to knock on doors, stuff envelopes and drive people to the polls on a wet and windy night, all for the love of the party. An army of volunteers is still an extremely useful asset, but a modern high-tech election campaign depends upon a coterie of specialists and a lot of expensive equipment. Computers must be bought, staff must be employed, offices must be rented, phone, fax and postage bills must be paid. There are opinion polls to be commissioned, videos to be produced, posters to be printed, campaign buses and helicopters to be hired, manifestos to be published, and so on.

Where does all this money come from? Until recently, the short answer to this question has been that nobody has known, precisely. As both Michael Gallagher (1985, p. 130) and Peter Mair (1987, p. 106) have noted, this matter has traditionally been 'shrouded in secrecy'. This was because, while most parties received some state support, most also received quite extensive contributions from private sources about which they were most unwilling to give any information at all. In addition, the larger parties organise 'national collections', which typically take place outside churches on Sundays, and these can result in the raising of considerable sums.

While the traditional perception was that Irish parties received little or no public funding, parliamentary party leaders have in fact long received public money in the form of 'leaders' allowances'. This system was reformed in 1996, to redress what had previously been systematic discrimination against smaller parties. The reformed system retained the traditional principle that, since government parties can draw upon the resources of the civil service, the distribution of leaders' allowances is weighted in favour of the opposition. The annual sums falling due after the 1997 election thus ranged from over £650,000 for Fine Gael, through about £540,000 for Fianna Fáil, just under £300,000 for Labour, to £100,000 for Democratic Left, about £65,000 for the Progressive Democrats and £50,000 for the Green Party.

In addition to the leaders' allowances, Irish parties have traditionally received benefits in kind at election time, in the form of free air time for 'party election broadcasts'. This air time is made available to parties on the basis of a formula used by the state broadcasting station, RTÉ, that takes account both of a party's current Dáil representation and of the number of candidates nominated. This is a very significant asset, though difficult to quantify. It would certainly cost a lot if it had to be paid for. Since so many Irish homes now have access to a range of non-Irish television stations, however, it is difficult to know how many voters switch channels or turn the sound down when party election broadcasts fill the screen. Nonetheless, this facility does offer even small and poor parties a chance to make a case directly to the entire Irish electorate, an opportunity fully exploited by such smaller parties as the Greens.

Notwithstanding these traditional public supports, the public funding of Irish political parties until very recently was at a much lower level than that to be found in many other European countries. However, the issue of party funding in Ireland came to a head in 1997 with reports of large sums of money being paid by businessmen to senior politicians. These reports led directly to the disgracing of a former Taoiseach, Charles Haughey, and to the resignation of senior cabinet ministers from two successive governments. The accompanying furore led to the Electoral Act 1997, a piece of legislation that is destined to have a fundamental impact on party politics in modern Ireland. This deals with public funding for political parties, the disclosure of political contributions and the strict regulation of campaign spending.

Public funding has two components. The first is a contribution to parties' annual running costs; the second concerns the reimbursement of election expenses (see Box 6.1). If the act had been in force for the 1997 Dáil election, then the public contribution towards running costs (over and above the leaders' allowances referred to above) would have been about £400,000 to Fianna Fáil, £300,000 to Fine Gael, £115,000 to Labour, £50,000 to the Progressive Democrats and a little under £30,000 each to the Green Party, Sinn Féin and Democratic Left. The act would also have allowed the reimbursement of election expenses of about £550,000 to Fianna Fáil, £400,000 to Fine Gael, £190,000 to Labour, £100,000 to the Progressive Democrats and of around £50,000 each to the Green Party, Sinn Féin and Democratic Left. A further £100,000 or so would have been payable to independents and smaller parties.

The total sums payable to Irish political parties from the public purse, in the wake of the 1997 Electoral Act, are thus quite considerable. They amount in an election year to over £1.5 million to Fianna Fáil, and almost £1.4m to Fine Gael. On the basis of the 1997 election results, the Labour Party would have been due about £600,000, and the Progressive Democrats and Democratic Left about £200,000 each. Smaller parties will benefit too under these arrangements, with over £100,000 falling due to both the Green Party and Sinn Féin, on the basis of an election with the same voting patterns as those in 1997.

Balancing the provision of substantial public funding for political parties and setting out to remove some of the potential for allegations of political 'sleaze', the 1997 act also deals with the disclosure of political contributions from private sources (see Box 6.1). No limit is set upon the size of political donations provided these are declared, and no distinction is made between donations from private individuals and donations from companies, businesses and other organisations. Thus the 1997 act relies entirely upon making political donations transparent, rather than upon regulating either the size or the source of acceptable donations.

The act also introduces strict regulation of spending by candidates and parties at Dáil and European Parliament elections (see Box 6.1). It goes to considerable lengths to prevent expenditure by people or groups friendly to political parties or candidates from escaping the regulatory net. It is not yet

Box 6.1 The Electoral Act, 1997

The Act came fully into force on 1 January 1998. It deals, among other important matters, with public funding for political parties, the disclosure of political contributions and the regulation of campaign spending.

Public Funding
Public funding goes to 'qualified parties': registered political parties winning over 2 per cent of the vote in the previous election.
This funding has two components. The first is a contribution to parties' annual running costs; the second concerns the reimbursement of election expenses.

- Payments towards parties' annual running expenses come from a fund with an initial value of one million pounds per year, inflated annually at the same rate as general pay increases to the civil service. This is divided and distributed tax-free to qualifying parties in proportion to their share of the first preference votes won by all qualifying parties in the previous election.
- The Act also provides for partial reimbursement of election expenses up to a maximum of £5,000 for every candidate who contested the election without losing his or her deposit (that is, who was either elected, or whose votes exceeded one quarter of a quota at some stage during the count).

Disclosure of contributions
The Act deals with a wide variety of benefits in kind as well as donations of cash, and prohibits any anonymous donation of more than £100.

- Unsuccessful candidates in Oireachtas or European Parliament elections must declare all donations over £500 within 56 days of the election, giving the value of the donation and the name, description and address of the donor.
- All members of the Oireachtas or European Parliament must make a similar declaration every year.
- Each political party must provide a donation statement every year, giving details of all donations over £4000.
- Companies, trade unions and building societies making donations of more than £4000 must declare these in their annual returns.

Regulation of campaign spending
The Act imposes clear limits on election spending by both candidates and national political parties.

- The limits on spending by parties flow indirectly from the limits on party candidates, which are fixed at £14,000 per candidate in three-seat constituencies, £17,000 per candidate in four-seat constituencies, and £20,000 per candidate in five-seat constituencies.
- Total election expenses for *a party and all of its candidates* are limited to the total expenses allowed for all of the candidates of the party in question.
- Parties must get the written permission of each candidate to cede up to half of the candidate's spending limit to the party organisation as a whole.

clear how successful it will be in preventing the use of the type of 'political action committee', friendly to but formally unconnected with a candidate, which has become so prevalent in the United States as a way of getting around spending regulations.

The act imposes clear limits on election spending by both candidates and national political parties. If it had been in force for the 1997 election, this would have limited total spending by Fianna Fáil and all of its candidates to about £2m, with corresponding sums for Fine Gael of £1.6m, for Labour of £760,000, the Progressive Democrats of £540,000 and Democratic Left of £240,000. These limits would have made little difference for small parties with limited resources, but for the larger parties they might well have been a real constraint on their electioneering activities. It is quite possible, therefore, that the act will change the nature of Irish political campaigning.

Overall, therefore, recent financial scandals have helped to create a radically new legal environment for party funding in Ireland. Much more public money is being provided, to reduce the dependence of parties on anonymous private donors. Much more regulation is in place to limit campaign spending and force the declaration of private donations. Since most parts of the 1997 act came into force only on 1 January 1998, we have yet to see their full impact on Irish party politics, but the signs are that this impact will be considerable.

Membership

As we have already seen, party branches can sometimes have a shadowy existence. It is indeed only recently that parties have kept records of how many members they have and Fianna Fáil still does not do so. In general, most party membership figures in Ireland remain a combination of guesswork and wishful thinking. Many party members, furthermore, are merely nominal and are certainly not active. Estimates of party membership, such as they are, are reported in Table 6.1. These figures were supplied by the parties themselves, and may well involve considerable over-estimates.

Table 6.1 Party members and voters, 1997

	Members in 1996	Voters in 1997	Voters per member
Fianna Fáil	65,000	703,682	11
Fine Gael	25,000	499,936	20
Labour	7,000	186,044	26
Democratic Left	1,400	44,901	32
Progressive Democrats	7,000	83,765	12
Sinn Féin	2,000	45,614	23
Greens	1,000	49,323	49
Total	108,400	1,613,265	15

Source: King and Gillespie (1998).
Note: The total excludes votes cast for 'other' parties and candidates.

Table 6.1 shows the memberships of the different parties at the time of the 1997 general election, the votes won by different parties and the ratio between these figures. Fianna Fáil claims roughly one member for every eleven voters. It is striking that the ratio is much lower in all other major parties, with Labour having only one member for every twenty-six voters. Thus, 60 per cent of all those belonging to an Irish political party seem to belong to Fianna Fáil. If this is indeed the case, then it clearly gives the party a real organisational advantage at election time.

Overall, however, relatively few Irish people belong to political parties. The figures above suggest that something like 110,000 people are party members, less than 4 per cent of the electorate and well below the European average of 13 per cent (Gallagher, Laver and Mair, 1995, p. 245). The smaller more radical parties, such as the Workers' Party in the 1980s and early 1990s, and Sinn Féin more recently, tend to place very heavy demands upon members and require a high level of year-round commitment. Most Irish parties, however, are essentially electoral organisations. Furthermore, party membership appears to be in decline in Ireland. Activists seem to be less active, judging by the results of recent national collections, while party members seem to be getting collectively older. The few thousand members picked up by newer parties have not been sufficient to offset the membership losses suffered by the traditional parties. Even so, many people are still active in parties, as Table 6.1 makes clear. This next section examines the impact they can have on their parties.

Party management

Selection of candidates and officials

Members of Irish parties can play a significant role in deciding who becomes a politician since the nomination of candidates for elections is for the most part a highly decentralised process, allowing considerable participation by rank and file members (Gallagher, 1988). In recent years, however, there are signs that party leaderships are trying to exert more control over this.

The process of candidate selection varies somewhat between the parties. Typically, candidates are selected by members delegated by the various local party branches in the area in which the election is to take place. For Dáil elections, each branch in a Dáil constituency sends delegates to a constituency convention, which decides both how many candidates to select and who these people are to be. In the case of the Green party, candidate selection is handled directly by the membership as a whole, and not via a delegate convention. Fine Gael now follows a similar practice, allowing all members of eight weeks standing who belong to a branch which has been registered for three months to attend and vote at the candidate conventions, a procedure which caused a few upsets during the selection of candidates for the 1997 elections (Galligan, 1999). The Progressive Democrats' rules are flexible, and allow for both one-member-one-vote and delegate selection conferences as appropriate, with the former most common. Direct membership participation in this process can be quite extensive. In 1997, meetings ranged in size from thirty to 1000 people, depending on party and location (Galligan, 1999).

The criteria for candidate selection in Ireland are essentially pragmatic. There are no formal grounds for eligibility. What is most valuable to an aspiring candidate is having a track record of winning votes. If an aspiring candidate has not stood for election before, the next best thing is to have a very solid local reputation. Neither the political views of the aspiring candidate nor his or her potential as a legislator seem to carry much weight. When several candidates are selected by the same party, there seems to be little concern to achieve any social balance, by age, gender or social class for example. In rural areas, however, candidates will almost always come from different parts of the constituency.

The nomination of candidates by local branches is subject to some control by central party organisations. The national executive or party leadership is typically able to veto a particular candidate, to nominate additional candidates, and to decide how many candidates should stand in any particular area: in fact, to take all key decisions on candidate selection. While it is quite common for the central party to determine how many candidates there should be in each constituency, other powers have generally been exercised more infrequently. Local members have become accustomed to choosing candidates and it is of course local activists who must do the gruelling legwork that helps to get any nominee elected. The local party, because of its knowledge of the constituency, also has the necessary expertise to identify the candidates best equipped to win.

Since the late 1970s, first Fianna Fáil and then Fine Gael and the other parties have sought to impose their nominal central control over local organisations more forcefully in practice. Attempts by central party organisations to 'parachute' prominent outsiders into a local constituency have, however, usually been deeply resented at local level. In the same way, vetoing a local candidate can be risky. Two prominent members of the two larger parties, Jackie Healy-Rae and Michael Lowry, responded to non-selection in 1997 by standing as independents and winning their seats at the expense of their former parties. While this is a relatively rare occurrence, it is a possibility that all party centres are aware of when deciding whether or not to intervene.

Local parties may in practice often be effectively under the control of local TDs, whose personal supporters may occupy all key posts. This has sometimes meant that candidate selection has favoured the interests of particular local incumbents at the expense of the party in general. In Fine Gael in particular, many deputies have been suspected of engineering the selection of a weak running mate, or of no running mate at all, in order to protect their personal position. In such cases, opportunities to win an extra seat have been lost because the incumbent feared the risk to his or her own position. The Fine Gael leadership intervened often in the 1980s to alleviate this danger, adding candidates to the list of those nominated (see O'Byrnes, 1986). Concern about the quality of deputies as legislators has also justified greater involvement by the party leadership, often informally and prior to the selection meeting. Fianna Fáil went one step further and established a committee in 1995 to prepare for the 1997 elections. This identified potential new candidates and supervised all stages of the process (Galligan, 1999).

In addition to candidates, members elect a number of other party officials. Branch members elect branch officials, as well as nominating delegates to constituency conventions and national conferences. A party's national executive committee also contains a number of people directly elected by the party conference. Although this committee is formally the decision making body within the party between meetings of the party conference, in most parties it defers in practice to the party leader. While rank-and-file members participate quite fully in the selection of local candidates and officials, they typically have no direct say in the choice of a national party leader.

Selection of leaders

It is arguable that the choice of party leader is the most important decision facing any party. Elections are as much about who governs as about what leaders do when they govern, so the party leader is a key figure in any party's campaign. In Fianna Fáil and Fine Gael, furthermore, the party leader is a potential Taoiseach, so that these parties, when they choose a leader, make a decision of major national significance.

In Fianna Fáil, Fine Gael and the Progressive Democrats, selection of the parliamentary leader (effectively the party leader, even when there is some other formal post such as party president) is made solely by parliamentarians. Fianna Fáil and the Progressive Democrats restrict the vote to members of the Dáil; Fine Gael allows senators and members of the European Parliament a vote as well. An internal party report did suggest that all members should be involved in electing the Fine Gael party leader, but this was resisted by the party leadership, largely on grounds of cost.

The Labour Party, however, has changed its method of leadership selection more fundamentally. It used to operate the system currently employed by Fianna Fáil but, under new rules adopted in 1989, the election of a Labour leader (who must be a member of the parliamentary party) may involve party members as a whole (Marsh, 1993). This change has the potential to alter the character of the election, given the need for candidates to campaign much more publicly than has been common in the past. However, it remains to be seen whether or not the new method will ever be employed. Dick Spring, who took over as leader in 1982, was never challenged as leader under these rules. When he resigned in 1997, the decision to appoint Ruairí Quinn rather than Brendan Howlin was made by a joint meeting of the General Council (a body of about sixty people broadly representative of members and affiliated bodies) and the parliamentary party. This followed a 1997 amendment to party rules which gave this body responsibility for electing a leader in the event of his or her predecessor not serving out the full term of six years. Even when Quinn's term is up (in 2002) the membership as a whole will vote on a new leader only if the election is contested.

Even where they have no formal role, however, rank-and-file members of any party have some indirect influence on who becomes leader. In the election of a new Fianna Fáil leader in 1992, for example, most deputies consulted their constituency members before the vote took place. Several local parties held meetings, following which clear messages were sent to local deputies. The voice of the ordinary party member was particularly evident in 1983, when the then Fianna Fáil leader, Charles Haughey, in 'the night of the long phone calls', used his popularity among the party rank and file to improve his standing with deputies on the eve of a challenge to his leadership.

When the decision on the party leadership is confined to parliamentarians, a single question seems to be uppermost in everyone's minds: who is most likely to boost party support in the next election? Most new leaders have been selected after a very muted campaign, and certainly not one that has put issues to the fore. As with candidate selection, it is the perception of a person's vote-winning ability that is decisive. However, if the electorate is extended to all party members, who may have little to gain directly from election victories and may be more concerned with certain core values of the party, then the policy positions of potential leaders may become more important.

Formation of party policy

While the ordinary member continues to have a real say in candidate selection, his or her voice may be no more than the faintest of whispers when it comes to deciding the policies on which these candidates fight elections. The formation of party policy in Ireland, as in most other democracies, presents some fascinating contrasts between theory and reality. In theory, as we have seen, the official policy of each of the main Irish parties is made at an annual or biennial conference involving a large number of party representatives, both local and national, as well as activists and ordinary members. In practice, this body is too large, too diffuse, and meets too rarely to make effective strategic decisions about party policy. A partial exception is the Labour national conference, which has in the past laid down the law on matters such as coalition, for example, binding the party leadership not to go into coalition without coming back to a special delegate conference for permission to do this. For the most part, however, national conferences that fill large halls are far too cumbersome to generate effective party policy documents. This task normally falls to the party's national executive, or to an even smaller group. Small teams of people responsible to the party leader, for example, generally drew up party manifestos for the 1997 election. Although there was some consultation with members, no party engaged in any widespread formal consultation on policy formulation (Garry and Mansergh, 1999).

When parties move into government, furthermore, policy making tends to become an even more centralised process. When only one party is in power, then the effective policy making body of the party is the cabinet; it is as simple as that. A national executive might make some decision that conflicts with a cabinet decision, but it would have very little real control over the individuals concerned, and its decisions would have relatively little effect. In the popular mind, party policy would certainly be cabinet policy, not some policy propounded by the government party's national executive. Because of this reality, a wise voter wishing to assess Fianna Fáil's policy on third level education would be well advised to examine the speeches of the minister for education alongside the party's election manifesto.

Even when a party is in opposition, its parliamentary party designates a set of senior politicians to 'shadow' cabinet ministers in the Dáil and act as party spokespersons on the policy areas concerned. These people make the party's public statements on these policies, attack the government ministers concerned, and are the ones to whom the media turn for official party reaction. Members of this shadow cabinet develop policy expertise in the areas for which they are responsible, and are in effect the main engines of policy development for their party, whatever the party rule-book might say.

Organisations and leaders: the balance sheet

Irish parties are often seen as being outside the European mainstream, but in many respects they are not very different from their counterparts on the continent. Many of the trends that we have identified in Ireland can be found elsewhere. In the most authoritative summary of current trends in contemporary democracies, Mair (1994) noted that, even if members are no longer as numerous as they once were, parties are no less attentive to their views in such areas as the selection of party officials and candidates. The decentralisation of candidate selection in Ireland is in line with the experience in other countries. Yet this is not incompatible with a tendency for parties to become more centralised in their pursuit of electoral advantage, and more dependent upon the state for the resources with which to fight elections. This is very apparent in Irish parties and goes some way to explain the increasing role of party elites. The prominent role played by the parliamentary leadership in Ireland in guiding the party is also typical. However, attempts to construct parties in which deputies are under the firm control of the party organisation have, for the most part, been unsuccessful.

In an attempt to buck this centralising trend, the Green Party in Ireland, like its counterparts elsewhere, has tried to construct a more democratic party organisation. There is no party leader, merely a 'co-ordinator' elected by the Co-ordinating Committee. Local groups elect 'facilitators'. Delegates to higher bodies should normally serve for a short, limited term to ensure rotation of office, and all members may attend any party meeting as observers. Decisions, according to the party's rules, should be reached by consensus wherever possible. Efforts are made to consult widely within the party before policy decisions are made. Yet, before the party can really claim to be different, these procedures will have to be tested when it has a significant governmental presence, something that is currently no more than an aspiration.

All this is not to say that modern Irish parties have no place for rank and file activity. Ordinary members do play a role, and this is not just confined to raising money. They can exercise considerable influence on the choice of candidates who bear the party label at election time. Furthermore, as we argued in the introduction, the power of the party leadership is made possible only by the fact that voters tend to give their support to national party labels rather than to individual local candidates. To a large extent, therefore, the internal affairs of Irish parties are determined by the voting behaviour of the Irish electorate – the matter to which we now turn.

Party support

When political scientists study patterns in the votes cast for different political parties, they usually have in mind some kind of 'model' that sets out to explain why people vote at all. Two different models of voting behaviour have become current in recent times. One of these assumes that voting is a form of self-expression; the other assumes that people vote in order to have an effect on how society is run. We briefly describe these models before discussing how much each of them can add to our understanding of voting behaviour in Ireland, and we go on to look at the importance of political issues, social background and personality factors as determinants of voting choice.

Two models of voting behaviour

The 'party identification' model of voting behaviour is based on the idea that voting is an act of self-expression. Every individual in society is 'socialised' into a set of beliefs and attitudes by a complex process involving parents, teachers, church, friends, peers and the mass media. As a result of this process of socialisation, people may come to 'identify' with a particular political party. Irish voters, according to this account, might come to identify closely with Fianna Fáil, Fine Gael or Labour. Such attachments change only very slowly, and go much deeper than a vote cast at any particular election. Thus a Fine Gael supporter may 'defect' and vote for Labour at a given election – under the influence of some particular candidate, issue, or scandal – but will continue to identify with Fine Gael and see a vote for Labour as a deviation from this. In the most boring election imaginable, with no hot issues, scandals or colourful candidates, according to this approach, every voter would vote according to his or her party identification.

While the 'party identification' model sees voting largely as an expression of identity, the 'rational choice' model is based on the idea that casting a vote is a purposeful act designed to achieve something. Every individual in society has a set of desires. Some of these may be very basic human needs: the desire for food, warmth and shelter, for example. Other aspirations are products of the socialisation process: the desire for a united Ireland, for example, or for nuclear disarmament. The rational choice model assumes that people vote in such a way as to bring their desires closer to fulfilment. A person thus votes for the party that seems most likely to guarantee food, warmth and shelter, or to bring about a united Ireland or nuclear disarmament, if these are the desires that he or she wants to satisfy. According to this approach, voters have no psychological loyalty to any given party, but rather pick the party that seems most likely to deliver what they want at each election. They may of course vote over and over again for the same party, but they do this because the same party is always their best choice, not because they are particularly loyal to it.

Popular accounts of party choice in Ireland have tended to set great store by traditional party loyalties, and thus to fit better with the party identification model. The origins of the two main Irish parties are typically traced to the civil war, and party loyalties are widely seen as having been handed down within families from that point onwards. It has been argued that very many Irish families can be thought of as 'Fianna Fáil families' or 'Fine Gael families', for example, and that Irish people who grow up voting in a particular way stay loyal, more or less regardless of the current policies of 'their' party (for an engaging and lucid presentation of this view, see Waters, 1991).

Some argue that the importance of such traditional loyalties is probably much less now than it might have been in years gone by. Observers in the 1990s expressed the view that there were no longer significant blocks of voters – Fianna Fáil, Fine Gael or whatever – on which parties could rely. Votes had to be campaigned for, and won afresh, at each election. Even if we accept that there are traditional loyalties to parties, it is common to assume that the hopes and fears of the electorate constrain Irish parties in the choice of policies that they offer. It would be seen by most people as electoral suicide in Ireland, for example, for a party to promote the introduction of abortion on demand. Thus most commentators feel that Irish parties cannot trade on the loyalty of their supporters to promote just any old policy on anything. In other words they feel that, at least in part, Irish voters choose whom to support on the basis of party positions on key policy issues.

Issues

While many people claim to see no difference between any of the parties, discussion of issues does play a major role in Irish election campaigns, as elsewhere. According to opinion polls, by far the most important issues in recent elections have been economic, with employment normally heading the list. Other socio-economic matters such as tax, health services and interest rates are also typically prominent (Laver, Marsh and Sinnott, 1987; Marsh and Sinnott, 1990; Marsh and Sinnott, 1993; Sinnott, 1995; Marsh and Sinnott, 1999). Interestingly, given media attention to such matters, purely 'social' issues such as abortion, divorce and contraception, as well as the Northern Ireland problem, have typically ranked very low in the priorities of most voters. The low rating of the abortion issue was particularly striking in 1992, since controversial referendums on the issue were held at the same time as the election: only 4 per cent of voters rated abortion as one of the main issues in the election (Marsh and Sinnott, 1993). Perhaps equally surprisingly, given the significance of the peace process negotiations then underway, only 13 per cent claimed the Northern Ireland issue was the most significant influence on their vote in 1997. Above all, therefore, Irish voters seem to be concerned at election time with economic policy.

Yet there are strong grounds for doubting claims that issues matter much to Irish voters. Asked during the 1992 campaign whether policies, leaders or local candidates were the most important factor in making up their minds how to vote, only 20 per cent of respondents cited 'the policies of the parties' (Marsh and Sinnott, 1993). This may of course be because voters felt that the economic policies of the main parties were so similar that there was nothing much to choose between them.

Voters in such circumstances, many of whom clearly regard economic policy as very important, may choose between parties on the basis of their perceived competence to run the economy, rather than their stated policies. One way in which voters can make this decision is to reward incumbent governments that have presided over an economy that has done well, and punish incumbents where it has done badly. One implication of this is that governments may attempt to manipulate the economy so that it appears to be performing well in the run-up to an election. This is certainly a popular perception among political commentators, in Ireland as elsewhere in Europe.

The impact of economic performance on political popularity in Ireland has been explored by two studies (Borooah and Borooah 1990; Harrison and Marsh 1998). Both examined the impact of key economic indicators on the opinion poll lead of successive Irish governments over the opposition since 1974 and found a strong relationship. However, while the earlier study argued that this relationship was essentially short term, with improvements in economic well-being almost instantly reflected in government support, the latter study suggested a different relationship, arguing that economic performance was reflected in a general level of long-term support for a government. Although support could deviate temporarily from this level, as a result of scandals, changes of party leader or occasional policy successes and failures, it would quickly move back towards an 'equilibrium' level of support set by overall economic well-being.

Another reason to be sceptical about the impact of issues is that many people often seem to have little knowledge of a party's position on a particular issue, a tendency mirrored in most other countries. There are more interesting things in most peoples' lives than politics, and they simply do not try to keep up with policy details, even at election time. In such circumstances, voters may simply guess party positions from what they happen to know anyway about a party. On economic matters, they may see a party as being generally 'left', 'centre' or 'right wing' on economic matters, and broadly approve one of these positions. Thus they may support a party because they see it as generally 'right wing' without being at all clear about the details of the particular policies being advocated.

It is commonly argued, particularly by supporters of Fianna Fáil and Fine Gael, that concepts of left and right are inappropriate to Irish politics. Most voters, however, are willing to describe themselves in such terms, and willing to use them to describe political parties. Table 6.2 shows the profile of support, expressed in terms of right and left, for the various Irish parties in 1997. Almost all parties win the votes of a very significant group of voters who see themselves as being in the centre. However, the table demonstrates quite clearly that supporters of some parties were much more likely to see themselves as being on 'the left' while supporters of others were more likely to place themselves on 'the right'. For Sinn Féin, the Greens, and Labour, all parties that would be placed on the left by experts, left wing supporters greatly outnumbered right wing ones. The reverse is true for those parties

Table 6.2 Ideological self placement by party support, 1997

	Left	*Centre*	*Right*	*Total*
Sinn Féin	49.3	40.8	9.9	100.0
Labour	36.0	47.8	16.1	100.0
Greens	37.8	40.0	22.2	100.0
Others	24.8	48.6	26.6	100.0
Fine Gael	10.9	54.2	34.9	100.0
Progressive Democrats	7.5	48.3	44.2	100.0
Fianna Fáil	6.2	44.9	48.8	100.0

Source: Lansdowne/RTE general election 1997 exit poll.
Note: Voters for Democratic Left and Labour have been combined.

on the right (Fianna Fáil, Fine Gael and the Progressive Democrats).

To sum up, government popularity in Ireland responds to economic indicators and opinion polls suggest that economic issues in general, most especially unemployment, are the most highly rated by the electorate. Furthermore, many voters appear to prefer a party that is located close to their own ideological position. Taken together, these findings suggest that many (though not necessarily most) Irish voters make explicit choices based on their views about economic policy, ideology or performance when they vote, rather than simply affirming a traditional partisan loyalty.

A changing pattern of voting behaviour?

We would be rash to turn our backs completely on the widely held view that support for the traditional 'civil war' parties is to some extent based upon enduring party loyalties. Baseline support for the traditional parties does, however, seem to be declining as folk memories of the bitterness of the civil war fade. The combined vote of Fianna Fáil and Fine Gael has declined from about 85 per cent in the two 1982 elections to about 67 per cent in 1997. Furthermore, 48 per cent of those intending to vote for Fine Gael, and 41 per cent of those intending to vote for Fianna Fáil claimed to have no very strong allegiance, or no allegiance at all, to their party. Only 29 per cent and 26 per cent respectively had a very or extremely strong allegiance to the two parties (analysis of IMS polls during 1997 election). Polls carried out for the European Commission since the 1970s suggest that the number of Irish people saying they 'feel close' to a particular party has declined markedly (Schmitt and Holmberg, 1995). Each generation of new voters is less strongly attached to a party, while attachment is also declining among older voters. It is reasonable to see these results as pointing to a decline in the appeal of the traditional parties.

This suggests that many people's identification, even with established parties, is not at all strong. In consequence we might expect the electorate to become more volatile. Certainly, general fluctuations in levels of party support were greater in recent elections than they had been since the 1940s. Opinion poll evidence suggests that around 25 per cent of voters at one election change their vote at the next (see Sinnott, 1995; Marsh and Sinnott 1999). New parties have also emerged, offering an alternative both to the civil war parties and to Labour, something that would be impossible if unchanging party loyalties determined the votes of everyone in the land. This might lead us to wonder whether the traditional pattern of Irish party loyalties is breaking down.

We can find further evidence that this might be the case if we contrast the patterns of party support for 'alternative' and 'traditional' parties, and for Labour, between rural and urban, between farming and non-farming and between young and old voters. Table 6.3 shows a very clear tendency for support for the 'alternative' parties, which have grown more prominent

Table 6.3 Electoral support for traditional and alternative parties, by various social groups, 1997

	'Civil war'	Labour	New	Total
Connacht/Ulster	82.1	6.4	11.5	100
Dublin	60.8	15.0	24.2	100
Farming	90.5	4.6	5.0	100
Industry/Services	68.9	13.8	17.4	100
Rural	86.5	5.3	8.2	100
Urban	61.8	16.0	22.2	100
Age 35+	74.2	12.4	13.4	100
Age 18–34	69.1	11.8	19.1	100

Source: Lansdowne/RTE general election 1997 exit poll.
Urban/rural figures from MRBI poll, May 27 1997.

since the 1980s, and Labour, to be concentrated among younger and more urban voters, and to be much lower among farmers and more rural voters. Support for the 'civil war' parties is at its highest among older and rural voters, and among small farmers. Indeed, the erosion of support for the traditional parties may be accounted for in part by the shifts from rural to urban areas and from the farming to the non-farming sectors. This is one major possible explanation. Since demographic trends and social mobility in Ireland continue to reduce the size of the more elderly, rural and farming sections of the electorate, the demographic profile of support for the traditional parties poses a stiff challenge to their future well-being.

This table also makes it clear that there is some social patterning in the party preferences of Irish voters. The relationship between social class and voting behaviour is, however, very weak in Ireland by comparison with that in almost every other European country. In particular, the contest between the two 'civil war' parties, still by far the biggest in the Irish party system, does not seem to be based to any great extent on social class. This is why

Table 6.4 Party support by social class, 1997

	Middle class	Lower middle	Skilled working	Unskilled working	Farmers
Fianna Fáil	36.1	34.9	42.8	42.2	48.3
Fine Gael	28.1	28.4	22.8	18.5	38.8
Labour	10.7	11.9	11.6	14.9	4.4
Progressive Democrats	8.2	6.8	3.5	2.4	4.0
Greens	4.3	5.4	4.9	2.4	0.0
Sinn Féin	1.8	1.2	3.7	5.2	0.8
Others	10.7	11.3	10.7	14.4	3.8
Total	100	100	100	100	100

Source: Lansdowne/RTE general election 1997 exit poll.
Note: Voters for Democratic Left and Labour have been combined.

many who have written about party competition in Ireland have agreed with John Whyte in describing it as 'politics without social bases' (Whyte, 1974). Writing several years later, R. K. Carty re-emphasised this line of argument with the bold claim that 'social characteristics do not structure voting behaviour in Ireland' (Carty, 1981, p. 24). In this sense the largest parties fit the label of 'catch-all' parties, because of their broadly based appeal.

These assertions are based on the sort of survey evidence that is reproduced in appendix 2i. Some evidence of this kind is summarised in Table 6.4, which depicts the vote of each social grade in 1997. This table shows that similar levels of support go to Fianna Fáil from most social groups, ranging only from 36 per cent of the middle class and 42 or 43 per cent of the working class to 48 per cent among farmers. It is this fairly uniform pattern of Fianna Fáil support, particularly between middle and working class groups, that has been cited since 1969 as evidence for the 'politics without social bases' thesis. Considering support for each of the three main parties, there is no major difference in the voting behaviour of middle class and working class voters in Ireland. Fine Gael tends to be more attractive to the middle class and Labour slightly more attractive to the working class, particularly the unskilled working class, among whom it won almost 15 per cent of the vote. The differences, however, are certainly not large, in contrast to the pattern to be found in many other western European countries. Knowing an Irish voter's occupation does not help us much in predicting how he or she is likely to vote (see Franklin, Mackie and Valen, 1992, p. 387).

Nonetheless the table does show some quite interesting features. As we have already noted, farmers are very much more likely to vote for either Fianna Fáil or Fine Gael than they are to vote for any of the other parties. The Progressive Democrats' support declines sharply across the table, from 8 per cent in the middle class to only just above 2 per cent in the unskilled working class category and 4 per cent among farmers. Middle class voters were more than three times as likely to vote for the Progressive Democrats as were working class ones. Sinn Féin's support was about twice as strong among unskilled workers as among the middle class. Despite the catch-all basis of Fianna Fáil support, furthermore, the party did receive somewhat more support from workers than from the middle class. The social bases of Irish voting behaviour may be weak, but they are noticeable nonetheless. We do get some limited clues about which party a voter is likely to support if we know his or her position in the occupational structure. Moreover, as we find elsewhere, the right wing parties are supported by more middle class people, and left wing parties by more of the working class.

Voting behaviour and personalities

While it may be necessary to examine the finer details of opinion polls to see the influence of social class on electoral behaviour, the importance of personalities is more obvious. Election campaigns tend to be dominated by party leaders. For the big parties, each leader is in effect its nominee for Taoiseach. This leads to an understandable focus on personalities that extends to the leaders of the smaller parties. Irish elections have always had a personality component, but many see the current emphasis as replacing rather than supplementing discussion of political issues. Certainly, media coverage does focus on party leaders, and most recent elections have culminated in a 'great debate' between the leaders of Fianna Fáil and Fine Gael. The parties have been as responsible for this as have been the media. Election posters frequently feature little more than the party leader's face. All local Progressive Democrat posters at the 1997 election, for example, featured the leader Mary Harney looking over the shoulder of the local candidate, while Fianna Fáil posters generally featured an artistically lit photograph of Bertie Ahern, seen by election strategists as the party's trump card, caught in a pensive mood. Slogans such as the Progressive Democrats' 'Dessie can do it', in 1987, have also personalised election campaigns. There is certainly a strong perception in many quarters that a popular leader is worth many votes to a party, and election strategies have frequently been built around this assumption.

Notwithstanding these perceptions, there is no conclusive evidence that party leaders have a big effect on voting behaviour. It is true that a leader's popularity may help the party in the polls, and this appears to be particularly the case in Fianna Fáil (Harrison and Marsh, 1994). There is evidence that an increase of 10 per cent in a leader's poll rating could be expected to deliver almost 2 per cent more support for the two big parties, and less than half of 1 per cent in the case of Labour. Poll support between elections, however, does not necessarily translate into votes on election day. When asked during the 1989 election campaign whether choice of policies, local candidates, ministers or choice of Taoiseach most influenced their vote only between 14 and 20 per cent of Irish voters claimed that the choice of Taoiseach was the most important (Marsh and Sinnott, 1990). In 1997, the choice of Taoiseach ranked behind various policy issues and local candidates in people's own explanations for their vote (Marsh and Sinnott, 1999). In addition, even when surveys show a high degree of consistency between respondents' voting intentions and their perceptions of who would make the best Taoiseach (Marsh and Sinnott, 1990), we cannot tell which of these two things, party choice and leader perception, follows from the other.

Our focus, like that of election campaigns, has so far been on national leaders, but it must be remembered that, when the electors finally go to the polls, the votes cast are given to individual local candidates under the single transferable system of proportional representation, as we have seen in chapter 4. Moreover, even though the emphasis in national election campaigns is on parties, much of the activity at local level revolves around the candidates. Activity within any given constituency is certainly aimed at increasing party votes, but most candidates are also concerned to maximise their individual performances. Because the Irish electoral system compels voters to indicate a preference for an individual candidate, many candidates are effectively in competition with others of their own party, as well as with candidates from other parties. Indeed, a third of the turnover of TDs from one election to the next happens because a TD from one party is beaten for the seat by a rival from the same party, rather than by an opponent from another party. There is thus rarely such a thing as a 'safe seat' in Ireland.

Once more, evidence about the effect of individual candidates on voting behaviour is difficult to assess. Certainly, when surveys ask about the extent to which the voting decision is affected by parties, issues, leaders and candidates, voters are more likely to claim that they make up their mind on the basis of the local candidates on offer than to mention any other single factor. Thus, 74 per cent claimed that the local candidates influenced their vote in 1997 (Lansdowne/RTE exit poll). When voters are asked which of several factors mentioned above (local candidates, sets of ministers, policies and choice of Taoiseach) most influenced their vote, the importance of local candidates normally overshadows that of choice of Taoiseach. In 1992, for example, 37 per cent of voters said that 'picking a candidate to represent the needs of the constituency' was the most important thing for them, a figure very close to that found in previous elections (Marsh and Sinnott, 1993, p. 98). Such responses need to be interpreted cautiously: 63 per cent, after all, opted for national factors, and, as was noted above, electoral casualty lists have often testified to the vulnerability of a TD who goes it alone and dispenses with the protection of a party label.

Detailed examination of STV election results provides quite convincing evidence that the party affiliation of candidates guides the choices of most voters. A majority give their second preference vote to a candidate of the same party as their first preference candidate, where this is possible (Gallagher, 1978). When a typical Fianna Fáil candidate was eliminated from a count in 1997, for example, on average 68 per cent of his or her votes went to another Fianna Fáil candidate, although 32 per cent of the vote did not transfer within the party (Gallagher, 1999). Transfer rates are lower for other parties, but were equally strong within alternative government coalitions in 1997. It thus seems likely that many of those who say that candidates are the most important factor in their voting choice mean that they first choose a party and then decide which of the chosen party's candidates to support on the basis of their local record or potential.

Even so, just as voting patterns imply that most people vote for party first and candidate second, they also reveal that some do not. Some candidates are able to attract at least some votes across party lines, and incumbents especially can expect to attract personal support to add to the support they attract by virtue of their party label. A 1989 survey found that one third of those who changed their minds about which party to vote for during the course of the campaign did so out of a desire to support a particular candidate (Marsh and Sinnott, 1990).

Conclusion

Elections in Ireland, as in all parliamentary democracies, are largely about parties. Parties nominate most of the candidates who stand in elections, and candidates with well known party labels attract the overwhelming majority of votes. Parties dominate the campaign with their manifestos, their media events and their press conferences. Their leaders provide the personal focus of most media attention. Yet parties are getting an increasingly bad press in Ireland. Nineteenth century commentators often saw them as private bodies that interfered with the public democratic process, and there are clear echoes of these complaints today.

Despite these reservations, there is no getting away from the fact that parties do organise and simplify much of the fundamental process of holding democratic elections. Without them, voters would have very little information about the choices on offer. They would have even less information about the link between the votes that they cast at an election and the political complexion of the government that was subsequently formed to run the affairs of the country. This is the basis of the argument that the vital role played by political parties in the essentially public processes of parliamentary democracy implies that they need substantial resources, the bulk of which should be provided from the public purse. This remains a controversial view in Ireland, with many arguing that public funding undermines the voluntarism that is also part of the essence of democracy. Scandals in the 1990s associated with secret private contributions to politicians, potentially in exchange for political favours, have tilted the balance away from the latter view, however, and in favour of more public funding and regulation.

Increased public funding may also have some negative effects on the internal life of Irish political parties, however. It may change the balance of power between the centre and the grass roots and further downgrade the importance of party membership. Irish parties do not have large memberships, but they do have enough members to give the larger parties a presence in most parts of the country. This provides a very important personal link between representatives in the Dáil and ordinary citizens. Party membership, furthermore, allows a relatively large number of people to get involved in politics, and to participate more fully in the political process than merely by filling in a ballot paper.

For voters, a party label provides at least one simple cue, enabling people to make sense of what is sometimes a complex choice at election time. Although votes can only be cast for individuals, most electors behave as if they are voting for parties. In the last analysis, political scientists still remain unsure as to why voters select one party rather than another. Much of the evidence is consistent both with the argument that party choices are based on habits learned early in life, and with the view that electors assess parties by what they say and what they do, particularly in relation to the economy.

There are of course some limits to the reach of political parties in

Ireland. Independent candidates do get elected to the Dáil at a typical Irish election and the number of these has been rising in recent years. Voters still decide which of their chosen party's candidates they would most like to have as their public representatives. Local party politicians can build a reputation and organisation that is essentially personal and can transcend their party labels. This allows local TDs some independence and offers us a glimpse of what politics might be like without political parties.

Ultimately, however, parliamentary democracy in Ireland works as it does because people vote for parties rather than individuals at election time, and do so in a way that is to some extent predictable. This makes the social patterns in party choice a fundamental basis of Irish party politics. It also suggests that, if such social bases are changing, we can expect change in the Irish party system. The rise of new parties and the modest decline of the old ones suggest that this process is already under way, but we may expect the old parties to make every effort to adapt to the changing circumstances and to maintain their central place in Irish politics.

References and further reading

Borooah, Vani K. and Vidya Borooah, 1990. 'Economic performance and political popularity in the Republic of Ireland', *Public Choice* 67:1, pp. 65–79.

Carty, R. K., 1981. *Party and Parish Pump: Electoral Politics in Ireland*. Ontario: Wilfrid Laurier University Press.

Farrell, David M., 1992. 'Ireland', pp. 389–457 in Richard S. Katz and Peter Mair (eds), *Party Organizations: A Data Handbook on Party Organizations in Western Democracies*. London: Sage.

Farrell, David M., 1994. 'Ireland: centralization, professionalization and competitive pressures', pp. 216–41 in Richard S. Katz and Peter Mair (eds), *How Parties Organize: Change and Adaptation in Party Organizations in Western Democracies*. London: Sage.

Franklin, Mark, Tom Mackie, Henry Valen *et al.*, 1992. *Electoral Change: Responses to Evolving Social and Attitudinal Structures in Western Democracies*. Cambridge: Cambridge University Press.

Gallagher, Michael, 1978. 'Party solidarity, exclusivity and inter-party relationships in Ireland, 1922–1977: the evidence of transfers', *Economic and Social Review* 10:1, pp. 1–22.

Gallagher, Michael, 1985. *Political Parties in the Republic of Ireland*. Manchester: Manchester University Press.

Gallagher, Michael, 1988. 'Ireland: the increasing role of the centre', pp. 119–44 in Michael Gallagher and Michael Marsh (eds), *Candidate Selection in Comparative Perspective: The Secret Garden of Politics*. London: Sage.

Gallagher, Michael, 1999. 'The election of the 28th Dáil', pp. 177–205 in Marsh and Mitchell (1999).

Gallagher, Michael, Michael Laver and Peter Mair, 1995. *Representative Government in Modern Europe*. New York: McGraw-Hill.

Gallagher, Michael and Michael Laver (eds), 1993. *How Ireland Voted 1992*. Dublin: Folens; Limerick: PSAI Press.

Gallagher, Michael and Richard Sinnott (eds), 1990. *How Ireland Voted 1989*. Galway: Centre for the Study of Irish Elections and PSAI Press.

Galligan, Yvonne, 1999. 'Candidate selection', pp. 57–81 in Marsh and Mitchell (1999).

Garry, John and Lucy Mansergh, 1999. 'Party Manifestos', pp. 82–106 in Marsh and Mitchell (1999).

Harrison, Michael and Michael Marsh, 1994. 'What can he do for us? The popularity of leaders and their parties in Ireland', *Electoral Studies* 13: 4, pp. 289–312.

Harrison, Michael and Michael Marsh, 1998. 'A re-examination of an Irish popularity function', *Public Choice* 94, pp. 367–83.

King, Simon and Gordon Gillespie, 1998. 'Irish political data 1997', *Irish Political Studies* 13, pp. 211–79.

Laver, Michael, Peter Mair and Richard Sinnott (eds), 1987. *How Ireland Voted: the General Election of 1987*. Swords: Poolbeg Press.

Laver, Michael, Michael Marsh and Richard Sinnott, 1987. 'Patterns of party support', pp. 99–140 in Laver, Mair and Sinnott (1987).

Mair, Peter, 1987. *The Changing Irish Party System: Organisation, Ideology and Electoral Competition*. London: Frances Pinter.

Mair, Peter, 1994. 'Party organisations: from civil society to the state', pp. 23–50 in Richard S. Katz and Peter Mair (eds), *How Parties Organise*. London: Sage.

Marsh, Michael, 1993. 'Selecting party leaders in the Republic of Ireland', *European Journal of Political Research* 24:3, pp. 295–316.

Marsh, Michael and Paul Mitchell, (eds) 1999. *How Ireland Voted 1997*. Boulder, Colo.: Westview and PSAI Press.

Marsh, Michael and Richard Sinnott, 1990. 'How the voters decided', pp. 94–130 in Gallagher and Sinnott (1990).

Marsh, Michael and Richard Sinnott, 1993. 'The voters: stability and change', pp. 93–114 in Gallagher and Laver (1993).

Marsh, Michael and Richard Sinnott, 1999. 'The behaviour of the Irish voter', pp. 151–80 in Marsh and Mitchell (1999).

Mockler, Frank, 1994. 'Organisational change in Fianna Fáil and Fine Gael', *Irish Political Studies* 9, pp. 165–72.

O'Byrnes, Stephen, 1986. *Hiding behind a Face: Fine Gael under FitzGerald*. Dublin: Gill and Macmillan.

Schmitt, Hermann and Søren Holmberg, 1995. 'Political Parties in Decline?' pp. 95–133 in H.-D. Klingemann and Dieter Fuchs (eds), *Citizens and the State*. Oxford: Oxford University Press.

Sinnott, Richard, 1995. *Irish Voters Decide: Voting Behaviour in Elections and Referendums since 1918*. Manchester: Manchester University Press.

Waters, John, 1991. *Jiving at the Crossroads*. Belfast: Blackstaff Press.

Whyte, John H., 1974. 'Ireland: politics without social bases', pp. 619–51 in Richard Rose (ed.), *Electoral Behavior: a Comparative Handbook*. New York: Free Press.

7 Parliament

Michael Gallagher

The Irish constitution, as we saw in chapter 3, provides for a parliamentary system of government. Ireland's parliament, the Oireachtas, is bicameral: the lower and directly elected house, the Dáil, has since 1981 consisted of 166 members (see appendix 2c) elected from forty-one constituencies, while the upper house, the indirectly elected Seanad, has sixty members. The power of the Seanad is very limited, and we shall concentrate on the Dáil in this chapter.

In classical liberal democratic theory, parliament plays a key role in the democratic process. It is elected by the people to decide how the country should be governed; the government, which is accountable to it, then carries out its decisions. This, in fact, is what enables democratic states to claim that they are democratic. Set against this theory, many people have found practice rather disappointing right across western Europe. Parliaments may still be elected by the people, and may even elect governments, but it seems that once a government gets into office it can go its own way largely unchecked. And, even in the context of these generally low expectations of how much control over a government a parliament can really exercise in any country, together with the notorious difficulty of measuring its power, it has frequently been argued that the Dáil stands out for its exceptional weakness. In the 1970s Ward described the Dáil as 'supine', in the 1980s Dinan adjudged it 'a woefully inadequate institution', and in the 1990s Chubb saw it as 'a puny parliament peopled by members who have a modest view of their functions and a poor capacity to carry them out' (Ward, 1974, p. 241; Dinan 1986, p. 71; Chubb, 1992, p. 189). In this chapter we shall look at what parliament is supposed to do and ask how well it does it.

The constitution assigns two main functions to the Houses of the Oireachtas. These are the appointment of the Taoiseach and the government (Articles 13 and 28), and law making, or more broadly policy making (Articles 15 to 27). The constitution also declares (Article 28.4.1) that 'The Government shall be responsible to Dáil Éireann'. This gives us three dimensions on which to assess the performance of the Dáil: the appointment of governments, policy making, and scrutiny of government behaviour.

Arend Lijphart (1984, p. 3) identifies 'two diametrically opposite models of democracy: the majoritarian model (or the Westminster model) and the consensus model'; when it comes to relations between parliament and government, and indeed in other ways too, Ireland displays features of both models. The Westminster model is characterised by, among other things, single-party and bare-majority cabinets, no effective separation of power between government and parliament, unbalanced bicameralism, a two-party system, a plurality electoral system, unitary and centralised government, and the absence of a written constitution that seriously checks administrative freedom of action (Lijphart, 1984, pp. 10–15). In contrast, among the characteristics of the consensus model are government by grand coalition, a genuine separation of powers between government and parliament, balanced bicameralism, a multi-party system, a proportional representation electoral system, and a written constitution that imposes real constraints on the executive's behaviour (ibid., pp. 23–30). Given the major impact of the British style of government on the Irish system at independence, it is no surprise that Ireland strongly displays some of the features of the archetypal Westminster system, such as bare-majority cabinets, no effective separation of power between government and parliament, unbalanced bicameralism, and unitary and centralised government. Yet, at the same time, other aspects of the Irish political system are quite different: Ireland has a multi-party system (see chapter 5), proportional representation (see chapter 4), and a judicially-interpreted written constitution (see chapter 3). As a result, Irish practice does not conform fully to either a majoritarian or a consensus model.

The profile of TDs (members of the Dáil) is similar to that in many west European parliaments. In the 28th Dáil, which was elected in June 1997, the average TD was aged 49, with two-thirds of TDs in their forties or fifties (details of members' backgrounds are based on O'Sullivan, 1999). Nearly half have a professional occupation, with school-teachers the most common category, although the great majority are in practice full-time politicians. Around half of Dáil members have a university degree. They have very strong local roots; nearly all live in their constituency, most were born and raised there, and around three-quarters were members of local government before being elected to the Dáil.

Parties and parliament

Before we discuss the relationship between government and parliament in Ireland, we should make the point that viewing the two as distinct bodies that vie with each other for supremacy would be quite unreal. Government and parliament are 'fused'. The government sits in parliament – in practice virtually all members of government are also TDs, as discussed in chapter 10 – as opposed to being a body external to it. The executive could be seen, as suggested by the nineteenth century writer Walter Bagehot, as a committee of parliament, elected by it and acting in its name and with its authority. From this perspective, it is more realistic to see parliament as wielding power *through* the government that it has elected than to see it as seeking to *check* a government that has come into being independently of it.

Parliament, like every other aspect of modern political life, is dominated by political parties. When deputies vote on issues, they do so as members of a party, not as 166 atomised individuals. All around Europe, deputies follow the party line in votes in parliament, and if anything parliamentary party cohesion is even higher in Ireland than the average. It is extremely rare for deputies not to vote with the party; the norm is that every TD votes in accordance with the party line on every issue. There are powerful incentives to stay in line: those voting against the party whip, or even abstaining, can expect to find themselves summarily expelled from the parliamentary party, with the prospect of remaining as independents until and unless the party agrees to readmit them. In addition, TDs know that rebellion will probably harm their chances of promotion within the party.

However, TDs' obedience to the party line is not just a matter of fear of draconian punishments if they stray. Parliamentary party rules, after all, are made by members of the parliamentary groups themselves, and these members choose voluntarily to bind themselves by such tight discipline. They do this because they believe such rules are in their and their party's interests. Deputies stay in line because they are reluctant to appear to be siding with the other side, and because the party line is in any case likely to be broadly acceptable to them since they have their say on it at meetings of the parliamentary party. Their instincts are always to remain part of the party bloc, out of a sense of loyalty and common purpose. Moreover, the tough penalties imposed on defectors – provided these are rigidly enforced – make life easier in some ways. They make TDs less vulnerable to pressure from outside the party; they cannot be picked off, one by one, by pressure groups or local interests, because everyone knows that any threats such bodies can make against a TD for not doing their bidding pale into insignificance against the punishment the party will impose for displeasing it.

Viewed in this light, to consider parliament and government as two separate bodies competing with each other is to ignore the reality of party domination of parliament and government. Any effective increase in the role or power of 'parliament' *vis-à-vis* the executive means, in effect, an increase in the role or power of the opposition, not of parliament as a collective body. The role of government backbenchers, willingly accepted, is to sustain the government rather than to act as independent scrutineers of it; government backbenchers do not seek additional means of holding their own ministers to account. The ongoing battle of government versus opposition is paramount and tangible; the notion of a contest for power between government and parliament bears little relation to political reality.

Appointment and dismissal of governments

The formal position, as laid out in Article 13.1 of the constitution, is that the Dáil nominates the Taoiseach and approves the composition of the government, whereupon the President appoints them. The Dáil can also dismiss a Taoiseach and a government, by passing a vote of no confidence (Article 28.10). In Westminster-model countries, the role of parliaments in appointing governments is negligible, because in practice the latter are chosen at elections, and the vote of parliament after the election merely puts the seal on what the voters have decided. In consensus model countries, in contrast, forming an government can be a more complicated and time-consuming process; coalition government is the norm, and weeks can elapse after an election before a government emerges, a process that entails lengthy negotiation and bargaining between prospective coalition partners (see Gallagher, Laver and Mair, 1995, ch. 12). Indeed, in some such countries governments might change frequently between elections.

Until the 1980s it was conventional to see government formation in Ireland as a variant of Westminster practice, with coalitions and minority governments, when they occurred, as relatively rare exceptions. Certainly, there were elections that conformed very well to the model. For example, at the 1977 election Fianna Fáil won a majority of the votes and eighty-four of the 148 seats, and when the new Dáil met, the party's leader, Jack Lynch, was duly elected as Taoiseach on the bloc vote of the Fianna Fáil TDs. But a closer look at the record shows that, in fact, single-party majority government was not as common prior to the 1980s as was sometimes assumed, while in the 1980s and 1990s it became a definite rarity. Over the whole period of the state, single-party majority governments have been in office for less than half the time. If we consider the period 1948–97, only four of the sixteen governments have been single-party majority ones, and they have held office for only about sixteen of the forty-nine years; majority coalition government has been more common in this period (see Table 7.1). No election since 1977 has produced a single-party majority administration. While majority government is the norm, minority governments, which have been markedly more short-lived (just under two years in office on average in the 1923–97 period compared with almost four years for majority governments), have been in office for more than a quarter of the time.

The growing infrequency of single-party rule means that elections are less likely to be the sole battleground that determines who forms a government. This does not necessarily mean that the Dáil has displaced elections as the place where governments are decided. There are, in fact, three ways in which government composition might be settled: by an election at which a single party or a pre-agreed coalition wins a majority of seats; by political parties which, after an unclear election outcome, put together a majority coalition; or by the Dáil itself, which elects a government whose own strength alone does not suffice for a majority. In the first two cases, the

Table 7.1 Number and duration of governments in Ireland, 1923–97

	1923–97			1948–97		
	Number of gov'ts	Days in office	% of total days in office	Number of gov'ts	Days in office	% of total days in office
Majority 1-party	8	12,198	45.3	4	6,026	33.4
Minority 1-party	9	6,232	23.1	4	3,488	19.4
Majority coalition	6	7,041	26.1	6	7,041	39.1
Minority coalition	2	1,463	5.4	2	1,463	8.1
Majority governments	14	19,239	71.4	10	13,067	72.5
Minority governments	11	7,695	28.6	6	4,951	27.5
Total	25	26,934	100.0	16	18,018	100.0

Source: details of governments from Appendix 3c.
Note: Governments are defined as lasting until either a change of partisan composition or an election. The three governments holding exactly 50 per cent of Dáil seats are classified as majority if the Ceann Comhairle (Speaker) was drawn from opposition ranks, as in 1965 and 1989, or minority when the Ceann Comhairle was a government TD (1937).

Dáil's role could be seen as nominal, in that it is merely ratifying either a verdict of the people or a deal made among parties. In the post-1948 period, only five elections have directly produced a government, while another six governments have resulted from post-election agreements among parties rather than being chosen directly by the electorate (see Table 7.2). This leaves six other occasions when the role of the Dáil has been decisive. In four of these cases, the Dáil elected minority Fianna Fáil governments; the other two occurred in 1981, when a minority Fine Gael–Labour coalition emerged, and in 1997, when a minority Fianna Fáil–Progressive Democrats coalition was formed.

The role of the Dáil was central after some of the elections of the 1980s

Table 7.2 Origins of governments, 1948–97

Government composition settled by	Number of cases	Cases
Election: single party or pre-declared coalition wins majority of seats	5	1957, 1965, 1969, 1973, 1977
Parties: parties controlling a majority of seats put together post-election majority coalition	6	1948, 1954, Nov 1982, 1989, 1992, 1994
Parliament: Dáil elects government that controls only a minority of seats	6	1951, 1961, 1981, Feb 1982, 1987, 1997

Source: details of governments from appendices 2c and 3c.

and 1990s. After the 1981 election, uncertainty as to who would form the next government persisted right up to the point when the vote was taken in the Dáil. Even though Fine Gael and Labour had agreed to try to form a coalition government, these two parties had only eighty of the 166 seats and thus needed the backing of independent TDs to secure a Dáil majority. After the February 1982 election, it was Fianna Fáil that needed support from the Workers' Party and independent deputies to enable it to form a minority government. In 1987, it seemed for a while after the election that no potential government would secure the Dáil's approval. When the Dáil met it was known that eighty-two of the 166 TDs would be voting for Charles Haughey as Taoiseach and eighty-two would be opposing him, with independent Tony Gregory uncommitted and the Ceann Comhairle (Speaker) in the chair. The suspense continued until Gregory declared that he would abstain on the crucial vote, thus enabling Haughey to be elected Taoiseach on the casting vote of the Ceann Comhairle.

In 1989, for the first time ever, the Dáil was unable to elect a Taoiseach at its first post-election meeting. It took a further two weeks and two meetings of the Dáil before Fianna Fáil and the Progressive Democrats agreed to form a government that controlled exactly half of the Dáil seats. This was the first occasion on which Fianna Fáil, hitherto a staunch defender of the principle that a party should be either in government on its own or in full-blooded opposition, agreed to share power with another party. Forming a government after the 1992 election was an even more protracted process; again, the new Dáil was unable to elect a Taoiseach at its first meeting, and the Fianna Fáil–Labour government was not installed until eight weeks after the election (Farrell, 1993). In 1997, neither of the competing coalitions commanded majority support, and both sought the support of independent and minor party TDs; the Fianna Fáil–Progressive Democrat combination was able to secure the backing of three of these TDs, enough to ensure its election by the Dáil (Mitchell, 1999).

When we look at the Dáil's role in dismissing governments, a similar picture emerges: compliance neither with the purest version of the Westminster pattern nor with the consensus model. It is not the case that the Dáil regularly brings down governments; in fact, it has dismissed them on only two occasions. The first was in November 1982, when the minority Fianna Fáil government was beaten by eighty-two votes to eighty on a confidence motion, precipitating its resignation and a general election. Even this could be explained away as an aberration caused by the recent death of one Fianna Fáil TD and the absence through illness of another. The second occasion was in November 1992, when the PDs left their coalition with Fianna Fáil and joined the opposition benches, whereupon a motion of no confidence in the government was passed by eighty-eight votes to seventy-seven (Girvin, 1993, p. 12). At first sight, then, the record might look like that of an archetypal Westminster system, where the support of parliament can generally be taken for granted by the government.

However, there have been eight other occasions when the Dáil has, in effect, terminated the life of a government, which has chosen to resign rather than continue when defeat on a confidence motion seemed only a matter of time. This happened in August 1927, 1938 and 1944, when the minority governments of the day were in a weak position and preferred to call a general election at a time of their own choosing rather than wait for the Dáil to pull the plug. Similarly, prior to calling the 1951 election the first Inter-Party government had been losing support from some of its own backbenchers in the wake of the traumatic 'Mother and Child' affair. Six years later the same fate befell the second Inter-Party government, and this factor was coupled with a weakening of its Dáil position due to by-election defeats. In January 1982 the minority coalition government was defeated in a vote on its budget, an item so basic to any government's programme that failure to get it through the Dáil is regarded as tantamount to losing a vote of confidence, and it resigned at once. In January 1987 Labour pulled out of a coalition, leaving Fine Gael with only sixty-eight seats and facing certain defeat had the Dáil met again. In 1994, Labour again ended a coalition, this time with Fianna Fáil, and the latter faced imminent defeat in a confidence motion; on this occasion, in an unprecedented development, the government resigned but the Taoiseach did not seek a dissolution, and several weeks later a new government, with a different partisan complexion, was formed. In other words, one reason why governments have so rarely been dismissed by the Dáil is that, when they have seen defeat staring them in the face, they have usually jumped off the cliff rather than waiting to be pushed.

The Westminster model, then, does not adequately capture the reality of the Dáil's role in appointing and dismissing governments. However, it remains true that Irish governments do not routinely fear dismissal by the Dáil; governments are not regularly made or broken on the floor of the house. In this, of course, the Dáil is in line with virtually every other parliament in Western Europe. The idea of parliaments constantly making and unmaking governments is neither realistic nor especially attractive. The classic example of a parliament wielding this power occurred in the French Fourth Republic, where there were twenty-eight governments in only thirteen years. Few would recommend 'strengthening' the Dáil so that this pattern could be replicated. If parliament has a role, it must lie in one of the areas to which we now turn.

Making policy

The constitution, by assigning law-making powers exclusively to the Oireachtas (Article 15.2.1), reflects one of the central tenets of classical liberal democratic theory: the legislature (parliament) makes laws and the executive (government) carries them out. This might lead us to expect that the latter is merely the striking arm of the former, carrying out parliament's will whether it likes it or not. However, no-one really expects to find this kind of relationship between government and parliament, and, as we have said, it is more common to find the view expressed that parliament, in Ireland even more than in many other countries, has come to be a mere 'glorified rubber stamp' (Dinan, 1986, p. 76) for whatever proposals the executive puts before it.

In the area of policy making, as in appointing governments, we can distinguish between the Westminster and consensus models. In the Westminster model, parliament is not seen as a real maker of laws. Rather, it provides a forum where the issues raised by a government proposal can be fully aired. The government is obliged to justify its measure and the opposition gets the chance to make the case against it (and, generally, to keep the government on its toes), but ultimately the government sees its plans approved by parliament pretty much as a matter of course. There is no feeling that the views of the opposition parties need to be taken into account or that their agreement is required for the passage of legislation; after all, they are in opposition precisely because they 'lost' the last election and the government won it. To bring the opposition into the policy making process could thus be seen as undemocratic, since it would reduce the significance of the choice made by the voters at elections. In the consensus model, in contrast, government is (or, at least, feels) obliged to take seriously the wishes of parliament, including the feelings of the opposition. While in the last resort it is the government that governs, governments prefer not to railroad their legislation through against strong resistance; they try to find a consensus within parliament for their proposals and are willing to take on board constructive suggestions from other parties.

Ireland's law-making procedure is closely based, in the letter and in the spirit, on that of Westminster. Bills can be introduced in either house (in the past, almost all government bills were introduced in the Dáil, but in recent years about one in every ten has been introduced in the Seanad). The formal progress of a bill is the same through each house, but since in the event of a disagreement between Dáil and Seanad it is the former that prevails (see p. 200 below), we shall concentrate here on the Dáil. A five-stage process is provided for bills, though most bills can bypass the first stage (see Box 7.1). The second stage is the general debate on the principle of the bill. The third (committee stage) involves a detailed examination of each of its sections. The fourth and fifth stages consist of tidying up the decisions made at the committee stage and formally passing the bill. After this, it goes to the other house and then to the President, who signs it into law or, very rarely, refers it to the Supreme Court for a verdict on its constitutionality (see p. 83–4 above). In effect, only the second and third stages offer the house any real opportunity to affect the content of a bill.

The second-stage debates are, at least in theory, the big events in the life of the Dáil, as it is here that the broad lines of bills are argued out. However, in practice debates have a very ritualistic quality about them. All

Box 7.1 The stages of a bill initiated in Dáil Éireann

Stage   Matters decided

First stage   Formal introduction of bill, securing agreement that the bill
               proceed to second stage. Virtually all bills (government bills,
               and private members' bills introduced by a 'group' of at least
               seven deputies), can be presented to the house without
               needing this formal agreement, and enter the process at the
               second stage.

Second stage   Debate on the broad principle of the bill. The details of the
               bill are not discussed at this stage, and the substance of the
               bill cannot be amended. The vote taken after the second
               stage debate (assuming there is one – a significant number
               of bills are passed by agreement of the house, without the
               need for a vote) determines whether the bill is allowed to
               proceed to almost certain acceptance or is rejected.

Third stage   Committee stage. The bill is examined in detail by a commit-
               tee (in the past, almost invariably, the 'committee' consisted
               of the whole Dáil; since 1997, specialist fourteen-member
               committees have undertaken this task). The bill is discussed
               section by section. Amendments may be proposed, pro-
               vided they do not conflict with the principle of the bill,
               since this was approved by the house at the second stage.

Fourth stage   Report stage. Usually a formal tidying up of amendments
               made at third stage. New amendments may be proposed
               provided that they are not substantively the same as amend-
               ments rejected at the third stage.

Fifth stage   The final and formal passing of the bill. Speeches at this
               stage tend to be shorter and more ritualistic versions of
               those on the second stage. The bill now goes to the Seanad
               for discussion.

Final stages   When it returns from the Seanad the Dáil discusses the
               changes, if any, proposed by the Seanad. If it accepts them,
               the bill is sent to the President, for signing into law or, in
               the President's discretion, for referral to the Supreme
               Court for a verdict on its constitutionality. If the Dáil does
               not accept the Seanad's suggested amendments, it sends
               the bill back to the Seanad for reconsideration. The
               Seanad may fall into line with the wishes of the Dáil or it
               may reaffirm its amendments, in which case it can delay but
               not veto the passage of the bill.

Note: Bills can also be initiated in the Seanad. In this case they then go to the
Dáil after being passed, but, in the event of the Dáil deciding to make amendments, they are treated as if they had been initiated in the Dáil (Article 20.2.2
of the constitution).

too often they are highly predictable affairs. The relevant minister opens the event by outlining the rationale for the measure to be introduced, after which a succession of opposition deputies use the occasion to pour cold water on the bill under discussion or, at best, to welcome the legislation but criticise the government for the delay in bringing it forward. There is little incentive for the opposition to offer constructive alternative proposals since the likelihood of any government deputy crossing the floor to vote for them is practically zero.

TDs are not supposed to read speeches from a prepared text, but they may use 'notes', which are sometimes very extensive. In recent years Dáil procedures have been reformed, and speeches are shorter and more to the point than prior to the 1990s, when much of the time in Dáil debates was taken by 'having people waffle on', as Bertie Ahern once put it (*Dáil Debates* 339: 658, 27 January 1983). Some speeches used to stretch to astonishing lengths simply in order to pad out the available time, but now ministers and opposition spokespersons can speak for a maximum of thirty minutes in the second stage debate and other TDs for at most twenty minutes. The Dáil usually meets for three days a week (from 2.30 to 8.30 on Tuesdays, 10.30 to 8.30 on Wednesdays, and 10.30 to 4.45 on Thursdays) for around thirty weeks of the year, for ninety to a hundred days in all. Table 7.3 shows that the Dáil met more frequently in the 1980s and 1990s than in either the 1930s or 1960s, but actually passed fewer bills than in the 1930s.

Not surprisingly, second-stage speeches, at least once the minister and the main opposition spokesperson have had their say, are not made to a packed and expectant Dáil chamber. It is not uncommon to find only a handful of TDs in the chamber for such speeches. If the opposition is feeling recalcitrant, one of its TDs will demand a quorum (twenty TDs), without which the Dáil technically cannot conduct its business. This means that

Table 7.3 Sittings and business of Dáil Éireann, 1930s–1990s

	1934–38 (average per year)	1964–68 (average per year)	1984–88 (average per year)	1992–96 (average per year)
Sitting days	72	78	92	96
Sitting hours	478	568	765	758
Bills considered by Dáil	66	52	63	53
Bills promulgated as laws	49	32	32	38
Bills carried over to following year	14	15	27	22

Source: For the 1930s, *Sittings of Dáil Éireann; Public Bills in the Dáil; Private Bills in the Dáil.* All published annually by the Stationery Office, Dublin. For the 1960s, *Returns relating to Sittings and Business of the 17th Dáil* (Dublin: Stationery Office, 1967) and *Returns relating to Sittings and Business of the 18th Dáil* (Dublin: Stationery Office, 1971). For the 1980s, *Returns relating to Sittings and Business of the 24th Dáil* (Dublin: Stationery Office, 1990) and *Returns relating to Sittings and Business of the 25th Dáil* (Dublin: Stationery Office, 1991). For the 1990s, information supplied by the Houses of the Oireachtas.

government backbenchers have to stream out of their offices and into the Dáil chamber to make up the numbers for a while, but they soon drift back again and hope that the opposition tires of the tactic. Attendance used to be particularly low when Friday sittings took place.

While some profess indignation at the low level of attendance in the Dáil chamber, it is hard to criticise those TDs and ministers who conclude that they have more useful ways of spending their time. Dáil debates are often dialogues of the deaf, set pieces with a strong element of theatre in which speeches are made for the record or in order to get publicity at local level. Dáil deputies, when they speak in a debate, wonder whether anyone is listening. There is far less newspaper coverage of parliamentary proceedings than twenty years ago, and TDs complain that unless they supply a script of their speech to journalists there is little or no chance of their words being reported in the press. Proceedings have been televised since 1991, but the rigid rules laid down for the broadcasters by parliament have made the result rather dull viewing. As a result viewing figures have been low, and 'Oireachtas Report' ended up at one stage in 1998 being broadcast at 2.30 am, which Pat Rabbitte TD of Democratic Left described as a time when 'only drunks and insomniacs' would be watching (as a result of such protests, its transmission was brought forward to midnight). The feeling among TDs that the world takes little notice of them is shared by backbench parliamentarians almost everywhere. Attendance in the chamber tends to be low in nearly all parliaments these days (especially on Friday afternoons), and a Danish joke has it that a deputy wanting to keep something secret should announce it from the rostrum of the Folketing, as then it is certain that nobody will hear it.

It is very rare for a government bill to be defeated at the second stage. Such a defeat will not happen because some of the government's backbenchers become convinced by the brilliance of the arguments from the opposition, but it may happen when there is a minority government. In January 1982, as we have already mentioned, the minority coalition government's budget was defeated. The 1987–89 minority Fianna Fáil government was defeated six times in the Dáil, though none of these defeats concerned legislation. More significantly, this government did not bring before the house a bill to approve the redrawing of constituency boundaries in a way that would have made life more difficult for the smaller parties at the next election, because of a well-founded fear that any such bill would be defeated.

The assumption made so far is that all bills are government bills because, with rare exceptions, only government bills can expect to pass into law. Indeed, the constitution states (Article 17.2) that no motion or resolution shall be passed, or law enacted, that involves spending public money unless the Dáil receives a written message, signed by the Taoiseach, recommending the measure on behalf of the government. This is a stipulation in many countries, clearly motivated by the fear that were it not in force, parliament might vote for the spending of money but against government efforts to raise it. When the 1987–89 Fianna Fáil government sustained Dáil defeats on motions apparently 'directing' it to take certain steps, it ignored the motions, dismissing them as being merely declaratory. The standing orders of the Dáil contain provision for 'private members' bills', which are usually introduced by an opposition deputy. From 1937 to 1988 only six such bills were passed, all in the 1950s (Morgan, 1990, pp. 103, 231). In the 1990s there were a small number of additional cases, along with some instances of governments accepting bills originating with the opposition. Such bills do not represent any temporary dominance of parliament over the executive, though, because they will be passed only if the government directs its own backbenchers to support them. Even unsuccessful private members' bills may have an impact, however, since the government sometimes secures the withdrawal or defeat of the bill by promising to take some action itself.[1]

The opposition, then, is unlikely to secure the defeat of a government bill or the passage of a bill of its own. If the Dáil is to make any impression on legislation, this must come at the third, 'committee', stage of a bill's progress, where the opposition can hope to have some influence on the final shape of the bill. Prior to 1993, the 'committee' that considered bills in practice normally comprised the whole house. After several reforms, the position in 1999 was that all bills went to a specialist fourteen-member Dáil committee; there are currently thirteen such committees, on which the parties are represented in proportion to their Dáil strengths. Although discussion on the broad principle of the bill is ruled out, this having been settled at the second stage, TDs can raise points about specific sections: they can point out anomalies, inconsistencies, loopholes, imprecise phraseology, and so on. If the points raised are consistent with the basic intention of the bill, the minister may well accept them and modify the bill accordingly. If the minister does not want to accept such amendments, then they will fail. The atmosphere in a small committee may be less confrontational than in the full chamber – even when the chamber is in practice nearly empty rather than full – and ministers may be readier to take opposition proposals on board.

The fact that the plenary discussion of the principles of a bill in the Dáil precedes the committee stage is more significant than is often realised. In many countries, a bill is examined in detail by a small committee of parliament *before* it goes to the whole house; in the Westminster model, the sequence is usually the other way around and 'the committee is bound by the principle of the bill to which the House has agreed' (Laundy, 1989, p. 73). This is a very important factor in deciding the significance of parliamentary committees in policy making: 'if a committee can consider a bill before it is taken up on the floor, the chances of the committee influencing or determining the outcome tend to be greater than when the lines of battle have been predetermined in plenary meetings' (Shaw, 1979, p. 417). Small committees of deputies who have acquired some expertise in a particular area are more likely to reach a consensus if the issues at stake have not been heavily politicised by partisan debates on the floor of the house, and the chances of the government's proposals getting through unaltered are correspondingly lower. For this reason, governments in Westminster model countries prefer to leave the committee stage until after the plenary discussion, so that any changes made by the committee are likely to be minor.

It is clear, then, that the Dáil cannot be seen as an active participant in the process of making laws, let alone broader policy. Governments are usually more concerned to bring the major interest groups round to their way of thinking (see chapter 11) than to placate the Dáil, whose backing they tend to take for granted. The Dáil is often seen as legitimising legislation rather than really making it, though the role of legitimation should not be dismissed out of hand. Norton (1990b, p. 147) points out that parliaments play an important symbolic role, and that for many people the fact that all legislation has to be passed by a parliament consisting of the elected representatives of the people is more important in making them feel that they are ruled demo-cratically than the question of how much real power that parliament wields.

It would be an exaggeration, though, to say that Ireland suffers from 'cabinet dictatorship' or an 'elected dictatorship' between elections. Quite apart from the extra-parliamentary checks on the executive, such as the constitution, the Dáil cannot be disregarded. It will do what the government wants provided, and only provided, the government has the backing of a majority of TDs. When there is a minority government, it will be able to get its legislation through only if it takes care not to introduce any proposals that would induce the opposition to combine against it. For example, the minority Fianna Fáil government of 1987–89 suffered no defeats on any of its legislative proposals, but this was because it took care not to introduce proposals that would have been defeated, not because the Dáil was certain always to do its bidding (Girvin, 1990, p. 7).

Moreover, even when the government parties have a Dáil majority, it is easy to overlook the fact that the government has to pay a price to retain the backing of its TDs. Relations between governments and their own back-benchers are central to any understanding of the relationship between government and parliament (King, 1976). Ministers have to show their backbenchers some respect in order to keep them trooping loyally through the lobbies. When the party is in power, weekly meetings of its parliamentary party (attended by TDs, senators and MEPs) hear from ministers about their plans, and they expect this to be a genuine process of consultation. If a member raises a doubt or a question, the minister would be unwise to brush this aside as dismissively as an opposition deputy might be dealt with in the Dáil chamber; ministers, after all, want to be personally popular with their own TDs, for a variety of obvious reasons. A sensible minister will 'wear a velvet glove, albeit having a mailed fist within it', when dealing with government backbenchers (Rose, 1986, p. 14).

The power of the parliamentary party should not be overstated; evidently, the initiative in making policy lies with the government, not with back-benchers. But no government has a completely free hand from its own party; if a proposed policy or item of legislation arouses broad antagonism from government TDs at a parliamentary party meeting, it is unlikely to be pressed further, as was seen early in 1991 when government proposals to make contraceptives available to sixteen- and seventeen-year-olds ran into Fianna Fáil backbench resistance. Similarly, in the extremely rare event that government TDs are persuaded of a measure's flaws by a critical speech from the opposition in the Dáil, this will be reflected not in votes against the measure in the chamber but in private pressure on the minister to amend or rescind the proposal. One of the few cases in Irish parliamentary history of a Dáil speech having such an impact occurred in 1985. A lone crusade by the then independent TD Des O'Malley against a bill (designed to protect a cartel of airlines) that was backed by both the Fine Gael–Labour government and the Fianna Fáil opposition sowed seeds of doubt in the minds of many Fine Gael backbenchers. As a result of the views they expressed in the privacy of parliamentary party meetings the minister significantly amended the bill. An awareness of what the parlia-mentary party will and will not stand for is bound to be a factor in determining what policies the government tries to introduce.

With this qualification, then, it is the government and not the Oireachtas that has the initiative in the shaping of laws and policies. Once again, the Irish pattern is not especially exceptional, even if the Oireachtas is less active in this area than are most parliaments. Of course, in presidential systems such as the USA, parliament can be quite strong, because the survival of a government is not at stake: if a presidentially-backed bill is defeated in Congress, the administration does not fall. But things are very different in the parliamentary systems by which Western European countries are governed. When a government is elected by, answerable to, and dismissable by par-liament, measures proposed by the government are very unlikely to be rejected. When bills go to a specialist committee before they reach the floor of the house, parliament can exercise significant influence over their final shape, but where the Westminster model prevails it would be unrealistic to expect a policy making role for parliament. All that we might hope for is that the Dáil keeps a vigilant eye on what government is up to, the topic that we now examine.

Scrutinising the behaviour of government

As we have just said, the initiative in making policy lies with government rather than with parliament. However, this does not freeze the Oireachtas out of the political process entirely. Even if it does pass virtually all the government's proposals, it still has a choice as to how to follow this up. Does it merely sit back and allow the government to act as it wishes? Or does it keep the government under careful scrutiny, checking on whether it has behaved as it said it would and on whether public money has been spent as promised, keeping the government on its toes and exposing its mistakes? How effective is the Dáil in making ministers answerable and accountable? The Dáil has three main methods of trying to compel the government to justify its behaviour: debates, parliamentary questions and committees.

Debates

As well as considering bills, as we have already discussed, the Dáil may debate other motions. Three that are relevant to the scrutiny function of the Dáil are: first, motions of confidence in the government; second, *ad hoc* motions on topical political issues; and, third, formal motions on topics such as the adjournment of the house. From time to time an opposition party is prone to table a motion of no confidence in the government, to which the government almost invariably responds by tabling a motion of confidence in itself. The resultant debate, naturally, ranges over the entire gamut of the government's activity, with opposition TDs using the occasion to obtain publicity for their criticisms of the government rather than really expecting to oust it; as we have already mentioned, only twice (in 1982 and 1992) has such a motion actually been passed. *Ad hoc* motions may be granted by the government to allow the opposition to air their grievances about some administrative action, or, alternatively, they may be occasions for the expression of broad consensus among TDs about some major development. The adjournment debate held at the end of some sessions (a debate ostensibly on a topic such as 'That Dáil Éireann do adjourn for the summer recess') is predictable in content, as various ministers defend the government's record while opposition TDs disparage it.

Parliamentary questions

On each Tuesday and Wednesday when the Dáil sits, one hour and three-quarters are set aside for parliamentary questions (PQs), with a further hour and twenty minutes on Thursdays. Ministers face questions in turn, on successive sitting days. In order to give the minister and departmental civil servants time to discover the information sought, questions must be put down three working days before they are due to be answered. Most PQs seek a written answer, which the TD receives within three working days, but others are put down for oral answer, which means that he or she must wait until the relevant minister's day for answering comes around. Questions may seek very detailed information about an individual constituent or the constituency of the TD asking the question (this is characteristic of questions for written answers), or they may ask about a topic of national significance or a matter of government policy (characteristic of those for oral answer).

TDs can respond to the minister's oral reply by asking a 'supplementary' question. If dissatisfied with the minister's reply, a deputy can raise and elaborate upon his or her grievance during the 'adjournment debate' that occupies the last fifty minutes of each day's sitting, and the minister is obliged to reply more fully. This, however, receives little media coverage because of its late hour, except in the relevant provincial newspapers.

A deputy may ask any number of questions for written answer, but can put down no more than two on any one day that seek an oral answer, The order in which the latter questions appear on the order paper is settled by lottery. This determines which ones will be reached, since time constraints mean that on average only about twenty questions are answered orally each day. A number of opposition TDs therefore put down identical or near-identical questions in order to boost the chances of the question being drawn in a high position.

The number of questions has risen greatly over the years. Over the sixty-year period covered in Table 7.4, the number of questions for oral answer doubled while the number of written questions rose fifty-fold. This may in part reflect an increase in constituency work, though it is worth noting that exactly the same pattern of a major increase over the years is found in several other west European countries (Gallagher, Laver and Mair, 1995, p. 48). The prominent recurrence of the same few names among those asking questions about individual constituents does suggest that many deputies find other less public ways of obtaining similar information. Any figure purporting to represent the average 'cost' of dealing with a PQ is obviously purely notional, but in 1993 it was stated that the Department of Finance estimated this at £65, a figure that several TDs suggested was unrealistically high

Table 7.4 Parliamentary questions, 1930s–1990s

	1934–38 (average per year)	*1964–68* (average per year)	*1984–88* (average per year)	*1995–96* (average per year)
Questions for oral answer	984	4,043	2,011	1,804
Questions for written answer	179	249	8,740	14,183
Private notice questions	1	3	39	74
Total questions	1,164	4,295	10,791	16,061

Source: For the 1930s, *Questions in the Dáil*, published annually by the Stationery Office, Dublin. For the 1960s, *Returns relating to Sittings and Business of the 17th Dáil* (Dublin: Stationery Office, 1967) and *Returns relating to Sittings and Business of the 18th Dáil* (Dublin: Stationery Office, 1971). For the 1980s, *Returns relating to Sittings and Business of the 24th Dáil* (Dublin: Stationery Office, 1990) and *Returns relating to Sittings and Business of the 25th Dáil* (Dublin: Stationery Office, 1991). For the 1990s, information supplied by the Houses of the Oireachtas.
Note: All figures are averages, so, due to rounding, columns do not necessarily add to the total figures. Private notice questions are questions of which the minister receives no prior notification: Dáil Standing Order 31 provides that questions 'relating to matters of urgent public importance' may be 'asked on private notice', subject to the permission of the Ceann Comhairle.

(*Dáil Debates* 435: 1906, 17 November 1993). The fact that most questions are tabled by opposition TDs affirms their political purpose; government deputies ask very few questions, even of a local nature.

Question time is highly politicised. TDs put down questions for oral answer not in an ingenuous search for information but, in most cases, as part of the ongoing war of attrition against the government, which they hope to be able to embarrass. Ministers treat question time in the same spirit, aiming to give away as little as possible. The culture is one of concealment, not of openness. The etiquette of PQs requires not that answers be helpful or informative but only that they not be untruthful (though it has been alleged that answers given by certain Fianna Fáil ministers in the late 1980s and early 1990s relating to the beef industry failed to meet even this minimal requirement; see FitzGerald, 1994). Answers to a number of possible supplementary questions are worked out in advance, but the information contained in them is not disclosed unless the relevant supplementary is asked. In February 1998 an opposition TD, Liz McManus, received a written answer mistakenly accompanied by a confidential memo that was not intended for her eyes and contained far more information than the bland official reply. The chairman of the long-running beef tribunal (discussed further in chapter 11) stated that if questions had been answered in the Dáil as fully as they had to be answered in the tribunal, the tribunal would not have been necessary. A senior civil servant appearing before the tribunal stated that in preparing responses, the policy was to answer the question but go no further; information, no matter how interesting it might be to the questioner, is not disclosed unless specifically sought (O'Toole, 1995, p. 257). Indeed, the former Taoiseach Garret FitzGerald sometimes found it necessary while in government to expand suggested answers to PQs, because the civil servants drawing up the reply had been 'too economical with the truth' (FitzGerald, 1994). A minister involved in the beef affair, Ray Burke, explained that if the opposition did not ask the right questions, they would not get the right answers (O'Toole, 1995, p. 256). Oppositions tend to deplore this approach, and John Bruton, while opposition leader, suggested that the Ceann Comhairle be given additional power to insist that ministers answer fully and properly. However, entering government usually diminishes such reforming zeal, and in February 1995, as Taoiseach, Bruton used exactly the same words as Burke when explaining on the radio that he had not disclosed a piece of information because the TDs questioning him had 'not asked the right question'. The opposition responded that they could not possibly have asked the right question unless they had already known the answer.

Logistically, the odds at question time are stacked in the ministers' favour. After all, they have at least three days to think of a reply and, besides, there is nothing to prevent them from giving an evasive reply. In addition, they need not answer supplementary questions at all, but can use the formula that 'that is a separate question', if by chance the supplementary asked is one that they did not anticipate and hence did not have their officials prepare for. At question time, ministers have civil servants sitting across the aisle waiting to pass them the relevant information or documents, while the TD asking the question does not have access to this kind of back-up.

However, there is a limit, in practical political terms, to the extent to which a minister can evade a question without giving the impression that he or she has something to hide. The stature of one who seems unable to give convincing answers to questions will drop, not only in the eyes of the opposition, whose negative opinion will not disturb the minister, but also among both government deputies and journalists. Question time is the liveliest part of the Dáil schedule, so it gets good media coverage. If a minister performs ineptly, this may well receive coverage on television news, and journalists' assessments of the minister are less likely to be favourable. Consequently, parliamentary questions can be quite effective in probing some alleged ministerial misdemeanour. However, they are not designed to enable the monitoring of government policies on a continuous basis. If this is to be done, the most appropriate mechanism is a system of committees.

Oireachtas committees

Committees are a feature of almost all modern parliaments, but their significance varies greatly. Where government is not directly accountable to the legislature, the latter may work mainly through committees: examples include the US Congress and the European Parliament. In parliamentary systems, committees tend to be more powerful in countries closer to the consensus pattern than where the Westminster model applies. In the traditional Westminster model, which Ireland took over in 1922, they have no great significance.

When a fully-fledged committee system is up and running, parliament has a number of committees, each consisting of around ten to thirty deputies depending on the size of the parliament. Some committees monitor the performance of government in broad policy areas, such as agriculture or education. Others might be assigned to review policy on some specific question, such as taxation or pensions, and to examine or suggest legislation. If committees are to be strong and effective, they will have the power to insist that ministers and civil servants appear before them to explain their decisions, and they will also need the resources to hire outside experts and research staff in order to examine subjects systematically. If they are to work properly they need to operate to some extent on non- or cross-party lines, as otherwise they will merely replicate the division on the floor of parliament. Sometimes 'small group psychology' creates an identification with the committee that rivals, though rarely displaces, identification with party. Ministers and civil servants know that they might one day have to give detailed justifications of the decisions they make and so, it is hoped, they take more care to make the right ones.

Because the idea of a strong committee system was not part of the Westminster system in 1922, it did not form part of the original procedures of the Oireachtas either. Until the 1980s, committees were few in number. The most important was the Public Accounts Committee, which has the function of considering the accounts of government departments in the light of the annual reports of the Comptroller and Auditor General, who checks that public money has been spent in the way that the Oireachtas decided it should be. However, a study of the operation of this committee from 1961 to 1980 criticised the unconscientious attitude of its members, superficial and unplanned questioning, and haphazard treatment of officials (O'Halpin, 1985, especially pp. 507–8). On the other hand, the Committee on State-Sponsored Bodies, which was created in 1978, soon established a reputation for thorough investigation of this sector of the economy, where information had previously been hard to come by (Chubb, 1992, pp. 202–3).

It is apparent to everyone that the only way in which the opposition – and government backbenchers – can be given a more meaningful role is through a well-designed committee system. Coming up with such a system is not so easy. The Fine Gael–Labour coalition government of the 1980s introduced an ambitious scheme entailing a multitude of committees but, despite some positive aspects such as increasing the expertise of back-benchers who subsequently became ministers, it was clear that this particular configuration was not the answer. There were far too many committees, several of them had vague remits, and some major areas of government escaped scrutiny (assessments of the 1983–87 committees can be found in O'Halpin, 1986; Arkins, 1988). Most of these committees were not re-established in the next two Dála (elected in 1987 and 1989), but after the 1992 election the committee system leapt into life again. This time, the range was more logical than in the 1982–87 Dáil, and there was a significant innovation in that for the first time committees played a part in the legislative process, as the 'committee stage' of bills was conducted not by the entire Dáil but by the appropriate committee. However, in a repetition of the 1983 mistake, too much was tried too soon. In 1993 TDs were required to fill 228 places on committees, yet there were only about 130 deputies eligible to fill them (given that the thirty or so TDs in full and junior ministries, along with certain other deputies, do not sit on such bodies). The result was that TDs were over-stretched. At certain times during the lifetime of the Dáil, some were on as many as five committees simultaneously, and a Dáil debate on the subject in October 1996 heard repeated complaints that there were simply far too many of them.

After the 1997 election, a new set of committees was established (see Table 7.5), including fourteen non-housekeeping ones. The principle underlying this arrangement is that the structure of these bodies should closely match the structure of government departments, so there is more or less one committee per department (in practice, some committees handle two departments). Each monitors the activities of its department and discusses its estimates, and deals with the third stage of any legislation within the area of the department. The committees normally comprise fourteen TDs and five senators, but when they take the third stage of legislation that is passing through the Dáil, only TDs may take part. There are seven government TDs out of the fourteen on each committee, but in addition the relevant minister is ex officio a member and has a vote. Even in the highly unlikely event of a government defeat on some matter, any committee decision can be overturned by the full Dáil. There is also one non-housekeeping committee which is not matched to a department. This is the Public Accounts Committee, whose role has been enhanced since a modernisation and extension of the remit of the Comptroller and Auditor General in 1993 (O'Halpin, 1998, p. 133; see also p. 267 below).

TDs are assigned by the party whips to committees, though they are able to indicate which they wish to serve on and, given that many deputies have no specific preference, those who want to be on a particular committee have a good chance of being selected for it. The system is also a vehicle of patronage: on each of the non-housekeeping committees, there are four paid positions (chairperson, vice-chairperson, 'government whip' and 'opposition whip'). The position of committee chair usually goes to a government TD,

Table 7.5 Oireachtas committees in 1999

Committee (type)	TDs	Senators	Total
Agriculture, Food and the Marine (Joint)	14	5	19
Education and Science (Joint)	14	5	19
Enterprise and Small Business (Joint)	14	5	19
Environment and Local Government (Joint)	14	5	19
European Affairs (Joint)	14	5	19
Family, Community and Social Affairs (Joint)	14	5	19
Finance and the Public Service (Joint)	14	5	19
Foreign Affairs (Joint)	14	6	20
Health and Children (Joint)	14	5	19
Heritage and the Irish Language (Joint)	14	5	19
Justice, Equality and Women's Rights (Joint)	14	5	19
Public Accounts (Dáil)	12	-	12
Public Enterprise and Transport (Joint)	14	5	19
Tourism, Sport and Recreation (Joint)	14	5	19
Housekeeping committees			
Consolidation Bills (Joint)	3	3	6
House Services (Joint)	9	9	18
Members' interests (Dáil)	6	-	6
Members' interests (Seanad)	-	7	7
Procedure and Privileges (Dáil)	17	-	17
Procedure and Privileges (Seanad)	-	11	11
Total	229	96	325

Source: Information supplied by the Houses of the Oireachtas.

and is undoubtedly used on occasions as a consolation post for those who have missed appointment as a cabinet minister or minister of state.

While it is too early for a full assessment of the post-1997 system, past experience shows that it would be unrealistic to expect dramatic consequences to flow from any such reorganisation. There are a number of fundamental reasons why, despite the extensive reforms introduced in the 1990s, relations between government and parliament may be slightly adjusted by a well-designed committee system but will never be fundamentally changed.

First, few governments have been keen to see a particularly probing committee system emerge. Ministers, like everyone else, would prefer not to have to work under close scrutiny. Second, those who would most benefit from such a system have ambivalent views on the matter. Opposition frontbenchers would like to see the government on the rack, but they look forward to being in office themselves in the future and are thus somewhat reluctant to see too many checks on ministers. Ambitious backbenchers likewise dream of one day being ministers, not of chairing committees. Because of the relatively small size of the Dáil, a high proportion of TDs become ministers – in the Dáil elected in 1997, for example seventy-six TDs (46 per cent of the total) were current or past cabinet or junior ministers – so able deputies who are capable of dealing with national political issues know that they have a good chance of gaining office some day. A strong committee system would be of most appeal to those who, while interested in some aspect of the policy process, do not hope or expect to be ministers, and such TDs are rare.

Third, there are questions as to how far a strong committee system can be reconciled with a parliamentary system of government, especially when the Westminster model operates. When government TDs must be loyal to the government in the Dáil chamber, they may be unlikely to criticise it within a committee, so cross-party agreement might be difficult to preserve unless committees refrain from too direct an assault on government. Comparisons with the strong committee system in the US Congress or the European Parliament are misleading since government survival is not at stake there. It is true that in many parliamentary systems committees are more significant than Oireachtas committees have traditionally been, but they do not come anywhere near to displacing government from its dominant position in the political process. A prudent backbencher who wants promotion might well decide that going along with the party line is a safer option than becoming a trenchant inquisitor of his or her own party leaders in government.

Fourth, TDs are not well equipped to enquire closely into the actions of government. Their basic facilities are modest – it was only in 1982 that each TD finally got his or her own secretary. Before then, many deputies had answered all their letters personally in longhand. Their salaries (around £38,000 a year) do not allow them to employ personal staff beyond, in some cases, a constituency secretary. Moreover, TDs have heavy demands on their time from other sources, especially constituency work (see chapter 8). In the past, many probably had more interest in their constituents' problems than in committee work. That may well have changed since the late 1970s, but even those who would like to devote themselves to parliamentary duties are reluctant to spend too much time on committee work. They fear that devoting their energies to Oireachtas committee work for four years, and thereby neglecting their clinics, would be a recipe for losing their seat at the next election. Committees are generally under-resourced, often having to share clerks and lacking research support. This may lead them to become captives of interest groups supplying apparently plausible arguments and data; for example, the Committee on Small Businesses of 1983–87 accepted uncritically the barrage of material fed to it by an umbrella business organisation and produced reports that were little more than small-business wish lists (O'Halpin and Connolly, 1999, p. 133). Certainly, the provision of more expert assistance and research advice for the committees would be needed to enable TDs to contribute effectively to committee work without feeling that they were placing their seats in jeopardy.

Overall, the Dáil's mechanisms for scrutinising the government are not as effective as they might be. However, the Dáil, while playing, as we have seen, little part in influencing policy, is not necessarily out of line with any European norm when it comes to keeping an eye on the executive. The French National Assembly is very ineffectual as a watchdog over government: 'the procedures for controlling executive power, for scrutinising or debating or questioning executive acts, are completely inadequate', and the only real checks on the executive are fear of violence in the streets or of losing the next election (Frears, 1990, p. 50). Governments in Greece, Italy and Sweden are also seen as able to operate without any effective scrutiny by parliament.

Seanad Éireann

Our discussion so far has concentrated mainly on the Dáil but, as we mentioned at the start of the chapter, the Oireachtas also has an upper house, Seanad Éireann. The lifespan of each Seanad matches that of the Dáil, except that Seanad elections take place a couple of months after the corresponding Dáil election. The house has sixty members, who are elected in a particularly convoluted manner (see Box 7.2). The election of forty-three members from quasi-vocational panels might give the impression that the Seanad consists largely of representatives of the main interest groups. However, even if this is what some expected in 1937 when the format of the new upper house was first outlined, the reality is otherwise because of the composition of the electorate (which is defined by law and not by the constitution). Not surprisingly, since the great bulk of the voters are practising party politicians, so are the people they elect, and, by and large, the senators elected from the panels are similar in background to TDs; indeed, they are often former or aspiring TDs, or both. The presence of the university senators has generated argument, with the principle of special graduate representation being criticised as elitist. The main argument in favour of the university seats is that these six senators, most of whom are not members of a political party, are often an innovative and independent force in an Oireachtas otherwise firmly controlled by the parties. The eleven senators appointed by the Taoiseach are usually chosen so as to ensure that the government has a secure majority in the Seanad, and to give a boost to politicians who have a chance of winning an extra seat for the party at the next Dáil elections.

The Seanad is by far the weaker of the two houses. A few of the powers of the Houses of the Oireachtas, it is true, are shared equally between the

---

Box 7.2 The composition of Seanad Éireann

Of the sixty senators, forty-three are elected from five 'panels', six are elected by university graduates and the other eleven are appointed by the Taoiseach.

- The five panels are Agriculture, Culture and Education, Industry and Commerce, Labour, and Public Administration, and those nominated for a panel are required to have 'knowledge and practical experience' of its subject (Article 18.7.1 of the constitution). The electors for the forty-three panel seats are members of county and major city councils, the Dáil and the outgoing Seanad; those qualified under more than one heading receive only one vote. At the 1997 Seanad election, the electorate for the panel seats comprised 992 people, of whom 794 were affiliated to one of the three main parties (Coakley and Manning, 1999).
- The six university senators are returned from two panels. Graduates of the National University of Ireland return three senators, with the other three elected by graduates of Trinity College Dublin. The details of representation give more weight to Trinity graduates than to the more numerous NUI graduates, not to mention graduates of other third-level institutions who are excluded from the election.
- The remaining eleven senators are appointed by the Taoiseach.

In 1997 the all-party Oireachtas Committee on the Constitution proposed that major changes should be made to the way in which the Seanad is elected. It recommended that fifteen of the sixty senators should be directly elected by the people, with a further fourteen elected by members of local authorities, fourteen by the incoming Dáil, and six by graduates of all third-level educational institutions, with eleven appointed by the Taoiseach as at present.

chambers; thus, the declaration of an emergency (see p. 78 above), the impeachment of a President or the removal of a judge need acquiescence from both Dáil and Seanad. In the area of legislation, the Dáil is unequivocally the superior chamber. Bills come before the Seanad, but at most it can delay them for ninety days. If it rejects a non-money bill, reaches no decision or suggests amendments that are unacceptable to the Dáil, the latter can simply overrule it (Article 23.1 of the constitution). In the case of a money bill, the Seanad is given only three weeks in which to make its 'recommendations', which again the Dáil may overrule (Article 21). If it rejects a bill (other than a bill to amend the constitution) and is overruled, it may invoke the 'Article 27 procedure'; under this a majority of senators and a third of the members of the Dáil may petition the President not to sign the bill but instead to submit it to a referendum. No such petition has ever been presented – indeed, the Seanad has not rejected a government bill since July 1964.

The government nearly always has majority support within the chamber, especially given the Taoiseach's right to nominate eleven of the senators. In December 1994 the change of government without an election left the incoming Rainbow government facing a Seanad in which it could rely on only a minority of members, with independent senators representing university graduates holding the balance of power. The independents were able to use this position to gain certain concessions from the government, for example on planned legislation concerned with regulating the affairs of the universities. The Seanad meets less frequently than the Dáil – for only seventy-three days in 1996 and sixty-one days in 1997 – and senators are paid only about 60 per cent of a TD's salary.

Not surprisingly, the Seanad is often dismissed as a mere 'talking shop', and some have called for its abolition, pointing out that comparable chambers were abolished, without noticeably adverse consequences, in Denmark (in 1953), New Zealand (1950) and Sweden (1970). Defenders of the Seanad argue that despite its lack of power, it plays a useful role in the legislative process, as debates on bills are usually conducted in a more reflective and constructive non-party spirit than in the Dáil. In addition, the task of setting up an effective Oireachtas committee system would be even more difficult without the sixty senators. In April 1997 the all-party Oireachtas Committee on the Constitution issued a report advocating both greater powers for the Seanad and a change in its composition, on the basis of an exhaustive discussion of the options by two academics (Coakley and Laver, 1997). The committee suggested that the Seanad be given an expanded legislative role, and be asked to report on statutory instruments, review government programmes, debate EU legislation and debate policy reports (All-Party Oireachtas Committee, 1997). It also recommended certain changes to the way in which senators are elected (see Box 7.1). There have been no subsequent developments, and it remains to be seen whether Seanad reform ever becomes a political priority.

Weakness of parliament

From what we have said so far, it is clear that the executive dominates parliament, though as its most powerful committee rather than a body that competes with it. In times of minority government, though, a situation quite common during the 1980s, the position is not quite so clear cut, and minority governments came into office after the elections of 1981, February 1982, 1987 and 1997. There are many reasons for executive dominance, some applicable to most parliaments – hence the frequent references to a 'decline of parliaments' during the twentieth century – and some specific to the Oireachtas.

For one thing, the role of the state, and hence of government, has grown considerably since the nineteenth century. Government business has become much more complex, and it is more difficult for all but those directly and continuously involved to monitor its work. The level of specialisation and expertise required is such that everyone else, including the backbench member of parliament, is effectively an amateur in the policy making process.

Second, the development of the mass media has provided an alternative and often more effective means of making governments accountable. Ministers cannot so easily wriggle out of awkward situations when being grilled by an interviewer on the television as they can in parliament.

Third, parliaments tend to be conservative institutions, slow to adapt to changes in the outside world. The Dáil has tended to look only as far as another notoriously conservative parliament, the House of Commons, when considering reforms. Thus an expanded committee system was introduced in 1983 only after Westminster had adopted one in 1979, and broadcasting of Dáil proceedings on radio (in 1986) and on television (in 1991) began several years after the Commons had taken these steps. The Oireachtas was very slow to demand that its members declare their interests in a register maintained for that purpose. Only with the passage of the Ethics in Public Office Act (1995) did this become necessary. TDs and Senators are now obliged to declare whether they have income or property above certain levels, and if so from what source, under a number of headings, though they are not obliged to declare the value of such income or property.

Fourth, new patterns of decision making virtually bypass parliament. In many European countries, including Ireland, the major interest groups, especially the employers' and farmers' organisations and the trade unions, play a central role in economic policy making (see chapter 11). When the government agrees a package with these interests (such as the 1994 'Programme for Competitiveness and Work' or the 1997 'Partnership 2000'), parliament can do little except retrospectively discuss a *fait accompli*. Interest groups naturally concentrate their lobbying efforts on government ministers and senior civil servants, who hold the real power, leaving ordinary TDs with few interests to represent other than those of their constituents. In addition, a growing number of policies are made at EU level, again undermining the traditional notion of domestic parliaments as law-making bodies (see chapter 13). The courts also, utilising their role as interpreters of the constitution, have become increasingly active in effectively changing the law in a number of respects (see chapter 3).

Fifth, as we have already observed, TDs have other demands on their time, especially from their constituency work (see chapter 8). Even the most nationally-oriented deputies cannot spend all their political lives on parliamentary work, because they are expected to service the needs of their constituents and fear losing their seats if they neglect this task.

Finally, and most importantly, as we observed at the start of the chapter, deputies behave not as individuals but as members of a party. When it comes to the crunch, backbenchers in most parliaments follow the party line; when political life is dominated by political parties, as is the case throughout Europe, deputies' orientation to party is stronger than their orientation to an abstract notion of 'parliament'. As we saw earlier, this is not necessarily a bad thing: to govern effectively, governments need to be able to rely on their own backbenchers to support them through thick and thin. In Ireland, government backbenchers have proved very reliable indeed.

The 'fusion' of government and parliament, with virtually all ministers simultaneously being TDs, greatly affects the way in which deputies, especially government backbenchers, see their role. Fusion is a characteristic feature of Westminster-model countries, and as such is by no means typical of European practice generally. While in Ireland all ministers must be members of parliament, in certain European countries (notably France, the Netherlands, Norway and Sweden) the offices of MP and government minister are incompatible. Whereas in Ireland only two of the approximately 150 ministers since 1922 have not previously been MPs, the average European figure is 25 per cent. In the Netherlands and Norway around half of all ministers have never been MPs (De Winter, 1991, pp. 48–50). In such countries, there are to some extent different parliamentary and governmental career structures, and a greater psychological separation between parliament and government. In Ireland, certainly as far as government backbenchers are concerned, there is little or no such separation.

Listing the reasons for the weakness of parliament as a check on government puts into perspective occasional calls for 'reform' to make the Oireachtas stronger. Ward (1996) deplores the Constitution Reform Group's ready acceptance of the dominant position of the government and suggests a number of reforms, such as having the Dáil sit for more days per year, increasing the size of the Dáil, and generally improving 'the performance of the Dáil in legislation, estimates or scrutiny of the executive' (p. 60). Yet, as O'Halpin (1998, p. 133) points out, 'the appropriate tools of enquiry and analysis are now to hand'; the Dáil seldom challenges the government, not because it meets for too few days or because its procedures are inadequate but because government back-benchers want to back the government – indeed, ultimately to become members of it – and not to harass it. Giving government TDs more teeth will not alter the role of the Dáil if they do not wish to bite.

Conclusion

The relationship between the executive and parliament is often seen in adversarial terms, and the question is asked: which controls which? We have argued in this chapter that the question makes little sense in the context of a political system where government sits in parliament and is backed, as a matter of principle rather than on an *ad hoc* basis, by a majority of deputies.

If government and parliament were seen as competing for power, then, clearly, we should have to conclude that government has the upper hand. Virtually all of its bills are passed, with opposition amend-ments taken on board only as it sees fit, while hardly any legislation originating with the opposition is passed, certainly not against the wishes of the government. Extracting information from the executive that it does not wish to disclose, through debates or parliamentary questions, is an uphill struggle. Other than in times of minority government or coalition break-up, the government need not fear being ejected from office by the Dáil.

None the less, Irish government does not amount to cabinet dictator-ship. The Dáil's provisions for scrutiny do allow the opposition to harass the government and bring into the light matters that it would prefer to keep concealed. The executive also has to pay a price for the continued loyalty of its own backbenchers; it usually has to clear its plans with its TDs in advance, and takes care not to introduce measures that they indicate they could not support. Even if its legislation is virtually certain to be passed, the opposition has plenty of opportunities to state its own criticisms.

If it were desired to make the Dáil a more significant actor, the most obvious step would be the establishment of an effective committee sys-tem, with committees that have the power to monitor the behaviour of government departments and to discuss legislation before rather than after it goes to the full parliament. The reforms instituted after the 1997 election implement some of these ideas, yet it is clear that changes to the rules alone will never transform the position of parliament. Parliament would become more powerful if TDs of the government parties ceased to see their main role as supporting the government and became, instead, quasi-neutral observers of the political process, ready to back or oppose the government depending on their view of the issue at hand. Such a development, which is improbable in the extreme, would undoubtedly transform the role not only of parliament but of the entire process of government – and not necessarily for the better.

Notes

1   Private members' bills should be distinguished from 'private bills'; the latter
differ from public bills in that they apply only to certain bodies or localities (an
example is the Altamont (Amendment of Deed of Trust) Act, 1993). Private
bills, of which there are only a handful per decade, must be introduced in
the Seanad and have a distinctive method of enactment (for detals see
Morgan, 1990, pp. 103–4; Dooney and O'Toole, 1998, pp. 60–1).

References and further reading

All-Party Oireachtas Committee on the Constitution, 1997. *Second Progress Report:
Seanad Éireann.* Dublin: Stationery Office.
Arkins, Audrey, 1988. 'The committees of the 24th Oireachtas', *Irish Political
Studies* 3, pp. 91–7.
Chubb, Basil, 1992. *The Government and Politics of Ireland,* 3rd ed. Harlow: Longman.
Coakley, John and Michael Laver, 1997. 'Options for the future of Seanad Éireann',
pp. 32–107 in *All-Party Oireachtas Committee on the Constitution* (1997).
Coakley, John and Maurice Manning, 1999. 'The Senate elections', pp. 195–214 in
Michael Marsh and Paul Mitchell (eds), *How Ireland Voted 1997.* Boulder, Colo.:
Westview, and Limerick: PSAI Press.
De Winter, Lieven, 1991. 'Parliamentary and party pathways to the government',
pp. 44–69 in Jean Blondel and Jean-Louis Thiébault (eds), *The Profession of
Government Minister in Western Europe.* Basingstoke: Macmillan.
Dinan, Des, 1986. 'Constitution and parliament', pp. 71–86 in Brian Girvin and
Roland Sturm (eds), *Politics and Society in Contemporary Ireland.* Aldershot: Gower.
Dooney, Seán and John O'Toole, 1998. *Irish Government Today,* 2nd ed. Dublin: Gill
and Macmillan.
Farrell, Brian, 1993. 'The formation of the partnership government', pp. 146–61 in
Gallagher and Laver (1993).
FitzGerald, Garret, 1994. 'Paying too high a price for techniques of obfuscation',
Irish Times 13 August, p. 10.
Frears, John, 1990. 'The French parliament: loyal workhorse, poor watchdog', pp.
32–51 in Norton (1990a).
Gallagher, Michael and Michael Laver (eds), 1993. *How Ireland Voted 1992.* Dublin:
Folens and Limerick: PSAI Press.
Gallagher, Michael, Michael Laver and Peter Mair, 1995. *Representative Government
in Modern Europe.* New York and London: McGraw-Hill.
Girvin, Brian, 1990. 'The campaign', pp. 5–22 in Michael Gallagher and Richard
Sinnott (eds), *How Ireland Voted 1989.* Galway: Centre for the Study of Irish
Elections and PSAI Press.
Girvin, Brian, 1993. 'The road to the election', pp. 1–20 in Gallagher and Laver (1993).
King, Anthony, 1976. 'Modes of executive–legislative relations: Great Britain,
France, and West Germany', *Legislative Studies Quarterly* 1:1, pp. 11–34.
Laundy, Philip, 1989. *Parliaments in the Modern World.* Aldershot: Dartmouth.
Lijphart, Arend, 1984. *Democracies: Patterns of Majoritarian and Consensus Government
in Twenty-one Countries.* New Haven and London: Yale University Press.
Mitchell, Paul, 1999. 'Government formation: a tale of two coalitions', pp. 243–63
in Michael Marsh and Paul Mitchell (eds), *How Ireland Voted 1997.* Boulder,
Colo.: Westview, and Limerick: PSAI Press.

Morgan, David Gwynn, 1990. *Constitutional Law of Ireland*, 2nd ed. Blackrock: Round Hall Press.

Norton, Philip (ed.), 1990a. *Parliaments in Western Europe*. London: Frank Cass.

Norton, Philip, 1990b. 'Conclusion: legislatures in perspective', pp. 143–52 in Norton (1990a).

O'Halpin, Eunan, 1985. 'The Dáil Committee of Public Accounts, 1961–1980', *Administration* 32:4, pp. 483–511.

O'Halpin, Eunan, 1986. 'Oireachtas committees: experience and prospects', *Seirbhís Phoiblí* 7:2, pp. 3–9.

O'Halpin, Eunan, 1998. 'A changing relationship? Parliament and government in Ireland', pp. 123-41 in Philip Norton (ed.), *Parliaments and Governments in Western Europe*. London: Frank Cass.

O'Halpin, Eunan and Eileen Connolly, 1999. 'Parliaments and pressure groups: the Irish experience of change', pp. 124–44 in Philip Norton (ed.), *Parliaments and Pressure Groups in Western Europe*. London: Frank Cass.

O'Sullivan, Mary-Clare, 1999. 'The 28th Dáil', pp. 181–94 in Michael Marsh and Paul Mitchell (eds), *How Ireland Voted 1997*. Boulder, Colo.: Westview, and Limerick: PSAI Press.

O'Toole, Fintan, 1995. *Meanwhile Back at the Ranch: the Politics of Irish Beef*. London: Vintage.

Rose, Richard, 1986. 'British MPs: more bark than bite', pp. 8–40 in Ezra N. Suleiman (ed.), *Parliaments and Parliamentarians in Democratic Politics*. New York: Holmes and Meier.

Shaw, Malcolm, 1979. 'Conclusion', pp. 361–434 in John D. Lees and Malcolm Shaw (eds), *Committees in Legislatures: a Comparative Analysis*. Oxford: Martin Robertson.

Ward, Alan J., 1974. 'Parliamentary procedures and the machinery of government in Ireland', *Irish University Review* 4:2, pp. 222–43.

Ward, Alan J., 1996. 'The Constitution Review Group and the "executive state" in Ireland', *Administration* 44:4, pp. 42–63.

8 The constituency role of TDs

Michael Gallagher and Lee Komito

In chapter 7 we looked at the legislative and scrutinising roles of Dáil deputies. In this chapter we concentrate on a different aspect of their work, looking at the business on which they spend a lot of their time, namely constituency work. Some question whether these constituency roles are really part of the duties of a TD at all; after all, as is often pointed out, the Irish constitution says nothing about TDs engaging in constituency work. Yet, judging by the large amount of time spent on constituency affairs, it seems in practice to be more important in the working life of a TD than narrowly-defined parliamentary duties such as speaking in the Dáil chamber or examining legislation. In most countries, it is taken for granted that parliamentarians will work assiduously to protect and further the interests of their constituents; constituency work forms part of an MP's parliamentary duties rather than existing in counterposition to them. In Ireland, however, there is a body of opinion that sees a constituency role as aberrant and outdated, criticises it as 'clientelism', or believes that it is taken to excess. We shall ask whether there is anything distinctive about Irish practice in this area, looking at the reasons why TDs do so much constituency work, and then consider the consequences it has for the political system.

The nature of constituency work

In all parliaments, members have both a formal, national, parliamentary role and a local, often more informal, constituency role. In the former they are expected to play a part in legislative business and in scrutinising the way in which the government is running the country, something that we discussed in the previous chapter. In their local role they keep in touch with the people who elected them, looking after the interests both of their constituencies generally and of individual constituents. This local role may be said to have several components (Searing, 1994, pp. 121–60; Norton, 1994, pp. 706–7). First, there is what has been termed a 'welfare officer' role, in which the deputy sorts out a problem on behalf of an individual or group, usually by interceding with the local or central civil service. Second, there is the 'local promoter' role, the deputy being expected to advance the interests of the constituency generally, by helping to attract industry to the area, to avert factory closures, to secure public investment, and so on. Third, the TD has the role of 'local dignitary', and will be invited to, and expected to attend, a variety of functions in the constituency, a time-consuming if not otherwise very demanding duty. The first two of these require some elaboration, though it is worth observing that, unlike in Britain where Searing concludes that most constituency-oriented MPs consciously choose the role either of welfare officer or of local promoter, in Ireland most TDs feel that they have little choice but to try to perform both tasks.

The Dáil deputy as welfare officer

Those labelled 'welfare officers' by Searing are those 'whose primary focus falls on individual constituents and their difficulties' (Searing, 1994, p. 124). The welfare officer role can involve, for instance, advising constituents about the benefits for which they are eligible (such as a grant, allowance, pension, or livestock headage payment), and how to obtain them; taking up with the civil service an apparently harsh decision or a case of delay; or helping, or seeming to help, someone to obtain a local authority house or even a job. Some of these activities allegedly involve pulling strings, as in the apocryphal threat to have a garda transferred or demoted unless a pending drink-driving case is stopped, or in smoothing the path for dubious planning applications. Such allegations lead some people to suspect that some constituency work has unsavoury connotations because it is regarded as using undue influence to give certain people unfair advantages. Whatever it entails, it is very time-consuming. A former TD, Máire Geoghegan-Quinn, graphically describes the way in which the welfare officer role imposes on the life of a TD:

> Once you get elected you instantly become public property. You are on call 24 hours a day, 365 days a year . . . As a TD you become responsible for whatever it is that any one of your 100,000 constituents wants you to be responsible for. They will raise these issues with you when you are out shopping, relaxing in the pub on Sunday night or at any other time they happen to run into you. Alternatively they might decide to, and indeed often do, call to your home to discuss their problems . . . the Dáil only really operates from Tuesday to Thursday. But working in the Dáil alone doesn't tend to get you re-elected. So on Friday, Saturday and Monday you will find TDs criss-crossing their constituencies holding clinics, attending meetings and dealing with local problems. If they are based in any of the larger constituencies they will put up more than a thousand miles a week in their cars. Their evenings are spent at a mixed bag of political and public functions.[1]
>
> (Geoghegan-Quinn, 1998)

Unquestionably, TDs do a lot of constituency work; indeed, they spend most of their time doing it. There are quite a few pieces of evidence on this over the years, all unfortunately now somewhat outdated, but all pointing in the same direction. Dick Roche (who later became a TD himself) found from interviewing 115 TDs in 1981 that they reported handling an average load of about 140 representations a week, though admittedly some of these were insignificant, such as a request for a form (Roche, 1982). Moreover, whichever way their work was measured it was clear that the volume of constituency work had gone up greatly since earlier surveys in the 1960s; the large increase in parliamentary questions in recent years (see Table 7.4 in the previous chapter) can be taken as a rough indicator of this. The main subject matter of representations was delay, usually concerned with the Department of Social Welfare or local authority housing.

In comparison with Roche's 1981 study, Kelly (1987, p. 139) reported a rather lower figure for the Labour TD Michael D. Higgins's load in 1982: about 3,000 cases in the year or sixty a week. This may be a more reliable figure since it was based on a count of actual cases as opposed to TDs' reports of what they do. In 1997 a Dublin TD estimated that he dealt with 1,000 to 1,500 cases a year (Ben Briscoe in *Dáil Debates* 480: 1519, 2 October 1997). Whatever the precise figure, it is clear that a lot of time and work is involved: in holding several clinics each week in the constituency, and in exchanging letters or phone calls with constituents and with officials to follow up these cases.

Unfortunately, we do not have full and up-to-date research about patterns of contact between constituents and TDs. Not only do we lack a precise figure for the volume of contacts, we do not know who contacts TDs in their welfare officer role. Impressionistic evidence suggests that working-class constituents make more use of their services than do middle-class people. One of the very few survey questions to touch on this area, carried out in 1991 and concerned with contact between respondents and *local* public representatives, found that 24 per cent of respondents said they had contacted a city or county councillor since the 1985 local elections. Contact had been higher among rural than urban dwellers and among working-class people than middle-class respondents (Irish Marketing Surveys, 1991, Table 12/1). It also seems that clinics as such are becoming less central to constituency work, as an increasing percentage of problems arrive via the telephone or by mail. We do not know what proportion of those who take a problem to one TD simultaneously take the same problem to others in the same constituency. Nor do we know what if any factors define the people who make up a particular deputy's caseload: is this composed primarily of people who gave their first preference vote to that TD, or of people who live near to the TD even if they didn't vote for him or her? In terms of the representation of interests through constituency work, we do not know whether deputies see themselves as representing the whole constituency and everyone within it, a geographical area of it, a social group within the constituency, or the people who voted for them.

Even without knowing the precise figure for contacts between TDs and constituents, we can be confident that there are a lot of them, and that a great deal of time is devoted to constituency work. Does all this activity serve any useful purpose; do people benefit from asking TDs for assistance? Early studies came to very different conclusions. Bax, whose research was in County Cork, maintained that deputies have considerable power, deriving in some cases from their influence over the appointment of senior county council officials; they could install an associate in a position of power and use him or her thereafter. He painted a picture of corruption, string-pulling and bribery (for example, Bax, 1976, pp. 49, 64). In contrast, Sacks, who conducted research in County Donegal, concluded that politicians could actually achieve very little. They none the less manage to create and retain bodies of support by dispensing what he calls 'imaginary patronage': that is, they convince people that they have achieved something for them even though in reality they haven't (Sacks, 1976, pp. 7–8). Nearly all this constituency work is carried out, he implies, solely to create the impression that the TD is making an effort. Certainly, some of it might be of this nature: many requests concern cases where the constituent will get the benefit anyway without anyone's help (such as an old age pension) or won't get it as he or she is simply not eligible.

From the civil service side of the fence, Dooney and O'Toole tend to share Sacks's perception. They write that 'officials are not impressed by representations' from politicians and that the 'elaborate and expensive' representations procedure 'very rarely has the effect of having administrative decisions reversed' (Dooney and O'Toole, 1998, pp. 236–7). The implication is that TDs are largely going through the motions in order to impress their constituents with their industry rather than genuinely expecting to have any impact on decisions already reached by the civil service. However, it might seem implausible that most or all of TDs' work falls into this category; it is doubtful whether they could build up, and preserve for many years, a reputation as hard-working and effective constituency politicians simply by dispensing imaginary patronage, unless their constituents are exceptionally gullible.

Moreover, *pace* Bax, there is not much evidence to back up claims of widespread 'string-pulling'. Such cases as reach the public domain are very small beer: for example, a TD using influence with a government minister to have a constituent appointed as a lock-keeper (Chubb, 1992, pp. 293–4; Gallagher and Komito, 1993, p. 153). Of course, it is possible that there is more such activity than meets the public eye. When a former minister, Michael Lowry, fell from grace in 1997, with a tribunal finding that he had been benefiting from the black economy since shortly after he was first elected to the Dáil, reporters found considerable local support for him from people who saw him as helpful in various though not precisely specified ways. In the words of one:

He will help secure finances for certain things. He will help you if you are buying land or setting up your own business. Whatever it is, you can go to Michael, he will be there and if he can he will sort it out.

(quoted in Ingle, 1997)

However, one supporter maintained that Lowry did not get people things to which they were not entitled; he was simply 'an absolute master at cutting through red tape' (ibid.).

Overall, though, politicians' scope for pulling strings is not great, and is certainly less than it once was. The principle of appointment on merit rather than through patronage was established early on, with the creation of the Civil Service Commission and the Local Appointments Commission. Over the years, the writs of these bodies have been progressively extended. Rate collectors were one of the last sizeable job categories excluded from their scope, and with their inclusion there are now very few types of civil service job where a politician's support can help an applicant. However, the army, the police and the boards of semi-state companies are exempted from the scope of these Commissions.

In other words, it is very unlikely that much constituency work involves pulling strings on behalf of constituents, if only because ordinary TDs do not have many strings to pull. It is true that government ministers have the power to make decisions that will benefit or damage individuals, and there have been allegations that string-pulling and corruption have surfaced at this level (see chapters 10 and 11 below). At local level, scope for enrichment exists because rezoning of land may result in a substantial financial gain for the landowner. Politicians have some power to permit exemptions from general planning rules, and there have been persistent suggestions that politicians sometimes benefit, directly or indirectly, from favourable planning decisions (Komito, 1983; see also a series of articles in *Irish Times* 12–16 July 1993). These allegations led to the establishment of a tribunal of inquiry, known after its chairman as the Flood Tribunal, in 1998. The absence until recently of laws compelling disclosure of political donations in Ireland, on the part of either the donors or the political parties, provided plenty of scope for rumour and suspicion to flourish (for fuller details of donations to parties see chapter 6 above).

Although it would be naive to assume that no improper string-pulling ever occurs, most reliable research suggests that the bulk of the constituency work conducted by ordinary backbenchers is more mundane and less ethically questionable than this. A consensus has emerged that TDs can be helpful to constituents, but not by getting people things to which they are not entitled. Instead, the value of contacting a TD lies in the fact that this can enable people to find out about the existence of – and/or how to obtain – benefits, grants or rights of which they would otherwise have been unaware.

This was the conclusion of research conducted in Dublin in the late 1970s and early 1980s. It found that the claim of politicians 'to power or influence rested on their ability to monopolise and then market their specialist knowledge of state resources and their access to bureaucrats who allocated such resources' (Komito, 1984, p. 174). Politicians could tell people what they were eligible for and how to secure it; this involved little work for the politician but saved constituents, many of whom are 'bureaucratically illiterate', a lot of work (ibid., pp. 182–3). Working-class constituents, it found, made much more use of the politicians' services than did middle-class people. In addition, a TD's intervention sometimes forced a case to be reviewed, a decision to be speeded up or a service to be provided (ibid., p. 183). Indeed, there is now a special exclusive 'hotline' in the Department of Social Welfare to enable deputies to enquire about individual cases (statement by Minister for Social Welfare – *Dáil Debates* 421: 778–9, 23 June 1992).

Kelly found much the same from her analysis of Michael D. Higgins's caseload. Despite the picture presented by Dooney and O'Toole (1998, pp. 235–7), according to which representations from politicians rarely have any effect, Kelly (1987, p. 145) found that in many instances the TD was able to secure a benefit for people after they had initially been turned down by the civil service, and he also got cases speeded up. He achieved this not by pulling strings but because of his expertise: his knowledge of how best to present the case and of the sort of supporting documentation that was needed. Some people had been corresponding with the wrong department, while others had omitted steps like quoting their social welfare number or obtaining a doctor's certificate to back up their case. The point that some people really do benefit from contacting a TD was put colourfully in 1997 by a renowned exponent of constituency work, Fine Gael's P. J. Sheehan, a TD for Cork South-West since 1981. During his successful re-election campaign, he posed the rhetorical question:

> In rural Ireland, many don't have the confidence, or the knowledge about where to go or how to fight for their rights . . . as long as we have the present system and bureaucracy exists, there will be a need for a helping hand and a friendly ear. If this service isn't needed, why are my clinics from the Head of Kinsale to the Dursey Sound overflowing with people every weekend?[2]
>
> (*Southern Star* 31 May 1997, p. 3)

The notion that the bureaucracy operates without problems and that constituents really have no need for help from a politician is also disputed by a Dublin TD, Róisín Shortall of the Labour party:

> I represent an area with a very high level of unemployment, poverty, housing problems, and people who spend their lives in queues, trying to sort out social welfare issues. I get up to 250 letters a week, and the follow-up on all these takes time. I wish it were not so. I wish people

were sufficiently empowered to sort out their own problems. I wish they could go to their citizens' advice bureau and get the help they need. But this doesn't happen.

(*Irish Times* 13 June 1995, p. 11)

So researchers have not found evidence of deputies interfering on a major scale with the equitable operation of the political or administrative system, but, equally, it is not true that TDs cannot achieve anything and that those who attend their clinics are suffering from a collective delusion. The picture to which most research points is that constituency work mainly involves rather routine activity, attending many clinics and local meetings, writing letters, helping people to sort out their social welfare problems and so on, rather than anything more corrupt or devious. The TD's welfare officer role, in fact, resembles that of a lawyer, who operates not by bribing the judge but by presenting the case better than the ordinary citizen could. In many ways, politicians' brokerage activities are similar to the activities of a range of professional mediators (such as priests, advice centre personnel and trade union officials); the difference derives from their special access to the state bureaucracy and their specific motives in carrying out brokerage functions.

The Dáil deputy as local promoter

The local promoter role is concerned primarily with making representations about 'the constituency's collective needs, which may be economic, environmental, or social' (Searing, 1994, p. 130). It may involve activity on behalf of a community, town, or residents' association, for example to persuade central or local government to improve water or sewerage services, street lighting, or roads. Much of this activity is in essence no different from the welfare officer role, in that the TD may be contacting civil servants to try to get a decision reversed or speeded up. Another aspect of the local promoter role is that a TD is expected to fight to increase the constituency's share of whatever cakes exist: that is, to attract new industries to the area, to prevent existing industries closing, to get state backing for local projects, and generally to ensure that the constituency does well out of the disbursement of government resources.

Voters in many if not most constituencies seem to feel that their constituency is hard done by, so at elections TDs and other candidates invariably stress their determination to rectify matters. For example, at the 1997 election, a newspaper advertisement of John McGuinness, one of the three Fianna Fáil candidates for the two-county constituency of Carlow–Kilkenny, read:

'Politicians should lead from the front and be accountable', says McGuinness. 'That is what people expect. They want action; they want results; they want politicians who can deliver significant benefits to the constituency. We are elected to provide leadership and we have to believe we can change things for the better, otherwise we should not be here'. McGuinness insists that it will not be difficult to represent both counties. 'Both counties are asking for the same things, both counties have been left behind', he says. 'We want our Ring Roads finished and our country roads improved. Our need for new industry has been ignored by successive Governments and we have the same concerns about hospitals, third level education, our old and weak, widening social divisions and, of course, unemployment. All the TDs in this constituency need to get together and form an Action Group in the next Dáil to ensure we get a proper share of the national cake.'

(*Carlow Nationalist* 23 May 1997, p. 6)

Essentially the same sentiments are expressed by many other candidates around the country at every election.

Given his or her very limited power, though, there is not a great deal that the ordinary TD can do in this capacity, except intensively lobby those, primarily ministers, who make the important decisions. If a TD becomes a minister, constituents' expectations will rise accordingly, as there is a belief that a minister who is sufficiently hard-working and adroit can 'deliver' in a big way for the constituency. Examples abound of ministers who are said to have secured largesse – 'pork', in American terminology – for their constituency, or at least for their own base within it (see Box 8.1). In this way, voters have an incentive, when choosing their TDs, to elect those of perceived ministerial ability. As we saw in chapter 4, the Irish electoral system provides for intra-party competition for electoral support, and supporters of the largest parties usually have a choice of candidates. It might be thought that voters' desire for good constituency representation might lead them to choose active locally-oriented representatives at the expense of people of national ability, and hence lower the calibre of parliamentarians (part of the argument of Carty, 1981, p. 137). In fact, however, voters making their choices purely on the basis of local considerations have a strong incentive to support candidates of ministerial ability, because a minister can deliver the goods locally on a much grander scale than a permanent backbencher. Ironically, then, a desire for good local representation does lead to the election of nationally-oriented politicians.

Constituency work and clientelism

Some people use the term 'clientelist politics' to describe politics in Ireland; journalists and politicians alike are prone to speak of 'our clientelist system'. The picture painted by Bax and Sacks, as we have outlined, is one of politicians doing favours (real according to Bax, imaginary according to Sacks) for people and in return being rewarded by a vote at the next

Box 8.1 Irish politicians and the delivery of largesse

Members of the Dáil are expected not just to deal with the individual problems of constituents but to secure largesse for their home base or for the constituency as a whole. Names such as Pádraig Flynn in Castlebar, Ray MacSharry in Sligo, and Michael Lowry in Thurles are cited in this context, along with Dick Spring, who held senior positions in governments from 1982 to 1987 and from 1993 to 1997. When Spring stepped down as Labour party leader in November 1997, a reporter found many testimonies to his ability to deliver 'pork' to his constituency and especially to his own base in Tralee, including a leisure centre, a heritage project, a marina, hotels, a new sewage treatment plant, a regional college, a technology park, and so on, all of which were attributed to his efforts and influence. The reporter concluded: 'Modern-day Tralee is almost unrecognisable compared to a decade ago. The town is on the crest of a wave. The man who made it happen is Dick Spring' (Hogan, 1997). Similarly, Michael Lowry, whose 'welfare officer' role was mentioned earlier in the chapter, was also credited with having brought benefits to his constituency at large, such as getting a planned educational institution off the ground and bringing about a project that would employ 700 people. He was described as 'the only minister for ages who has actually done things for North Tipperary' (Ingle, 1997).

election. The suggestion is that politicians gradually build up a sizeable and fairly stable body of people who are under some obligation to them; the politicians are able to 'call in the debts' at election time. Most voters, it is implied, are part of some politician's clientele.

However, this term is not very apposite to describe those who give a first preference vote to a particular Dáil candidate. TDs simply do not possess 'clienteles'. Many, perhaps most, people have never contacted a politician at all. In the early 1970s, only 17 per cent of those questioned in a Dublin survey had ever contacted a politician for any reason (Komito, 1989, p. 185), and, as we noted earlier, only 24 per cent of those surveyed in 1991 had contacted a local councillor in the previous six years. Moreover, even those who are helped by a politician cannot be taken for granted. For one thing, some of them 'do the rounds' of the clinics, hoping to improve their chances by getting several TDs to chase up their case. For another, even if a TD does do something for a constituent, the secrecy of the ballot means that he or she has no way of knowing whether the favour is returned at the ballot box. Many of the key characteristics of clientelism, such as the solidarity binding 'clients' and 'patrons', are simply not present in Irish electoral politics (Farrell, 1985, p. 241).

Thus, an earlier study concluded that 'politicians believed that they were inevitably dependent on the votes of anonymous constituents with whom they could have no direct links' (Komito, 1984, p. 181). Far from resting comfortably atop pyramids of loyal supporters, they come across as 'professional paranoids', permanently insecure, always busy at constituency work but never sure that any of it will pay electoral dividends. They promote a high community profile, advertise clinics, turn up at residents' association meetings and so on, not to build up a clientele – which is impossible – but simply to earn a reputation as hard-working people. They hope that even people who never actually need their services are impressed and will conclude that the TD will be there if they ever need help. Much as TDs might wish that they could build up solid clienteles by their constituency work, its rewards are much less certain than this.

This being so, the word 'clientelism' does not seem very appropriate to describe what TDs do in their role as constituency representatives. It is more realistic to see them as being engaged in 'brokerage', a distinct concept. A broker deals in access to those who control resources rather than directly in the resources themselves; there might be situations in which a person wants something but is unable or unwilling to obtain it from the person who has it, in which case the services of a broker may be useful. Once the service has been provided, the brokerage relationship ends. The main difference between brokerage and clientelism is that clientelism implies a more intense, more permanent relationship. It involves 'clients', people who are in some way tied in to the person who does things for them, whereas 'brokerage' implies a relationship that is not institutionalised. Thus to say that Irish politics are characterised by clientelism would suggest that TDs have sizeable bodies of people who are linked directly to them and who are in some way in their debt. 'To describe a political system as clientelistic is to imply persistent and diffuse relations of exchange in a closed system where all participants are either leaders or followers, and never simply uninvolved' (Komito, 1984, p. 176). To argue that Irish politics are characterised by brokerage would imply that there are many people who do not have any dealings with TDs, and that even the people who do use them as brokers are not under any direct obligation to them as a result. Although the loosely-used term 'clientelism' has caught on in some circles as a way of describing constituency work, most reliable research suggests that brokerage rather than clientelism, as defined above, is the appropriate term to characterise the constituency activities of members of parliament in Ireland.

The term 'clientelism' may be used by some commentators partly because of its pejorative and nefarious connotations; it has overtones of manipulation and string-pulling, of a mode of behaviour that some feel Ireland should be moving away from, in contrast to the more neutral 'brokerage'. Eisenstadt and Roniger (1984, p. 18) observe that the tendency develops in many societies to perceive less formalised relations of this kind as 'slightly subversive to the institutionalised order, to fully institutionalised relationships or to membership of collectivities'. As we shall see later, constituency work in Ireland has been criticised on precisely these grounds.

Constituency work in comparative perspective

Before going on to examine the reasons why TDs engage in so much constituency work, we will look briefly at patterns in other countries; this should dispel any illusion that the constituency role of Irish parliamentarians is somehow unusual. The reality is that constituency work is not, as some people seem to imagine, a peculiarly Irish phenomenon. In fact, 'grievance chasing' is part of the role of the parliamentarian virtually everywhere: 'members of every type of legislature say that they are subjected to an incessant flow of such [casework] demands, and they indicate that coping with them requires a substantial portion of their time and resources' (Mezey, 1979, p. 159). More broadly, relationships (which may or may not be of the patron–client form) based on personal linkages tend to exist in all types of society, modern or traditional, western or eastern, developed or pre-modern (Eisenstadt and Roniger, 1984).

For example, in France the role of the *député* is seen by voters as 'interceding with central government on behalf of individuals or councils, rather than as a legislator or watchdog over executive power or debater of the great issues of the day', and so deputies spend most of their time on constituency work (Frears, 1990, p. 46). In Australia, MPs 'complain of the pressure of electoral work and the constant requests for help from their constituents' (Rydon, 1985, p. 99).

Even members of the British House of Commons, sometimes seen as relatively nationally oriented, are on the receiving end of a sizeable volume of constituency demands; just as in Ireland, the leisurely pace of the past has been replaced by a pattern of frenetic activity. One study of MPs described them as 'self-generating workaholics' who actively seek constituency work because they find it more satisfying than the pointlessness of life on the backbenches: 'Members of Parliament are preoccupied with endless meetings, ceaseless letters, difficult constituency problems . . . There is the sense of an "endless treadmill" of late nights and early mornings, perhaps allowing little time for reflection' (Radice, Vallance and Willis, 1990, p. 154). This is particularly the case for constituencies in the Celtic peripheries, where voters expect their MPs 'to display a commitment to constituency service, perhaps above all other responsibilities', and the role of 'local promoter' is all-important (Cody, 1992, pp. 351–2).

Wood and Young, directly comparing recently-elected British MPs with Irish TDs on the basis of a 1995 survey, found that the MPs did indeed do less constituency work than the TDs, but not very much less. MPs spent 1.8 days a week in their constituency compared with 2.5 days for TDs; MPs devoted thirty-five hours a week to constituency work compared with forty-nine hours for TDs; MPs spent 47 per cent of their time on constituency work compared with 58 per cent for TDs (Wood and Young, 1997, p. 221). Most TDs believed that their re-election prospects would be damaged if they cut back on their constituency work, but most MPs did not believe this. Why, then, do MPs in Britain do so much constituency work? The main factor, another study concludes, is the psychological satisfaction that comes from doing it, 'combined with a general sense that casework is an important public duty of representatives' (Norris, 1997, p. 47).

Given this pattern, it would be very surprising if Irish members of parliament did *not* have heavy constituency workloads. The constituency work of TDs may at one time have been seen as a role peculiar to Ireland, but such a perspective was never really sustainable. Defending and promoting the interests of one's constituents to the best of one's abilities is 'part of the job' for a member of parliament, and it is hard to imagine a job specification for deputies that does not include this role. The argument that because neither the Irish constitution nor nineteenth-century constitutional theory makes any mention of this role, it is therefore one that TDs should not really be performing, makes no more sense than it would to maintain that because the Irish constitution makes no mention of political parties, parties should not play a central role in Irish politics. Perhaps, indeed, what requires explaining is not so much why TDs do a lot of constituency work but, rather, why anyone should think it strange that they do so. However, this question, interesting as it is, falls outside the scope of the present chapter.

Causes of constituency work

Even though, as we have seen, members of parliament almost everywhere have a heavy constituency load, the perception of Irish politics as 'clientelist' and somehow anomalous seems to be so widespread that it is worth trying to explain the high volume of casework descending on TDs. It may be, after all, that even if the role of constituency worker is virtually universal, the intensity of contact is still exceptionally high in Ireland, though the comparative statistics to support any such claim are lacking. Four factors in particular are frequently mentioned: political cultural attitudes to the state, the small scale of society, the electoral system, and the nature of the Irish administrative system.

A historically developed suspicion of the state

In all peasant societies, the capital city and the machinery of central government tend to be looked on with some suspicion. In Ireland, this factor was reinforced by the non-indigenous nature of the ruling elite. In the words of Chubb, brokerage is

deeply rooted in Irish experience. For generations, Irish people saw that to get the benefits that public authorities bestow, the help of a man with connections and influence was necessary. All that democracy has meant is that such a person has been laid on officially, as it were, and is now no longer a master but a servant.

(Chubb 1992, p. 210)

The argument is that the political culture of the nineteenth century and before, when central government was for obvious reasons perceived as alien, remote and best approached via an intermediary, has carried on into the post-independence state. Former Taoiseach Garret FitzGerald comments that Dublin 'is still widely perceived in rural Ireland as if it were even today a centre of alien colonial rule' (FitzGerald, 1991, p. 364). Given that so many other aspects of pre-independence political culture have a bearing on contemporary politics (see chapter 2), this is perfectly plausible. It is hard to avoid some cultural explanation when seeking reasons as to why people in some countries (such as Ireland and France) approach deputies on matters that people in other countries (such as, perhaps, those in Scandinavia) would take elsewhere. Surveys testify to people's belief that a TD is the best person to approach if one wants to be sure of getting one's entitlements (Farrell, 1985, p. 243; Komito, 1992).

This cultural explanation would become dubious, however, if linked too closely with the notion of a 'dying peasant culture' or with a suggestion that people's tendency to approach their TDs springs from an atavistic misconception of the way in which the civil service works and of how to interact with it. After all, the volume of brokerage seems to be increasing rather than decreasing as urbanisation and the decline of agriculture proceed. Political culture and the legacy of the past are part of the explanation, but we need to look also for causes in present-day Ireland: 'rather than an outmoded style of behaviour, brokerage is an effective solution to a particular set of problems' (Komito, 1984, p. 191). This also means that there is no reason to expect brokerage work to go away as 'modernisation' continues.

Small size of society

In all societies, informal networks of trust exist within and alongside formal structures. While such networks exist in large industrial societies (Komito, 1992, p. 143), they may be particularly significant in small societies where, even if it would be an exaggeration to say that 'everybody knows everybody else', it is at least true that many people have some kind of direct or indirect access to decision makers that bypasses the formal structure. The Republic of Ireland is clearly, in relative terms, a small society, with only 3.7 million people, and the small scale of Irish society has an impact on people's perceptions of their deputies' role. At the 1997 election, for example, there was one deputy for every 16,514 electors and for every

10,777 valid votes. Very few other countries have as high a ratio of deputies to voters.

In one sense, one might expect that the fewer people each member of parliament represents, the lower members' constituency workload will be. Yet, at the same time, the fewer people each member represents, the more contact voters are likely to expect with him or her. In the USA, it has been found that the smaller the number of people represented by each Senator, the more those people are likely to define the politician's role in pork-barrel terms and the more contact they are likely to have with their Senators (Hibbing and Alford, 1990). With such a small number of voters to represent, it is hardly surprising that deputies find themselves asked to play the role of 'mediator-advocate vis-à-vis the local and national administrative bureaucracies', as Farrell (1985, p. 242) puts it. A reinforcing factor in Ireland is the high degree of centralisation of decision making, nearly all of which takes place in Dublin. Local government is weak, with very few powers, and there are no intermediate (regional or provincial) tiers of government. The upshot is that national parliamentary representatives get requests for assistance with what in many other countries would be purely local matters.

The electoral system

The electoral system is sometimes suggested as a cause of brokerage since, as we saw in chapter 4, PR-STV puts candidates of one party in competition with each other and thereby forces them to establish an edge over their so-called running mates. Running mates are a definite danger. Between 1923 and 1997, 34 per cent of all TDs who suffered defeat at an election, and 56 per cent of defeated Fianna Fáil TDs, lost their seat not to a rival party's candidate but to one of their own. Moreover, given that the Oireachtas is not very strong, backbench deputies cannot easily establish a reputation as outstanding parliamentarians and fight internal party battles on this terrain. So, once the demand for brokerage activity arises, they feel they have to respond to it, even though many of them wish there was less of it. When surveyed by Wood and Young (1997, p. 221), 60 per cent of recently-elected TDs said they felt they could lose their seat if they reduced their constituency work.

TDs are probably right to believe that their electoral fortunes are affected by their reputations as constituency workers. Surveys have consistently shown that voters, when asked to rank a number of factors as determinants of their votes, attach more importance to 'choosing a TD who will look after the local needs of the constituency' than to anything else, such as choosing a Taoiseach, choosing between the policies of the parties, or choosing a representative who will perform well on national issues in the Dáil (Marsh and Sinnott, 1990, pp. 120–1; Dooney and O'Toole, 1998, p. 236). Even if some of those who say they want a TD who will look after the constituency are in fact expressing a choice *within* party rather than a choice regardless of party, it is clear that voters attach importance to this role. Newly-elected deputies, as part of their informal socialisation process in the Dáil, learn the conventional wisdom among politicians that ignoring constituency work is electoral suicide. Perhaps this wisdom is wrong. In the early 1980s, a Dublin TD, Professor John Kelly, ceased doing any clinics, and his vote increased at following elections. However, few would want to take the risk of testing the theory.

The electoral system gives deputies a strong incentive to respond with alacrity to the demand that they do constituency work, but it doesn't really explain where this demand comes from in the first place. If requests for assistance come in every week, TDs must deal with them, but PR-STV itself does not explain why they come in. Even allowing for the fact that TDs eagerly advertise their availability and actively seek problems to solve, and maybe thereby generate more constituency work than would arise otherwise, this still leaves a lot that arises from other causes.

Emphasis on the electoral system as a significant cause of the volume of constituency work seems to imply that under a different electoral system it might diminish significantly. This is very doubtful (Gallagher, 1996, pp. 512–18). As we saw earlier, members of parliament in countries with a range of completely different electoral systems undertake a lot of constituency work. A particularly interesting case in this regard is Belgium, where the electoral system is based on party lists. These lists are in effect 'closed'; whether a particular candidate is elected is determined not by the preference votes cast by the voters but by the candidate's position on the list, something that is decided by party members, not by the public. Yet Belgian MPs carry out a great deal of constituency work, each dealing on average with over 2,000 cases a year (this account of Belgian MPs' constituency roles is based on De Winter, 1997, pp. 141–2). Like TDs in Ireland, Belgian MPs hardly dare venture out of doors because of the demands that are continuously pressed upon them: 'when MPs participate in local social life, they return home with their pockets full of beercards on which they have noted down the requests of people they met at these social gatherings' (ibid.). Two reasons are offered as to why Belgian MPs work so assiduously at a task for which the electoral system seems to provide no incentive. The first is the familiar one of discharging what is felt to be a duty, together with the gratification that comes from achieving something tangible for a constituent, while also establishing one's position as a VIP in the constituency, in contrast with the anonymity of life as a back-bencher. The second is that the candidate selectors, who are the local party members, when deciding how to order the candidates on the party list, favour candidates who are active in dealing with casework. Tempting as it undoubtedly is for many TDs to believe that a new electoral system would reduce or remove the burden of constituency work, the evidence does not support such a belief.

Administrative structures

The argument here is essentially that some citizens need brokers to obtain their entitlements. This is the conclusion of Roche and implicitly of others, such as Komito and Kelly, as well as TDs such as Róisín Shortall and P. J. Sheehan whom we quoted earlier. As Roche (1982, p. 103) puts it: 'Irish complaint behaviour is a manifestation of a breakdown at the interface level between Ireland's public institutions and the Irish public'. In other words, some people turn to TDs to help them because of the frustration that results from their own direct dealings with the state apparatus.

This arises because of the nature of the machinery with which citizens come into contact. All bureaucracies tend to develop certain characteristics, such as inflexibility, obsession with precedent, secretiveness, rigid adherence to the rules, and perhaps impatience with people who do not fully understand the system. In Ireland, there is also very little occupational mobility between the public service and the wider economy, or even between the different public service departments. Thus the 'culture' that develops within a department is not tempered by the introduction of new personnel at middle or upper levels. There may be a bureaucratic tendency to send out standard replies that do not address a specific query, or not to explain fully what someone is entitled to or why some application has been turned down, and inevitably there will be cases of delay.

The problem was exacerbated in the 1960s and 1970s by the rapid growth in state intervention: the number of services being provided increased rapidly, as did the number of people looking for these services. Long delays in processing social welfare claims, for instance, were the result of increases in the number of people applying for assistance and of an increasingly complex application procedure to decide eligibility. Structural improvements (such as computerisation) have reduced processing delays; the result may not suit the applicant, but at least the answer is known more quickly. For example, the number of complaints made to the Ombudsman about Telecom Éireann dropped by two-thirds between 1987 and 1992 following the introduction of itemised billing (Ombudsman, *Annual Report 1992*, p. 5), which suggests that when people know how a decision has been reached, they are less likely to complain about it. Similarly, the need for assistance simply to find out where in the queue an application sits is somewhat less. This has, to some degree, lessened the scope for brokerage interventions by politicians; their ability to get fast answers is now a less valuable commodity. New technology and the advent of the 'information society' might, in theory, reduce the need for politicians' assistance still further (Komito, 1997). Citizens will be better able to monitor progress on their applications, and freedom of information legislation (see chapter 10) will make more information available to the citizen.

Unfortunately, the increase in efficiency has not been matched in most areas by any marked increase in transparency: the rules for determining

222 Politics in the Republic of Ireland

eligibility remain complex, and thus the need for the assistance of someone who understands the system remains. Those citizens whose resources for dealing with the bureaucracy are fewest are also the least likely to be able to make meaningful use of the information society. Furthermore, there has been no great increase in the amount of trust extended to civil servants and their activities, and thus there is still a need for someone who can be trusted to act on one's behalf.

All of this leaves many people wanting assistance from someone willing to help them. When this happens, contacting a TD often seems the most suitable mechanism by which a grievance might be redressed. The civil service has an appeal procedure, but those whose problems spring from 'bureaucratic illiteracy' are unlikely to be able to make much use of this. In the past some appeal procedures have been viewed more as extensions of the bureaucracy that made the initial adverse decision than as independent structures (Hogan and Morgan, 1998, pp. 275–82). A more promising step is to seek assistance from a Citizens Information Centre (CIC). There are eighty-five such centres around the country; they operate under the auspices of the state-funded National Social Service Board (NSSB) but are run by volunteers (a little over 1,000 of them). Their services are used much more by women than by men (NSSB, *Annual Report* 1994, p. 13; NSSB, *Annual Report* 1995, p. 9). They not only give information on social welfare entitlements but, where appropriate, also take up cases with the relevant office or department. In 1996 they dealt with around 124,000 queries (NSSB, *Annual Report* 1996, p. 11). This is clear evidence of public demand for assistance in dealing with the state bureaucracy. However, the restricted opening hours of CICs, and perhaps the limited ability of their volunteers to persuade public officials to reverse a decision, mean that these centres clearly do not meet the full demand.

One potentially valuable channel for obtaining rectification of grievances is the office of the Ombudsman, which was established in January 1984 (see Hogan and Morgan, 1998, pp. 337–93, for the powers and operation of the office). The Ombudsman has the role of investigating complaints from members of the public who feel that they have been treated unfairly by public bodies. He or she has the power to demand any information, document or file from a body complained against and can summon any official of that body to give information about a complaint. The number of cases dealt with is not large. Leaving aside those cases that fall outside the Ombudsman's jurisdiction, the 3,126 complaints received in 1997 marked the first time the figure had exceeded 3,000 since 1987, and the number dropped to an all-time low of 2,250 in 1995. The office has been able to assist a significant proportion of those whose cases fall within its jurisdiction: of the cases dealt with in its first ten years, 21 per cent were resolved in favour of the complainant and assistance was provided in a further 27 per cent of cases. The respective figures in 1997 were 18 per cent and 27 per cent (Ombudsman, *Annual Report* 1993, p. 1; Ombudsman, *Annual Report*

1997, p. 4). Moreover, details of some of the cases outlined in the annual reports of the office show how difficult it has sometimes been even for the Ombudsman, endowed as the office is with statutory powers to demand all the files relating to a case, to persuade the bureaucrats concerned that they should review a decision, highlighting the difficulties that ordinary citizens can encounter.

However, given the earlier estimates of TDs' caseloads, Dáil members collectively receive anything from a quarter of a million to half a million cases a year, or even more, and clearly most of these do not come to the Ombudsman. One reason, no doubt, is that TDs seem more available and accessible than the Ombudsman, despite the latter's willingness to be of assistance. A survey carried out in October 1996 discovered that only 34 per cent of adults seemed to be aware of the office of Ombudsman (*Annual Report* 1997, p. 8). Another reason why most people do not use it is that many cases coming to TDs result from a lack of information as to how best to utilise the administrative system (or just disgruntlement with a decision) and do not involve possible maladministration; as John Whyte (1966, p. 16) put it, they are problems on 'a humbler scale' than would warrant the attention of the Ombudsman. In the words of the NSSB, 'the problem for most people in writing to the various Departments seems to be (i) not knowing exactly which section to address their letter to and (ii) the standard letter of reply may not deal satisfactorily with their enquiry' (NSSB, *Annual Report* 1991, p. 7).

When the Ombudsman's 1996 annual report was debated in the Dáil in 1997, a number of TDs were quite critical of the way the office was performing. Several made the point that with a staff of forty-one, the Ombudsman seemed to be handling hardly any more cases than the average TD, who worked alone with a secretary. One commented that when the Ombudsman solves someone's problem, his work is praised, yet when TDs do the same their activities are denigrated and dismissed as 'an antiquated practice of parish pump politics' and not something that they should be doing (Michael Noonan, *Dáil Debates* 480: 1483–4, 2 October 1997). Dick Roche, an academic authority on the office of the Ombudsman internationally, maintained that the Irish Ombudsman was uniquely 'fettered' in what he could look into, and lamented 'the failure of this important public office to make an impact on public administration'. He drew attention to a client review undertaken by the office, showing that 67 per cent of those who responded were happy with the way their complaint was handled, implying that a third were unhappy (*Dáil Debates* 482: 927–8, 6 November 1997). More forcefully, Michael D'Arcy said that he had simply stopped referring certain cases to the Ombudsman because he believed they were not being treated fairly: 'I question whether he is impartial because he seems to side more with Department officials than with complainants' (*Dáil Debates* 482: 927, 6 November 1997). Although the Ombudsman responded to some of these points in his next report (Ombudsman, *Annual Report* 1997, p. 13), it is clear that the office has, to say the least, not established itself in the public mind as the first port of call when assistance in dealing with the bureaucracy is needed.

So, almost by default, people wanting assistance turn to public representatives, who cannot afford to be abrupt or offhand: TDs' jobs, unlike those of civil servants, may depend on how helpful and approachable they are. Moreover, because of their experience they probably can be of genuine assistance: as one TD put it, 'there is hardly a Deputy in this House who is not at least as conversant with the supplementary welfare allowance scheme as are the community welfare officers' (Proinsias De Rossa, *Dáil Debates* 428: 834, 25 March 1993). TDs are very much available, highly responsive, and possessed of relevant expertise.

To suggest that the nature of the Irish administrative system is part of the explanation for the high volume of brokerage demands made to TDs might seem to imply that civil servants are not doing their jobs perfectly. In one sense this is true, in that if the Irish public service dealt with all cases effectively, promptly and to the complete satisfaction of the citizen, there would be no need for brokers. But no large organisation does or ever will work this way, so such a standard is unrealistic. It would be unfair to put all the blame on civil servants. Individual civil servants may not have enough training to be as helpful to the public as they would like to be and, as in most bureaucracies, the most junior people are placed across the desk from the applicants; promotion means getting away from the public.

The only way in which civil servants could stifle the brokerage system would be by refusing to entertain any representations from politicians. They do not do this, partly because the brokerage system suits both politicians and civil servants, especially at the local level (Komito, 1984, pp. 188–9). For one thing, it protects the bureaucrats to some extent, since politicians form a barrier between them and the public. Without politicians acting as brokers, many more people would be tackling them directly; as it is, politicians form an unofficial complaints tribunal. In this capacity politicians also provide an unpaid monitoring service; they can assess whether people really have been dealt with harshly, or have lost out on the benefit of the doubt. If a TD or councillor then makes a firm complaint about a particular case, the civil servant or local official can be fairly sure that it is a valid complaint, since the politician does not want to jeopardise an ongoing relationship with the official on behalf of an undeserving constituent. So politicians in effect do some preliminary screening of cases and then present the strongest among them in a manner tailored to the expectations of the civil service, which helps the officials. In return, civil servants may well give special priority to representations from TDs and respond more sympathetically than to letters of complaint or injury from ordinary members of the public (cf. the special TDs' 'hotline' mentioned on p. 211 above). In addition, officials consider politicians to be more 'trustworthy'. Politicians have a stake in maintaining good relations with them, so officials can rectify errors without any adverse comment. Members of the public, having no stake in the status quo, cannot be similarly trusted; officials are less likely to admit errors, which means that they are also less likely to rectify them.

Consequences of TDs' constituency work

Some of the consequences of the constituency role of TDs are highly tangible, while others are less so. Brokerage work affects the operation of the political and administrative systems, and some suggest that it plays a part in shaping political culture. We shall look at its impact on the Dáil, the government and the civil service, and consider its effects on people's attitudes towards politics generally.

Impact on the Dáil and the government

This is the most obvious and tangible area in which brokerage has an impact. Dealing with casework reduces the time available for formal parliamentary duties, such as examining legislation and discussing policy. Many TDs believe that to devote time to work in the Dáil chamber or in parliamentary committees, at the expense of constituency work, could be electorally fatal. The effect is to weaken the Dáil's ability to provide effective scrutiny of government and to contribute to policy formation, and for these reasons some have deplored TDs' immersion in constituency duties. However, as we saw in chapter 7, there are obviously many other reasons why the Dáil is weak, and it is open to question how much stronger it would be if deputies had less constituency work. Moreover, there is no reason why, with an adequate provision of support staff, politicians should not be able both to provide a service for constituents and to be active parliamentarians (Chubb, 1992, p. 210).

It is also sometimes suggested that even ministers are overburdened with constituency work and are unable to devote enough time to government business. However, in recent years ministers have used civil servants to do most of their constituency work for them. A series of parliamentary questions tabled in March 1993 asked about the size of each minister's private office and constituency office. It turned up the information that the fifteen cabinet ministers collectively had 127 civil servants in their private offices and eighty-one in their constituency offices, while the figures for the fifteen ministers of state were eighty-one and sixty respectively (*Dáil Debates* 427: 1804–96, 11 March 1993 and 428: 519–20, 24 March 1993). The distinction between the 'private office' and the 'constituency office' may be more apparent than real; indeed, one minister acknowledged that 'staff are not formally divided between constituency and other duties. The situation varies from day to day in each office and staff carry out appropriate duties as the need arises' (Joe Walsh, Minister for Agriculture, *Dáil Debates* 427:

1854, 11 March 1993). Given that each cabinet and junior minister has, therefore, an average of eleven civil servants, paid for by the taxpayers, to assist in his or her constituency and political work, it is hard to believe that brokerage can be a major burden on the shoulders of ministers.

Impact on the work of the civil service

The constituency work of TDs serves many useful functions for citizens, but this does not mean that all of its consequences are beneficial, or that there is no such thing as excess. We noted earlier that deputies may do some preliminary screening of cases before deciding which ones to take up with officials. However, even if a TD can see that a constituent's chances are negligible, he or she may not want to say this to the constituent. It is less risky electorally to forward the case to the civil service, perhaps even putting down a parliamentary question, though of course without using up credit with contacts in the civil service by claiming that it is a deserving case. When this happens on a large scale, there is an obvious cost in terms of time and money, and indeed in 1962 a senator characterised the constituency work of TDs as 'going about persecuting civil servants', a phrase that was later used as the title of a very influential article (Chubb, 1963). Each question has to be followed up fully and all the details have to be investigated, even if the answer turns out to be something straightforward such as the person simply not being eligible. If, as sometimes happens, the person has not even applied for the grant they complain they have not received, or there is some confusion over their social welfare number, the search is much longer. Tales abound of civil servants or ministers, faced with even minor decisions, finding that the matter is the subject of correspondence from several TDs and perhaps councillors too. The cost is virtually impossible to quantify. Examining these representations also costs civil servants time that could be spent dealing with other things, so, ironically, some TDs, by clogging up the works with pointless representations, may exacerbate the delays they complain about (Dooney and O'Toole, 1998, p. 237). Whether it really follows that citizens would get a better service were it not for TDs taking up the cudgels on their behalf is, of course, another matter.

Individualisation of social conflict

Higgins (1982, p. 133) argues that clientelism 'disorganises the poor'; it encourages them to seek an individual solution to a problem such as poverty rather than to see the problem as fundamental to society and take part in collective action to try to redress it. It encourages vertical links, from the TD to the constituent, rather than horizontal ones between people in the same position, such as the poor or the unemployed. It promotes competition rather than cooperation between people in similar vulnerable positions. It reinforces and perpetuates individualism – social conflict is individualised. Thus, he concludes (p. 135), clientelism is 'exploitative in source and intent'. Its origins lie in the dependency of the poor, 'the structural fact of poverty', and in the uneven distribution of resources such as wealth, knowledge and access, and it perpetuates this dependency by heading off any demand for more fundamental changes. Hazelkorn also argues that clientelism redirects incipient class conflict into channels that emphasise the role of individuals rather than of classes: 'the effect has been to retard the political development and consciousness of the economically dominated classes' (Hazelkorn, 1986, p. 339). She suggests that for left-wing TDs 'to operate in constituencies through clinics could be politically disastrous in the long-term', as this would reduce the chances of horizontal class links building up among the dominated classes (Hazelkorn, 1986, p. 340).

This is all very well, but what exactly is meant by 'clientelism' in these accounts? Hazelkorn seems to regard all the constituency work of a TD as clientelism: 'Irish clientelism involves individuals who seek out their TD . . . in order to acquire some benefit or service which they feel they would not receive by their own, or their group's efforts' (Hazelkorn, 1986, p. 327; cf. Higgins, 1982, pp. 118–19). If politicians who help sort out problems with the bureaucracy that the constituents could not sort out by themselves are behaving in a 'clientelistic' fashion, then clientelism exists in virtually every country in the world, and cannot explain much about Ireland specifically. Higgins later became a TD, and was once asked on television whether he now engaged in the clientelistic practices that he had earlier deplored. His answer drew a distinction between, on the one hand, politicians attempting to give the impression that they were achieving results through manipulation, and, on the other hand, politicians helping people to obtain their rights (RTÉ 1, 'Prime Time', 25 February 1997). The feeling remains that the term 'clientelism' is being used very loosely in these arguments.

TDs' readiness to offer helpful advice to constituents would come well down the list as an explanation for the absence of socialism in Ireland. It may well be that politicians' brokerage work reduces the level of alienation among those who seek their assistance, and thereby acts as a force for the stability, rather than the radical transformation, of a social structure marked by clear inequalities. However, it is far-fetched to imagine that if politicians refused to help their constituents with their problems, the result would be a unstoppable build-up of demand for collective action that would rectify all of society's ills. It is hard to see how, say, a widow concerned about a delay in her pension payment can tackle the immediate problem except in individual terms, and it is not necessarily irrational for individuals to seek to solve their own short-term problems rather than to try to transform society first. Although it is true that the 'welfare officer' role of members of parliament involves solving the problems of individuals – as it does in every country – the 'local promoter' role entails work on behalf of groups or communities. The case against constituency work as a barrier to the left in Ireland remains unproven.

Impact on perceptions of the political system

There is general agreement that constituency work affects perceptions of the political system, but some disagreement about exactly how it does this. Some, such as Bax (1976, pp. 51–2) feel that it has an integrative effect; it brings citizens and the central state machinery closer together. TDs, by providing a 'helping hand and a friendly ear', in P. J. Sheehan's words (p. 211 above), can serve the functions of humanising the state in the eyes of people who would otherwise see it as remote and would feel alienated from it, and countering the cynicism that attaches to 'politicians' en masse. As has been noted in Britain, the effect is to build support for the political system generally by making people feel that there is at least someone who will listen to their problem and is 'on their side' (Norton and Wood, 1993, pp. 50–5). Moreover, through constituency work, information is transmitted in both directions; politicians are kept fully in touch with their constituents, and will be quickly alerted to any general problems, for example about the way in which a department is implementing a policy.

Others, however, believe that constituency work perpetuates a mistaken belief that government and the civil service do not work in a fair and rational manner. For Dooney and O'Toole, the making of representations by politicians creates the 'impression among the public that everything can be fixed' (Dooney and O'Toole, 1998, p. 237). Similarly, Dick Roche, a public administration specialist as well as a TD, argues that the practice of approaching a politician with complaints about the civil service has 'a corrosive impact on political life. It undermined the confidence in the administrative system and its impartiality, and it also gave rise to the view that just about everything could be fixed' (*Dáil Debates* 482: 929, 6 November 1997). Sacks (1976, pp. 221–5), also believes that much constituency work propagates the notion that a citizen has a better chance of getting something from the state if he or she approaches it via a TD, and this perpetuates citizens' negative and suspicious views of the political system. In turn this reinforces personalism and localism, the tendency to trust only those with whom one has some personal or local connection, which Sacks sees as being important elements in Irish political culture. However, as we pointed out earlier, the bureaucratic view according to which people's use of TDs is irrational has been disputed by detailed research, according to which TDs can be of genuine help to constituents, not by 'fixing' matters improperly but by securing the legitimate redress of grievances or, at least, obtaining a satisfactory explanation of a decision.

Conclusion

Irish citizens expect their members of parliament to be active constituency representatives, taking up their personal or communal problems or grievances with the relevant government department. Although some have sought distinctively Irish explanations for this, a heavy constituency workload is the norm for parliamentarians around the world, and the main reason tends to be the same everywhere: quite simply, representing one's constituents is a central part of the job of a member of parliament in every country. The volume of constituency work takes time that TDs could, at least in theory, devote to their formal parliamentary responsibilities, and also has an impact on the functioning of the civil service. Among some observers of Irish politics, constituency work tends to be regarded as a negative phenomenon. It is often branded 'clientelism', a term with a multitude of unfavourable connotations (largely due to the private and individual, rather than public and collective, nature of politician–voter interactions), yet it is clear that Irish politics are not clientelistic in the conventional sense of the term. As in other countries, constituency work has both negative and positive consequences: it may weaken the ability of parliament to provide effective scrutiny of government and to make an input to policy making, yet it provides a vital link between citizen and state, reduces alienation, and provides feedback on the effects of government policies. The constituency role of TDs is a central aspect of the Irish political system, and its consequences continue to generate argument and discussion.

Notes

1   Máire Geoghegan-Quinn was a Fianna Fáil TD for Galway West from 1975 to 1997. In the 1990s the constituency, with a population at the 1997 election of 100,251 people, was represented by five TDs. Most TDs hold 'clinics' in their constituency, setting aside a certain amount of time at designated places where constituents can come and discuss their problem.
2   The Head of Kinsale and the Dursey Sound are approximately eighty miles apart.

References and further reading

Bax, Mart, 1976. *Harpstrings and Confessions: Machine-style Politics in the Irish Republic.* Assen: Van Gorcum.
Carty, R. K., 1981. *Party and Parish Pump: Electoral Politics in Ireland.* Waterloo, Ontario: Wilfrid Laurier University Press.
Chubb, Basil, 1963. '"Going about persecuting civil servants": the role of the Irish parliamentary representative', *Political Studies* 11:3, pp. 272–86.
Chubb, Basil, 1992. *The Government and Politics of Ireland*, 3rd ed. Harlow: Longman.
Cody, Howard, 1992. 'MPs and the peripheral predicament in Canada and Britain', *Political Studies* 40:2, pp. 346–55.
De Winter, Lieven, 1997. 'Intra- and extra-parliamentary role attitudes and behaviour of Belgian MPs', pp. 128–54 in Wolfgang C. Müller and Thomas Saalfeld (eds), *Members of Parliament in Western Europe: Roles and Behaviour.* London: Frank Cass.
Dooney, Seán and John O'Toole, 1998. *Irish Government Today*, 2nd ed. Dublin: Gill and Macmillan.

Eisenstadt, S. N. and L. Roniger, 1984. *Patrons, Clients and Friends: Interpersonal Relations and the Structure of Trust in Society.* Cambridge: Cambridge University Press.

Farrell, Brian, 1985. 'Ireland: from friends and neighbours to clients and partisans: some dimensions of parliamentary representation under PR-STV', pp. 237–64 in Vernon Bogdanor (ed.), *Representatives of the People? Parliaments and Constituents in Western Democracies.* Aldershot: Gower.

FitzGerald, Garret, 1991. *All in a Life: an Autobiography.* Dublin: Gill and Macmillan.

Frears, John, 1990. 'The French parliament: loyal workhorse, poor watchdog', pp. 32–51 in Philip Norton (ed.), *Parliaments in Western Europe.* London: Frank Cass.

Gallagher, Michael, 1996. 'Electoral systems', pp. 499–520 in Constitution Review Group, *Report.* Dublin: Stationery Office.

Gallagher, Michael and Lee Komito, 1993. 'Dáil deputies and their constituency work', pp. 150–66 in John Coakley and Michael Gallagher (eds), *Politics in the Republic of Ireland,* 2nd ed. Dublin: Folens and Limerick: PSAI Press.

Geoghegan-Quinn, Máire, 1998. 'Loss in salary and privacy price of becoming a TD', *Irish Times* 28 March, p. 14.

Hazelkorn, Ellen, 1986. 'Class, clientelism and the political process in the Republic of Ireland', pp. 326–43 in Patrick Clancy, Sheelagh Drudy, Kathleen Lynch and Liam O'Dowd (eds), *Ireland: a Sociological Profile.* Dublin: Institute of Public Administration.

Hibbing, John R. and John R. Alford, 1990. 'Constituency population and representation in the US Senate', *Legislative Studies Quarterly* 15:4, pp. 581–98.

Higgins, Michael D., 1982. 'The limits of clientelism: towards an assessment of Irish politics', pp. 114–41 in Christopher Clapham (ed.), *Private Patronage and Public Power.* London: Frances Pinter.

Hogan, Dick, 1997. 'Spring's influence can be seen in north Kerry', *Irish Times* 6 November.

Hogan, Gerard and David Gwynn Morgan, 1998. *Administrative Law in Ireland,* 3rd ed. Dublin: Round Hall Sweet and Maxwell.

Ingle, Róisín, 1997. 'Tipperary voters stand by their man despite damning report from tribunal', *Irish Times* 30 August, p. 9.

Irish Marketing Surveys, 1991. *Irish Independent/IMS poll, 30 May–7 June.* Dublin: Irish Marketing Surveys.

Kelly, Valerie, 1987. 'Focus on clients: a reappraisal of the effectiveness of TDs' interventions', *Administration* 35:2, pp. 130–51.

Komito, Lee, 1983. 'Development plan rezonings: the political pressures', pp. 293–301 in John Blackwell and Frank J. Convery (eds), *Promise and Performance: Irish Environmental Policies Analysed.* Dublin: Resource and Environmental Policy Centre, University College Dublin.

Komito, Lee, 1984. 'Irish clientelism: a reappraisal', *Economic and Social Review* 15:3, pp. 173–94.

Komito, Lee, 1989. 'Voters, politicians and clientelism: a Dublin survey', *Administration* 37:2, pp. 171–96.

Komito, Lee, 1992. 'Brokerage or friendship? Politics and networks in Ireland', *Economic and Social Review* 23:2, pp. 129–45.

Komito, Lee, 1997. 'Politics and administrative practice in the Irish information society', *Economic and Social Review* 28:3, pp. 295–300.

Marsh, Michael and Richard Sinnott, 1990. 'How the voters decided', pp. 94–130 in Michael Gallagher and Richard Sinnott (eds), *How Ireland Voted 1989.*

Galway: PSAI Press.

Mezey, Michael L., 1979. *Comparative Legislatures.* Durham, NC: Duke University Press.

National Social Service Board (NSSB), *Annual Reports.* Dublin: National Social Service Board.

Norris, Pippa, 1997. 'The puzzle of constituency service', *Journal of Legislative Studies* 3:2, pp. 29–49.

Norton, Philip, 1994. 'The growth of the constituency role of the MP', *Parliamentary Affairs* 47:4, pp. 705–20.

Norton, Philip and David M. Wood, 1993. *Back from Westminster: British Members of Parliament and their Constituents.* Lexington: University of Kentucky Press.

Ombudsman, *Annual Reports.* Dublin: Stationery Office.

Radice, Lisanne, Elizabeth Vallance and Virginia Willis, 1990. *Member of Parliament: the Job of a Backbencher*, 2nd ed. Basingstoke: Macmillan.

Roche, Richard, 1982. 'The high cost of complaining Irish style: a preliminary examination of the Irish pattern of complaint behaviour and of its associated costs', *IBAR – Journal of Irish Business and Administrative Research* 4:2, pp. 98–108.

Rydon, Joan, 1985. 'Constituents and their MPs in Australia', pp. 86–102 in Vernon Bogdanor (ed.), *Representatives of the People? Parliaments and Constituents in Western Democracies.* Aldershot: Gower.

Sacks, Paul M., 1976. *The Donegal Mafia: an Irish Political Machine.* New Haven and London: Yale University Press.

Searing, Donald, 1994. *Westminster's World.* Cambridge, Mass: Harvard University Press.

Whyte, John, 1966. *Dáil Deputies: Their Work, its Difficulties, Possible Remedies.* Dublin: Tuairim pamphlet 15.

Wood, David M. and Garry Young, 1997. 'Comparing constituent activity by junior legislators in Great Britain and Ireland', *Legislative Studies Quarterly* 22:2, pp. 217–32.

9   Political leadership

The President and the Taoiseach

Robert Elgie

As we have seen in chapter 3, the political life of the Republic of Ireland is, according to the constitution, overshadowed by two figures: the President of Ireland, who is now the head of state, and the Taoiseach, who has been the head of government since the enactment of the constitution in 1937 and who has exercised executive power since then. The presidency is a largely symbolic office with few powers. By contrast, the Taoiseach has consistently been a powerful political actor.

This chapter explores the foundations of executive power in the Republic of Ireland. It begins by assessing the role of the President. Why is the presidency such a weak institution and should the office be reformed or even abolished? It then considers the dominant position of the Taoiseach. What resources can the Taoiseach mobilise and what obstacles are placed in the way of individualised political leadership?

The President

In terms of protocol, the constitution indicates that the President takes 'precedence over all other persons in the State' (Article 12.1). In practice, though, the Irish presidency has been perceived in a European context as 'the weakest presidency to be filled by direct election' (Gallagher, 1999). There is no doubt that the presidency is a secondary political office and there are no expectations that the President should exercise political leadership. Indeed, any attempt to do so would be treated as an unnatural interference in the normal workings of the political process. Why is the presidency so weak? There are several reasons, including the party-dominated method of election, the absence of constitutional powers and the tradition of limited presidentialism which has been the norm since 1937.

Why is the presidency so weak?

The constitution provides for the election of the President by a direct vote of the people every seven years. In order to stand for office candidates must be nominated by at least twenty members of the Oireachtas or four county or county borough councils (Article 12.4.2; in addition, former or retiring presidents may nominate themselves, Article 12.4.4). The effect of the nomination process has been to place the selection of presidential candidates almost exclusively in the hands of Fianna Fáil, Fine Gael and Labour Party elites. In general, these parties have tended to choose elderly candidates (although this was not the case in 1997) or candidates from amongst the second-ranking set of politicians, rather than senior – as opposed to retirement-age – figures with a strong political base. In this way, presidents have come to office either without ambition or without the party political means to achieve what few goals they might have set themselves in the first place. Moreover, party elites can collude to prevent an election from taking place at all. The constitution states that where 'only one candidate is nominated for the office of President it shall not be necessary to proceed to a ballot for his election' (Article 12.4.5). In such a case, presidents are deprived not just of political authority but popular legitimacy as well. Since the office was instituted, there have been five uncontested elections (1938, 1952, 1974, 1976 and 1983) and six have been contested (1945, 1959, 1966, 1973, 1990 and 1997). Whatever the nature of the contest, though, successful candidates have been in no position to claim a mandate for leadership even if they had ever wished to do so. In this way, one of the conditions for presidential leadership has been absent from the system.

Arguably, though, the context in which presidential elections take place may be changing, albeit marginally. First, parties have tended recently to nominate rather younger and more dynamic candidates. Moreover, in the elections of 1990 and 1997 the Labour Party chose a candidate whose links with the party organisation were relatively weak. The selection of Mary Robinson in 1990 was quite significant. She certainly had a history of Labour Party politics, having been a Labour senator and an unsuccessful Labour candidate at two Dáil elections. However, she resigned from the party in 1985 and during the 1990 election campaign stressed that she was an independent candidate. As a result, in office she was relatively unconcerned with maintaining close relations with her sponsor party and there were persistent rumours about the difficulties between her and the then Labour leader, Dick Spring. All told, if the trend towards nominating younger, more independent-minded candidates continues, then the likelihood is that at some stage in the future a party may find that it has helped to elect someone who wishes to maintain and perhaps even promote his or her own separate political agenda while in office.

Second, the 1997 election set an important precedent in that for the first time ever candidates were able to obtain sufficient support from county councillors to be validly nominated. The fact that two candidates managed to mobilise so many county councils served to loosen the grip of party elites on the nomination process. Local councillors failed to follow the strictures of party central offices and were willing to let the names of two independent candidates go forward for election. It might be argued that this innovation opens the way for non-party, even populist, candidates to be nominated in the future. If successful, such candidates would probably cause problems for the traditional view of the President as figurehead. Currently, though, it is this vision of the presidency which, despite these changes, still prevails.

Over and above the context of the election process, presidents have very few constitutional powers to call upon. Indeed, so limited are these powers that a populist, reformist or even mildly independent-minded president would soon come up against the constraints of the office. The President has both non-discretionary roles and discretionary powers (Ward, 1994, pp. 286–95). Regarding the former, the President has no room for independent action whatsoever. For example, Article 13.1.1 states that the 'President shall, on the nomination of Dáil Éireann, appoint the Taoiseach . . .'; the President must accept the Dáil's nominee. The same principle applies to all other roles under this heading. In addition, the President may not even leave the state without the express agreement of the government (Article 12.9). Beyond this, the President is likely to heed any advice from the government not to take a certain course of action if that would create a risk of political controversy. Thus, in 1991 the government asked President Robinson not to deliver the Dimbleby lecture in London, and in 1993 it asked her to decline an invitation to chair a Ford Foundation committee on the future of the United Nations; on each occasion the President accepted this advice without forcing a confrontation (O'Leary and Burke, 1998, pp. 153, 220–2). The Taoiseach must keep the President informed on matters of domestic and international policy (Article 28.5.2), but there is no indication of how often the two must meet or how detailed the information must be. Indeed, Liam Cosgrave is reported to have seen President Ó Dálaigh only four times in two years in 1974–76. In all of these ways, then, the President's room for manoeuvre is not just limited, it is altogether absent.

In the case of discretionary powers, the President has a somewhat greater degree of freedom. That said, the scope of these powers is very small. There are six such powers, three of which are of minor significance relating to the President's role as an arbiter in the case of disputes between the Dáil and the Seanad. In fact, so far only one discretionary power has been invoked with any degree of significance (Article 26.1.1) and only one other remains potentially important (Article 13.2.2).

Article 26.1.1 allows the President, after consultation with the Council of State, to submit a bill to the Supreme Court to test its constitutional validity (see chapter 3). The Council of State comprises the Taoiseach, Tánaiste, Chief Justice, President of the High Court, the chairs of both the Dáil and the Seanad and the Attorney General, as well as any former President, Taoiseach or Chief Justice who is willing to serve, plus up to seven presidential nominees. Its role in this as in any other matter on which the President consults it is purely advisory; the President need not follow its recommendations. From 1938 to 1998 this power was used on twelve occasions and on one occasion it was the cause of a major controversy (Gallagher, 1977). In September 1976, President Ó Dálaigh referred the Emergency Powers Bill to the Supreme Court. This bill was designed to give additional power to the state authorities when dealing with suspected IRA members. On its referral, the bill was declared constitutional by the Supreme Court, but shortly afterwards the Defence Minister, Patrick Donegan, described President Ó Dálaigh as 'a thundering disgrace' for having referred the bill at all. The Taoiseach, Liam Cosgrave, refused to sack the minister for his comment and a Dáil motion of no confidence in Donegan was narrowly defeated. Following the vote, President Ó Dálaigh tendered his own resignation.

Article 13.2.2 states that the 'President may in his absolute discretion refuse to dissolve Dáil Éireann on the advice of a Taoiseach who has ceased to retain the support of a majority in Dáil Éireann'. In fact, this power has never been exercised. However, it remains controversial because at times of extreme political tension it draws the President into the party political process whether or not the article is actually invoked. Either to grant or to refuse a dissolution might lay the President open to charges of favouring one political party over another. Moreover, this article is doubly controversial because it politicises the presidency in circumstances that are not clearly spelt out in the constitution. Who is to say when the Taoiseach has actually lost the support of the Dáil? Is it simply when the government has lost a vote of confidence, or when it has been defeated over a single item of legislation, or when a party announces that it is leaving the governing coalition, or even when an independent TD withdraws his or her support? On several occasions the significance of this article has been apparent. In 1944 President Hyde agreed to dissolve the Dáil upon a request from the Taoiseach after a government defeat on a minor piece of legislation, because he considered that there was no alternative administration in waiting. In January 1982 President Hillery again agreed to dissolve the Dáil after a government defeat on a part of the annual budget, even though this time the leader of the opposition, Charles Haughey, was apparently willing to try to form a government without recourse to an election. Finally, President Robinson made it known that she would have refused a dissolution had Albert Reynolds requested one following the fall of the Fianna Fáil–Labour coalition in 1994 (Gallagher, 1999).

These examples illustrate the ambiguities that surround Article 13.2.2. As a result, the recent Constitution Review Group stated in its final report that 'the introduction of a constructive vote of no confidence would be preferable to the involvement of the President in the government-formation process' (Constitution Review Group, 1996, p. 98). In other words, it recommended that the constitution be changed so as to oblige the Dáil to nominate an alternative Taoiseach at the same time as it voted on a motion of confidence. This would prevent the President from participating in any such political controversies and put an end to any lingering problems associated with this article.

Against this general background, the tradition of a limited presidency was established from the first incumbent, Douglas Hyde, onwards. The fact that he was the sole nominee, that he was associated with the cultural rather than the party political world, that he was aged seventy-eight at the time of his election and that de Valera, as Taoiseach, was at the peak of his political authority all went to ensure that power continued to reside with the head of government. This tradition was then reinforced by Hyde's successor, Seán T. O'Kelly. In contrast to Hyde, he was elected (at least in 1945) and he had previously enjoyed a long party political and ministerial career. However, he made no attempt to break the mould that had just been set. Indeed, Hussey comments that O'Kelly held office 'safely and unremarkably' until 1959 (Hussey, 1994, p. 11). Thereafter, most presidents appear to have been happy with a role as figurehead. For example, President Hillery has written that he wanted to do the job with 'the minimum of self-projection' and, in an oblique reference to the events of January 1982, stated that 'the most important use of [presidential] powers was sometimes not to employ them at all (*Irish Times*, 12 November 1997). All told, the desire to exercise presidential leadership has generally been absent from the system.

In fact, there have been only two presidents who have had the will to test the limits of the office. The first, Erskine Childers, enjoyed considerable political authority and public affection. However, his attempts to reform the office were met with outright resistance from the Taoiseach of the day, Liam Cosgrave. For example, Garret FitzGerald reveals that Cosgrave vetoed the President's desire to fulfil a campaign pledge to set up a 'think-tank' to examine the long-term needs of the country (FitzGerald, 1991, p. 254). In the event, Childers' presidency was brought to an abrupt end by his sudden death. The second, Mary Robinson, was the most popular and, arguably, most successful president to date. She demonstrated that it was possible for a president to shape the political agenda at least at the margins. Most notably, on a visit to West Belfast in 1993 she shook the hand of Sinn Féin president, Gerry Adams, at a time when the first IRA cease-fire had yet to be called and when the party was still treated as a pariah. Equally, she made a series of high-profile visits to Rwanda and alerted the public, not just in Ireland but also elsewhere, to the atrocities that were being perpetrated there. Needless to say, there was a great deal of opposition to some of her actions. In 1995, for example, her comments in a US television interview were interpreted as a call for a 'yes' vote in the divorce referendum and, hence, were criticised by those who were campaigning on the opposite side and by elements of the media. At the same time, though, she was truly able to incarnate the concerns of many sections of Irish life in her championing of women, the disadvantaged, travellers and the diaspora.

Abolish or reform?

The weakness of the presidency is such that its very existence has periodically been called into question. In 1967, the Committee on the Constitution identified two arguments in favour of abolishing the office, stating that the Taoiseach could quite happily exercise the few powers that the President does enjoy and that abolition would bring about budgetary savings (Committee on the Constitution, 1967, p. 8). However, the Committee also identified three counter-arguments: that it would not be realistic for the Taoiseach to act as guardian of the constitution, that it would be a severe burden for one person to carry out the duties of both head of state and head of government and that the amount of budgetary savings would be minimal (ibid.). More than that, it is generally felt that there is a real need for a non-political figure to personify in a disinterested manner the aspirations of the people as a whole. In this vein, the 1996 Constitution Review Group concluded that 'there is no public demand or good reason for abolition of the office' (Constitution Review Group, 1996, p. 28).

What about reforming the presidency? According to one writer, the basic problem is that as things stand the presidency is neither truly political nor truly non-political (Gallagher, 1977, p. 382). As the above examples demonstrate, there are occasions when presidents cannot avoid being drawn into the political process. At the same time, on the occasions when they might wish to make their mark presidents do not have the powers with which to do so. It might be argued, therefore, that the presidency should be reformed either to increase the set of presidential powers so as give the incumbent the potential to be a significant political player or to reduce them even further so as to place the institution completely above the political fray. In fact, if there is to be reform then it is likely that it will take the second of these two courses. All countries require a symbolic figure to personify the state. This is the role that the President is currently in a position to perform successfully, while the Taoiseach is already charged with exercising political leadership. There is therefore a case for further reduction of the President's powers with a view to eliminating the lingering suspicion that the presidency is anything other than a purely symbolic office. Indeed, this logic led the Constitution Review Group to recommend that executive authority should be reserved for the government and that the President should be placed 'above politics' altogether.

The Taoiseach

If the Irish presidency is perceived to be one of the weakest of all directly-elected heads of state, then the Taoiseach is usually considered to be one of the strongest of all heads of government. For example, Anthony King places the Taoiseach alongside the British, German, Greek, Portuguese and Spanish prime ministers in the category of heads of government who have the highest degree of influence within their own systems of government (King, 1994, p. 152). Brendan O'Leary goes one further. He states that: 'Within his own political system the Irish prime minister is potentially more powerful than any other European prime minister, with the exception of his British counterpart' (O'Leary, 1991, p. 159). However, the key word here is 'potentially'. In practice, the power of the Taoiseach varies from one office holder to another. Even if the Taoiseach is usually pre-eminent amongst his colleagues, the 'precise degree of this pre-eminence . . . may well vary from Taoiseach to Taoiseach' (Chubb, 1974, p. 13). The reality, then, is a system in which there are several constitutional, administrative and political resources at the disposal of the office. However, it is also a system in which the Taoiseach faces a number of constraints. Most notably, the power of the Taoiseach is shaped by party political factors, and these go a long way towards accounting for the strength of an individual Taoiseach.

Constitutional, administrative and political resources

The constitution officially designates the Taoiseach as head of government (Article 13.1.1 and Article 28.5.1). In this capacity, the Taoiseach meets and negotiates with heads of state and heads of government throughout the world, attends meetings of the European Council on behalf of the state, pays particular attention to the situation in Northern Ireland and is the government's main spokesperson at home. In all, the Taoiseach is the person upon whom the responsibility for leadership is most visibly incumbent.

The constitution also provides the Taoiseach with a considerable power of appointment. For example, Article 13.1.2 gives the Taoiseach the right to appoint the other members of the government, subject, of course, to Dáil approval. Although the appointment of junior ministers, or ministers of state, is vested by law in the government, in practice the Taoiseach plays no less significant a role here. In addition, Article 30.2 provides the Taoiseach with the right to appoint the Attorney General, who has a seat at the cabinet table. It should be noted, though, that there are formal limits to the Taoiseach's power of appointment: the number of cabinet ministers is limited to fifteen, the choice of ministers is restricted to members of the Oireachtas and no more than two ministers at any one time can be members of the Seanad (Article 28.7.2). There are also informal limits which are outlined below. Despite these limits, there is no doubt that heads of government have used the power of ministerial appointment to shape the membership of the cabinet to their own advantage. This was particularly noticeable in February 1992 when Albert Reynolds declined to appoint a number of senior Haughey supporters to his first cabinet. Moreover, Article 28.9.4 states that the 'Taoiseach may at any time, for reasons which to him seem sufficient, request a member of the Government to resign', and that, if the minister refuses to comply, the Taoiseach may simply dismiss him or her. Accordingly, Jack Lynch dismissed Charles Haughey and Neil Blaney during the 'arms crisis' in 1970, while Haughey himself dismissed Albert Reynolds and Pádraig Flynn for refusing to back his leadership in 1991. All other things being equal, then, the Taoiseach has the opportunity to determine the composition of the cabinet not just at the beginning of an administration but at any time throughout its life.

As well as having the power to select the government, the Taoiseach nominates eleven members of Seanad Éireann (see chapter 7). This is usually sufficient to guarantee that the government of the day has a majority in the upper house. So, in 1997 Fianna Fáil won only twenty-three of the forty-nine elected seats to the Seanad but the incoming Taoiseach, Bertie Ahern, was then able to use his power of appointment to ensure that the Fianna Fáil–Progressive Democrat coalition enjoyed a comfortable majority in the sixty-seat chamber. Finally, Article 13.2.1 provides the Taoiseach with the power to dissolve the Dáil and call a general election. Use of this power depends on the likelihood that the government will win the ensuing election, but it was successfully used by de Valera in the 1930s to maintain and reinforce his position in office. In short, when the circumstances are right the head of government, who comes to office thanks to the favour of the lower house, has the right to determine the parliamentary lifetime of its members.

In addition to the power of appointment, the Taoiseach also has the capacity to shape the day-to-day process of policy making. The Taoiseach has important prerogatives with regard to the operation of the cabinet, even though coalition government is now the norm and has somewhat restricted the head of government's powers in this respect (see p. 243 below). In general, as Farrell states: 'The Taoiseach determines the order in which items on the cabinet agenda are taken, the time given to consideration of each item, who is to speak, and when a decision should be reached – or postponed . . . in practice, ministers do not challenge the Taoiseach's control of the agenda' (Farrell, 1993, p. 176). In this context, Farrell quotes an anonymous cabinet minister as saying: 'Really you can't get an item discussed for five seconds at a cabinet meeting if the Taoiseach isn't with you' (Farrell, B., 1994, p. 80). Outside the cabinet, the number of permanent cabinet committees is small. In one sense, though, this factor further strengthens the position of the Taoiseach. It obliges the head of government to be personally concerned with all departmental policy matters and requires the Taoiseach to be more than just a policy co-ordinator. As such, although the head of government must bear in mind the sensitivities of coalition partners, the Taoiseach is in a position to direct rather than simply manage the flow of governmental business and is thus able to follow the full course of policy making from inception through to approval at the cabinet table.

The Taoiseach is in a similar position with regard to the legislative aspect of the policy making process (see chapter 7). For example, Article 25 of the Dáil's standing orders allows the Taoiseach to determine the order in which government business will be taken each day. In this sense, the Taoiseach controls not just the cabinet's business but the Dáil's agenda as well. In addition, the Taoiseach regularly defends the government's record during question time and on other occasions. Since the office of the chief whip is formally part of the Department of the Taoiseach (see below), the head of government has a strong, direct relationship with the parliamentary party. Overall, the Dáil is one of the least influential legislatures in Western Europe (Norton, 1990). It is the Taoiseach who is the main beneficiary of this situation.

The head of government's position is further strengthened by the administrative support that the office commands. The most important institution in this respect is the Department of the Taoiseach. The Department comprises approximately 300 people in a number of different sections or divisions. Their role is to co-ordinate government policy and contribute to its formulation. There are separate sections in various areas such as Economic and Social Policy, European and International Affairs and Northern Ireland (see Department of the Taoiseach, 1999). The Department also includes the Taoiseach's private office, the office of the chief whip, the government secretariat and the Government Information Service. Collectively, these institutions carry out many of the essential tasks of government on the Taoiseach's behalf. For example, one of the pivotal organisations is the government secretariat, the main task of which is to prepare meetings of the cabinet and to execute its decisions. In this capacity, the Secretary General to the Government attends cabinet meetings in a non-voting capacity to take the minutes.

More generally, though, the secretariat co-ordinates the work of the government as a whole. It liaises with government ministers to ensure that decisions are being made and deadlines are being met. In this way, it is central to the working of the cabinet system. As O'Leary notes, its existence 'is no proof of overweening monocratic power' (O'Leary, 1991, p. 155). However, to the extent that the Secretary General to the Government is one of the Taoiseach's closest interlocutors, it allows the head of government to maintain a privileged overview of the cabinet system. As Morgan argues, it 'equips the Taoiseach to exercise better-informed powers of surveillance over his government's activity' (Morgan, 1990, p. 55). Also significant in this respect is the Government Information Service, which is headed by the government press secretary. The press secretary is a political appointee chosen for his or her loyalty and knowledge of the media. There is no doubt that the press secretary is privy to the most sensitive of all government discussions (see, for example, Duignan, 1996). There is also no doubt that the presence of an experienced and skilled individual at this post can be of enormous public and political benefit to the Taoiseach personally.

The final resource upon which a Taoiseach may draw is electoral and party political. As will be shown below, party politics is also the main reason why the power of the Taoiseach varies. However, when the party situation allows, the head of government can draw upon three electoral and party-based resources. First, the Taoiseach derives authority from the electoral process. General election campaigns are highly personalised. In the words of Basil Chubb, they 'often take the form of gladiatorial contests between two designated party leaders' (Chubb, 1992, p. 185). In 1997, Bertie Ahern clearly won the battle of the photo opportunity. As a result, he could claim that the party's (admittedly slim) victory was at least partly a personal one and insist on a degree of loyalty from both cabinet and parliamentary party colleagues. Second, the Taoiseach can benefit from the fact that the formation of the government is approved by a vote in the Dáil. As Coakley notes, this forces 'parliament to define at the outset its attitude to any new prime minister and compels would-be dissidents within his party to choose between open rebellion and conformity' (Coakley, 1984, pp. 413–4). There is no equivalent of the so-called *franchi tiratori* ('secret snipers', or defectors) who, taking advantage of the provision for secret voting in parliament, used to be a disruptive element of Italian politics. Thus, after the 1997 election the incoming government led by Bertie Ahern successfully marshalled its own troops and won the support of sufficient independent deputies to muster a very narrow but working majority. Finally, the Taoiseach is not just head of government but also party leader (John A. Costello, Taoiseach in 1948–51 and 1954–57, is the single exception to this rule). This is a significant power because Fianna Fáil and Fine Gael are highly centralised political parties (Farrell, D., 1994). The leader has the power to appoint staff members at party headquarters, influence candidate selection and, hence, create the conditions for party support (see chapter 6).

Structural and conjunctural constraints

All of the above points might suggest that there is a system of prime ministerial government in the Republic of Ireland. And yet, such a conclusion would be premature. Although it is certainly the case that the Taoiseach is the principal political figure within the executive, it is also the case that there are distinct limits to the Taoiseach's powers. Some of these limits are structural, others are conjunctural. That is to say, some are built into the system and are inescapable, whereas others depend on the particular context within which the head of government has to operate. With regard to the latter, the most important variable is the nature of the party political situation with which the government is faced.

As a result of structural factors, the Taoiseach's position within government is always less than absolute. Most notably, running the business of government is an extremely complicated and time-consuming affair. Even in his experience as a minister, Garret FitzGerald was struck by the workload that government representatives face. He states: 'At times, I found it difficult even to get time to read through the very often extensive cabinet memorandums, and even more difficult to undertake the study, and in some cases personal research, needed to ensure that I could contribute usefully to cabinet discussions on domestic affairs' (article in *Irish Times*, 28 January 1995). While the Taoiseach is freed from the need to master details of policy at this level, there is pressure to prioritise some policy areas, such as foreign and European policy, Northern Ireland policy and social and budgetary policy, at the expense of others (see FitzGerald, 1991, p. 425).

Moreover, the Taoiseach's power of ministerial appointment is, in effect, quite restricted. In addition to the constraints of coalition government (see p. 243 below), the pool of potential ministers is always relatively small. For example, in December 1994 there were forty-six Fine Gael deputies from whom the Taoiseach was able to choose and in 1997 there were only seventy-seven Fianna Fáil TDs; not all of these were necessarily available to serve as ministers. Furthermore, the Taoiseach must pay attention to both the loyalty and seniority of party colleagues when making appointments. There are certainly times when it is best to appoint potential dissidents so as to bind them to the principle of collective governmental responsibility. There are also times when a Dáil newcomer may be appointed to ministerial office, as was Niamh Bhreathnach, Minister for Education, in 1992, and evidence indicates that TDs are being promoted more quickly to ministerial office than in the past (Farrell, 1987, p. 146). However, in general terms the Taoiseach will wish to reward loyalty and there may be certain long-standing deputies whose presence at the ministerial table is almost a given. In these ways, the Taoiseach's freedom of choice is further restricted.

Equally, there may be pressure to appoint ministers from particular geographical areas in the hope of reaping future electoral reward. So, there will be strong pressure to appoint a number of deputies from Dublin and from the other major cities to ministerial office. Indeed, the Taoiseach ignores such pressure at his own peril. For example, the absence of a high-profile minister from Cork was put forward as a reason for the relatively poor electoral performance in that area by the parties of the outgoing government at the 1997 election. Again, this limits the room for manoeuvre in appointments to the cabinet. Finally, the Taoiseach must at least bear in mind the policy expertise of potential appointees. This is not to say that the Minister of Education has to be a former teacher, or the Minister of Health a former doctor. It is simply to suggest that the Taoiseach may wish to take into account the role played by junior ministers or opposition party spokespersons when appointing people to full cabinet posts. For example, Bertie Ahern was mindful of the reputation that had been built up by both John O'Donoghue and Brian Cowen during their periods as opposition spokespersons on Justice and Health respectively when he appointed them to the corresponding positions in cabinet in 1997. Overall, there is certainly a sense in which the Taoiseach's power of ministerial appointment is always more restricted than a simple reading of the constitution might suggest.

In addition to structural limitations the head of government's power is subject to conjunctural constraints. In terms of the Taoiseach's power within government, the most important conjunctural variable is party political. As O'Leary asserts, 'the Taoiseach's ability to fulfil his policy-initiating role within the government is primarily determined by party–government variables' (O'Leary, 1991, pp. 159–60). The Taoiseach is a professional party politician who comes to power by way of a party-dominated process and who remains in power only for as long as party support can be maintained. Thus, party politics pervades the political process. At times, the Taoiseach can be relatively unrestricted if the conjunction of party forces is favourable. At other times, though, the Taoiseach can be imprisoned by party politics if the conjunction of these forces is disadvantageous. Accordingly, his or her power and freedom to manoeuvre is shaped by whether there is a coalition or a single-party government, whether there is a majority or a minority government and whether the main governing party is united or divided.

All other things being equal, the position of the Taoiseach is stronger during periods of single-party government than when there is a coalition. All told, from 1922 to 1998 single-party governments held power for fifty-two years and coalitions for twenty-four. For the most part, then, heads of government have not had to operate within the confines of coalition constraints. This is one reason why commentators such as Anthony King (as quoted above) have classified the Taoiseach as such an influential domestic actor in a comparative context. However, there has been a coalition government of one sort or another since 1989 due to the fact that Fianna Fáil has been unable to win an overall majority on its own and that it no longer refuses to envisage a coalition agreement (see chapter 5). As coalition government has become the norm, the overall position of the Taoiseach has become weaker and judgements of the kind cited above may need to be revised accordingly.

The impact of coalition government can be seen in four ways. First, the Taoiseach's power of appointment is restricted; it is shared with the leaders of other parties participating in the coalition. The head of government must accept ministerial nominations that are made by the coalition partner, and may even be forced to make imaginative compromises. For example, the agreement which sealed the formation of the so-called Rainbow Coalition in 1994 included the understanding that an additional junior minister would be allowed to attend cabinet meetings as Democratic Left's second representative, even though the constitutional limit of fifteen cabinet ministers had already been reached. Second, in office representatives of the coalition partner may be in a position to shape the policy of the departments that they head. So, for example, Ruairí Quinn was a high profile Labour Party finance minister in 1994–97. Third, it may also mean that the Tánaiste becomes a significant political actor. There is a convention that the Taoiseach appoints the leader of the main coalition partner to this post. From this vantage point, the Tánaiste is in a position to participate in the most important decisions of the government and it is certainly the case that Dick Spring's influence on foreign and Northern Ireland policy from 1993 to 1997 was greater than that of the typical foreign minister. Indeed, during this time he headed a specially-created Office of the Tánaiste which was agreed as part of the January 1993 coalition agreement with Fianna Fáil and which was designed to provide the incumbent with administrative support along the lines of the Department of the Taoiseach. The Labour leader thus received all government papers and not simply those relating to his own ministerial portfolio of foreign affairs. Overall, such was the position of Dick Spring during this time that Brian Farrell wonders whether there was a subtle shift from the role of Tánaiste as deputising Taoiseach to the Tánaiste as deputy Taoiseach (Farrell, 1993, p. 179). This experiment, though, did not continue after 1997, when the Office of the Tánaiste was abolished. Finally, if the Taoiseach rides roughshod over the concerns of the coalition partner, then the government runs the risk of collapse. There is nothing inherently unstable about coalition governments, but circumstances can conspire to render them extremely fragile, as the coalition break-ups of 1992 and 1994 showed.

Over and above the number of parties in government the power of the Taoiseach is also affected by the government's position in the Dáil: whether or not it enjoys majority support. Again, in general terms, the position of the Taoiseach is stronger during periods of majority government than minority government (where government parties command fewer than 50 per cent of the seats in the Dáil). From 1922 to 1998, there were fifty-eight years of majority government (single-party and coalition majority governments combined) and eighteen years of minority government (again, single-party and coalition minority governments combined). Most heads of government, then, have benefited from the support of a parliamentary majority. This provides a further reason why most commentators have categorised the Taoiseach as such an influential political actor. Nevertheless, some minority governments have remained in office for a considerable period of time. This was particularly the case with the de Valera government of 1951–54 and the Lemass government of 1961–65. These were both single-party Fianna Fáil administrations which capitalised on the lack of cohesion amongst the opposition parties in order to remain in office. Moreover, it is also the case that governments which are only just short of a majority have encouraged non-aligned TDs to give them their ongoing support. This happened in 1982 in the case of the so-called 'Gregory deal' (Joyce and Murtagh, 1983). It also happened in 1997 when the minority Fianna Fáil–Progressive Democrat administration looked for the support of independents, such as Harry Blaney and Mildred Fox. This indicates that a minority government need not necessarily be a fragile government.

At the same time, though, the absence of a parliamentary majority does constrain the power of the Taoiseach. This is because the government constantly runs the risk of being defeated. Its head must then negotiate more, bargain more and compromise more. In this way, the ability to shape the legislative process is weakened. Moreover, if negotiations break down, bargaining positions are inflexible and compromise cannot be reached, then the government runs the further risk of being forced out of office altogether. Thus, for example, the short-lived 1981–82 Fine Gael–Labour minority coalition was brought down when an independent deputy decided on the spur of the moment to vote against the government. Overall, despite the fact that minority governments can exist for a considerable period of time, the Taoiseach's position is still somewhat less comfortable when the government does not enjoy majority support in the Dáil than when it does.

Finally, the power of the Taoiseach depends on the extent to which the main governing party is united. Generally speaking, the position of the Taoiseach is stronger under a unified party than under a divided one. In this respect, the experience of the historic leaders of both Fianna Fáil (de Valera and Lemass) and Cumann na nGaedheal/Fine Gael (William T. Cosgrave), who were the subject of a certain 'cult of leadership' and were capable of inspiring not just followership but also an amount of devotion in some cases, contrasts starkly with the experience of John A. Costello, who was not even the leader of Fine Gael when he held office and who had to share power with the party leader Richard Mulcahy. That said, at least until the mid-1960s most heads of government enjoyed the almost unqualified support of their own parties. This is yet another reason why commentators have traditionally described the Taoiseach as a powerful leader. In recent times, though, the degree of party discipline has generally weakened. For example, although John Bruton was never openly challenged during his period as Taoiseach, neither was he a charismatic figure who had the unquestioning support of all his party colleagues. Furthermore, on occasions internal party problems have found expression not so much in rebellions against the parliamentary party whip but more in behind-the-scenes scheming and public 'heaves' against the leadership. In Fianna Fáil, the level of intra-party disaffection was particularly significant from the election of Jack Lynch in 1966 to the accession of Bertie Ahern in late 1994 (see the account in Marsh, 1993). Overall, the result is that the link between the Taoiseach and the party is more conditional now than in the past. As with the trend towards coalition government, this suggests that the overall position of recent heads of government is now weaker than was previously the case and requires King's view of the power of the office to be further qualified.

Chairman or chief?

The Taoiseach, then, occupies an office which can call upon many political resources but which also faces both structural and conjunctural constraints.

In practice, the incumbent's power is potentially great but it is also subject to considerable variation. In this context, how do we make sense of the role of the Taoiseach? One useful approach has been outlined by Brian Farrell (1971; 1993). He distinguishes between 'chairman' and 'chief' images of the office. He defines a 'chairman' as someone who is 'prepared to allow others to share resources, responsibilities and publicity, reluctant to move beyond established procedures and slower to act' (Farrell, 1993, p. 180). By contrast, he defines a 'chief' as someone who is distinguished 'by a tendency to accumulate political resources, concentrate decision making or control of decision making in their own hands, and – above all – make use of their strategic position to mobilise the machinery of government for action' (ibid., pp. 179–80). Although in practice a Taoiseach may exhibit a mixed set of characteristics, these 'ideal-type' images capture two of the main ways in which incumbents can exercise power.

Whether or not the Taoiseach emerges as a 'chairman' or a 'chief' depends on a number of factors. In the first place, the Taoiseach is an individual political actor and so each incumbent 'will bring their own policy concerns and preferences to the office; they will enlist new supports, acquire new debts, recruit new men, confront new political situations' (Farrell, 1971, p. 8). Thus, the office is at least partly shaped by the person who holds it. So, for example, Haughey's instinct was to be a chief, whereas Lynch preferred the chairman role (Farrell, 1993, pp. 184–6). At the same time, though, as Farrell also correctly indicates, it is 'his position, not his personality, which puts him into the centre of the electoral stage' (Farrell, 1971, p. 3). In other words, the office enjoys considerable powers and even reluctant heads of government have leadership responsibilities thrust upon them. Thus, Lynch was obliged to assert his and the government's authority during the 'arms crisis' of 1970. And yet, even if the office enjoys considerable political resources and public attention, the incumbent also has to operate within the 'value systems of the community' (Farrell, 1971, p. 83) and 'to switch roles according to circumstance' (Farrell, 1988, p. 45). This serves to limit the role of the office holder. In this way, de Valera, whom most people might consider to be the epitome of the 'chief' image, was 'more cautious and less assertive than the title suggests' (Farrell, 1993, p. 181). Similarly, even if Haughey's instinct was to be a 'chief', this was 'curtailed by factionalism within his party, failure to secure a parliamentary majority, and economic circumstance' (ibid., p. 186). By virtue of the combination of these factors, Farrell argues that only Seán Lemass

> exhibited a wide range of behaviour associated with the 'chief'. He was assertive in advancing policies in the cabinet and in public, prepared to use ministers to float ideas, to circumvent normal procedures on occasion and to chair cabinets with decisive consequences.
>
> (ibid., p. 183)

Conclusion

The President and the Taoiseach stand at the apex of the state. The former is there in a symbolic capacity as the representative of the nation. As such, though, the President has little or no opportunity to control decision making and scarcely any power even to act as a 'guardian' of the constitution, one of the roles de Valera initially suggested that the incumbent would play (see Gallagher, 1988, p. 75). And yet, there is still a need for at least one high-profile public representative to be 'above politics' and to incarnate in a disinterested way the legitimacy of the state. In this way, the President performs an important function. In contrast to the symbolic presidency, the Taoiseach is a 'working' part of the constitution. The Taoiseach has the potential to control decision making and there is the expectation that the incumbent will do so in order to address the pressing issues of the day. However, there sometimes exists a gap between the potential to shape public opinion and the actual ability to do so. In this context, a Taoiseach must sometimes be content simply to articulate popular concerns, to administer party relations and to facilitate the business of government. Depending on the context, then, the Taoiseach may act as either leader or manager.

References and further reading

Chubb, Basil, 1974. *Cabinet Government in Ireland.* Dublin: Institute of Public Administration.

Chubb, Basil, 1992. *The Government and Politics of Ireland,* 3rd ed. Harlow: Longman.

Coakley, John, 1984. 'Selecting a prime minister: the Irish experience', *Parliamentary Affairs* 37:4, pp. 403–17.

Committee on the Constitution, 1967. *Report of the Committee on the Constitution.* Dublin: Stationery Office.

Constitution Review Group, 1996. *Report of the Constitution Review Group.* Dublin: Stationery Office.

Department of the Taoiseach, 1999. *Department of the Taoiseach – Government of Ireland,* available http://www.irlgov.ie/taoiseach/ [1999–02–02].

Duignan, Seán, 1996. *One Spin on the Merry-Go-Round.* Dublin: Blackwater Press.

Farrell, Brian, 1971. *Chairman or Chief? The Role of Taoiseach in Irish Government.* Dublin: Gill and Macmillan.

Farrell, Brian, 1987. 'The road from February 1987: government formation and institutional inertia' , pp. 141–52 in Michael Laver, Peter Mair and Richard Sinnott (eds.), *How Ireland Voted: The Irish General Election 1987.* Galway: PSAI Press.

Farrell, Brian, 1988. 'Ireland: the Irish cabinet system: more British than the British themselves', pp. 33–46 in Jean Blondel and Ferdinand Müller-Rommel (eds), *Cabinets in Western Europe.* London: Macmillan.

Farrell, Brian, 1993. 'The government', pp. 167–89 in John Coakley and Michael Gallagher (eds), *Politics in the Republic of Ireland,* 2nd ed. Dublin: Folens and Limerick: PSAI Press.

Farrell, Brian, 1994. 'The political role of cabinet ministers in Ireland', pp. 73–87 in Michael Laver and Kenneth A. Shepsle (eds.), *Cabinet Ministers and*

Parliamentary Government. Cambridge: Cambridge University Press.

Farrell, David M., 1994. 'Ireland: centralization, professionalization and competitive pressures', pp. 216–41 in Richard S. Katz and Peter Mair (eds), *How Parties Organize: Change and Adaptation in Party Organizations in Western Democracies*. London: Sage.

FitzGerald, Garret, 1991. *All in a Life*. Dublin: Gill and Macmillan.

Gallagher, Michael, 1977. 'The presidency of the Republic of Ireland: implications of the "Donegan Affair"', *Parliamentary Affairs* 30:4, pp. 373–84.

Gallagher, Michael, 1988. 'The President, the people and the constitution', pp. 75–92 in Brian Farrell (ed.), *De Valera's Constitution and Ours*. Dublin: Gill and Macmillan.

Gallagher, Michael, 1999. 'Republic of Ireland', in Robert Elgie (ed.), *Semi-presidentialism in Europe*. Oxford: Oxford University Press.

Hussey, Gemma, 1994. *Ireland Today: Anatomy of a Changing State*. London: Viking.

Joyce, Joe and Peter Murtagh, 1983. *The Boss: Charles J. Haughey in Government*. Dublin: Poolbeg Press.

King, Anthony, 1994. '"Chief executives" in Western Europe', pp. 150–63 in Ian Budge and David McKay (eds), *Developing Democracy: Comparative Research in Honour of J. F. P. Blondel*. London: Sage.

Marsh, Michael, 1993. 'Selecting party leaders in the Republic of Ireland', *European Journal of Political Research* 24:3, pp. 295–316.

Morgan, David Gwynn, 1990. *Constitutional Law of Ireland: the Law of the Executive, Legislature and Judicature, 2nd ed.* Dublin: Round Hall Press.

Norton, Philip (ed.), 1990. *Parliaments in Western Europe*. London: Frank Cass.

O'Leary, Brendan, 1991. 'An Taoiseach: the Irish prime minister', *West European Politics* 14:2, pp. 133–62.

O'Leary, Olivia and Helen Burke, 1998. *Mary Robinson: The Authorised Biography*. London: Hodder and Stoughton.

Ward, Alan J., 1994. *The Irish Constitutional Tradition: Responsible Government and Modern Ireland, 1782–1992*. Blackrock: Irish Academic Press.

10 The government and the governmental system

Eileen Connolly and Eunan O'Halpin

In several chapters of this book, most notably chapter 7, we have seen that the government is a very powerful actor. It tends to dominate parliament, and, as we shall see in chapter 11, it has a central role in the policy making process. In this chapter, rather than emphasise its dealings with other actors, we look inside the administration itself. This chapter thus provides an outline of how Irish government actually works, and of the forces, values and assumptions that influence its operation. That involves both an outline of the main structural and operational features of the system, and consideration of its decision making processes. It requires examination of the roles both of the titular masters of the machinery of state – members of the cabinet and junior ministers – and of their officials in the national bureaucracy, the civil servants sometimes described in the media as the 'permanent government' because, while ministers and parties enter or leave power every few years, civil servants remain at their posts at the heart of the administrative machine. It also necessitates consideration of recent developments in the way that Irish cabinet government operates.

Cabinet government

After independence Ireland adopted a system of government that broadly followed the British 'Westminster model', in a set of arrangements that ensure that the executive will in practice predominate over the legislature (see chapter 7). While the Irish and British systems have diverged considerably over the years, this basic relationship remains unaltered. The relationship is not entirely one-sided. The government is not directly elected by the people: rather, it is chosen by the Dáil, through the election of a Taoiseach and the approval of his choice of ministers who are collectively responsible to the Dáil for every aspect of the administration's activities. The government cannot survive if it loses the support of the Dáil.

Article 28 of the constitution lays down the basic powers, functions and responsibility of the government (the term 'cabinet' is frequently used colloquially instead of 'government', though this term has no legal basis). While the constitutional provisions do not adequately describe the process of government formation and operation, they remain the bedrock upon which the day to day conduct of national affairs is based, and as such they require enumeration.

The constitution fixes the size of the government at not less than seven and not more than fifteen members, all of whom must be members of the Oireachtas. Up to two ministers may come from the Seanad, but the Taoiseach, the Tánaiste (deputy prime minister) and the Minister for Finance must all be TDs. In practice, almost all ministers have been TDs: only three senators have been appointed since 1922. All members of the government have 'the right to attend and be heard' in both Houses of the Oireachtas: a minister from the Dáil can participate in Seanad debates and, similarly, a minister from the Seanad can attend the Dáil.

The constitution places the Taoiseach in a very powerful position as the head of the government, as we saw in chapter 9. In a single-party government at least, all ministers are nominated by him for formal appointment by the President following approval by the Dáil. The Taoiseach decides on the distribution of responsibilities amongst ministers, and can sack them. If the Taoiseach resigns, all ministers are deemed to have resigned also. The Taoiseach alone can approach the President to request a dissolution of the Dáil, and the President is bound to accept such a request other than in the specific circumstances discussed in chapter 9 (see p. 235 above).

Making the government

The constitution provides a basic framework under which governments are formed: the Dáil votes a government into existence by first choosing a Taoiseach and then endorsing the new incumbent's choice of ministers. In practice the process is more complex than the constitution's provisions suggest, because government formation is usually the result of post-election bargaining between the various political parties and sometimes, as in February 1982 and in 1997, on negotiations with independent TDs who may hold the balance of power. For many years after 1932, the issues underlying such negotiations were simple: could an anti-Fianna Fáil majority be found in the Dáil and a coalition government formed, or would a minority Fianna Fáil government, supported by independents, emerge? Although no party has won an overall majority of seats in the seven elections since 1977, it was only in 1989 that the rules of the government formation game changed dramatically. This happened because Charles Haughey of Fianna Fáil then ditched his party's so-called 'core value' of never entering a coalition by concluding an unlikely alliance with his most bitter political enemies in the Progressive Democrats (PDs), as we saw in chapter 5. Haughey's embrace of coalition as a means of staying in personal power was a contributory factor in his eventual ousting as party leader, but neither of his immediate successors was any more successful in getting the party into government without the support of other groups.

Fianna Fáil's pragmatic conversion to coalition politics, just at a time when the state's acute public financial problems were fading and when the first evidence of economic improvement was emerging after a decade of disaster, helped to remove the aura of perpetual crisis management that had surrounded previous coalitions. The unprecedented growth of the 'Celtic Tiger' economy, together with the dramatic achievements of the Northern Ireland peace process in the 1990s, were overseen by a succession of coalition governments. These successes disposed of the old argument that coalitions were simply a poor substitute for single party government and could not provide strong and resolute direction of national affairs.

In late 1994 another stock assumption about government formation, that there would not be a change of Taoiseach and of the party composition of the government without an intervening general election, was shown to be outdated. A month after the collapse of the Fianna Fáil–Labour coalition in November 1994, the Dáil installed a three-party 'Rainbow coalition' under John Bruton of Fine Gael, which included Reynolds's previous coalition partners Labour. After the 1997 election, Fianna Fáil and the PDs were able to form a minority coalition government by dint of careful courtship of a number of independent TDs who held the balance of power in the Dáil. While there may be no way of predicting which parties will end up in government together following the intense and lengthy post-election negotiations that now characterise coalition formation, the absorption of Democratic Left into Labour, and the possible disappearance of the Progressive Democrats, may eventually see the re-emergence of the 'Fianna Fáil versus the rest' paradigm that dominated government formation for almost six decades after 1932 (see chapter 5 for a fuller discussion).

The succession of coalitions since 1989 has altered the nature and perception of cabinet government. The PDs discovered that, having forced Fianna Fáil into coalition, they could exert considerable leverage and were able to push through action on taxation and other issues close to their hearts; more significantly, they found that the Taoiseach took the threat of PD withdrawal from government so seriously that he was willing to antagonise his own party in order to maintain the coalition. The PDs won major concessions on a succession of issues including the reappointment of the Ombudsman in December 1989, the establishment of a judicial enquiry into the beef industry in 1991, the eventual dismissal in 1990 from the government of Brian Lenihan (the Tánaiste and Fianna Fáil candidate for the presidency), and the withdrawal of the nomination of Dr James McDaid to be Minister for Defence in 1991. Ultimately, they were even able to force Mr Haughey's resignation as Taoiseach (Arnold, 1994, pp. 245–77). As one Labour party official commented admiringly, 'most of us had watched as the PDs took one scalp after another in the course of their relationship with Fianna Fáil' (Finlay, 1998, p. 145). For the first time in a coalition, a small determined party had shown itself able to stick to its defining principles rather than simply securing piecemeal concessions on constituency or policy questions as the price of continued participation.

The PDs' visible success in coalition was largely a result of their realisation of how desperate their Fianna Fáil partner under Charles Haughey was to remain in office, and was not the result of any significant innovations in government or civil service organisation. Once Haughey was forced to resign as Taoiseach, however, the PDs found themselves virtually ignored by the new Fianna Fáil leadership under Albert Reynolds, and their influence on government policy diminished dramatically. This lesson was not lost on other parties. In particular, the Labour party, which went into coalition with Albert Reynolds's Fianna Fáil following the 1992 election, adopted an innovative approach to participation. This involved both the agreement in advance of detailed policy proposals across the spectrum of government responsibilities, and the establishment of coordination and review mechanisms to ensure their implementation. These mechanisms, notably that of the 'programme manager' (see p. 261 below), enabled the party to maximise its strength in coalition across a range of issues and policies, including those where Labour ministers had no direct responsibility but where the party itself had definite views (O'Halpin, 1997, pp. 81–2; Finlay, 1998, pp. 156, 165–7).

The appointment of ministers

The process of deciding who is to be included in the government, and who gets what department, is always sensitive. In a single party government, the party leader will have made many of the decisions prior to the election result. In the case of coalition governments, the allocation of ministerial portfolios becomes part of the negotiation process. The outcome of this aspect of negotiations is linked to the policy ambitions of the parties involved; comparative research confirms that within coalition governments in European countries the party affiliation of a minister has a definite bearing on the policy programme pursued in a given department, although allowances must always be made for the fact that some ministers are more effective than others in bringing their policy ideas to fruition (Laver and Shepsle, 1994, p. 308). The coalition bargaining process can often see the reorganisation of government departments and the redistribution of functions between them in order to balance out the portfolios assigned to ministers of different parties. For example, as a result of the formation of the Fianna Fáil–PD coalition in 1997 the Department of Equality and Law Reform established by the 1993–94 Fianna Fáil–Labour coalition was merged with the Department of Justice (from which some of its divisions had been transferred on its foundation) to produce a Department of Justice, Equality and Law Reform. In addition, a Department of Public Enterprise was formed from parts of the Department of Enterprise, Trade and

Employment and of the Department of Transport, Energy and Communications; and a Department of the Marine and Natural Resources emerged through the transfer of responsibility for forestry and other matters from the Department of Agriculture and Food. It is fair to say that there is a degree of cynicism within the civil service about such innovations, which are carried out entirely without reference to their impact on civil service effectiveness and often disappear with the government that introduced them.

There is a clear ranking in the perceived importance of ministerial portfolios, with Finance generally accepted as the most important (after the Taoiseach, of course) because of its responsibility for economic management and for public expenditure. Foreign Affairs is also considered a senior department, given its key role in European Union business (Laver, 1994, p. 157). Establishing a ranking of departments is made more difficult by the way in which departments are frequently chopped and changed when a new government is formed. In addition to the natural desire of all parties in a coalition to have good seats at the cabinet table, individual parties will be influenced by their particular policy priorities in the coalition bargaining process. For example, the position of Minister for the Environment, while not a glamorous portfolio, is considered a strategic one because of the opportunities it offers to allocate public investment in physical infrastructure such as roads and housing (Finlay, 1998, p. 8). Fairly or not, it is taken for granted that the constituency and region from which the incumbent minister hales will benefit disproportionately from public policy decisions during his or her term of office.

A Taoiseach's selection of ministerial colleagues will be influenced by a number of factors. There are always more aspiring ministers than there are cabinet seats available, and so some hearts are likely to be broken. Among probable calculations will be the need to have competent colleagues in key departments and to make sure that all sections of the party are represented as far as possible so as to prevent the growth of factions. There may also be electoral considerations, whether to reward colleagues whose efforts have produced a premium of seats for the party in their constituencies, or to avoid the charge that some region is under-represented and by implication disadvantaged; this is often where the less important departmental portfolios are useful. Finally, since 1982 every government has included at least one woman minister, and it is highly unlikely that any Taoiseach would entirely ignore gender representation in constructing a government.

Once the personnel and the allocation of portfolios have been finalised – in the case of a single party government by the Taoiseach, in the case of a coalition by the Taoiseach and the other party leader or leaders – the Dáil will be asked to confirm the nominees *en bloc*. This is usually a formality, since a government could not be formed if it could not command a Dáil majority for such a vote. The same usually applies when a minister leaves office and is replaced. We should note, however, the important case of the withdrawal of Dr McDaid's nomination as Minister for Defence in 1991 under pressure from Fianna Fáil's coalition partners, the Progressive Democrats, who objected to his nomination.

Following the appointment of the government, the Taoiseach will in due course nominate up to seventeen 'Ministers of State' (junior ministers) outside the cabinet. With the exception of the Chief Whip, these are not entitled to attend government meetings unless invited specifically to talk about some matter affecting departmental responsibilities (although during the Rainbow Coalition of 1994–97 the Democratic Left junior minister Pat Rabbitte was allowed to attend all meetings, and the same facility was extended to the PD junior minister Bobby Molloy in the following government). Even more than in filling government posts, a Taoiseach will be mindful of regional and constituency considerations when appointing junior ministers, and may also wish to bring in new blood who in time will graduate to the cabinet. In coalitions junior ministries are also deployed in key departments so as to provide a balance of representation between the participating government parties.

While problems often arise between ministers and junior ministers within departments, such tensions appear to stem more from personal competition for publicity and credit for policy successes than from genuine party or policy differences. It is said that ministers of state are commonly starved of high profile work by their senior colleagues, although some have established considerable reputations for themselves in areas such as European Affairs, where the workload is so heavy – and, arguably, the constituency payback so low – that a cabinet minister is glad to have a junior colleague to share the burden. Furthermore, in coalitions it may be that ministers of state from the smaller parties have a greater chance of carving out a niche for themselves than those from the largest coalition party. Precisely because they are so few, they can afford to hold out for substantive roles, knowing that the larger party can afford to placate them. Thus, for example, the Progressive Democrat junior minister Liz O'Donnell played a very public role in the Irish team that negotiated the 1998 Good Friday Agreement at Stormont.

The functioning of the government

The cabinet

Like most of its European counterparts, the Irish constitution is fairly vague on the actual organisation of cabinet government, concentrating instead on the conditions under which governments may be formed or may fall (Blondel, 1988, pp. 5–6). In practice the cabinet determines the overall policy programme and aims of the government, it takes all major policy decisions and approves the budget and all other legislation to be submitted to the Dáil. It is the decision-making body of an executive structure composed of the Department of the Taoiseach, which includes the office of the Chief Whip, and the various ministerial departments with their attendant ministers of state.

The constitution describes the government as 'collectively responsible' to the Dáil for all its decisions and actions. This principle lies at the heart of cabinet government. In theory, it means that all members of the cabinet are bound by, and must uphold, all cabinet decisions. Farrell (1994), in his examination of government practice, found that ministers did not regard the cabinet as a 'mere rubber stamp' for departmental decisions. Rather, it was considered to be a considerable restraint on individual ministers. Gemma Hussey (1990, p. 12), a former minister for education, said that the Department of Finance 'rarely agreed to any spending proposal and fought the battles out at full cabinet'. The negotiations for the Partnership 2000 agreement (see chapter 11) also give an indication of the active role played by the cabinet, which certainly went well beyond a rubber stamp for decisions taken elsewhere. One participant in the talks recalled that issues identified as 'bottom line' for the voluntary and community sector were agreed only after consideration at two cabinet meetings and were included in the final text only hours before it went to print (Crowley, 1998, p. 78). Perhaps the clearest indication that cabinet meetings, in spite of their crowded agenda, do produce debate and conflict and are not merely an official stamp for an already agreed position is the care with which party leaders in both single party and coalition governments seek to manage the cabinet agenda. Depending on the issues and the personal style of the Taoiseach involved, meetings can be brisk or 'staggeringly interminable' (Finlay, 1998, p. 15).

Once a decision has been taken by cabinet it becomes a government position to which all members must give public support. The doctrine of cabinet confidentiality also requires that all cabinet discussions remain confidential and that all policy proposals and initiatives by individual ministers are discussed and approved by their colleagues before being made public. Such confidentiality permits free discussion of policy issues among ministers unconstrained by the impact that the espousal of particular views may have on the electorate. It also allows for the free discussion of sensitive material. If the cabinet is to maintain a united front and unanimously support all policy decisions taken by the government, it cannot make disagreements at cabinet public knowledge. Cabinet minutes, because of the requirement of confidentiality, are very brief, being little more than a record of decisions taken. Individual ministers are circulated only with the decisions relevant to their departments, not with the full minutes.

The absolute nature of cabinet confidentiality was called into question during the beef tribunal in 1992, when the Tribunal wished to ask ministers about cabinet discussions (Hogan, 1993, p. 131). The issue was taken to the Supreme Court, which ruled that collective cabinet responsibility and hence cabinet confidentiality were absolute constitutional principles and the Tribunal could not hear reports of cabinet debates. A referendum in

October 1997 on cabinet confidentiality explicitly enshrined the principle in the constitution, while relaxing the strict Supreme Court judgment very slightly.

The confidentiality of government decision-making more generally was liberalised to a significant degree in the 1997 Freedom of Information Act, which we discuss further later in the chapter. This Act creates for the first time a general right of access to government documents, qualified by a number of exemptions including diplomatic and security material. Hitherto such papers were covered by the Official Secrets Act and were generally not made available. Indeed, even historical documents were made widely available only under the National Archives Act of 1986, which released most government papers once they were more than thirty years old. The Freedom of Information Act, by allowing access to contemporary papers, clearly has a more immediate impact on the policy process. Cabinet papers are exempt but background and factual briefing papers must be made available as soon as a government decision is announced. Other government papers must be released after five years unless exempt under some other provision such as security. The precise impact of the legislation remains to be seen but international experience, while varied, does suggest that such legislation tends to improve standards of administration, as civil servants respond to the fact that documents could be made public quite quickly (Doyle, 1996, p. 77).

The cabinet customarily meets weekly in Government Buildings on Upper Merrion Street in Dublin (on Tuesdays when the Dáil is sitting, on Wednesdays at other times of the year). In principle, all ministers are required to attend; in practice, depending on the agenda and on ministers' other commitments, some may be missing. There is no quorum for the meetings. Additional meetings may also be convened, if required, at short notice. In addition to ministers, the government chief whip and the Attorney General also attend, while the Secretary General to the Government (a civil servant) takes the minutes and advises the meeting on aspects of procedure and precedent. Papers relating to the agenda are circulated beforehand to ensure that all ministers' departments will have had the opportunity to comment on any matters for decision that might affect them. Ministers of state and even some officials may be invited to attend to assist in the discussion of particular items. The Secretary General to the Government manages the government secretariat with a staff of civil servants; its role is a coordination one. Prior to 1979, the secretary of the Taoiseach's office also served as secretary to the government. Since then, the Secretary General has had the primary role of making sure that the business of government is properly coordinated.

In one respect Irish government does depart markedly from the European norm. This is in the area of cabinet committees to help reduce the workload of the grossly overburdened cabinet agenda. Blondel (1988, p. 10) describes the use of such committees as widespread – but not universal –

Box 10.1 How do we know how the government works?

Finding out how the government works entails drawing upon a number of sources. There are basic documents such as the constitution and laws, which describe the formal outlines of the system; in addition, there are off-the-record comments by officials and politicians giving their personal perceptions of how the system actually works. In between is a range of official sources: official publications; the reports of tribunals; the records of government meetings and of departments. As well as these, there are informal sources, including academic studies, the published recollections of former ministers and officials, and newspaper reporting.

Furthermore, it is likely that the Freedom of Information Act, which came into operation in April 1997, will significantly add to our knowledge of the workings of government. Finally, a great deal of information about government organisation and procedures is now available via the internet (see http: //www.irlgov.ie/irlgov/Contents.htm).

It is important to realise that no single kind of source sufficiently describes the way Irish government works, and that sources often conflict on matters of fact and interpretation. Take the example of the drive to eradicate human tuberculosis that began in the late 1940s. The Minister generally credited with responsibility for this, Noel Browne, gave his account in his celebrated autobiography, *Against the Tide*. His department's chief medical officer recalled affairs very differently, while a respected academic study also offered an altogether more complex story (Browne, 1986, pp. 110–24; Deeny, 1989, pp. 165–73; Barrington, 1987, pp. 15–61).

---

and as having widely varying functions and status in the different European states. In general their function 'is to propose (or in some cases even "take") decisions for the cabinet meeting. Often the result is that they tend to take decisions and filter to the cabinet meeting only those matters on which agreement has been achieved' (Blondel, 1988, p. 10). Although Ireland lacks an institutionalised system of cabinet committees comparable to European practice, it does make some use of more informal or *ad hoc* sub-committees, especially during coalition governments.

Such committees have been constituted from time to time, but have often been transient in nature rather than developing into permanent features of the cabinet landscape. Even those that have lasted in one form or another for decades under different administrations – for example on Northern Ireland and on Security – have never developed their own secretariats or pools of official expertise independent of the succession of ministers who serve on them over the years. They thus remain genuine subsets of each government, rather than forces for continuity in analysis and policy from one administration to the next. In coalition governments cabinet committees have been used to oil the wheels of inter-party government. In 1994, during the disagreements between the Fianna Fáil and Labour coalition partners over the appointment of Attorney General Harry Whelehan to the High Court, it was agreed that a cabinet sub-committee be set up 'to defuse the conflict' (Garry, 1995, p. 194). However, the general lack of a committee structure means that the majority of questions facing the government, major and minor, come to the cabinet table for discussion and decision.

During coalition governments a system of informal meetings between the party leaders has sometimes operated to circumvent unnecessary argument at cabinet. These meetings finalise the cabinet agenda and generally ensure that issues that are not capable of immediate resolution between the parties do not appear on the agenda until a compromise has been reached (Farrell, 1993, p. 158). However, there have been times when the junior party in a coalition has been 'left largely in the dark about key aspects of government business' by the Taoiseach, usually at times of strain between the parties (O'Halpin, 1997, p. 79; Finlay, 1998, pp. 70–1). Zimmerman (1997, p. 538), drawing on interviews with former ministers and civil servants, also reports that rules governing cabinet meetings and procedures relating to the circulation of material have on occasion been quite deliberately broken over the years.

The cabinet exerts a considerable degree of control over the Dáil through its ability to control parliamentary business. The Dáil may debate and enact legislation, but the cabinet decides what it will debate and the time allocated to different topics. In Ireland the cabinet's control over parliamentary business is almost total (Laver and Shepsle, 1994, pp. 294–5). This contrasts with practice in many other European states, for example Austria and Norway, where the parliamentary agenda is partly determined by a body within the legislature (Laver and Shepsle, 1994, p. 294). Cabinet supervision of the work of ministers is equally tight; all policy proposals by individual ministers require the cabinet's approval, and procedures are in place to ensure that all relevant ministers and departments have been properly consulted about any policy initiatives before these come to cabinet for a final decision. This is spelt out in the official guidelines for ministers, which are given to all cabinet members upon appointment: 'where proposals for legislation relate to matters on which government policy has not already been laid down, or where they include a new development or a material departure from existing policy, they should first be submitted to the Government [Cabinet] by way of a memorandum for a decision in principle' (Department of the Taoiseach, 1998a, p. 26). The Taoiseach's power as chairman of the cabinet is reflected in the rule that no item can be put on the government agenda without his approval.

The Department of the Taoiseach

In 1988 Jean Blondel observed that the role of the prime minister in most European states had grown substantially in importance since the early 1970s, and as a result prime ministers had also become more dominant figures in cabinet (Blondel, 1988, p. 9). In Ireland as elsewhere, that trend has continued for a combination of reasons, amongst them the growing emphasis on meetings of heads of government in European Union affairs and the increasing complexity of public business. The power of the Taoiseach, as we saw in chapter 9, stems from the control he has over the composition of the government and over the conduct of cabinet business, and usually also his influence as the leader of a political party, as well as from his position as actual and symbolic head of government. Officially the role of Taoiseach is described as one of providing leadership; he is responsible for 'setting the strategic direction of government, for the development of overall policy and for the coherent implementation of government policy' and must 'co-ordinate the efforts of his/her colleagues in the development and implementation of national and international policy' (Department of the Taoiseach, 1998, p. 3). From this, three primary functions can be distinguished: a general leadership role, especially important in key policy areas such as Northern Ireland, European Union affairs and international negotiations; an agenda setting role; and the overall management of the business of government. These roles are given organisational expression in the structure of the Department of the Taoiseach.

The department is organised essentially by function. The Taoiseach's private office coordinates the day to day official activities of the Taoiseach, and also liaises with the Government Information Services, which act as a public relations arm of the department. The Office of the Chief Whip is responsible for organising and coordinating government business in the Oireachtas. As well as keeping government deputies and senators in line, the chief whip acts as a channel of communication between government and opposition parties. The office also monitors the preparation of draft legislation within the bureaucracy.

Under the Secretary General to the Government are three divisions – the government secretariat, protocol, and European and international affairs – providing for interdepartmental coordination and the smooth and efficient functioning of government (Department of the Taoiseach, 1998, p. 5). The government secretariat services all government meetings, drawing up the agenda, circulating documentation to ministers and communicating decisions to government departments. The protocol division provides state protocol services, and also advises the government on its constitutional relationship with the President. The European and international affairs division supports the Taoiseach as a member of the European Council of the EU and in any other international responsibilities. The work of this division reflects the high degree of penetration of EU policy and administration into the process and outcomes of the Irish government's policy programme. The division works closely with the Department of Foreign Affairs in particular in identifying and responding to issues at EU level that affect Ireland's core interests. In such matters tensions can sometimes arise between the Department of the Taoiseach and other departments, which may resent what they perceive as interference in their policy areas.

Under the direction of the Secretary General to the Department of the Taoiseach there are, in addition to two divisions dealing essentially with routine administrative matters, three divisions dealing with policy areas in which the Taoiseach plays a key leadership role: Northern Ireland, Economic and Social Policy, and the Irish Financial Services Centre. The Northern Ireland division supports the essential input of the Taoiseach as leader of the state. All recent taoisigh have appointed special advisors on Northern Ireland to work in the Department of the Taoiseach, the most prominent of whom has been Martin Mansergh, who has worked for all Fianna Fáil taoisigh since Charles Haughey. Officials of the department have played a key role in the development of state policy on Northern Ireland.

The Economic and Social Policy division deals with the management and renegotiation of the social partnership agreements that have become a cornerstone of domestic policy since the Programme for National Recovery was negotiated in 1987. Since the negotiation of that first partnership agreement, the policy scope of such understandings has broadened beyond their initial focus on macro-economic policy parameters and pay bargaining to include a wide range of social issues. The centrality of the Department of the Taoiseach to the management of relations with and between the social partners reflects both its coordinating role and the imperative that the Taoiseach must take a leadership position on this funda-mental and central aspect of the overall policy programme of the state. In the Partnership 2000 negotiations the core of the government's negotiating team came from the Department of the Taoiseach, 'supplemented by ministers and senior civil servants from various departments, depending on the issue that was being discussed' (O'Donnell and Thomas, 1998, p. 132).

The three policy divisions under the Secretary General of the department, and the European and international affairs division under the Secretary General to the Government, give the Taoiseach and the officials of his department a central role in policy development in almost all the key areas of the government's policy programme.

The role of the Tánaiste

The constitutional role of the Tánaiste is a limited one, that of deputising for the Taoiseach in circumstances where the latter may be temporarily incapacitated or outside the state. Traditionally this was the role assigned to the Tánaiste even in coalition governments, although as a minister he or she had plenty of departmental work to do. The Tánaiste's role was, however, radically recast during the 1993–4 Fianna Fáil–Labour coalition. This was because the Labour leader Dick Spring, who was also Minister for Foreign Affairs, insisted on the creation of an Office of the Tánaiste that in some respects resembled, and was designed to shadow, the Department of the Taoiseach in its leadership and policy oversight role. This development was perceived partly as a response to the way in which the previous Fianna Fáil–PD coalition had ended amidst recriminations about alleged failures to follow cabinet procedures, and partly to provide the Tánaiste with a proper overview. As one Labour official put it, the Tánaiste 'must have the same breadth of understanding as the Taoiseach – but the Taoiseach has a hundred or more civil servants to help him do his job' (Finlay, 1998, p. 156). While the Fianna Fáil–PD coalition that formed the government in 1997 abandoned this and other innovations, it is possible that further efforts will be made to bolster the role of the Tánaiste in future coalitions.

Government departments

The role of the minister

Ministers are the political heads of government departments. They are charged with setting the policy parameters of their departments and with making all policy (rather than administrative) decisions. The minister takes decisions, but civil servants play a key role in the detailed development and implementation of policy.

Ministers' work loads are extremely heavy: as well as having departmental duties, they are members of the cabinet, leading figures in their political parties, and prominent constituency politicians. The time constraints on an individual minister may result in there being little political input into ongoing policy development even in key areas, with such matters being dealt with mainly by civil servants. Yet, there has been no attempt to develop the ministerial *cabinets* that are a feature of policy making and of political control of administration in many other European states, with the partial exception of the successful 'programme managers' experiment between 1993 and 1997. At that time, officials from inside and outside the public service were given the job of ensuring the implementation of the programmes for government agreed between the parties forming both the Reynolds–Spring government of 1993–94 and the Rainbow coalition of 1994–97. The originator of the programme managers concept had in fact planned a full blown *cabinet* system, but, in the words of a Labour official, 'to our surprise, there was immediate opposition' from the Department of the Taoiseach and the proposal was dropped (Finlay, 1998, p. 156). It is significant that, despite general acceptance that the innovation worked very well, once Labour left office the programme manager experiment was virtually ended (O'Halpin, 1997, pp. 81–2).

Even for the most energetic and innovative of ministers, policy innovation is limited by the need to get prior approval from the cabinet. The general policy direction and practical control of government business is exerted by the Taoiseach through the cabinet, while the Department of Finance keeps a nervous eye on any policy proposals that would involve additional expenditure (as almost every policy development does). Farrell points out that 'the concentration on the cabinet itself as the clearing house for information and the centre of all government decision-making severely restricts the independence of individual ministers'. On the basis of interviews with former ministers he concluded that 'with the rarest exceptions' ministers 'will always seek cabinet approval in policy matters', a necessary discipline if collective responsibility is to be maintained (Farrell, 1994, p. 77). The four categories of decision-making in which they felt unable to act on their own initiative were: issues involving cost, innovation, or coordination with other departments, or those regarded as politically sensitive. Cabinet ministers are bound into a formal system of consultation on policy initiatives and in the preparation of legislation that gives both the Department of the Taoiseach and the Department of Finance an oversight role, allows for consultation with other departments, and gives cabinet the final voice on the output and shape of policy. To be effective, a minister must therefore, in addition to being a convincing advocate for his or her department, be an influential member of the wider cabinet team. Within these constraints, however, cabinet ministers are ultimately judged by their colleagues, by the media and by the public to a large degree on their perceived performance in charge of a department, responsible not only for policy development and new legislation but also for the efficient and fair execution of existing law and policies.

The decisive role of ministers at crucial moments, as well as their ultimate responsibility for decisions reached, is indicated in a study by an Irish official of the crucial negotiations of the 1997 Treaty of Amsterdam. This highlights the degree to which even the most intricate EU agreements, for which committees of officials from the member states, the Council of Ministers and the European Commission make the most painstaking and intricate preparations, are ultimately concluded virtually unaided by ministers of the member states in marathon meetings (MacDonagh, 1998, pp. 190–5).

The civil service

Senior officials of government departments in legal terms have no independent role in policy making: under the Ministers and Secretaries Act of 1924 each minister is a 'corporation sole', the effect of which is that (with a few stated exceptions) civil servants can act only in the name of the minister (O'Halpin, 1991, pp. 295–6; Garvin, 1991, p. 51). The 1985 White Paper *Serving the Country Better*, the first sustained attempt since the 1924 Act to change the way that the civil service worked, did not propose to alter the basic corporation sole principle. Instead, it placed new emphasis on

changing the administrative process, invoking concepts such as quality of
service, accessibility, improved management of resources within departments,
and the imaginative use of information technology, as well as encouraging
staff mobility between departments at every level (Department of the Public
Service, 1985; Boland, Dowling and O'Halpin, 1986). These concepts were
elaborated on in the 1994 Strategic Management Initiative, which in turn
led on to the 1997 Public Service Management Act.

This Act recast the role of the most senior official in each department
– now styled the Secretary General – giving clearer powers to manage than
had been the case under the 1924 Ministers and Secretaries Act, the linch-
pin of the administrative system since independence. The impact of the
1997 Act can be assessed only in the longer term, although there is
already evidence that departments are uncertain about what strategic
management actually entails (McKevitt and Keogan, 1997). We may also
note the cautionary words of the then Taoiseach in introducing the measure:
its success would depend on ministers 'releasing their grip' to some
extent, an attitude that runs counter to the 'clientelist nature of much
Irish politics' which 'puts significant pressures on politicians to involve
themselves in detailed matters' (Boyle *et al.*, 1997, p. 6).

The degree of influence over policy outcomes that is exerted by the
civil service is a matter of debate. Research by Zimmerman reveals conflicting opinions from the former ministers and civil servants whom he
interviewed. Overwhelmingly, interviewees believed that ministers did not
play a 'direct role in the internal management of their departments': this
function was left entirely to the civil servants (Zimmerman, 1997, p. 540).
Former ministers did not view the department secretaries as their principal
advisors (even in the absence of an outside ministerial advisor or programme
manager), although it would be general practice to consult departmental
secretaries on major policy issues, where their experience would make
their advice invaluable (ibid., p. 538). Retired department secretaries,
while they corroborated this view, also played down the frequency with
which 'major policy issues' arose. They laid stress on the incremental,
continuous nature of policy making, with major changes in policy occurring only rarely (ibid., p. 538). It was this incremental approach that the
Labour party set out to change with its new approach to policy development and implementation in government between 1992 and 1997, so that
there would be far greater party political input into national affairs
(Finlay, 1998, p. 149).

It is probably in the incremental dimension of policy making that civil
servants exert their greatest influence, not only through their preparation
of information and the evaluation of policy alternatives, but also through
their ongoing contact with a wide range of interest groups concerned with
policy development in a particular department. Although interest groups
may occasionally get to meet the minister or minister of state (see chapter
11 for a fuller discussion), their usual point of contact is with civil servants

in the department, working on policy areas that are of concern to them. Such dealings between interest groups and the civil service are growing and becoming more systematic (O'Halpin and Connolly, 1999). Contacts of this sort are a two-way exchange of information, and the civil servants directly involved pass material that they consider significant up the line within their departments. Ultimately a senior official will determine how much material should reach the minister.

The position of the senior officials in a department allows them, should they choose, both to block policy with which they disagree and to promote policy of which they are in favour. The extent to which these tactics are employed by the civil service is a matter of some dispute. Farrell (1994, p. 83) found diverse views. Although only a handful of ministers thought that the obstruction of particular policy initiatives was 'usual', a larger number thought it occurred sometimes. There was more support from former ministers for the idea that civil servants were inclined to promote their own policy preferences, with varying assessments as to how successful this strategy was. These assessments ranged from the view that ministers in general had only a small impact on eventual legislation, to the opinion that ministers could easily detect, and therefore take into account, the overselling of particular lines of policy by civil servants (Farrell, 1994, p. 84).

The question of how much influence the higher civil service does and should exert on policy is not unique to Ireland. Laver and Shepsle state that the 'power of the civil service is acknowledged almost everywhere' in European states, particularly with regard to 'routine decisions, dealing more with the implementation of policy'. However in France, the Netherlands, Norway and Sweden, the senior civil servants have comparatively more power, as their 'professional knowledge' in certain policy areas is acknowledged (Laver and Shepsle, 1994, p. 303). In Ireland, by contrast, the relationship between the ministers was until 1997 defined by the Ministers and Secretaries Act of 1924, under which ministers were legally responsible for everything done by their officials, from the formulation of policy to the administration of departments, and to the most basic and routine clerical duties. Ministerial responsibility acted like a shield, behind which the actual policy roles of senior civil servants were hidden from public view. This position has now been somewhat altered by the Public Service Management Act 1997, which for the first time identified the role and responsibilities of senior civil servants and distinguished their responsibilities from those of the minister. The Act gave a public, legal accountability to the Secretary General of each government department and acknowledged the key strategic and managerial role that holders of this office play.

The Public Service Management Act of 1997 is part of a two-pronged change in the culture of government departments, aimed at making their operation both more efficient and more transparent. A process of public sector reform, strengthened by commitments in Partnership 2000, together with the drive towards open government embodied in the

Freedom of Information Act 1997, is significantly altering the ethos of government. Departments are now required (also under the Public Service Management Act) to produce detailed strategy statements as freely available public documents. This is a further development of the Strategic Management Initiative (SMI) introduced by the government in 1994 'as an attempt to enhance strategic capabilities in the civil service' (Boyle *et al.*, 1997, p. 3). The strategy statements detail the goals and objectives of the individual departments and set out how the department will achieve them. The Secretary General at the Department of the Taoiseach expressed the view that not only would the strategy statement provide 'a blueprint' for the work of the department but it would also provide 'the basis for formal delegation of responsibility and accountability' (Department of the Taoiseach, 1998a, p. 7). Also arising from the 1997 Act, and the recommendations of Partnership 2000, is the introduction of 'partnership committees' in the departments. These allow management, unions and staff to come together to facilitate the process of change and reform in the civil service 'by empowering staff at all levels to engage in a continuous process of improvement' (Link newsletter, 1999). This process is still at the experimental stage. There does appear to be a strong commitment to civil service reform, which aims to increase the effectiveness of the service but also more openly acknowledges the actual role played by the upper echelons of the civil service in policy making.

This wider process of public service change is placing a new emphasis on the effective management of resources, on the incorporation of strategic planning as a dynamic element of management, on customer consciousness, and on openness and transparency in policy formulation and decision making (Murray and Teahon, 1998, pp. 55–8). Interestingly, senior civil servants must observe the provisions of the 1995 Ethics in Public Office Act concerning the submission of an annual statement of personal interests, including gifts or benefits of one kind or another, that might influence them in the performance of their duties. Whether or not this is evidence of a possible problem of influence buying and corruption within the higher civil service is a moot point: while very few cases of public service corruption at any level have come to light, the proceedings of the 1991–94 beef tribunal raised some disturbing questions about official favouritism for some commercial interests over others.

Monitoring Irish government

Over the past two decades, the degree to which the government and the administrative system can be subjected to public scrutiny and held accountable for their actions has been greatly enhanced, with the pace of change accelerating in the 1990s. Four pieces of legislation are primarily responsible for this change: the Ombudsman Act of 1980, the National Archives Act of 1986, the Comptroller and Auditor General Act of 1993, and the Freedom of Information Act of 1997 (which has already been briefly discussed). Together, these have greatly increased external oversight of administrative practices and decision making, and cumulatively they represent a sea change in public knowledge of the activities of central government.

Individual citizens have been able to have their grievances against central government departments (and from 1986, also against local authorities and the health boards) investigated by impartial officials from the Office of the Ombudsman since 1984, when the *Ombudsman Act of 1980* came into operation (see also chapter 8 for discussion of the role of this office). This has put the actions and administrative practices of officials under unprecedented review. Since the Ombudsman began his work, investigations have uncovered not only individual cases of unfairness, maladministration, or mistakes by civil and public servants, but systemic problems with the decision making processes within the public service. For example, the Ombudsman has discovered serious anomalies in pensions regulations, which resulted in great unfairness to some individuals. Again, the investigations of a host of individual complaints of overcharging by Telecom Éireann in the mid-1980s disclosed the complete inadequacy and inaccuracy of the company's billing system. The office continues to face some problems in increasing awareness amongst both the general public and the political system of its capacity to help people. As in other countries, the Ombudsman has found that it is the least well off in society and those most dependent on the state's social services who are the least likely to seek his help, while a recent study reported that only a minority of TDs ever refer cases of possible error or maladministration to the Ombudsman (Martin, 1998). Nevertheless, there can be no doubt that the office has had a considerable impact on the approach of national, local and health board officials to their dealings with the public.

The *National Archives Act of 1986* came into operation in January 1991. It has transformed the way that students of Irish policy making and political history do their work. Under the Act, departments are obliged to make all records more than thirty years old available to the public for research (subject to a few exceptions where records dealing with sensitive matters such as state security can be withheld). This act has provided a wealth of material for people studying every aspect of politics and administration, and has transformed the study of Irish politics and public affairs since independence. It has enabled the writing of systematic and detailed studies of all aspects of Irish government from foreign policy to the development of local government (Kennedy, 1996; Skelly, 1997; Daly, 1997). It has also seen the uncovering of unpleasant truths about aspects of policy making and administration in the past, most notoriously in relation to the treatment of Jewish immigration and of the state's complicity in the unethical and sometimes illegal transport of Irish children for adoption in the United States without the consent (or even the knowledge) of their natural parents

(Keogh, 1998, pp. 207–8, 210; Milotte, 1997, pp. 94–122). Although such studies are necessarily historical, they inform and can have a considerable impact on public debate about contemporary challenges and problems in such areas.

The *Comptroller and Auditor General Act of 1993* is another crucial piece of legislation. The Comptroller and Auditor General (C&AG) is responsible for ensuring that all public money is properly handled and accounted for by the state. Although the C&AG is protected by Article 33 of the constitution, historically holders of the office were severely hampered in their work by three factors. The first was a lack of resources, linked to civil service dislike of their activities. The second was a lack of Oireachtas interest, which is probably explained by the winner takes all, majoritarian culture of the Dáil. The third was archaic legislation: the C&AG's powers came principally from the Exchequer and Audit Departments Act of 1866, a British measure introduced by the Chancellor of the Exchequer William Ewart Gladstone in the rather different circumstances of mid-Victorian Britain. Attempts by successive C&AGs to interpret their powers of audit and review in a more modern fashion ran into civil service obstruction for years (O'Halpin, 1985, pp. 506–7). In the late 1980s and early 1990s, however, under the guidance of an unusually assiduous chairman, the Fine Gael TD Gay Mitchell, the Dáil Committee of Public Accounts belatedly took an interest in these problems. A consensus emerged on the desirability of radical change. As well as closing crucial loopholes, the resulting 1993 Act empowered the C&AG to carry out Value for Money (VFM) audits, including comparative studies across the public sector. These have already occasioned much embarrassment for the institutions whose financial practices come under scrutiny, for example Irish universities whose sometimes questionable purchasing practices have been exposed (Comptroller and Auditor General, 1996). They also have an important exemplary function, encouraging other public sector institutions to handle state funds with due care so as to avoid criticism in the future.

The *Freedom of Information Act of 1997*, which came into operation in April 1998, is a powerful measure that confers three new legal rights on individuals: the right to consult official records held by government departments and other state agencies, subject to some security, commercial confidentiality, privacy and other provisos; the right to have personal information held on them corrected or updated if incomplete, inaccurate or misleading; and the right to be given reasons for decisions, taken by public bodies, that affect them. While it is too early to assess the long term impact of the Act, it is clear that it represents a reversal of the presumption of secrecy that has underpinned Irish government since independence (Doyle, 1996, pp. 78–81). It is, for example, in practice a far more powerful investigative instrument than a parliamentary question, until now the main overt means by which information could be dragged out of a government unwilling to release it voluntarily (see chapter 7). Furthermore, the Act is underpinned by a number of provisions designed to ensure that public bodies do not dodge their responsibilities by obfuscation, and officials are required actively to help enquirers to frame their questions in a way that ensures they find the material they are seeking. Significantly, among the earliest users of the measure have been opposition politicians wishing to find out what the government is up to.

Conclusion

This chapter has looked at the Irish government system undergoing a process of change. How fundamental or significant that change will be remains to be seen, but it is undeniable that the 1990s saw real developments. The Freedom of Information Act has ensured greater openness in government, while the Ethics in Public Office Act was a belated acknowledgement that corruption is a problem in the Irish as in all other European political and administrative systems. The Public Sector Management Act has altered the relationship between top civil servants and ministers in a way that may make the internal workings of the departments more transparent and that, by defining the responsibilities of senior civil servants more clearly, may encourage ministers to concentrate more on policy questions. Other measures have strengthened oversight of government. These changes have been driven by a number of diverse forces: the experience of coalition government, the need to deal with political scandals, public pressure for more openness in government, the development of social partnership as an energising force in public policy development, and the impact of new approaches to public management in the public service. The Irish government system is in some respects transforming itself following the trauma of scandals and the unsettling shifts in voter behaviour. However, in spite of the many welcome changes that are taking place the fundamentals of the system have remained intact. The Taoiseach and the cabinet will remain in an overwhelmingly dominant position, and their deliberations will continue to be secret; the degree of control, of innovation and of integrity exhibited by ministers of all parties will continue to vary widely; and senior civil servants will continue to play a crucial and largely unseen role in policy development.

References and further reading

Arnold, Bruce, 1994. *Haughey: His Life and Unlucky Deeds*. London: Harper Collins.
Barrington, Ruth, 1987. *Health, Medicine and Politics in Ireland, 1900–1970*. Dublin: Institute of Public Administration.
Blondel, Jean, 1988. 'Introduction', pp. 1–15 in Jean Blondel and Ferdinand Müller-Rommel (eds), *Cabinets in Western Europe*. Basingstoke: Macmillan.
Boland, John, John Dowling and Eunan O'Halpin, 1986. 'Serving the country better: a debate', *Administration* 34:3, pp. 287–301.
Boyle, Richard, Tony McNamara, Michael Mulreaney and Anne O'Keeffe, 1997. 'Review of developments in the public sector in 1996', *Administration* 44:4, pp. 3–41.

Browne, Noel, 1986. *Against the Tide.* Dublin: Gill and Macmillan.

Comptroller and Auditor General, 1996. *Procurement in Universities: Value for Money Audit no. 12.* Dublin: Stationery Office.

Crowley, Niall, 1998. 'Partnership 2000: empowerment or co-option?', pp. 69–81 in Peadar Kirby and David Jacobson (eds), *In the Shadow of the Tiger: New Approaches to Combating Social Exclusion.* Dublin: Dublin City University Press.

Daly, Mary, 1997. *The Buffer State: the Historical Roots of the Department of the Environment.* Dublin: Institute of Public Administration.

Deeny, James, 1989. *To Cure and to Care: Memoirs of a Chief Medical Officer.* Dublin: Glendale Press.

Department of the Public Service, 1985. *Serving the Country Better.* Dublin: Stationery Office.

Department of the Taoiseach, 1998. *Strategy Statement, 1998–2001.* Dublin: Stationery Office. [Also available at http://www.irlgov.ie/taoiseach/publication/smi/smi.htm].

Department of the Taoiseach, 1998a. *Cabinet Handbook.* Dublin: Stationery Office. [Also available at http://www.irlgov.ie/taoiseach/publication/cabinethandbook/contents.htm].

Doyle, John, 1996. 'Freedom of information: lessons from the international experience', *Administration* 44:4, pp. 64–82.

Farrell, Brian, 1993. 'The formation of the partnership government', pp. 146–61 in Michael Gallagher and Michael Laver (eds), *How Ireland Voted 1992.* Dublin: Folens and PSAI Press.

Farrell, Brian, 1994. 'The political role of cabinet ministers in Ireland', pp. 73–87 in Michael Laver and Ken Shepsle (eds), *Cabinet Ministers and Parliamentary Government.* Cambridge: Cambridge University Press.

Finlay, Fergus, 1998. *Snakes and Ladders.* Dublin: New Island Books.

Garry, John, 1995. 'The demise of the Fianna Fáil/Labour "Partnership" government and the rise of the "Rainbow" coalition', *Irish Political Studies* 10, pp. 192–9.

Garvin, Tom. 1991. 'Democracy in Ireland: collective somnambulance and public policy', *Administration* 39:1, pp. 42–54.

Hogan, Gerard, 1993. 'The Cabinet Confidentiality case of 1992', *Irish Political Studies* 8, pp. 131–7.

Hussey, Gemma, 1990. *At the Cutting Edge: Cabinet Diaries, 1982–1987.* Dublin: Gill and Macmillan.

Kennedy, Michael, 1996. *Ireland and the League of Nations, 1919–1946: International Relations, Diplomacy and Politics.* Dublin: Irish Academic Press.

Keogh, Dermot, 1998. *Jews in Twentieth-Century Ireland: Refugees, Anti-semitism and the Holocaust.* Cork: Cork University Press.

Laver, Michael, 1994. 'Party policy and cabinet portfolios in Ireland 1992: results from an expert survey', *Irish Political Studies* 9, pp. 157–64.

Laver, Michael and Ken Shepsle, 1994. 'Cabinet government in theoretical perspective', pp. 285–309 in Michael Laver and Ken Shepsle (eds), *Cabinet Ministers and Parliamentary Government.* Cambridge: Cambridge University Press.

Link Newsletter, 1999. [http://www.irlgov.ie/taoiseach/publication/link/frmain.htm, 30 June 1999].

MacDonagh, Bobby, 1998. *Original Sin in a Brave New World: An Account of the Negotiation of the Treaty of Amsterdam.* Dublin: Institute of European Affairs.

Martin, Shane, 1998. 'The ombudsman: unwelcome competition or a helping hand for Irish parliamentarians?', paper presented at 3rd Workshop of Parliamentary Scholars and Parliamentarians, Wroxton, 8–9 August.

McKevitt, David and Justin F. Keogan, 1997. 'Making sense of strategy statements: a user's guide', *Administration*, 45:3, pp. 3–25.

Milotte, Mike, 1997. *Vanished Babies: the Secret History of Ireland's Baby Export Business.* Dublin: New Island Books.

Murray, Frank and Paddy Teahon, 1998. 'The Irish political and policy making system and the current programme of change', *Administration* 45:4, pp. 39–58.

O'Donnell, Rory and Damien Thomas, 1998. 'Partnership and policy making', pp. 117–46 in Seán Healy and Brigid Reynolds (eds), *Social Policy in Ireland: Principles, Practice and Problems.* Dublin: Oak Tree Press.

O'Halpin, Eunan, 1985. 'The Dáil Committee of Public Accounts, 1961–1980', *Administration* 32:4, pp. 483–511.

O'Halpin, Eunan, 1991. 'The civil service and the political system', *Administration* 38:3, pp. 283–302.

O'Halpin, Eunan, 1997. 'Partnership programme managers in the Reynolds–Spring coalition, 1993–4: an assessment', *Irish Political Studies* 12, pp. 78–91.

O'Halpin, Eunan and Eileen Connolly, 1999. 'Parliaments and pressure groups: the Irish experience of change', pp. 124–44 in Philip Norton (ed.), *Parliaments and Pressure Groups in Western Europe.* London: Frank Cass.

Skelly, Joseph Morrison, 1997. *Irish Diplomacy at the United Nations, 1945–1965: National Interests and the International Order.* Dublin: Irish Academic Press.

Zimmerman, Joseph F., 1997. 'The changing roles of the Irish department secretary', *Public Administration Review* 57:6, pp. 534–42.

11   The role of interest groups in the policy making process

Gary Murphy

Defining interest groups is a perennial problem, especially given the proliferation of organisations that have attempted to influence the policy
process in recent years. As one commentator has asked, should we conclude
that 'any organisation which seeks to any degree to influence public policy
is to be regarded as an interest group?' (Wilson, 1991, p. 7). Such a broad
definition would embrace political parties. A satisfactory definition will
stipulate two criteria: that the organisation has some autonomy from
government, and that it tries to influence policy (Wilson, 1991, p. 8). Thus
as a formal definition, the view of Kimber and Richardson that a pressure
group or interest group 'may be regarded as any group which articulates
demands that the political system or subsystem should make an authoritative
allocation' (Kimber and Richardson, 1974, p. 1) is amongst the most useful.
Adding the rider that such groups do not themselves seek to occupy the
position of authority has the effect of excluding political parties.

A feature of policy making in Ireland in recent years has been the
increasingly vigorous lobbying on behalf of individual or private business
interests, in an attempt to influence government policy. Thus any discussion
of interest groups has now to take into account private business interests as
well as the cause centred and sectional groups with which interest group
study has been traditionally associated. Interest group politics in essence
means influencing the formation, passage through the legislature, and
implementation of public policy by means of contact with ministers, civil
servants, political parties, individual politicians and the public. It can also
mean attempting to change existing legislation by lobbying within the
relevant area of public policy (Punnett, 1994, p. 142). Ultimately the existence of interest groups places constraints on governments in that the
'process of governing societies always involves some accommodation of the
wishes of pressure and interest groups' (Richardson, 1993, p. 11).

Interest groups and the political process

The centrality of interest groups to the political process is thus clear, as
much of the process of governance can be seen as the management of the

'interface between governments and groups' (Richardson, 1993, p. 10). This can be vividly seen in western Europe. While modern European states have a tradition of strong political parties or administrative elites, which in theory could insulate them from particularist private demands (Aspinwall and Greenwood, 1998, p. 1), in practice governments interact extensively with interest groups right across the continent. A central element of west European democracy has been the so-called 'co-optation' of interest groups into the policy process; the interrelationship between governments and interest groups, depending on the specific policy area, can often be of greater significance for policy outcomes than general elections (Richardson, 1993, p. 12). Thus notwithstanding the strength of political and administrative elites, interest groups have a substantial role to play in western European polities. As Heisler and Kvavik emphasise, a common denominator of the European polity is 'a decision making structure characterised by continuous, regularised access for economically, politically, ethnically, and/or subculturally based groups to the highest levels of the political system, i.e. the decision making subsystem' (Heisler and Kvavik, 1974, p. 48).

Models of interest group activity

Where does Ireland fit into such a model? Within the decision making subsystem as outlined by Heisler and Kvavik, two distinct models of interest group behaviour are particularly useful: corporatism and pluralism. The *corporatist* model suggests that interest groups are closely associated with the formal political process and play a critical role in both formulating and implementing major political decisions. Thus large and powerful interest groups monopolise the representation of the interests of a particular functional section of the population. This usually encapsulates organised labour, the farmers and employers. Moreover, these interest groups are organised in a hierarchical manner, each typically having a powerful peak organisation. In the Irish case, for example, these would probably include the Irish Congress of Trade Unions (ICTU), the Irish Business and Employers Confederation (IBEC) and the Irish Farmers' Association (IFA), coordinating strategy at the apex of a pyramid of organisations (Gallagher, Laver and Mair, 1995, p. 360). These organisations negotiate with each other and with government to produce agreed outcomes that minimise social and economic disruption.

They are also, however, ready to oppose each other if they perceive that their interests are threatened. For instance the IFA maintains that in many cases it is up against well-resourced pressure groups, which might be environmental, animal welfare, consumer or politically related. To resist these pressures, it insists, farmers must present a strong united voice. Thus it perceives itself to be at the forefront in defending the farmers' interests. Indeed, its motto claims it is 'fearlessly representing' the interests of Irish farmers to government, European Commission, agri-business, the media and social partners as well as internationally.[1]

Thus even within a corporatist model, the ability of interest groups to present their case forcefully is an important consideration. What is more important is that agreements made within a true corporatist system entail a comprehensive role for the social partners in the implementation of policy and are applicable in wide policy domains, not simply in the economy (Cawson, 1986, p. 37; Gallagher, Laver and Mair, 1995, p. 362). Economic policy formulation that involves government, industry, trade unions and perhaps farmers is better described as tripartite. Some scholars have also used the term meso-corporatism to describe those countries where corporatist practices take place only for some groups or issues, with pluralism prevailing for other groups and issue areas (Cawson, 1985; Regan and Wilson, 1986, p. 394).

The *pluralist* model maintains that individual interest groups apply pressure on political elites in a competitive manner, and attributes power in policy making to individual groups operating in particular areas at particular times. This competition is usually disorganised and its essence is to exclude other interest groups from the policy process. Unlike corporatism, pluralism offers no formal institutional role to interest groups in decision making or the implementation of policy. Interest groups are assumed to be self-generating and voluntary. This allows government a critical role in mediating between groups that are competing with each other to represent the interests of the same classes of people in similar areas of economic and social activity. Indeed, group activity may be fragmented and group membership may only be a small proportion of the possible total. Moreover, groups in the same field of interest may be poorly coordinated by peak organisations, resulting in a pluralist rather than a corporatist model of behaviour emerging. In the pluralist model, better organised interest groups with more resources and more strategic social, economic and political positions than others can be relatively powerful influences on government (Budge *et al.*, 1997, p. 159).

Interest groups in Ireland

Given the difficulty of measuring degrees of corporatism and pluralism, there has been no consensus on the application of these models to the policy process, either generally or in relation to the Irish case. Beyond doubt, interest groups play a major role in policy formulation and implementation in Ireland. For the purposes of this chapter they can be divided into two broad categories. On the one hand are those with a *sectional* base, such as trade unions, farmers' associations and business organisations, as well as professional bodies such as the Irish Medical Organisation and the Institute of Chartered Accountants of Ireland, which are self regulating. The second category comprises *cause centred* groups such as Conradh na Gaeilge and Youth Defence, which lobby to promote a particular cause: in these cases, the promotion of the Irish language and the anti-abortion agenda respectively.

Those interest groups that we classify as sectional are increasing in number. In 1998 there were twenty-five agricultural organisations, twenty-seven teaching organisations, nine civil service associations, four different Garda (police) representative bodies, three defence force representative bodies, seventeen local government associations, sixty-three trade unions affiliated to the Irish Congress of Trade Unions, two unions not affiliated to ICTU, and over 250 other trade and professional bodies that were organised to represent the interests of their members. Within these there were a number of distinct business organisations, with IBEC having over fifty separate sector associations affiliated to it (Institute of Public Administration, 1998, pp. 296–334).

There is a similarly impressive number of cause centred groups. Again in 1998 there were sixty-one different arts organisations, eighty-nine health organisations, twenty-two Irish language organisations, forty-six youth organisations, and over 250 other organisations that espoused various social, political and cultural causes (Institute of Public Administration, 1998, pp. 335–81). Although this conveys the impression that there are a lot of cause centred groups, membership of voluntary organisations in Ireland is in fact low by west European standards, and Ireland's proliferation of cause centred groups is not unusual. In a world values survey conducted at the beginning of the 1990s, 49 per cent of people in Ireland belonged to a voluntary organisation. This placed Ireland below Austria, Belgium, Britain, Denmark, Finland, Iceland, the Netherlands, Sweden and Germany, but ahead of France, Italy, Portugal and Spain (Therborn, 1995, p. 307). In terms of sectional groups, Ireland's main economic interests can usefully be compared with those in Germany, where there are only seventeen major trade unions, all of which belong to the German Trade Union Federation, which represents over 80 per cent of all unionised workers. This peak organisation can be compared to ICTU in the Irish context. Moreover while there are hundreds of employers' organisations, these again are part of a larger umbrella body, the Confederation of German Employers' Associations, which deals with social policy, including collective bargaining. There are two other peak organisations in Germany – the Association of German Chambers of Industry and Commerce and the Federation of German Industries (Gallagher, Laver and Mair, 1995, pp. 374–5) – but the key point is that all three organisations coordinate their activities and often function as a single entity, similar to IBEC in Ireland.

Sectional groups

Tripartite agreements

Ireland has had a tradition of tripartite consultation in the public policy sphere since the early 1960s. It was during this era that the economic interests (farmers, trade unions and business associations) were invited to participate in the work of a number of national bodies that were concerned with formulating a new approach to economic management (Lee, 1989, pp. 399–404; Horgan, 1997, pp. 228–49). This whole approach, coordinated by the Taoiseach, Seán Lemass, had as its ultimate aim entry to the European Economic Community, which the government of the day assumed would happen sometime in 1963–64. It was with this goal in mind (and the perceived need to show a united front to western Europe) that the economic interest groups were co-opted into this tripartite approach to economic management (Murphy, 1997, pp. 57–68).

In the 1970s, however, the focus of state policy shifted; corporatist policies in the economic sphere were dropped, and the process was no longer directly aided by government financial support. Notwithstanding this, the continuing high level of state intervention in the economy ensured a continuing and important role for the Confederation of Irish Industry (McCann, 1993, p. 51). To a lesser degree, this was also the case with the trade unions and the farmers' organisations. While the sectional groups were not central to economic decision making, they were far from isolated voices in the wilderness. The tripartite approach to governance took centre stage again in 1987 with the coming to power of the minority Fianna Fáil government. The approach has since evolved into a system that aims to keep all the major interests reasonably happy by giving them a role within the broad economic approach of the state, which in turn will perpetuate a national economic and social coalition of sorts. This social partnership cements these economic interests, now known as the 'social partners', to a coherent and consistent policy framework. This consensual approach mirrors that of northern European social democracies such as Sweden, Norway and Denmark; indeed, since the mid-1990s Ireland has experienced the kind of economic success that was previously associated with such countries. In this respect the Irish approach has been markedly different to the dismissive tone sometimes taken by British governments in regard to organised labour in particular.

It was during a period of deep depression in the mid-1980s that the social partners, acting in the tripartite National Economic and Social Council, agreed a strategy to overcome Ireland's economic difficulties. The NESC's *Strategy for Development* (1986) formed the basis upon which, in 1987, the new Fianna Fáil government and the social partners negotiated the Programme for National Recovery (PNR), which was followed by three further agreements (see Box 11.1). What made these agreements different from the agreements of the 1960s onwards was that they were not simply centralised wage mechanisms but agreements on a wide range of economic and social policies such as tax reform and the evolution of welfare payments (O'Donnell and Thomas, 1998, pp. 118–19).

With the development of the Partnership 2000 agreement a watershed was reached, as for the first time agencies from the voluntary sector, includ-ing charities and self help groups, were included in consultation and

---

Box 11.1 Social partnership agreements in Ireland since the 1980s

A number of broadly tripartite agreements have been made between governments and the main economic interest groups since the mid-1980s, under the auspices of the NESC (the National Economic and Social Council, an advisory body through which employers, trade unions, farmers and senior civil servants analyse policy issues). The first of these represented a strategy to escape from the circle of economic stagnation, rising taxes, increasing debt and massive unemployment that surrounded the Irish economy in the mid-1980s. Its success paved the way for further agreements in the 1990s, and these agreements were widely seen as a major explanation for the rapid economic growth that Ireland enjoyed in the 1990s (the so-called 'Celtic tiger' economy). The main agreements have been:

- The Programme for National Recovery (PNR), running from 1987 to 1990
- The Programme for Economic and Social Progress (PESP), running from 1990 to 1993
- The Programme for Competitiveness and Work (PCW), running from 1994 to 1996
- Partnership 2000, running from 1997 to 2000.

The negotiation of each of these social partnership agreements was preceded by a NESC strategy report, which set out the shared perspective of the social partners on the achievements and limits of the previous programme and the parameters within which a new programme would be negotiated.

---

ultimately negotiations. This new initiative resulted from complaints that the government and the economic partners were missing an opportunity to tackle social exclusion in an integrated fashion by ignoring the voices of other interest groups. The most graphic illustration of this widening of the social partnership parameters was the inclusion of the Irish National Organisation of the Unemployed (INOU) in the negotiations, the first time that the unemployed had been seen by the government as an actor with something to offer to social partnership negotiation. In all, eight organisations were involved in what was known as the 'second tier' of interest groups in the negotiations leading up to Partnership 2000: the INOU, the Conference of Religious in Ireland, the National Women's Council, the National Youth Council of Ireland, the ICTU unemployed centres, the Society of St. Vincent de Paul, Protestant Aid and the Community Platform, which included the travelling community and people with disabilities. The inclusion of such groups shows that while the main sectional groups (farmers, employers and trade unions) remain the critical players in the realm of social partnership, the development of a 'social pillar', in terms of economic and social development, has come to be accepted as intrinsic to the conclusion of any national development plan. Partnership 2000 looked forward to nothing less than the enactment of a new social contract. For the first time in the history of centralised bargaining in the state it provided an integrated package of pay rises and tax cuts that enabled trade union leaders, for example, to calculate the real value of the deal, in order to sell it to their members.

Other sectional group activity

Of course, the interest groups involved in social partnership are also frequently in competition for favourable decisions from government. For example, following a number of fatalities on building sites, the trade union concerned has lobbied for a scheme that would give workers more protection, while the employers' organisation argues that existing legislation is adequate. Moreover, it should be borne in mind that not all sectional groups are involved in social partnership. An example of a sectional group that is outside the realm of social partnership is the Vintners' Federation of Ireland, which lobbies on behalf of the publicans of the country, and played a very important role in opposing the plans of the Minister for the Environment during the 1993–94 Fianna Fáil–Labour coalition to reduce the drink-driving limit. Another example is the Law Society of Ireland, which, despite its best lobbying attempts, was compelled in 1991 to change its admission and examination procedures for aspiring solicitors.

The question of access is crucially important for sectional interest groups, which pursue their aims and exercise their influence on policy through public or private channels, directly or indirectly. Thus the major economic interest groups have representatives on the boards of state companies, on various advisory and review bodies, and at the European level. They have adequate resources to carry out their own research and analysis of decisions, to be taken at various levels, that could affect them. They have excellent access to the bureaucracy at both the national and international level and they lobby continuously (O'Halpin, 1993, p. 200). As an illustration, we will look at the main sectional interest groups: the IFA, ICTU and IBEC.

The major sectional groups in action

The IFA spends nearly half of its income from farmers every year on its European lobbying efforts. While Ireland has only 1.2 per cent of the European Union's nine million farmers, the IFA claims that its influence in Europe is far greater than its numerical strength would indicate. This influence is achieved by maintaining a permanent office in Brussels which is manned by the association's director of European affairs, who plays a vital role in promoting and defending Irish farmers' interests in Europe and acts as an effective communications link with EU decision makers. The Brussels office provides advice and research of a technical and political nature, which again is vital to IFA representatives when lobbying abroad. It has the back-up of twenty expert staff in its head office in Dublin, who are well versed in European policy, and attempts to ensure that all IFA policies are drafted so as to command the support of EU farm organisations across member states.

The key point about lobbying is that the structures put in place by organisations such as the IFA are of little benefit unless they can be used effectively to influence the decision makers in the government, the European Union and agri-business. Central to the effectiveness of such a pressure group is to have good communication links with sympathetic parties. The IFA has both formal and informal links with Fianna Fáil and Fine Gael at professional and voluntary levels. This ensures that when governments change, the association's influence on the parties in government is not diminished. Fundamental to its success as a pressure group, then, is well researched and professionally documented policy formulation. Intrinsic to the success of any such policy is the implementation of a strategy to deliver for its members. Since its foundation as the National Farmers' Association in 1955, the IFA has developed a very professional and flexible approach to political pressure. It lobbies decision makers and politicians on all relevant issues, and its national representatives meet with the Taoiseach, the Minister for Agriculture, department officials, agri-business and, indeed, any political actor who can bring about a favourable result.

At local level, the IFA uses its voluntary officers and links with individual political party representatives, whether backbenchers or county councillors, to lobby on various issues, using these political representatives to try to secure its objectives. If this is not enough to deliver its aims, other strategies such as national demonstrations will be considered to keep the pressure on decision makers. Ever since a ground-breaking march in Dublin by the NFA in 1966, the IFA has been the foremost interest group engaged in demonstrating outside government offices.

The other main economic interest groups, the trade unions and the business organisations, have similar access to the decision making process and employ lobbying techniques akin to those of the farming organisations. While the trade union movement was substantially weakened during the early 1980s (Weinz, 1986, p. 100), its re-emergence as a central player in the social partnership context since 1987 has made it an intrinsic part of the fabric of public policy in Ireland. As a social partner, ICTU has represented unions in the negotiation of national agreements on social and economic issues, as well as on pay and conditions of workers. ICTU is the central authority for the trade union movement in Ireland, with 97 per cent of trade union membership in the country affiliated to it. It has sixty-three affiliated unions, forty-nine of them in the Republic, where about two-thirds of the membership of around 725,000 is based. Its main function is to coordinate the work of trade unions operating in Ireland. It is represented on government advisory bodies and it proposes and names representatives of labour for nomination to a number of bodies, such as the Labour Relations Commission and the Labour Court. It also coordinates union action through industrial committees and groups and assists unions in the resolution of industrial disputes.[2]

The business community is represented through IBEC, which believes that the industry's bargaining position is strengthened through representation of the widest range of members across the fullest range of issues in a single organisation (McCann, 1993, p. 52). IBEC represents and provides economic, commercial, employee relations and social affairs services to about 4,000 companies and organisations, from all sectors of economic and commercial activity. It attempts to shape policies and influence decision making in a way that develops and protects its members' interests, and it does this by representing these interests to government, state agencies, trade unions, other national interest groups and the general public. It is also active on the European level, and works through its Brussels office, the Irish Business Bureau, on behalf of business and employers to ensure that European policy is compatible with IBEC's own objectives for the development of the Irish economy.[3] This access to the structure of decision making gives both IBEC and ICTU powerful leverage in their attempts to protect their members' interests. Any semblance of a threat from any of the social partners to withdraw from one of the partnership agreements is usually met with an urgent round of discussions to ensure that the demands of the sector are met without jeopardising the remit of the agreements.

Cause centred groups

Cause centred groups have been significant players in the policy process since the early 1980s. Whether they are *ad hoc* groups formed to press for a single measure, as has become prevalent in the area of moral politics, or organisations with a permanent mission such as Greenpeace or the Simon Community, their activities and influence have become much more visible. Groups that formed in the hope of getting a single piece of legislation enacted have become quite vocal in recent years, particularly where moral controversies are concerned for, without doubt, the politics of morality have been conducted in the domain of the interest group. The classic example is the divorce referendum of 1995. The campaign was primarily fought by concerned interest groups, as the government deliberately pursued a low key approach, with one minister claiming that by doing so the hysteria associated with the 1986 divorce campaign would be avoided (Girvin, 1996, p. 179). The fact that all the political parties stood back let the various interest groups involved come to the fore in the debate.

In the abortion and divorce referendums of the 1980s, the forces of moral conservatism had shown themselves to be far better skilled in modern pressure group techniques than those who sought to modernise Irish society. By the time of the 1995 divorce referendum, however, those groups in favour of the amendment, such as the Divorce Action Group and the Right to Remarry Group, had become efficient operators in the game of pressure politics. In the words of one journalist who followed the campaign closely: 'without the efforts of members of voluntary organisations with direct experience of marriage breakdown who . . . felt it necessary to campaign for divorce independently of the government, the amendment would have been lost' (Coulter, 1995).

Prior to this campaign it was those groups who wished to impose a distinctly Catholic view of morality on the state who were the acknowledged kingpins in the field of pressure group politics. The Society for the Protection of the Unborn Child sprang up completely unannounced in 1981 and campaigned along with other like-minded groups under the umbrella of the Pro-Life Amendment Campaign. Within two years, their campaign successfully persuaded the government of the day to call a referendum with the purpose of introducing an amendment which would in effect guarantee the rights of the unborn child and constitutionally outlaw abortion (Girvin, 1986). This referendum was primarily due to the incessant lobbying of a number of highly vocal interest groups, which argued that the legal ban on abortion could be overturned in the courts and that a constitutional ban on abortion was imperative. The Fine Gael–Labour government of the day appeared to be ill equipped to deal with such a highly organised pressure group, and the result was a decade of social division, whose effects have not yet disappeared.

While interest groups have come to the fore in fighting various referendum campaigns, it should be stressed that women's interest groups have been at the centre of political life since the early 1970s. Organisations such as AIM (Action, Information, Motivation) and Cherish (a single mothers' organisation) became important lobbying agencies for changes in family law and the status of women. Moreover the National Women's Council of Ireland, which represented established women's organisations, sought to influence government policy in a wide range of areas affecting women (Galligan, 1998, p. 54). Both AIM and the Rape Crisis Centre were successful in having their demands accepted by policy makers, and each group was closely involved in shaping the detail of legislation as it impacted on its interests. The Rape Crisis Centre ran a sustained lobbying campaign between 1981 and 1990 in its attempts to reform the Criminal Law (Rape) Act of 1981. As Galligan notes, 'they presented a case for policy changes to government advisory bodies and to parliamentary committees; raised public awareness of the need to reform the legislation through use of the media; and finally negotiated with the Minister for Justice and government administrators on the reform proposals' (Galligan, 1998, p. 119). The ultimate result was the passage of the Criminal Law (Rape) (Amendment) Act of 1990. AIM, for its part, was involved in a number of policy initiatives, most notably in its lobbying over a number of years for the introduction of divorce. As a cause centred group it also had an input into such legislation as the Family Law (Maintenance of Spouses and Children) Act of 1976, the Family Home Protection Act of 1976, and the Judicial Separation Act of 1987 (Galligan, 1998, pp. 104–5). It is not all a story of success, however, as regards women's interest groups; for instance, they have had little success in the area of employment equality (Galligan, 1998, p. 170).

While moral interest groups have had a heightened public profile, due to the important role they have played in various referendum campaigns, it is important to stress that cause centred activity in the policy process stretches well beyond the politics of morality. For instance there are twenty-two different Irish language associations, ranging from educational groups to organisations that simply promote the development of Irish culture. All, in one form or another, aim to promote the use of the Irish language. The objective of Comhhdháil Náisiúnta na Gaeilge (CNG), for example, is to strengthen and consolidate goodwill and support for the Irish language and its use as a living language, so that Irish may come to be used more widely. For CNG this entails strategic planning for the promotion of Irish in both the political arena and public life, through increased status for the Irish language and the rights of Irish speakers and the maintenance and development of the language and the Irish community in general. Likewise Gael-Linn Teoranta sees its aim as the promotion of Irish language culture throughout Ireland. While CNG is theoretically a coordinating body for the numerous Irish language organisations, each of these sees itself as promoting different aspects of the same objective (the strengthening of the Irish language). Consequently, each looks out for its own interest in terms of lobbying and seeks funds, in various guises, from different government departments, most notably the Departments of Education and of Arts, Heritage and the Gaeltacht. The result of this is that CNG is not really a coordinating body at all, but simply one of many competing individual organisations, all of which have similar objectives. While all these organisations attempt in some shape to promote the Irish language, they can differ dramatically over the means of achieving that aim. For instance there was no unanimity over the objectives of the Irish language television station, Telefís na Gaeilge, which was launched in October 1996. Some groups wanted it to concentrate on local Gaeltacht issues, while others wanted the station to have a wider remit to appeal to a larger countrywide audience.

Influencing public policy

Interest groups pursue their goals through a number of different channels. These include public and private pressure on government, individual politicians and other interest groups, and use of the mass media. Yet, despite all the other avenues open to various groups, it is still the Oireachtas and its members who remain the prime focus, principally because parliament is the centre for information, access and publicity for such groups. TDs have access to inside information, can generate publicity (particularly given the televising of Dáil proceedings) and are in a position to put pressure on governments and individual ministers by tabling parliamentary questions. In fact all the political parties as well as TDs and county councillors report that they receive an ever increasing amount of material from interest groups and lobbyists (O'Halpin and Connolly, 1999, p. 132).

The ability of interest groups to extract concessions from government was evident in the difficulties experienced by the 1973–77 Fine Gael–Labour coalition over its introduction of a wealth tax. This tax was part of the Labour party's price for participation in government and was part of a wider initiative in tax reform, intended to increase the tax burden on the better off (Sandford and Morrissey, 1985, p. 61). It was accepted with great reluctance by Fine Gael as, besides being open to legitimate technical criticism, it was inherently unattractive to most Fine Gael members of the government. With the government fundamentally divided on the issue, the main interest groups involved – the farmers and the business organisations – launched a wave of attacks on the proposal in an attempt to obtain concessions for their members (Sandford and Morrissey, 1985, pp. 71–81). The result was that the government came under increasing pressure from a number of directions. The agricultural lobby was represented by about twenty-five different organisations, which all made detailed submissions to the government and encouraged their members to lobby their local TDs. All these organisations in their various forms argued that Irish agriculture was under-capitalised and that farmers did not have the income to pay the wealth tax (Sandford and Morrissey, 1985, p. 76). While the agricultural lobby was the most vocal pressure group, the government also came under assiduous pressure from business interests, with the hotel lobby being particularly outspoken. In reply to this wave of pressure, the government made concessions to the agricultural lobby, the commercial lobby and the tourist lobby, with the result that the proposed tax ultimately became 'an ineffectual tax with limited support' and yielded less than a quarter of what had been originally anticipated (Morrissey, 1990, pp. 33–5).

For their part, cause centred groups, in their attempts to influence policy, have used a variety of methods to raise public consciousness. Some have run candidates at elections, in the hope of having a disproportionate influence on government should their candidate get elected and hold a pivotal position in parliament. A good example of this was the election of the Roscommon hospital candidate Tom Foxe in Longford–Roscommon in 1989. Foxe, a member of the Roscommon Hospital Action Committee, stood and was elected solely on a platform of opposition to the health cuts then being implemented by the minority Fianna Fáil government (Neville, 1990, p. 74). The potential reward for interest groups of getting one of their members elected can be seen by the fact that a motion of no confidence in the Minister for Health in early 1990 was defeated only when Foxe switched his vote after receiving guarantees about the status of Roscommon hospital. Foxe was seen by his constituents as having done such a good job that he was re-elected in 1992.

The 1997 general election saw success for another interest group candidate when Tom Gildea, running as a 'television deflector' candidate on behalf of a group concerned that their ability to watch British television channels at low cost was under threat, was elected in Donegal South-West (Murphy, 1998, p. 132). While Gildea originally voted against the minority Fianna Fáil–Progressive Democrat government on a number of issues, in November 1998 he reached 'an understanding' with the government under which a number of issues in the constituency would receive sympathetic treatment, and he announced that he would henceforth support the government.

While cause centred groups have only recently discovered the advantages of having representatives elected to the Dáil, some of the main sectional interest groups have had links to various political parties going back many years. The Labour party, indeed, was conceived by the Irish Trades Union Congress in 1912 to act as the political voice of organised labour and came into being in 1922 as a party committed to defending workers' rights. Over the years the trade union movement has played an important financial role within the Labour party through affiliation fees. The links were strengthened in the 1960s when the number of unions affiliated to the party increased. In 1999, ten trade unions were officially affiliated to the Labour party; these include SIPTU (Services Industrial Professional Technical Union) and the Amalgamated Transport and General Workers' Union, which between them account for about 44 per cent of union membership in the Republic. Moreover, the trade union movement has long been a breeding ground for politicians on the left, with many Labour TDs having been trade union officials. However, despite its close ties with the trade union movement, the Labour party has remained historically weak. Indeed, Fianna Fáil has also had traditionally close links with the organised trade union movement, which has often preferred dealing with Fianna Fáil governments rather than with coalition governments involving Labour in a minor role.

For its part, the Irish Farmers' Association has had links with both Fianna Fáil and Fine Gael. Former Fine Gael leader Alan Dukes was at one stage an economist with the IFA, while Alan Gillis (who was elected as a Fine Gael MEP in 1994) and Paddy Lane (elected as a Fianna Fáil MEP in 1989) were both former leaders of the IFA. It is also clear that the major political parties have all received substantial donations from business interests, amongst others, although as yet no definite link has been uncovered between any financial contributions made and administrative decisions taken (see chapter 6 for more on donations to parties). The link between business contributions to political parties, and by extension the political process, and favourable treatment for such business interests can at this stage only be said to be 'not proven'.

The influence of private interests

One concern about interest group activity is that much of it takes place out of the public view, leading to suggestions that nefarious activity might be taking place behind closed doors. In this section we will look at political corruption, allegations of which have recently begun to surface in Irish political life, at the extent of lobbying, and at relations between parliament and interest groups.

Political corruption

Concern about political corruption – which we can define as the abuse of public power for private profit or political gain – in Ireland has been expressed since the nineteenth century, if not before. In independent Ireland, particular concern was expressed towards the end of the 1960s, when Fianna Fáil began to accept large donations out of which the organisation Taca (Aid) was born. The original idea behind Taca was to bring together 500 large subscribers whose money would be invested for a year and then transferred into the Fianna Fáil election account (Keogh, 1994, p. 270). The creation of Taca sprang from a realisation by Fianna Fáil that the financial support of the entrepreneurial class could be substantial and would become vital as the business of running a large political organisation became more expensive. Taca, however, soon acquired a reputation for influencing ministerial decisions, and it was wound up within a few years (Collins and O Raghallaigh, 1995, p. 707). In the 1990s, evidence and allegations of wrong-doing involving some political and business interests prompted the establishment of a number of tribunals of inquiry to investigate these matters. Some of these tribunals, in particular the Hamilton tribunal of inquiry into the beef processing industry and the McCracken tribunal of inquiry into payments to politicians, revealed that certain large businesses regularly make substantial contributions, particularly at election time, to political parties that they consider to be sympathetic to them.

The McCracken tribunal of 1997, for instance, uncovered a whole host of payments from the wealthy businessman Ben Dunne to politicians of various parties. While the McCracken tribunal was most successful in tracking down payments from Dunne to the former Fine Gael minister Michael Lowry and the former Fianna Fáil leader Charles Haughey, its conclusions that 'there was no political impropriety' on the part of Lowry and 'there appears in fact to have been no political impropriety' on the part of Haughey reflect the lack of evidence before the tribunal to support any claim that payments were made in exchange for political action (Tribunal of Inquiry, 1997, pp. 70, 73). The conclusions of the McCracken tribunal, however, did force the Oireachtas to establish a further tribunal to examine whether business interests might have secured favourable policy decisions by any action taken by Lowry or Haughey in their respective ministerial careers.

The vexed question of political donations reared its head again with the case of the Fianna Fáil politician Ray Burke, who resigned in October 1997 from his position as Minister for Foreign Affairs when he became embroiled in allegations about controversial rezoning of land in north county Dublin. Land rezoning, to allow the construction of private houses, particularly in Dublin, has in recent decades been a source of bitter friction between various interest groups. On the one hand, property developers and building interests claim that such rezoning creates and maintains jobs in the building industry and provides citizens with the opportunity to live in modern housing at reasonable prices. On the other hand, opponents claim that the real beneficiaries are the landowners, whose holdings increase exponentially in value as a direct result of councillors' decisions; they also argue that areas of natural beauty in the state are being destroyed by rapacious developers. In the mid-1980s Burke had been chairman of Dublin County Council, which carried out numerous rezonings, usually against the advice of its own planning officials. No charges were ever brought against him in relation to any rezoning questions and he went on to have a long and successful political career, being a government minister on no fewer than six occasions. However, in September 1997, Burke admitted having received £30,000 in cash during the 1989 general election campaign at a meeting in his home with two property development figures, one of whom he had never previously met. He maintained that there was nothing unusual or sinister in this and that the money received was simply an election contribution, of which he passed on £10,000 to Fianna Fáil headquarters. The familiar argument that this was a case of 'payments for no political response' was used; Burke insisted that 'at no time during our meeting were any favours sought or given' (*Dáil Debates* 480: 617–18, 15 September 1997). In the light of the Burke revelation, the Oireachtas set up another tribunal, the Flood tribunal, to examine some of the more contentious rezoning decisions.

Lobbying

A further development in interest group politics has been the growth of professional lobbyists, or 'public affairs consultants' as they like to be known. As one political journalist put it: 'the rise of the lobbyist is one of the most striking developments of Irish political life in recent years' (Collins, 1998). The list of lobbyists in Ireland now includes former government press secretaries, former officials of all the major parties, some ex-TDs, and a host of former journalists. While these lobbyists originally catered primarily for foreign interests wishing to operate in Ireland, they are now involved in much more mainstream lobbying. Politicians argued in the past that private companies made donations to political parties not to achieve a particular outcome but simply for the access to government that such donations provided. It would appear that companies and others are paying lobbyists for the same purpose, though now on a more formal footing. In general, lobbyists claim that what they are doing is providing advice and access to the decision making process for business people who are unfamiliar with it and who need a specialist to introduce them to the complex workings of government. Most lobbyists now working in Ireland have long experience of how the political and administrative system works and claim that the people they represent, in practically all cases large business interests, have no such knowledge. As one lobbyist pointed out: 'We represent the interests of corporate Ireland to the government of the day. Our job is to get access to the system for people who want their case to be heard because if they don't get that access they can end up getting the wrong end of the stick when decisions are made' (quoted in Collins, 1998).

Lobbyists talk of trying to convince their clients that sometimes there is no point in talking to the relevant government minister and it is more important to talk to the senior civil servant who is handling the particular file. This is where their role is questionable in a parliamentary democracy. While they all claim that the lobbying system is above board, there are no guidelines governing the interaction between lobbyists and civil servants, who are after all servants of the state and are supposed to offer advice impartially without regard to any interest group pressure.

In any case, advice from the civil service can be ignored by the minister, as was shown by evidence given at the beef tribunal in the early 1990s. This tribunal found that Albert Reynolds, as Minister for Industry and Commerce, was legally entitled to make all the decisions he had done in relation to export credit insurance and had done so in good faith. Reynolds, however, through the whole period under investigation by the tribunal had systematically overruled the advice of his senior civil servants in relation to export credit insurance (O'Toole, 1995, pp. 79–85). The tribunal could find no link between such decisions and the relationship between highly powerful beef industry figures and either individual politicians or political parties in general. What the tribunal did find was that one such beef figure, Larry Goodman, profited from advance business information which he had acquired because he was on the 'inside political track'. Goodman, the tribunal found 'had reasonably ready access to members of the government . . . for the purpose of discussing his plans for the development of his companies and his exports. It is clear that he had similar access to previous governments' (Collins and O Raghallaigh, 1995, p. 706).

The close relationship between business and government was also illustrated by the case of stockbroker Dermot Desmond, who was embarrassed by the revelation that, while acting for a large French firm in a distillery take-over bid, he had mentioned in a letter that one of his advantages was his ready access to very senior politicians (Collins and O Raghallaigh, 1995, p. 705). The close relations between senior members of various governments and the business community would seem to cast doubt on the claim of many lobbyists that dealing with the civil servant, not the minister, is what counts. One Irish lobbyist, indeed, is of the opinion that access to the minister is the key. He maintains that politicians are swamped with paperwork and that the case has to be made to them in a personal way: 'Our job is to get our client into a position to make their case but at the end of the day the decisions are made by the politicians themselves' (Collins, 1998). While lobbyists deny that it matters who is in power, many major companies are now covering their options by having different lobbyists cover approaches to different political parties; this is now quite easy as there are so many former officials and government press secretaries involved in the lobbying business.

A good example of the problems associated with access occurred in March 1996, when two Labour ministers, Ruairí Quinn, the Minister of Finance, and Eithne Fitzgerald, Minister of State at the Department of the Tánaiste, were forced to apologise to the Dáil for invitations issued to business people on semi-official government notepaper. The invitations were to a £100 a plate lunch to 'gain access' to Quinn and promised a 'rare opportunity' to question him in a 'semi-formal' environment prior to the publication of the Finance Bill. The invitations were sent out by Fitzgerald's office, with the proceeds to benefit the Labour party organisation in her Dublin South constituency. However, the opposition queried the propriety of 'selling private briefings to selected business people' for the benefit of a constituency organisation and asked whether it was 'morally and ethically acceptable' that a select few, on a payment of £100 to the Labour party, could have direct access to Quinn (*Irish Times,* 7 March 1996). While fund-raising is to an extent the lifeblood of politics, what seems even more curious is the idea of ministers actually selling access to themselves. More embarrassing again was the fact that Ms Fitzgerald was the minister of state who pioneered and steered the Ethics in Public Office Act through the Oireachtas.

Interest groups and parliament

The Ethics in Public Office Act of 1995 provided for the first time for a register of interests of members of Dáil Éireann. The publication of this register for the period February 1998 to January 1999 does not shed much light on interest group activity in the policy arena. Only one interest group is mentioned in the whole of the register as remunerating a TD, namely the Irish Music Rights Organisation (IMRO). IMRO is the national body that administers the performing rights in copyright music in Ireland on behalf of its members – songwriters, composers and music publishers – and on behalf of the members of the sixty-one overseas societies affiliated to it. It works by attempting to highlight what it sees as the inadequacies of copyright legislation, not only in Ireland but in other countries too, and has worked closely with the Irish government on drafting a Copyright Amendment Bill. At a European level, it lobbies the European Commission on intellectual property issues and claims to have been instrumental in getting the Commission to lodge a complaint against the US authorities regarding inadequate copyright protection. One TD, Eoin Ryan, states in the register that he has a remunerated position with IMRO (Register of Interests, 1999). In the register for the previous year, Ryan had made the same declaration, and also stated that he had occupational income from this position. In the 1998 register, two other Fianna Fáil TDs, David Andrews and Noel Davern, had declared themselves to be respectively 'Consultant/Advisor' and 'Advisor' to IMRO, until they were appointed to ministerial positions in the summer of 1997. Thus, from the declarations of the 166 TDs, only three Dáil members were remunerated by an interest group at any time during 1997 and 1998. In addition, four Labour TDs declared that they had been given the use of premises by trade unions to hold constituency clinics, and a further five TDs (two from Fianna Fáil, two from Fine Gael and one from Labour) described themselves as 'consultants' in one or both of the 1998 and 1999 registers. This information apart, the register of interests throws no light on the scope and nature of contacts between interest groups and politicians.

The committee system of the Oireachtas has increasingly become a forum for interest groups to articulate their concerns to the legislature. While the record of Oireachtas committees in recent years may not make for inspired reading (there have been four major overhauls since the early 1980s, as discussed in chapter 7), these committees have at least provided an avenue for interest groups to attempt to influence public policy. The Joint Committee on Small Businesses, for example, which sat from 1983 to 1987 and produced sixty-eight reports in all, most of which were mere wish lists for small business, was largely dependent for research support and topics for inquiry on a unit of the Confederation of Irish Industry (O'Halpin and Connolly, 1999, p. 133). While the defects in the committee system continue to hamper their work (see chapter 7 above), the system itself is useful as a conduit between the Oireachtas and various interest groups. The practice of Oireachtas committees in receiving representations from interest groups provides what could be seen as a valuable forum for such groups to air their grievances, but this should be tempered with a word of warning. As O'Halpin and Connolly point out:

> Given the shortage of research and administrative support for
> Oireachtas committees of all kinds, it is probable that they will remain

exceedingly soft targets for any coherent pressure group, however selective its data or outlandish its case, wishing to set the agenda and to influence thinking and ultimately policy.

(O'Halpin and Connolly, 1999, p. 133)

While this is substantively true, it should be said that when interest groups deal officially through such committees, and government channels in general, this would seem to be a far more open and accountable way of influencing government than the lobbying of individual ministers and senior civil servants, which as we have seen is becoming increasingly prevalent in Ireland today.

Interest group activity assessed

A strong case can be made for or against the involvement of interest groups in the policy process. Realistically, interest groups are certain to be involved, but we can identify the advantages and disadvantages this entails (see Box 11.2). In an Irish context, one can find numerous examples to exemplify both the benefits and the dangers. In the 1980s many interest groups were criticised for looking for ever more resources from the over-stretched state. A former secretary of the Department of Finance complained that such behaviour by sectional groups over a number of years had had disastrous consequences for the national finances (Doyle, 1987, p. 72). Regarding cause centred groups, the anti-abortion groups' tactics in rela-tion to the Maastricht treaty of 1992 can be viewed as a good example of the dangers of interest group activity. As a result of their behind-the-scenes representations, the government persuaded its European counterparts to accept an Irish protocol to the treaty, which stipulated that nothing in any of the European treaties would affect the application in Ireland of the eighth amendment to the constitution (the so-called 'pro-life', or anti-abortion, amendment that had been passed by referendum in 1983). As one commentator has asked about the pro-life lobby's activities: 'what right did they have to make demands and seek consultations when the elected repre-sentatives of the people, the opposition parties, did not even know what was going on?' (O'Reilly, 1992, p. 139).

There can be little doubt, however, that interest groups have also played a beneficial role in Irish politics and society. IMRO, which, as we have seen, has employed a number of public representatives as advisors, plays an important role in protecting its members' interests in respect of copyright of work. Likewise, the INOU has filled an important gap in representing the unemployed, a group that was for many years without a formal voice in relation to policy making. For their part, while the main sectional interests have often been criticised by outsiders, and more often than not by each other, there is no doubt that they play an important role as a conduit to government for their members, who otherwise would not

---

Box 11.2 The benefits and disadvantages of interest group activities

Andrew Heywood (1997, p. 259) summarises the balance sheet as
    follows:
On the positive side, interest groups may:

- provide some kind of check on government power; they help to
  ensure that the state is balanced by a vigorous and healthy civil
  society;
- articulate interests and advance views that may be overlooked by
  political parties;
- provide an alternative to conventional party politics and offer
  opportunities for grass roots activism;
- constitute an additional channel of communication between
  government and the people.

On the negative side, interest groups:

- exercise non-legitimate power, in that their leaders, unlike
  politicians, are not publicly accountable and their influence
  bypasses the representative process;
- are divisive, given that they advance minority interests against
  those of society as a whole;
- entrench political inequality by strengthening the voice of the
  wealthy and privileged in particular;
- create an array of vested interests that are able to block government
  initiatives and make policy unworkable.

---

have any ready access to the decision making process. Moreover, cause
centred groups, through their activities in consciousness raising, create a
better informed electorate. In this way, interest group behaviour may
benefit society generally, and not just the membership of the organisations themselves.

Conclusion

Is there a specific model of interest group activity that is applicable to
Ireland today? As far back as 1986, Regan and Wilson came to the conclusion
that interest group activity in Ireland was neither corporatist nor pluralist
and argued that a new theory had to accommodate both corporatist and
pluralist features, while allowing for practices and structures that groups and
governments might evolve as part of the policy making debate (Regan and
Wilson, 1986, p. 410). In the decade after 1987, when the Programme for

National Recovery was launched, interest group activity in Ireland attained centre stage, with the tripartite agreements of the 1990s cementing social partnership. With the implementation of Partnership 2000, with its unique social pillar, the number of interest groups associating with government has grown quite substantially. Moreover, these agreements, originally tripartite but now more inclusive, were driven by various governments, to the extent that the Taoiseach told a meeting of the social partners in July 1998 that there was 'no alternative' to Partnership 2000 (*Irish Times*, 29 July 1998).

Given the various definitions of interest group involvement in the policy process, it would seem that all countries in western Europe are nationally specific, with none of them fitting any model of interest group activity precisely. Some countries, such as Austria, tend more towards corporatist ideas of policy making and others, such as Britain, towards more pluralistic versions. In Ireland, from the mid-1980s major sectional interest groups gained access to government and an input into public policy that brought the political process to a position where the Taoiseach talked of full-blown social partnership as the way forward to economic success and social inclusiveness. Yet this seems to be a sort of hybrid partnership; while there is now a comprehensive role for the social partners, Partnership 2000 came under various strains as individual interests pressed their claims on the government in a way that was practically pluralistic. In this respect Ireland finds itself now very much in the mainstream of west European politics in relation to interest group influence, having experienced a blurring of the distinction between corporatist and pluralist models of group behaviour. It is now pretty much redundant to ask whether a particular system is corporatist or pluralist, as behaviour is more concentrated on policy making within particular sectors (Gallagher, Laver and Mair, 1995, p. 384). It is within these parameters that interest group activity finds itself in Ireland today, but there can be little doubt that this activity is growing as the Oireachtas and its members come under more pressure from an increasing number of interest groups attempting to influence policy.

Notes

1   See the IFA's web site at http://www.farm.ie/ifa.
2   See the ICTU's web site at http://www.iol.ie/ictu/.
3   Information on IBEC can be found at its web site at http://www.ibec.ie.

References and further reading

Aspinwall, Mark and Justin Greenwood, 1998. 'Conceptualising collective action in the European Union: an introduction', pp. 1–30 in Justin Greenwood and Mark Aspinwall (eds), *Collective Action in the European Union: Interests and the New Politics of Associability*. London: Routledge.

Budge, Ian, Kenneth Newton et al, 1997. *The Politics of the New Europe: Atlantic to Urals*. London: Longman.

Cawson, Alan (ed.), 1985. *Organised Interests and the State: Studies in Meso-Corporatism.* London: Sage.

Cawson, Alan, 1986. *Corporatism and Political Theory.* Oxford: Basil Blackwell.

Collins, Neil and Colm O Raghallaigh, 1995. 'Political sleaze in the Republic of Ireland', *Parliamentary Affairs* 48:4, pp. 697–710.

Collins, Stephen, 1998. 'Do you want your old lobby washed down, sunshine?', *Sunday Tribune,* 12 July.

Coulter, Carol, 1995. 'Government owes yes victory to voluntary groups', *Irish Times,* 27 November.

Doyle, Maurice, 1987. 'Comment', pp. 71–6 in Seán Cromien and Aidan Pender (eds), *Managing Public Money.* Dublin: Institute of Public Administration.

Gallagher, Michael, Michael Laver and Peter Mair, 1995. *Representative Government in Modern Europe,* 2nd ed. New York: McGraw-Hill.

Galligan, Yvonne, 1998. *Women and Politics in Contemporary Ireland: From the Margins to the Mainstream.* London: Pinter.

Girvin, Brian, 1986. 'Social change and moral politics: the Irish constitutional referendum 1983', *Political Studies* 34:1, pp. 61–81.

Girvin, Brian, 1996. 'The Irish divorce referendum, November 1995', *Irish Political Studies* 11, pp. 74–81.

Heisler, Martin O. and Robert B. Kvavik, 1974. 'Patterns of European politics: the "European polity" model', pp. 27–89 in Martin O. Heisler (ed.), *Politics in Europe: Structures and Processes in Some Post Industrial Democracies.* New York: David McKay and Co.

Heywood, Andrew, 1997. *Politics.* Basingstoke: Macmillan.

Horgan, John, 1997. *Seán Lemass: The Enigmatic Patriot.* Dublin: Gill and Macmillan.

Institute of Public Administration, 1998. *Administration Yearbook and Diary, 1999.* Dublin: Institute of Public Administration.

Keogh, Dermot, 1994. *Twentieth Century Ireland: Nation and State.* Dublin: Gill and Macmillan.

Kimber, Richard and Jeremy J. Richardson (eds), 1974. *Pressure Groups in Britain.* London: Dent.

Lee, J. J., 1989. *Ireland 1912–1985: Politics and Society.* Cambridge: Cambridge University Press.

McCann, Dermot, 1993. 'Business power and collective action: the state and the Confederation of Irish Industry 1970–1990', *Irish Political Studies* 8, pp. 37–53.

Morrissey, Oliver, 1990. 'Scanning the alternatives before taxing with consensus: lessons for policy making from the Irish wealth tax', *Administration* 38:1, pp. 21–40.

Murphy, Gary, 1997. 'Government, interest groups and the Irish move to Europe: 1957–1963', *Irish Studies in International Affairs* 8, pp. 57–68.

Murphy, Gary, 1998. 'The 1997 general election in the Republic of Ireland', *Irish Political Studies* 13, pp. 127–34.

NESC, 1986. *A Strategy for Development, 1986–1990.* Dublin: National Economic and Social Council, Report No. 83.

Neville, Pat, 1990. 'The 1989 general election in the Republic of Ireland', *Irish Political Studies* 5, pp. 69–76.

O'Donnell, Rory and Damian Thomas, 1998. 'Partnership and policy making', pp. 117–46 in Seán Healy and Brigid Reynolds (eds), *Social Policy in Ireland: Principles, Practice and Problems.* Dublin: Oak Tree Press.

O'Halpin, Eunan, 1993. 'Policy making', pp. 190–206 in John Coakley and Michael Gallagher (eds), *Politics in the Republic of Ireland,* 2nd ed. Dublin: Folens and

Limerick: PSAI Press.

O'Halpin, Eunan and Eileen Connolly, 1999. 'Parliaments and pressure groups: the Irish experience of change', pp. 124–44 in Philip Norton (ed.), *Parliaments and Pressure Groups in Western Europe*. London: Frank Cass.

O'Reilly, Emily, 1992. *Masterminds of the Right*. Dublin: Attic Press.

O'Toole, Fintan, 1995. *Meanwhile Back at the Ranch: The Politics of Irish Beef*. London: Vintage.

Punnett, R. M., 1994. *British Government and Politics*, 6th ed. Aldershot: Dartmouth.

Regan, Marguerite C. and Frank L. Wilson, 1986. 'Interest-group politics in France and Ireland: comparative perspectives on neo-corporatism', *West European Politics* 9:3, pp. 393–413.

Register of Interests, 1999. *Register of Interests of Members of Dáil Éireann, 1 February 1998 to 31 January 1999*. Dublin: Houses of the Oireachtas.

Richardson, Jeremy J., 1993. 'Pressure groups and government', pp. 1-15 in Jeremy J. Richardson (ed.), *Pressure Groups*. Oxford: Oxford University Press.

Sandford, Cedric and Oliver Morrissey, 1985. *The Irish Wealth Tax: a Case Study in Economics and Politics*. Dublin: Economic and Social Institute, ESRI paper 123.

Therborn, Goran, 1995. *European Modernity and Beyond: The Trajectory of European Societies 1945–2000*. London: Sage.

Tribunal of Inquiry, 1997. *Report of the Tribunal of Inquiry (Dunnes Payments)*. Dublin: Stationery Office. [This tribunal was chaired by Mr Justice McCracken.]

Weinz, Wolfgang, 1986. 'Economic development and interest groups', pp. 87–101 in Brian Girvin and Roland Sturm (eds), *Politics and Society in Contemporary Ireland*. Aldershot: Gower.

Wilson, Graham K., 1991. *Interest Groups*. Oxford: Basil Blackwell.

12 Women in politics

Yvonne Galligan

Women's political participation has become a central theme in discussions of Irish politics. The high media profile of both President Mary Robinson, who took office in 1990, and her successor as head of state, Mary McAleese, together with the strong public image of women parliamentarians such as Mary Harney, leader of the Progressive Democrats, have served to heighten popular interest in women's political involvement. Political parties have sought to develop policies that attract women voters specifically. In addition, parties have become aware of the desirability of selecting women candidates as part of the electoral package presented to voters. As an academic study, too, the political behaviour of women has attracted attention. Today, no textbook on politics is complete without a contribution that considers the relationship between women and the political system.

Much of this interest in women and politics is based on concepts of democracy and on the nature of interest representation within a polity. Women constitute about half of the citizenry of any nation. Their absence from the decision making arenas of a state has come to signify a failure on the part of democratic institutions to represent the major interests in society. Exploring the reasons for the dearth of women in political life deepens our understanding of the political system and of the opportunities and constraints for the representation of interests other than those of middle class males. It exposes the underlying bias of a political system and facilitates a recognition of prejudice that otherwise might remain unrecognised. A study of the factors contributing to the under-representation of women in electoral politics offers an understanding of the nature of power and how it is distributed in a society. The insights gained from this analysis can contribute to the development of strategies and policies that encourage greater equity, justice, and indeed public confidence in political institutions.

Studying women and politics also allows us to deconstruct the nature of the political agenda at any one time in order to analyse whose interests are being reflected in policy priorities. There is clear evidence to show that while women and men agree on many important political issues, they have different priorities. In terms of the labour market, for instance, women are more likely than men to highlight the low provision of child-care facilities for working parents. This representation of interests carries over into political life where women parliamentarians are likely to inform legislative debates from a distinct starting point.

We study women and politics in order to deepen our insights into the party, institutional and policy processes that constitute the political system. As we shall see, women's political behaviour is as complex and multi-layered as that of men; the challenges that women face in seeking political representation are in some instances similar to, but in other instances different from, those of men. In policy terms, women have placed many issues on the political agenda that would not have arisen if men retained a monopoly on the representation of interests in a society.

In order to assess the relationship between women and politics in Ireland, we will first look at the pattern of women's representation in political and social decision making. We will then explore possible causes of the under-representation of women before assessing the consequences, for women and for society, of providing one half of the population with a little over one-tenth of the political voice. The concept 'parity democracy' is used to describe the goal of equal participation by women and men in all aspects of decision making in a society. In this chapter, we will measure the extent to which Ireland has moved towards becoming a democracy that gives equal voice and equal power to all its citizens, women and men alike.

Women in political institutions

Head of state

In 1990 the Irish electorate chose Mary Robinson as the country's President, making Ireland only the second country in Europe (after Iceland) to have a woman head of state elected by popular vote. In 1997, President Robinson was succeeded by another woman, Mary McAleese. Indeed, Robinson's election victory, and the success of her presidency, seemed to influence the parties to nominate women as candidates for the 1997 presidential election: four of the five candidates were women, representing diverse strands of political opinion. To an outside observer, this could give the impression that women are strongly represented in all aspects of Irish political life. Yet this is not the case. Women have always been under-represented in Ireland's political institutions, as we shall see when we look at their record in government, parliament, local government and the political parties.

Government

With the exception of the appointment of Countess Markievicz as Minister for Labour in the government elected by the first Dáil in 1919 (a largely symbolic appointment in the circumstances of the time), no woman held a cabinet post until December 1979 (see Box 12.1). Of the 151 people who held full ministerial positions from 1922 to 1998 inclusive, only eight (5 per cent) were women. However, if we examine more closely the composition of governments from 1979 onwards, we can detect a clear increase in the number of women holding government office. In the nine administrations formed between 1979 and 1997 inclusive, sixteen women politicians held full ministerial positions or junior ministries. In the government formed in 1997 there were three women out of fifteen ministers at the cabinet table, one of whom held the position of Tánaiste (deputy prime minister), as well as two women among the seventeen junior ministers. Thus, at government level, the overall representation of women in ministerial positions increased from one out of twenty-five (4 per cent) in December 1979 to five out of thirty-two (16 per cent) in June 1997. In this respect, Ireland was not far off the average of 19 per cent representation of women in government in the EU member states (European Commission, 1997, pp. 19–20).

Parliament

During the half century after the beginning of the state in 1922, the average Dáil contained only four women (3 per cent of all TDs). Over the twenty-six elections held between 1922 and 1997 inclusive, only sixty-one individual women were elected to the Dáil. The figures for women TDs and candidates in 1977, low as they were (see Table 12.1 and appendix 2d), represented record levels at the time, highlighting women's near invisibility in parliamentary politics up to that point. In recent years there has been some increase: on average, twelve women were elected to each Dáil from 1977 to 1997. In 1998 a by-election saw the return of an additional woman to the Dáil, and this brought the total number of women in the lower house of

Table 12.1 Women candidates and TDs at elections, 1977–97

	Candidates			Deputies		
Election	Total	Women	%	Total	Women	%
1977	376	25	6.6	148	6	4.1
1981	404	41	10.1	166	11	6.6
1982 (Feb)	366	35	9.6	166	8	4.8
1982 (Nov)	365	31	8.5	166	14	8.4
1987	466	65	13.9	166	14	8.4
1989	371	52	14.0	166	13	7.8
1992	482	89	18.5	166	20	12.0
1997	484	96	19.8	166	20	12.0

Source: Author's calculations.
Note: The actual number of women candidates contesting the 1987 general election is distorted due to the fact that one Independent candidate, Barbara Hyland, ran in thirteen constituencies.

Box 12.1 Leading women politicians

Irish government has been largely male-dominated since the foundation of the state. Only since the start of the 1980s have women politicians gained access to any of the levers of power, but they still remain very much in a minority in the governmental system. Since 1922, only eight women have been members of an Irish government:

Máire Geoghegan-Quinn (born 1950), Fianna Fáil. In 1979 became the first female cabinet minister, and served in subsequent Fianna Fáil administrations in the 1980s and 1990s.

Eileen Desmond (born 1932), Labour. Appointed Minister for Health and Minister for Social Welfare in 1981.

Gemma Hussey (born 1938), Fine Gael. Appointed Minister for Education in 1982.

Mary O'Rourke (born 1937), Fianna Fáil. Appointed Minister for Education 1987, and a senior figure in Fianna Fáil during the 1990s.

Niamh Bhreathnach (born 1945), Labour. Appointed Minister for Education in 1993.

Nora Owen (born 1945), Fine Gael. Appointed deputy leader of her party in 1993, became Minister for Justice in 1994.

Mary Harney (born 1953), Progressive Democrats. Became leader of her party in 1993 (the first female leader of a party), became Tánaiste and Minister for Enterprise, Trade and Employment in 1997.

Síle de Valera (born 1954), Fianna Fáil. Appointed Minister for Arts, Heritage, Gaeltacht and the Islands in 1997.

In addition, the country has had two female Presidents:

Mary Robinson (born 1944). Elected President 1990 with the backing of Labour, the Workers' Party and the Green Party.

Mary McAleese (born 1951). Elected President 1997, standing as the Fianna Fáil candidate with the support also of the Progressive Democrats.

parliament at that time to twenty-one (13 per cent). This placed Ireland among the lowest in terms of gender balance in the lower houses of parliament of the EU member states. In 1998 it shared eleventh place out of the fifteen EU member states, alongside Belgium and ahead only of France, Italy and Greece. This marks a significant relative disimprovement, as Ireland had held sixth position among the twelve member states in 1993. Since then, three countries – Austria, Finland and Sweden – with high proportions of women in parliament have joined. Even leaving these new entrants aside, women's representation in the national parliaments of other EU member states has tended to increase since the early 1990s while in Ireland it has remained static. Ireland, then, has some way to go to reach the 1998 EU average of 22 per cent of parliamentary seats that are held by women.

The pattern of women's representation in the Seanad, the upper house, is not very different. Over the forty-year period from 1937 to 1977, there were only nineteen female senators in total in the second chamber. There was a perceptible increase in the number of women senators after 1977, when Jack Lynch, as Taoiseach, included three women among his eleven appointees (for the composition of the Seanad, see Box 7.2). The 1997 Seanad election resulted in eight women being elected to the upper house, and a further three were appointed by the Taoiseach, bringing the representation of women in the Seanad to its highest level, eleven out of sixty (18 per cent).

Women's overall representation on parliamentary committees does not differ much from that of men. Thirteen (81 per cent) of the sixteen

Table 12.2 Women on parliamentary committees in 28th Dáil, 1999

Committee	Type	Size	Number of women	% of women
Agriculture, Food and the Marine	Joint	19	0	0.0
Education and Science	Joint	19	4	21.0
Enterprise and Small Business	Joint	19	3	15.8
Environment and Local Government	Joint	19	2	10.6
European Affairs	Joint	19	1	5.3
Family, Community and Social Affairs	Joint	19	3	15.8
Finance and the Public Service	Joint	19	1	5.3
Foreign Affairs	Joint	20	3	15.0
Health and Children	Joint	19	5	26.3
Heritage and the Irish Language	Joint	19	3	15.8
Justice, Equality and Women's Rights	Joint	19	7	36.8
Public Accounts	Dáil	12	1	8.3
Public Enterprise and Transport	Joint	19	0	0.0
Tourism, Sport and Recreation	Joint	19	1	5.3
Total		260	34	13.1

Source: From information made available by the Clerk of Dáil Éireann, 1999.
Note: This list excludes the 'housekeeping' committees that regulate the internal affairs of the Oireachtas (see Table 7.5).

women TDs available to serve on committees in 1998 did so, compared with 116 (97 per cent) of their male counterparts. The average committee membership of women and men parliamentarians (TDs and senators) was also similar: women served on an average of 1.6 committees each, men on 1.7. What was striking, however, was the pattern of male and female representation on the various committees (see Table 12.2). Women parliamentarians constituted a sizeable proportion of the membership of the Committee on Justice, Equality and Women's Rights (37 per cent) and were also represented in significant numbers on the committees on Health and Children and on Education and Science. In contrast, they were noticeably absent from the committees dealing with Agriculture and Public Enterprise, and had minimal representation on a number of others, including European Affairs, Finance, and Public Accounts. As parliamentarians generally volunteer for positions on various committees (see p 196), this suggests that women TDs and senators have, as a group, specific policy interests and priorities, just like their British counterparts, who have been found to have a distinctive policy agenda (Norris, 1996, p. 93).

Local government

The pattern of women's representation in local government has been similar to that in the national parliament. Studies show that women generally fare better in terms of their representation at local level than in national assemblies. A study of women and decision making in the EU, for instance, found that in 1994 women made up 20 per cent of the membership of local assemblies across the Union, compared with a representation of 15 per cent in national assemblies (European Commission, 1996, pp. 3, 5). However, the differences are not always significant in individual countries, and Ireland is a case in point. The 1991 local elections saw a modest increase in women's representation from 8 per cent to just under 12 per cent. When elections to the smaller councils and town commissions were held some time later, the total level of women's representation in local government increased to 15 per cent. This figure places Ireland in ninth position among the EU member states (European Commission, 1996, p. 5).

Political parties

Women, then, are largely absent from the electoral arenas, and are similarly under-represented in the political parties, which is particularly important given that the parties dominate the candidate selection process (see chapter 6 above). The level of women's participation in party politics has increased over the last two decades, with women comprising between a third and a half of the membership of Irish parties. In Fianna Fáil and Fine Gael women constitute 33 per cent of party members, 40 per cent of Labour members are women, and the Progressive Democrats have equal numbers of men and women in their membership (information supplied by the political parties). But this growing activism within the formal party political structures has not been reflected in the numbers of women holding positions on the national executives of the major parties (see Table 12.3). The pattern is such that it is unlikely that women will ever be represented in significant numbers at senior party decision making levels unless there is a strong commitment to balancing gender representation at the top.

The form that this commitment to providing for gender equality takes and the extent to which it is acted upon varies from party to party (Galligan and Wilford, 1999). In Fianna Fáil, for instance, the practice has been to rely on exhortation to increase the supply of women candidates and party office-holders. There exists a reluctance to contemplate any measures that would favour the advancement within the party of women specifically. Not surprisingly, Fianna Fáil's record on the selection of women candidates is the poorest of all the parties. Fine Gael, in contrast, has progressed to a positive action strategy, adopting a voluntary 33 per cent quota for women candidates, particularly for local elections. The party's record on women's office-holding has been more positive than Fianna Fáil's. This can be attributed, in some measure at least, to two waves of party modernisation: one in the 1980s, the second a decade later. The Progressive Democrats, formed in 1985, eschew any commitment to gender equality within their ranks, pointing instead to the successful integration of women party members into office-holding positions and electoral politics. This view, which essentially ignores the gendered nature of power within an organisation, is shared by other European centre-right parties, such as the Swedish Centre Party. On the left of the political spectrum, the Labour party implements a modest gender quota of 25 per cent for party office-holding and electoral politics. However, as we shall see, an

Table 12.3 Women's representation on national executives of the main political parties, 1983–98

	Fianna Fáil %	Fine Gael %	Labour %	Progressive Democrats %
1983	16.6	23.5	8.3	—
1985	11.1	12.5	13.8	—
1987	16.6	21.6	16.2	n.a
1989	21.0	n.a	15.4	37.5
1991	7.9	27.0	17.0	27.5
1993	12.6	23.7	21.0	n.a.
1995	16.8	28.0	22.0	32.0
1998	30.0	21.4	26.3	46.6

Source: For 1983–89, Farrell (1992, p. 444); 1991–98, data supplied by the political parties.

examination of the distribution of women in constituency officer positions in Labour points to the continuation of traditional divisions of power within the party organisation.

Given the low representation of women on the national executives of the main parties, one might expect them to be proportionally better represented in party office-holding at constituency level. Yet, this is not entirely the case (Table 12.4). There are proportionately more women on the national executives of Fianna Fáil and the Labour Party than hold constituency positions. Only in Fine Gael can women be found in greater proportions at constituency officer level. This is an interesting pattern and has two possible explanations. One is that the higher representation of women in national party affairs is a result of the operation of a gender quota in the case of the Labour Party. In the case of Fianna Fáil, we must look for a more subtle explanation. Party members are not in favour of quotas or other forms of positive discrimination measures. Yet, the recurring debate on the under-representation of women in political life appears to have created an awareness among party activists of this issue. The fact that it is deemed important for the party's image to have at least some women participating at national level facilitates the election of increasing numbers of women to the national executive. In addition, party leaderships are generally more progressive than their rank and file membership and, in the case of Fianna Fáil, the leadership displays a positive attitude towards the involvement of women in national party affairs. Although support for women does not stretch beyond rhetoric, even rhetoric sends an encouraging signal to women seeking national office, and to party activists, that results in a modest representation of women on the national executive. The above influences do not operate to the same degree at local level, with the result that constituency politics remains firmly in male hands.

There is a second possible reason for the unexpected discrepancy between women's involvement in national and local party organisations. The holder of a constituency office is in a strong position to build support for his or her electoral ambitions within the party organisation. As the candidate

Table 12.4 Women's constituency office-holding by party, 1998

	Fianna Fáil %	Fine Gael %	Labour %	Progressive Democrats %
Constituency chair	32.6	10.0	9.5	28.6
Constituency secretary	4.3	69.2	40.5	42.8
Constituency treasurer	15.2	34.6	14.3	40.0
Average women's office holding at constituency level	16.8	37.0	21.4	37.7

Source: Information supplied by the political parties.
Note: While the Green Party does not adopt this form of organisation, 40 per cent of its constituency coordinators are women.

selection process is highly localised, party office-holding at this level offers an aspirant the opportunity of staking a claim for a nomination at election time. Thus, one of two things happens with constituency office positions. Either they are filled by members loyal to the incumbent deputy or the leading party representative, or they are held by potential candidates, or both. In essence, office-holding at constituency level can be seen as an arena in which electoral challenges are rehearsed. These conflicts are more likely to focus around the ambitions of aspiring or incumbent males than those of females because, as we shall see, the existing attitudes and structures facilitate male political aspirants over women.

It is not surprising, then, to find that the position of constituency secretary is the one most associated with women's office-holding in party organisations. While the reasons for this dichotomy in position-holding are complex and deserving of further study, the general consensus among party insiders questioned on this matter is that the position of constituency secretary entails a range of skills and demands that have traditionally been more available among women than men. Thus, the office demands secretarial and administrative skills, flexibility in terms of time, attention to detail, and continuity over the long term. The constituency secretary is seen as being a key position in the smooth running of the constituency, supporting the elected representatives, liaising with the central party organisation and keeping in touch with party members in the constituency.

The role of constituency chairperson, on the other hand, is distinctly male-dominated, and invested with greater significant political content and status. It is also one that requires a knowledge of the rules and procedures of meetings, generally seen as being a skill more associated with the life experiences of men. We can tentatively conclude, in the absence of hard data, that the patterns of constituency office-holding reflect the gender-related patterns of power in society, where women are more likely to be found in supportive roles and men dominate the overt decision making positions. This idea will be explored more fully in the next section.

Women in society

The dearth of women in positions of power in parties and political life is, of course, only part of the wider pattern of women's absence from decision making centres generally. In this section of the chapter we shall provide a brief summary of the levels of women's representation on state boards and in the civil service, the judiciary, trade unions and other economic interest groups, and discuss the extent of women's participation in the paid workforce.

In a survey of the numbers of women serving on state boards in 1970, the Commission on the Status of Women noted that there was only one woman among the board members of the ten leading state-sponsored bodies. Matters changed gradually over the next twenty years, and in 1993 the Fianna Fáil–Labour government stated its intention to increase the gender balance on state boards to 40 per cent by 1997. In 1998, 812 of 2,814 members (29 per cent) were women, and sixty-five of the 211 state boards (31 per cent) exceeded the 40 per cent gender-balance threshold (National Women's Council of Ireland, 1998). Some progress, then, has been made towards redressing the shortfall of women in public decision making positions, though the survey revealed a serious under-representation of women on the eight regional health boards.

The poor record of women's representation in the senior levels of the civil service has been consistently highlighted. In the early 1990s there were no women among the senior positions of secretary and deputy secretary, only 2 per cent of the assistant secretaries and 3 per cent of the principal officers were female, and the majority of women employed in the civil service filled the lower clerical and typing grades (Eager, 1991, p. 19). Some improvements have been recorded since then. In 1996 there was one woman holding the position of secretary general (formerly secretary) out of a total of thirty-four positions of this kind. At the same time, 10 per cent of assistant secretary posts and 13 per cent of principal officer positions were held by women (Department of Finance, 1999). While women made up almost half (49 per cent) of the civil service workforce in 1996, they were still concentrated in the lower clerical grades despite the existence of an equal opportunity policy dating from 1986.

This pattern is repeated in the judicial arena. In December 1992 Ms Justice Denham became the first woman on the Supreme Court bench. Table 12.5 shows the levels of gender representation in the judiciary. The total number of women working as justices has doubled over the 1990s, with significant increases in the proportion of women serving at high court, circuit court and district court levels. Yet women still constitute a minority among the judiciary (17 per cent), even though about half of all solicitors and one quarter of barristers are women (Connelly and Hilliard, 1993, p. 232).

The numbers of women in decision making positions in the organisations of the 'social partners' – the trade union, employer and agricultural interests influential in shaping government economic policy – are also low. Women have consistently formed over a third of trade union membership

Table 12.5 Women in the judiciary, 1998

Court	Total number of judges	Number of women	%
Supreme Court	8	1	12.5
High Court	23	4	17.4
Circuit Court	25	4	16.0
District Courts	51	9	17.6
Total	107	18	16.8

Source: Department of Justice.

since the 1980s, and in 1997 comprised 39 per cent of union members. However, women held only 30 per cent of the places on the executive committees of the twenty-three unions that represented 84 per cent of the female membership. In 1997, only five (18 per cent) of the twenty-eight executive committee members of the Irish Congress of Trade Unions (ICTU) were women (with four of these holding reserved positions) even though, according to the ICTU women's committee, there should be eleven women on the executive to effect a gender balance in representation on that body (ICTU, 1998). None of the senior official positions in the Irish Business and Employers Confederation (IBEC) or the Irish Farmers' Association (IFA) was held by a woman in 1998. Yet the prospect for women's inclusion in economic decision making is not one of unrelieved gloom. There are signs that the issue is being addressed in some occupational sectors. The under-representation of women in business, in the state transport service, in local government, and in careers such as medicine and accountancy has been the subject of investigative reports by the associations regulating these professions, and growing attention is being paid to the under-representation of women in science and technology.

It has been noted in other countries that the level of women's participation in employment affects the extent of their participation in other areas of public life. Traditionally, women have made up 30 per cent of the total workforce in Ireland. During the 1990s, this proportion increased substantially and by 1998 half of the workforce consisted of women (OECD, 1998, p. 193). This figure hides significant changes in the composition of the female labour force. In 1926, over three-quarters of women in employment were single, but in 1997 45 per cent of them were married (CSO, 1998). When placed in an international context, the proportion of women at work in Ireland (50 per cent) still falls short of the EU average of 58 per cent and the OECD average of 59 per cent. Women's labour force participation in Ireland in 1998 was the fourth lowest in the EU: only Spain, Italy and Greece had a lower percentage of women participating in the workforce (OECD, 1998, p. 193). Despite the dramatic rise in the numbers of married women engaging in economic activity in Ireland, such workers are concentrated in lower-paid and part-time jobs and are not represented in management positions in proportion to their numbers in the workforce. Women at work, then, are less subject than men to the socialising experiences that come with holding authority positions in employment.

Causes of the under-representation of women

The previous pages have examined the extent of the under-representation of women in politics and in decision making centres. We must now look at the reasons for this under-representation. In doing so, we will discuss some of the factors that have acted as barriers to women's participation in public life, beginning with attitudes towards women's role in society and ending with a focus on obstacles inherent in the Irish political system that have developed from social expectations and practices.

Social attitudes

The main factor inhibiting women's participation is generally recognised as being the degree to which a society holds negative attitudes towards the involvement of women in politics. In a study of obstacles to women's political participation in Ireland, Randall and Smyth noted that:

> Irish women have until the very recent past been subject to a particularly intense, if complex, process of socialisation, through the agency of family, school and the Church, into an acceptance of an extremely traditional division of labour between the sexes and its implications for women's political role.
>
> (Randall and Smyth, 1987, p. 200)

For these authors, the socialisation process, which transmits traditional assumptions about women's role in society (a feature, to varying degrees, of all societies in the liberal democratic world), has been reinforced in Ireland through the Roman Catholic church, which continues to prioritise a home- and family-based role for women. This leads to women in predominantly Roman Catholic countries having less interest in politics than do men, and so being less inclined to participate in the political process and its institutions.

This view is modified by later surveys measuring changes in men's and women's attitudes towards gender roles over a period of time. These studies pinpoint the existence of two contradictory sets of attitudes regarding women and politics held by the Irish public. On the one hand, there is evidence that suggests increasingly favourable attitudes towards women and men having equal status in society (European Commission, 1996, p. 72). However, there are indications that attitudes in Ireland towards women's participation in public life are less egalitarian than in other EU countries. In addition, Irish men and women appear least willing to favour equality in gender roles within the home and family, in contrast to attitudes in Denmark, Spain and the Netherlands, whose citizens are among the most supportive of equality in a family context (European Commission, 1992, pp. 85–6; European Commission, 1995, pp. 71–2). This finding was confirmed by Whelan and Fahey who found that

> While Irish attitudes [on sex roles] are not significantly more tradi-tional than European views, the pattern of results does point to the continuing influence of values that underpin sex role differentiation. Thus, while attitudes to women's employment are generally positive, substantial proportions of the adult population consider that there are negative effects for children. Furthermore, significant majorities

consider that women can be fulfilled in the role of housewife and indeed that this, rather than jobs outside the home, is what they really want.

(Whelan and Fahey, 1994, pp. 51–2)

Thus, two views of women's role in society, which are difficult to reconcile with each other, coexist in Ireland. On the one hand, participation of women in public activity, be it employment, politics or other public functions, is viewed with greater equanimity now than it was fifteen years ago. Yet women are expected to combine their 'traditional' home responsibilities with their activities in the public sphere. The expectation held by a majority of the population is, therefore, that women wishing to become involved in activities outside the home will combine both public and domestic responsibilities, leading them to assume the responsibility of a 'dual burden' that men do not need to assume to the same extent.

Although Ireland still has the highest family size in the EU, women TDs have significantly smaller families than their male counterparts. This suggests that for women with political ambitions the practicality of pursuing this time-consuming career in tandem with child-rearing is an issue of greater significance than it is for their male colleagues. The issue of family size is related to the access of women to family support systems, which male politicians can in general avail themselves of more readily than women. While family demands may not deter politically ambitious women, they none the less appear to constitute a factor that women seeking political opportunities have to consider to a greater degree than do men.

However, the socially determined constraints on women wishing to engage in a political career are not as all-encompassing in the twenty-first century as they have been in earlier times. The greater acceptance of a broader role for women, the availability of contraception enabling them to limit family size, the higher level of education they enjoy, and the more extensive occupational opportunities open to them all suggest that women and men should have similar access to political careers. None the less, certain obstacles have remained more salient for women than for men.

Local base

If, as research has repeatedly shown, both education and occupation are relevant factors in the development of a political career for both women and men, then one must ask in what way they are significant. The standard of education of the average parliamentarian has increased over time, and the business of being a member of parliament has become a full-time occupation in its own right. Given the significance of localism in Irish politics, the building of a personal support base or 'bailiwick' in a constituency is a matter of considerable importance for both aspiring candidates and incumbents (Randall and Smyth, 1987, pp. 204–5). One of the most effective methods of doing this is through local government service. However, as we have seen, there are relatively few women in local government due to the persistence of conservative party selection practices.

One way of overcoming this disadvantage is through the development of local networks based on occupation. Professions such as teaching, medicine, law and business are generally seen as conferring status within a local community. They involve extensive interaction with the local electorate, and can be used as a foundation for personal bailiwick-building. In addition, these occupations bring economic independence and relative flexibility of time, two additional advantages for a person ambitious to hold political office. It is no accident that teaching is the occupation of the majority of women in the Dáil, as it combines the security of a salaried profession with opportunities for local contact and time in which to pursue support-building activities.

Local voluntary activity presents another method of building a public profile, yet an impressionistic view would lead one to conclude that this route to a political career is under-utilised by women. If this is the case, then the question arises: do women who are involved in local voluntary community activity choose not to engage in the political party process, or do they not see their participation in local issues as being of a political nature? The conclusions of research by O'Donovan and Ward suggest that women's groups in particular do not perceive their activities as political, although group members were receptive to the possibility of conducting ostensibly political campaigns:

> 36 per cent of the total sample reported that they were unsure as to whether they viewed their network as being political, suggesting that the networks were still in the process of defining their role and functions. Despite this, a significant proportion of women felt their network should be involved in campaigning, particularly on issues concerning the environment, education and child care.
>
> (O'Donovan and Ward, 1999, p. 98)

It appears that women with political ambitions try to follow the common routes of entry into political life. However, the influence of localism is one that many aspiring women politicians find difficult to counteract if they have not had the opportunity to break into a brokerage network through local authority service or through occupational activity. In other words, the opportunities for building recognition and credibility as a candidate are more limited for women than for men. Women political hopefuls are more likely to look to party elites for 'sponsorship' at the candidate selection stage in order to compensate for a lower degree of access to local networks.

Finally, while family connections have been important in determining routes to political power in Ireland, this has traditionally been a more significant factor for women than for men. From 1927 to 1973, the majority of women elected to the Dáil were related through family or marriage to former TDs. While it appeared that the significance of family in contributing to women's electoral prospects was on the wane in the early 1990s, the results of the 1997 election indicated a return to the traditional pattern. Comparing the 1992 and 1997 elections, we find that in 1992, seven (35 per cent) women deputies were related in varying ways to former members of the Dáil while the corresponding figure in 1997 was ten (50 per cent). In other words, while in 1992 almost two-thirds of the women TDs had no previous connections with earlier TDs or senators, in 1997 the family connection was relevant for exactly half of the successful women candidates. The proportions of men with family connections to politics did not change as dramatically as that of women over the same period. In both elections, only about one fifth of male TDs (22 per cent in 1992 and 21 per cent in 1997) were related to a previous incumbent.

Candidate selection

However, the above explanations, which focus on social and socio-political factors, do not fully account for the small number of women in politics. We must also look at the barriers embedded in the political system itself, and particularly at the selection processes of the political parties.

During the 1980s, the record of the parties in selecting women candidates improved. Since 1977, the party executives have played an increasing role in promoting women candidates, removing some of the almost complete discretion previously held by local party units over the candidate selection process (see chapter 6, pp. 160–2 above). Research confirms the critical role of party officials when it comes to the participation and selection of women candidates and their perceived opportunity for success (Fawcett, 1992). However, this involvement of the parties' central authorities, while being important for individual women, has not significantly redressed the gender imbalance in candidate tickets (Galligan, 1999). Although the proportion of women selected as candidates has increased over time, in 1997 it still remained stubbornly below 20 per cent of all those standing for election. As long as significantly fewer women than men are selected to contest elections, the opportunities for women to secure a place in the political process will continue to be limited. As Darcy (1988, p. 74) notes: 'Growth in the short term depends on increasing the proportions of women among new candidates . . . creating more opportunities for new people and increasing the re-election chances of women incumbents'.

One of the reasons for the low selection rate of women candidates traditionally put forward by party activists has been that voters prefer men. Evidence from survey research was unclear: indications that Irish people were not hostile to the idea of women TDs existed alongside other findings that suggested a modest bias existed among voters against women. The question of whether voters prefer male to female candidates was tested in relation to voter preferences in the 1997 general election. It was found that voter attitudes had become more positive than hitherto towards women as parliamentary representatives. When factors such as age, incumbency and previous political experience were controlled, it was clear that there was no significant gender bias among voters, suggesting that the parties – Fianna Fáil and Fine Gael in particular – can afford to be more adventurous in their selection of women candidates (Galligan, Laver and Carney, 1999).

Consequences of the under-representation of women

Public policy

There is no doubt that for much of the state's history, the law and public policy have treated women in a discriminatory fashion. Public policy was constructed within a constitutional context which, in Article 41.2 of the 1937 constitution, prescribed a homemaking role for women:

1   In particular, the State recognises that by her life within the home, woman gives to the State a support without which the common good cannot be achieved.
2   The State shall, therefore, endeavour to ensure that mothers shall not be obliged by economic necessity to engage in labour to the neglect of their duties in the home.

From this clear statement of the role of women, shaped by the values of conservative Catholic social thinking and accepted by the majority of men and women alike, public policies were enacted that reinforced the socially inferior position of women and their dependence on men as providers. As Scannell notes in summing up the relationship between women, the law and the constitution:

> For almost thirty years after the constitution was adopted, the position of women in Irish society hardly changed at all. The common law relegation of women to domesticity and powerlessness continued. Laws based on the premise that women's rights were inferior to those of men survived in, and indeed even appeared on, the statute books.
>
> (Scannell, 1988, p. 127)

Scannell outlines a long list of examples of discrimination against women in law and public policy from the 1930s to the 1960s. These included a ban on the employment of married women in the civil and public service, and unfavourable treatment as compared with men in employment, unemployment allowances, the tax code, family law, health, and social policies relating to fertility, family property, legal aid and social security matters.

From 1957, some of the more obvious manifestations of gender inequality in law began to be redressed. The Married Women's Status Act of 1957 was the first attempt to accord some measure of equal treatment for female spouses in the context of family policy. It gave married women the right to sue and be sued, to enter into contracts and to hold property in their own name, rights already enjoyed by unmarried women and by all men, irrespective of their marital status. In 1957 also, the ban on the employment of married women teachers, which had existed since 1932, was removed by a ministerial order, although the prohibition on the employment of married women remained in operation in the civil service until 1973. The Guardianship of Infants Act, which was passed in 1964 and came into force in 1967, gave mothers an equal say in all decisions relating to the upbringing of their children. Prior to this, fathers had had sole rights in child-rearing matters. The 1965 Succession Act gave a widow a legal entitlement to a share in her husband's estate on his death, ending the state of affairs in which a wife could be completely disinherited by a husband in his will.

However, major discriminatory policies against women remained in operation. During the 1970s, pressure for changes in legislation and other aspects of public policy began to emerge from three main sources: the judiciary, the feminist movement and the European Community. According to Scannell (1988, pp. 129–30), these agencies were more important catalysts in the initiation of change in the status of women than either politicians or parliament, suggesting that the political system was forced to respond to external pressures rather than being prepared to initiate change. While EC directives and judicial decisions acted as important catalysts for specific legislative changes, the re-emergence of the women's movement in the early 1970s prompted a public discussion of gender-based discrimination in law and public policy.

Evidence suggests that women's lobby groups have had a more immediate influence on specific aspects of law than the efforts of women TDs (Galligan, 1998). In 1972, the Commission on the Status of Women, established by the government two years earlier, recommended that action be taken to remove discrimination in the areas of the home, employment, social welfare, taxation, family law, jury service, public life and education. This report provided government with a blueprint for legislative reform, particularly in the areas of employment and social welfare policies, much of which was implemented in the course of the 1970s.

The Commission on the Status of Women was dissolved on production of its report, and the task of lobbying for legislative change was taken up by a range of women's interest groups that had grown out of the women's movement. For example, the National Women's Council of Ireland (NWCI, formerly known as the Council for the Status of Women), a non-partisan interest group formed in 1972 from a core of traditional women's organisations, is now regularly consulted by government and makes frequent submissions on a variety of issues directly affecting the position of women in society (Fitzsimons, 1991). In the 1990s, NWCI representatives were admitted to the highly corporatised economic decision making network, enabling them to make a direct contribution to policy making in this area. The family law reform group AIM (Action, Information, Motivation), established in 1972 as an offshoot of the women's movement, was instrumental in lobbying for changes in legislation relating to the family, which materialised during the 1970s and early 1980s. The Rape Crisis Centres succeeded in having the legislation dealing with sexual violence against women radically amended in 1990. The status of children born outside marriage was finally regulated with the abolition of the concept of illegitimacy and the enactment of provisions giving equal rights, as far as possible, to all children in the Status of Children Act (1987) after a decade of lobbying by Cherish and other single-parent support groups. These are some instances of the work of feminist issue groups in securing legislative reform that reflected the needs and demands of women (see chapter 11 for more discussion of the role of interest groups).

If lobbying efforts were not sufficient to secure change, national and European judicial systems served as agencies of progress. The McGee (1973), de Búrca (1976) and Airey (1979) cases, which respectively established the right of married couples to import contraceptives for their own use, the right of women to serve on juries, and the right of women to free legal aid, are seen as important cases leading to legislative reform of benefit to women. The principle of equality for women in social welfare entitlements was conceded by the government in 1990 following a judgement from the European Court of Justice in a case brought by two women, Cotter and McDermott, against the state. In the early 1990s, a confluence of three sets of judicial findings on aspects of abortion – from the European Court of Justice in 1991, the European Court of Human Rights in 1992 and the Supreme Court in the 'X' case of 1992 – led to constitutional referendums in November 1992 that showed clear majorities against an absolute ban on abortion and in favour of affirming a right to travel and to information about abortion (Kennelly and Ward, 1993).

Despite the advances in women's rights, there remain many important issues relating to women's lives that legislators have shown a reluctance to tackle. These range from the relatively non-contentious area of providing in law for equal rights and status between women and men to legislating on emotive and politically difficult issues such as abortion and new reproductive technologies.

The differential treatment of women and men demonstrated in the previous section raises the question of whether public policy might have been altered had there been more women in politics, and whether a greater number of women in future could make a difference. We can approach this by examining the extent of male–female differences in political attitudes and priorities.

Women as voters

On most issues, no marked policy differences between women and men have surfaced. For instance, in the 1997 general election there were at most minor differences in political priorities. While 42 per cent of women and 38 per cent of men considered unemployment the most important political issue, the pattern was reversed for concerns about crime and justice; 45 per cent of men prioritised crime as an electoral issue as compared with 37 per cent of women. Men were slightly more concerned about taxation policies and peace in Northern Ireland, women placed a slightly higher priority on education and poverty (King and Gillespie, 1998, p. 240). During the 1990 and 1997 presidential elections, there was again little evidence to support the theory of a gender gap in voting behaviour. A comprehensive survey of gender attitudes in Ireland from 1983 to 1997 reveals that gender gaps in voting intentions for the main political parties are 'neither consistent nor long lasting' (Donoghue and Devine, 1999, p. 241). However, although women and men broadly agree on the importance of a number of core issues, there is room for investigating whether they perceive those issues differently.

Surveys of social attitudes and voting intentions towards the two major controversies that Irish society faced in the 1980s, namely abortion and divorce, revealed that women clearly adopted a more conservative position than men on these matters. Polls taken during the 1986 debate on divorce indicate that there was a distinct gender gap in voting intentions towards the end of the campaign. Women's support for removing the constitutional ban on divorce dropped by 27 per cent between April and June 1986, in comparison with the 8 per cent decline in men's support for divorce, and the last pre-referendum poll found that while 49 per cent of men favoured legalisation of divorce, only 31 per cent of women did so (MRBI, 1986, Table 1). The issue of divorce was the subject of a second referendum in November 1995. In the period since the first referendum, polls indicated that support for the removal of the ban on divorce had grown, with approximately two-thirds of the electorate favouring this initiative. There were few detectable gender differences in this nine-year period, with the most significant gap occurring just prior to the referendum in November 1995. Men adopted a more liberal position than women, with 55 per cent supporting the removal of the ban, while only 49 per cent of women adopted this view (Donoghue and Devine, 1999, pp. 250–2).

Women were significantly more supportive than men of a 'Yes' vote in the closing stages of the 1983 campaign on the 'pro-life' (anti-abortion) amendment, with 75 per cent stating an intention to vote in favour as against 62 per cent of men (Girvin, 1986, p. 79). This gender gap recurred in a less clear-cut fashion prior to the November 1992 referendums on abortion, travel and information. There was some degree of difference in the opinions of men and women, with men being slightly more in favour of the right to travel than women (68 per cent as against 62 per cent).

There was no real difference in opinions on the 'right to information' question. However, when asked a general question on the availability of abortion, women indicated a greater preference for the range of conservative options presented than men (Donoghue and Devine, 1999, pp. 253–6). Thus we are led to conclude that when a question exploring general attitudes to abortion is asked, women will adopt a less liberal position than men. This appears to be carried through to voting behaviour, as a post-referendum survey found that, on the issue of the limited availability of abortion, women were more likely to have voted 'No' for conservative reasons while men were more likely to have voted 'No' for liberal reasons (Kennelly and Ward, 1993, pp. 129–30).[1]

Women as representatives

The growing body of literature on women's parliamentary activity offers no definite conclusion as to whether women make a distinctive contribution to the legislative process. Some studies suggest that women bring a particular style and policy agenda to political office, others highlight the similarities between women and men legislators, while still other research points to the significance of the institutional context in shaping gender debates in politics (Norris, 1996, pp. 93–5). The nature of the participation of women in the Dáil remains to be assessed, but there is an indication that women TDs bring distinctive perspectives to bear on legislative debates that spring from their personal and observed experiences of womanhood. In a June 1993 debate on the legalisation of condoms for sale in retail outlets, for instance, it was women TDs who placed this measure in the wider context of family planning and who were critical of the absence of a comprehensive, country-wide family planning service.

As matters stand, there are limits to how far women parliamentarians can go in promoting a feminist agenda or in challenging the dominant agenda without becoming politically marginalised. After all, party discipline dictates that members of the Oireachtas need to present a unified front in parliament and dissension from the party position is seldom tolerated. In addition, few women enter parliament with the intention of promoting women's issues alone; women representatives contribute to the same broad range of policy debates as their male parliamentary colleagues. This view was confirmed in a study of candidate attitudes towards policy issues in Britain which found that

> while women politicians were more likely to express concern about issues like welfare services, poverty and health . . . only two or three women politicians spontaneously mentioned issues which related more specifically to the agenda of the women's movement, such as equal opportunities for women, the provision of nursery schools or tax relief for child care.
>
> (Norris, 1996, p. 100)

If this finding is applicable to Ireland, it may appear that women TDs are less than effective in representing women's rights. To adopt this view, though, would be to judge female and male parliamentarians by different standards. Having expectations of women TDs that are different from, and arguably higher than, those applied to their male counterparts is ultimately a discriminatory act in itself.

There is a view that gender differences do not become part of parliamentary discourse while women remain in a distinct minority in the legislature. Evidence from countries in which the numbers of women parliamentarians have increased to significant proportions suggests that women legislators can effect change in the direction of women's rights only when they begin to constitute a substantial minority, perhaps about a third, of parliamentary representatives (Dahlerup, 1988). In other words, so long as women remain in a minority, we should not expect them to advance an agenda challenging the dominant, male-defined political consensus. Thus, we could say that without a substantial increase in the number of women elected to the Dáil, women's issues and policy priorities will not become part of the mainstream political agenda.

This line of thinking has been advanced by observers of Scandinavian and northern European politics. It is a very persuasive argument, but its relevance to Irish political circumstances remains unproven. There are two factors that might militate against the fulfilment of this thesis in an Irish context. The first relates to the consciousness of parliamentarians, particularly women TDs, of gender difference in policy issues. The 'large minority' thesis appears to work in Scandinavian countries partly because there is a generally high level of social and political awareness of gender issues. This perspective has been highlighted since the late 1970s by the activities of a strong women's movement in the case of Denmark and Norway, and the pursuit of an egalitarian social policy by successive Swedish governments. Legislators' awareness of the gender dimension was given a further impulse with the election of parliamentarians sympathetic to feminist demands. In Ireland, legislators have not been particularly conscious of feminist issues, the women's movement was a weak and short-lived phenomenon, and few feminists have been elected to the Dáil. To date, then, there has been little expression of an organised feminist voice in the Oireachtas apart from some notable individuals, both men and women. The advent of a larger number of women parliamentarians, then, may not in itself change policy priorities unless their political agenda is one of gender equality.

A second reason is the dominance of party discipline, which, as already noted, regulates the policy positions of all deputies, both women and men. But, although this is an important constraint, we must also take the gender composition of the various parliamentary parties into consideration. As we have seen, these bodies are at present heavily male dominated, and it is possible that the parliamentary party line, which all TDs must toe, might be different if a higher proportion of their membership were women. Party discipline could then become an instrument for advancing woman-friendly policies.

While there may be little prospect of a feminist agenda taking hold in the Dáil, there is more scope for the representation of women's perspectives on all political concerns. Indeed, with the requirement from 1993 onwards that all legislation be 'gender-proofed', the opportunity for advancing a woman-centred perspective on policy issues has increased. This government rule has had the effect of introducing a measure of gender balance into legislation: for example, the 1997 Universities Act stipulates that gender equality must be provided for in all aspects of the work of a university, while the 1999 Sports Act prescribes a 40 per cent gender balance on the board of the Irish Sports Council.

The institutionalisation of women's interests

Gradually, as issues of women's rights and status in society became part of the political agenda, political structures evolved that institutionalised the expression of these demands. First, the Women's Representative Committee was established by the Fine Gael–Labour coalition government in 1974 to oversee the implementation of the recommendations of the Commission on the Status of Women. It was replaced in 1978 by two organisations, the Employment Equality Agency (a statutory body) and the NWCI. The establishment of the junior ministry for Women's Affairs and Family Law Reform in 1982 and the Joint Oireachtas Committee on Women's Rights in 1983 brought a woman-centred focus on policy and legislation into the mainstream of the political system. The report of the Second Commission on the Status of Women, suggesting extensive public policy reforms, was received in a positive way by government (Galligan, 1993). The Oireachtas Committee on Women's Rights became an important advocate for women's issues within the framework of parliamentary institutions. However, in a restructuring of the committee system in 1997, the women's affairs committee was subsumed into the activities of the committee on justice and equality. This new arrangement shows that the institutionalisation of gender interests has yet to set down firm roots in the parliamentary structure.

A renewed political commitment to the principle of equality was indicated in 1993 with the appointment of a Minister for Equality and Law Reform. On this occasion, the concept of equality was given a generic definition. Gender equality was a significant component, but not the only concern, of this ministry. In 1997 the office was amalgamated with the Department of Justice and once again given junior status. As with the parliamentary Committee on Women's Rights, this points to some lack of stability within the decision making machinery attaching to women's affairs as a government concern. On the positive side, it is significant that governments since the early 1980s have considered gender interests and related equality concerns to be of sufficient importance to specify them in a ministerial portfolio.

The achievements of successive equality ministers include reforming the laws on domicile and domestic violence, initiating a voluntary code on sexual harassment in the workplace and introducing an all-embracing statute providing for equal status treatment of citizens in public policy. The results of the efforts of successive ministers in this area have been to strengthen the protections afforded to women in the workplace, in the home and in society. In keeping with the expanded concept of equality dominant in government thinking since the early 1990s, many of these rights are not exclusively focused on women. The legislation on domestic violence, for instance, applies not only to women but also to parents, children at risk of violence, and men. The equal status legislation covers a range of minority groups in society as well as women. The code on sexual harassment recognises that both men and women can be victims and perpetrators of the abuse of power in the workplace.

If successive governments have shown some desire to incorporate women's demands into the governmental and legislative process, individual political parties have not shown the same degree of enlightenment. In terms of candidate selection, parties have been quick to recognise the advantage of attracting the support of women voters but slow to adopt measures that would facilitate the selection of women in significantly greater numbers, as we saw earlier in the chapter. In policy terms, however, parties recognise that women and men may hold diverse views on policy issues and are coming round to accommodating women-specific issues and women's perspectives on general policies in their manifestos.

None the less, the more enduring structural adaptations that have incorporated the 'women's agenda' have involved a minimal disruption, if any, to the political system. The mainstreaming of women's issues has proceeded apace, but the price to be paid for integration into policy priorities is a sharing of government attention with other groups. The challenge for women's interest organisations and for feminists within the political system is to ensure that women's perspectives on women's affairs are not lost as equality issues assume a wider dimension.

Conclusion

The relationship between women and politics in Ireland has become more complex over time. Women considering a career in public life do so in a social environment that expects them also to fulfil traditional home-based duties. Ireland ranks close to the bottom of the European scale in terms of women's representation in political life, yet there is no discernible bias among the electorate against women candidates. Women remain under-represented as election candidates, although parties are making some progress towards redressing this imbalance. The number of women candidates has increased over the years, but is still fewer than 20 per cent of all candidates in national elections. This is due to a combination of social and structural factors that inhibit women's political activity, and to a resistance within the parties to giving serious consideration to providing gender balance on candidate tickets. While the role models presented by Mary Robinson, Mary McAleese and Mary Harney may encourage more women to present themselves for selection as candidates, the prognosis for a greater level of active participation by women in political life remains poor unless parties adopt strong affirmative action strategies similar to those successfully employed in some parties elsewhere in Europe, such as the German Social Democrats, the Norwegian parties, and the Austrian and German Greens.

Some progress has been made in policy terms. A range of issues raised by women since the 1970s, particularly those relating to women's rights within the family and in employment, were incorporated into the political process and legitimised in the 1980s and the 1990s. A political resolution of the abortion conflict, however, has proved more difficult to achieve. A skeletal institutional framework exists that initially focused on women's status but now pays attention to the legislative rights of a number of minority groups. This structure did not exist in 1980, but its legislative powers can vary in accordance with the priority attached to these concerns by government. Women's interest groups have been incorporated into policy networks in specific areas, with varying degrees of success. In some areas, progress has been substantive but in key policy areas, such as the economy, there has been little progress in resolving women's concerns. In addition, Ireland still has a long way to go before women are elected to the Dáil in the same proportions as men. A serious commitment by political leaders to progress is required in order that the voice and needs of one half of the population are adequately catered for in the political system.

Note

1   This referendum followed the Supreme Court's judgment in the 'X' case, whose effect was that abortion was now legal in certain circumstances (for the 'X' case, see Box 3.2). The proposal put to the people in the November 1992 referendum would have reduced, but not eliminated, the circumstances in which abortion would be legal. This proposal was opposed both by liberals (who did not want any further restrictions imposed) and by conservatives (who wanted abortion outlawed completely). For a full discussion of this complex issue, see Kennelly and Ward (1993).

References and further reading

Central Statistics Office (CSO), 1998. *Quarterly National Household Survey: September–November 1997*. Cork: Central Statistics Office.

Connelly, Alpha and Betty Hilliard, 1993. 'The legal system', pp. 212–38 in Alpha Connelly (ed.), *Gender and the Law in Ireland*. Dublin: Oak Tree Press.

Dahlerup, Drude, 1988. 'From a small to a large minority: women in Scandinavian politics', *Scandinavian Political Studies* 11:4, pp. 275–98.

Darcy, R., 1988. 'The election of women to Dáil Éireann: a formal analysis', *Irish Political Studies* 3, pp. 63–76.

Department of Finance, 1999. *Equality of Opportunity in the Civil Service, 1996: Tabular Statement to Accompany the Ninth Annual Report on the Implementation of the Equal Opportunity Policy and Guidelines for the Civil Service*. Dublin: Department of Finance.

Donoghue, Freda and Paula Devine, 1999. 'Is there a gender gap in political attitudes in Ireland?', pp. 240–68 in Galligan, Ward and Wilford (1999).

Eager, Clare, 1991. 'Splitting images – women and the Irish civil service', *Seirbhís Phoiblí* 12:1, pp. 15–23.

European Commission, 1992. *Eurobarometer* No 38. Brussels: European Commission.

European Commission, 1995. *Eurobarometer* No 42. Brussels: European Commission.

European Commission, 1996. *Women in Decision-making: Facts and Figures on Women in Political and Public Decision-making in Europe*. Brussels: European Commission, 4th edition.

European Commission, 1997. *Equal Opportunities for Women and Men in the European Union: Annual Report 1997*. Brussels: European Commission.

Farrell, David M., 1992. 'Ireland', pp. 389–457 in Richard S. Katz and Peter Mair (eds), *Party Organizations: A Data Handbook on Party Organizations in Western Democracies, 1960–90*. London: Sage.

Fawcett, Liz, 1992. 'The recruitment of women to local politics in Ireland: a case study', *Irish Political Studies* 7, pp. 41–55.

Fitzsimons, Yvonne, 1991. 'Women's interest representation in the Republic of Ireland: the Council for the Status of Women', *Irish Political Studies* 6, pp. 37–51.

Galligan, Yvonne, 1993. 'The Report of the Second Commission on the Status of Women', *Irish Political Studies* 8, pp. 125–30.

Galligan, Yvonne, 1998. *Women and Politics in Contemporary Ireland: From the Margins to the Mainstream*. London: Pinter.

Galligan, Yvonne, 1999. 'Candidate selection', pp. 57–81 in Michael Marsh and Paul Mitchell (eds), *How Ireland Voted 1997*. Boulder, Colo.: Westview Press and PSAI Press.

Galligan, Yvonne, Michael Laver and Gemma Carney, 1999. 'The effect of candidate gender on voting in Ireland, 1997', *Irish Political Studies* 14.

Galligan, Yvonne, Eilís Ward and Rick Wilford (eds), 1999. *Contesting Politics: Women in Ireland, North and South*. Boulder, Colo.: Westview Press and PSAI Press.

Galligan, Yvonne and Rick Wilford, 1999. 'Gender and party politics in the Republic of Ireland', pp. 149–68 in Galligan, Ward and Wilford (1999).

Girvin, Brian, 1986. 'Social change and moral politics: the Irish constitutional referendum 1983', *Political Studies* 34:1, pp. 61–81.

ICTU, 1998. *Congress Affiliated Union Membership*. Dublin: Irish Congress of Trade Unions.

Kennelly, Brendan and Eilís Ward, 1993. 'The abortion referendums', pp. 115–34 in Michael Gallagher and Michael Laver (eds), *How Ireland Voted 1992*. Dublin: Folens and Limerick: PSAI Press.

King, Simon and Gordon Gillespie, 1998. 'Irish political data 1997', *Irish Political Studies* 13, pp. 211–79.

MRBI, 1986. *Irish Times*/MRBI Poll 3450/86. Dun Laoghaire: Market Research

Bureau of Ireland.

National Women's Council of Ireland, 1998. *Who Makes the Decisions in 1997? A Review of Gender Balance on State Boards in Ireland.* Dublin: National Women's Council of Ireland.

Norris, Pippa, 1996. 'Women politicians: transforming Westminster?' pp. 91–104 in Joni Lovenduski and Pippa Norris (eds), *Women in Politics.* Oxford: Oxford University Press.

O'Donovan, Órla and Eilís Ward, 1999. 'Networks of women's groups in the Republic of Ireland', pp. 90–108 in Galligan, Ward and Wilford (1999).

OECD, 1998. *Employment Outlook, June 1998.* Paris: Organisation for Economic Cooperation and Development.

Randall, Vicky and Ailbhe Smyth, 1987. 'Bishops and bailiwicks: obstacles to women's political participation in Ireland', *Economic and Social Review* 18:3, pp. 189–214.

Scannell, Yvonne, 1988. 'The constitution and the role of women', pp. 123–36 in Brian Farrell (ed.), *De Valera's Constitution and Ours.* Dublin: Gill and Macmillan.

Whelan, Christopher T. and Tony Fahey, 1994. 'Marriage and the family', pp. 105–28 in Christopher T. Whelan (ed.), *Values and Social Change in Ireland.* Oxford: Oxford University Press.

13 Ireland

A small open polity

Patrick Keatinge and Brigid Laffan

Ireland, according to Article 5 of its constitution, is a 'sovereign, independent, democratic state'. This reference to the state's legal right to conduct its
own affairs without outside interference can hardly be seen as an adequate
description of the Irish state's political relationship with the rest of the
world. For that purpose it makes more sense to adapt the terminology often
used by economists, and to think of Ireland as a 'small open polity'.

Such an approach reminds us that the national political system is not
self-contained but is subject to complex influences from its external environment. In the first part of this chapter we identify the main
characteristics of that environment, and show how changes at this 'macro-
political' level have affected Ireland's political development during the
first eighty years of the state's existence. A significant example is the
evolution of Ireland's single most important diplomatic connection, that
with the United Kingdom. This 'special relationship', covered in the
second part of the chapter, centres on the often contested issue of
Northern Ireland. The ensuing difficulties came to be mediated through
unique international arrangements, first under the Anglo-Irish
Agreement of 1985 and then through the complex institutional framework arising from the Northern Ireland peace process in the 'Good Friday
Agreement' of 1998.

A second element in Ireland's international setting also merits a
detailed analysis. The European Union – or European Community, as it
was known when Ireland joined in 1973 – is a complex political system with a
unique structure. Its influence on its members is pervasive. EU membership
is not just a 'foreign policy' issue; in many respects it is an extension of
national (or 'domestic') politics. The rest of this chapter thus concentrates
on the Union's impact on Irish political activity, and on the way in which
Ireland's European policy is formed.

In this context we ask whether Ireland really has a 'foreign policy', in
the sense implied in the constitutional claim to independence quoted
above. To what extent, and employing what means, do Irish governments
pursue their values and interests in international politics in general? We
shall see that much of this activity now takes place in conjunction with

other EU states and through the complex web of multilateral networks that have been developed since the Second World War. This raises questions about the viability of specific policies, such as neutrality, and even about the continued existence of the 'sovereign, independent state'.

The external environment

Any state's external environment consists of all other states together with the nature of the international system formed by their relationships. Writers in the field of international relations have disagreed when it comes to identifying the most important characteristics of the international system (Little and Smith, 1991). We do not have to go very far into their contending theories to appreciate the complexity of the external environment, but one of their basic distinctions provides a starting point for an analysis of Ireland's position in world politics.

Followers of what is often called the 'realist' school stress the state as the focus of international politics, and look to 'power' as a major explanatory factor. Given the anarchic nature of the international system – there is no authority above states – the ever present tendency to resort to force is seen as the most pressing problem of international life. In this view the foreign policy of a small state such as Ireland is above all a struggle for survival in a Hobbesian world of predatory great powers.

On the other hand, 'interdependence' theorists have argued that economic forces are generally more important than the formal prerogatives of statehood. International actors other than states, including international organisations and non-state ('transnational') bodies such as multinational corporations, may wield as much influence as states, if not more. In the eyes of these theorists, the politics of 'security' is less significant than the characteristics of the international political economy. In this context, it is Ireland's small open economy that puts it at risk, rather than any lack of diplomatic or military power.

Ireland in a world of Realpolitik, 1922–45

From the establishment of the Irish Free State as a member of the British Commonwealth until 1945, the international system approximated the realist model all too closely. Although the League of Nations provided the new state with the opportunity to establish and develop its international credentials (Kennedy, 1996), the attempt to organise an international rule of law through the League failed dramatically, and international stability was eventually established only by force of arms. At first sight it seems paradoxical that Ireland's political independence was steadily consolidated during this period, but given that it was independence from British domination this result is not so surprising. British decline was a constant theme, giving Irish governments the leverage to obtain a somewhat ambiguous statehood in the first place, and then to remove most of the ambiguities by a variety of means.

These started with multilateral negotiations within the Commonwealth and the League, allowing for coalitions with the other dominions, and providing the basis for de Valera's unilateral revision of the 1921 Treaty in the form of the 1937 constitution. By this time the British government's policy of appeasement of Germany implied the appeasement of Ireland, in handing over the naval facilities at the ports, which in turn was a prerequisite of Irish neutrality throughout the Second World War (Keatinge, 1986).

This achievement – and in Irish political culture neutrality acquired the status of a 'core value', as the touchstone of independence – should not blind us to the limitations of Ireland's international position coming into the postwar era. Formal political independence had not been matched in economic terms; the economy remained almost wholly dependent on the fortunes (or more usually the misfortunes) of one of Europe's least successful economies. Partition was if anything consolidated, in spite of attempts to make it an international issue. Playing the (Irish-) American card was supposed to mobilise Washington against London, but that would always be a doubtful proposition when the exigencies of a great power alliance were at stake. Even wartime neutrality had not been played strictly according to the rules (Salmon, 1989; Fisk, 1983). It had been played quite skilfully, but in the end its viability owed more to geopolitical realities than to government policy. Irish neutrality was not tested to the extent experienced by, for example, Finland, which was located between the Soviet Union and the Third Reich, the least scrupulous of the great powers.

Ireland in an interdependent world, 1945 to the present

A very different international system existed between 1945 and 1989. This 'bipolar' system, although marked by a major international conflict (the cold war between the United States and the Soviet Union), came to acquire a much greater degree of stability than its predecessor. In the western world this permitted the development of a type of international politics that looks much more like the model of the interdependence theorists. Against a background of unprecedented economic growth, 'international regimes' (a term that covers both formal organisations and looser arrangements) became the norm. Traditional distinctions between 'foreign' and 'domestic' policy tended to lose much of their meaning, especially among the countries forming the core of west European integration.

Ireland, like the other small peripheral states in western Europe, was slow to adapt to this process. In the late 1940s traditional concerns with Anglo-Irish relations and partition seemed at least as important as the new issues, such as the cold war, and geopolitical irrelevance again permitted the continuation of an even less clearly defined neutrality policy. Economic dependence on the United Kingdom inhibited a close involvement in the integration process, as British governments remained aloof from 'Europe'. However, a fundamental reappraisal of economic policy in the late 1950s brought about a more active interest in European integration. This led to an application to join the European Economic Community (EEC) in 1961, when the United Kingdom turned in this direction, only to be blocked by the veto on EEC enlargement in 1963 imposed by French President Charles de Gaulle.

Nevertheless, the state's internationalisation did make some tentative progress. A founding member of the Organisation for European Economic Cooperation (OEEC) and the Council of Europe in the late 1940s, Ireland was at last admitted to the United Nations (UN) in 1955. The delay had more to do with cold war politics than with Irish policy, which had aimed at membership since 1946. Participation in the UN provided the basis of a peacekeeping role which became one of the constants of Irish foreign policy, and it also allowed the formation of policies towards the emerging third world countries (Skelly, 1997).

'Europe' – that is, the European Community that evolved from the EEC and its associated treaties – was, however, the focal point of government policy from the early 1960s onwards, mainly for economic reasons. When enlargement again became feasible in 1969 membership was negotiated and was approved in a referendum in 1972, by a majority of 83 per cent to 17 per cent in a turnout of over 70 per cent (see appendix 2h). Thus from 1973 the state's involvement in international affairs became much more intensive, and its direct effects reached far into Irish public life (Keatinge, 1991). The economy experienced a faster rate of growth than would otherwise have occurred. Financial support, initially mainly through the Common Agricultural Policy (CAP) and then more broadly through the structural funds (whose function is to promote development, especially in the less wealthy parts of the Union), contributed significantly to Irish growth. As of the late 1980s it still seemed a moot point whether Ireland's position as a net beneficiary had been exploited to maximum advantage through national economic policies, but the dramatic increase in Irish growth rates in the second half of the 1990s (the so-called 'Celtic tiger' phenomenon) led to more optimistic assessments. EU membership is not of itself a panacea for all economic ills, but at the very least it has provided a systematic way of influencing the collective EU response to global forces that are beyond the control of even the largest European economies.

The revival of momentum towards west European integration in the late 1980s confirmed the significance of Ireland's membership of the EC, which was transformed into the European Union (EU) following the Maastricht Treaty of 1992. At the same time the state's international position was also affected by a separate, and even more fundamental, change in world politics: the collapse of the Soviet Union as one of the world's two 'superpowers' between 1989 and 1991. The new global political system is characterised by major uncertainties: the strains of fundamental democratic and free market transition in the former communist world, and especially in the Russian Federation; the capacity and will of the USA to play the role of 'global policeman'; and the proliferation of military technology of all sorts, especially weapons of mass destruction.

The extent of change in Ireland's external environment at this level has been greater than at any time since the immediate aftermath of the Second World War. However, there is one important difference between these two transitional phases. In the late 1940s the complex networks of multilateral organisations – the UN and its agencies, alliance systems, and economic institutions – were at a formative stage, as were the conventions of modern multilateral diplomacy. Now they are mature, and while this maturity has eased the current transition there remains a major task of adaptation of institutions and attitudes alike. The European Union is a central element in all this, and thus Ireland is much more directly involved in the making of the global and regional systems than was the case in the late 1940s. As well as impinging constantly on the formation of national policy, adaptation to the external environment reaches into 'domestic' politics in a number of different ways. No fewer than four referendums have been held on European integration. Following the accession referendum in 1972, the Irish electorate voted on the Single European Act in 1987, the Maastricht Treaty in 1992 and the Amsterdam Treaty in 1998. The last of these coincided with a referendum on the 'Good Friday Agreement' on the Northern Ireland peace process. This served as a reminder of the significance of that other distinctive element in the state's external environment: the relationship between the governments in Dublin and London over the question of the conflict in Northern Ireland.

A special relationship: Ireland and Britain

As we have seen, Anglo-Irish relations were the predominant theme in Irish foreign policy from the founding of the state to the formative years of the cold war system in the late 1940s. In the critical period of 1948–49, while the western alliance system was being established under the North Atlantic Treaty, the Irish government was more concerned with the issues of constitutional status, Commonwealth membership and partition (McCabe, 1991).

Even when 'Europe' assumed the central place in the state's external relations, Anglo-Irish relations retained an important position. Ireland's negotiations to join the European Community coincided with the collapse of political authority in Northern Ireland, and the subsequent conflict there has been a constant element in the state's external relations. While it goes against the grain of nationalist ideology to conceive of the North as 'foreign policy', certain political and legal realities place this issue on the boundary between foreign and domestic politics. In attempting to influence political behaviour outside the jurisdiction of the state, Irish governments are inevitably brought into contact with the sovereign government in whose jurisdiction Northern Ireland actually lies.

Anglo-Irish relations, dominated by the issue of Northern Ireland, have thus served both as a touchstone of nationalist ideology in domestic politics and as an important dimension of the state's diplomacy. Yet attitudes in the Republic towards the northern conflict have not always led to clear or consistent policy. A refusal to accept the partition of the island as a socio-political reality (Girvin, 1999, pp. 220–1) was accompanied by a combination of occasional rhetorical posturing and neglect, until the outbreak of violence in the late 1960s. Subsequently policy was based on two needs: first, to defend the legitimacy of the state against the extremist nationalism of the IRA, and then to ensure that the nationalist case for change in Northern Ireland was pursued within the constraints of consti-tutional rather than violent nationalism (Ruane and Todd, 1996).

For Dublin governments, northern policy was traditionally seen as the prerogative of the Taoiseach, but in operational terms the Department of Foreign Affairs deals with most of the business. Since 1969 that has been considerable (Keatinge, 1986). The original neglect of Northern Ireland by both British and Irish governments was followed by Dublin's often painful attempts to persuade London that an 'Irish dimension' had any legitimacy or utility. The negotiation of the Sunningdale Agreement in 1973 achieved that objective but proved to be a false dawn for Northern Ireland. It satisfied neither the majority of unionists nor extreme nationalists, and it was not until 1985 that a formal institutional basis for Anglo-Irish relations was established in the Anglo-Irish Agreement.

For students of both Irish and international political processes, this bilateral 'regime' possessed several interesting features. Following a period of acute adversarial party politics it had been necessary to build an unusually detailed nationalist consensus in the New Ireland Forum of 1983–84. This extra-parliamentary consultation between the Dáil parties and the northern SDLP produced a sufficient level of agreement and political will for the government of the day to engage in prolonged and intensive negotiations with its British counterpart. The commitment of the Taoiseach, Garret FitzGerald, and the involvement of a small group of senior civil servants contrasted with the rather marginal role of the government as a whole (FitzGerald, 1991, pp. 460–575).

Once the agreement was signed a pattern of regular and quite frequent meetings of a newly-created Anglo-Irish Intergovernmental Conference took place, at which the Irish representative, the Minister for Foreign Affairs, could raise issues pertaining to the government of Northern Ireland with his counterpart, the British Secretary of State for Northern Ireland. This was not joint decision-making, but as an opportunity to influence policy in another jurisdiction, on matters of considerable sensi-tivity, it was an unusual form of international relationship.

Irish governments, including those of Fianna Fáil (which originally

opposed the agreement in 1985), have argued that it reduced the vulnerability of constitutional nationalists in Northern Ireland, and replaced
'megaphone diplomacy' between Dublin and London by a more ordered,
less tense and more sensitive relationship. Ireland acquired leverage in the
northern conflict, in a context of acknowledged partnership between the
two sovereign governments (Girvin, 1999, p. 228). The agreement's critics
maintained that it did not achieve its primary aim of a lasting resolution of
the conflict, and some of them – particularly the northern unionists –
regarded it as part of the problem rather than as part of the solution.
There were clearly limits to this experiment in 'coercive consociationalism'
(O'Leary and McGarry, 1996).

Yet from 1985 the momentum behind the search for a political rap-
prochement in Northern Ireland remained high on the agenda of
Anglo-Irish relations. The more focused bilateral effort was supplemented
by an increasing 'internationalisation' of the issue, a process that the Irish
government deliberately promoted, often in the face of British resistance.
This strategy aimed to achieve the 'greening' of both Europe and the
United States. In the early 1970s there had been expectations that
European integration would have an ameliorating influence, but for a long
time the basic antagonism remained impervious to external influences
(Guelke, 1988). EC membership did have some positive effects: it brought
the British and Irish governments into constant contact on less contentious
issues, and at the same time helped the Irish government to mobilise international support. The EC itself was a source of modest financial aid, in the
form of cross-border projects and a contribution to the fund established
alongside the Anglo-Irish Agreement. But the hope that the weakening of
the economic border in the European single market, together with moves
towards political union, would make the Northern conflict more 'anachronistic' than ever did not of itself suggest a resolution of the conflict (Ruane
and Todd, 1996, pp. 279–88). Being seen as anachronistic has rarely worried
the extremes of Irish politics, and the borders to be crossed are psychological as well as economic.

The engagement of the United States was ultimately more important
and, in the short term, more pressing (Ruane and Todd, 1996, pp. 273–9).
From the early 1970s the support of Irish-American opinion had to be
channelled towards the constitutional approach rather than in the direction
of extreme nationalism. This involved the Dublin government in mobilising both congressional opinion and the administration itself. The
policy first bore fruit with President Carter's public acknowledgement of
Dublin's role in 1977, and was an important factor in both the negotiation of and subsequent support for the agreement of 1985; the
traditional American preference for their main cold war ally was not
allowed to stand in the way of an independent view of the Northern
Ireland issue. But it was under President Bill Clinton, who came into
office in 1993, that American activism reached the point where Northern

Ireland was seen as 'an issue of legitimate American concern' (Ruane and Todd, 1996, p. 278).

By this time there was a distinct, though very convoluted, 'peace process' in Northern Ireland (Tonge, 1998, pp. 126–71). Irish policy consisted of the promotion of dialogue between constitutional and paramilitary nationalists in an effort to persuade the latter to abandon violence, alongside a concerted attempt by both Irish and British governments to bring all the northern political parties to the negotiating table. After several false starts the process was formalised in the intergovernmental Downing Street Declaration of December 1993, which paved the way for paramilitary ceasefires in the late summer of 1994. These did not prove sufficient in themselves to engage the parties in substantive negotiations, and the following eighteen months exposed serious tactical differences between Dublin and London before the IRA ended its ceasefire in February 1996. Yet the common strategic purpose of both governments, and the basic framework of the peace process itself, survived these setbacks (and changes to the composition of the governments in both countries). A renewed IRA ceasefire in July 1997 led to substantive negotiations under the chairmanship of the American 'peace envoy', former senator George Mitchell, and included intensive direct input by both heads of government; the outcome was the 'Good Friday Agreement' of 10 April 1998. This was endorsed by an unprecedented combination of referendums in both the Republic and Northern Ireland on 22 May.

The immediate political problems associated with the Good Friday Agreement had to do with the demilitarisation of the conflict: the early release of paramilitary prisoners, the decommissioning of their arms and the marginalisation of the still active diehard factions. In the longer term, the agreement allowed for the establishment of a complex system of institutions: an elected assembly in Northern Ireland, with an executive authority responsible for devolved legislation; a north–south ministerial council to 'develop consultation, cooperation and action within the island of Ireland'; and a British–Irish Council representing both the Irish and British governments together with the new devolved institutions in the United Kingdom: Scotland and Wales as well as Northern Ireland (and the Isle of Man and the Channel Islands). Finally, as a reminder of the conventional location of political authority, a new standing British–Irish Intergovernmental Conference replaces the arrangements of 1985.

The most immediate implication for politics in the Republic lay in the referendum of 22 May 1998, which authorised amendments to Articles 2, 3 and 29 of the Irish constitution, contingent on the overall implementation of the Good Friday Agreement. The vote – 94 per cent in favour – was decisive for such a break with the orthodoxy of traditional nationalism, though some disappointment was expressed at the turnout of only 56 per cent. The amendment of Articles 2 and 3 marked a significant evolution in public opinion, reflecting a recognition of unionist sensitivities, a revulsion towards IRA methods and a readiness to see Irish unity as a relatively

Box 13.1 The Good Friday Agreement, 1998

The Agreement was signed in Belfast on Good Friday (10 April) 1998.

The actors
- the British and Irish governments
- the political parties in Northern Ireland representing both unionists and nationalists (including paramilitary groups), except for two unionist parties (the Democratic Unionist Party and the United Kingdom Unionist Party).

Constitutional change
- the Republic abandons territorial claim (in Articles 2 and 3 of the Irish constitution)
- the United Kingdom repeals the 1920 Government of Ireland Act
- 'Consent' becomes the new constitutional imperative.

'Interlocking and interdependent' institutions
- Strand 1: Northern Ireland Assembly (based on PR-STV) and Executive Committee.
- Strand 2: 'North-South' Ministerial Council, responsible for functional cooperation.
- Strand 3: 'East/West' structures: (a) British–Irish Council, representing both governments, new devolved assemblies in Northern Ireland, Scotland and Wales, the Isle of Man and the Channel Islands; (b) British–Irish Intergovernmental Conference.

Policy changes
- disarmament of all paramilitary groups by 22 May 2000
- early release of paramilitary prisoners
- phasing out of emergency provisions and security deployments
- reform of policing and criminal justice systems.

Legitimacy
The Agreement was endorsed by simultaneous referendums in Northern Ireland and the Republic on 22 May 1998.
- the vote in the north was 71 per cent in favour and 29 per cent against
- in the south, 94 percent voted in favour.

remote aspiration. However, the broader implications of the Good Friday Agreement were far from clear. What policy content will eventually be covered by the North–South and British–Irish institutions? More importantly, what influence will northern interests have over policies which have up to now been decided mainly within the Republic, and how will this affect the legitimacy of what is in any case likely to be for some time a fragile settlement within Northern Ireland?

One thing is clear, however. The Agreement adds a new complexity and new levels of governance to the Irish political system. Yet in doing so it is not altogether without precedent. As a member state in the European Community (later European Union) since 1973, Ireland has already demonstrated the capacity to adapt its national policy system to an external source of political authority.

The European Union

The European Union is a very distinctive organisation in the international system, being much more than a traditional international organisation but not a fully fledged state. In fact, the Union is unlikely ever to assume the properties of traditional statehood. Within the Union, fifteen sovereign states agree to pool their sovereignty over a wide range of policy areas. By joining the EU, a state becomes part of a regional polity, above the level of the state, but one in which states play a pivotal role. Membership of the EU does not mean a negation of the national; rather the national is embedded in a wider set of political and legal processes.

The EU differs from traditional forms of interstate cooperation in five main respects. First, the founders of the EU in the 1950s set out to lay the foundations of a federal Europe. After the war, there was a strong movement favouring European unity. Although the European Union has failed to live up to the expectations of the founding fathers, the notion of an 'ever closer union among the peoples of Europe' – a phrase used in the preamble to the 1992 Treaty of Maastricht – is part of the rhetoric of EU policies and provides an ideological underpinning to European integration. Moreover, when a country decides to opt for EU membership, it is accepting an open-ended commitment to participate in an evolving political entity (Laffan, O'Donnell and Smith, 1999).

Second, the Union has a quasi-constitution in the form of a set of treaties (see Box 13.2). These treaties establish the range of public policies that the Union may engage in and make provision for a set of institutions to manage collective governance among the member states. Law plays a central role in the workings of the Union, and EC law in effect represents an 'external constitution' for the Irish political system. Three characteristics of Community law are particularly important: direct effect, direct applicability, and its supremacy over national law. The principle of *direct effect* means that Community law is not just a matter for public agencies but may be directed towards individuals and companies. *Direct applicability* of EC law, on the other hand, means that once a regulation is passed by the legislative process it immediately becomes part of national law. The practical implication of these principles is that Community law involves not only governments and public agencies but also individual citizens or private bodies, and that Community law can override national law. When joining the Union, states must accept the entire *acquis communautaire*, a term used to describe the bundle of obligations that arise from Community law, convention and practice.

Third, the Union is endowed with a set of institutions to make and implement policy (see Box 13.2). The Union involves both traditional or orthodox intergovernmental co-operation (that is, co-operation between fully sovereign states) and, at the same time, elements of supranational authority, in the form of institutions that are largely independent of the member states (Nugent, 1994). Intergovernmental relations are formalised in the Council system, while supranational authority is represented by the

---

Box 13.2 EU treaties, pillars, and institutions

Treaties
The main treaties are
- the Paris Treaty (establishing the European Coal and Steel Community) of 1950
- the Rome Treaties (European Economic Community and Euratom) of 1957
- the Merger Treaty of 1965
- the Budget Treaties of 1970 and 1975
- the Single European Act of 1987
- the Treaty on European Union (Maastricht Treaty) of 1992
- the Treaty of Amsterdam (1997)

Pillars
The Treaty on European Union organised the work of the Union into what are called the three pillars:
- Pillar I: EC pillar, including economic and monetary union
- Pillar II: Common Foreign and Security Policy (CFSP)
- Pillar III: Justice and Home Affairs (JHA).

Institutions
The EU has five main institutions. These are
- the Commission
- the Council of the EU (formerly known as the Council of Ministers)
- the European Parliament
- the European Court of Justice
- the Court of Auditors, which was elevated to the status of a full institution in the Treaty on European Union.

In addition, there are a number of Union bodies, such as the Economic and Social Committee, the Committee of the Regions and the Ombudsman.

legal system, the Commission, the Court and the European Parliament (EP). The Union's policy processes are a delicate balance between the powers of all of these institutions.

The fourth respect in which the EU differs from traditional forms of interstate co-operation is that it has an extremely ambitious policy reach. The treaties set out in considerable detail just what the Union should be doing, and the substance of much of what it does is economic. The EEC Treaty established the goal of integration as the creation of a customs union and a common market, in which there would be a free flow of goods, capital, workers and services. A large part of the Union's later policy developments flowed from the need to fulfil this goal. In addition, the treaty made provision for a common policy on agriculture and transport. Over time the Union's policy scope has widened to meet new problems such as the environment and regional development. The central thrust of the Single European Act was the '1992 programme', which aimed by the end of 1992 to create an internal market in which economic exchange between states would resemble economic exchange within a state. This involved nothing less than the abolition of border controls, the harmonisation of technical standards, the creation of a framework in which banks and insurance companies from one member state may set up in any member state, liberalising the rules governing air transport, and achieving a degree of convergence in rates of indirect taxation. The Treaty of Maastricht established the framework for a single currency (the Euro), which came into effect on 1 January 1999, with Ireland as one of its first eleven members (the rate fixed was that one Euro equalled 0.787564 Irish pounds).

Fifth, the Union has a presence in world politics. Some 156 states are accredited to the Community, with embassies in Brussels. The Union's international role has led to development cooperation with other countries, a number of association agreements with European and non-European states, the common commercial policy that makes the Community an important actor in the World Trade Organisation (WTO), and the system of foreign policy co-operation that is described below.

Since the mid-1980s, the EU has experienced a particularly dynamic period of development characterised by two big economic projects (the single market and the single currency), a series of additional treaties, and the accession of new states. The Treaty of Maastricht (1992) established the constitutional framework of the Union within a single treaty for the first time. It defined the European Union as resting on three 'pillars'; this structure was maintained in the 1997 Treaty of Amsterdam (Tonra, 1997). In practice, this means that there are three frameworks for policy making and a host of different decision rules within each pillar. The roles and powers of the four institutions differ from one framework to another. The Commission, the Court of Justice and the Parliament have a far greater role in the first pillar (the EC) than in either of the other two. Put simply, the supranational element of the policy process is strongest in the

Community pillar. Co-operation on foreign policy and judicial affairs takes place essentially within an intergovernmental format, although the role of the so-called supranational institutions has been strengthened in pillars two and three (Keatinge, 1992; see also discussion below). As a consequence of an intensive period of treaty change, the Union's governance structures are very complicated, with a myriad of rules and differing institutional roles. The debate on the future of the system has become highly politicised, with considerable conflict about the future shape and purpose of the Union as it tries to adjust to the prospect of enlargement to the east and south.

EU institutions and Ireland

Given the importance of the Union to the economies and societies of the member states, 'voice' and representation in the Brussels system are very important.

The Commission

The Commission, originally conceived of as the EU's embryonic government, has twenty members drawn from the member states. Since 1973, there have been six Irish commissioners (see Box 13.3). Although in principle the incoming president of the Commission should have a say over national nominees, in practice the government of the day decides who should get the Irish nomination.

Apart from the College of Commissioners, the Commission as the Union's central bureaucracy interacts with the Irish political system in a variety of ways. Irish civil servants and the representatives of interest organisations participate in Commission advisory bodies and working parties when legislation is being prepared for submission to the Council of the EU. They are also involved in what are called the 'comitology' committees which oversee the implementation of EU policies. The Commission plays a very important role in managing the flow of Brussels money to the member states. Its officials sit on national monitoring bodies to ensure that EU money is being well spent. In its capacity as guardian of the treaties, the Commission is responsible for ensuring that the member states implement, observe and enforce Community laws, and that private companies adhere to competition policy and to legislation on mergers. The Commission can issue proceedings against a member state for failure to implement EC law. Ireland, which had a reasonably good record on implementation in the mid-1980s, then fell behind in the incorporation of legislation on the internal market directives; a Commission report of December 1991 showed that only Italy and Luxembourg had a higher rate of non-implementation (European Commission, 1991, p. 57). The reasons for this included the lack of legal expertise within Irish government departments, reliance on the over-burdened parliamentary draftsman, staff shortages in some departments and

Box 13.3 Ireland's EU Commissioners, 1973–99

Commissioners are appointed by the respective national governments, and to date all the commissioners appointed by Irish governments have been politically established figures. Up to 1999, all Irish commissioners apart from Peter Sutherland were former ministers and senior politicians within their political parties. A commissioner is assigned a 'portfolio' in the Commission, much like a cabinet minister at national level, and there is considerable competition for the plum positions. Peter Sutherland was given Competition when he joined the first Delors Commission in 1985, an important portfolio because of its significance for the 1992 programme. Agriculture, for which his successor Ray MacSharry was given responsibility in the second Delors Commission in 1989, is also much sought after because the CAP commands a sizeable proportion of the Community budget. Pádraig Flynn's brief included Social Affairs which is regarded as a middle-ranking portfolio. In July 1999 it was announced that Ireland's seventh commissioner, with responsibility for Health and Consumer Protection, would be David Byrne; like Peter Sutherland, he was the Attorney General at the time of his appointment.

Commissioner	Appointing government	Period	Portfolio
Patrick Hillery	FF	1973–76	Social Affairs
Richard Burke	FG–Lab	1977–80	Transport, Consumer Affairs, Taxation, Relations with EP
Michael O'Kennedy	FF	1981–82	President's delegate, Administration
Richard Burke	FF	1982–84	Greek renegotiation
Peter Sutherland	FG–Lab	1985–88	Competition
Ray MacSharry	FF	1989–92	Common Agricultural Policy
Pádraig Flynn	FF	1993–99	Social Affairs

the sheer weight of the Community's legislative programme in the run-up to 1992. With pressure from the Commission to complete the 'single market' programme and increased monitoring of the implementation of EC law, Ireland's performance improved somewhat, and by the end of 1996 it was in the middle ranks of the league table for the transposition of EC law (see Table 13.1). Ireland appears to have particular difficulties in implementing directives in the fields of transport, the environment, and food legislation.

The Council of the EU

The Council of the EU is at the centre of the legislative process and is the juncture where the Union meets with the national political systems.

Table 13.1 Implementation of European Community directives

Member state	Directives applicable as of 31 December 1996	Measures notified as having been applied	% applied
Denmark	1310	1285	98.0
Netherlands	1310	1275	97.3
Spain	1314	1245	94.7
UK	1309	1233	94.2
Sweden	1308	1227	93.8
Germany	1313	1227	93.5
Luxembourg	1309	1223	93.4
Ireland	1310	1218	93.0
Belgium	1311	1215	92.7
Portugal	1311	1204	91.8
France	1310	1203	91.8
Greece	1304	1189	91.2
Italy	1310	1181	90.2
Austria	1306	1153	88.3
Finland	1306	1057	80.9

Source: European Commission, 1997, p.17.

Although the Council is legally just one body, in practice the appropriate national ministers (such as Foreign Affairs, Agriculture or Transport) meet to negotiate on Commission proposals that fall within the ambit of their responsibilities at national level. All Irish ministers (apart from the Minister of Defence) meet with their counterparts from other member states in Council. The Taoiseach has direct contact with the heads of government of other member states in the European Council. The Ministerial Council has a vast and complicated substructure made up of some 250 working parties and committees. During a typical working week in Brussels, Irish ministers, civil servants and officials from state-sponsored bodies will be attending working-party meetings in the Commission or in the Council. The frequency of flights from Dublin to Brussels (fifty-seven per week on winter schedules, as compared with thirty to Amsterdam, for example) underlines the impact of this additional layer of government on Irish government and politics.

The presidency, which was originally envisaged simply as a convenient mechanism to provide chairpersons for Council meetings, has become an important source of political direction within the Union. Member states hold the presidency on a rotating basis for a period of six months. Since joining the EU, Ireland has held it on five occasions: in 1975, 1979, 1984, 1990 and in the latter half of 1996. In 1996, the Irish Presidency held 1,216 meetings or seminars in Dublin, and chaired forty Council meetings and 2,000 working group meetings in Brussels. One aspect of the presidency system is that it allows small states to play a central role in the Union and provides a limited check on the dominance of the larger states. During the presidency, a small state such as Ireland can enhance its status and involvement in international politics. Successive Irish governments have taken the presidency very seriously, seeing it as an opportunity to run the affairs of the Union in a businesslike fashion so as to build up a stock of goodwill in other member states.

The European Parliament

The European Parliament is the Union's representative institution. It was conceived as a consultative body rather than a legislature by the founding fathers, and so it could only give its views on legislative proposals, though it could dismiss the entire Commission by a two-thirds majority of its members. In 1975, the Parliament gained some budgetary powers. After 1979, when for the first time it was directly elected, its search for new powers was underpinned by its democratic credentials. During the negotiations on the Single European Act, the Maastricht Treaty and later the Treaty of Amsterdam, the Parliament pressed for increased powers for itself, both in the legislative process and in relation to the Union's international role. It was partially successful on each occasion and the Council now has to take more heed of its views.

The Parliament has 626 members, of whom fifteen represent the Republic and a further three Northern Ireland. While fifteen seats might not appear that many, Ireland is generously represented in per capita terms: each of the Irish MEPs represents some 235,000 voters whereas their German counterparts represent some 806,000 voters (Gallagher, Laver and Mair, 1995, p. 90). The number of Irish MEPs will be reduced following the forthcoming enlargements of the Union as the parliament's overall size was capped at 700 in the Treaty of Amsterdam. There are currently eleven further states wishing to join the EU, and as these are admitted, the existing member states will lose a number of MEPs to accommodate their need for representation. MEPs do not sit in national delegations but as part of political groupings that are largely based on Europe's traditional party families.

Irish MEPs are divided among five of the Parliament's groups (see table 13.2). When Ireland became a member of the Community in 1973, its political parties had to decide which EP group to join. This was relatively straightforward for Labour, which joined the Socialist group. For Fianna Fáil and Fine Gael the decision was more difficult; for one thing, they could not both join the same group because of electoral competition at national level. Fine Gael joined the largest of the conservative groups, the European People's Party (the Christian Democrats). Participation in the christian democratic movement has widened the horizons of Fine Gael and has brought its senior members and some of its activists into contact with their counterparts in other countries. Fianna Fáil was left without a political grouping for its first six months in the Parliament. The advantages of belonging to a group – including secretarial and research backup, speaking time and membership

Table 13.2 Irish party membership of EP groups, June 1999

EP group	Total	Ireland	
European People's Party	224	4	(Fine Gael)
Socialist	180	1	(Labour)
Liberal Democratic and Reformist	50	1	(Pat Cox)
Greens	38	2	(Greens)
United Left / Nordic Greens	35	0	
Europe of the Nations	21	0	
Union for Europe	17	6	(Fianna Fáil)
European Radical Alliance	13	0	
Non-attached and undecided	48	1	(Dana Rosemary Scallon)
Total EP	626	15	

Source: Figures supplied by EP Office, Dublin.

of committees – forced it to link up with the French Gaullists in what became the Union for Europe group. This was always an uneasy partnership, and Fianna Fáil from time to time considered other options. The alliance with the Gaullists was limited to the Parliament; there were no party-to-party links of the sort found in the christian democratic group or the socialists. The Progressive Democrats joined the Liberal grouping in 1989. The Green Party won two seats in the 1994 and 1999 elections; its MEPs sit in the Green group.

The five-yearly direct elections to the European Parliament constitute an additional contest in the Irish electoral cycle (for the results of past elections see Appendix 2e). The Republic is divided into four large constituencies for the purposes of European elections: Leinster (4 seats), Dublin (4 seats), Connacht–Ulster (3 seats) and Munster (4 seats). Election is by PR-STV, like Dáil elections (see chapter 4), though this could well change in the future since a common electoral system for all member states remains on the agenda. A uniform system would probably involve some type of list system of PR (see p. 100 above) rather than STV. Irish MEPs inhabit a rather different world from that of their counterparts in the Dáil. They must travel a lot and spend two or three weeks of every month outside Ireland at plenary sessions of the Parliament, attending committee meetings and dealing with the work of their political grouping. This makes it difficult for them to maintain contact with their very large constituencies and to maintain a profile in their political parties.

The Court of Justice

Since its inception, the European Court of Justice (ECJ) has played a key role in providing the legal cement for integration. It has interpreted the treaties in a dynamic fashion rather than in a static manner, and its legal activism has strengthened the federal character of the Community. The Irish judicial system now feeds into the Community's legal order because of the principles of Community law outlined above. Irish courts may seek rulings from the Court of Justice on the correct interpretation of Community law, and the Irish government and private citizens may find themselves before the court in Luxembourg. Between 1973 and 1996, seventy-six actions were taken against Ireland in such diverse areas as agriculture, fisheries, internal market, taxation and the environment (*Official Journal*, C 250, 1998). EC law endows Irish citizens and groups with rights that they can pursue in the Irish courts and also at the Court of Justice in Luxembourg. The Irish courts are obliged to ask the ECJ for a preliminary ruling on matters of EC law, if these are raised by cases in the Irish system. Rulings from the ECJ have meant, for example, that the Irish state has had to pay compensation to women for discrimination in social security legislation and late implementation of EC directives (cf p. 311 above). Issues of constitutional law and the compatibility of EC treaties with the Irish constitution were raised by the Supreme Court judgment in 1987 on the Crotty case, when it deemed that title three of the Single European Act was incompatible with the constitution, meaning that a referendum had to be held on the SEA.

The Court of Auditors

The Court of Auditors was given full institutional status in the Treaty of Maastricht. The main task of the Auditors is to monitor the management of EU finances by EU institutions and the member states. This means that its officers have the right to investigate EU expenditure by Irish public and private agencies. It works closely with the Irish Comptroller and Auditor General. The Court was particularly critical of Ireland's management of the beef regime, a matter that came to public attention during the 1991–94 beef tribunal.

The EU and the Irish political system

The management of EU policy in Ireland

The EU's complex policy process is but the tip of an iceberg that extends deep into the national political and administrative systems. Each member state must service the policy process in Brussels, the constant round of meetings held under the auspices of the Commission and the Council. Outside the formal legislative process, there are frequent informal meetings at various levels. During each set of negotiations and at all stages, Irish civil servants prepare briefing material and instructions for those going to Brussels to represent the Irish interest. The preparation of positions requires consultation and co-ordination both within and between departments. Moreover, Irish interest groups will seek to influence those formulating the Irish position. The farming organisations are active on all issues dealing with the CAP, and the employers and trade unions debate labour law issues within a European framework. Other groups such as the Irish National Organisation of the Unemployed, women's groups and environmentalists all seek to lobby in the Union's multilevel system. Politics may begin at home, but it no longer ends there (Laffan, 1996).

The Department of Foreign Affairs, being responsible for keeping a watching brief over the flow of legislation through the policy process and over the main lines of policy development, is the centre of day-to-day and week-to-week co-ordination. It has built up an extensive expertise on the Union, which gives it a key role in the management of EU business in Ireland, and its responsibility for EU matters means that its importance within the administrative system has increased. In addition, the extensive nature of the Union's policy interests brings a European dimension to the work of all of the domestic departments, which are responsible for those areas of EU policy that fall within their normal duties. The Departments of Finance, Enterprise, Trade and Employment, and Agriculture are heavily involved in EU business. With the growing importance of the European Council, the Department of the Taoiseach also plays a major role. In October 1998, following an informal European Council during the Austrian Presidency, a communications network called Prime-Net was established linking the prime ministers' offices in the member states. EU matters, then, have been added on to the process of domestic public policy making. EU policies determine national policies in many instances and act as a constraint on policy options.

All member states of the Union have established coordinating mechanisms to manage EU business, in order to ensure that the Brussels process is adequately serviced and that national priorities are highlighted. There are a number of different levels of coordination in Ireland. The cabinet, as the arena at which major policy issues are resolved and legislation is processed before it goes to the Oireachtas, deals with EU matters much as it deals with domestic policy. From time to time cabinet sub-committees have been set up to deal with particular areas of EU policy, but there is no standing committee on Europe. The European Communities Committee, which predated Ireland's membership, was the main centre of interdepartmental coordination and was responsible for formulating national strategy and deciding priorities. This committee was chaired by the Department of Foreign Affairs from 1973 until 1987, when its composition changed somewhat. In that year, Máire Geoghegan-Quinn was appointed Minister of State in the Department of the Taoiseach with responsibility for coordinating EU matters. She was given the task of chairing the EU Committee, which added the authority of the Taoiseach's department to the committee and changed it from being purely administrative. At the end of the presidency in 1990, its work fell into abeyance and it was not replaced immediately by any new mechanism to ensure political and administrative coordination. When Albert Reynolds became Taoiseach in February 1992, he gave Tom Kitt (a minister of state) responsibility for EU coordination and reactivated the European Communities Committee. This was replaced in 1994 by a Ministers' and Secretaries' Group (MSG), chaired by the Taoiseach, which is responsible for working out Ireland's strategy for the major negotiations on the future finances of the Union. The work of the MSG is prepared by a committee of senior civil servants and a number of interdepartmental groups on discrete areas of EU policy. The system of administrative coordination in Ireland is less institutionalised than those in other member states.

Since 1973 Irish policy makers have adopted a very pragmatic approach to the development of the EU and to the promotion of Irish interests. For many years there was little sustained thinking about the overall development of the Union and the needs of small states within it. The decision in the late 1980s by the Taoiseach, Charles Haughey, to ask the National Economic and Social Council (NESC) to undertake an extensive review of Ireland's membership of the Community, and the subsequent publication of the NESC report (NESC, 1989), marked an important move away from the *ad hoc* approach of the past. A further attempt to develop a more considered approach was the establishment in 1991 of an Institute of European Affairs, a non-governmental organisation that promotes interdisciplinary Irish research on EU matters.

The role of the Oireachtas

Following membership of the Union, the Oireachtas lost the 'sole and exclusive power of making laws' bestowed on it by Article 15.2.1 of the constitution. Like other parliaments in the member states, the Oireachtas sought to qualify its loss of law-making powers by establishing mechanisms to oversee the government's behaviour in the Union. Besides being to some extent accountable through the traditional mechanisms of parliamentary questions and debates (see chapter 7), the government is also committed to placing a report on developments in the EU before the Houses of the Oireachtas twice yearly. These reports generally arrive too late for parliament to give serious consideration to the issues they raise.

In addition, in 1973 the Oireachtas established the Joint Committee on the Secondary Legislation of the European Communities, as a watchdog committee on EC matters. Since Ireland does not have a strong tradition of parliamentary committees, as we saw in chapter 7, this committee was something of a novelty at the outset. It had twenty-five members (eighteen deputies and seven senators), with the political parties represented in proportion to their strength in the Oireachtas. Its terms of reference allowed it to examine and report to the Oireachtas on Commission policy proposals, legislative proposals, EC laws, regulations made in Ireland under the European Communities Act 1972, and all other legal instruments that flow from EC membership.

The Joint Committee suffered from a number of constraints that impede the work of all parliamentary committees. Its terms of reference were very restricted, so it concentrated most of its energies on secondary legislation and did not maintain a systematic overview of the flow of EU policies through the legislative process. Nor could it examine major changes in the European landscape, notably the collapse of communism and German unification, that were certain to shape the Community of the 1990s. In the work that it actually did, it was hampered by a weakness of both financial and human resources. Neither the members nor the secretariat of the committee had the legal or technical expertise to examine many of the complex issues involved in EC law and policies; the time pressures on Irish politicians do not allow them to develop the kind of expertise required for a thorough examination of EU policies.

In response to these difficulties the Fianna Fáil–Labour government established a new Joint Oireachtas Committee on Foreign Affairs in the spring of 1993. This subsumed the work of the previous Committee on Secondary Legislation, and also covered a much broader agenda encompassing the state's foreign relations as a whole. The establishment of a Foreign Affairs Committee brought Irish parliamentary practice into line with other parliaments in Western Europe. A separate Joint Committee on European Affairs was established in March 1995, because the work of the Foreign Affairs Committee left it with inadequate time for the scrutiny of European law, and both committees were re-established after the 1997 election. Neither committee has adequate research and administrative back-up to develop independent thinking on foreign and European issues. The committees are heavily dependent on briefing papers from the Department of Foreign Affairs and on external consultants. Moreover, attendance at the committees is patchy, given the constituency duties of Irish parliamentarians. There is some overlap and hence tension between the two committees on areas such as the common foreign and security policy. That said, the committees have contributed to greater openness on foreign policy matters; the meetings are usually held in public, and successive ministers and officials have attended and given evidence. The committees have also provided a focus for the attentive public in this domain. A small coterie of deputies and senators have become engaged in foreign policy matters. The involvement of the European Affairs Committee in the Conference of Parliamentary Committees on European Affairs (COSAC) has exposed Irish parliamentarians to practices in other member states.

Public opinion, referendums and politics

The emphatic endorsement of membership in the 1972 referendum demonstrated that Irish public opinion was largely in favour of EU membership. The Irish electorate has endorsed major developments in European integration on the three further occasions when referendums were held to allow for constitutional change to accommodate Euro-politics. Acceptance of Ireland's involvement in European integration appears well rooted in the

Irish body politic; in surveys over many years, well over 80 per cent of respondents believe that membership has been good to Ireland. In *Eurobarometer 50* (conducted in autumn 1998), 85 per cent of Irish respondents felt that Ireland had benefited from membership, a far higher proportion than for any other member state (see Table 13.3). Support for Ireland's membership of the Union is not accompanied by a high level of knowledge about EU affairs, however. Ireland ranks just above the Union average in knowledge of EU affairs, with 59 per cent of Irish respondents to Eurobarometer surveys displaying low or very low knowledge of the EU (Sinnott, 1995, p. 34).

In 1972, Fianna Fáil and Fine Gael both supported entry, along with the employers' and farmers' organisations, while Labour and the trade unions opposed it, in a campaign dominated by economic issues. Although integration itself faltered in the 1970s and early 1980s, the reform of the EC in the Single European Act (SEA) was approved by a second referendum in 1987. However, the result – 70 per cent to 30 per cent in a poll of only 44 per cent – reflected a measure of disillusionment, or at least of indifference. It may also indicate a degree of bewilderment concerning a very complex political system; what is certain is that none of the major parties came out of the ratification process of the SEA with any distinction (Gallagher, 1988). Again Fianna Fail and Fine Gael supported the treaty whereas the Labour party did not take an official stance.

The SEA was followed by the Treaty on European Union (the Maastricht Treaty) which again required a change in the constitution, and was thus the subject of another referendum on 18 June 1992 (Holmes, 1993). This was complicated by the issue of abortion: the government had inserted a protocol in the Maastricht treaty, in order to protect Ireland's constitutional ban on abortion (Article 40.3.3), but the Supreme Court's

Table 13.3 Perceived benefits of EU membership among public in EU member states, 1998, in per cent

	Austria	Belgium	Denmark	Finland	Germany	Greece	France	Ireland
Benefited	41	44	70	39	39	76	53	85
Not benefited	34	32	20	44	36	17	27	5
Don't know	25	24	10	17	25	7	21	10
Total	100	100	100	100	100	100	100	100

	Italy	Luxembourg	Netherlands	Portugal	Spain	Sweden	UK	all EU
Benefited	51	69	67	67	58	27	37	49
Not benefited	27	14	22	18	25	53	42	31
Don't know	22	18	12	15	18	20	21	20
Total	100	100	100	100	100	100	100	100

Source: European Commission (1999, p. B22).
Note: The figures represent responses to a question as to whether respondents believe that their country has benefited from EU membership. The survey was conducted in autumn 1998.

subsequent interpretation of that Article in the 'X' case (see Box 3.2 above) led to confusion about the meaning and remit of the protocol. Both feminist and anti-abortion lobbies opposed the treaty, alongside traditional nationalists and supporters of neutrality. On the other side was almost the whole political establishment (with the exception of Democratic Left, the Workers' Party and the Green Party) and the major economic interests. The turnout of 57 per cent was noticeably higher than that in the SEA referendum, while the distribution of votes cast was similar, with 69 per cent in favour and 31 per cent against (see appendix 2h). In the circumstances this was a strong endorsement of Ireland's participation in the mainstream of European integration. In the event, neither abortion nor neutrality proved to be decisive, but the difficulty for governments of making something as complicated as the Maastricht Treaty intelligible to the voters was plain to see.

Although in 1992 there had been much uncertainty about the achievement of economic and monetary union, one of the main points of substance in the Maastricht Treaty, by 1998 it was clear that Ireland would be a founding member when the plan came to fruition. In May of that year the electorate was asked to give its verdict on a further revision of the EU's legal base, the Amsterdam Treaty of 1997. The outcome may suggest some hesitation among the Irish electorate about the continuing process of Treaty change in the Union. Whereas 69 per cent supported the Maastricht Treaty in 1992, just 62 per cent voted for Amsterdam, with a turnout of 56 per cent (see appendix 2h). Yet, by 1998 all the main Dáil parties, with 156 of the 166 seats between them, supported the treaty. A degree of fatigue with referendums on Europe is apparent among the Irish electorate.

The development of the EU is not merely a political issue in Ireland; it has a continuing impact on a host of public policy matters. The expanding scope of EU policy has had an increasingly important impact on the domestic political agenda in Ireland. Irish agricultural policy is almost entirely made in Brussels. Since 1989, the Irish government has had to deal with the MacSharry proposals for fundamental reform of the CAP, and these in turn impinged on trade talks, notably the GATT round. Irish governments must seek to protect the interests of Irish agriculture not only within the Council of the EU in Brussels but also in a wider international context. Financial flows from the CAP have meant that the subvention of farm incomes has been paid for by the EU budget. Any return of responsibility for the agricultural policy to national governments could well exacerbate urban–rural tensions in Ireland, as the Irish exchequer would be under considerable pressure from farmers to increase its spending on farm incomes.

Financial transfers from the European Union have become part and parcel of distributive politics, especially since the 1980s. The structural funds represented a very significant transfer from the EU budget to Ireland. EU largesse was channelled to Ireland in the form of two Community Support Frameworks (CSF) which ran from 1988 to 1993, and from 1994 to the end of 1999. The 1994–99 CSF pledged 5.4 billion ECU to Ireland in addition to monies from the Cohesion Fund. The Economic and Social Research Institute (ESRI) has described this as a notable success story because it enhanced medium-term financial planning and represented a quantum leap in the provision of public infrastructure (Honohan, 1997). Central government invested heavily in the implementation of the various EU programmes, and Ireland is generally regarded as a state that uses structural funds well. This is reflected in the fact that Ireland receives the highest per capita transfer from the funds. (Transfers to Ireland amounted to 1600 ECU per head for the period 1994–99, compared with 1400 ECU to poorer Portugal and Greece.) Whereas the first CSF was developed and controlled by the Department of Finance, different regions, localities and community groups fought for influence over the second CSF. Local development became a significant feature of the second CSF.

The single currency project is another area that has had a significant impact on Irish public policy. Following the ratification of the Maastricht Treaty, successive Irish governments signalled their desire to join the single currency in the first wave. This had a direct bearing on the framing of the annual budget from 1992 onwards, as the goal of policy was to meet the criteria for membership of EMU. This implied tight control over the public finances and a fiscal policy designed to promote low inflation. The position of the Central Bank and the Department of Finance was enhanced *vis-à-vis* the spending ministries, as Finance could hide behind the criteria in the annual budget round. Once the new currency, the Euro, is fully established, EU economic governance will become even more important as there will be considerable pressure to coordinate macro-economic policies, including taxation, at an EU level. The long-term consequences of this for Irish politics are difficult to predict, other than to say that there will be increasing constraints on Irish government and a further narrowing of policy options.

The EU and Irish foreign policy

If membership of the EU impinges to such an extent on what is conventionally thought of as the internal policy process, it might be asked whether we can expect a member state, especially a small one such as Ireland, to conduct its own foreign policy. Not surprisingly, this activity does indeed largely take place in a collective setting, the Common Foreign and Security Policy (CFSP). Yet although it involves intensive consultations with the other fourteen member states, this 'second pillar' of the Union is a less closely integrated form of policy making than exists in the supranational first pillar described above. In spite of attempts to introduce a token measure of qualified majority voting in the Maastricht and Amsterdam Treaties, a consensus among all the member governments is required for any move beyond consultation to the expression of a common view ('declaratory policy') or the taking of common action, such as imposing economic sanctions (Keatinge, 1997).

National foreign policies have thus resisted the logic of integration to a considerable extent. Decisions on Irish foreign policy still rest with the government in Dublin, and the whole apparatus of national diplomacy – the Department of Foreign Affairs and its embassies abroad – grew in both size and political importance following Ireland's accession to the Community. When it takes its turn for six months in the rotating EC presidency, the Irish government is actually responsible for the management of CFSP, giving both the Foreign Minister and the Taoiseach an opportunity to play the role of 'statesman' in public. Routine access to their counterparts in the major European states, on top of the vastly enhanced information available to the Department of Foreign Affairs, is arguably as much a national resource as it is a form of exposure to external influences. Moreover, in so far as EU positions on major international issues are consistent with Ireland's interests and values, if they are advanced on behalf of 325 million people they are likely to bear more weight than statements on behalf of a society of 3.7 million (Keatinge, 1991).

At this level of generalisation it may seem that, so far, an acceptable balance has been found between the way in which Irish governments see their national foreign policies and the rather loosely framed obligations of the CFSP. This may not remain the case, though. Up to 1993 Irish governments arrived at many foreign policy decisions with the minimum input from political parties, and enjoyed relatively large domestic freedom of manoeuvre so long as the Oireachtas was the only western European parliament without a standing foreign affairs committee. But two factors have changed in this policy environment. First, the Treaty of Maastricht, by introducing the possibility of a European defence policy, may clash with a long standing element of Irish foreign policy: the stance of neutrality. We shall return to this question at the end of the chapter.

A second change occurred closer to home: what might be called the 'democratisation' of the foreign policy process (Keatinge, 1998). In addition to the introduction of parliamentary committees, which we discussed earlier, the Labour Party leader, Dick Spring, as Minister for Foreign Affairs, launched an elaborate consultative process prior to publishing the first ever comprehensive white paper on foreign policy in 1996 (Department of Foreign Affairs, 1996). These developments have been matched by the emergence of a proliferation of nongovernmental organisations (NGOs), suggesting at least the potential for the advocacy of 'bottom-up' foreign policies that may be at odds with those of Irish governments or an EU consensus.

Nevertheless, Ireland's participation in the CFSP (and its predecessor, European Political Cooperation) over the last twenty-five years does on the whole support the proposition that opportunities to pursue foreign policy objectives were enhanced by EC and later EU membership. Some examples may illustrate the point. So far as East–West relations were concerned, the

EC states jointly were an important positive influence in the Conference on Security and Cooperation in Europe (the 'Helsinki process'), which maintained a modicum of diplomatic engagement with the USSR during the tension of the 'new cold war' of the early 1980s. In the Middle East, the Irish government's position on the Arab–Israeli conflict was mirrored in the EC's gradual receptiveness to the Palestinian case. For most of this period Ireland remained, as it had been before joining the EU, a consistent and credible contributor to United Nations peace-keeping operations, and governments developed a more substantial and systematic approach to relations with the third world (Holmes, Rees and Whelan, 1993).

This is not to suggest that Ireland's policy (or that of the EC/EU as a whole) was an unequivocal success story. Trying to influence the unruly game of international politics is best approached in the Olympic spirit: 'it is not to have won but to have taken part'. Indeed, for a small state, taking part may be what it really is all about. Ireland's activism on the question of sanctions against South Africa was resisted by other EC governments, but it answered at least some of the demands of the anti-apartheid lobby at home (Laffan, 1988).

Repositioning Ireland in the European Union

Ireland is now confronted with transition and change in its continental environment and the wider international environment. It faces the prospect of further treaty change, enlargement of EU membership, and the evolution of the global system itself. This raises several broad questions about the future direction of Irish policy and politics.

The first question is a very general one, which up to now has been largely avoided in Irish debate on EU membership: is the European Union a decisive step closer to the creation of a single federal state? If it were, the prospect of a radical transformation of the Irish political system would be on the horizon. At present the Maastricht and Amsterdam Treaties seem to fall well short of the federal mark, and it may be some years before their effects can be accurately gauged. Nevertheless, the long-running British controversy over the 'f' word could well make an appearance on the Irish political agenda before long, with suitable adjustments to cater for the different political culture. The future shape of the Union and the relationship between statehood and EU membership are matters of continuing debate and controversy, which are unlikely to go away.

A second issue is the continuing impact of European integration on Irish politics. Even if Europe does not move in a federal direction, national and European politics are likely to become even more intertwined. National budgetary policy has already been greatly influenced by the goal of striving to meet the criteria established for membership of the Economic and Monetary Union. Participation in the single currency locks Irish budgetary policy into Europe-wide processes, including strict rules about deficit spending. There is also the question of how Ireland will adjust to becoming a net contributor to the Union budget. An eastwards enlargement (the admission of poorer countries from central and eastern Europe) means that Union support will flow not to Ireland but elsewhere in Europe. The absence of budgetary transfers could make it harder for Irish governments and parties to convince the Irish electorate of the benefits of membership. There is also the challenge of how a weak parliamentary system can hold Irish representatives in the Council accountable as Brussels becomes involved in a wider range of policies. Moreover, the use of the principle of 'subsidiarity' (meaning that policy should be executed at the lowest effective level of government) in European politics will draw attention to the centralised nature of the Irish system of government. It is likely, therefore, that the Irish political system, or, to be more precise, the parties in parliament, will have to pay more attention to the state's external environment.

Although there are differences among the political parties in their attitudes towards European integration, up to now a distinctive Irish approach has been discernible. Ireland's experience as a small, peripheral, less developed economy, together with its traditional policy of neutrality, shaped attitudes towards integration. The defence of the CAP, the politics of redistribution and the need to ensure that European laws are appropriate to Irish circumstances have dominated Ireland's EU agenda. A recurring concern in Ireland's European policy has been the need to ensure that political integration advances on the basis of balanced economic integration. Irish policy makers have adopted a strongly federalist approach towards financial transfers from the richer to the poorer parts of the Community, favouring larger EU budgets. This may change when the budgetary benefits decline. In addition, calls for a harmonisation of taxation systems could well run counter to Ireland's reliance on low levels of corporate tax to attract foreign investment to Ireland.

Irish attitudes have been less federalist concerning institutional development in the Union. Ireland did not lend active support to very significant increases in the powers of the European Parliament, although the latter is now taken more seriously. The Council of the EU is seen as the main arena for the protection of national interests; the presence of one Irish minister in the Council is regarded as a source of more influence than fifteen MEPs in the 626-member European Parliament. This said, Fine Gael and the Progressive Democrats tend to espouse more federalist policies than their counterparts in either Fianna Fáil or the Labour Party. Labour party activists and a number of TDs remain sceptical about the benefits of European integration for Ireland. Fianna Fáil, when in opposition, tends to be cautious about a deepening of integration but always supports treaty change when in office.

A third issue is the more sharply focused debate on neutrality. Not that Irish neutrality itself can be said to be a sharply focused concept; indeed, in the most detailed study made to date, applying rigorous criteria, it is interpreted as 'non-belligerence' at best, and at worst an exercise in self-delusion (Salmon, 1989). Yet it clearly retains an important place in Irish political culture (Marsh, 1992), whether it is associated with quasi-pacifist or with nationalist values. In the emerging international system the basis of neutrality policy, like most other diplomatic orientations coloured by the cold war, is being subjected to reappraisal. This is true of those European neutrals, such as Austria, Finland, Sweden and Switzerland, which have had a more clearly defined (and more militarised) policy than Ireland. However, by joining NATO's Partnership for Peace (PfP) – a form of association with NATO that falls short of a full alliance commitment – the continental neutrals have adapted more readily than Ireland. In practice the PfP represents the inclusion of nearly all European states in a network of military cooperation that emphasises peacekeeping, an activity in which Ireland has a long experience in the UN context. Ireland's idiosyncratic hesitation on this issue owes more to domestic party politics than to the substance of the external commitments involved (Keatinge, 1996). In fact Irish troops do participate in the NATO-led peacekeeping operation in Bosnia, and the possibility of making similar types of commitment has been accepted by ratifying the Treaty of Amsterdam. The difficulty that politicians seem to have with explaining and justifying adaptations to international security issues does not bode well for their ability to come to terms with other issues that reflect the tension between the forces of economic interdependence and the ethos of independent statehood.

Conclusion: a small open polity

Ireland's external environment has been an important influence on the state's political development. In the turbulent international system up to the end of the Second World War, the British connection provided the main focus, in which the new state's political independence was demonstrated by the policy of neutrality during the war. After 1945 Ireland was gradually drawn into a broader, more stable and increasingly interdependent international system. The eruption of political violence in Northern Ireland ensured a continuing emphasis on Anglo-Irish relations, which entered a new phase with the Good Friday Agreement of 1998. This Agreement, together with constitutional devolution within the United Kingdom, is set to alter relations between these neighbouring islands. Nevertheless, involvement in European integration now represents the most significant source of external influence on the Irish state.

Membership of the European Union since 1973 has had a major impact on the political life of Ireland. The EU differs from traditional interstate cooperation because its founders aspired to create a new political entity. Member states thus agreed to pool their sovereignty over a wide range of public policy within a system of law that interacts directly with national legal systems. Ireland, along with the other EU members, has representation in the main Union institutions: the Council of the EU, the Commission, the European Parliament and the Court of Justice. Irish trade unions, employer groups, producer groups and many other representative organisations see Brussels as an important arena for politics. EU membership has made it even more difficult than before for the Oireachtas to hold the executive accountable for its actions.

Since 1989, there has been a major change in the state's external environment, with the unexpected end of the relatively stable bipolar system of the cold war era. So far this has led to a greater emphasis on the process of European integration. Questions about the nature of European union, the effects of integration on Irish politics, and the future of neutrality are being raised in the new, and much less stable, world system. In order to understand the future evolution of Irish politics, it will be essential to see the state as a 'small open polity'.

References and further reading

Department of Foreign Affairs, 1996. *Challenges and Opportunities Abroad: White Paper on Foreign Policy*, Pn. 2133. Dublin: Stationery Office.

European Commission of the EU, 1991. *Report on the Implementation of Measures for Completing the Internal Market*, 2491 final, 19 December. Brussels: European Commission.

European Commission, 1997. *Fourteenth Annual Report on Monitoring the Application of Community Law*, Com (97) 299 final. 29 May.

European Commission, 1999. *Eurobarometer No 50*. Brussels: European Commission.

Fisk, Robert, 1983. *In Time of War: Ireland, Ulster and the Price of Neutrality 1939–1945*. London: Andre Deutsch.

FitzGerald, Garret, 1991. *All in a Life: an Autobiography*. Dublin: Gill and Macmillan.

Gallagher, Michael, 1988. 'The Single European Act referendum', *Irish Political Studies* 3, pp. 77–82.

Gallagher, Michael, Michael Laver and Peter Mair, 1995. *Representative Government in Modern Europe*. New York: McGraw–Hill.

Girvin, Brian, 1999. 'Northern Ireland and the Republic', pp. 220–41 in Paul Mitchell and Rick Wilford (eds), *Politics in Northern Ireland*. Boulder, Colo.: Westview Press and PSAI Press.

Guelke, Adrian, 1988. *Northern Ireland: the International Perspective*. Dublin: Gill and Macmillan.

Holmes, Michael, 1993. 'The Maastricht Treaty referendum of June 1992', *Irish Political Studies* 8, pp. 105–10.

Holmes, Michael, Nicholas Rees and Bernadette Whelan, 1993. *The Poor Relation: Irish Foreign Policy and the Third World*. Dublin: Trócaire.

Honohan, Patrick (ed.), 1997. *EU Structural Funds In Ireland: a Mid-Term Evaluation of the CSF 1994–99*. Dublin: Economic and Social Research Institute.

Keatinge, Patrick, 1986. 'Unequal sovereigns: the diplomatic dimension of Anglo-Irish relations', pp. 139–60 in P. J. Drudy (ed.), *Ireland and Britain since 1922*. Cambridge: Cambridge University Press.

Keatinge, Patrick (ed.), 1991. *Ireland and EC Membership Evaluated*. London: Pinter.

Keatinge, Patrick (ed.), 1992. *Maastricht and Ireland: What the Treaty Means*. Dublin: Institute of European Affairs.

Keatinge, Patrick, 1996. *European Security: Ireland's Choices*. Dublin: Institute of European Affairs.

Keatinge, Patrick, 1997. 'Strengthening the foreign policy process', pp. 97–105 in Ben Tonra (ed.), *Amsterdam: What the Treaty Means*. Dublin: Institute of European Affairs.

Keatinge, Patrick, 1998. 'Ireland and European security: continuity and change', *Irish Studies in International Affairs* 9, pp. 31–7.

Kennedy, Michael, 1996. *Ireland and the League of Nations, 1919–1946: International Relations, Diplomacy and Politics*. Dublin: Irish Academic Press.

Laffan, Brigid, 1988. *Ireland and South Africa: Irish Government Policy in the 1980s*. Dublin: Trocaire.

Laffan, Brigid, 1996. 'Ireland', pp. 291–312 in Dietrich Rometsch and Wolfgang Wessels (eds), *The EU and Member States: Towards Institutional Fusion?* Manchester and New York: Manchester University Press.

Laffan B., R. O'Donnell and M. Smith, 1999. *Europe's Experimental Union: Re-thinking Integration*. London: Routledge.

Little, Richard and Michael Smith (eds), 1991. *Perspectives on World Politics*, 2nd ed. London: Routledge.

McCabe, Ian, 1991. *A Diplomatic History of Ireland, 1948–49: the Republic, the Commonwealth, and NATO*. Dublin: Irish Academic Press.

Marsh, Michael, 1992. *Irish Public Opinion on Neutrality and European Union*. Dublin: Institute of European Affairs, Occasional Paper 1.

NESC, 1989. *Ireland in the European Community: Performance, Prospects and Strategy*. Dublin: National Economic and Social Council, Report no. 88.

Nugent, Neill, 1994. *The Government and Politics of the European Community*, 3rd ed. London: Macmillan.

O'Leary, Brendan and John McGarry, 1996. *The Politics of Antagonism: Understanding Northern Ireland*, 2nd ed. London: Athlone Press.

Ruane, Joseph and Jennifer Todd, 1996. *The Dynamics of Conflict in Northern Ireland: Power, Conflict and Emancipation*. Cambridge: Cambridge University Press.

Salmon, Trevor, 1989. *Unneutral Ireland: an Ambivalent and Unique Security Policy*. Oxford: Oxford University Press.

Skelly, Joseph Morrison, 1997. *Irish Diplomacy at the United Nations, 1945–65: National Interests and the International Order*. Dublin: Irish Academic Press.

Sinnott, Richard, 1995. *Knowledge of the European Union I – Irish Public Opinion: Sources and Implications*. Dublin: Institute of European Affairs.

Tonra, Ben (ed.), 1997. *Amsterdam: What the Treaty Means*. Dublin: Institute of European Affairs, Occasional Paper 5.

Tonge, Jonathan, 1998. *Northern Ireland: Conflict and Change*. London: Prentice Hall Europe.

14 Democratic politics in independent Ireland

Tom Garvin

Having considered the mechanics of Irish politics in considerable detail, it is important for us to stand back and look critically at the achievements of the Irish state. To what extent was the promise of the new state fulfilled? What future does the new Europe hold for an Ireland in whose history a nationalist struggle played so important a part?

The pursuit of democracy

Modern Irish democracy is the result of a long process of political agitation, argument and conflict. In this, it is typical of the democracies that have emerged, mainly in the west, in the past two hundred years. Irish democracy was the result of a revolution which occurred between 1879 and 1923, the final, violent phase being in the last decade of this period. This revolution was a struggle for national independence rather than a classic social revolution as that of France after 1789 is often claimed to have been, and as that of Russia between 1917 and 1921 certainly was. It was an attempt to assert, by a mixture of political agitation, propaganda and armed struggle, the national identity and political independence of an Ireland conceived of, often rather vaguely, as being both republican and democratic. The analogy commonly used by the Irish leaders themselves was the American Revolution of 1776–83. Other possible analogies are the Finnish campaign for national independence after the collapse of tsarism, the Baltic states' escape from Soviet rule in 1989–90 or the insurgencies against British, French and Portuguese power in Africa and Asia in the generation after the Second World War.

The Irish civil war of 1922–23 had a profound impact on the form post-independence public life was to take. It was nominally fought over the issues of republicanism and democracy, and Irish politics for a generation after independence came to centre as much on a profound set of constitutional questions concerning the right relationships between the state and the citizenry as over questions of economic well-being, church versus state issues, or the interests of various sections of society. Nominally, the conflict was between a new British dominion, the Irish Free State, and a Republic of Ireland which had been formally brought into existence by the first Dáil in January 1919 (Curran, 1980; Thompson, 1969; Garvin, 1981; Garvin, 1988, 1996; Mair, 1987; Hopkinson, 1988).

Lloyd George and the Irish lawyers alike had spotted that the Irish-language rendering of the title 'Republic of Ireland' used by the first Dáil was not the *Poblacht na hÉireann* of the 1916 Proclamation, but rather *Saorstát Éire-ann*, a newer coinage. The official notepaper used by de Valera in giving the 1921 plenipotentiaries their letters of credence during the treaty negotiations was headed *Saorstát Éireann/Respublica Hibernica*. In the Irish language, continuity of nomenclature survived the 1921–22 constitutional shift from Republic of Ireland to Irish Free State (Kennedy Papers, P4/196). Both sides in the civil war saw themselves as republican and democratic, yet they killed each other over different interpretations of these terms.

A brief survey of the two key words *democracy* and *republicanism*, so often invoked and so little examined in Irish public life, is appropriate before offering a general assessment of the Irish record of democratic and repub-lican government two generations after independence.

Democracy

Democracy is a form of government that has been, historically, very rare. It is only in the past hundred years that a significant proportion of mankind has come to be governed by democratic or quasi-democratic regimes. Furthermore, democracy has commonly proved to be a fragile plant and has often failed. The destruction of the infant Russian democracy by Lenin in January 1918 and Hitler's murder of the Weimar democracy in 1933 are two of the better-known failures. Oligarchic government has been the norm for post-tribal mankind over millennia.

Formidable intellectual enemies have historically ranged themselves against the idea of popular government. The intellectual origins of modern fascism and authoritarian communism are in the heart of nineteenth century European culture. Anti-democratic thought has very old roots. Direct democracy, as tentatively experimented with in ancient Athens, was looked upon unfavourably by the founders of political theory. Plato and Thucydides saw the democracy of Athens, with much justification, as going hand-in-hand with greed and the imperialist aggression of the armed, land-hungry poor who manned the navy. Plato's condemnation of democracy as the rule of the unwise has echoed down the centuries, as has Aristotle's more measured and possibly more justified scepticism about the pure forms of democracy and aristocracy alike (Thucydides, 1910; Plato, 1960; Klosko, 1986; Aristotle, 1962).

The representative democracies that have evolved in western Europe and its new-world extensions since 1776 are intellectually related to, but structurally quite different from, the small-scale direct democracies of the classical era. The crucial difference is one of scale. Modern democracies have populations of millions, whereas in ancient Greece the privileged band of voting citizens was commonly less than 10,000. Large-scale representative democracy in our time has somewhat oligarchical tendencies and goes hand-in-hand with a private, commercialised economic order which also tends to favour the few over the many. However, it is relatively the most egalitarian and genuinely popular type of political system ever to evolve in the world, and is far more so than its most conspicuous recent challenger, Marxist-Leninist oligarchical communism, which has now largely disappeared.

Modern representative democracy has several historical roots. One is the medieval tradition of representative assemblies which survived the absolutist era to re-emerge in the late eighteenth century. Another important source was a tradition of political thought that can loosely, but usefully, be described as *republicanism*. A third source is the tradition of philosophical individualism sometimes labelled liberalism, but not quite coterminous with that word (Huntington, 1968, pp. 93–140; Montesquieu, 1989; Dahl, 1971, 1989).

Republicanism

In Ireland, republicanism has come to refer not just to a particular form of political organisation but to a strongly nationalist political movement and ideology. This use of the term is rather parochial; it does, of course, have a broader meaning in the western intellectual tradition. Modern European and American republicanism was heavily influenced by the classical experience of Greece and Rome, by the writings of the Renaissance and by the English and French Enlightenments. It came to involve the idea of the law-bound polity, where both rulers and ruled were equally subject to the laws. Another central republican idea was the making of government policy in public, as distinct from behind closed doors: the creation of a public space in which citizens could engage in political participation, rather than being obedient and passive subjects and courtiers of an absolute monarch (Barker, 1951).

Republics need not be democratic. An aristocratic republic, such as that of eighteenth century Poland, where only the nobility or the rich have the vote, is perfectly feasible and has often occurred historically. A democratic republic, where the right of participation in political life is shared by all adults, is merely one of several possibilities. The aristocratic and democratic options can usefully be seen as 'right' and 'left' versions respectively of republicanism. Parenthetically, a state such as the modern United Kingdom or the Kingdom of Denmark, where the monarch reigns but does not rule, is best described, not as a monarchy, but as a 'crowned republic'.

'Left' or democratic republicanism has tended to win out in the last century in the west. Increasing democratisation and the development of large, popular electoral organisations such as political parties and single interest organisations have ensured this. A general move away from British-style plurality electoral systems to proportional representation and run-off ballot systems has also been part of this general long-term process (see chapter 4). The growing use of referendums to settle issues is an important democratic development.

Another central republican idea was that of the citizen as moral actor in the polity, an idea that has classical roots, and which has been put forward by political thinkers such as Hannah Arendt in the modern era. In practice, of course, the mundane activity of counting voters' heads in elections involving the suffrages of millions has become the norm in modern democracies. The older republican tradition has, however, survived, often as an inchoate, instinctive sense of the inadequacy of simple vote-counting as a basis for civic life. The concept of the fully participant citizen survives, for example, in the concept of trial by jury, in traditions of political activism and organisational agitation, in the institution of the referendum and in even the little thought-of but vital activity of discussing political events and what has been seen in the papers, heard on radio or seen on television with one's fellow citizens in a routine and daily fashion.

Democracy and republicanism in independent Ireland

For Ireland, the democratisation of the franchise coincided with the coming of independence for most of the island in 1922. The election of August 1923 was the first to be fought on the basis of a universal franchise in Ireland whose specific purpose was to decide which group of people was to form a government, as distinct from deciding which particular hundred mendicants would be sent to Westminster. As suggested earlier, the civil war of 1922–23 had divided the Sinn Féin movement into those who accepted and those who rejected a compromise agreement with London, involving a constitutional settlement for the twenty-six counties which was republican and democratic in essence but which retained much of the symbolism of monarchy in an uneasy blend with that of popular sovereignty (Kohn, 1932).

Although few admitted it publicly, neither side had any real idea what to do about Northern Ireland, whose existence predated the Irish Free State. Tacitly, it came to be set aside as unfinished business, or even to be written off until relatively recently. De Valera used it as a stick with which to beat the Cumann na nGaedheal government, but ended up conclusively demonstrating that he had no idea what to do about it either (Bowman, 1982). The party system came to divide republican moralists from crypto-republican pro-Treatyites, a general post-revolutionary pragmatism eventually winning an undeclared but overwhelming victory as the first generation of leaders died out and were replaced by younger and clearly post-revolutionary men and women (Cohan, 1972).

The new state had some oligarchical trappings, in particular the existence of special Dáil seats for graduates, but these were soon swept away in favour of formal electoral democracy. In local government, however, the trend was to some extent the other way; local democracy was seen as inefficient and corrupt, and a bureaucratisation of local government occurred, apparently with the acquiescence of local people. The introduction of the bureaucratic county manager system more or less coincided with the abolition of the property qualification for the local franchise in 1934. Irish political culture has commonly blended authoritarian and democratic forms in a character-istic way (see chapter 2), and the restructuring of local government illustrates this rather well (Mansergh, 1934, pp. 225–50).

The elimination, in 1928, of provisions for popular initiative and refer-endum illustrates another tendency for native governments to retreat shamefacedly to the more authoritarian traditions of pre-independence Ireland under pressure of party rivalries and fear of public disorder. The idealistic intentions which lay behind the extern ministry idea, by which the Dáil could have some input into government, were soon abandoned as power was centralised in the cabinet and the prime minister and party lines hardened. The referendum, but not the initiative, was restored in 1937 by de Valera's constitution. Power continued to be concentrated in the Taoiseach and the cabinet (see chapters 3 and 9).

In independent Ireland, fear of insurgency has, historically, discouraged moves towards truly republican, that is, open and law-bound, govern-ment. The activities of the IRA and similar anti-democratic organisations have given governments the excuse to step around the normal legal processes under both the 1922 and 1937 constitutions. The problem was recognised by government advisors at the very beginning. In July 1923, Senator J. G. Douglas begged the Attorney General to persuade the government, now that it had won its war, to move from the principle of militarily-enforced obedience to that of voluntary civic compliance as quickly as possible:

> All the time that arrests and imprisonments, etc. were taking place as a result of the armed resistance to the Government it has been a source of great satisfaction to me, and I am sure to you also, that slowly and steadily the Government were building up a structure of order which was winning the respect of the people. The sending out of an unarmed police force was an act of courage and wisdom on the part of the Government, and I believe did a good deal to add to public confidence and hope for the future. The promised creation of a new judiciary at an early date together with an unarmed police force with only the military in case of extreme disorder or organised violence, all pointed towards a speedy establishment of an Irish State . . . My idea is that the aim of the Government should be to slowly and steadily withdraw the military rule with its abnormal powers and substitute the civil authority acting strictly in the spirit of the Constitution.
>
> (Kennedy Papers, P4/1002)

Unfortunately, a certain tendency toward authoritarian law-enforcement and censorship in the name of keeping public order and also as a way of furthering state policy has persisted in Irish public life and detracts somewhat from the republican character of Irish political institutions even today, although the tradition has admittedly weakened as the judiciary has begun to flex its muscles and as Irish public opinion has become more articulate. By and large, the Republic's record on civil rights has been good.

The growing role of the judges has been important. Since the 1960s, the courts have shown an increased willingness to assert not only the human rights enshrined rather conditionally in the 1937 constitution but also unasserted rights which the judges have derived from them. A tradition of judicial review inspired by the American prototype has grown up to balance the older reliance on executive power, as we saw in chapter 3. The EC's Court of Justice has begun to perform a similar function in recent years. The Republic has gradually moved away from the British tradition of parliamentary supremacy and executive discretion and towards a pattern that characterises both the USA and certain European countries – such as Germany and Austria – and that is more consonant with the principle of the supremacy of the constitution over parliament, executive and judiciary alike (see Chubb, 1991). By European standards, moreover, the Irish judiciary is relatively activist. Its activism is not only shaped by the discretion allowed by the constitution; the judiciary has also elaborated extensively on the meaning of the constitution itself (see chapter 3).

Electoral democracy in Ireland

The most important long-term general check on authoritarian tendencies in both state and church has, however, turned out to be the mechanism of electoral democracy. The founders of the state do not seem to have completely appreciated the importance of the new party organisations which were rising from the ruins of British rule. Certain provisions of both the 1922 and 1937 constitutions attempted to ignore the reality of party power. Highly disciplined organisations controlling the votes of substantial proportions of a newly enfranchised electorate installed themselves in local councils, took over the Dáil and penetrated the legal and teaching professions, the post office and other public and private organisations in the early decades.

The coming of the mass, voter-directed and disciplined political party, exemplified in particular by Fianna Fáil, surprised and dismayed some. The framers of the 1922 constitution had anticipated that PR-STV would generate a large number of small parties. However, Ireland was spared the fragmentation that plagued the parliaments of France, Germany and eastern Europe in the inter-war years. In turn, the new parties owed the adeptness of their activists at fighting elections to a tradition of public contestation which dated back to Daniel O'Connell (Carty, 1981; Garvin, 1981).

The securing of the adhesion of the bulk of the anti-Treaty forces to the institutions of the state in the form of Fianna Fáil in 1927 represented a real breakthrough in the process of legitimising the new system. It was an extraordinary triumph for William Cosgrave's statesmanship, and one that is frequently underrated. Were it not for this tacit and sullen acceptance of Free State democracy by de Valera, the long-term viability of democratic rule in Ireland would have been seriously menaced, and authoritarian tendencies would have been greatly encouraged. The years 1922–23, 1927, 1932 and 1937 are crucial in the evolution of Irish democracy. The armed defence of the majority's right to decide who was to govern, the acceptance of majoritarianism by the defeated minority in 1927, the transformation of that minority into a ruling majority, and the enactment of de Valera's non-Commonwealth constitution are all events that were not inevitable. The inexperienced politicians of the fledgling democracy managed to pass the test each time. Looked upon from a long historical perspective, the emergence and consolidation of what became the Republic of Ireland in 1949 is a formidable achievement; it constitutes the first regime ever to emerge in Ireland in which no significant group disputed the right of the regime to rule (Prager, 1986).

Fianna Fáil became the master of the applied science of winning elections very early in its history. Most of the vote-managing techniques which have fascinated observers of Irish politics were perfected by the party before 1932. A despairing private letter from a Cumann na nGaedheal activist in Waterford in 1932 mourned the defeat of the government party, but expressed admiration for the unrivalled efficiency of the Fianna Fáil electoral machine, against which Cumann na nGaedheal was helpless. The anti-Treatyites had lost the war but won the peace by means of a 'wonderfully worked Organised Campaign', he said:

> Outside the school wall [at Ballyduff] were two FF Cars and posters all over them, telling us to vote for Goulding, Little and Mansfield . . . there were two FF cars plying to and from the booth laden with voters, most of them illiterate and well tutored how to vote.
>
> (Mulcahy Papers, P7B/89 (53))

Fianna Fáil, he reported, had systematic lists of voters, and had partitioned the constituency so as to maximise local loyalties and party preferences in a style that has now become a textbook classic (Sacks, 1976; Bax, 1976). Similar stories could have been told of most other counties, and the Fianna Fáil challenge forced other parties to imitate it; Fine Gael, Labour and other parties all had to take lessons from de Valera's party.

Policy making in a small democracy

Party democracy in a country as small as the Republic of Ireland has always been liable to overwhelm the structures of impersonal bureaucratic administration in favour of a generalised spoils system, as happened in the United States in 1828 with the advent of Jacksonian democracy. In Ireland, the separation of function between politician and civil servant has been maintained, but it has often been endangered. A confusion of the two roles was evident in the minds of the early Sinn Féiners. The famous 1919 oath to the Republic itself refers to Dáil Éireann as the government (though it was in reality a parliament, not a government). In the Dáil government and in the first year of the Free State, members of parliament were commonly given administrative positions in defiance of the administrative/political distinction. The chief of staff of the army and the commissioner of the civic guards were, for example, Dáil deputies when appointed. This practice soon ceased, however. The formation of the Civil Service Commission and the Local Appointments Commission in the mid-1920s reflected the government's sensitivity to the potential hazards of interpenetration of the political and administrative spheres. Civil servants came to be recruited on meritocratic and non-political grounds, a major achievement. By and large, the separation of function has been maintained. In some ways, the situation has improved; the growth of public service unions has, for example, made it more difficult for a politician to prevent a garda from doing his duty in enforcing the law. However, the beef tribunal, 1991–94, demonstrated that civil servants were sometimes constrained to obey their political masters even when the legality of their instructions was in question.

Issues of this kind are rather difficult to explore in Ireland, partly because of a tradition of stifling secrecy in government. This tradition derives in part from the practices of the old British system, partly from the conspiratorial style of the first Irish Republican government and partly from a general secretive streak in the political culture. Most of the Irish governmental archives, for example, were kept closed to the public for seventy years after independence, a level of secretiveness that is almost Soviet in its intensity. Casual inspection suggests that many of the files that have been opened have been well weeded. The recent freedom of information legislation (see p. 267), coupled with a liberalisation of official attitudes and the development of stronger parliamentary committees, has begun to change the situation.

Policy making, then, has proceeded in a rather indirect relationship to electoral politics, which tended to be fuelled by local economic, welfarist and nationalist passions. These then had to be translated or, rather, transformed into symbolic, constitutional and socio-economic policy outputs by an often secretive governmental process. The oligarchical relationships that evolved between the executive and parliament made this process irrational in many cases, subject not so much to an informed public opinion, as to veto from ecclesiastical and lay interest groups and local pressure in the context of a highly competitive electoral process. The growth of corporate collective bargaining structures since 1945 has further removed much policy making from both public opinion and the market, making for policies that are often not obviously in the public interest and are certainly arrived at by means that are not democratic (see chapter 11 and Hardiman, 1988).

An ideological preference for state monopoly and distrust of private enterprise in the 1930s acted together with the natural ease of monopoly formation in a small country to make Irish government big and interventionist in the economy. Electoral competition ensured that grants and hand-outs were spread around the country evenly even when it was obvious that this dissipation of resources did not make economic sense. Furthermore, the power of local interests ensured that such irrationalities long outlived their original purposes and arguably were contrary to the public interest.

A good example is afforded by the historical underdevelopment of the Irish road system. By the mid-1980s, the Republic of Ireland was said to have the worst main road system in western Europe, while having the greatest density of side roads. A preference for state transport systems and a dislike of the motor car as a vehicle of the rich combined with the natural inclination of the local councils to spread a labour-intensive type of road-mending activity evenly around their electoral areas. County engineers were forced to go along with this archaic system. A modern main road system could not be built by such methods nor with the kind of resources commanded by the local authorities. Small-town traders feared for the passing trade and blocked the making of bypasses. In 1948–49, a proposed dual carriageway bypass of Bray was blocked by the Taoiseach. The projected building of a new postwar road network was killed off by pressures from other departments on the Department of Finance to divert the money into more popular and apparently charitable areas such as social welfare and public housing (Department of Taoiseach, S12895, S13061, S13527, S14297).

It was not until the advent of European subventions in the 1980s that the blockages caused by Irish political structures started to be overcome, and a modern road system of an international standard began to be put in place. It is impossible to say how much the generation's delay in supplying a modern transportation infrastructure has cost the Irish economy, but the price has certainly been high. In other areas, political structures have not prevented successful reforms. A good example is the preventive medicine campaigns of the post-war period, which greatly improved the general health of the population in an efficient, humane and inexpensive way. Another example is the brilliant reconstruction of the primary school curriculum carried out during the 1970s.

Two generations of self-government

It is commonly said that independent Ireland started out life in 1922 with considerable advantages. Certainly this is true. Infrastructure was tolerably well-developed, the civil service was honest and fairly well-trained, and the agricultural economy had received a considerable fillip from the wartime boom in food prices. As argued above, the new state was also fortunate in that republican democratic institutions survived the bloody transition of 1921–23. An IRA victory in 1922 would have meant the eclipse of Dáil Éireann in favour of some kind of military directorate, and the ending of the principle of decision-making by the electorate, as it was exactly that principle that the IRA denied. Furthermore, the British would very probably have intervened, with horrendous consequences.

The legacy of British rule was, however, by no means as benign as it is sometimes permitted to appear. Irish slums were among the worst in Europe, and Irish agriculture was underdeveloped, being at least a generation behind that of Denmark (Lee, 1989, pp. 513, 519). More subtly, the lack of a tradition of self-government and the experience of insurrection and revolution rendered many Irish people psychologically unready to think about the mundane but vital problems of self-government. The civil war perpetuated a tradition of hate-filled and self-righteous rant which often drowned out any attempt at coherent and informed discussion of the new possibilities afforded by independence. As in other post-revolutionary societies, the culture developed an aspirational twist which prompted the noisy berating of the government for not immediately achieving the visions of the revolutionary martyrs.

The new party system, generated by a civil war that was itself a *lusus naturae*, was an oddity, in some ways a benign one. It forced the old Sinn Féiners to compete against each other and submit themselves and their often peculiar ideas to popular judgement. On the other hand, it may have encouraged much irrationality. For example, Fianna Fáil-led governments and Fine Gael-led governments have shown about the same aggregate propensity to spend public money; Fine Gael's more thrifty tradition has tended to be balanced by other, more spending-oriented allies in coalition governments.

Another long-term consequence of the split of 1922–23 was a chronic alienation between Fianna Fáil, because of its electoral prowess the natural governing party in the system, and the universities, which were quickly taken over in the early 1920s by Cumann na nGaedheal and its pro-Treaty clerical allies. The difficulties any government has with the media were compounded by the hostility between the anti-Treatyites and the over-whelmingly pro-Treaty press in 1922–23. Despite Fianna Fáil's developing a house newspaper, the *Irish Press*, the dislike of free journalism persisted until the 1990s in a willingness to gag the electronic media, which were in any case largely controlled by the state. The demise of the *Irish Press* and the explosion of non-state controlled media in the 1990s has transformed the situation.

Much of the opinion-forming process in Irish society is shaped by third-level institutions in which the Fianna Fáil tradition is relatively weak and those of both Fine Gael and the left are relatively strong. The relative weakness of the usual left–right polarisation in the party system has encouraged a pragmatism that sometimes veers into incoherence, opportunism or an intellectually and otherwise corrupt know-nothingness.

Irish political culture was, until very recently, post-peasant, and exhibited a tendency that I have labelled 'communalism', or a propensity to fear the achievement by others of their particular interests on the ground that it might damage one's own interests and those of the collectivity; no one should be too successful. Opportunism could lurk behind such 'groupthink'. The party system communicated this general cultural propensity to the political system.

Despite structural and cultural problems of the kind I have outlined, policy does get made. Between 1922 and 1948, the new state experimented, at first tentatively and then boldly, with different economic and social policies. A low-tariff and non-dirigiste policy was followed in the 1920s. The government streamlined the local government system, imposed a puritan clean-up of prostitution and clamped down on literature and film. It also abolished the hated workhouses and replaced them by a more at-home relief system, started the electrification of the country and standardised quality and branding of exported agricultural goods.

Under Fianna Fáil, economic interventionism, state-led industrialisation, discouragement of foreign investment and import substitution industrialisation behind high tariff walls were given a determined trial between 1932 and 1959. It could be argued that the economic isolationists were unlucky because of the depression and the Second World War; as against this, it might be argued that the policy of isolationism was more a by-product of the depression than a strategy that was adopted for its own sake. One's overall impression is of relatively little economic success between 1932 and 1948 (Lee, 1989, pp. 184–201).

The opening up of a new European order and the coming of Marshall Aid transformed the objective situation. What is important is how slow the Irish were to react to the new situation and get on the developmental bandwagon. Ireland missed out on the first fifteen years of the post-war thirty-year boom, the greatest such boom in history. Pre-war protectionism and discouragement of foreign investment were clung to for a decade and a half too long. The country took a long time to 'go developmental'. Education, for example, which had been seen as a means of producing patriotic, pious and obedient citizens, only very slowly became also a means of producing skilled and competent workers who might contribute to the gross national product (GNP). The idea that Ireland might have an economy as well as be a country was routinely derided by journalists. The political system was seen primarily as a means of redistribution and the Catholic church, as late as the early 1960s, had, in the minds of the many, a greater moral and even political legitimacy than did the elected leaders of the state.

Economic and social progress (and much regression) did occur in the first thirty years after independence, but progress was piecemeal and sluggish compared with the distance the country has covered since the mid-1950s. GNP per head has more than doubled, and this growth rate has approximated to that of the OECD countries during the last generation. Ireland has been damaged in this league table by its late start, due to the old revolutionaries who passively and even actively prevented change between 1945 and 1960. Its relatively poor performance is, however, mainly due to the phenomenal economic growth rates of the defeated countries of 1939–45 (the Axis countries plus France and Finland). The success of these countries gives superficial credence to Olson's well-known thesis that defeat of a nation's ruling group unleashes energies that had previously been bottled up (Olson, 1982).

Clearly, Ireland's progress, although impressive in comparison with its own past, was not spectacular by the standards of the 'top twenty-four' economies. In part, this is a product of the population figures. Irish people chose in the 1957–80 era to have a large number of children, and even the country's much lamented high emigration rate could not reduce its dependency ratio – the proportion of the population who, because of youth or age, are out of the labour market – to average west European levels. On top of this, because of the baby boom, a generous unemployment relief scheme, obsolescence of many skills and economic sluggishness, unemployment was chronically high until 1990. Since then, there has been an extraordinary transformation, involving annual GNP growth rates of over 6 per cent.

Quite apart from that, enormous progress has been made in many areas. In particular, a true revolution in public health took place after 1945. The life expectancy of women increased by more than ten years, and diseases such as tuberculosis, polio, diphtheria and rickets were stamped out (Garvin, 1989). In education, an equally sweeping transformation occurred. Between 1922 and 1957, educational participation rates scarcely changed, a scandalous symptom of the hands-off posture enforced by jealous churches on a timid government which, in any case, saw education primarily as a means of cultural defence, much as did the churches themselves. Since 1957, Irish education has been revolutionised. In 1922, scarcely 4,000 privileged young people received third-level education. By 1957, the figure was not all that much higher. It is now over 60,000, a tripling since the mid-1960s. The proportion going to some kind of third-level education now surpasses its United Kingdom equivalent, an important historical landmark, but both countries lag well behind mainland European countries (Garvin, 1989).

Progress in many areas was associated with the elite generational change that occurred between 1957 and 1965, when old revolutionaries, often begrudgingly and with great foreboding, gave way to younger people. De Valera's last fifteen years as leader of Fianna Fáil (1944–59) resemble faintly Brezhnev's last fifteen as general secretary of the Communist Party of the Soviet Union (1968–83). In the Irish case, turning things around was relatively easy, once the dead hand of the old revolutionaries was absent, because the Irish revolution was one of national separatism rather than one of social transformation. Old revolutionaries make the most implacable reactionaries, and with luck it takes only a generation to recover from a successful revolution. The fact of the matter is that the Irish revolution was an expensive business, and that expense was borne disproportionately by the poor. Given the fact of independence, the Irish state has some impressive achievements to its credit. The central achievement was, however, the establishment of a free political order, essentially republican and democratic, in a society with a long tradition of primitive hatred of government. Success in this has been so total that Irish people do not realise what an achievement it has been.

Envoi

The passions that dominated the struggle for independence from the British Empire two generations ago are not quite dead. The coming of the European Union has led some to argue that Ireland is throwing away its much longed-for and dearly-bought sovereignty for a new version of the Act of Union of 1800. This is, actually, a poor analogy. The Act of Union ensured that Ireland would be perpetually in opposition within the joint Irish-British political system and would be perpetually an under-governed mendicant. The European Union gives Ireland, a tiny country, a veto over policy and preserves her domestic democracy (see chapter 13). Irish sovereignty is not being thrown away; it is being pooled with that of the largest and richest multinational commonwealth ever seen. European union may, however, mean that Ireland's separate history is coming to an end and is becoming part of the general history of Europe. In this sense, Irish independence may indeed be over.

References and further reading

Aristotle, 1962. *Politics.* Harmondsworth: Penguin.
Barker, Ernest, 1951. *Principles of Social and Political Theory.* Oxford: Clarendon Press.
Bax, Mart, 1976. *Harpstrings and Confessions: Machine-style Politics in the Irish Republic.* Assen: Van Gorcum.
Bowman, John, 1982. *De Valera and the Ulster Question.* Oxford: Clarendon Press.
Carty, R. K., 1981. *Party and Parish Pump: Electoral Politics in Ireland.* Waterloo, Ontario: Wilfrid Laurier University Press.
Chubb, Basil, 1991. *The Politics of the Irish Constitution.* Dublin: Institute of Public Administration.
Cohan, Al, 1972. *The Irish Political Elite.* Dublin: Gill and Macmillan.
Curran, J. C., 1980. *The Birth of the Irish Free State, 1921–23.* Tuscaloosa, Ala.: University of Alabama Press.
Dahl, Robert A., 1971. *Polyarchy: Participation and Opposition.* New Haven: Yale University Press.
Dahl, Robert A., 1989. *Democracy and its Critics.* New Haven: Yale University Press.
Department of Taoiseach. Papers, D/Taoiseach, National Archives, Bishop St, Dublin.

Garvin, Tom, 1981. *The Evolution of Irish Nationalist Politics.* Dublin: Gill and Macmillan.

Garvin, Tom, 1988. *Nationalist Revolutionaries in Ireland.* Oxford: Oxford University Press.

Garvin, Tom, 1989. 'Wealth, poverty and development: reflections on current discontents', *Studies* 78:311, pp. 312–25.

Garvin, Tom, 1991. 'Democracy in Ireland: collective somnambulance and public policy', *Administration* 39:1, pp. 42–54.

Garvin, Tom, 1996. *1922: The Birth of Irish Democracy.* Dublin: Gill and Macmillan.

Hardiman, Niamh, 1988. *Pay, Politics and Economic Performance in Ireland 1970–1987.* Oxford: Oxford University Press.

Hopkinson, Michael, 1988. *Green against Green: the Irish Civil War.* Dublin: Gill and Macmillan.

Huntington, Samuel P., 1968. *Political Order in Changing Societies.* New Haven: Yale University Press.

Kennedy Papers. Archives Department, University College, Dublin.

Klosko, George, 1986. *The Development of Plato's Political Theory.* New York and London: Methuen.

Kohn, Leo, 1932. *The Constitution of the Irish Free State.* London: Allen and Unwin.

Lee, J. J., 1989. *Ireland 1912–1985: Politics and Society.* Cambridge: Cambridge University Press.

Mair, Peter, 1987. *The Changing Irish Party System: Organisation, Ideology and Electoral Competition.* London: Pinter.

Mansergh, Nicholas, 1934. *The Irish Free State.* London: Allen and Unwin.

Montesquieu, 1989. *The Spirit of the Laws.* Cambridge: Cambridge University Press.

Mulcahy Papers. Archives Department, University College, Dublin.

Olson, Mancur, 1982. *The Rise and Decline of Nations.* New Haven and London: Yale University Press.

Plato, 1960. *Gorgias.* Harmondsworth: Penguin.

Prager, Jeffrey, 1986. *Building Democracy in Ireland: Political Order and Cultural Integration in a Newly Independent Nation.* Cambridge: Cambridge University Press.

Sacks, Paul, 1976. *The Donegal Mafia.* New Haven and London: Yale University Press.

Thompson, William, 1969. *The Imagination of an Insurrection.* Oxford: Oxford University Press.

Thucydides, 1910. *The History of the Pelopennesian War.* London: Dent.

Appendices
John Coakley

Appendix 1: Demographic data

1a Population and social indicators, 1841–1996

Year	Population	Urban population %	Dublin population %	Males in agriculture %	Catholics %	Other denominations %	Irish-speakers %
1841	6,528,799	16.7	3.7	74.3	–	–	–
1851	5,111,557	22.0	5.8	68.8	–	–	29.1
1861	4,402,111	22.2	6.7	64.6	89.3	10.7	24.5
1871	4,053,187	22.8	7.4	63.1	89.2	10.8	19.8
1881	3,870,020	23.9	8.4	62.6	89.5	10.5	23.9
1891	3,468,694	25.3	9.6	61.4	89.3	10.7	19.2
1901	3,221,823	28.0	11.2	61.7	89.3	10.7	19.2
1911	3,139,688	29.7	12.3	59.5	89.6	10.4	17.6
1926	2,971,992	31.8	13.7	58.9	92.6	7.4	19.3
1936	2,968,420	35.5	15.9	55.9	93.4	6.6	23.7
1946	2,955,107	39.3	17.1	54.1	94.3	5.7	21.2
1961	2,818,341	46.4	19.1	43.1	94.9	4.9	27.2
1971	2,978,248	52.2	26.9	31.9	93.9	4.3	28.3
1981	3,443,405	55.6	29.1	21.7	93.1	3.7	31.6
1991	3,525,719	57.0	29.1	19.1	91.6	4.2	32.5
1996	3,626,087	58.1	29.2	15.1	–	–	43.5

Source: Calculated from *Census of Ireland* and *Statistical Abstract of Ireland*, various dates, and from David Fitzpatrick, 'The disappearance of the Irish agricultural labourer, 1841-1912', *Irish Economic and Social History* 7, 1980, pp. 66-92.

Notes: All data refer to the present area of the Republic of Ireland. Urban areas are defined as those with a population of 1,500 or more, but figures for these and for Dublin are difficult to compare over time due to changes in boundary definition criteria. The data on involvement in agriculture are also difficult to compare over time due to varying classification criteria, and it has been possible to compute comparable data for men only. Data on religion are expressed as percentages of the total population (which includes those refusing to give information on this matter). Data on Irish speakers from 1926 onwards refer to the population aged over three years, but the form of the question changed in 1996, so the data for this year are not strictly comparable with the earlier ones. In all cases, knowledge of the language is self-assessed.

1b Emigration, 1841–1996

Period	Total emigration	Annual average
1841–51	1,132,000	108,000
1852–60	791,648	87,961
1861–70	697,704	69,740
1871–80	446,326	44,633
1881–90	616,894	61,689
1891–00	377,017	37,702
1901–10	266,311	26,631
	Net emigration	
1911–26	405,029	27,002
1926–36	166,751	16,675
1936–46	187,111	18,711
1946–61	528,334	35,222
1961–71	134,511	13,451
1971–81	–103,889	–10,389
1981–91	206,053	20,605
1991–96	–8,302	–1,660

Source: computed from W. E. Vaughan and A. J. Fitzpatrick (eds), *Irish Historical Statistics: Population, 1821–1971* (Dublin: Royal Irish Academy, 1989), Commission on Emigration and Other Population Problems 1948–1954, *Reports* (Dublin: Stationery Office, [1956]) and *Statistical Abstract of Ireland*, 1997.

Note: The data for 1841–51 are estimates based on the assumption that the proportion of Irish emigrants coming from the present territory of the Republic was the same as in the 1852–60 period (the data begin in mid-year 1841). Net emigration refers to out-migration less inmigration, and the negative values in 1971–81 and 1991–96 indicate a surplus of immigrants over emigrants in these periods.

Appendix 2: Electoral data

2a Distribution of parliamentary seats by party, 1801–1918

Year	Southern Ireland Tory/ Unionist	Whig/ Liberal	Nat. etc.	Other	Total	All Ireland Tory/ Unionist	Whig/ Liberal	Nat. etc.	Other	Total
1801	23	16	–	39	78	34	16	–	50	100
1802	27	26	–	25	78	43	28	–	29	100
1806	34	34	–	10	78	50	36	–	14	100
1807	37	32	–	9	78	54	33	–	13	100
1812	43	28	–	7	78	59	30	–	11	100
1818	41	32	–	5	78	61	34	–	5	100
1820	44	29	–	5	78	63	32	–	5	100
1826	38	37	–	3	78	56	41	–	3	100
1830	34	41	–	3	78	49	48	–	3	100
1831	26	48	–	4	78	40	56	–	4	100
1832	14	26	42	–	82	30	33	42	–	105
1835	22	26	34	–	82	37	34	34	–	105
1837	14	38	30	–	82	32	43	30	–	105
1841	23	39	20	–	82	43	42	20	–	105
1847	20	21	36	5	82	31	25	36	13	105
1852	21	11	48	2	82	40	15	48	2	105
1857	26	43	13	–	82	44	48	13	–	105
1859	33	49	–	0	82	55	50	–	0	105
1865	24	58	–	0	82	47	58	–	0	105
1868	19	63	–	0	82	39	66	–	0	105
1874	16	4	60	–	80	33	10	60	–	103
1880	7	10	63	–	80	25	15	63	–	103
1885	2	–	76	–	78	18	–	85	–	103
1886	2	–	76	–	78	19	–	84	–	103
1892	4	–	74	–	78	23	–	80	–	103
1895	4	–	74	–	78	21	1	81	–	103
1900	3	–	75	–	78	21	1	81	–	103
1906	3	–	75	–	78	20	1	82	–	103
1910–11	3	–	75	–	78	21	1	81	–	103
1910–12	2	–	76	–	78	19	1	83	–	103
1918	3	–	2	70	75	26	–	6	73	105

Sources: Calculated from Henry Stooks Smith, *The Parliaments of England from 1715 to 1847*, 2nd ed, edited by F. W. S. Craig (Chichester: Political Reference Publications, 1973), and Brian M. Walker, *Parliamentary Election Results in Ireland, 1801–1922* (Dublin: Royal Irish Academy, 1978).
Notes: 'Southern Ireland' refers to the present territory of the Republic of Ireland. Before 1832 party affiliations are approximate only. 'Tories/Unionists' includes Liberal Unionists; 'Nationalists, etc.' includes the Repeal Party (1832–47), the Independent Irish Party (1852–57) and the Home Rule or Nationalist Party, including breakaway factions and independent nationalists (1874–1918); 'others' includes nonaligned MPs (1801–32), Peelites (1847–52) and two Irish Confederates in the South (1847); in 1918 it refers to Sinn Féin MPs.

2b Distribution of first preference votes in Dáil elections by party, 1922–97

Year	Fianna Fáil %	Fine Gael %	Labour Party %	Farmers' parties %	Republican parties %	Others %	Turnout %
1922	21.7	38.5	21.3	7.8	–	10.6	45.5
1923	27.4	39.0	10.6	12.1	–	10.9	61.2
1927–1	26.1	27.5	12.6	8.9	3.6	21.4	68.1
1927–2	35.2	38.7	9.1	6.4	–	10.7	69.0
1932	44.5	35.3	7.7	3.1	–	9.4	76.5
1933	49.7	30.5	5.7	9.2	–	5.0	81.3
1937	45.2	34.8	10.3	–	–	9.7	76.2
1938	51.9	33.3	10.0	–	–	4.7	76.7
1943	41.9	23.1	15.7	11.3	0.3	7.7	74.2
1944	48.9	20.5	8.8	11.6	–	10.2	67.7
1948	41.9	19.8	8.7	5.5	13.2	10.9	74.2
1951	46.3	25.8	11.4	2.9	4.1	9.6	75.3
1954	43.4	32.0	12.1	3.1	3.9	5.6	76.4
1957	48.3	26.6	9.1	2.4	7.0	6.6	71.3
1961	43.8	32.0	11.6	1.5	4.2	6.8	70.6
1965	47.7	34.1	15.4	–	0.8	2.1	75.1
1969	45.7	34.1	17.0			3.2	76.9
1973	46.2	35.1	13.7	–	2.0	3.0	76.6
1977	50.6	30.5	11.6	–	1.8	5.5	76.3
1981	45.3	36.5	9.9	–	2.5	5.9	76.2
				PDs	*SF*		
1982–1	47.3	37.3	9.1	–	1.0	5.3	73.8
1982–2	45.2	39.2	9.4	–	–	6.3	72.9
1987	44.1	27.1	6.4	11.8	1.9	8.7	73.3
1989	44.1	29.3	9.5	5.5	1.2	10.4	68.5
1992	39.1	24.5	19.3	4.7	1.6	10.9	68.5
1997	39.3	27.9	10.4	4.7	2.6	15.1	65.9

Source: Michael Gallagher (ed.), *Irish Elections 1922–44: Results and Analysis* (Limerick: PSAI Press, 1993); Brian M. Walker (ed.), *Parliamentary Election Results in Ireland 1918–92* (Dublin: Royal Irish Academy and Belfast: Institute of Irish Studies, 1992).
Notes: Fianna Fáil includes Anti-Treaty Sinn Féin (1922–23). Fine Gael includes Pro-Treaty Sinn Féin (1922) and Cumann na nGaedheal (1923–32). 'Farmers' parties' includes the Farmers' Party (1922–32), the National Centre Party (1933), and Clann na Talmhan (1943–61). 'Republican parties' refers to Sinn Féin, including the original party before 1970 (1927–1, 3.6%; 1954, 0.1%; 1957, 5.3%; 1961, 3.1%), 'Official' Sinn Féin in the 1970s (1973, 1.1%; 1977, 1.7%), and the following parties: Córas na Poblachta (1943, 0.3%), Clann na Poblachta (1948, 13.2%; 1951, 4.1%; 1954, 3.8%; 1957, 1.7%; 1961, 1.1%; 1965, 0.8%), Aontacht Éireann (1973, 0.9%), the Irish Republican Socialist Party (1977, 0.1%; 1982–1, 0.2%) and the National H-Block Committee (1981, 2.5%). 'Others' includes the National League (1927–1, 7.3%; 1927–2, 1.6%), National Labour (1944, 2.7%; 1948, 2.6%), the National Progressive Democrats (1961, 1.0%), and the Green Party (1987, 0.4%; 1989, 1.5%; 1992, 1.4%; 1997, 2.6%), as well as smaller groups and independents. From 1981, Sinn Féin the Workers' Party and its successor, the Workers' Party, have been grouped with 'others' (1981, 1.7%; 1982–1, 2.2%; 1982–2, 3.1%; 1987, 3.8%; 1989, 5.0%; 1992, 0.7%; 1997, 0.4%), as has Democratic Left (1992, 2.8%; 1997, 2.3%).

2c Distribution of seats in Dáil by party, 1922–97

Year	Fianna Fáil	Fine Gael	Labour Party	Farmers' parties	Republican parties	Others	Total
1922	36	58	17	7	–	10	128
1923	44	63	14	15	–	17	153
1927–1	44	47	22	11	5	24	153
1927–2	57	62	13	6	–	15	153
1932	72	57	7	4	–	13	153
1933	77	48	8	11	–	9	153
1937	69	48	13	–	–	8	138
1938	77	45	9	–	–	7	138
1943	67	32	17	14	–	8	138
1944	76	30	8	11	–	13	138
1948	68	31	14	7	10	17	147
1951	69	40	16	6	2	14	147
1954	65	50	19	5	3	5	147
1957	78	40	12	3	5	9	147
1961	70	47	16	2	1	8	144
1965	72	47	22	–	1	2	144
1969	75	50	18	–	–	1	144
1973	69	54	19	–	–	2	144
1977	84	43	17	–	–	4	148
1981	78	65	15	–	2	6	166
				Prog. Dems	Sinn Féin		
1982–1	81	63	15	–	–	7	166
1982–2	75	70	16	–	–	5	166
1987	81	51	12	14	–	8	166
1989	77	55	15	6	–	13	166
1992	68	45	33	10	–	10	166
1997	77	54	17	4	1	6	166

Source: As for appendix 2b.
Notes: Fianna Fáil includes Anti-Treaty Sinn Féin (1922–23). Fine Gael includes Pro-Treaty Sinn Féin (1922) and Cumann na nGaedheal (1923–32). 'Farmers' parties' includes the Farmers' Party (1922–32), the National Centre Party (1933), and Clann na Talmhan (1943–61). 'Republican parties' refers mainly to Clann na Poblachta (1948–65) but includes also Sinn Féin (1927–1, 5 TDs; 1957, 4 TDs) and the National H-Block Committee (1981, 2 TDs). 'Others' includes the National League (1927–1, 8 TDs; 1927–2, 2 TDs), National Labour (1944, 4 TDs; 1948, 5 TDs), the National Progressive Democrats (1961, 2 TDs), Sinn Féin the Workers' Party and its successor, the Workers' Party (1981, 1 TD; 1982–1, 3 TDs; 1982–2, 2 TDs; 1987, 4 TDs; 1989, 7 TDs), the Green Party (1989 and 1992, 1 TD; 1997, 2 TDs) and Democratic Left (1992 and 1997, 4 TDs), as well as smaller groups and independents.
      The first Dáil was convened on the basis of the British general election of 1918; at this election Sinn Féin won 73 seats (all except three of these in the south; two of the northern seats were won by candidates who were also successful in the south and one candidate was returned for two constituencies in the south, leaving Sinn Féin with 70 MPs), the Unionists 26 (all except three in the north) and the Nationalists won six (four in the north and two in the south). The second Dáil was convened on the basis of the elections in 1921 to the proposed Houses of Commons of Southern Ireland and Northern Ireland; at this, Sinn Féin won 130 seats (all except six of these in the south; five of the northern seats were won by candidates who were also successful in the south, leaving Sinn Féin with 125 MPs), the Unionists 40 (all in the north), the Nationalists six (all in the north) and independents won four (all in the south).

2d Distribution of men and women in the Oireachtas, 1922–97

	Dáil Éireann				Seanad Éireann		
Year	Men	Women	Total	Year	Men	Women	Total
1922	126	2	128	–	–	–	–
1923	148	5	153	1922	56	4	60
1927–1	149	4	153	1925	56	4	60
1927–2	152	1	153	1928	55	5	60
1932	151	2	153	1931	55	5	60
1933	150	3	153	1934	57	3	60
1937	136	2	138	1938–1	56	4	60
1938	135	3	138	1938–2	57	3	60
1943	135	3	138	1943	57	3	60
1944	134	4	138	1944	57	3	60
1948	142	5	147	1948	57	3	60
1951	142	5	147	1951	57	3	60
1954	142	5	147	1954	57	3	60
1957	142	5	147	1957	56	4	60
1961	141	3	144	1961	57	3	60
1965	139	5	144	1965	56	4	60
1969	141	3	144	1969	55	5	60
1973	140	4	144	1973	56	4	60
1977	142	6	148	1977	54	6	60
1981	155	11	166	1981	51	9	60
1982–1	158	8	166	1982	52	8	60
1982–2	152	14	166	1983	54	6	60
1987	152	14	166	1987	55	5	60
1989	153	13	166	1989	54	6	60
1992	146	20	166	1993	52	8	60
1997	146	20	166	1997	49	11	60

Notes: The data refer to the position immediately after general elections to Dáil Éireann (1922–97) and Seanad Éireann (1938–97). The earlier data on Seanad Éireann refer to the position immediately after the initial installation of the first Seanad under the Free State constitution (1922) and after the triennial elections which renewed a portion of its membership (1925–34).

Only one woman was returned from the 105 Irish seats in the British general election of 1918; of the 73 Sinn Féin seats, 72 were occupied by men (since three of these seats were double returns, the full potential membership of the first Dáil was 69 men and one woman). Eight women were returned from the 180 seats to the Houses of Commons of Southern Ireland and Northern Ireland in 1921, two Unionists in the north and six Sinn Féin members in the south (since the 130 Sinn Féin seats were occupied by only 125 people due to double returns, the full potential membership of the second Dáil was 119 men and six women).

2e Distribution of first preference votes in European Parliament elections, 1979–99

Year	Fianna Fáil %	Fine Gael %	Labour Party %	Workers' Party %	Progressive Democrats %	Others %	Turnout %
1979	34.7	33.1	14.5	3.3	–	14.4	63.6
1984	39.2	32.2	8.4	4.3	–	15.9	47.6
1989	31.5	21.6	9.5	7.5	11.9	17.9	68.3
1994	35.0	24.3	11.0	1.9	6.5	21.3	44.0
1999	38.6	24.6	8.7	–	–	28.0	50.2

Notes: 'Workers' Party' includes Sinn Féin The Workers' Party; 'Others' includes Sinn Féin (1984, 4.9%; 1989, 2.3%; 1994, 3.0%; 1999, 6.3%), Democratic Left (1994, 3.5%) and the Green Party (1989, 3.7%, 1994, 7.9%; 1999, 6.7%).

2f Distribution of first preference votes in local elections, 1967–99

Year	Fianna Fáil %	Fine Gael %	Labour Party %	Workers' Party %	Progressive Democrats %	Others %	Turnout %
1967	40.2	32.5	14.8	–	–	12.5	69.0
1974	40.1	33.7	12.8	1.5	–	11.9	61.1
1979	39.2	34.9	11.8	2.3	–	11.8	63.6
1985	45.5	29.8	7.7	3.0	–	14.0	58.2
1991	37.9	26.4	10.6	3.7	5.0	16.4	55.1
1999	39.0	28.1	10.8	0.5	2.9	18.7	49.5

Notes: These figures relate to the results in county and county borough elections only. 'Workers' Party' includes Sinn Féin (1974) and Sinn Féin the Workers' Party (1979); 'Others' includes Sinn Féin (1979, 2.2%; 1985, 3.3%; 1991, 1.7%; 1999, 3.5%) and the Green Party (1991, 2.0%; 1999, 2.5%).

2g Distribution of votes in presidential elections, 1945–97

Year	Candidate	Count 1 No.	(%)	Count 2 Transfers	Result	(%)	Comment
1945	McCartan, Patrick	212,834	(19.6)				Ó Ceallaigh elected;
	MacEoin, Seán	335,539	(30.9)	+117,886	453,425	(44.5)	turnout: 63.0%
	Ó Ceallaigh, Seán T.	537,965	(49.5)	+27,200	565,165	(55.5)	non-transferable: 67,748
1959	de Valera, Eamon	538,003	(56.3)				de Valera elected;
	MacEoin, Seán	417,536	(43.7)				turnout: 58.4%
1966	de Valera, Eamon	558,861	(50.5)				de Valera elected;
	O'Higgins, Thomas F.	548,144	(49.5)				turnout: 65.4%
1973	Childers, Erskine	635,867	(52.0)				Childers elected;
	O'Higgins, Thomas F.	587,771	(48.0)				turnout: 62.2%
1990	Currie, Austin	267,902	(17.0)				Robinson elected;
	Lenihan, Brian	694,484	(44.1)	+36,789	731,273	(47.2)	turnout: 64.1%
	Robinson, Mary	612,265	(38.9)	+205,565	817,830	(52.8)	non-transferable: 25,548
1997	Banotti, Mary	372,002	(29.3)	+125,514	497,516	(41.3)	McAleese elected;
	McAleese, Mary	574,424	(45.2)	+131,835	706,259	(58.7)	turnout: 46.8%
	Nally, Derek	59,529	(4.7)				non-transferable: 66,061
	Roche, Adi	88,423	(7.0)				
	Scallon, Rosemary	175,458	(13.8)				

Note: In 1938, 1952, 1974, 1976 and 1983 no contests took place as only one candidate was nominated.

2h Referendum results, 1937–99

Date	Subject (article altered)	For %	Against %	Turn-out %	Spoiled %
1.7.37	Approve new constitution	56.5	43.5	75.8	10.0
17.6.59	Replace proportional representation by plurality system (*3rd amendment; 16*)	48.2	51.8	58.4	4.0
16.10.68	Permit flexibility in deputy–population ratio (*3rd amendment; 16*)	39.2	60.8	65.8	4.3
16.10.68	Replace proportional representation by plurality system (*4th amendment; 16*)	39.2	60.8	65.8	4.3
10.5.72	Permit EC membership (*3rd amend't; 29*)	83.1	16.9	70.9	0.8
7.12.72	Lower voting age to 18 (*4th amend't; 16*)	84.6	15.4	50.7	5.2
7.12.72	Remove 'special position' of Catholic church (5th amendment; 44)	84.4	15.6	50.7	5.5
5.7.79	Protect adoption system (6th amend't; 37)	99.0	1.0	28.6	2.5
5.7.79	Permit alteration of university representation in Senate (7th amendment; 18)	92.4	7.6	28.6	3.9
7.9.83	Prohibit legalisation of abortion (8th amendment; 40)	66.9	33.1	53.7	0.7
14.6.84	Permit extension of voting rights to non-citizens (9th amendment; 16)	75.4	24.6	47.5	3.5
26.6.86	Permit legalisation of divorce (*10th amendment; 41*)	36.5	63.5	60.5	0.6
26.5.87	Permit signing of Single European Act (10th amendment; 29)	69.9	30.1	43.9	0.5
18.6.92	Permit ratification of Maastricht Treaty on European union (11th amend't; 29)	69.1	30.9	57.3	0.5
25.11.92	Restrict availability of abortion (*12th amendment; 40*)	34.6	65.4	68.2	4.7
25.11.92	Guarantee right to travel (13th amendment; 40)	62.4	37.6	68.2	4.3
25.11.92	Guarantee right to information (14th amendment; 40)	59.9	40.1	68.1	4.3
24.11.95	Permit legalisation of divorce (15th amendment; 41)	50.3	49.7	62.2	0.3
25.11.96	Permit refusal of bail (16th amendment; 40)	74.8	25.2	29.2	0.4
30.10.97	Guarantee cabinet confidentiality (17th amendment; 28)	52.5	47.5	47.2	5.2
22.5.98	Permit ratification of Amsterdam Treaty (18th amendment; 29)	61.7	38.3	56.2	2.2
22.5.98	Permit changes agreed in Good Friday Agreement (19th amend't; 29 (and 2, 3))	94.4	5.6	56.3	1.1
11.6.99	Strengthen position of local government (20th amendment; 28A)	77.8	22.2	51.1	7.6

Notes: Amendment numbers in italics refer to constitutional amendment bills rejected at a referendum. The first amendment bill (state of emergency, affecting article 28) and the second amendment bill (emergency provisions and various matters, affecting articles 11–15, 18, 20, 24–28, 34, 40, 47 and 56) were passed by the Oireachtas without a referendum in 1939 and 1941 respectively (see p. 78 above).

2i Opinion poll support for parties by social group, 1969–97

Party	Year	All	Middle class	Working class	Large farmers	Small farmers
Fianna Fáil	1969	43	45	42	38	53
	1977	49	46	50	48	48
	1981	44	39	43	42	53
	1985	42	37	45	41	46
	1989	38	35	38	39	47
	1993	36	35	34	40	44
	1997	36	32	37	40	40
Fine Gael	1969	25	28	16	46	26
	1977	28	30	21	42	38
	1981	32	41	28	43	32
	1985	28	37	21	38	23
	1989	23	25	17	43	21
	1993	16	14	15	29	15
	1997	23	22	19	36	35
Labour Party	1969	18	14	28	2	5
	1977	9	7	15	1	5
	1981	10	4	14	1	4
	1985	5	6	5	0	2
	1989	6	5	9	3	2
	1993	15	16	18	3	8
	1997	9	9	12	1	7

Notes: The figures relate to the percentage of each occupational group that expressed an intention to vote for the party in question. The occupational groups are defined as follows: middle class, ABC1 (professional, managerial and clerical); working class, C2DE (skilled and unskilled manual workers); large farmers, F1 (farmers with 50 acres or more, except in 1969, when the cutoff was 30 acres); small farmers, F2 (farmers with less than 50 acres, except in 1969, when the cutoff was 30 acres). Poll dates were April 1969 (Gallup), May–June 1977 (IMS), May 1981 (IMS), February 1985 (MRBI), June 1989 (MRBI), July 1993 (MRBI) and 28 May 1997 (MRBI). Percentages for a given occupational group will not necessarily total 100 across parties due to the omission of supporters of other parties or of none.

Appendix 3: Political office holders

3a Heads of state, 1922–99

Dates of office	Name
	King
6.12.22 – 20.1.36	George V
20.1.36 – 11.12.36	Edward VIII
11.12.36 – 18.4.49	George VI
	Governor-General
6.12.22 – 1.2.28	Timothy Healy
1.2.28 – 1.11.32	James MacNeill
26.11.32 – 12.12.36	Dónal Ó Buachalla
	President
25.6.38 – 25.6.45	Douglas Hyde
25.6.45 – 25.6.59	Seán T. Ó Ceallaigh
25.6.59 – 25.6.73	Eamon de Valera
25.6.73 – 17.11.74	Erskine Childers
19.12.74 – 22.10.76	Cearbhall Ó Dálaigh
3.12.76 – 3.12.90	Patrick Hillery
3.12.90 – 12.9.97	Mary Robinson
11.11.97 –	Mary McAleese

Note: The King continued to represent the state in external affairs until 1949. The President's role was exclusively domestic until then.

3b Heads and deputy heads of government, 1922–99

Date	Head of government	Deputy head of government
	President of the Executive Council	*Vice President of the Executive Council*
6.12.22	William T. Cosgrave	Kevin O'Higgins
		Ernest Blythe (10.7.27)
9.3.32	Eamon de Valera	Seán T. Ó Ceallaigh
	Taoiseach	*Tánaiste*
29.12.37	Eamon de Valera	Seán T. Ó Ceallaigh
		Seán Lemass (14.6.45)
18.2.48	John A. Costello	William Norton
13.6.51	Eamon de Valera	Seán Lemass
2.6.54	John A. Costello	William Norton
20.3.57	Eamon de Valera	Seán Lemass
23.6.59	Seán Lemass	Seán MacEntee
		Frank Aiken (21.4.65)
10.11.66	Jack Lynch	Frank Aiken
		Erskine Childers (2.7.69)
14.3.73	Liam Cosgrave	Brendan Corish
5.7.77	Jack Lynch	George Colley
11.12.79	Charles Haughey	George Colley
30.6.81	Garret FitzGerald	Michael O'Leary
9.3.82	Charles Haughey	Ray MacSharry
14.12.82	Garret FitzGerald	Dick Spring
		Peter Barry (20.1.87)
10.3.87	Charles Haughey	Brian Lenihan
		John Wilson (13.11.90)
11.2.92	Albert Reynolds	John Wilson
		Dick Spring (12.1.93)
15.12.94	John Bruton	Dick Spring
26.6.97	Bertie Ahern	Mary Harney

3c Composition of governments, 1922–99

Date	Government	Fianna Fáil	Fine Gael	Labour	Other	Total	Dáil support
14. 1.22	Collins	–	8	–	–	8	49.0
22. 8.22	Cosgrave 1	–	9	–	–	9	49.0
9. 9.22	Cosgrave 2	–	11	–	–	11	45.3
6.12.22	Cosgrave 3	–	10	–	–	10	45.3
19. 9.23	Cosgrave 4	–	11	–	–	11	41.2
23. 6.27	Cosgrave 5	–	10	–	–	10	30.7
11.10.27	Cosgrave 6	–	9	–	–	9	40.5
2.4.30	Cosgrave 7	–	9	–	–	9	40.5
9.3.32	de Valera 1	10	–	–	–	10	47.1
8.2.33	de Valera 2	10	–	–	–	10	50.3
21. 7.37	de Valera 3	10	–	–	–	10	50.0
30. 6.38	de Valera 4	10	–	–	–	10	55.8
1.7.43	de Valera 5	11	–	–	–	11	48.5
9.6.44	de Valera 6	11	–	–	–	11	55.1
18. 2.48	Costello 1	–	6	2	5	13	45.6
13. 6.51	de Valera 7	12	–	–	–	12	46.9
2.6.54	Costello 2	–	8	4	1	13	50.3
20. 3.57	de Valera 8	12	–	–	–	12	53.1
23. 6.59	Lemass 1	13	–	–	–	13	53.1
11.10.61	Lemass 2	14	–	–	–	14	48.6
21. 4.65	Lemass 3	14	–	–	–	14	50.0
10.11.66	Lynch 1	14	–	–	–	14	50.0
2.7.69	Lynch 2	14	–	–	–	14	52.1
14. 3.73	Cosgrave	–	10	5	–	15	50.7
5.7.77	Lynch 3	15	–	–	–	15	56.8
12.12.79	Haughey 1	15	–	–	–	15	56.8
30. 6.81	FitzGerald 1	–	11	4	–	15	48.2
9.3.82	Haughey 2	15	–	–	–	15	48.8
14.12.82	FitzGerald 2	–	11	4	–	15	51.8
10.3.87	Haughey 3	15	–	–	–	15	48.8
12.7.89	Haughey 4	13	–	–	2	15	50.0
11.2.92	Reynolds 1	13	–	–	2	15	50.0
12.1.93	Reynolds 2	9	–	6	–	15	60.8
15.12.94	Bruton	–	8	6	1	15	50.6
26.6.97	Ahern	14	–	–	1	15	48.8

Notes: The first three governments were provisional governments. 'Fine Gael' includes also the Pro-Treaty party or Cumann na nGaedheal (1922–33). 'Others' include two Clann na Poblachta, one Clann na Talmhan, one National Labour and one independent in 1948, one Clann na Talmhan in 1954, two Progressive Democrats in 1989 and 1992 and one in 1997, and one Democratic Left in 1994. 'Dáil support' refers to Dáil seats held by parties participating in government as percentage of total Dáil membership immediately after the formation of the government; independent deputies committed to supporting the government are not included (even though one of these was actually a member of the government in 1948); the first two figures in this column are estimates.

3d Ceann Comhairle of Dáil and Cathaoirleach of Seanad, 1922–99

Date	Ceann Comhairle	Date	Cathaoirleach
9.9.22	Michael Hayes (CnG)	12.12.22	Lord Glenavy (Ind)
9.3.32	Frank Fahy (FF)	12.12.28	Thomas Westropp Bennett (CnG)
		27.4.38	Seán Gibbons (FF)
		8.9.43	Seán Goulding (FF)
		21.4.48	T. J. O'Donovan (FG)
13.6.51	Patrick Hogan (Lab)	14.8.51	Liam Ó Buachalla (FF)
		22.7.54	Patrick Baxter (FG)
		22.5.57	Liam Ó Buachalla (FF)
7.11.67	Cormac Breslin (FF)	5.11.69	Michael Yeats (FF)
		3.1.73	Micheál Cranitch (FF)
14.3.73	Seán Treacy (Lab)	1.6.73	James Dooge (FG)
5.7.77	Joseph Brennan (FF)	27.10.77	Séamus Dolan (FF)
16.10.80	Pádraig Faulkner (FF)	8.10.81	Charlie McDonald (FG)
30.6.81	John O'Connell (Ind)	13.5.82	Tras Honan (FF)
14.12.82	Tom Fitzpatrick (FG)	23.2.83	Pat Joe Reynolds (FG)
10.3.87	Seán Treacy (Ind)	25.4.87	Tras Honan (FF)
		1.11.89	Seán Doherty (FF)
		23.1.92	Seán Fallon (FF)
		12.7.95	Liam Naughten (FG)
26.6.97	Séamus Pattison (Lab)	27.11.96	Liam T. Cosgrave (FG)
		17.9.97	Brian Mullooly (FF)

3e Leaders of political parties, 1922–99

Fianna Fáil	*Fine Gael*	*Labour Party*
Eamon de Valera (1926–59)	Eoin O'Duffy (1933–34)	Thomas Johnson (1918–27)
Seán Lemass (1959–66)	William T. Cosgrave (1935–44)	T. J. O'Connell (1927–32)
Jack Lynch (1966–79)	Richard Mulcahy (1944–59)	William Norton (1932–60)
Charles Haughey (1979–92)	James Dillon (1959–65)	Brendan Corish (1960–77)
Albert Reynolds (1992–94)	Liam Cosgrave (1965–77)	Frank Cluskey (1977–81)
Bertie Ahern (1994–)	Garret FitzGerald (1977–87)	Michael O'Leary (1981–82)
	Alan Dukes (1987–90)	Dick Spring (1982–97)
	John Bruton (1990–)	Ruairí Quinn (1997–)

Progressive Democrats	*Cumann na nGaedheal*	*Democratic Left*
Desmond O'Malley (1985–93)	William T. Cosgrave (1922–33)	Proinsias De Rossa (1992–99)
Mary Harney (1993–)		

Note: The party to which the Democratic Left deputies belonged was originally Sinn Féin, after 1970 known as 'Official' Sinn Féin; it became Sinn Féin the Workers' Party in 1977 and The Workers' Party in 1982. Six of its seven deputies left in 1992 to form Democratic Left. The original party had been led by Tomás Mac Giolla (1962–88) and Proinsias De Rossa (1988–92).

Appendix 4: Biographical notes on major political figures

The following notes give basic information on all those who have held the post of Governor-General, President, President of the Executive Council, Taoiseach, Vice President of the Executive Council or Tánaiste. For further information on most of these, see Louis McRedmond (ed.), *Modern Irish Lives: Dictionary of 20th-Century Biography* (Dublin: Gill and Macmillan, 1996), Henry Boylan, *A Dictionary of Irish Biography*, 2nd ed. (Dublin: Gill and Macmillan, 1988), Ted Nealon's *Guides to the Dáil and Seanad*, various years, and *Who's Who, What's What and Where in Ireland* (London: Geoffrey Chapman, in association with *The Irish Times*, 1973).

Ahern, Bertie. Born Dublin, 12 September 1951; educated Christian Brothers, Whitehall, Dublin, and College of Commerce, Rathmines; worked as an accountant; Fianna Fáil TD since 1977; leader of Fianna Fáil since 1994; minister of state, 1982; government minister, 1987–94; Taoiseach since 1997. A very popular deputy and committed constituency worker, he also developed an outstanding reputation as a negotiator and compromise broker; although he has been accused of vacillation and indecisiveness, his skills and commitment were displayed particularly impressively during the negotiation of the Good Friday Agreement of 1998.

Aiken, Frank. Born Camlough, Co Armagh, 13 February 1898; educated Christian Brothers, Newry; worked as a farmer; active in Gaelic League and in Irish Volunteers; leading figure in IRA during war of independence and civil war; anti-Treaty Sinn Féin and Fianna Fáil TD, 1923–73; government minister, 1932–48, 1951–54, 1975–69; Tánaiste, 1959–69; died 18 May 1983. One of the last IRA divisional commanders to take sides in the civil war, was associated with the pursuit of neutrality also in international affairs; as Minister for External Affairs, guided Ireland along an independent line in the United Nations.

Barry, Peter. Born Cork, 6 August 1928; educated Christian Brothers, Cork; worked as a tea importer and wholesaler; Fine Gael TD since 1969; government minister, 1973–77, 1981–82, 1982–87; Tánaiste, 1987. A popular and respected elder statesman in Fine Gael, built up a positive image as foreign minister; nevertheless, did not succeed to the party leadership in a 1987 contest where youth appeared to take precedence over experience; Tánaiste only for a few weeks after the collapse of the Fine Gael–Labour coalition in 1987.

Blythe, Ernest. Born Lisburn, Co Antrim, 13 April 1889; educated locally; worked as a clerk in the Department of Agriculture; active in the Gaelic League, IRB and Irish Volunteers; Sinn Féin MP/TD, 1918–22; pro-Treaty Sinn Féin and Cumann na nGaedheal TD, 1922–33; lost his seat, 1933; minister in Dáil government, 1919–22; government minister, 1922–32; Vice President of the Executive Council, 1927–32; died 23 February 1975. A northern Protestant, was strongly associated with the Irish language movement and with Irish cultural activities, going on after his retirement from politics to become managing director of the Abbey Theatre; as Minister for Finance, won notoriety for reducing the old age pension from ten to nine shillings (from 50 pence to 45 pence!).

Bruton, John. Born Dublin, 8 May 1947; educated St Dominic's College, Dublin, Clongowes Wood College, Co Kildare, University College Dublin, and King's Inns; qualified as a barrister; Fine Gael TD since 1969; leader of Fine Gael since 1990; parliamentary secretary, 1973–77; government minister, 1981–82, 1982–87; Taoiseach, 1994–97. Noted as a sincere, hard-working politician with an abiding interest in parliamentary reform; his distinctive perspective on Northern Ireland politics placed him close to the unionist position, and made him an object of some suspicion to nationalists; his political skills were challenged when his first budget was defeated in the Dáil in 1982, precipitating a general election; showed considerable flexibility and skill in heading a 'rainbow coalition' that took over following the collapse of the Reynolds government in 1994.

Childers, Erskine. Born London, 11 December 1905; educated Norfolk and Cambridge University; worked in Paris for an American travel organisation; advertising manager, *Irish Press;* Fianna Fáil TD, 1938–73; government minister 1951–54, 1957–73; Tánaiste, 1969–73; President of Ireland, 1973–74; died 17 November 1974. He was a son of Robert Erskine Childers (1870–1922), a Clerk in the House of Commons who had Irish connections, became involved in the Irish nationalist movement, took the anti-Treaty side during the civil war and was executed in 1922.

Colley, George. Born Dublin, 18 October 1925; educated Christian Brothers, Dublin, and University College, Dublin; worked as a solicitor; Fianna Fáil TD, 1961–83; parliamentary secretary, 1964–65; government minister, 1965–73, 1977–81; Tánaiste, 1977–81; died 17 September 1983. Contested the leadership of Fianna Fáil against Jack Lynch in 1966 and against his long-time rival and former school classmate, Charles Haughey, in 1979; intensely suspicious of Haughey since the arms crisis of 1970, insisted during Haughey's first government on being given a veto on appointments to the security ministries (Defence and Justice).

Collins, Michael. Born Clonakilty, Co Cork, 16 October 1890; educated local national school; worked in London as a clerk in the post office and for a firm of stockbrokers; participated in 1916 rising as IRB member; Sinn Féin TD/MP, 1918–22; minister in Dáil government, 1919–22; Chairman of Provisional Government and Commander-in-Chief of the new national army, 1922; killed in an ambush at Béal na mBláth, Co Cork, by anti-Treaty forces during the civil war on 22 August 1922. He was a charismatic leader during the Anglo-Irish war of 1919–21 and a very effective director of intelligence for the IRA; his influence helped to swing the IRB (of whose Supreme Council he was President) and many members of the IRA into support for the Anglo-Irish Treaty, which he had negotiated as one of the representatives of the Irish side.

Corish, Brendan. Born Wexford, 19 November 1918; educated Christian Brothers, Wexford; worked as a local government official; Labour TD, 1945–82; leader of the Labour Party, 1960–77; parliamentary secretary, 1948–51; government minister, 1954–57; Tánaiste, 1973–77; died 17 February 1990. Though a popular party leader, was relatively unassertive in his later years and allowed strong-willed colleagues considerable latitude when the party was in government, 1973–77.

Cosgrave, Liam. Born Dublin, 13 April 1920; educated Christian Brothers, Castleknock College and King's Inns; called to bar, 1943; Fine Gael TD, 1943–81; leader of Fine Gael, 1965–77; parliamentary secretary, 1948–51; government minister, 1954–57; Taoiseach 1973–77. A son of William T. Cosgrave; his period as Taoiseach was marked by a strong emphasis on the maintenance of law and order.

Cosgrave, William T. Born Dublin, 6 June 1880; educated Christian Brothers, Dublin; joined the early Sinn Féin movement and the Irish Volunteers and participated in 1916 rising; Sinn Féin MP/TD, 1917–22; pro-Treaty Sinn Féin, Cumann na nGaedheal and Fine Gael TD, 1922–44; leader of Cumann na nGaedheal, 1923–33 and of Fine Gael, 1935–44; minister in Dáil government, 1919–22; President of Executive Council, 1922–32; died 16 November 1965. Despite his background as a revolutionary in 1916, was associated with conservative policies during the first decade of the new state.

Costello, John A. Born Dublin, 20 June 1891; educated University College, Dublin; called to bar, 1914; worked in Attorney General's office, 1922–26; Attorney General, 1926–32; Cumann na nGaedheal and Fine Gael TD, 1933–43, 1944–69; head of first and second Inter-Party governments and Taoiseach, 1948–51 and 1954–57; died 5 January 1976. Associated with a striking about-face in Fine Gael when he moved in 1948 to sever Ireland's links with the Commonwealth and declare the state a republic; did not support his Minister for Health, Noel Browne, whose 'Mother and Child' health care proposals in 1950 were strongly opposed by the Catholic church and led ultimately to the collapse of Costello's first government.

de Valera, Eamon. Born New York city, 14 October 1882; brought up Bruree, Co Limerick; educated Christian Brothers, Charleville, Blackrock College, Dublin, and Royal University; teacher of mathematics; involved in early Gaelic League and Irish Volunteers and participated in 1916 rising; senior surviving commandant of rising; leader of Sinn Féin, 1917–22, of anti-Treaty Sinn Féin, 1922–26 and of Fianna Fáil, which he founded, 1926–59; Sinn Féin TD/MP, 1917–22; anti-Treaty Sinn Féin and Fianna Fáil TD, 1922–59; President of Dáil government, 1919–22, President of Executive Council, 1932–37, Taoiseach, 1937–48, 1951–54 and 1957–59; President of Ireland, 1959–73; died 29 August 1975. An enigmatic figure who played a leading role in Irish politics from 1916 to 1973, and a controversial one at certain times, such as 1921–23 and 1926–27; was largely responsible for leading the bulk of the anti-Treaty side into operating within a constitutional framework in the 1920s; though committed to Irish unity and the Irish language, made little progress on the former and saw the latter weaken further; was more successful in the area of foreign relations, where he succeeded in greatly enhancing the state's independence.

FitzGerald, Garret. Born Dublin, 9 February 1926; educated Belvedere College, University College, Dublin and King's Inns; worked as a research and schedules manager in Aer Lingus and later as lecturer in Political Economy, University College, Dublin; Fine Gael senator, 1965–69 and TD 1969–92; leader of Fine Gael, 1977–87; government minister, 1973–77; Taoiseach 1981–82 and 1982–87. Led his party to its largest ever share of electoral support in 1982; his liberal agenda was undermined by conservative outcomes in referendums on abortion (1983) and divorce (1986), but his Northern Ireland policy was significantly advanced by the signing of the Anglo-Irish Agreement (1985).

Griffith, Arthur. Born Dublin, 31 March 1871; educated Christian Brothers, Dublin; worked as a printer and then as a journalist; editor of a number of nationalist periodicals and pamphlets; founder of Sinn Féin party and member of Irish Volunteers, but did not participate in 1916 rising; Sinn Féin MP/TD, 1918–22; minister in Dáil government, 1919–22; President of Dáil government, 1922; died 12 August 1922. Was responsible for popularising the Sinn Féin policy of economic self-reliance after 1905; this also envisaged following the Hungarian model of 1867, by which an independent Irish state would be established as part of a dual monarchy, linked to Britain only by the crown.

Harney, Mary. Born Ballinasloe, Co Galway, 11 March 1953; educated Convent of Mercy, Goldenbridge, Dublin, Coláiste Bhríde, Dublin, and Trinity College, Dublin; employed as research worker; Fianna Fáil senator, 1977–81; Fianna Fáil TD, 1981–85; Progressive Democrat TD since 1985; leader of the Progressive Democrats since 1993; minister of state, 1989–92; Tánaiste since 1997. The youngest ever member of the Seanad, the first woman leader of a political party and the first woman Tánaiste, she has fought hard to maintain the identity of the Progressive Democrats (of which she was a founding member) in unfavourable circumstances.

Haughey, Charles J. Born Castlebar, Co Mayo, 16 September 1925; educated Christian Brothers, Dublin, University College, Dublin, and King's Inns; worked as an accountant; Fianna Fáil TD, 1957–92; leader of Fianna Fáil, 1979–92; parliamentary secretary, 1960–61; government minister, 1961–70 and 1977–79; Taoiseach 1979–81, 1982, 1987–92. A son-in-law of Seán Lemass; was dismissed as Minister for Finance by Jack Lynch in 1970 in the course of the 'Arms Crisis', but was acquitted in court of all charges; fought his way back to emerge as party leader in 1979 with the support of the party's backbenchers; led his party into its first ever coalition government in 1989; following his retirement his financial affairs were subjected to rigorous examination by tribunals established to enquire into allegations of irregularities during his time as Taoiseach.

Healy, Timothy. Born Bantry, Co Cork, 17 May 1855; educated local Christian Brothers; worked in England as a railway clerk and later as a nationalist journalist; Nationalist MP 1880–86, 1887–1910 and 1911–18 (anti-Parnellite, 1890–1900, then an independent Nationalist); Governor-General, 1922–28; died 26 March 1931. Noted as a lively and witty debater, but divisive as a political figure.

Hillery, Patrick. Born Miltown Malbay, Co Clare, 2 May 1923; educated Rockwell College and University College, Dublin; practised as a medical doctor; Fianna Fáil TD, 1951–72; government minister, 1959–72; Irish member of EC Commission, 1973–76; President of Ireland, 1976–90, a post for which he was an unopposed nominee. As Minister for External Affairs, was responsible for handling Irish foreign policy in the difficult period coinciding with the outbreak of the Northern Ireland troubles and with the negotiation of EC membership.

Hyde, Douglas. Born Castlerea, Co Roscommon, 17 January 1860; educated Trinity College, Dublin; collector of Irish folklore, of which he published many volumes; professor of Modern Irish, University College, Dublin; founder member of Gaelic League, of which he was first president (1893–1915); maintained a non-political role, and resigned as president of the League when it began to follow a more political path; independent member in Senate of Irish Free State, 1925, but failed to secure election in 1925 Senate general election; senator (Taoiseach's nominee), 1938; President of Ireland, 1938–45, a post for which he was an all-party choice; died 12 July 1949. Son of a Protestant rector in Co Roscommon, was much loved by language revivalists for his work for their movement, and was the author of the first play in Irish ever to appear on a professional stage (1901).

Lemass, Seán. Born Dublin, 15 July 1899; educated Christian Brothers; worked in his father's drapery shop; joined Irish Volunteers and participated in 1916 rising; active in IRA, 1919–23; anti-Treaty Sinn Féin and Fianna Fáil TD, 1924–69; government minister, 1932–48, 1951–54, 1957–59; Tánaiste, 1945–48, 1951–54, 1957–59; Taoiseach 1959–66; died 11 May 1971. Associated with the shift in Fianna Fáil, of which he was a founder member, from traditional nationalist policies to support for rapid economic development, especially in the 1960s, and with normalisation of relations with Britain and Northern Ireland.

Lenihan, Brian. Born Dundalk, Co Louth, 17 November 1930; educated Marist Brothers, Athlone, University College, Dublin and King's Inns; worked as a barrister; Fianna Fáil TD, 1961–73, and since 1977; lost his seat, 1973; Fianna Fáil senator, 1973–77; parliamentary secretary, 1961–64; government minister, 1964–73, 1977–81, 1982, 1987–90; Tánaiste, 1987–90; died 1 November 1995. An enormously popular politician, was a casualty of an incident during the 1990 presidential election campaign in which he appeared to be giving contradictory versions of an event in 1982 involving an alleged attempt to bring undue pressure to bear on the President; though he sought to explain the incident away in terms of his medical condition (he was seriously ill at the time and under heavy medication), it is believed to have cost him the presidency and it brought about his dismissal as Tánaiste.

Lynch, John (Jack). Born Cork, 15 August 1917; educated Christian Brothers, Cork, University College, Cork, King's Inns; worked in civil service and later as a barrister; Fianna Fáil TD, 1948–81; parliamentary secretary, 1951–54; government minister, 1957–66; Taoiseach, 1966–73 and 1977–79. His sporting background (in Gaelic football and hurling) and personable character won him immense popularity; his qualities as a leader were severely tested in the early years of the Northern Ireland troubles (1969–70), as his party sought to come to terms with the state's impotence in the face of attacks on nationalists in the North; in 1977, led his party to its greatest ever size in the Dáil and largest share of the vote since 1938, but ironically was forced to step down as leader two years later.

McAleese, Mary. Born Belfast, 27 June 1951, as Mary Leneghan; educated Falls Rd convent secondary school, Belfast, and Queen's University, Belfast; Reid Professor of Law at Trinity College, Dublin, 1974–79 and 1981–87; journalist and television presenter, 1979–81; Director, Institute of Professional and Legal Studies, Queen's University, Belfast, 1987–97, and Pro Vice-Chancellor, Queen's University, Belfast, 1994–97; President of Ireland since 1997. Though associated with Fianna Fáil, was seen as an outsider within the party; during her election campaign her Northern origins and links were used against her, apparently counter-productively; despite a lukewarm relationship with the media at the beginning of her presidency, her popularity improved following a number of very successful visits abroad.

MacEntee, Seán. Born Belfast, 22 August 1889; educated St Malachy's College, Belfast, and Belfast Municipal College of Technology; worked as a consulting electrical engineer and registered patent agent; active in Irish Volunteers; participated in 1916 rising, sentenced to death but reprieved; active in IRA; Sinn Féin MP/TD, 1918–22; Fianna Fáil TD, 1927–69; government minister, 1932–48, 1951–54, 1957–65; Tánaiste, 1959–65; died 10 January 1984. Noted as a poet in his early life, later devoted himself fully to politics.

MacNeill, James. Born Glenarm, Co Antrim, 27 or 29 March 1869; educated Belvedere College, Dublin, and Cambridge University; worked in Indian civil service; on early retirement joined Sinn Féin; Irish high commissioner in London, 1923–28; Governor-General, 1928–32; died 12 December 1938. Though with a less political past than his elder brother, Eoin (Professor of History at University College, Dublin, leader of the Irish Volunteers and government minister, 1922–25), became fully immersed in political conflict in 1932 following the change of government; de Valera forced his resignation as Governor-General within a few months.

MacSharry, Ray. Born Sligo, 29 April 1938; educated locally and Summerhill College, Sligo; worked as a haulier, auctioneer and farm owner; Fianna Fáil TD, 1969–89; minister of state, 1977–79; government minister, 1979–81, 1982, 1987–89; Tánaiste, 1982. Rated very highly as minister for finance, went on to become an extremely successful EC commissioner for agriculture, a position from which he retired in 1992.

Norton, William. Born Dublin, 1900; educated locally; worked in the post office and as a trade union official; Labour TD, 1926–27, 1932–63; lost his seat, 1927; leader of the Labour Party, 1932–60; Tánaiste 1948–51, 1954–57; died 4 December 1963. Though he built up the support base of his party until 1943 and led it into government for the first time ever in 1948, in his later years was more preoccupied with trade union affairs and with his own constituency than with the leadership of the party.

Ó Buachalla, Dónal (also known by the English form of his name, Daniel Buckley). Born Maynooth, Co Kildare, 3 February 1866; educated Belvedere College and Catholic University School, Dublin; owner of a shop in Maynooth; member of the Gaelic League and IRB; participated in 1916 rising; Sinn Féin MP 1918–22; Fianna Fáil TD, 1927–32 (lost his seat in 1922 and again in 1932); Governor-General, 1932–36; died 31 October 1963. Achieved early prominence when prosecuted for painting his name in Irish on his cart; as Governor-General avoided meeting the King, never left the state and resided in a house in Dun Laoghaire rather than in the Viceregal Lodge in the Phoenix Park.

Ó Ceallaigh, Seán T. (also known by the English form of his name, Seán T. O'Kelly). Born Dublin, 25 August 1882; educated Christian Brothers; active in Gaelic League, Celtic Literary Society, IRB and Sinn Féin; participated in 1916 rising; Sinn Féin MP/TD, 1918–22; anti-Treaty Sinn Féin and Fianna Fáil TD, 1922–45; Ceann Comhairle of first Dáil; government minister, 1932–45; Vice President of Executive Council, 1932–37; Tánaiste, 1937–45; President of Ireland, 1945–59; died 23 November 1966. Though personally popular, was in effect 'pushed upstairs' to the presidency in 1945, making way for Seán Lemass, 17 years his junior, to take over as Tánaiste and heir apparent to de Valera.

Ó Dálaigh, Cearbhall. Born Bray, Co Wicklow, 12 February 1911; educated Christian Brothers and University College, Dublin; called to the bar, 1944; active in Fianna Fáil; Attorney General 1946–48, 1951–53; Supreme Court judge, 1953; Chief Justice, 1961; Irish member of European Court of Justice, 1972; President of Ireland, 1974–76, a post for which he was an unopposed nominee; died 21 March 1978. A lover of the Irish language; his resignation from the presidency was precipitated by a chain of events that began when the Minister for Defence, speaking at a military function, described him as 'a thundering disgrace' for referring an Emergency Powers Bill to the Supreme Court to test its constitutionality.

O'Higgins, Kevin. Born Stradbally, Co Laois, 7 June 1892; educated Clongowes Wood and University College, Dublin; early member of Sinn Féin; Sinn Féin MP/TD, 1918–22; pro-Treaty Sinn Féin and Cumann na nGaedheal TD, 1922–27; government minister, 1922–27; Vice President of the Executive Council, 1923–27; assassinated on 10 July 1927 while walking to mass by a group of anti-Treaty IRA members of the 1922–23 period who came upon him by accident. As Minister for Home Affairs during the civil war, was associated with the strong measures taken by the government to ensure victory, including the execution of seventy-seven of the anti-Treaty side.

O'Leary, Michael. Born Cork, 8 May 1936; educated Presentation College, Cork and University College, Cork; worked as a trade union official; Labour TD, 1965–82; Fine Gael TD, 1982–87; leader of the Labour Party, 1981–82; government minister, 1973–77, 1981–82; Tánaiste, 1981–82. Associated with his party's move to the left in the late 1960s and initially an opponent of coalition, his switch of allegiance to Fine Gael in 1982 was one of the more spectacular somersaults in Irish politics.

Reynolds, Albert. Born Rooskey, Co Roscommon, 3 November 1932; educated Summerhill College, Sligo; worked as director of his own petfood company; Fianna Fáil TD since 1977; government minister 1979–81, 1982, 1987–92; Taoiseach 1992–94. Though regarded as one of the more conservative members of his party, negotiated a coalition agreement with Labour following his defeat in the 1992 general election; noted as a risk-taker, he played a crucial role in paving the way for the Good Friday Agreement, 1998, by facilitating Sinn Féin's entry into negotiations.

Robinson, Mary. Born Ballina, Co Mayo, 21 May 1944, as Mary Bourke; educated Mount Anville, Paris, Trinity College, Dublin, and Harvard University; Reid Professor of Constitutional and Criminal Law, Trinity College, Dublin; independent senator, 1969–76, 1985–89; Labour party senator, 1976–85; President of Ireland 1990–97. Resigned the Labour whip in 1985 over the party's support for the Anglo-Irish Agreement, but was nominated and supported by Labour in her successful presidential election campaign in 1990; an extremely popular and assertive President, she played a subtle but significant political role; she resigned shortly before the expiry of her term of office to assume the position of United Nations High Commissioner for Human Rights.

Spring, Dick. Born Tralee, Co Kerry, 29 August 1950; educated Christian Brothers, Tralee, St Joseph's, Roscrea, Trinity College, Dublin and King's Inns; worked as a barrister; Labour TD since 1981; leader of the Labour Party since 1982; Tánaiste 1982–87 and 1993–97. Enjoying an enormously high rating with the voters as leader of his party, his victory in 1992 placed him in a much stronger position than any previous Labour leader in hammering out a coalition deal and in giving Labour a more powerful position in cabinet than ever previously; resigned following the defeat of Adi Roche, the candidate sponsored by his party in the 1997 presidential election.

Wilson, John. Born Kilcogy, Co Cavan, 8 July 1923; educated St Mel's College, Longford, University of London and University College, Dublin; worked as a teacher and university lecturer; Fianna Fáil TD, 1973–92; government minister, 1977–81, 1982, 1987–92; Tánaiste, 1990–92. One of the more popular elder statesmen within Fianna Fáil, took over as Tánaiste when the politically wounded Brian Lenihan was dismissed during the presidential election campaign; a witty contributor in the Dáil, and a Latin scholar.

Appendix 5: Chronology of main political events

The following lists a selection of the main events in Irish political history. For further information, see *A Chronology of Irish History to 1976: A Companion to Irish History Part 1*, Volume 8 of *A New History of Ireland* (Oxford: Clarendon Press, for the Royal Irish Academy, 1982); J. E. Doherty and D. J. Hickey, *A Chronology of Irish History since 1500*, (Dublin: Gill and Macmillan, 1989); Jim O'Donnell (ed.), *Ireland: The Past Twenty Years: an Illustrated Chronology* (Dublin: Institute of Public Administration, 1986); and the annual chronology appearing in *Irish Political Studies*, beginning in Volume 8 (1993).

1169, May	Norman invasion of Ireland begins; most of Ireland subsequently subdued.
1264, June 18	First Irish parliament meets at Casteldermot, Co Kildare.
1541, June 18	King of England declared also to be King of Ireland.
1607, September 4	'Flight of the earls': Earl of Tyrone (Hugh O'Neill) , Earl of Tyrconnell (Rory O'Donnell) and others sail from Co Donegal for continental Europe, symbolising the end of the Gaelic social and political order and the near-completion of the English conquest.
1608, July 19	Initiation of 'survey' of ownership of six counties of Ulster (followed by the 'plantation' of these counties with English and Scottish settlers).
1641, October 22	Beginning of rebellion of Catholics (who subsequently organised as the 'Confederation of Kilkenny', but whose rebellion had been largely crushed by Oliver Cromwell by 1650).
1688, November 5	William of Orange lands in Devon to become King of England (war

between Willliam and the deposed James II follows in Ireland, 1689–91, with the Irish defeat at the Battle of the Boyne, July 1 1690 (July 12, old calender) and the Treaty of Limerick, 3 October 1691, as its most noted events).

1798, May 23	Beginning of 'United Irish' rebellion, which was defeated within a few weeks.
1800, August 1	Act of Union passed; came into effect 1 January 1801.
1845, September 9	First report of arrival of potato blight, which led to famine in Ireland over the next four years, with deaths reaching a peak in 1847.
1848, July 29	'Battle of Widow McCormack's cabbage-patch': principal event in short-lived 'rebellion' of the Young Ireland movement.
1858, March 17	Foundation of Irish Republican Brotherhood (IRB) in Dublin (popularly known as the Fenians, it was the principal republican organisation until 1916, and continued to exist for some years after 1922).
1867, February 12	Beginning of Fenian rebellion; skirmishes took place over the following month.
1884, December 6	Representation of the People Act passed; this greatly extended the franchise, permitting the development of mass electoral politics.
1886, April 8	First Home Rule Bill introduced in parliament; defeated in the House of Commons on 8 June.
1893, February 13	Second Home Rule Bill introduced in parliament; passed in House of Commons on 2 September, defeated in House of Lords on 9 September.
1905, November 28	First use of term 'Sinn Féin' by radical nationalists; the Sinn Féin League was formed on 21 April 1907 through an amalgamation of existing organisations.
1912, April 11	Third Home Rule Bill introduced in parliament; passed in House of Commons on 16 January 1913; defeated in House of Lords on 30 January 1913; passed in House of Commons a third time, thus overriding the Lords' veto, 25 May 1914; implementation suspended.
1913, January 31	Foundation of Ulster Volunteers.
1913, November 25	Foundation of Irish Volunteers.
1916, April 24	'Easter rising' (IRB-led rebellion in Dublin that ended on 29 April).
1918, December 14	General election, at which Sinn Féin won 73 of the 105 Irish seats, going on to call a meeting of the 'First Dáil' for 21 January 1919.
1919, January 21	Opening shots in war of independence, which lasted until a truce on 9 July 1921.
1920, February 25	Government of Ireland Bill introduced in parliament; passed 23 December; House of Commons of Northern Ireland meets, 7 June 1921, giving effect to partition; Act largely ineffective in south.
1921, December 6	Signing of Anglo-Irish Treaty by representatives of Dáil and of British government; approved by Dáil, 7 January 1922; formal transfer of power to provisional government on 16 January 1922.
1922, June 16	General election for Dáil; pro-Treaty parties win substantial majority.
1922, June 28	Provisional government attack on Four Courts marks beginning of civil war, which lasted until 27 April 1923.
1922, October 25	Constitution of Irish Free State approved by Dáil; approved by British parliament, 5 December 1922; into effect 6 December 1922.
1926, March 11	Split in Sinn Féin at ard-fheis; de Valera withdraws; Fianna Fáil founded on 16 May.
1927, July 10	Assassination of Kevin O'Higgins, Minister for Justice; government responds with a legislative package that has the effect of forcing Fianna Fáil deputies to take their seats in the Dáil on 11 August.
1932, February 9	Formation of Army Comrades Association; renamed National Guard on 20 July 1933; popularly known as the Blueshirts.
1932, March 9	Fianna Fáil forms government after becoming largest party in general election.
1933, September 2	Foundation of United Ireland Party through merger of Cumann na nGaedheal, the National Centre Party and the National Guard; in later years the party became known as Fine Gael.

1936, May 29	Senate abolished by constitutional amendment.
1936, December 11	Abdication of Edward VIII; constitutional amendment to remove remaining references to King and Governor-General; King allowed to retain external functions.
1937, July 1	Referendum approves new constitution; comes into effect 29 December.
1938, April 25	Anglo-Irish agreements covering 'treaty ports', financial relations and trade.
1948, February 4	Fianna Fáil loses power in general election; replaced 18 February by 'Inter-Party' government.
1948, September 7	Taoiseach John A. Costello announces that Ireland is to become a republic; Republic of Ireland Act passed, 21 December; in effect, 18 April 1949.
1958, November 11	Programme for Economic Expansion published; formed basis for shift from protectionist policies to more open policy on industrial development and trade.
1965, December 14	Anglo-Irish free trade agreement signed; in effect, 1 July 1966.
1968, October 15	Clash between civil rights marchers and police in Derry marks escalation of civil unrest in Northern Ireland.
1970, January 11	Split in Sinn Féin, with secession of supporters of 'Provisional' IRA (who had seceded from the 'Official' IRA in December 1969).
1970, May 6	Dismissal of Charles Haughey and Neil Blaney from government in connection with alleged illegal importation of arms for supply to Northern Ireland; resignation of Kevin Boland.
1972, May 10	Referendum on Ireland's membership of EEC; this came into effect on 31 December.
1973, March 14	Coalition government takes office after 16 years of Fianna Fáil rule.
1979, March 13	Republic joins European monetary system; break in parity of Irish currency with sterling follows.
1983, May 30	First meeting of New Ireland Forum, representing Fianna Fáil, Fine Gael, Labour and the SDLP; reports on 2 May 1984 endorsing Irish unity as a solution to the Northern Ireland problem.
1985, November 15	Anglo-Irish Agreement on government of Northern Ireland signed.
1985, December 21	Foundation of Progressive Democratic Party.
1987, May 26	Referendum on Single European Act.
1989, July 12	Fianna Fáil enters coalition government for the first time, with the Progressive Democrats.
1992, February 22	Resignation of six of the seven Workers' Party TDs; formed party named New Agenda, 3 March; name changed to Democratic Left, 29 March.
1992, June 18	Referendum on Maastricht Agreement on European unity.
1993, January 12	Fianna Fáil and Labour Party form coalition government, changing nature of interparty relations in Ireland.
1993, December 15	Downing Street Declaration by British and Irish prime ministers lays down parameters for a Northern Ireland settlement.
1994, November 17	Resignation of Albert Reynolds as Taoiseach following withdrawal of Labour from government; 'rainbow' coalition of Fine Gael, Labour and Democratic Left takes office under John Bruton without an election, 15 December.
1998, April 10	Good Friday Agreement signed in Belfast; approved by referendums North and South, 22 May.
1998, December 12	Democratic Left agrees to merge with Labour Party; merger in effect, 24 January 1999.

Web addresses

Because of the volume of source material now available on the world wide web, no introduction to Irish politics would be complete without a reference to material available on this medium. Since, however, web addresses are still very unstable (in that they change very frequently, and in many cases disappear altogether), we have confined the present set of web addresses to a small number of especially important resources. From these, links to a large number of other sources of web material are available.

We list below, then, only certain key resources: a general guide to Irish politics material on the web (which provides links to parties, official bodies, newspapers, documents such as the constitution and other sources) and a similar guide that can be used to find comparative material on politics. These are followed by links to major institutions, including the Irish government, the Dáil debates, and the *Irish Times*, which maintains an exceptionally valuable archive. The last site, that of the European Union, provides links to other government sites. The list is intended to provide an introduction only; for further information and for updated material, see the first item on the list.

Document	*Address*
UCD Politics Department: Irish politics resources	www.ucd.ie/~politics/irpols.html
Richard Kimber's political science resources	www.psr.keele.ac.uk/
Information on the Irish state (Irish government)	www.irlgov.ie/
Oireachtas debates (1997–)	www.irlgov.ie/oireachtas/frame.htm
Ireland.com [*The Irish Times*, 1996–]	www.ireland.com/
Welcome to Europe (central European Union server)	europa.eu.int/index-en.htm

Index